# LOUIS

Master of Modernism

# ARMSTRONG

# LOUIS

## Master of Modernism

# ARMSTRONG

## Thomas Brothers

W. W. NORTON & COMPANY
New York • London

For information about permission to reproduce selections from this book,
write to Permissions, W. W. Norton & Company, Inc.,
500 Fifth Avenue, New York, NY 10110

For information about special discounts for bulk purchases,
please contact W. W. Norton Special Sales
at specialsales@wwnorton.com or 800-233-4830

Manufacturing by RR Donnelley Harrisonburg
Book design by Charlotte Straub
Production manager: Julia Druskin

Library of Congress Cataloging-in-Publication Data

Brothers, Thomas David.
Louis Armstrong, master of modernism / Thomas Brothers.
— First edition.
pages cm
Includes bibliographical references and index.
ISBN 978-0-393-06582-4 (hardcover)
1.  Armstrong, Louis, 1901–1971. 2.  Jazz musicians—United States—
Biography.  I. Title.
ML419.A75B776 2014
781.65092—dc23
[B]
2013037726

W. W. Norton & Company, Inc.
500 Fifth Avenue, New York, N.Y. 10110
www.wwnorton.com

W. W. Norton & Company Ltd.
Castle House, 75/76 Wells Street, London W1T 3QT

1 2 3 4 5 6 7 8 9 0

# FOR

Olly Wilson,
Samuel A. Floyd Jr.,
AND
T. J. Anderson

# CONTENTS

Preface  *ix*

Introduction  *1*

1. "Welcome to Chicago"  *13*

2. Oliver's Band and the "Blues Age"  *40*

3. Opposites Attract: Louis and Miss Lil  *70*

4. The Call from Broadway  *116*

5. "This Is What Really Relates to Us": The Dreamland Café, the Vendome Theater, and the First Hot Five Records  *165*

6. Melody Man at the Sunset Café  *222*

7. "Some Kind of a God"  *276*

8. The White Turn  *326*

9. The Rosetta Stone  *377*

10. Sleepy Time Down South  *417*

Discography  *463*

Bibliography  *465*

Endnotes  *489*

Source Notes  *521*

Index  *571*

# PREFACE

**Louis Armstrong produced, during the glory years of the mid-1920s through the** early 1930s, a musical legacy of tremendous richness and joy. Armstrong, to our great fortune, was also prolific in documenting his life through letters, interviews, and memoirs. To this material we may add autobiographies of and interviews with his contemporaries, as well as a vibrant collection of archival sources, including African-American newspapers of the day, some rare and some now available for web-based searching. The result is an extremely rich body of documentary evidence that allows us to view Armstrong, his life and his musical legacy, from the inside.

To draw attention to the details of this legacy, I sometimes refer to specific timings in his recordings, indicated in parentheses (e.g., CD: 1:10). A brief discography of reissued CDs is published in the back for those who wish to listen along as they read. And since one of the aims of this book is to place Armstrong's music within a broader historical context. I also include a detailed bibliography of my sources, divided into two parts, one for archival material and the other for general publications. The former are distinguished by an abbreviation for the archive where the document is held, inserted after the author and before the date (e.g., Keppard HJA 1957).

The book provides two types of notes. Superscript numbers in the text alert the reader to explanatory material that appears in the

Endnotes section in the back of the book. The Source Notes include brief citations, keyed to the main body of the book by page number and key phrase.

## Acknowledgments

Compelled to make frequent research trips to New York City, I remain grateful for the hospitality of Giuseppe Gerbino, Krin and Paula Gabbard, and Jeff Taylor; I am equally indebted to Lewis Erenberg and Susan Hirsh in Chicago. At Duke, Roman Testroet, Karen Cook, Jason Heilman, and Dan Ruccia provided excellent assistance. No less important has been the archival help of Michael Cogswell (Louis Armstrong House Museum), Bruce Boyd Raeburn (Hogan Jazz Archive), Alfred Lemmon (Williams Research Center), Dan Morgenstern (Institute of Jazz Studies), Kelly Martin (University of Missouri, Kansas City), Deborah Gillaspie (University of Chicago), Linda Evans (Chicago History Museum), and David Sager (Library of Congress). Duke's library staff—Laura Williams, Tom Moore, and staff at the Music Library and the staff at Perkins, Lilly, and Interlibrary Loan—has supported my work with precision and care for many years. Likewise I have constantly relied on Jos Willems's amazing *All of Me: The Complete Discography of Louis Armstrong*; my thanks to Jim Farrington for introducing me to it. In William Howland Kenney's indispensable *Chicago Jazz: A Cultural History*, a splendid field of research was opened up for me. Now that it is gone, the amazing achievement that was Redhotjazz seems more special than ever. My thanks to Steven Lasker, who supplied me with material he collected on Armstrong's California year, and to Chris Albertson and Ron L'Herault for photos. Two leading specialists in jazz of this period, Bruce Boyd Raeburn and Brian Harker, shared their knowledge and offered help at a number of turns. Without a fellowship from the John Simon Guggenheim Memorial Foundation, combined with a Dean's leave from Duke University, this book would not have been possible. Likewise without the support of my family, Leo and Roger, and especially Tekla, whose patience with my work habits has been immense. Maribeth Anderson Payne provided, once again, invaluable advice and editing, such as no musicologist can take for granted. At Norton, I am also grateful for the thorough and professional help of Michael Fauver and Harry Haskell. This book is dedicated to Olly Wilson, Samuel A. Floyd Jr., and T. J. Anderson, three musicians who have offered me so much support over the years, insights and mentoring that got me started, and encouragement and inspiration that have kept me going.

# LOUIS

Master of Modernism

# ARMSTRONG

# INTRODUCTION

*He was just an ordinary-extraordinary man.*
—Doc Cheatham

## October 1931, Memphis, Tennessee

**Louis Armstrong and His Orchestra are performing at the Peabody Hotel, giving local** jazz fans a chance to finally see and hear in person the singer-cornetist whose records they have been collecting and whose radio broadcasts they have been tuning in to. "Master of Modernism and Creator of His Own Song Style" is how he is billed, and no one dismisses it as mere marketing hype. Few performers, black or white, are more exciting or innovative. Armstrong has been packing them in on this tour of the South, in city after city, segregated white hall after segregated black hall, with an occasional thrill of mixed patronage now and then, carefully guarded by the police.

Everyone in the audience is white, the ten musicians black. The modern master himself is very black—which is to say, first, that he has very dark skin, and second, that he is culturally very black. He does not disguise this cultural allegiance. To the contrary, he has found ways to glorify it while reaping tremendous financial rewards.[1]

Armstrong announces that he would like to dedicate the next song to the Memphis Police Department. Turning to the band, he sets the tempo and they are off with their arrangement of *I'll Be Glad When You're Dead You Rascal You.*

Trombonist Preston Jackson reacts with a nervous jolt, and with good reason. "I'll be glad when you're dead, you rascal you!" Armstrong sings. "I'll be tickled to death when you leave this earth, you dog!" he grins, shucks, and jives. He's dedicating this song to the

1

Memphis police? Not a bunch known for their sense of humor, and many are members of the Ku Klux Klan. What saves the moment is that while the band knows the words, the audience cannot easily make them out. For part of Armstrong's modern song style is a weird way of mixing words and nonsense syllables, sometimes blurring the line between the two, just as the melody he sings is part original tune, part radical transformation of that tune, and part free invention. The policemen come up afterwards to thank Armstrong, and Jackson relaxes. No other band coming through town has ever honored them like this, they tell him.

Some of the musicians were reluctant to take this southern tour. They would have agreed with the New Orleanian banjo player Danny Barker, who explained that "Chicago was considered to be the safest place near New Orleans . . . getting off a Chicago-bound train . . . before it reached its destination was like a ship's captain, in mid-ocean, putting someone on a small raft to drift without provisions." But this is the Depression, which causes people to do things they would not do under normal circumstances.

The relationship of Armstrong's band to the Memphis police was already loaded with tension, for the night before the Peabody Hotel gig they had all been thrown in jail. Their crime: Armstrong was discovered sitting next to his white manager's white wife on the chartered bus, the two of them talking over business. "Why didn't you shoot him in the leg?" one officer demanded from his colleague when he witnessed this provocative scene. On stage, Armstrong displays a persona that is alternately confident, even cocky, with his powerful trumpet virtuosity, and seductive, with his innovative style of singing ballads. Artistically, he is at the top of his game, yet he is crippled by a society that seethes with brutally racist ideologies, laws, and practices.

And thus it was that one of the most important musicians of the twentieth century made his living in 1931. Race was the ever-present elephant in the room. It affected Armstrong every day and every moment of his life, on different levels simultaneously. Today we live in a country that yearns for "postracial" harmony, which makes it comfortable to ignore this distant reality and concentrate instead on the astonishing splendor of his music.

Armstrong's career, the most successful jazz has ever known, spanned half a century. From the time he left New Orleans in 1922, at age twenty-one, until he died as one of the most famous people in the world in 1971, he trumpeted and sang his way through some of the greatest dramas in the nation's history—nascent Jim Crow, the Great Migration of African Americans from the South to the urban North, the Great Depression, World War II, the civil rights era, and the Cold War. To see how a dark-skinned musician from the Deep South, whose formal education ended at age twelve, accomplished all of this is to witness one of the most compelling life stories of the twentieth century. A small man who controlled a powerful instrument, Armstrong first internalized and then transformed the African-American musical vernacular.

*Louis Armstrong, Master of Modernism* aims to tell this story for the period that includes the crowning glories of his musical achievement. It picks up where my *Louis Armstrong's New Orleans* left off, with his arrival in Chicago in 1922, and ends ten years later. My main thesis is that the success of this nimble-minded musician depended on his ability to skillfully negotiate the musical and social legacies of slavery. Indeed, his career can be understood as a response to these interlocking trajectories. His quickness and sureness, so evident in his music, served him well in his encounters with racism. This played out both directly, through daily events in the life of a highly visible figure, and indirectly, through expectations imposed on African-American entertainers that conditioned many of their professional decisions. As black and white Americans responded to the ongoing drama of racial oppression, Armstrong's music was in turn shaped by those responses.

The legacies of slavery are sometimes hard to see. There is a long tradition of simply not wanting to look, of hiding in a kind of historical amnesia that has its own manipulative utility. One thing is clear: emancipation was followed by a century and more of systematic subjugation of people of African descent. The cultural legacy bequeathed by enslaved African Americans to their descendants may be hard to identify precisely, too. Yet most people, over the centuries, have intuitively sensed how music has occupied the thriving center of that legacy. During the decades after Emancipation, the African-American musical vernacular was bursting out of the plantations, from which it spread through the Deep South and then eventually to the urban North, laying the groundwork for the spectacular success of ragtime, blues, jazz, gospel, and other African-American idioms in the twentieth century.

Armstrong was born in 1901 into a community of New Orleanians who were transforming vernacular culture in an urban setting that was hardly paradise but still carried a sense of possibility. By "vernacular" I mean the orally based traditions that were formed on the slave plantations of the Deep South and continued to provide the everyday basis for cultural expression among lower-class blacks. Armstrong was surrounded by and closely tutored in this culture, as it was transformed in New Orleans, for the first 21 years of his life. These traditions promoted resilience and flexibility, which was one reason he was able to hold strong to vernacular values until the very end, even when he was singing songs like *Zippity Do Dah* and *Chimchimery*.

His earliest musical experiences were in church, where his mother took him as a boy and where he first learned to sing. Here he was exposed to music designed to invoke the Holy Spirit, characterized by rhythmic intensity, pitch bending, strained and emotional vocal production signaling release, and communal participation. Heterophony (multiple versions of a single tune, sung simultaneously) kept the community together while accommodating individual expression. The church gave the young musician a nourishing and enjoyable way to learn music.

Armstrong's early years also found him hanging out in the streets with a toothless man named Larenzo, who held him spellbound with his talk of music and with the blues that he played on a long tin horn. Larenzo had a lot of soul, he remembered later. Larenzo's blues brought children running with scraps of tin and rags that they exchanged for small toys. Blues were everywhere, in the simple honky tonks on the block where Armstrong lived and in the casual singing of people he knew. Blues could be performed by ensembles, but it was primarily a solo idiom, a way for an individual to publicly identify himself or herself. It was no accident that when Armstrong eventually got a cornet, the first thing he learned to play was blues.

He often skipped school to follow parade bands, which circulated daily. Funeral processions moved slowly through the streets for hours, broadcasting a range of musical expression, from deep mourning through the famous New Orleanian rejoicing after the body was "turned loose." The rough heterophony of one marching band gave way to the polished sheet-music playing of another, but all wore uniforms and tried to look sharp. Sometimes the cornetist Joe "King" Oliver let Armstrong carry his horn, which was the license he needed to follow the band through neighborhoods that otherwise would have been dangerous for him. When there wasn't a parade there was a funky advertising band, perched on a horse-drawn wagon and playing as audaciously as possible, in an effort to lure people out to look at the signboards on the side of the wagon. Spontaneous contests between bands on different wagons were routine.

At age eleven Armstrong was sent to a home for juvenile delinquents and stayed there for 18 months. He loved playing various instruments in the marching band, working his way up to the cornet under the tutelage of the director, Peter Davis. After he left the home he started hanging around older musicians, asking if he could sit in and play with them. Eventually he knew enough tunes to substitute in a pinch. Oliver became his idol. Like Armstrong, Oliver had dark skin, was raised with church music and blues, and had no father in his life. Oliver noticed his progress and invited him to his house for lessons at his kitchen table, teaching him "the modern way of phrasing on the cornet," as Armstrong described it. Oliver taught by example and by verbal instruction how to play a strong lead and not get lost in "figurations," how to play second and thus contribute to collective improvisation, how to attack notes with punch and sustain them with fire.

He gradually learned more repertory and made a place for himself in the New Orleans dance-band scene. His blues got fancier and more impressive. He learned to "fill in" and create obbligato lines that were the heart of collective improvisation. Earlier he enjoyed singing with his buddies in a little vocal quartet, improvising harmonies in the African-American tradition; now his ear for harmony led him to greater precision and experimentation. Cornetist Buddy Petit was doing this, too, playing second lines that were harmonically imaginative and gaining control of advanced formations like diminished chords. That was one way for a cornet player in this community to distinguish himself. Others played faster or higher, or made elaborate "freak music"—the talking effects produced by growls, mutes, and timbral distortion. This rich and multidimensional environment, competitive and with lots of low-paying jobs, was perfect for a developing talent.

This complex musical culture thrived independently of musical notation; in fact, non-notatable features were emphasized. This was partly a matter of "taking advantage of the disadvantages," as the old African-American saying goes, and partly a matter of using music to strengthen group identity, since it was clear to everyone that these features had come from Africa. Armstrong grew up surrounded by freak music, pitch bending, heterophony, and collective improvisation. Most important was the format I refer to as "fixed and variable," a musical model that is still ubiquitous in sub-Saharan Africa, from which enslaved people brought it to the New World. The model works like this: one instrument (or group of instruments) plays a repeated rhythmic figure. This "fixed" level orients the listener or dancer, while the "variable" instrument or group brings the music to life by departing from the repeated figure in interesting ways.

Music in this multilayered format is easy to hear, but harder to talk about. It was poorly understood by early jazz scholars, who focused on the plurality of rhythms (or polymeters) instead of the rhythmic hierarchy based on a fixed pattern. This misconception obscured African music's connection to the New World and to jazz. But the model is there, plain as day.

The fixed and variable model became the key ingredient in Armstrong's mature style. He internalized it so completely that he was able to think creatively in these terms, in the intuitive way that all great artists come to once they have mastered central forms of expression. This cannot be stated too strongly: all of his mature solos during the period covered in this book are governed by the fixed and variable model; furthermore, his creative extensions of it account for the most distinctive features of his style. No one in the 1920s wrote about this model. They simply understood it tacitly, then rejected or accepted its legitimacy. Even today it is rarely discussed in scholarly literature, and as a result the deep connections of Armstrong's music to sub-Saharan Africa and to racially conditioned culture in the United States have not been properly understood. The model, as Armstrong uses it, applies to melody and harmony as well as rhythm. For this reason it must establish the ground for musical analysis, and ultimately social analysis, as well.

The implications of this line of analysis are startling: by making the fixed and variable model so central to his music, Armstrong *intensified the audible presence of his African heritage.* It is obvious today that cultural practice has no basis in biology. But given the strong associations between race and culture in the 1920s, Armstrong's musical practice cannot be separated from the story of race. Aspects of the fixed and variable model are key to hearing his music, as well as understanding how it was socially conceived. When race is downplayed by jazz historians who prefer to think of the music in a unified "American" way—with whites and blacks both contributing, and with more or less equal debt to Europe and Africa, making jazz a kind of golden multiculturalism *avant la lettre*—these fundamental points are obscured. They are also obscured by those who treat jazz as a rhetorical text, attending to its social complexities but, for one reason or another, disregarding socially conditioned details of sonic practice.

Trumpeter Adolphus "Doc" Cheatham, who knew and admired Armstrong during the late 1920s in Chicago, described his hero as "an ordinary-extraordinary man." There are several ways to think about that paradox. To say he was ordinary could mean that he accepted, without hesitation, apology, or compromise, the social and musical values of the people he grew up with, who were pegged as the lowest of the low. The extraordinary side of the paradox may be related to Armstrong's musical accomplishments. He was not only a great trumpeter, but also a great singer and entertainer; further, he was a great melodist, who invented a melodic idiom of jazz solo playing that became tremendously influential. That's a lot of greatness in one person. It all fell into place in the decade or so after 1922, which was also the period that found him at his peak.

When Armstrong arrived in Chicago in August 1922, no one was thinking so grandly. Oliver had sent for him because he was suffering from gum disease that made it increasingly difficult for him to play his horn. He needed the support of a second cornetist, and Armstrong was not even the first player he thought of. His assignment was to play second to Oliver's lead, which he did for almost two years. Oliver kept his maturing apprentice out of the spotlight and extended the mentoring he had begun in the mid-1910s. Among other things, he taught Armstrong how to design a memorable solo; the impact of that instruction can be clearly heard in Armstrong's earliest recorded solo, from *Chimes Blues* in 1923. There also must have been lessons about the texture of collective improvisation, and perhaps composition as well. King Oliver's recordings with Armstrong during 1923 and 1924, a treasure comprising some 30 different sides, make this phase of his career a true delight.

An important part of Armstrong's maturation in Chicago was the enthusiastic patronage of other African Americans who had recently moved from the Deep South and were eager to discover a new cultural identity, one that incorporated the vernacular principles they cherished, yet was also forward-looking and competitive with white culture. The urban sophistication of Chicago played out musically in places like the Vendome Theater, where Armstrong first made his mark. The spotlight there was normally on operatic overtures and symphonic arrangements. Armstrong was able to match that kind of sophistication while making music that "relates to us," as one African-American observer put it. He did not stand up and shout, "I'm black and I'm proud," but his music said so in no uncertain terms.

Without Armstrong's early commercial recordings, we would have far less reason to engage with his accomplishments from this period. Nevertheless, that legacy is at best a partial and potentially misleading representation of what was happening. Not all recordings were created equally. Some were generated in the studio, on a moment's notice, to satisfy the demand for one more side. A smaller number reflect what was going on in venues where Armstrong played regularly. We should not expect uniformly excellent results from such a varied profile. One purpose of this book is to work through the recorded legacy with an eye toward what it tells us about contexts beyond the studio. The irony is that commercial recordings were merely a sideshow for Armstrong, while for us they are the main event.

"Master of modernism and creator of his own song style" is a good way to sum up Armstrong's accomplishments from this period. The word "modern" is an easy term of abuse for the lazy historian, but the 1920s was a decade when the reach of the modern was extending in all directions. "Modernism will always rule," wrote Dave Peyton, the most important African-American critic of music from this period, in a 1925 review of a Chicago battle of bands that was won by Sam Cooke's orchestra. Modernism meant progress, the articulation of fresh forms, sophistication, something of consequence. It meant inventions of daring and speed, the Chrysler Building in New York City, talking movies, flappers, jazz, consumerism, and distance from Victorian conventions. The degree to which modernism in the black community took white accomplishment as a standard depended on how one was positioned socially and how one imagined future progress for the race. The astonishing thing about Armstrong is that he invented not one but two modern art forms, one after the other, both of them immensely successful and influential, and that he did this with vigorous commitment to means of expression derived from the black vernacular he had grown up with.

Armstrong's first modern style, created around the years 1926–28 and based on the fixed and variable model, was pitched primarily to the black community. These people enjoyed his entertaining singing, but they were in awe of his carefully designed trumpet solos, which helped articulate the modern identity they were looking for. They might have been satisfied with the dazzling display of his increasingly impressive chops—the big round tone, quick fingers, and high-note playing. But he was driven to create a new melodic idiom, which made him different from almost everybody else. His compositional skills led him to craft solos of enduring melodic beauty, and that is how they should be regarded.

His second modern formulation was the result of efforts to succeed in the mainstream market of white audiences. The key here was radical paraphrase of familiar popular tunes. The basic idea was nothing new: when, during the late nineteenth century and probably long before, African-American musicians spoke of "ragging the tune," they meant creating their own stylized version of a known melody by adding all kinds of embellishments and extensions. This technique was part of Armstrong's early musical training. In the early 1930s, with the assistance of the microphone, he invented a fresh approach to this old tradition, creating a song style that was part blues, part crooning, part fixed and variable model, plastic and mellow, the most modern thing around. In 1931 and 1932, Armstrong's recordings made him the best-selling performer in the country, regardless of genre, style, color, or pedigree, and his live performances were regularly beamed across national radio networks.

Jazz à la Paul Whiteman and George Gershwin, made by whites

with the assistance of musical notation, was conceived as a modern art form infused with distinctly American energy, "the free, frank, sometimes vulgar spirit of the bourgeoisie," in the words of one writer, clearly referring to the white bourgeoisie. Notation allowed composers like Gershwin and arrangers working for bands like Whiteman's to create works of formal sophistication and artistic complexity. Although this white modernism was inspired by the African-American vernacular, it was so thoroughly transformed that its origin was obscured.

Modern jazz as Armstrong presented it was something altogether different. It was just as sophisticated as white jazz, but its terms of expression could not be transmitted through musical notation. Armstrong's music was a unique transformation and extension of the African-American vernacular. That was the key to his success as a modernist who appealed both to blacks in the mid- and late 1920s and to whites in the early 1930s.

Few composers can claim to have made significant innovations in musical style; Armstrong did it twice. Like Beethoven, Stravinsky, and The Beatles, he had a remarkable ability to move through different conceptual formations and offer a musical response that, in turn, helped define his surroundings. He learned northern showbiz ways and adapted them to foundational principles he had internalized in New Orleans. "You'll swing harder if you learn to read music," one musician told him around 1920, and he took the advice to heart. In Chicago he studied with a German music teacher, woodshedded the "classics" with his piano-playing wife, and learned to play higher, faster, and with more precision in the scales and chords of Eurocentric music. This project was very much in step with the agenda of the typical southern African-American immigrant who was "doing something to improve myself," as it was often phrased.

Armstrong played the naïve Negro, as whites expected him to. But a genuine historical appreciation of his accomplishment exposes a formidable intellect totally absorbed in music. We still live with the image of an untutored musician who didn't think too much about his music, which simply poured out of him intuitively. Few white people who admired Armstrong in the 1930s were prepared to discover in him the kind of artistic discipline that we associate with Beethoven,

Stravinsky, and even The Beatles. Most assumed that Armstrong was led "only by the sincere unconsciousness of his genius," as one sympathetic writer said about the dancer Bill "Bojangles" Robinson, just as "inspiration has always come to tribal man." We have not completely left that kind of garbage behind.

Like all great artists, Armstrong was so thoroughly immersed in his art that he thought in purely musical terms, with no need for verbal translation. His creative genius expressed itself in abstract forms, the fixed and variable model, blues archetypes, and the transformation of popular songs. Armstrong used what he learned from Eurocentric music to infuse the African-American vernacular with new intensity and possibilities. This process produced, in the mid-1920s, a style that served as the basis for jazz solos for the next decade and beyond. After that, the combination of creative drive and hustle for the rewards of the white marketplace led Armstrong to create an equally innovative modern song style. These twin accomplishments make him the greatest master of melody in the African-American tradition since Scott Joplin, the central figure in virtually the entire tradition of jazz solo playing and singing, and arguably the most important American musician of the twentieth century. For that reason they are the main focus of this book.

When Armstrong left New Orleans behind on a teary day in August 1922, there were no hints of the magnificence that would soon unfold in the North. He had played for whites on Mississippi riverboats, but only as a soloist who could carry a strong lead, not as a blues-based specialist in collective improvisation. He had played for tips in the prostitution district of New Orleans. But most of his musical experience had been in front of African-American audiences, playing the kind of music they liked and he liked. That was precisely what he was called upon to do in Chicago. At Lincoln Gardens, on the South Side, he was eager to step into a band of musicians who thought the way he did and attracted enthusiastic audiences. That band was led by none other than Joe Oliver, who had, since the last time Armstrong saw him, been crowned "King."

# ONE

# "Welcome to Chicago"

## August 8, 1922

Twenty-one-year-old Louis Armstrong is riding on a train bound for Chicago, having boarded at the Illinois Central Railroad station in New Orleans. He sits next to a lady with three children. The lady recognizes him, says she knows his mother. This comforts him, not least because she has packed a large basket of fried chicken, enough to last all the way to California in his estimation. Trains in "Galilee"— African-American slang for the South—do not include dining facilities for Negroes, so passengers must bring their own food. His mother bagged a trout sandwich for him, but it feels good to be sitting next to the overflowing basket of chicken. Underneath his long coat and clothes he wears long underwear, even though it is August, and he is lugging a small suitcase in one hand, a little case for his cornet in the other.

Armstrong, the lady, and her children are following a well-worn path that took shape as an imposing phenomenon half a dozen or so years earlier. They are part of what will later be called the Great Migration, the movement of African Americans from the countryside and cities of the South into the urban North. The trend picked up large numbers with the shutting down of European immigration in 1914; it was spurred along by floods and a boll weevil epidemic—"Hey hey boll weevil, don't sing them blues no more, boll weevil here, boll wee-

*The South Side, Chicago*

1. Pekin Theater and Cabaret
2. Elite Café
3. Grand Theater
4. Vendome Theater
5. Ed Victor's Barber Shop
6. Mecca Flats
7. Jones Music Store
8. Monogram Theater
9. Fiume Café
10. Dreamland Café
11. Musicians' Union
12. Lil and Louis rental, 1924
13. Lil's mother
14. Eighth Regiment Armory
15. Apex Club
16. Plantation Café
17. Sunset Café
18. Lincoln Gardens
19. Alpha Smith
20. Earl Hines
21. House purcchased by Lil and Louis, 1925
22. Metropolitan Theater
23. Regal Theater
24. Savoy Ballroom
25. Warwick Hall

vils everywhere you go," goes the blues song. Lynchings are on the rise, and the force of vigilante terror—"the tremendous shore of southern barbarism," as songwriter-poet-novelist James Weldon Johnson described it—seems inexorable. And there is the lure of money, with jobs in the North paying much more than anything available anywhere in the South. African-American musicians are as touched by this set of magnetizing and repelling forces as everyone else is.

The thousands of New Orleanians who go north consider only one destination seriously. By 1922, so much is known about Chicago and so little about the alternatives that there is no need for deliberation. The immigrants find work in the meatpacking industry, in steel yards, and as porters, janitors, and domestics.

The *Chicago Defender*, a nationally circulating newspaper produced by and for African Americans, plays a large role. *Defender* headlines radiate across the South like a lighthouse beam of safety proclaiming the benefits of northern living, printing letters from happy newcomers, and listing timetables for northbound trains. During the first wave of the Great Migration, some 50,000 African Americans are relocating to the Windy City, greeted at the train station by huge signs that spell out "Welcome to Chicago."

On the day of his departure, Armstrong accepted a funeral job at the last minute, thinking the cash might come in handy, but it caused him to miss the train he had told Joe Oliver he would be taking. Now he isn't sure if Oliver will be at the station to greet him. As he disembarks at the 12th Street Station, the excitement of so many people waiting for taxi cabs, the vigorous hustling in all directions—it all leaves him stunned. He says goodbye to his traveling companion and her children and looks around for some help, getting more and more nervous.

Finally, a redcap offers assistance. "Oh, you are the young man who's to join King Oliver's band at Lincoln Gardens," he says. This gives the twenty-one-year-old pause, for he has never heard his mentor called "King." The redcap flags a cab and directs the driver to Lincoln Gardens, where the evening show is already in progress.

Through three seasons of playing cornet on excursion boats up and down the Mississippi River, Armstrong has drifted through a lot

*Louis, mother May Ann, and sister Beatrice, ca. 1922 (The William Russell Photographic Collection, MSS 520 F. 2041, Willliams Research Center, The Historic New Orleans Collection)*

of towns. But he has never seen a city like this, with its tall buildings, bright lights, and paved streets. The cab pulls out from the station and heads down South State Street, the most famous street in the so-called Black Belt of Chicago.

It is 10:30 p.m. and the action is just starting to crank up. Young

African-American adults live in eager anticipation of the sparkling night life. Some are known to work from 7:00 in the morning through 4:00 in the afternoon, followed by dinner and an early bedtime, only to wake up at 2:00 in the morning and head for South State Street to hang out until dawn, when they start the cycle again.

The drive takes Louis past the red-light district, just a few blocks from the train station, around 22nd Street. At 2630 South State Street is the Savoy Bar, where the legendary Tony Jackson from New Orleans used to dazzle audiences with flamboyant piano playing and falsetto singing of his composition *Pretty Baby*, the big hit of 1916. On the same block the Pekin Theater and Cabaret has also discovered the potential of New Orleans musicians to pack in audiences, having hired Oliver and pianist Jelly Roll Morton at different times, and also clarinetist Sidney Bechet, who worked the Cabaret in 1918 in a duo with Jackson. Further down the block is the apartment Oliver shares with his wife Stella, perched strategically above Jackson's Music Shop.

Now the cab approaches the hub of the 3100 block of South State, the home of Elite Café #1, the Vendome Theater, and the Grand Theater, an 800-seat stop on the TOBA circuit—Theater Owners Booking Association, also known as "Tough on Black Artists" (and also known with the word "Artists" switched to a cruder word). This is where the Creole Band from New Orleans, managed by bass player Bill Johnson and featuring cornetist Fred Keppard, made a big splash in 1915 as the first to bring what the *Defender* described as the "weird effects" of New Orleans jazz to Chicago. The Grand's offerings include a steady stream of famous blues divas.

The driver hangs left on 31st Street, heading east toward Cottage Grove Avenue. He passes the Schiller Café, where the white band from New Orleans who immodestly named themselves the "Original Dixieland Jazz Band" became popular in 1915. ("They were the first to record the music I played," wrote Armstrong in carefully chosen words.) And suddenly, a few blocks later, there it is, at 459 East 31st Street—Lincoln Gardens (formerly Royal Gardens). It is already well on its way to becoming one of the most famous venues in jazz history.

## The House That Oliver Built

As he steps out of the cab to gaze across 31st Street, music pours through the open front door, Oliver and his band playing "some kind of a real jump number." Suddenly he is in direct contact with the sound that mesmerized him during his mid-teenage years, when the Oliver–Ory band was at its popular peak in New Orleans. The moment overwhelms him and he is reluctant to go inside. Maybe he isn't good enough to join this band, he says to himself. Oliver's status exceeds even what he had achieved in New Orleans, where he was the dominant figure in Armstrong's life. Now he is the larger-than-life King of Lincoln Gardens.

A canopy stretches from the front door of the hall to the street, and along its front is a painted canvas sign spelling out the main attraction: "KING OLIVER AND HIS CREOLE JAZZ BAND." As Armstrong enters the crowded lobby, he notices how the space amplifies the music, increasing the excitement. Florence Majors, the white owner of the hall, greets him, and so does Bud Redd, the "colored" manager who works for her.

From the lobby he steps into the largest dance hall on the South Side of Chicago, which holds, according to various estimates, between 700 and 1,000 people. Tables sit along the sides, and halfway up each wall is a balcony wrapped around the interior, seating about 100 people. Benches pushed against the walls are occupied by shy ladies who lack escorts. Bright colors give the hall a festive feeling. Artificial maple leaves dangle from chicken wire strung across the ceiling, and at the very center hangs a large crystal ball, the "Ball of Fire," imported from Europe for $5,000. The hall is generally dim, with a single light above the bandstand cutting through the smoke and haze. But when the band turns to slow blues, around midnight, multicolored spotlights strike the Ball of Fire as it rotates, scattering light unpredictably over the dancers, who grind away in an embracing dance known as the Bunny Hug.

The musicians sit in a row across a four-foot-high bandstand, in traditional New Orleans format. At far (house) right is Bill Johnson, string bass and banjo. Johnson was the one who opened up this whole

*Lincoln Gardens (The William Russell Photographic Collection, MSS 520 F. 87, Willliams Research Center, The Historic New Orleans Collection)*

scene when he brought the Creole Band to Chicago in 1915. He is the oldest player (b. ca. 1874) in this band, and he's been around. In New Orleans, he sometimes played at Lulu White's legendary house of prostitution, sometimes with the Eagle Band, sometimes with the Excelsior Brass Band (tuba). Louis has never seen Johnson before, and he is fascinated because Johnson looks so much like a white person.

Next to Johnson is pianist Bertha Gonsoulin. In New Orleans, very few of the bands Armstrong knew had pianists, for the simple reason that very few of the venues they played had pianos. There was a small group of women pianists active on that scene, however, and Oliver has continued that tradition in Chicago. One role of the pianist is to respond to requests by pulling out some sheet music and reading through it, leading the rest of the band, which stumbles along, playing by ear. Violin players usually filled this role in New Orleans, but in Chicago pianos and pianists are more common. More women than men have Eurocentric training on the piano and can read music well. A female pianist also adds sex appeal, which is appreciated by the patrons and the musicians, too.

To the left of the piano sits clarinetist Johnny Dodds. Armstrong played with him in the Ory band after Oliver left New Orleans. In that band, Louis was playing lead cornet; now he will be playing second cornet, which means that he and Dodds will work closely together. Dodds is quiet, serious, and professional. He avoids alcohol, doesn't curse, and wears gloves to protect his fingers. He has little interest in material things, but likes to keep track of the Chicago White Sox every day through box scores in the newspaper. His reserved manner seems incompatible with the intensity of his funky blues playing, which has earned the nickname "toilet." He hates clowning by musicians on stage and he tries to avoid playing music he considers trivial, which he thinks of as "prostituting" himself.

Alongside Dodds sits Oliver himself, "Papa Joe," as Armstrong calls him, radiating authority. "If anyone ever looked good in front of a band it was Joe Oliver," said drummer George Wettling. "He had a way of standing in front of Johnny and Baby Dodds and the other cats that was just too much." Oliver occasionally discharges big slurps of tobacco juice into a brass cuspidor. On the other side of his chair is a bucket of sugar water with a big piece of ice in it, from which band members freely fetch drinks for themselves whenever they get thirsty. Sugar water is not a typical feature of jazz bands in Chicago, but Oliver encourages it while discouraging boozing.

To Oliver's left is trombonist Honoré Dutrey, whom Louis used to follow around when Dutrey played in parades. A good reader, Honoré played with the Excelsior band and with John Robichaux's orchestra before he joined the Navy in 1917. A ship accident seriously damaged his lungs, and Dutrey now suffers from asthma that compromises his playing and leaves him short of breath. Occasionally he scoots behind the bandstand to inhale a nasal spray the doctor has prescribed for him before he takes a solo. Dutrey is businesslike and saves his money so that he can buy property around town.

And on the far left side of the stage sits drummer Warren Dodds, Johnny's younger brother, known to all as "Baby." Louis and Baby know each other very well from their time on the riverboats, a job that Dodds lost due to a serious drinking problem. Armstrong is delighted to see that things are now going better for Baby. After the riverboat job, Dodds hung out in New Orleans until he got a surprising summons from Oliver—surprising because just a few years earlier Oliver had been one of the musicians in the Ory band who humiliated Baby by collectively walking off the stage, leaving him behind to play by himself; they repeated the stunt until Dodds got the message and stopped showing up. When the call came from Oliver to join his band in San Francisco in the middle of a tour, Dodds felt like his world had suddenly been born anew.

Oliver landed this highly visible leadership position through a formidable combination of talent, hard work, and force of will. He left New Orleans with clarinetist Jimmie Noone in the summer of 1918 to join Johnson's band at Royal Gardens. Meanwhile, a band led by New Orleans clarinetist Lawrence Duhé was thriving at the Dreamland Café, in the 3500 block of South State Street. The big draw in Duhé's band was the hand-cupping, growling cornet work of Thomas "Sugar Johnny" Smith. But Smith was dying from tuberculosis. So Duhé convinced Oliver to double up with his band. Oliver was the perfect replacement since he, too, was an expert in creatively manipulating timbre to produce freak music.

But before Duhé knew it, Oliver was stepping out and making deals for the band on his own. This might seem like a helpful gesture, but it was actually a power grab. In New Orleans there was always one person designated "manager," whose responsibility it was to contract the job, collect the money, and pay the musicians. It was a position of real advantage, especially since managers were not always straightforward about dividing up the pay. This was not the first time Oliver had hijacked the manager's responsibilities. A few years earlier, in New Orleans, Kid Ory had strategically invited Oliver to join his band; before he knew it, Oliver was contracting jobs for the "Oliver–Ory Band." Ory was shrewd enough to recognize Oliver's popularity and acquiesce.

At Lincoln Gardens, Oliver's freak style has become the main focus of his playing, and he rarely plays with an open horn. Partly as a matter of showmanship and partly as a matter of technique, he rotates through an assortment of mutes, hats, bottles, and buckets. "He'd put his hand over the mouth of the [cornet] and it would sound like a mouth organ. We used to call him 'harmonica,'" said Baby Dodds. "With an ordinary mute, [he] could make the horn talk," remembered Buster Bailey. "I never saw anyone in my life use mutes the way he did," said Barney Bigard. Oliver's talking-cornet version of *I'm Not Rough* was so compelling on his first night in Chicago that Calwell "King" Jones, master of ceremonies at Royal Gardens, placed a paper crown on his head and proclaimed him King while men in the hall threw their hats into the air in celebratory delight.

In May 1921, a little over a year before Armstrong's arrival in Chicago, management decided to renovate Royal Gardens, so Oliver took the band to California for an extended stay. In Los Angeles they worked at a multiracial "black-and-tan" cabaret that received them well and paid them nicely. Baby Dodds noted how it was during this West Coast stay that the band was first presented as "King Oliver's Creole Band." Oliver started to speak in terms of "my" rather than "our" band, and Dodds sensed a distinct change in atmosphere.

Dodds also described a lively incident in San Francisco that reveals a crucial dimension of how the new music from New Orleans was received. At a matinee performance in the California Theater, some "little smart guy" called out from the audience, "I thought you said those guys were Creoles. Those guys are no Creoles. Those are niggers!" Oliver and Dutrey immediately started chattering in French patois. "The people just stared," said Dodds.

What was Oliver thinking when he identified himself and his musicians as Creoles? Certainly no one in New Orleans had ever mistaken him for a Creole; people there thought of him as belonging to the opposite end of the social spectrum reserved for people of color—field hands from the plantations who had recently immigrated to the city. The word "Creole" pops up again and again in Chicago during the late teens and early twenties in names like the Original Creole Band, the New Orleans Creole Band, King Oliver's Creole Jazz Band, and Charlie Elgar's Creole Band. This may have begun as an attempt to siphon off some of the heavy notice granted to the Creole Band. Perhaps it was easy to confuse the public about whether or not they were going to hear the band that had moved through town with so much publicity a few years back.

But "Creole" held other kinds of appeal, too. The word instantly conjured up the sexual legends of New Orleans, with its spicy images of octoroon mistresses, available to French settlers in antebellum times, as well as their modern-day counterparts in the city's famous prostitution district. Light-skinned African Americans were regarded by many whites as highly charged with eroticism. Almost all of the skimpily clad female dancers at black-and-tan cabarets fit this profile, for example. Musicians from New Orleans found it useful to project these connotations of risqué sexuality onto the new dance music as a way to highlight its visceral, kinetic energy.

"Creole" could play out on the national stage in yet a different way. People of mixed ancestry did hold a special place in the white imagination, but according to the simplified biracialism of the United States, to be of mixed race simply meant that one was "colored" and therefore locked into the same social and legal categories that all other colored people belonged to. According to this logic, "Creole" connoted black authenticity from New Orleans, and that was, in some quarters, becoming a desirable musical identity to have. "Creole" helped Oliver and his band separate themselves from white "imitators," which was something black minstrel bands had been trying to do for a long time. The nationwide success in 1917 of the Original Dixieland Jazz Band, the white group that raked in financial rewards for ripping off black music, gave this logic an urgent punch.

In any event, Armstrong must have chuckled when he heard the story about Oliver pretending to be a Creole and chattering patois in California. Many Creoles in New Orleans lived a snooty life apart, clinging to their ethnically defining ways. As an acknowledged master of the new music that had developed in *his* section of town and was now becoming popular elsewhere, the old Creole arrogance must have mattered to Oliver very little. To borrow a phrase Oliver sometimes used, he could "make some good jack" on the word "Creole." I doubt that it meant anything more to him than that.

By summer 1922, King Oliver's Creole Jazz Band was back in Chicago, with renovations complete and Royal Gardens reopened as Lincoln Gardens. Intent on hiring Oliver, the owner paid moving expenses for the band's return from California. On June 21 she took out an advertisement in the *Defender*: "Dance to the Music of JOE OLIVER'S CREOLE JAZZ BAND/JUST BACK FROM A GREAT YEAR ON THE COAST/ Entertainers Refreshments." One report has the band making a weekly salary of $1,000 (the figure seems high, since Baby Dodds said his take was $55 per week). Oliver wrote to Little Louis, the only student he ever took, to come and join him, and he dipped into his stash of jack to buy a one-way train ticket. "You can stick your stinkin' feet in my bed," he wrote.

Oliver's soaring popularity boded well for Armstrong, who must have seen the opportunity as one that would bring him to a higher level of compensation and also artistry. The job would allow him to resume the apprenticeship that had been interrupted when Oliver left for Chicago in 1918; that is one way to think of his 1922–24 stay with Oliver's band. On the other hand, it's not clear that he still needed any apprenticing, since his cornet playing was now impressing a lot of people. Paul Mares, a white cornetist from New Orleans who liked to hang around the bandstand at Lincoln Gardens, teased Oliver about the "kid" he had heard back home: "If he ever gets here, you're dead." Oliver's own band members asked him, perhaps innocently or perhaps not, whether Louis was being brought in to play first cornet or second, to which Oliver could only stammer in response: "It's my band. What am I going to do, play second?"

*Interior of Royal Gardens, ca. 1919 (University Library of Southern Denmark)*

## The Floor Show

The hall at Lincoln Gardens is crowded, and Oliver doesn't notice his protégé's arrival until he gets close to the bandstand. He stops the set to make introductions. "Have a seat, son, we're going to do our show," he says. "You might as well stick around and see what's happening because you start work tomorrow night." Those who haven't seen Louis for a while are surprised by his appearance. Wearing a brown, box-back, double-breasted suit with padded shoulders, a pair of wide pants, a straw hat, and tan shoes, he weighs 226 pounds, his stomach protruding noticeably and his clothes too small. They greet him as "Dipper Mouth" and "Little Louis," names from his childhood, the latter now with a laugh due to his expanding bulk. He combs his hair in bangs.

With the introductions complete, the band returns to the floor show, already in progress.

The canvas sign at the front entrance makes clear that Oliver is the main draw; his band follows in second place, and the floor show follows that. Yet a floor show is still part of a ticket holder's expectations, still part of a fun night on the town. Armstrong has seen this kind of entertainment before, but never with Papa Joe Oliver's band playing the most inspiring music he has ever heard in the background. Similar blends of music and entertainment will remain part of his professional activity for decades.

Oliver's band played mainly for dancing back in New Orleans. The music had a few additional uses there, such as the famous "funeral with music," but jazz did not become heavily entangled with vaudeville until it left the city. When that happened it was immediately tainted by the trappings of blackface minstrelsy. Jelly Roll Morton, for example, masked himself with black grease paint for comic performances in the early 1910s. A reviewer from 1912 described him as "grotesque in his makeup," an impression that is confirmed by a surviving photograph of the great bandleader-composer-pianist.

The success of the Creole Band, which left New Orleans in 1914 for extensive tours, crisscrossing the Midwest and Northwest and dipping into Canada, alerted other New Orleanian musicians to the potential of vaudeville. At the center of the Creole Band's act was a skit described by one newspaper as "the familiar 'Uncle' and 'the boys' [routine] which has been a part of colored shows and touring minstrels for years." It was through this bit of racist theater that the nation was first exposed to the exotic new music from New Orleans.

The Creole Band's skit was performed in front of a backdrop painting of a plantation, with log cabin, the master's big house, and "many little darkie huts" scattered amidst blossoming cotton fields. The musicians dressed as slaves. After a long work day they decided to wander over to the cabin of Old Black Joe, portrayed by Morgan Prince, who wore black grease paint, a long coat, simple hat, gray beard, and a wig. With a full moon rising slowly in the background, Bill Johnson began to play *My Old Kentucky Home* on his string bass, his music magically putting "vigor into the old man's rheumatic knees," as one reviewer put it. After this, Prince and the entire band performed Stephen Foster's *Old Black Joe*, the infectious ragtime rhythms loosening up Joe's arthritic knees and causing him to dance in a way that held tremendous comic appeal. The musicians then sang the song in close, barbershop-style harmony, according to the improvising, African-American vocal tradition that was especially strong in New Orleans.

For a reviewer in Peoria, the *Old Black Joe* skit revealed "the southern plantation darky as he really is in his sportive hours." In Dubuque the scenery was felt to be "romantic in its picturesqueness and appealing in its charm." For a student newspaper at Purdue University, the whole production was "good, clean, wholesome and enjoyable." Entertainment like this was an essential part of how the nation was still trying to reconcile itself to the Civil War, still trying to heal wounds that had been festering for five decades. This was accomplished by romanticizing slavery. Late minstrelsy was doing what minstrelsy had always done—helping the white nation define blacks as inferior. It served the new project of locking blacks into the "separate but equal" place that was being mapped out through the expanding legal system of Jim Crow.

Thinking of the darkies on stage as authentic was an important part of the wholesome fun. Their syncopating skill was so strong that it could only have been "born in the bone," in one writer's estimation. "The mask of minstrelsy is torn off," said another from Sioux City, meaning that in contrast to white imitators, the Creole Band offered the real thing; they performed songs that, he believed, had been passed down from antebellum times. "They all hail from New Orleans and were working on the levee there when they were picked up by a café owner, who engaged them to play in his restaurant," wrote another in full-blown fantasy. More knowingly came this from an African-American weekly: "It is an act that shows very clearly what the white theatre patrons like the colored performer to do."

At least one member of the Creole Band was a descendant of the middle-caste *gens de couleur libres* of antebellum New Orleans. None had ever worked a levee or lived on a plantation. Their new white audiences believed that they represented the plantation culture of old, not the urban transformation of that culture that had so gloriously emerged in New Orleans. And represented it in pathetic terms, as a culture of subservience, superstition, illiteracy, ignorance, and inferiority, one that belonged to people who were formerly in chains and who now took their "natural" place at the economic bottom of society, happily and innocently generating wealth for those above.

For three extended vaudeville seasons, middle America flocked to see the Creole Band strum and strut and sing in full-on displays of minstrelsy. Jazz was surrounded by plantation imagery as soon as it left New Orleans, and the theme would keep crowding in on Armstrong for the rest of his life. In the early 1930s he picked up *When It's Sleepy Time Down South* as his signature song, with its imagery of "darkies crooning under a pale moon" in blissful ignorance. In 1942 he performed the song for a movie short by the same name, seated on a cotton bale in plaid shirt with a farmer's hat—the full dress of the authentic plantation darky, displayed for a new generation of white Americans. In the early 1950s, as the fervor for civil rights started to take hold, African Americans burned his recordings of the song in protest, forcing him to reissue it with revised lyrics. "Louis is the plantation character that so many of us . . . younger men . . . resent," explained Dizzy Gillespie in 1949. Gillespie and Armstrong later became close friends, but others found it difficult to loosen his image from these degrading fantasies.

But in 1922, King Oliver and his bandmates are not slicked out in blackface, and they are not trying to convey a sense of retrogressive plantation authenticity. Indeed, the floor show at Lincoln Gardens differs from the Creole Band's in a fundamental way: the audience here in Chicago is overwhelmingly black. The very name of the hall telegraphs the demographics of the place. Venues that are mainly black take less in at the box office than cabarets with substantial white patronage, and that accounts for the relatively slender dimensions of the floor show here. But the patrons prefer dancing anyway, so the emphasis on Oliver and his band works for everybody.

King Jones, master of ceremonies, directs the floor show. He leads the good time by having one himself, or at least appearing to. He dances in front of the band and sometimes pretends to conduct it, making a farce out of his obvious lack of connection to the music. The band pays no attention to him and the people love it. Jones is from the Caribbean and puts on a show of pompous British mannerisms, announcing the acts with tremendous projection, "Ladies and Gentlemen . . ."

One or perhaps two singers are featured; someone named

"Bodidly" has been associated with the place, and so has Ethel Waters. As with virtually all floor shows during this period, the centerpiece of the presentation is a row of light-skinned dancing girls; we know of one group named Miss Cleo Mitchell and Her Fast Steppers. Ma Rainey's traveling troupe is the exception to the rule of café au lait skin, reportedly because the singer doesn't want to perform with women who are lighter than she is, a policy that wins her favor with southern audiences.

Armstrong already knows one part of the floor show very well—drummer Baby Dodds doing his "shimmy beat," a bit of musical comedy that has Dodds shaking his stomach muscles in time with his drumming. Always a hit, Dodds's shimmy routine may have even been the reason Oliver invited him to join the band. Oliver had been reluctant, but Dave Jones, who was with both Dodds and Armstrong on the riverboat band, insisted he give Baby the call, despite his known liabilities. "That fellow is just as big a drawing card as Louis Armstrong," said Jones. Armstrong might have agreed with that, since he later wrote that Baby's shimmy "was in my estimation the whole worth of the price of admission."

For the climax of the floor show the band performs a piece known as *Eccentric*, based on *That Eccentric Rag*. Oliver used to perform the piece in New Orleans, and now for Lincoln Gardens he has discovered its vaudeville potential. The focus is on the "breaks"—brief moments at the ends of phrases where the background accompaniment stops and a soloist offers a little bit of dazzle. Usually a break is one or at most two measures (a measure defined as four beats), but Oliver's arrangement of *Eccentric* includes breaks of four full measures, alternating with four measures of activity from the band.

The unusual format leaves room for a dash of racially inflected comedy during the last chorus. In the break, Oliver imitates a baby with his wah-wah cornet, and as he does, bassist Bill Johnson walks over to pet the instrument. The first time they do this, Oliver's cornet is identified as a white baby, and Johnson soothes it, "Don't cry, little baby." The last time the baby is "colored"—"Baaaah! Baaaaaaaaah!" it bawls, causing Johnson to yell, "Shut up, you li'l so and sooooooo." This brings down the house with thunderous laughter and applause.

Perhaps it surprises Louis at least a little to see Oliver's skill and

*Oliver's orchestra in San Francisco, 1921 (Courtesy of the New Orleans Jazz Club Collections of the Louisiana State Museum)*

creativity being channeled into a racially charged bit of minstrelsy. Johnson's almost-white appearance is part of the skit. "You would swear he was a white boy," remembered Armstrong. "He had all the features, even the voice—yes he really did look like an o'fay (southern boy)." It is a fresh twist on black-faced masking—a person of racial ambiguity who can change his identity right before your eyes. Johnson has a nice comic touch, an "unlimited" sense of humor in Armstrong's estimation, honed no doubt during his years of touring with the Creole Band. *Eccentric* is thus built on a felicitous blend of talents, Oliver's skillful and creative freak music combined with Johnson's white appearance and comic timing. The package is completely new to Armstrong, and he stares in fascination.

A publicity photograph of Oliver's band taken on their California tour earlier that year shows the musicians posed in plantation outfits, the same kind of farm clothes that the Creole Band used earlier in its authentic rendition of *Old Black Joe*. But at Lincoln Gardens, Oliver and his men are tricked out in tuxedoes. These are some of the terms of presenting jazz in the various venues where it is performed. Armstrong has only been in the city for a few hours, but he is already getting a sense of what the long trip from New Orleans to Chicago might mean.

## The Dance

After intermission comes the dance segment of the evening. Dancing is difficult when the hall is crowded, but everyone has a good time anyway. "The people came to dance. One couldn't help but dance to that band," remembered Baby Dodds. "The music was so wonderful that they had to do something, even if there was only room to bounce around." Bud Freeman described the dance floor as "a picture of rhythm such as I had never seen."

Oliver directs the music with very few words. To let the musicians know what tune is coming, he turns around and softly toots a few notes. He sets the tempo by beating his foot against the foundation of his brass cuspidor. Musicians admire his knack for determining just the right speed, one appropriate for the piece and for the audience, a skill considered to be the mark of a good bandleader in New Orleans. That attitude still holds in Chicago, and it will continue into the swing era and beyond; musicians would praise both Ellington and Basie, for example, for an uncanny sense of judging the mood of a hall and responding with the right tempo.

Yet, even though Oliver has had a great deal of experience, he has been forced to adjust to a different set of expectations in Chicago. There is a demand for tempos faster than the typical pace of New Orleans. African-American dance halls in the uptown section of New Orleans featured blues played at an extremely slow tempo to accompany the "slow drag." Most other dances were moderate. In Chicago, tempos all around are noticeably ratcheted up. "The fastest numbers played by old New Orleans bands were slower than the Chicago tempo," said guitarist Johnny St. Cyr.

There are several reasons for this regional difference. For one thing, it is easier to generate excitement and disguise musical inadequacies with a fast tempo, just as low-quality beer is more drinkable when it is ice-cold. "When musicians from other places . . . played hot, they just played fast," said Emmanuel Sayles. "That's what people called playing hot." New Orleans musicians, on the other hand, could "play hot and at the same time be playing in a groovy tempo where you [could] dance or clap your hands or join him."

The fast tempos also have something to do with a different conception of what dancing is about. The famous team of Irene and Vernon Castle promoted dancing as exercise, which helped legitimize the peppy ragtime dances of the 1910s that gave way to the peppy jazz dances of the early 1920s. "We are making ourselves lithe and slim and healthy, and these are things that all reformers in the world could not do for us," wrote Irene. It's hard to know if this idea reached the patrons of Lincoln Gardens, but one thing is certain: the idea of dance as health-inducing exercise had never occurred to the patrons of Funky Butt Hall in New Orleans, which was named after a grinding dance, moving the "rear end like an alligator crawling up a bank," in one observer's description.

But in Chicago, dancing for health is a good way to brush back charges of immorality. An article in the *Defender* from September 1, 1923, notes approvingly how King Jones is "in charge of the dance floor" at Lincoln Gardens and how "correct dancing is insisted upon." Behind that remark stands the work of white reform organizations like the Juvenile Protective Association, which takes as its mission the hiring of chaperones to go out on the town and inspect the dance halls firsthand. When a chaperone sees a couple staying in one spot too long he barks out, embarrassingly, "Get off that dime, man. Let's move it around." The ultimate threat is forced closure of the hall. This kind of intervention is also completely alien to the transplanted New Orleanians.

Faster tempos alter both the dancing and the music. Tempo guides an improviser's approach to musical design and shapes the listener's sense of sonic patterning. Isolated gestures stand out and carry more weight at a leisurely tempo. There is also a greater sense of the independence of melodic lines, which happens to be a central feature of Oliver's band. Since African-American jazz from New Orleans did not get recorded until the musicians migrated north, the earliest sonic documents we have of this music are conditioned by the faster Chicago tempos. It is bracing to think of this skewed situation as determined by an attempt to banish sexualized movement.

The tempos may be new to Armstrong, but the repertory is not. *High Society*, one of the favorites, was an old New Orleans standard brought from street marches into dance halls early on. A recording by the Oliver band in 1923 clocks in at the standard length for all recordings of vernacular music during this period—around three minutes. But at Lincoln Gardens the band likes to stretch out with *High Society*. King Jones steps in front, turns to look back at the leader, and shouts, "Oh! One more chorus, King!" When Oliver eventually decides it is time to finish, he signals the final chorus with a single stomp on the floor. Having brought the heady rush of one driving chorus after another to its end, he pulls the cornet away from his lips, glances down at a young admirer, and winks while he says, "Hotter than a 45." (Or, more colorfully: "We were hotter than a pussy with the pox.") A few patrons dance the entire time, but many find a way to move in time with the music while they listen. And some of those listening at Lincoln Gardens are a bit surprising to Armstrong on his first evening in Chicago.

## The Alligators

Around the bandstand are clustered a set of ten tables or so, seating about 50 people. Sometimes referred to as "ringside" seating, the area forms a sort of barrier between the musicians and the dancers. It feels like a special place, one that marks a unique kind of participation in the musical event. It is a zone where the participants do not dance but listen. Ringside at Lincoln Gardens is often populated by musicians. And not just any musicians—white musicians.

By the time of Armstrong's arrival in August 1922, Lincoln Gardens has become well established as a hangout for young white players who are in awe of Oliver and his group. "There were *lots* of the musicians from downtown Chicago—hurrying from their jobs—to *dig* us every night that we played at the Lincoln Gardens," wrote Armstrong. Louis Panico, cornetist in Isham Jones's prestigious band, is there on Armstrong's first night. Drummer Dave Tough, saxophonist Bud Freeman, and cornetist Jimmy McPartland attend regularly. Cornetist Wingy Manone will soon acquire the honor of being the "first white boy musician" Armstrong will ever meet. Paul Mares and his colleagues in the future New Orleans Rhythm Kings like to hang around, and so do guitarist Eddie Condon, drummer George Wettling, and cornetist Muggsy Spanier. A young Benny Goodman will eventually make his appearance, and even the lofty Paul Whiteman stops by now and then.

"Well it looks like the little white boys is here to get their music lessons"—that is how the 300-pound bouncer, half teasingly, half menacingly, likes to greet the young musicians at the door. Condon, a little nervous, rides his bike to the hall and recruits older acquaintances to come with him. "A nod or a wave of [Oliver's] hand was all that was necessary," remembered Condon. "Then the customers knew that the kids were all right. Night after night we made the trip." Wettling claims his favorite place at the table on the far side, right in front of Baby Dodds. Spanier and a few others are brave enough to ask if they can play with the band from time to time.

The scene is totally new for Armstrong. In New Orleans he rarely heard white musicians play, and never got to know any of them. The reason was simple: it was "because New Orleans was so disgustingly segregated and prejudiced at the time—it didn't even run across our minds," as he bluntly explained. He made some acquaintances during his time on the riverboats, but that, too, was unusual and fraught with the tension of enforced segregation on a floating object. Here at Lincoln Gardens, white musicians have their own ringside seating in front of the bandstand. Nothing in his previous experience of race resembles this.

Management has good reason to accommodate the eager guests. Simply put, far more money is to be made from whites than can ever be made from blacks. Lincoln Gardens is thriving as a place for African-American dancers, but why not expand a little bit and see what happens? A black-and-tan cabaret like the Sunset Café, which is much pricier, makes it a point to attract whites, and the higher income benefits both the owners and the blacks who work there. The white clientele at Lincoln Gardens is mainly musicians and other entertainers.

With the venue packing in crowds of up to 1,000, it can afford to pay musicians pretty well. But if a step can be taken in the direction of the black-and-tan cabarets, this is surely something to explore. Hence the best seating in the house, right under the tips of the musicians' fingers. A few of the youngsters have convinced themselves that the preferential seating is offered as a sign of respect, but others are more realistic. "They were always happy to see white people come . . . because we had the money," remembered Wild Bill Davison. "So there was no bad treatment. You got the best of it, really, whether they liked you or not."

At some point in 1923 management will experiment with a whites-only night on Wednesdays. Known as the "midnight ramble," the format calls for the band to quit playing at 11:00 p.m., at which point black customers are asked to leave the hall so that whites can enter for a midnight show that carries a ticket price bigger than usual. The experiment does not appear to have gathered many customers beyond the musicians who had been coming all along. "We'd just sit and listen to these guys," pianist Tom Thibeau remembered. "White musicians mainly, just sitting around listening to these Negroes play." In separate discussions, Paul Barbarin, Baby Dodds, and Bud Freeman concurred: "I never saw any white people outside of our own clique," Freeman remembered.

Everyone knows that it is not simply a thirst for entertainment that draws them in. They are there for their lessons. "All of us white boys were coming and borrowing from King Oliver," remembered Hoagy Carmichael. Oliver and his colleagues have had prior experience with white musicians ripping them off and taking credit for their inventions, but now the situation involves bigger numbers of participants, sustained exposure, and higher stakes. Whites in New Orleans showed little interest in early jazz, so there was not really much of an engine to drive the project of white musicians stealing black music. In Chicago, that project is gaining strength. The New Orleanians have a name for the white predators, one suited with certain irony to their Louisiana homeland: they call them "alligators." "They were guys who came up to swallow everything we had," explained clarinetist Buster Bailey.

There are stories about ringside musicians transferring what they hear into musical notation that they scribble on their cuffs. "The white man can write down the black man's musical riffs and chord changes on his shirt cuff, but he will never be able to capture the black man's rhythm on paper," insisted one observer. The image serves as a symbol of cross-racial appropriation, the on-the-fly attempt to capture the slippery essence of largely unnotatable music. With repetition, good musicians can memorize what they hear, just as Armstrong did when he listened to Oliver in New Orleans. "It got so that I knew every phrase and intonation they played, just from listening," said Spanier. "In spite of myself, I was doing the same things—as nearly as possible, of course." A few weeks after Armstrong's arrival, Paul Mares and the New Orleans Rhythm Kings released their very first recording, on Gennett Records, a version of *Eccentric* that is full of the freak inflections that Mares and everyone else were admiring at Lincoln Gardens.

Baby Dodds appreciated the social interaction that was possible in Chicago, but he also acknowledged the exploitation: "We gave those fellows the time [i.e., rhythm] in music that they have now. In a way we gave something away." What makes the situation so exploitive is the fact that the best-paying jobs—not just in Chicago, but everywhere in the United States—are open only to whites. Blacks have no reason to even think of playing at places like the Drake Hotel and the resorts at Edgewater Beach. And in the back of everybody's mind looms the monster success of the Original Dixieland Jazz Band recording in 1917. "Should have been Freddie's," said Louis, referring to Fred Keppard's decision to turn down an offer to record, thus missing fame that instead went to white imitators who called themselves "original" nevertheless.

The little white boys are motivated to learn the music and cash in, but there is more to it than that. This music touches them deeply, in ways they may not fully understand. People their age all across the nation are attracted to the fresh sounds of jazz, but most of them are able to hear only white musicians. The bicycling youngsters in Chicago feel like they have stumbled on the authentic, original source. "We never went back to the New Orleans Rhythm Kings after hearing the King Oliver band, because we realized that in hearing the King Oliver band we were listening to the real thing," said Bud Freeman. White musicians from New Orleans who learned from blacks are often ambivalent or deny the relationship altogether; here, it is freely acknowledged.

Some of the alligators are children of immigrants from Europe. As they turn away from the Old World culture of their parents, in the American pattern, up pops African-American jazz. The alarming

*King Oliver's Creole Jazz Band: Johnny Dodds, Baby Dodds, Honoré Dutrey, Armstrong, Joe Oliver, Lillian Hardin, Bill Johnson (The William Russell Photographic Collection, MSS 520 F. 3339, Williams Research Center, The Historic New Orleans Collection)*

trend gives rise to a growing opposition, full of shrill and desperate rhetoric. The music appeals to the lower instincts. It threatens the civilizing power of reason. "The statistics of illegitimacy in this country show a great increase in recent years," writes one newspaper, and jazz is the cause. "Jazz brought about the downfall of 1,000 women in Chicago alone," hysterically writes another. No wonder the *Defender* nods approvingly at King Jones's efforts to control the dance floor.

For it is clear to everyone that the matter extends beyond taste, morals, and instincts: it is also about race. Jazz is putting the country in danger of "falling prey to the collective soul of the Negro." Some of the ringside alligators are aware of how their musical fascination blends into a fascination with Negroes. They represent the first fully documented linkage of teenage rebellion with black music, a pattern that would become a twentieth-century archetype. Youths turning from Old World culture and those rejecting the "broad lawns and narrow minds" (Ernest Hemingway's phrase) of bourgeois America, find in jazz a liberating release from inhibition, a breakthrough embrace of sexuality, a feisty rejection of parental control. As he watches the black dancers and listens to the black music, saxophonist Freeman sees "this freedom of spirit that we whites didn't have." Drummer Dave Tough would marry a black woman, and so would clarinetist Mezz Mezzrow (born Milton Mesirow), another alligator who eventually developed a special friendship with Armstrong.

Someone once quipped that whites in the United States imitate Indians as children and blacks as teenagers. Music supplies the magnetic energy for the latter embrace. In their pull toward jazz at what they imagine to be its point of origin, the alligators are ahead of the curve. The wellspring flowing freely on the South Side of their hometown beckons them with unmatched excitement and creative brilliance. "I was not only hearing a new form of music but was experiencing a whole new way of life," gushed Freeman.

The contrast between the way these young musicians engage with King Oliver's Creole Jazz Band and the way the average vaudeville patron engaged with the Creole Band's *Old Black Joe*, just a few years before, is complex and revealing. Both groups orient themselves toward the music as a sonic-visual phenomenon rather than as a kinetic one; this in itself marks a shift for the New Orleanians, who have been deeply trained, as members of the African diaspora, to associate virtually all music they make with moving bodies. Both of these northern groups take a reflective attitude toward the music. The earlier vaudeville audience found a confirmation of racist ideology through the performance, a glimpse of what the slaves were really like, and a reassurance that, in essence, the situation had not changed during the intervening decades. The spectacle confirmed what they had been told so often and in so many different ways—that blacks really are fundamentally different and absolutely inferior. They may have emerged with some appreciation for the music, but that is largely unexamined. In contrast, white musicians are drawn to Lincoln Gardens by enthusiasm for the music, along with a mysterious conceptual blend of what the music represents socially, what it can do for them emotionally, and what it has to do with their emerging adult identity.

The numbers are dramatically disproportionate: thousands

watched the *Old Black Joe* routine during the Creole Band's tours, but only a small handful, probably fewer than 50 altogether, sit ringside at Lincoln Gardens. As we watch Armstrong's career unfold during the next decade or so, we will see these proportions shift. It will not happen right away, but eventually the kind of appreciation cultivated by the alligators will spread until, in the mid-1930s, it lights up the nation, a phase of musical energy known as the swing era. Yet the more degrading view will never completely disappear, and the two will mix together in subtle ways. Armstrong's national success will be heavily conditioned by these styles of white engagement—indeed, he will be a primary agent shaping the phenomenon.

One writer in the 1920s described African-American migration from the South to the North as movement from a medieval world to a modern one. Armstrong hardly thought of his train ride in that way. Indeed, one comfort of the relocation was the strong network of New Orleanian colleagues in Chicago; what attracted him, in other words, were the familiar ways of home, musical and otherwise. Nevertheless, August 8, 1922, was an important day in jazz history. He and his friends from New Orleans made something new in the chilly urban North, spurred on by their fellow immigrants who came looking for a better life and wanted music to go along with it. Chicago would become his home, and from there he would make his mark.

# TWO

# Oliver's Band and the "Blues Age"

Everybody from New Orleans can really do that thing.
— Louis Armstrong, *Gut Bucket Blues*

**We do not have a lot of information about the patrons who threw their hats in the air** to proclaim Joe Oliver the King of Lincoln Gardens. It was not a black-and-tan club, for the only whites were youngsters who came for their music lessons, along with the occasional celebrity stopping by while in town for a gig.[2] Drummer Paul Barbarin said that African-American patrons at the hall "had come up to Chicago from all over the South, and a lot of them were in there every night . . . people from Georgia or New Orleans, you know, people moving up for better conditions." They dressed up and paid 25 cents (plus coat check) to enter a hall that was not especially fancy but was certainly a step up from anything they had known back home.

"In Chicago an opportunity is offered musicians," wrote music columnist Dave Peyton in the *Chicago Defender*, "and we must make good if humanly possible." To understand the environment that nurtured Armstrong's musical maturity, it is important to consider this burgeoning black population; in a sense, Armstrong and his musical friends were responding to the situation the immigrants had created. The biography of Milton Hinton, who was born in Vicksburg, Mississippi, in 1910 and moved to Chicago in 1919, illustrates the immigrant experience and expectations. Hinton eventually established a career for himself as a bass player, and even toured with Armstrong a bit in the 1950s.

Hinton's family was inspired to leave Mississippi by a complex

40

*Cotton pickers, Pulaski County, Arkansas, 1944 (Library of Congress)*

mixture of fear and hope, idealism and practicality, collective allegiance and the urge to step out as individuals. The move took nine years for the family to complete, and it demanded a degree of secrecy. They were driven by a combination of extreme poverty and deadly barbarism. The move meant more to them than it did to Armstrong, who moved mainly to expand his career options, which were already solid in New Orleans.

Milt spent his first nine years in his grandmother Hetty's three-room house, along with Hetty's five surviving children. Hetty had been born a slave, and in the 1910s she washed, ironed, and cooked for a white family for $3.50 per week. Milt's mother Hilda, the only one of Hetty's children to receive schooling, worked for churches as a pianist most of her life. (It is often the case that our best sources for the history of African-American life during this period come from people who were positioned relatively high on scales of income and education. The fact that Hinton's mother was the only person in her family to be educated accounts, ultimately, for the fact that we have a lot of information about him and far less about people who were less educated. This widespread historical problem skews the historical record in many ways.) The church choir rehearsed at Hetty's house because she owned a piano. Booker T. Washington wrote about dining with sharecroppers in Alabama who lacked cutlery, but somehow managed to scrape together payments for an organ. "[Hetty] must have paid 50 cents a week on it for like a hundred years," Hinton imagined.

Walking home one day, Hinton witnessed a lynching. Flames roared up around the body of a black man hanging from a wire attached to a tree limb, while a group of men made a sport of firing bullets into it. The next day the tree was cut down, its stump painted red. Hinton remembered his grandmother putting black pepper in his socks, a desperate tactic designed to keep away tracking dogs used for lynching hunts.

The move to Chicago was inspired by the local preacher. As the tide of emigration began to swell and white businessmen could plainly see the implications of a dwindling supply of cheap labor, *Defender* sales were banned in some locations, while pastors were bribed to discourage departure. Reverend Jones took the opposite stance and praised the glories of Chicago. When word of his activism eventually leaked out, he was run out of town.

"In 1910 a black man could not just leave Mississippi and go North," insisted Hinton. "He had to have some excuse." His uncle Bob lied to his employer about needing to visit a sick relative in Memphis; instead he moved directly to Chicago and found work as a hotel porter. Hinton explained that porters were typically southern immigrants who knew how to dish out the "yes sirs"—"what we consider Uncle Tom." The family followed Bob gradually, Milt finally leaving with his grandmother and aunt in 1919, dressed in a little suit and cap his mother had sent.

When the Hintons arrived in Chicago, perhaps they shared with novelist Richard Wright the disorienting experience of looking around in vain for the "White" and "Colored" signs they knew from Mississippi. Perhaps they hesitated, as Wright did, to sit next to a white man on a streetcar. If they gathered courage to take that seat, perhaps they were disturbed by the icy anonymity of their new surroundings, as Wright was. The family settled in an apartment on 36th Street, around the corner from cornetist Fred Keppard. Hinton recalled a "beautiful childhood" in Chicago. His aunts and uncles all held jobs while Hetty watched over him. Uncle Matt was "crazy" about Louis Armstrong and liked to pick out popular songs by ear on the piano, a cigarette dangling from his lips. His mother and her boyfriend led group singing around the piano.

Hinton's mother joined a club of former residents from Vicksburg. For Hinton, Chicago was a place where adults looked out for other people's children and where neighbors helped when someone took sick. Men worked in meat-packing and steel industries or on the railroad, women in the garment industry and as domestics. A neighborhood man called "Pappy," also from Vicksburg, asked if he could join the family on Sundays; since he worked in the stockyards, he always brought meat for dinner. Milt was fascinated by his hands, stained white from his job salting pork, in contrast with the dark skin on the rest of his body. After dinner with the family, Pappy got comfortable in a living room chair and took a nap.

Life on the South Side was not flawlessly peaceful. The 1919 race riots, provoked by the murder of a hapless African-American youth who had wandered into a white swimming area, were the most obvious reminders of that. The riots were violent and shocking; at least one musician from New Orleans (pianist-composer-publisher Clarence Williams) dodged a bullet and immediately dashed to New York. But their impact was different from that of the so-called Robert Charles riots in New Orleans in the summer of 1900, a year before Armstrong's birth. African Americans in Chicago gave as much as they got and showed an ability to defend themselves. And the Chicago riots were followed by a nonpartisan Interracial Commission on Race Relations that ended up recommending increased city services in black neighborhoods, the elimination of segregation at places of public accommodation, and capitalization of the word "Negro."

On the South Side it was possible to shop in Negro-owned stores, be assisted by Negro policemen, be represented by a Negro state senator—and even, in 1928, by a Negro in the House of Representatives of the United States of America. Black achievement was everywhere, the world of white exploitation somewhat hidden. "Anybody I saw was black in the metropolitan area," Hinton remembered. "There was no white–black problem because our whole community was black." People called themselves "colored," which "sounded a

*Selling the* Defender *(Library of Congress)*

little soft and pleasing to our ears," he said. " 'Negro' was an academic word, and "black" was considered offensive."

"There was no thought of integration back there in Chicago," he explained, "they just wanted to live nice amongst themselves." The *Defender*'s claim that migration was a "second Emancipation" did not seem like an exaggeration. The phrase most often used by those who moved north, when asked about personal goals, was "to better my position," which meant, at the least, education, voting rights, facilities that were truly equal, and good-paying jobs. "A thousand percent better than we had in Mississippi," was Hinton's view. Mahalia Jackson, a year younger than Hinton and arriving in Chicago in 1927, said it was possible for someone there to "lay down his burden of being a colored person in the white man's world and lead his own life."

The word "freedom" was often heard—freedom from humiliation, freedom to vote, freedom to quit a job, freedom to walk around town. Freedom could mean reinventing a personal identity. Tony Jackson, the great pianist, songwriter, and entertainer, moved from New Orleans to Chicago early in part because of the liberation it offered him as a homosexual (*macommère* in New Orleans). "He felt more free in Chicago than in his hometown," explained Jelly Roll Morton. There must have been a broad sense that in Chicago it was possible to escape social restrictions and blossom in a place where the new and forward-looking was popping up everywhere you turned.

## Blues People

After the gig at Lincoln Gardens was finished, Oliver escorted Louis to his apartment at 31st and State Streets, where Oliver's wife Stella served up a late meal. Louis's mind jumped back to his mid-teenage years, when he visited Oliver's house for cornet lessons and meals in exchange for running errands. Sitting down to the spread of red beans, rice, bread, and lemonade made him feel secure. "They were a happy family and I became one of them," he remembered.

Oliver then took him to a nearby boardinghouse where he had arranged a room. He mentioned that the room had a private bath, but Louis didn't know what that meant, prompting some edgy teasing from Oliver. "He had forgotten that he must have asked the same question when he first came up from New Orleans," wrote Armstrong. "In the neighborhood where we lived we never heard of such a thing as a bathtub, let alone a *private bath*." His hostess was a woman from New Orleans named Filo. "Is this my home boy?" she asked as he stepped inside. Filo made money on the side brewing strong beer.

A guy from New Orleans named Nicholas lived there, too, and

the next day Filo cooked the two of them a Creole dish with shrimp, chicken, and oysters. Armstrong spelled the dish phonetically as "Feefay" ("I give you the sound and you go on from there," he wrote; probably *étouffée*). He ate so much that it hurt. He understood at this moment that he was not going to get homesick. In the afternoon Nicholas showed him around town. They stopped first at Ed Victor's Barber Shop, on South State Street between 33rd and 34th Streets. Ed was another New Orleanian, and his shop was full of gambling and camaraderie. Surrounded by men from home, Louis forgot where he was. Jelly Roll Morton liked to roll up in front of the place in his chauffeur-driven Cadillac, his entourage right behind in a Stutz Bearcat that he also owned. It is difficult to track the comings and goings of the musicians from New Orleans precisely, but it has been estimated that some 20 to 30 were in town around this time.

For some, the old caste distinction between downtown Creoles of color and uptown Negroes no longer mattered, it being more important to stick together and solidify common advantages, which were considerable. That attitude was not universally shared, and Fred Keppard, for one, urged his fellow Creoles to speak in French dialect as a gesture of exclusion. But for the most part, the New Orleanian musicians, Negro and Creole, were known as a cliquish society that excluded musicians from other places. "The only time a New Orleans leader hired a musician who was not from . . . Louisiana, was when he couldn't get one from there," explained Preston Jackson. Just as Hinton's mother enjoyed the company of people who had relocated from Vicksburg, so did the transplanted New Orleanian musicians find comfort in their familiar ways.

The neighborhood was full of excitement. Jack Johnson, boxing champ and hero to African Americans everywhere, had a mansion nearby. From the barbershop, Nicholas pointed across the street to Mecca Flats, a huge apartment building that took up a whole block and was full of so-called buffet flats. In Nicholas's opinion, they compared favorably with the famous prostitution halls of Storyville and served "everything from soup to nuts." "He could see from the expression on my face that I could hardly wait [to visit]," Armstrong wrote. Pianists who worked in Mecca Flats sometimes camped out for days without leaving the building.

*Mecca Flats, 34th and South State Streets (The William Russell Photographic Collection, MSS 520 F. 730, Williams Research Center, The Historic New Orleans Collection)*

Back at home he took a nap, and when he got up Filo offered a ham sandwich covered with pineapple and brown sugar. "You got to do a lot of blowing and you need something to hold you up," she said. He put on his "roast beef" ("that was what we called an old ragged tuxedo"), satisfied that the wear spots and patches would be noticed only by people standing very close. At 8:30 p.m. a cab arrived to take him to Lincoln Gardens for showtime at 9:00, when he would take his place as second cornet player in King Oliver's Jazz Band.

He was nervous, of course. The musicians were sitting on the bandstand, warming up their instruments and smoking cigarettes, and he was in awe of these men. He settled in quickly when the patrons demanded an encore of the first number.

After the floor show came the dance section of the evening, and someone in the crowd, sensing the moment, called out, "let the youngster blow." Oliver nodded and his protégé ignored the butterflies in his stomach and played his "rendition of the blues." "I was really in heaven at that particular minute," he remembered. It was not by accident that the choice for the moment was the blues.

In a study of how social class is coordinated with cultural taste, sociologist Pierre Bourdieu came to the conclusion that "noth-

ing more clearly affirms one's 'class,' nothing more infallibly clas-
sifies, than tastes in music." The African-American population of
early-1920s Chicago was hardly an exception to that claim. When
Armstrong stepped into Lincoln Gardens, he already had a feeling
for different kinds of social-musical configurations, and whatever he
didn't know about his new town would come into focus soon enough.
No one was bashful about proclaiming allegiances, and a working
musician knew better than anyone who was listening to what and for
what reasons.

Many of the newcomers were entranced with the blues. Their
interest was so strong that they lay good claim to Amiri Baraka's
famous phrase "blues people." F. Scott Fitzgerald thought of the
1920s as the jazz age, but for African Americans in Chicago—at least
during the first half of that decade—it would be more appropriate to
speak of a blues age.

There has long been controversy about where jazz came from,
but no one has ever seriously doubted the origins of blues. "Blues
come out of the fields, baby," was the pithy historical analysis of sing-
er-guitarist Lightning Hopkins. Especially the fields belonging to the
large plantations of Louisiana and the "delta" region of western Mississippi. "They were singing the blues in Mississippi and Louisiana
ever since there were colored peoples living there to my way of knowing," explained Albert Luandrew, also known as Sunnyland Slim.
From these areas came huge numbers of the Chicago immigrants, and
many others from cities like New Orleans had strong connections—
Armstrong's mother, for example, came to New Orleans directly from
a plantation, as did the families of Joe Oliver and Mahalia Jackson.
These demographic facts made the association of blues with the
Great Migration almost inevitable. "Everybody from New Orleans
can really do that thing," Armstrong said at the beginning of *Gut
Bucket Blues*, and everyone understood what he meant.

The rural, southern stamp that was imprinted on the idiom from
the very beginning was never fully shaken off, even as it underwent
a series of transformations over the course of the twentieth century.
Other parts of the African cultural legacy were strong as well on
plantations, yet blues, along with the ecstatic style of religious music,
could seem to represent the entire range of African-American ver-

nacular culture all by itself. The unequivocally black identity of blues marked a cultural boundary with whites, which in turn promoted the idiom as a way of asserting independence and strength.

At its points of origin in the fields, levee camps, and loading docks, blues was a vocal idiom full of ornamentation. The practice of bending pitch, a way of sliding from one pitch to another and of featuring pitches that are slightly lower than those of the conventional Western scale, gave rise to the term "blue notes." The idiom was marked by casual, conversational delivery, with ambiguous definition of pitch and rhythm. A blurred boundary between speech and song, one of the foundations of African-American vernacular culture, encouraged performers to take advantage of the expressive potential of both and of fluid movement between the two. "Louis swings more telling a joke than most others do playing a horn," insisted saxophonist Bud Freeman. Growls, moans, and blue notes indicated heightened emotion, as performers explored a range from detached, cool, and ironic through heated, passionate, and intense.

Blues phrasing often included a sense of darting in and out of synchrony with a steady, "fixed" foundation to make the music automatically danceable. Fleeting rhythmic patterns, forming and dissolving quickly, peppered the melodic flow, and the practice of dragging behind a steady beat was common. An ancient melody-type was very strong: a leap up to a high, strained pitch followed by gradual and indirect descent, a jagged contour of falls and rises outlining a "sawtooth" design. A feeling of improvisational suppleness conditioned the entire flow of pitch, rhythm, and tone quality, communicating qualities of resilience. None of this can be captured in musical notation. Blues became emblematic of African-American vernacular culture because it fit so precisely the twin sides of what vernacular practice was all about: it was clearly a practice that belonged to ordinary African Americans, and it foregrounded performer-centered techniques that could only be learned by ear.

When Armstrong arrived in Chicago, he could hear the plantation tradition on the streets in pretty much its pure form. Hinton remembered one Mr. Hoskins, who shoveled coal for a living and liked to sit on his front stoop after dinner, playing bottleneck guitar in the delta tradition and singing blues with a nasal tone. Professional blues heard in theaters, cabarets, and dance halls could be audibly connected to the plantations, too, depending on the individual musician. This was one key to the idiom's success: it could be adapted to different circumstances without losing a blues identity and all of the social-historical dynamics associated with it. It was easy to have things both ways, according to any number of stylistic and social permutations.

Because of its associations with cornfields, cotton bales, and cane brakes, blues was opposed by the "old settlers," those African Americans who had made Chicago their home before the onset of the Great Migration, and by assimilative immigrants. "They wanted to forget all about the things for which the southern Negro was noted," observed pianist Willie "The Lion" Smith. Leaflets pasted around town and articles printed in the *Defender* advised new arrivals to avoid head scarves, aprons, and other "marks of servitude" in public. Scorn was heaped on iconic foods like watermelon and barbecue. "It's no difficult task to get people out of the South, but you have a job on your hands when you attempt to get the South out of them," complained the Chicago *Whip* in 1922. Some churches negotiated compromises as a way to woo the plantation immigrants: let them "shout a little" while gently turning toward the preferred path of racial progress. It is not surprising that a taste for blues was not shared by everyone.

But the attack on blues was mitigated by various adaptations that were already under way. One of the strongest came when blues found a home in published sheet music marketed to "people of color," as some advertisements explicitly say. W. C. Handy was the most successful of the composer-entrepreneurs who found a way to conjure up blues feeling through the dots and dashes of musical notation. His 1912 *Memphis Blues* demonstrated the commercial possibilities, which then expanded dramatically in 1914 with the publication of *St. Louis Blues*, the song recorded more often than any other during the years between World War I and World War II. Armstrong himself recorded *St. Louis Blues* some 75 times, the most famous version being the very first, with Bessie Smith in January 1925.

Handy's success depended on his ability to highlight a few salient gestures from the vernacular, especially, in the case of *St. Louis Blues*, these two: descending melodic lines that pass through a blue note on the third degree of the scale, and the habanera rhythm that was circulating during these years as part of the tango fad. Compared to everyday blues, Handy's songs have more melodic, harmonic, and textural variety. More formal variety, too, though the standard blues form—successive choruses, each in an AAB pattern of words, phrases, and chords—is always placed in a central position.

Handy's songs circulated more extensively through African-American society than any single performer possibly could. The *Pittsburgh Courier*'s description of him as "organizer of the blues" is felicitous in both a compositional and a social sense. The prestige and popularity of his songs helped put blues in a fresh position, out of the cornfields and into a broader social range. The songs are about Memphis and St. Louis, not about barefoot shouters harvesting cotton. There are charming references in the black press to blues songs as "colored folks' opera," an indicator of their social importance and of the emotional power and theatricality of professional performers. The swelling popularity of published blues coincided with the expanse of the Great Migration during the mid-1910s, which allowed the songs to serve as unifiers valued by people living almost anywhere one might move from or to. "Some time ago 'blues' . . . appealed only to the lower classes of Race folks," wrote Peyton in the *Defender* in June 1926. "Handy is the man who revolutionized their construction, eradicated vulgarities, commercialized them. . . ."

Blues were taken up in minstrel shows, circuses, and vaudeville circuits, where Ma Rainey was one of the first to make the idiom her specialty. On one tour her troupe consisted of eight dancing girls, some singing and dancing boys, a couple of comedians, a female ballad singer and a male one, a tap dancer, a juggler, a bicycling man dressed in Japanese costume, and a little band of strings, piano, and drums. At the climax of the two-hour show Rainey made her entrance, starting a song from behind a curtain and then strutting onto the stage in a flash of costumed splendor, with gold silk gown, rhinestone walking cane, and high hat with feathers, her gold teeth sparkling.

Singers like Rainey performed colored folks' opera, and they looked and acted like divas. "She possessed her listeners; they swayed, they rocked, they moaned and groaned," remembered accompanist-composer Thomas Dorsey. She took *St. Louis Blues* at a very slow tempo, and she excelled at the vernacular touches that Handy could not possibly capture in notation, dragging behind the beat, growls, and dramatically slurred blue notes. She and others thus completed the loop that the songwriters had initiated, from vernacular practice to notated composition and back.

The blues divas made a niche for themselves in vaudeville circuits like the Theater Owners Booking Association. TOBA theaters eliminated the humiliation blacks experienced when they were forced to enter white theaters by trekking down an alley, through a back door, and up five or six flights of stairs. Whites rarely attended TOBA outside of the occasional "whites-only" night.[3] The 3100 block of South State Street offered three theaters catering to blacks—the Phoenix, the Vendome, and the Grand, with the Monogram a few blocks away. When Rainey and Bessie Smith appeared in these venues, they sang gutbucket blues with southern diction and a complete absence of dicty pretense, to the delight of the newcomers ("dicty" meaning imitation of whites).

Slow tempos and narrow vocal range directed attention toward the melismas, slides, moans, and blue notes. Smith's regal presence and musical intensity led to analogies with preaching. "She, in a sense, was like people like Billy Graham are today," said Danny Barker. "Bessie was in a class with those people. She could bring about mass hypnotism." Smith walked onto the stage of the Grand Theater to thunderous applause, head bowed and eyes turned to the floor. After the applause faded, she stood in silence for what seemed like several minutes, finally releasing *Backwater Blues*, her powerful voice filling the theater and tingling the spine of the enraptured patron who later wrote about it. Dorsey was in an excellent position to understand the similarities between blues and church: "It [blues] gets down into the individual to set him on fire, dig him up or dig her up way down there 'til they come out with an expression verbally. If they're in the church, they say, 'Amen.' If they're in the blues, they say, 'Sing it now.'"

No one mistook Ma Rainey or Bessie Smith for preachers, just as no one mistook them for farm laborers. Composers like Handy organized blues into opera arias, and divas like Rainey and Smith were exceptionally good at "digging, picking, pricking at the very depth of your mental environment and the feelings of your heart," as Dorsey put it. Highly paid professionals acquired the aura of a life lived under special conditions, with licenses of behavior afforded by wealth and status. They represented an image of what everywoman or everyman could become, a fantastic range of experience, wealth, and fame granted to "one of us"—musically this was clear. In this way they became part of the hopeful vision of the immigrants. Their success was part of the equation that established blues as the music of the Great Migration.

In 1920, OKeh Records decided to expand its business to include the African-American vernacular, leading to yet another intervention in blues sociology. The key figure here was pianist and composer Perry Bradford, who convinced the company to take a chance and record cabaret singer Mamie Smith. Her August 1920 recording of *Crazy Blues* proved him right: it has been estimated that sales topped one million. "We'd get in 500 of those records, the clerk wouldn't even put them in a bag," said a seller in Atlanta. "Just take a dollar and hand them out—just like you were selling tickets." "You couldn't walk down the street in a colored neighborhood and not hear that record," recalled Alberta Hunter. "It was everywhere." Smith was soon commanding $1,000 per appearance. Eighteen thousand people heard her sing in Norfolk, Virginia, on a December evening in 1920. For a performance in Atlantic City, she donned a $3,000 ostrich-plumed cape. After *Crazy Blues* there would no longer be any doubt about the commercial potential of "race records," sold on designated labels and marketed explicitly to African Americans.

Mamie Smith belonged to a tradition of northern show-style singing that had little in common with plantation singing. She was not a "rough, coarse shouter," as *Defender* columnist Tony Langston wrote approvingly. She did not bend pitch; as clarinetist Garvin Bushell put it, "she didn't get in between the notes the way Bessie did." But her success opened up the recording industry to performer-centered vernacular blues.

Bessie Smith was initially rejected because she was precisely the rough, coarse shouter that Mamie Smith was not. Again, the white businessmen—and, in this case, the black businessman Harry Pace of Black Swan Records, as well—were surprised when Smith proved to be the most successful diva of all, beginning with her 1923 recording of *Down Hearted Blues*. The limitations of these primitive, tinny records did not hinder the enjoyment of African Americans across the nation. "The Negro is naturally musical and will often buy music before he will buy bread," crowed the trade magazine *Talking Machine World* in 1920, echoing in a celebratory way Booker T. Washington's earlier lament about the misguided priorities of sharecroppers who valued pedal organs more than cutlery. Observers in 1925 estimated that African Americans in the South were buying five to six million records per year; more recent estimates suggest ten million. Along with institutions like the *Defender* and national Baptist conventions, blues tied the African-American South to the African-American North. Handy, Bradford, Rainey, and Smith understood the dynamics of this social-musical loop and used it to build their careers.

One could sing along with Bessie Smith, but that did not contradict the fact that she was a skilled performer who held pride of place in an elaborate commercial structure. In the early 1920s, blues stood triumphant as one of the most modern and popular articulations of working-class African-American identity, a musical identity that drew a boundary between blacks and whites on the one hand, while combining vernacular tradition with urban sophistication on the other. The ongoing African-American experience of coming together in changing social formations was now manifesting the sense of a larger black community that extended beyond any person's local experience of place. Blues helped define what that community was all about.

Handy, Rainey, Smith, and Bradford professionalized blues through sheet music, vaudeville, and phonograph recordings, and the transplanted New Orleanians were doing the same thing in dance halls. Their music was perceived as a transformation of the bluesy vernacular, accomplished in such a way and at such a high level that they could not be matched by dance-band musicians from any other part of the country. Armstrong's solo debut with the Oliver band was a matter of marking his place in this musical-social network.

How uptown New Orleanians in general and Armstrong in particular came to this position of advantage is a key part of the story of early jazz. In the last decade of the nineteenth century, musicians in New Orleans developed a regional specialty of blues on wind instruments, especially cornet and clarinet. Anybody who had access to a wind

*Armstrong and Oliver, 1922 (The William Russell Photographic Collection, MSS 520 F. 1018, Williams Research Center, The Historic New Orleans Collection)*

instrument could experiment with blues, and part of what made New Orleans so special was that a good number of people did exactly that.

Around age ten, Armstrong found an unlikely tutor in a so-called rags-bottles-and-bones man named Larenzo, who played blues on a long tin horn. Jelly Roll Morton insisted that men like Larenzo played "more lowdown, dirty blues . . . than the rest of the country ever thought of." Just before Armstrong was born, they inspired cornetist Charles "Buddy" Bolden, whose ability in blues made him the most famous player in early jazz; Kid Ory accused Bolden of stealing ideas from the ragmen. Like the blues divas, Bolden took gestures made by ordinary people and stylized them with his powerful horn. He was immensely popular among uptown African Americans, a population that included some 40,000 immigrants from the plantations.

Oliver (b. ca. 1885) was in his formative years when Bolden reached the peak of local celebrity. Stella said that her husband listened to rail- and dockworkers and figured out how to play their songs on his cornet. Armstrong said that Oliver taught him "the modern way of phrasing" on the cornet, which must have meant conversational inflections, shadings of loud and soft, and the microscopic suppleness of come-and-go rhythmic patterning that communicated resilience. Oliver could demonstrate how to play blue notes, "the strongest notes you can play," in bass player Pops Foster's view.

Armstrong's first musical job at a local honky tonk, around age fifteen, required him to play nothing but blues, all night long. The idiom fundamentally shaped his conception of music. He may have been exceptional in his talent and in the opportunity to work closely with someone like Oliver, but he was not exceptional in the centrality of the blues-based vernacular to his musical upbringing. For all of these reasons, no musician who knew him was surprised to hear him play blues for his solo debut at Lincoln Gardens. That was his strength, and it was what the audience wanted to hear. When he finished, he must have been even more convinced that he would not be getting homesick in his new town.

Music can be heard in many different ways, and we have now seen three different types of reception encountered by musicians from New Orleans as they moved around the country in the late 1910s and early 1920s. Whites could look at the Creole Band and see "the southern plantation darky as he really is." Bicycling white teenagers at Lincoln Gardens heard in Oliver's band a liberation from bourgeois narrow-mindedness and parental control. And in that same location, African-American immigrants found satisfaction for their immense appetites for blues. They crowned Oliver "King" on his first night there (when it was called Royal Gardens) in 1918. A man known as "Memphis" walked around Chicago playing Oliver's solos on a comb covered with wax paper, thus completing yet another vernacular loop, from the rags-bottles-and-bones men and the levee and railroad workers into the repertory of professional wind players and back into everyday music making by ordinary people.

In one sense, blues was the foundation for everything the uptown New Orleanians played. In another, the word meant a slow-tempo dance, and with that we step into some confusing terminological territory. The three key words for understanding African-American secular genres during this period—jazz, blues, and ragtime—were alive with various types of usage, even within the discourse of a single community. These categories have been simplified today, so we need to carefully attend to the ways in which they were used.

Of these three terms, "jazz" was the most foreign to the New Orleanians. Armstrong and many others said that they did not call their music jazz in their hometown. "'Jazz,' that's a name the white people have given to the music," insisted Sidney Bechet. As I have explained in *Louis Armstrong's New Orleans*, the word these musicians were most likely to use for early jazz was "ragtime." With the national success of the (white) Original Dixieland Jazz Band in 1917, they willingly adopted "jazz." In the 1920s "jazz" was used interchangeably with "hot music" to mean any up-tempo music for dancing. "It was ragtime, Dixieland, gut-bucket, jazz, swing—and it ain't nothin' but the same music," Armstrong wrote, with a degree of frustration, in 1955.

"Blues" had similar flexibility. For musicians from New Orleans its primary meanings were, first, a very slow tempo, second, a musical form or pattern. Musicians need some kind of shared formal convention in order to improvise as a group, and blues provided this without requiring anyone to say a single word or have a single rehearsal. "Blues" could also mean a style, the emphasis of the present discussion, defined by blue notes, conversational phrasing, and so on. A

musical performance in the 1920s might have one of these attributes—
blues tempo, blues form, or blues style—but not the other two and
still be thought of as blues. But the marketing potency of the word was
so strong that it was often applied to music that lacked all three.

Pops Foster remembered W. C. Handy's band from Memphis
during the 1910s and highlighted the absence of non-notatable techniques of the vernacular: Handy's band "was called a blues band but
they didn't really play any blues," he said. "They just played everything straight. . . . With him it all came out like it was written in the
book." Discussing *Dipper Mouth Blues,* the most famous record made
by Oliver's 1923 band, drummer Zutty Singleton said, "That was a rag.
Just because they named it blues don't make it a blues"; for Singleton,
"blues" meant a tempo slower than *Dipper Mouth* and a musical form.

As for the word "jazz," George Gershwin summarized the problem in 1926: "The word has been used for so many different things
that it has ceased to have any definite meaning." Isham Jones, a white
dance-bandleader in Chicago, argued in 1924 for a precise definition
that actually excluded his own band, insisting that jazz was a "down
South Negro type" of blues. Jones felt that "American dance music"
was the phrase that fit his own band best.

What Jones rejected, Oliver was happy to embrace. The New
Orleanians' most compelling asset in Chicago was blues. When Willie "The Lion" Smith came through town in 1923, he was surprised
by the dominance of wind instruments and by how well those winds
played blues. "We hadn't heard groups in the East that could play
the blues and stomps like these guys in the Middle West," he said.
Dominance of the New Orleanians accounted for both distinctions.
"There wasn't an eastern performer who could really play the blues,"
explained Garvin Bushell. "We didn't put that quarter tone pitch in
the music the way the southerners did. Up north we leaned toward
ragtime conception—a lot of notes."

With blues in their pockets, "the New Orleans musicians had Chi-
cago locked up," as trombonist Preston Jackson put it. Singer Alberta
Hunter agreed that "the New Orleans boys had something that the
Chicago musicians couldn't get at that particular time." Their impact
was felt on nearly every instrument. Bubber Miley visited from New
York and studied Oliver's freak technique from a distance; he even-

tually personalized Oliver's approach and became the central force in Duke Ellington's maturing orchestra. Before Miley it had been clarinetist Sidney Bechet who brought the sound of New Orleans to Ellington's attention. "I had never heard anything like it," Ellington remembered of his first hearing of Bechet; "it was a completely new sound and conception to me." Clarinetists Dodds and Jimmy Noone shaped famous white clarinetists Benny Goodman and Frank Teschemacher. Cornetist Johnny Dunn from Memphis had blues talent, but even he, said Bushell, was not as soulful as the New Orleanians. Bass player Bill Johnson was the model for Hinton and others. Drummers Baby Dodds, Zutty Singleton, and Tubby Hall influenced George Wettling, Dave Tough, and Gene Krupa; the New Orleanians did things other drummers had never heard before, remembered Glover Compton from Kentucky. Even in the early 1930s, when saxophonist Leon Washington and Hinton were breaking into the professional scene, the New Orleanians still dominated. Hinton felt "surrounded" by them; "they controlled the real hotbed of jazz," he said. When he finally got a regular job playing in a band led by Singleton, he believed that it was this association with a New Orleanian that helped him enter the local network of musicians.

The New Orleanian advantage came from the fact that they carried a tradition that had, over the course of several generations, packed more and more of the plantation vernacular into dance-band music. This was partly a matter of ear-playing ensemble style. It was not just for self-protection and camaraderie that they clannishly stuck together: their way of playing by ear depended on knowledge and experience. And it was partly a matter of improvising solos: the "get off men"—players who "get off" the composed melody and onto an improvised solo—were "strictly" from New Orleans, according to clarinetist Ralph Brown. The musical legacy of slavery had been folded into professional dance music in New Orleans as it had nowhere else. It could all be summarized in the word "blues," if the speaker was so inclined, or "jazz," if inclined differently.

Many felt that Oliver was the best, both as bandleader and as soloist. On the South Side of Chicago, in 1922, Oliver stood at the top of the local dance-band pyramid, just as W. C. Handy was at the top of the list of composers who published blues, and just as Bessie

Smith would soon be in the forefront of the blues divas. Oliver's success was largely local, however, in contrast with Handy's and Smith's.

Alberta Hunter suggested to Columbia Records that they record Oliver's band in early 1923, but since she was not available to join them, the company refused. White businessmen could not yet imagine the phonograph market for black dance bands without a vocalist, no matter how bluesy. A small label took a chance. In doing so, Gennett Records launched Oliver's fame beyond the reach of those who could hear him in person and provided the earliest documentation of what his band sounded like. "When Joe Oliver went up [to Chicago], he made it bigger than any of them because he started to make records," acknowledged Pops Foster. This was one of the transitions the New Orleanians faced as they left behind the preindustrial South for the industrialized North. Gennett Records gave Oliver and his band a bigger spotlight than they previously could have imagined.

## Blues and the First Recordings from Oliver and Armstrong, April 1923

In the spring of 1923, Oliver's engagement at Lincoln Gardens came to an end, as all location jobs eventually must. Somehow he arranged a tour of one-night stands in dance halls through Illinois, Indiana, and Ohio. Indiana was a stronghold of the Ku Klux Klan, with 250,000 members, more than any other state, so it was not a place African-American musicians looked forward to visiting. Cornetist Punch Miller found Indiana to be worse than Mississippi or Georgia for prejudice. Trombonist Clyde Bernhardt remembered a tour of the upper Midwest in 1927, and how difficult it was to find food. "If the town was all white we knew not to stop. When we be starving, and that was frequently, we take a chance and pull up behind some white food store. . . . Ask if they feed us in the back or maybe allow us to take food out. Most of the time they wouldn't, so we move on."

While dealing with challenges like these, the band made its way to Richmond, near the Ohio border, where Gennett Records had its home base. The location was remote, so the company liked to sign up bands on the spot as they came through town on tour. A low-budget

*Gennett studios, Bix Beiderbecke and His Rhythm Jugglers (Collection of Duncan Schiedt)*

enterprise, Gennett looked for relatively unknown groups that had not yet recorded and were willing to do so for little or no money up front. The Oliver band entered the Gennett studios on April 5 and 6, and from these sessions nine sides were eventually issued. Four of the nine were called blues—*Canal Street Blues*, *Mandy Lee Blues*, *Chimes Blues*, and *Dipper Mouth Blues*.

The humble Gennett studio measured 125 feet long and 30 feet wide, with the performing space separated from the control room by a double pane of glass. Noise from trains frequently interrupted the recordings. A large Mohawk rug, a lot of draperies, and some towels hung from the walls helped with soundproofing, and sawdust filled the cavities between the walls. The room's resonance was so poor that musicians often had trouble hearing each other.

Recordings were made with the "acoustic" technique, which required the players to direct their instruments into the conical center of a large megaphone that popped out of the control room wall. The technology had severe limitations. Drums and string bass caused the recording needle to jump out of its grove, so they were usually abandoned. For the April 1923 sessions, Bill Johnson played banjo instead of bass and Baby Dodds tapped on a woodblock. A good portion of each session was dedicated to searching for balance. Banjo players usually sat directly in front of the megaphone on a high stool, since the instrument was difficult to pick up. When two musicians played the same instrument, as was the case with Oliver and Armstrong, the engineer experimented with different ways of positioning them; two cornets were known to create special problems with distortion. All of this fussing with balance was not just a matter of prettiness, since too much volume bounced the stylus and too little would not be recorded. Dozens of preliminary recordings were usually made to test the various combinations and positions.

When the testing began, Oliver and Armstrong stood side by side as usual, but the engineer soon remarked that Armstrong was overpowering Oliver's lead. The solution was to move Oliver up, closer to the horn, and Armstrong back, toward a corner of the room. Since Oliver was playing lead and Armstrong second, the basic logic of the decision was clear. Nevertheless, Armstrong took up his corner position with a frown. He must have been eagerly anticipating this moment, his first chance to record. He himself later said that the main problem with the 1923 recordings of the Oliver band was that the cornet pair together was not prominent enough, thus distorting the sound of the band as a whole.

Recordings were limited to around three minutes, so there could be no stretching out to 40 or more hot choruses. A red light flashed at two minutes and 30 seconds into every recording, signaling that it was time to wrap things up. Three masters were usually made for each piece. To keep the wax soft, the temperature was set around 85 degrees; pianist Earl Hines said that the Gennett studio felt like "sort of a steam room." The heat, the standing around, and the general anxiety about making a mistake made for a long day at work. "We were all very nervous," said Baby Dodds, who found relief in habitual fashion—with a bottle.

In these brief, tinny recordings, we have the best glimpse we will ever get of what Armstrong sounded like at age twenty-one, what Oliver's band at Lincoln Gardens sounded like, and even what jazz from uptown African-American neighborhoods of New Orleans sounded like before the musicians moved to Chicago. Yet the documentation is hardly direct. The inferior technology and the difficulties of instrumentation and balance automatically distance these recordings from what was happening in Lincoln Gardens, and so does Oliver's reluctance to put his best material on record. A few years earlier, Fred Keppard had passed up an opportunity to record because he was afraid someone would steal his ideas; Victor made the offer, and when Keppard refused they turned to the Original Dixieland Jazz Band, which hit the big time.

Keppard's reluctance is easy to understand. The biggest advantages in the performer-centered musical world the New Orleanians brought with them to Chicago were their unique creations, which they relied on week after week, year after year. It must have been worry enough for Oliver to look down from the stage of Lincoln Gardens and see the hungry alligators, studying his fingers and scribbling on their shirt cuffs. How much more damage they could do with a recording they could play over and over. Oliver never recorded *Eccentric*, and that may have had something to do with the fact that the New Orleans Rhythm Kings beat him to it with their own Gennett version some eight months before he arrived in Richmond. "I'd never heard any white band come so close to the New Orleans style before," said Mezz Mezzrow about the Rhythm Kings. "They stole Joe Oliver's riffs and they stole them good." Before entering the Gennett studios, Oliver told a friend, "I ain't gonna give these white boys my best stuff, you better believe it."

Alberta Hunter remembered hearing Oliver and Armstrong at Lincoln Gardens play a duet based on the celebrated anthem *Holy City* (music by Stephen Adams with words by Frederick Weatherly) that "would make the hair on your head rise."[4] They played it without the other band members, "just the two of them floating along," she said. Two of the four blues titles from these April sessions, *Canal Street Blues* and *Chimes Blues*, prominently display the main theme of *Holy City*. Compositional credit for *Canal Street Blues* went to Oliver and Armstrong jointly, credit for *Chimes Blues* to Oliver.

It is easy to imagine the hair-raising power of *Holy City* in this context. Oliver and Armstrong were both brought up with church music, and New Orleans dance-band music was filled with inspiration from that source. There were a few dissenters to this kind of mixing, and even Oliver's wife Stella admitted that she was opposed, early on in New Orleans, to the way he mixed the sacred with the secular. But most people loved it. Oliver majestically plays the main theme of *Holy City* in the second strain (CD 0:37–1:07) of *Canal Street Blues*, while Armstrong harmonizes below him. In *Chimes Blues* something very similar happens (CD 0:42–1:16). The pastiche approach to creating blues numbers, pursued so successfully by Handy, was an easy model to follow. The main theme from *Holy City* as originally composed does not match blues form precisely, but it is close enough that Oliver only needed to tweak it slightly so that it fit the standard pattern of 12 measures with conventional harmonies. It was easy to drop the tune into these two pieces.

Co-compositional credit to Armstrong for *Canal Street Blues* must mean that he created a melody for one of the strains, probably the first one. The theme for the third strain (CD 1:08–1:22 and repeated at 1:53) holds the strongest appeal for most listeners today, and it is very much in Oliver's style, with a simple but effective riff (a short musical idea repeated many times), rhythmic clarity, and punch. Johnny Dodds, a close follower of the great Sidney Bechet, provides another highlight with his funky solo.[5] Dodds repeatedly leaps and lands with an accent on blue notes that are then stretched and bent. His brother's counterrhythms behind the solo are clear and varied, livening up the texture. Also behind him is Bill Johnson, playing the banjo in a way that probably resembles the slap-pizzicato, four to the bar, that he and other bass players from New Orleans sometimes used to give a chorus special force.

These April 1923 sessions document very well how Oliver and Armstrong each conceived a solo. On *Dipper Mouth Blues* Oliver plays the solo that quickly became identified with him and is now his most famous. On *Chimes Blues*, Armstrong displays the cautious efforts of a young apprentice. The solos are a world apart. At first glance, the comparison hardly suggests that the younger player regarded the older one as the central musical influence in his life.

*Dipper Mouth Blues* is one of the best representations we have of the freak style that made Oliver famous in Chicago. When the band recorded the piece again ten weeks later, on the OKeh label, Oliver played the solo almost exactly the same. (The OKeh version is technologically superior to the Gennett and more widely reproduced.) It was, in fact, standard practice in New Orleans to craft a solo over time and then stick to it. "Once you got a certain solo that fit in the tune, and that's it, you keep it," explained Armstrong.

In three consecutive blues choruses, Oliver demonstrates freak wah-wah effects with the business end of a toilet plunger—or perhaps simply his hand—manipulated over the muted bell of his horn (the effect is more pronounced on the Gennett version). It is unusual to have a solo go for three choruses like this. The stretch encourages Oliver to craft a nice sense of expansion from the first chorus to the second and then into the third, giving the entire sweep of melody a feeling of fluidity and breadth. Oliver in this solo shares two basic values of melodic design with Bessie Smith: his range from low note to high note is relatively narrow; also, the solo keeps moving through the same limited selection of pitches. A melody like this puts emphasis on the bluesy details of expressive timbre, pitch bending (for example, the beginning of the first chorus), and dragging behind the beat (for example, the beginning of the second chorus).

This is the kind of playing that could "hit you inside," as Bushell said about Oliver's best music, and "make people jump out of their seats." Oliver scorned elaborate melodic contours, which he called "snakes," and advised two of his protégés, Armstrong and trombonist Clyde Bernhardt, to get rid of them. "All them snakes you makin' loses the flavor," he told Bernhardt, "it don't mean a damn thing." Armstrong first got that advice around age fifteen. "He'd hang around and he'd listen to me play a while. He'd tell me, 'Listen boy, play some more lead. Stop so much of that variation. Play some lead.'" What Oliver liked was a "phrase that stayed with you," as Armstrong put it.

Bushell said that the eastern players could not match the New Orleanians in blues because they were caught up in a "ragtime" conception with "a lot of notes." "Hot" music depended on heavy vibrato, aggressive attack, rhythmic drive, and strength. The successful blues singers from the early 1920s made their careers without microphones in venues that required tremendous vocal projection. They had to belt it out, and an abundance of hot features helped.

Preachers developed the same kind of projection and used the same means of expression.

*Chimes Blues* is one of those pieces that is removed from the plantation vernacular even though it has the word "blues" in its title. The title may be an ironic comment on social distance: on the plantations, one would not have heard blues played on chimes, which are imitated by the piano in the middle of the piece. Lillian Hardin Armstrong said that she lifted the effect out of a classical composition in a bid to carve out a solo place for herself in the band. Later she was surprised to learn that Oliver had put his name on it as composer.

Armstrong's solo on *Chimes Blues* (CD: 1:52–2:27) is his moment to shine in the April sessions. The situation must have been unnerving. As his solo approached, he had to advance from his corner position up to the recording horn, right in the middle of the performance. It is obvious that he had worked up the solo long in advance, getting it just like he wanted in the time-honored New Orleans tradition. He has two blues choruses to cover, but instead of developing the melody to create a sense of expansion, as Oliver did in *Dipper Mouth*, he simply plays the same theme twice, with slight changes for the endings. The solo feels stiff, and there is no sign of the marvelous imagination that would come to dominate the field of jazz in just a few years. It is certainly not the kind of playing that caused patrons at Lincoln Gardens to throw their hats into the air.[6] There are few bluesy effects, though the solo is harmonically precise and well balanced. He is striving for precision and order, a phrase that stays with you.

Armstrong's solo shows that he had internalized Oliver's instructions to stick to a strong lead. Though not exactly singable, it is repetitive and fairly simple. The solo also reveals his command of harmony, as he winds his way precisely through a variety of chords, with carefully chosen pitches. "As a kid it just came natural," he said about his understanding of chords, which he experimented with in a vocal quartet as a child. There were a few people in his musical community who could show him things about harmony, and cornetist Buddy Petit, who liked to experiment with diminished chords and other advanced formations, was an important influence in the late 1910s.[7] With a good ear, a quick mind, and a knack for precision, all the teenage Armstrong needed was strong role models and a few timely tips. Working on riverboat excursions during the summers of 1918–21 gave him a chance to learn more, allowing his natural ability to develop even further.

In fact, Armstrong's command of harmony in *Chimes Blues* distinguishes him from his colleagues. His chorus has more harmonic variety than the others, including the more colorful diminished chord in measure 6. When the same moment comes around in earlier choruses, the other musicians play simpler blues harmonies instead of complex chromatic harmonies. Indeed, one of the earlier choruses is marked by conflict, with some of the musicians playing a major chord and others a minor chord, signaling a bit of confusion about what was called for.

Armstrong's command of harmony set him apart, and this would become a key to his success in the later 1920s. The full significance of that observation emerges when it is placed in a broader context. Jazz as it flourished in early New Orleans, as a music made for the blues-loving former residents of the plantations of Mississippi and Louisiana, did not necessarily put a high value on harmonic precision. There was undoubtedly a substantial place for heterophony, with simultaneous variations of the same tune creating random dissonance and without any harmonic thinking whatsoever. That would have been the norm in church congregational singing, and it would have been the norm for vernacular dance music on the plantations (but not the dance music of slave musicians who were trained to play for the people who claimed ownership of them). It is important to realize that slaves and then former slaves on the plantations of the Deep South created a rich and expressive musical culture that did not require any familiarity with Eurocentric harmony.

When King Oliver and His Creole Jazz Band filled up Lincoln Gardens, they were not playing heterophony, but neither were they overly concerned with harmonic precision. Outsiders often complained about the harmonic funkiness of New Orleans jazz. James "Rosy" McHargue, for example, a white clarinetist active in Chicago, didn't like the Oliver band because they were "kind of raucous and rough . . . they weren't always in tune, there were wrong notes." White clarinetist Voltaire DeFaut was perplexed by cornetist Fred Keppard, who "had terrific range and good tone and you couldn't fault him in many ways, but it was the *harmony* that he played that grated on your nerves . . . it sounded so funny coming from such a good trumpet." The first time Lillian Hardin Armstrong sat down to play with the New Orleanians, she asked what key they were about to play in. A snarl came back: "We don't know what key. When you hear two knocks start playing." Keys and the harmonic precision that goes along with them were secondary concerns.

To complain about weak harmonic control in early jazz from New Orleans is to apply foreign terms of evaluation. What we want to understand is why Oliver and his colleagues were so tremendously popular on the South Side of Chicago, in spite of the clinkers that irritated McHargue, DeFaut, Dave Peyton, and others. What was played in the Gennett recording studio was not necessarily what was played in Lincoln Gardens, but it is safe to assume, I think, that the thousands of patrons who flocked to hear Oliver and his band week after week for several years were not bothered by occasional conflicts between major and minor chords. The musical style these musicians worked out was a success; it was not trapped by an opaque set of limitations that only those on the outside could see. Oliver's band flourished for the simple reason that it foregrounded, with more skill than anyone else, a set of musical values that appealed to the South Side population.

It is essential to recognize how, for the ear-playing specialists in the African-American vernacular from New Orleans, harmony was less important than other things. Their exposure to Western theory was either spotty or nonexistent. What they knew—and they *really knew it*—were the dynamics of on-the-spot musical interaction, the allure of music that was conceived as an integral part of moving bodies, the deep expression of blue notes and pitch bending, the power and fluidity of speechlike music, the vitality of strong initial attacks and intense vibratos, and the centrality of the fixed and variable model.

One can sometimes find a sense in historical writings that jazz needed to progress. Jazz musicians themselves spoke about their own individual progress, and they explicitly mention greater harmonic control. The progress of an individual, however, is not the same as the progress of an art form. The point is critical given the intense social pressures that have surrounded jazz from its inception. To say that jazz progressed in the hands of white musicians, or black musicians who were intent on reaching white audiences, puts the discussion on a par with discredited theories of cultural evolution.

From the point of view of Oliver and the patrons at Lincoln Gardens, harmonic precision was a secondary value that easily yielded to other considerations. Armstrong absorbed the specialized sounds of the Oliver band—some of it more and some of it less, as we shall see—and added his own "natural" sense of harmony. In the next few years, happy rewards would come his way when he developed that sense further. What is notable, then, in *Chimes Blues* from April 1923, is his slight step away from the stylistic package that made the band what it was.

Phonograph recordings from 1923 give composer credit for *Dipper Mouth Blues* to Oliver and Armstrong jointly. The piece probably began as a blues composition by Armstrong—was this "his rendition of the blues," his first solo at Lincoln Gardens?—and this probably survives as the first strain, to which Oliver added his three choruses and Johnny Dodds another two.[8]

Blues as a musical style had a range of possibilities, from Oliver's full-throated preaching style to the intricately carved phrases of Armstrong's *Chimes Blues*. "They were both good but Louis he could get over his trumpet more," acknowledged cornetist George Mitchell. "Louis he had a different style that was good, very good . . . but it was different from Joe's." The differences extended beyond technique and included emotional ambience. Neither Bolden nor Oliver was limited to the intense preaching style, but each made it his specialty. Armstrong eventually found a way to incorporate blues into a solo idiom that had some speechlike effects without the freak technique and without the preaching persona. The legacy of the African-American vernacular from New Orleans remained central for him, but with a different emotional configuration and with new openings for expression.

His musical rise depended on superior technical skill, natural musical sense, the late apprenticeship with Oliver, and a lot of hard work. He also had help from an unexpected source, a sort of Trojan horse who had popped up in the Oliver band and would contribute to its undoing—his future wife, Lillian Hardin.

# THREE

# Opposites Attract:
# Louis and Miss Lil

*But who was I to think that a big high-powered chick like Lillian Hardin, who came to Chicago from Memphis, Tennessee, the year of 1917, right out of Fisk University, the valedictorian of her classes—"Who me?" I thought to myself. I just couldn't conceive the idea.*

*—Louis Armstrong*

**After Armstrong got settled in his new town, Oliver offered to take him over to the** Dreamland Cabaret (name changed to Dreamland Café in 1924), one of the largest venues on the South Side. "Louis, do you want to go over and meet Lil?" he asked. The reference was clear. Oliver had sent him a photograph of Lillian Hardin as incitement to come to Chicago. "Tell Miss Lil I like her," Armstrong wrote back. In 1922 at the age of twenty-four, Hardin was easing out of a bad marriage, so it is possible that Oliver was seriously matchmaking, not just teasing his protégé.

They were not an obvious couple. Lil was slender, weighed around 85 pounds, and was trained to play classical piano. Singer Alberta Hunter knew them both in 1922, and she said that Lil might have been spending as much money on clothes as she herself was—quite a statement since Hunter's extravagant tastes included an $1,800 tailor-made coat and cape. Hunter described Louis as a "big overgrown kid." The initial meeting between future husband and wife left Lil unmoved. She didn't like the secondhand and ill-fitting clothes he was wearing, and his hair was combed in unfashionable bangs that stuck out. "I was very disgusted," she remembered.

He responded with understandable shyness, given the dramatic differences between Lil and his previous romantic partners. Around age fifteen in New Orleans he had pimped for a prostitute named Nootsy. Nootsy "wasn't very much to look at, but she made good

70

*Lillian's band at the Dreamland Cabaret, ca. 1921 (Courtesy of Chris Albertson)*

money," he explained. The relationship soured when Nootsy stabbed him in the shoulder; when his mother found out, she tracked down the woman and nearly choked her to death. He married a prostitute named Daisy Parker a few years later, and their relationship was also marked by violence. Daisy pushed him to the edge when she cut up his Stetson hat with a razor, and she eventually discovered a real point of vulnerability: if she attacked his mouth she could jeopardize his musical career. After that, a job that required extended time floating up and down the Mississippi River started to look pretty good.

Once in New Orleans Armstrong had a crush on a light-skinned girl, but he was too shy to talk to her and felt he was not good enough. How much more reluctant he must have been to approach this fancy-dressed pianist who claimed to be valedictorian from legendary Fisk University. In spite of her small size, he thought of her as a "big high-powered chick." Some of the other musicians were making a play for her, but it took a while before that thought occurred to him. "I just couldn't conceive the idea," he later wrote. After their first meeting, he didn't see her again until she joined Oliver's band in November 1922.

Lillian's point of entry into the musical scene in Chicago had been very different from Armstrong's. Just after arriving with her mother,

Dempsey, in 1917, she got a job at Jones Music Store, at 3409 ½ South State Street, demonstrating sheet music to customers. This was her reward for years of keyboard lessons in Memphis, beginning with the organ around age six. She won a piano competition at age sixteen, and from there she enrolled in the college preparatory program at Fisk University for 1915–16. That year of study was apparently the extent of her relationship with Fisk.

In Memphis her musical upbringing was highly focused—"dicty" is the word Armstrong and his friends would have used to describe it. She had little exposure to vernacular music. A cousin sitting on the front porch once played the rag *St. Louis Tickle* on his guitar, but her grandmother wouldn't let her near him; "that's vulgar music, get away," she said. Lil later purchased a piano-roll version of the piece, and when her mother found out, she beat her with a broomstick. "I hadn't heard any jazz, no piano players, no bands, anything in Memphis," she remembered.

Through practicing and studying in the Eurocentric tradition, she developed skill in sightreading, the ability to sit down and play through printed music on the first reading. This, along with her good looks, made her perfectly suited for the Jones Music Store, where she earned three dollars per week. The proprietors booked jobs on the side, so musicians sometimes hung out there. She remembered Jelly Roll Morton coming by and playing the piano in a way she had never heard before. Clarinetist Lawrence Duhé brought his band into the store one day for an audition. Jones found them a job at a Chinese restaurant. The venue was known for frequent requests from the audience, so Duhé asked if Jones might recommend a piano player. When Hardin accepted, her career with the improvising New Orleanians began.

She had memorized a good number of songs—"I just took the job [at the music store] so I could learn all the music," she said—and her efforts now paid off with Duhé. Pianist Willie "The Lion" Smith emphasized how much demand there was for popular music on request in Chicago around this time, with patrons wanting to hear the music they had purchased on records for their windup phonographs at home. Requests ranged through popular songs of the day, tunes like *Love Will Find a Way* from the Broadway show *Shuffle Along*, by Noble Sissle and Eubie Blake. In New Orleans, there had been some incentive to keep up with current repertories, but in Chicago that demand was extended considerably.

Given Lil's lack of exposure to vernacular music, she was rather brave to take the job with Duhé. When she sat down to rehearse, she asked what key the piece would be in and the response assured her that the question was irrelevant. It didn't take long for her to find her way. The repertory had a limited range of chords, which she could easily identify by ear. Besides, as we have seen in Chapter 2, harmonic precision was not the highest priority for the uptown, ear-playing musicians from New Orleans.

Rhythmically, her job was simple. When not leading the band in a tune requested from the audience, her role was to play a chord on every beat with no variation whatsoever—four beats per measure, with the chords usually changing every measure. The chords helped hold the texture together, and the steady beat was part of the rhythmic foundation upon which melody players could spring vigorous counterrhythms.

Hardin managed to hide the situation for a while from her mother, telling her that she was working late at a dance studio. The nice pile of cash she was bringing home must have helped bring her mother around when she eventually found out. At first her mother insisted on meeting her every night at closing, at the exit door of the cabaret, but eventually she let Lil come home at one o'clock, accompanied by drummer Tubby Hall, with mother waiting at the door to greet them.

When Oliver took over Duhé's band and they moved to Royal Gardens, Lil went along. She accompanied the band to California in May 1921, while Royal Gardens was being remodeled and transformed into Lincoln Gardens. In September she returned to Chicago without the others to take the job at the Dreamland. Oliver returned to Chicago in late spring of 1922, and with the departure of pianist Bertha Gonsoulin in November, he persuaded Lil to rejoin. She chorded on the beat and taught the band new pieces from sheet music.

Her engagement with the music was minimal. The improvising New Orleanians failed to excite her. "From a musical standpoint jazz didn't mean too much to me," she later admitted. The terms of expression were so different from the music she had been immersed in that she had no context for appreciating quality. She ignored Armstrong's cornet work, which was, after all, in second place, not first. "I was interested in the money," she explained. "You tell me he was good or that one was good, it wouldn't make any difference. I wouldn't know any difference, you know?"

But she perked up when Oliver, in a quiet aside, mentioned that Louis was a better player than he was. Then came the reckless follow-up that has since been repeated many times by many musicians, including Louis himself: "But as long as I keep him with me he won't be able to get ahead of me." The immediate effect of this startling confession was that Lil began to notice the pudgy second cornetist. The two grew closer on the spring 1923 tour that brought the band to the Gennett studios in Indiana. As she watched the shuffling around in the studio, with Louis being positioned further away from the recording horn, she thought that this, too, must be an indication of superior ability. He looked sad, and she flashed a reassuring smile. Louis was now more than simply another one of the home boys.

He was certainly a bit of a rube, and it is hardly surprising that it took her a while to warm up to him. One night he came to work with a new fragrance sprinkled on his clothes, something a friend from the rooming house had given him. Bud Redd, the manager at Lincoln Gardens, noticed the cheap scent right away and gave him a hard time. As it turned out, the boarder worked at the stockyards and the perfume was made from fertilizer. The ingredients were explained to Louis and "that ended the smelling session," he said.

In spite of their differences, the two musicians started to have long conversations during down time at Lincoln Gardens. This led to nighttime wanderings on the "stroll," the main thoroughfare for entertainment on the South Side, a stretch of State Street that had its center between 31st and 39th Streets.

The stroll offered round-the-clock sociability and excitement that few American cities today come anywhere close to matching. "You could stand on 35th and State and see just about anybody you wanted to see in Chicago," said clarinetist Darnell Howard. Stores, barbershops, and restaurants stayed open 24 hours a day. Nighttime service was enhanced by the installation of electric streetlights in

1922. "I made it my business to go out for a daily stroll and look this 'heaven' over," said Lil. "Chicago meant just that to me—its beautiful brick and stone buildings, excitement, people moving swiftly, and things happening."

The dense concentration of black-owned businesses ranged from small shops to illustrious enterprises like Anthony Overton's Victory Life Insurance Company, Half Century Magazine, and the Columbia Hotel, where visiting black musicians often stayed. Here also was the bank owned by Jesse Binga, who had risen from the humble position of Pullman porter many years ago. The stroll was "Wall Street and Broadway," a "Bohemia of the Colored Folks," a "Mecca for Pleasure," where, according to the *Defender*, there was no threat of "racial embarrassment."

Black musicians never "even thought about going downtown, we had too much in our own neighborhood," said Earl Hines, recently arrived from Pittsburgh. "You'd start out in the afternoon by making your first stop at a barber shop near the hotel," said Willie "The Lion" Smith. "They would give you a relaxing shave, and it was the policy of the shop to give each customer a half pint of gin to sip on. It got you off to a nice start. And then you went on, down the stroll." Inevitably, the stroll would be the main scene for the courtship of these two young musicians, with Lil leading the way since, in Louis's estimation, she "knew Chicago like a book."

At first, Armstrong started dropping by to see her at Edelweiss Gardens, at 41st and State Streets, where she kept an after-hours job. Fred Keppard, Oliver's rival from New Orleans, played there, too. This may have been Armstrong's first sight of Keppard, though he had heard him from a distance in New Orleans. Trumpeter Adolphus "Doc" Cheatham thought that Keppard was a cruder musician than Oliver, "but good." Lil's opinion was that Keppard had better tone.

Louis's first encounter with Keppard was a letdown. Keppard directed him to the bandstand and gruffly ordered him to play, which Louis cautiously did. He was put off by what he perceived as a lack of seriousness on Keppard's part. Keppard enjoyed bantering with the customers, and on this night an attractive blonde walked by the bandstand. "'Oh *Hello*,' he said in a real *high* voice," Armstrong recalled. The woman smiled and returned the greeting in a very heavy voice, which caused everyone to break up in uncontrollable laughter, especially Lil. Keppard liked to create an air of intrigue by covering his cornet-playing fingers with a handkerchief.

Louis and Lil started dropping by cabarets and after-hour spots after their 1:00 a.m. finish at Lincoln Gardens. His personal preference was a toss-up between Edelweiss Gardens and the Fiume Italian Café and Restaurant, at 3440 South State Street. The Fiume sometimes featured a combination that astonished him: white musicians playing for black patrons.[9] "I had just come up from the South, where there weren't anything as near beautiful as that happening," he wrote. "*White* musicians, playing all of that good 'Jump' music, making those Colored people (mostly colored) *swing like mad*." Willie "The Lion" Smith played at the Fiume Café around this time and described a visit from the white cast of a musical who, after they finished their show downtown, requested songs and gathered around the piano, "singing like a choir."

A little further down State Street at 27th Street was the Pekin Café, another after-hours place. Here, too, the crowd was racially mixed, with gangsters and prostitutes heavily represented; the *Defender* referred to the Pekin as "the house of a thousand crimes." A report on a dance act performed while Oliver was playing there, a year or so earlier, describes an African-American shimmy dancer who kept her feet perfectly still while vibrating her hips and breasts, "much to the amazement of the audience." "Lawless liquor, sensuous shimmy, solicitous sirens, wrangling waiters, all the tints of the racial rainbow, black and tan and white, dancing, drinking, singing, early Sunday morning at the Pekin café," ran a horrified review in a white newspaper. "At one o'clock the place was crowded. Meanwhile a syncopating colored man had been vamping cotton field blues on the piano. A brown girl sang. . . . Black men with white girls, white men with yellow girls, old, young, all filled with the abandon brought about by illicit whisky and liquor music."

One day in late 1922 Armstrong and Bill Johnson bought tickets for a matinee performance at the Erlanger Theater, where Bill Bojangles Robinson was the headliner. Armstrong had heard a lot about Robinson, and the famous entertainer did not disappoint on this Sunday afternoon. A spotlight flashed as he entered from the side of

Bill "Bojangles" Robinson (Collection of Duncan Schiedt)

the stage, dressed in a light-tan gabardine summer suit and brown derby hat—"so *sharp* he was *bleeding*," Armstrong wrote. After the long applause died down, Robinson called out, "Give me a light my color," causing every light in the house to go dark and the audience to roar with laughter. Louis laughed so hard that Johnson thought he would have to take him home. Robinson imitated a trombone with his walking cane, told a few jokes, and then shifted into his famous tap dance. He ended the performance with a silent skating routine. Until the last days of his life, Armstrong felt that Robinson was "the greatest showman that we've ever had in our Race."

The musical couple's favorite place was the Dreamland Cabaret at 3520 South State Street. Bill Bottoms, the proprietor, was one of the few African-American owners of entertainment spots on the South Side. The dance floor was laid out with floor boards in a circle, big enough to hold 800 people. A large dome dominated the ceiling, with red, white, and blue electric lights mixed into green foliage dangling down, and hanging lights on the edge of the dome forming the letter D. In the middle of the dance floor was a patch of glass flooring brightly lit from below. The musicians played from a balcony on the west end of the building and electric lamps brightened every table.

Each solo entertainer took a turn with an "up," which meant first performing on the stage and then circulating through the crowd, responding to requests. Letha Hill's specialty was a shimmy routine that she delivered on the glass spot in the middle. Two of the featured entertainers at the Dreamland would play a role in Louis's future. Ollie Powers had very light skin ("looked like an ofay boy," said Alberta Hunter) and was rather large. He sang in a high, sweet voice that carried a tremendous distance, a requirement for these large and boisterous venues. Armstrong remembered him "rocking the whole house" with Irving Berlin's *What'll I Do* in "fox-trot time." Mae Alix, another singer with very light skin ("an attractive, high yellow gal," according to Armstrong), had a routine that included splits for every dollar bill thrown by a tipping customer. Some patrons got a kick out of lining up dollars across the floor, challenging her to pick up all the bills in one running split. During one visit when the hall was not very crowded, Lil invited Ollie and Mae over to their table to meet Louis. Louis shyly asked her if it would be okay for him to give them each a dollar if they sang his requested song. She said, "Sure, it is perfectly all right." He later told the story to Oliver, who just snorted at Louis's lack of sophistication.

The turning point in their relationship came during an unexpected intervention. "We did not really get together until my Mother came to Chicago," Armstrong wrote. During the summer of 1923, Armstrong looked up one night from his chair at Lincoln Gardens and was stunned to see his mother, May Ann Albert, fervently advancing through the crowd toward the bandstand. He had no idea why she was there. "How is my boy, how are you doing?" she asked anxiously. He stared at her, mouth open, and the show was delayed for 20 minutes while she greeted him with obvious relief and met his colleagues.

Someone back home had mischievously told her that Louis was out of work, out of money, hungry, and sick. Even though he had been writing regularly (though any son might make that claim, Armstrong was so fond of letter writing that it is hard to doubt him), she panicked and took off on a rescue mission. It was the first time she met Joe Oliver. At intermission Armstrong started teasing his mentor about how he had been joking that he was actually Louis's father. "Shall I tell her what you've been saying?" Louis whispered, and Oliver blushed. After the show the two of them took her to the Arlington Restaurant, at 35th and State Streets, for a "good Southern cooked breakfast." Louis was so happy that he couldn't take his eyes off her.

It was clear that Louis was thriving, so the next day May Ann started talking about returning home. She was nervous and kept referring to all the "new fangled gadgets" of the modern city. But Louis wanted her to stay for a while, and he enlisted Lil to persuade her. They located an apartment at 43rd and St. Lawrence Streets. He had the feeling that this was the first opportunity in his life to treat his mother well. "Now was my turn to prove how thankful I was for the sacrifices she had made for me," he wrote.

He and Lil met the realtor to check out the three-room apartment, and as the other two talked, Louis slipped into a daydream—he called it a "trance"—about the old days in New Orleans and Nootsy, how she had stabbed him in the shoulder with her "chib," and how May Ann had defended him. Not having seen May Ann for a year and suddenly having her here in Chicago, at the same time that he and Lil were deepening their relationship—the whole conflation of emotions overwhelmed him. Whether he thought about it or not, the dramatic vectors of the scene were symbolic of the Great Migration. It was a clarified moment of transition in the twenty-two-year-old's life. Just a few years earlier he had fully embraced the image of a "low-class hustler" ("that's what Louis wanted to be in those days," said Baby Dodds). Now a completely different set of possibilities was coming into view, a world of class and money and fast-paced fancy entertainment with a woman who seemed far above him, yet increasingly within reach. The distance from New Orleans to Chicago could be measured in many ways, and the contrast between May Ann and Lil was one of them.

It didn't really matter that Lil had exaggerated her credentials. What mattered was that she knew things he didn't know and was willing to bring him into her world. One could say that their relationship emerged from the possibilities of the Great Migration, a set of interactions that made it possible for a home boy from New Orleans, one of the leading experts in the African-American musical vernacular from the Deep South, to mingle with a savvy pianist who had been hanging around Fisk University. The Great Migration brought them together in a city lit up by electric lights, where wealth and celebrity were flaunted, with dollar bills spilling across the floor. It was a new world fresh in the making, heaven indeed.

What was possible for him? What was possible for dark-skinned people, generally? How could African-American music be developed and where would his musical imagination lead? Whether Armstrong was aware of it or not, these were the questions that lay before him in Chicago in the autumn of 1923.

## Staying Under: The Rupture of the Break

While he was courting Lillian, he continued to hang out with his musical buddies, of course, including Oliver. Oliver had an authoritative manner, and with Armstrong especially he liked to strike a paternal pose. The two of them occasionally made the rounds of after-hours clubs, and Oliver continued to shape his apprentice's thinking, musical and otherwise. "It was real kicks—listening to music, diggin' his thoughts, comments," Armstrong wrote. "His conception of things—life, music, people in general, were really wonderful. . . . All Joe Oliver had to do was to just talk to me, and I'd feel just like I had one of those good old music lessons of his."

We don't have a lot of details about what Oliver expected from him on the bandstand, but stray remarks and the evidence of recordings make it possible to speculate. Armstrong was brought to Chicago to bolster his mentor's failing chops, and that is precisely what he did. His role was to support and "stay under" the lead, as musicians sometimes phrase it.

The problem of identifying precisely what Armstrong played on the 1923 recordings cannot be blamed solely on inferior recording technology. The situation was created by design. Oliver wanted to channel Armstrong's strength through a particular vision of how the band should sound, a vision that included Oliver as the featured cornetist. As someone trained to be deferential to older people, especially older musicians, and as the only student Oliver ever took, Armstrong understood this better than anyone. When we strain to hear him, we are right in the midst of where he was in 1923—under the protective arm of his mentor, and doing whatever he could to boost Oliver's success. "I felt that any glory that should come to me must go to him—I wanted him to have all the praise," he plainly wrote.

Professional musicians know what it means to support a featured soloist. Earl Hines described his strategy for accompanying Ethel Waters in Chicago around this time: "When a person's in the spotlight, and you're accompanying, you're always supposed to be *under* what the artist is doing," he said. "I'd always listen to what she did, and listen to the changes she made, so that the next time I could really follow the channel she was in." Armstrong brought that same spirit to his work with Oliver. Staying under had a literal meaning—playing with less volume and lower in range. And it also meant the kind of sensitivity described by Hines, so that the creative energy of the musician who is under follows the one who is above.

"I was so wrapped up in him and lived his music that I could take second to his lead in a split second," wrote Armstrong. Usually that meant matching Oliver's melodic contour and rhythm in a lower range so that the two harmonized. With the two cornets in close synchrony, they sounded like one voice, a voice that the public identified as Oliver's. *Snake Rag*, from their first trip to the Gennett studio in April 1923, shows the two of them in tandem, as do many other recordings.

They became famous for using this blended approach in the phrase-ending "breaks" that are ubiquitous in early jazz. A break is a brief solo passage, usually one or two measures (four or eight beats) at the end of a phrase, in which all accompaniment stops while a designated player spins out a brief and lively musical idea. The regular pulse and phrasing are suspended, and the soloist inserts a moment of intensity and surprise. The effect is like winding up a coiled spring, which then releases its energy to launch the next phrase for the full ensemble.

Pianist Richard Jones said that the only time he ever heard the word "jazz" used in New Orleans was to identify the "jazz stop," or break. "Only that ending was called 'jazz,'" he said, "the music that went with the bumps of the dancer at the end. All the musicians heard about that jazz stop at the end and came to hear it." The early history of the break is not well documented, but Jones indicates a connection to dancing and a moment that everyone waits for. ("Break" must be related to the "break-away," when couples parted and briefly performed steps that were both creative and individual.) Jelly Roll Morton was adamant about breaks: "Without breaks and without clean breaks, without beautiful ideas in breaks, you don't need to even think about doing anything else. If you can't have a decent break, you haven't got a jazz band or you can't even play jazz. . . . Without a break you have nothing."

Because the break was a rupture in the normal flow of the music, it fostered a kind of solo utterance very different from the beautifully constructed lead so dear to Oliver. The lead melody organized the listener's perception of the musical flow for the entire piece; the break was a suspenseful eruption of that regular flow. Baby Dodds liked to use a mix of cowbells, ratchets, and cymbals for his solo breaks. Oliver was admired for his ability to create an endless stream of them. Doubting, perhaps, his ability to improvise, white musicians at Royal Gardens offered him a dollar for every new break he could play. "Joe broke them that night, took all their money, and was still playing breaks afterwards," remembered Fess Williams.

Now his apprentice was here to support him, staying under all the while. For most bands, solo breaks were the norm. The Oliver-Armstrong duet breaks seemed to come out of nowhere, splendidly synchronized, and many observers commented on them. Armstrong alluded to a secret system of communication, with Oliver cueing what was coming next and his student scrambling to match it. "The crowd would go mad over it!" he wrote.

In uptown New Orleans, the break was both an energizing moment and an opportunity to make a personal statement. The success of the performance hung on the prominent statement of the known tune, whether it was *Maple Leaf Rag* or *What a Friend We Have in Jesus*. The break split the seams of that statement with a flash of idiosyncratic brilliance from the performer. It was a brief spotlight on personal identity, regional identity, class identity, or racial identity, depending on how the situation was configured.

Oliver took control of *Eccentric* (discussed in Chapter 1) by adding breaks and expanding them to four measures, each filled with his award-winning freak music. Armstrong's slightly older rival, clarinetist and soprano saxophonist Sidney Bechet, also used the break to good advantage, for example, in his first successful recording, made on July 30, 1923, with Clarence Williams's Blue Five. Williams arranged *Wildcat Blues* to give Bechet no fewer than seven breaks, and he takes every one of them with complete authority. As a group, they are nicely varied in range, contour, and rhythm. Barney Bigard said that it was impossible to walk down the street where he lived in New Orleans without hearing phonograph machines, positioned next to open windows, broadcasting *Wildcat Blues* into the open air.

It may not be mere coincidence that Armstrong recorded, just a few months later on October 26, 1923, a piece that is even showier in its use of multiple breaks. *Tears*, with the Oliver band, features Armstrong in not seven but nine breaks packed into a stretch of some 40 seconds during the middle of the piece. No duets—it is all Armstrong. He and Bechet, the greatest soloists ever to come from New Orleans, had already established a budding rivalry during their teenage years before Bechet left the city. Both were reared in the competitive environment of improvising cutting contests, each trying to outplay or cut out the other, and neither was known to back down from a challenge.

*Tears* was co-composed by Armstrong and Hardin. Bechet's performance would have been the only incentive the engaged couple (wedding plans were made in August) needed to design a piece that would display Armstrong's growing powers of invention and technical skill in a series of breaks. He is perhaps not yet able to match Bechet's soaring confidence and precision—few could. But his nine breaks, taken as a whole, convey slightly more variety in design. One of them (CD 1:49–1:52) would still be useful to him four years later, in his famous solo for *Potato Head Blues*. In *Tears* the caution of *Chimes Blues* has been put aside, and it is clear that Armstrong, after one year of late apprenticeship with Oliver, felt well qualified to fill the rupture of the break on his own. The recording documents a breakthrough, a proper format for presenting his creativity and intensity.[10]

## Staying Under: Collective Improvisation

Anthropologist and novelist Zora Neale Hurston discussed the high value African Americans placed on ornamentation in the 1930s. She described a cabin in Alabama where the walls were enriched by calendars, scarves, colorful ads from the Sunday newspaper, crepe paper, and a lithograph showing the Treaty of Versailles. "Decorating a decoration . . . did not seem out of place to the hostess. The feeling back of such an act is that there can never be enough of beauty, let alone too much. . . . Whatever the Negro does of his own volition he embellishes."

Louis Armstrong was surrounded by this attitude for the first 21 years of his life. At home in the 1960s, as he scaled down his touring career, he enjoyed making collage decorations on the little boxes that stored his collection of reel-to-reel tapes. His will to adorn comes through again in his prose writings, where he routinely spins out wild displays of hyperpunctuation, capitalization, underlining, and commentary. But it was in music, of course, that the decorating passions of his community shaped him most profoundly, especially the ensemble styles of church and early jazz.

The musical texture of early jazz was connected to congregational singing in Sanctified churches, and the southern audiences who heard the Oliver band in Chicago certainly recognized this. Armstrong and the other musicians he knew probably grew up with a practice that is called heterophony. This is the simultaneous performance of two or more variations of a single melody; the number of variations is limited only by the number of participants. Outsiders hear congregational heterophony as chaotic and primitive, while insiders delight in richness that is both socially organized and uncompromisingly individual. It is one of the most welcoming, participatory musical practices ever invented, one designed to foster intense emotional involvement within the firm support of the community.

The distinctive texture of early jazz from New Orleans, derived from church heterophony, is known as collective improvisation. The

*Collage (Collection of Duncan Schiedt)*

closest musicians from New Orleans got to naming this rich practice was with the phrase "every tub on its own bottom." The connection between heterophony and collective improvisation is one basis for Armstrong's assertion that "it all came from the old Sanctified Churches." Jazz bands learned how to create an atmosphere of abundant ornamentation with fewer people but no drop in intensity.

Collective improvisation must be based on a prominent lead melody. "The melody is supposed to be heard distinctly from some instrument—the trumpet, trombone, clarinet or violin," as Baby Dodds put it. "At all times." The lead anchors the listener's perception amidst a swirl of musical activity. Collective improvisation probably grew out of heterophony, with several melody instruments simultaneously ornamenting the tune, as can be heard in recordings of 1950s street bands in New Orleans. Heterophony requires no harmonic regulation whatsoever. Early jazz musicians, like singers in Sanctified churches, created a musical world that did not depend on harmony. Given the importance that harmony would later take on in jazz, it requires an effort of historical imagination to understand the implications of this. When professional jazz musicians deepened their harmonic understanding and started to create supplemental parts with true melodic independence (as opposed to simultaneous variations on the same melody), collective improvisation pulled away from church practice. Yet, as we have seen in Chapter 2 in the discussion of *Chimes Blues*, harmonic precision was still a secondary concern for the Oliver band in 1923. Their main priority was the intensity of individual lines and their combined textural effect.

Out of standard practices come personal visions, and there was plenty of incentive for those, too, in New Orleans. The success of Oliver's bands depended on doing things his way. At times his authoritarian streak stood in tension with collective practice. He fired musicians when he saw benefit, leading to protests and even sympathy departures from those who regarded the band as more of a club. In California he started speaking of "my" band rather than "our" band, and Baby Dodds detected a distinct change in atmosphere. In recording sessions Oliver picked the pieces to be recorded and decided how to adapt them. "He started being a writer" in the studio, said Armstrong. The other New Orleanian to whom that comment might also apply is Jelly Roll Morton, who came at the matter from a very different direction. Yet Morton, commonly regarded as the first great composer in jazz, was said to give soloists more opportunity and freedom than Oliver did.

"Joe was always making suggestions for the improvement of the band," said Dodds. When he wanted Dodds to play more lightly, he bought him a pair of wire brushes. Dodds had trouble with them, but he eventually learned to lighten up with regular drumsticks. When Lil Hardin joined the band, she quickly got the message that her role was limited to chording on the beat. "Sometimes I'd get the urge to run up and down the piano," she remembered. But Oliver growled, "We [already] *have* a clarinet in the band."

The band's success was due partly to the excellence and experience of the musicians and partly to Oliver's vision. Dodds explained how tight the musicians were, how they had such a good sense of playing with each other. They were all experts in the ear-playing tra-

*Joe "King" Oliver (The William Russell Archive at the Historic New Orleans Collection, accession no. 92-48-L.108)*

dition from New Orleans, yet Oliver found ways to intervene. Clarinetist Albert Nicholas said that Oliver "wanted everyone to blend together. . . . He had discipline in that band." "The Oliver band was traditional and Joe was always doing things according to the New Orleans tradition," Dodds insisted, yet it was his version of that tradition that was being advanced, bit by bit.

Oliver's instruction to Hardin points to the details of how collective improvisation works, with a designated role for each instrument. A summary of those roles will provide a deeper sense of what this music is all about, as well as a better idea of what was expected from Armstrong.

The rhythm section kept the beat steady and articulated the chord changes. The bass played the main pitch of each chord on beats one and three; for special effect he played all four beats, with a plucking slap of the string against the fingerboard. The pianist and banjo (or guitar) hit the full chord on each of the four beats. "She would . . . *lay that good 4 beat under Papa Joe,"* who could "really *give* out," wrote Armstrong about Lil. The drummer played all four beats on the snare drum, beats one and three on the bass. This was the basic format, though a degree of variety was valued.

When Armstrong wrote about the "good ol' New Orleans 4 beat," he meant the even articulation of all four beats, with no difference in accent. In Eurocentric music, stress accents typically produce a hierarchy, with beat one emphasized the most, beat three slightly less, and beats two and four receding into the background. The lack of accentual differentiation in the good old New Orleans four beat may be thought of as "flat," yielding the flat 4/4. In the Oliver recordings from 1923 this is produced by pianist and banjo player. Later recordings document four-beat slap-picking in the bass; Ed Montudie Garland called this "doubling up." When, alternatively, string bass and bass drum play only beats one and three, the flat profile of piano and banjo is overlaid with a two-beat feeling.

The historical record does not reveal completely when and where the flat 4/4 was invented, how often it was used during the 1920s, and how it eventually became standard in dance-band music by the 1930s, in time to launch the swing era.[11] But it is clear that the four-beat style was used sometimes in uptown New Orleans, before Oliver left, and that this tradition had an impact in Chicago. Eddie Condon bought a ticket for Lincoln Gardens and was struck by the music flowing through the entryway "like a muscle flexing regularly, four to the bar."[12] The eventual domination of the flat 4/4 in commercial dance music in the 1930s signals the growing impact of that vernacular on the popular music of the United States, in tandem with vernacular dancing. It was a kind of territorial conquest, the spread of a cultural invention far from its place of origin. New Orleans was the point of entry into commercial dance-band music and the travel of New Orleanian musicians the means of distribution.

A drummer could make or break a band, and Baby Dodds was highly valued. The routine withdrawal of drums and bass in recording studios could be crippling; "the rhythm tended to get ragged," confessed Garvin Bushell. Dodds sometimes used the less invasive woodblock on the 1923 recordings, and his playing shows inventiveness and precision, a way of keeping things fresh that made him a crowd pleaser at Lincoln Gardens. He was known to mischievously roll off rhythms anticipating what a soloist was about to play, just to keep things interesting.

The rhythm section is the anchor that holds the basic layers of time and pitch with clear beat patterns and chords. The lead melody, played all the time by at least one instrument, provides another kind of anchor. Armstrong's comment that the 1923 recordings do not give sufficient prominence to the cornets has everything to do with this principle. Oliver liked to have a strong, clear lead that was not too heavily ornamented, playing "few notes and with good rhythm," as Muggsy Spanier said; "he was a 'feeder,' helping the others in the band." The main reason Oliver wanted Armstrong to join him was that he felt that his ability to deliver a strong lead was slipping, due to a gum disease that would eventually bring him down.

Lead melodies in this repertory inevitably unfold regularly, in an easy-to-follow way that the listener can effortlessly predict without even thinking about it. Trombonist Roy Palmer gave the standard New Orleanian critique of bebop when he said, "The new stuff they got now ain't got no foundation. Everybody's jumping up, and you can't tell, you can't get the significance of the piece. You don't know what they're playing. There ain't no lead." New Orleans jazz was created with an eye toward excitement and richness, but also accessibility. "There's people all over the world, they like to hear that lead," noted Armstrong.

Trombone, clarinet, and cornet fill out the "front line" of main melody instruments. With cornet on lead, the other instruments enrich but do not challenge its primary status. They treat the lead "like a girl," in Eddie Condon's colorful description, "they hang around it, doing handsprings and all sorts of other tricks, always keeping an eye on it and trying to make an impression." The trombonist has some choices. At times he reinforces the bass notes of chords on beats one and three, duplicating the bass. He can also fill in between phrases of the lead melody. Clarinetist Mezz Mezzrow called this playing "in the windows."

Armstrong claimed to admire trombonist Honoré Dutrey's ability to fill in (less appreciative commentators have derided Dutrey's "mooing"). An easy way to begin hearing fill-ins is in blues form, which is built on a regular flow of four-measure groups that divide into two parts; traditionally, a call and response between instruments or between voice and instrument follows from this division. In *Dipper Mouth Blues* (OKeh, June 1923), listen to Dutrey entering with a prepared "response" on a strong high note as a way to build momentum into the next "call" (CD: 0:09; 0:23; 1:05; 2:00).

Johnny Dodds was good at all of it—breaks, leads, fill-ins, and obbligatos, which are melodies that remain independent of the main melody in both contour and rhythm. The clarinet moves easily through its wide range, so Dodds freely dips below and above the cornet in a constant buzz of activity, blurring the distinction between filling in and obbligato. He accounts for some of the great moments from the Oliver band. For example, he rises to a dramatic, independent climax that seems to come out of nowhere and then quickly dissolves back into the flow in the first strain of *Chimes Blues* (CD 0:07–0:42). He is even more exposed in the second strain of *Canal Street Blues* (CD 0:37–1:07): with Oliver and Armstrong playing the theme from *Holy City* in steady long notes, Dodds's melody stands out.

In these ways, the adornments that distinguish collective improvisation come from obbligatos and fill-ins produced by the clarinet and trombone. With the cleanness of this format in mind, Oliver commanded Lillian to drop her clarinet-like runs. But there was one additional part to play—second cornet, which did not always support the lead from below, in parallel. Sometimes Armstrong plays fill-ins and obbligatos, to wonderful effect. His experience in this technique had considerable impact on his emerging solo style, so the topic is important.

It has often been noted that it was rare for dance bands in New Orleans to carry two cornets, suggesting that Armstrong lacked models to look to. But in fact there were plenty. Oliver provided one back in the early 1910s when he played second cornet—making "monkeyshines" and "barrelhouse," as observers described it—to Manuel Perez's lead in the Onward Brass Band. Cornetist Buddy Petit provided another with his skillful second playing, and so did Bunk Johnson. Even the legendary Buddy Bolden, who attracted so much attention, may have done so by playing second rather than lead. And when you realize that Fred Keppard and Sidney Bechet were also great second players, it becomes clear that virtually *all* of the great soloists to come out of New Orleans excelled not only at lead but also at second. Armstrong played second in the Tuxedo Brass Band, just before he left for Chicago in 1922, staying soft and under the leader, cornetist Oscar "Papa" Celestin. One band member insisted that he should have played lead. But it was Celestin's band, Armstrong countered. "I can't be a boss on that, man. I just want my money," he joked.

Oliver probably gave sparse but pithy instructions regulating the texture. A few comments here and there and a few nonverbal cues were pretty much all he needed. In jazz it has always been important to make room for performer-centered specialties that cannot possibly be dictated and controlled in the traditional way of a composer or arranger. The details of collective improvisation depend on the experience and alertness of the ear-playing musicians; there is no way to micromanage them.

It is possible that the band used commercial arrangements—"stocks," as they are called—but that was probably rare. Preston Jackson and Lillian both said plainly that the band did not use written arrangements. The band's stately rendition of *Riverside Blues* was based on a composition by Richard Jones and the young Thomas Dorsey, who made an arrangement of the piece for Oliver's recording in autumn 1923.[13] Most likely, he and Jones produced a set of melodies with simple harmonic accompaniment, thus defining the "composition"; Dorsey then added notated details for the introduction, the coda, and parts of the accompaniment for the "arrangement," including rhythmic punctuations supporting the second-strain solos by clarinet and trombone (CD 1:02–1:54), repeated again when Armstrong takes the final statement of the same melody (CD 2:20–end).[14]

It was standard practice in New Orleans to take a piece of sheet music and tweak it to produce a head arrangement that existed nowhere but in the memory of the players. The arrangement could take shape gradually, night after night, the band getting things the way they wanted them. But the bands also rehearsed. Armstrong remembered the tough winter of 1922–23, when Mrs. Majors turned off the heat at Lincoln Gardens on "bad nights." The musicians wore overcoats and Johnny Dodds even wore gloves. Armstrong noticed a few ice crystals on his mouthpiece. "The only good thing about it was that we got a chance to do a lot of rehearsing," he said, "and that kept us right on the ball."

An unprescribed sequence of experimenting and rehearsing produced a head arrangement that foregrounded the African-American musical vernacular from New Orleans; eventually the arrangement became set. Of course, spontaneity was still possible, but the important thing was the *appearance* of spontaneity. The music sounded fresh and alive because the texture and details could not possibly be produced through notation, only through flexible give and take as guided by the players' ears.

"Once you got a certain solo that fit in the tune, and that's it, you keep it," explained Armstrong, and the same principle held for group playing. This is why the phrase "collective improvisation" is a misnomer: the musicians were not actually improvising when they performed in public. Their music was shaped by a potentially four-fold process that included the use of notated arrangements, a traditional formulaic sense of how each instrument should participate, head arrangements formed by ear, and spontaneous improvisation. We are stuck with the term "collective improvisation," which should be understood to mean not the process but the glorious results.

Viewed in another way, collective improvisation intersects with the fixed and variable model described in the Introduction. This practice may be one of the more imaginative transformations of this model in the New World. In blues we discovered the first great legacy of slavery that conditioned Armstrong's music; collective improvisation is the second. Both were central to the development of African-American vernacular music and to Armstrong's mature style.

In the Caribbean, where drum ensembles remained surprisingly stable through slavery up to the present day, the fixed and variable model works just as it does in Africa, down to details of identical rhythmic patterns played by identical instruments. One group of instruments, or simply a single instrument, repeats a rhythm that orients the listener or dancer. The pattern is usually divisible by two beats. This is the fixed group. The variable group, while always maintaining some connection to the fixed group, brings the music to life by departing from the pattern in interesting ways. Complexity comes from the way these two groups go in and out of phase with each other.

The changing activity of the variable group, as it interacts with the foundation, going back and forth between agreement and tension, is made more obvious through instrumentation. Timbral diversity—using instruments with contrasting sound qualities such as bell, drum, and gourd rattle in West Africa; or stick, harmonica, guitar, and fife on a Mississippi porch; or cornet, trombone, and clarinet in the front line of collective improvisation—makes it easy for the ear to pick out the layers. The emphasis is not on blending the timbres, as happens, say, in a classical string quartet, but on *differentiating* them, creating a stratified texture that makes it easy to pick out the distinct voices of fixed and variable activity.

Early Western scholars were often misled by the complexities of African drumming. What is now clear is that no matter how intricate the entire ensemble is, all of it must be understood *in terms of the fixed rhythmic group*. This is not merely an analytical matter, but a very real matter of perception. The movement of dancers teaches everyone how to hear the music, how to track the fixed layer as the primary one, and therefore how to recognize the variable group and internalize its relationship to the fixed in a natural, relaxed way.

The human ear's ability to synthesize sonic events that sound simultaneously is one basis for the miracle of music. Music all over the world takes advantage of this ability to hear multiple patterns and maintain a sense of their independence as well as their unity. European harmony may be explained in this way: we hear chords that serve as the foundation for textural complexity. Music of the African diaspora exploits the same auditory potential in a different way.

In African drum ensembles, the fixed group of instruments may create a rhythmic web that, in itself, is considerably complex. Compared to this, the fixed group in early jazz is stark and simple. Drum ensembles were routinely suppressed during slavery in the United States (those heard in Place Congo, or Congo Square, in New Orleans being a famous exception), so it is not surprising that specific details of the African model were lost while the general principles were retained and applied to different instruments, techniques, repertories, and styles.

Though details of West African drum ensembles did not survive in the American South, the fixed and variable model not only survived, it flourished. Musicians transformed it in countless, imaginative ways. Their creative search often meant incorporating Eurocentric harmony and melody into the model, and Louis Armstrong's mature solo style in the 1920s was the product of precisely this kind of synthesis.

In other words, the fixed and variable model, created in Africa and transmitted to the New World by enslaved people, accounts for central qualities of jazz as Armstrong learned it, transformed it, and propagated it.

The rhythm section keeps the beat and forms basic patterns. Eddie Condon, who liked metaphors, said that the "rhythm section provides transportation, everything floats on its beat." Another way of saying that is that the rhythm section provides a foundation that is analogous to the fixed rhythmic group in Africa.

In the 1923 Oliver recordings, the variable group usually departs from the fixed in four ways: dragging behind the beat, syncopation, additive rhythm, and irregularly placed accents. The first two are common in blues, the middle two in ragtime. Improvising wind players from New Orleans favored the final method—using irregular accents to form phrases that build tension against the fixed foundation. The variable group is connected to the fixed both rhythmically and harmonically: the improvised lines of clarinet, cornet, and trombone prominently feature the chord tones of each measure, and they are in phase rhythmically, to a degree.[15] The listener does not need this all spelled out in order to hear the form, for the ear will recognize it effortlessly and unconsciously. Pointing it out, however, leads to a more complete understanding of what the New Orleanians did with this basic structure, since it is the key to their distinctive sound.

The instrument playing the lead melody, usually the cornet, participates in both the fixed and the variable groups. The lead melody clearly articulates the tune's two-bar pattern. Then, with syncopation, dragging behind the beat, and irregularly placed accents, the trumpeter creates a rhythmic clash. Meanwhile, the trombonist plays the lowest notes of chords on the beat. He also shifts to the variable side of things with fill-ins and obbligato, but it's the clarinetist who is the variable specialist. Trombone and clarinet stagger their phrases against the regular pattern of the tune, unpredictably cutting, dipping, and rising. "Notes I had never heard were peeling off the edges and dropping through the middle," said Condon. The players clash on the level not only of rhythm, but of phrasing as well, with the fixed group following the established pattern and the variable constantly challenging it with irregular points of entry and irregular accents. This extensive clashing is not typical of ragtime and blues, and seems to have been a special achievement of New Orleans.

Uptown African Americans in Armstrong's community took two principles that do not necessarily go together—the will to adorn, and the fixed and variable model—and synthesized them to create music that was new and exciting. The *New York Clipper* (Sept. 14, 1923) reviewed four recordings by Oliver's band, including *Dipper Mouth Blues*, and referenced "barbaric indigo dance tunes played with gusto and much ado that leaves very little doubt as to their African origin." "In west Africa the superposition of two different, related pulse schemes is common and is like a grid in the mind," according to Gerhard Kubik, a scholar who has spent a lifetime studying African music south of the Sahara. African Americans in Armstrong's community, many recently arrived from the vast plantations of Louisiana and Mississippi, where African legacies were strong, carried this mental grid to New Orleans and then to Chicago; phonograph recordings took it from there.

Collective improvisation balances total order with total chaos. Other kinds of music do the same thing, but this one invites uncompromised intensity, which is precisely where the Oliver band excelled. They were oblivious to old settlers, dicty writers, and unappreciative whites who turned up their noses at rough dissonances and harmonic confusion. We can see more clearly now why it was not such a big deal to miss a chord and why the musicians had nothing to say when Hardin asked what key they would be playing in. It is not that harmony was irrelevant, only that it was less important here than the fixed and variable model, which extended an invitation to move. "One couldn't help but dance to that band," said Baby Dodds, and again the connection with West Africa is clear.

Without emphasis on the fixed and variable model, jazz would

*Louis and Lillian (Collection of Duncan Schiedt)*

have become a very different kind of music. In fact, the model became a defining characteristic of the idiom. When watered down, the music drifts toward pop. Bebop embraced the model and extended it; modal jazz retained aspects and free jazz abandoned it. Intensifications and departures like these were calculated, for complex historical reasons.

Oliver did not want Hardin interfering on the variable side, but Armstrong plays some attractive fill-ins in the 1923 recordings. Sometimes he breaks out with an extended obbligato, as he was known to do during the early days in New Orleans. "I didn't never understand Louis Armstrong, because that son of a gun, he didn't care what you played," remembered trombonist Charles "Sunny" Henry. "He would play a obbligato all the time, be off you understand; he wouldn't play straight with you. But every thing he put in there worked."

The classic representation of Armstrong's obbligato is the October 1923 recording of *Mabel's Dream*. In the third strain (CD 1:24–1:46) the ensemble is reduced, and for some reason Armstrong is close to the recording horn. Against the rules, he is louder than his mentor's lead. Yet the lead remains clear thanks to his skill in design; he keeps his obbligato out of the way. He balances the two lines while capturing just the right degree of independence in phrasing, very much in the tradition of filling in. The mandate to stay under Oliver generated this kind of sensitivity, no doubt.

Condon succinctly described the ensemble at Lincoln Gardens: "Everyone was playing what he wanted to play and it was all mixed together as if someone had planned it with a set of micrometer calipers." Condon had no way of knowing that he was witnessing modern masters of an ancient tradition of communal music making, one distributed to the New World through the African diaspora.

Garvin Bushell remembered the Dodds brothers feeling "very highly about what they were playing, as though they knew they were doing something new that nobody else could do." Intense urban competition lifted the vernacular to a sophisticated level of professional practice, first in New Orleans and now in Chicago. Armstrong was the emerging talent who was finding ways to express himself while staying under. Such was the nature of his late apprenticeship with Papa Joe, and even though it seemed to some that he could easily have skipped this stage in his training, the evidence of his mature solo style suggests that the control of musical order he was perfecting was extremely important.

## Stepping Out: Marriage and *Cornet Chop Suey*

The summer of 1923 was a lot of fun for Louis, Lil, and the rest of the band. When he wasn't feeling well, Oliver gave Louis some featured solos. These were token gestures; in general, Oliver was still holding him back, even in after-hours jam sessions. Willie "The Lion" Smith witnessed this at Schiller's Café, a favorite place for cutting contests in the early-morning hours. "Oliver would refuse to let Louis get off on his own sometimes," Smith remembered. "Louis at that time was beginning to out blow his boss and so Oliver would try to keep them both working on those famous cornet duets so Armstrong couldn't outshine him." Smith liked to tell Armstrong to step out and play a solo while slipping him five bucks. He showed his stuff one night in a contest against cornetist Bobby Williams, dashing off 40 choruses on *The Sheik of Araby*. Williams responded with a version of *Bugle Blues* that was gaining him a reputation. "The thing that seemed to get the listeners was Bobby's sweet tone and the way he made chords—something like Sidney Bechet later handled the soprano saxophone," said Smith.

Lil bought a used car and took her friends for rides. She and Louis attended an "all-colored" auto race, billed as the first of its kind and heavily advertised. Everyone had a hip flask and the place was buzzing with excitement. A pileup put a damper on things, and the event fell apart when a pedestrian wandered onto the track and got blasted into the air by a speeding car. "From now on I don't want to see a foot race let alone an automobile race," Louis told Lil as they hastily left the scene.

The couple attended picnics, including one at St. Thomas Episcopal Church, East 38th Street and Wabash Avenue, where John Henry Simons, a rector who enjoyed occasional write-ups in the *Defender*, gave strong sermons. St. Thomas's was known for elaborate performances of classical pieces like Haydn's oratorio *The Creation*. Lil wanted to expose Louis to a classy way of doing things, but the results were mixed. He watched "all the big wigs . . . each trying to out do the other," and decided "they was a pack of fools." "The big wigs in New Orleans acted differently when they were supposed to be the big wigs," he joked. Lil confided to him about her troubled marriage to a singer named Johnny and his heavy drinking; they were still married but no longer living together. He in turn told her about problems with his wife Daisy, whom he hadn't seen since he left New Orleans.

In early June the band was hired for the Music Trades Convention at the Drake Hotel, downtown on the "Gold Coast," as the only African Americans amidst a bunch of white units. Local bandleader Sig Meyer described the event as a "festival of recording bands." "The 'dark horse' orchestra of the whole bunch was sure dark," quipped *Talking Machine World*, which also singled out "the little frog-mouthed boy who played cornet." With Louis getting special notice at an event that was overwhelmingly white, Oliver must have seen the writing on the wall.[16]

Louis and Lillian helped May Ann find an apartment, and he entrusted the selection of furniture to Lil, since "she was really *up* on things, the *modern* things," he said, "and she had such wonderful *taste*." They set up the furniture and paused to look around. Lil may have made the first move; he later claimed that even now he did not suspect that she was romantically interested in him. "We both looked at the bed at the same time," he remembered. "And Lil, being the master mind of the two . . ." They played "a little tag" and finally got down to the business of "making violent but beautiful love. And from that moment, until the day we were married, we fell in love with each other"—an interesting and perhaps precise assessment.

Other, unnamed members of the band had been making a play for Lil, and there was some bafflement and even hostility in response to the blossoming of this relationship. "For a while they all gave she and I a lot of 'ice,' meaning they treated us rather cool when we went to work," Louis wrote. On June 23 the band recorded a piece cowritten by the two of them, *Where Did You Stay Last Night?*, which must have generated a few snickers.

On the June sessions Armstrong also played slide whistle, a common novelty instrument of the day, on *Sobbin' Blues*. Early August saw the co-composition of *When You Leave Me Alone to Pine*, music by Louis Armstrong and words by Lillian Hardin. An August 18 article in the *Defender* bragged that *Sobbin' Blues* and *Sweet Lovin' Man* were selling well all over the country. An August 22 notice in *Talking Machine World* mentioned Oliver's "trick" cornet playing, which is featured on both of these recordings. On September 1 the *Defender* reported that the Oliver band was filling up Lincoln Gardens close to capacity, night after night.

In early August 1923 Lil and Louis decided to get married. Each initiated divorce proceedings with their respective spouses.[17] She started to take a more active role in his life. He mentioned that Oliver had been keeping his money for him, dishing it out periodically as an allowance. (Armstrong would later duplicate that arrangement with Joe Glaser, who managed him for the last 35 years of his life.) Lil objected and told him that he should keep his own money. "You know, Mr. Joe sent for me and he looks out for me," he insisted. She replied that she would be looking out for him from now on.

When he showed up at work in a new gray overcoat and velour hat, the manager, Budd Red, cut him down to size, saying he knew that "if you fool around with that chick she was gonna change your appearance." Oliver angrily told him that Lil was spoiled and would waste his money on clothes and ice cream. Early in August Louis was switching to fashionable Chicago dress as a way of signaling his alignment with Lil, which meant taking a step away from his hometown friends. "He liked the [new] way he looked," insisted Lil. The two of them composed *Tears*, which made it into the October recording sessions with OKeh, and Armstrong showed the record-buying public what he could do. From the first recording sessions with Gennett in April through the October 25 sessions with OKeh, the Oliver band recorded 22 different pieces that feature dozens of breaks; but the first solo break for Armstrong on record comes in *Tears*. This moment represents an assertion by Armstrong and Hardin and a concession from Oliver: Lil was clearly advising him on more than clothing.

We have already seen two musical manifestations of Lil's ambition for Louis—their co-composition of *Where Did You Sleep Last Night?* and *Tears*, with its multiple breaks. The completion of *Cornet Chop Suey* in January 1924 marked an even more important milestone. We do not have much detail about the path to this impressive piece, which Louis composed as a solo vehicle for himself. But we do know about various streams contributing to his progress around this time. Some of this information comes without specific chronology and may describe slightly later events, but the general trends are firmly established. In their search for fame and lucre, Lil and Louis were exploring two main avenues—compositions that they could copyright and a more prominent space for Louis as a soloist. *Cornet Chop Suey* is a splendid synthesis of both.

Lil said that the two of them practiced once a week. She played the piano while he struggled to master Oliver's solo for *Dipper Mouth Blues*. Oliver's freak music had earned him a king's crown at Royal Gardens, and the Gennett recording of *Dipper Mouth Blues* extended his fame beyond Chicago. Freak music was the thing, and not just with Oliver. Keppard was featuring it, and so was fellow Louisianan Tommy Ladnier, whose solo on *Play That Thing* with Ollie Powers's Harmony Syncopators, recorded in September 1923, is a fine example. Lil said that Louis couldn't coordinate the wah-wah effects with his right hand as he manipulated the plunger over the bell of his horn. "I'm not much with a plunger, man," he said much later. "Well I mean I like it at times, but I don't have time to get to mine." It is easy to understand his frustration: if he couldn't play freak music, how was he going to make a name for himself?

Meanwhile, Bobby Williams was presenting an alternative voice on cornet. Soon after he arrived in Chicago, Armstrong heard Williams playing with Carroll Dickerson's Orchestra at the Sunset Café. He described Williams as a "nice looking, stout, brown skin man, a little on the heavy side and rather short," with a "pleasant smile and a very good looking personality. Always had a kind word for anyone whom he should meet." Williams had served in World War I as a military trumpeter. Armstrong believed him to be the composer of *Bugle Blues*, which Williams featured every night at the Sunset.

*Bugle Blues* belonged to a set of interrelated pieces that included *Bugle Call Rag*. The various titles were frequently confused; most likely these pieces had fluid musical identities. They all feature some kind of military call, usually *reveille*, mixed in with jazzy ensemble sections. Whether or not Williams thought up the idea, he was doing well with it at the Sunset Café, thus presenting Armstrong with an alternative solo model that was enjoying success.[18] Here was idiomatic cornet playing, based on the arpeggiated chords typical of bugle calls, heard now in a jazz context. It was a novelty that people obviously enjoyed.

Hoagy Carmichael remembered hearing Armstrong play *Bugle Call Rag* at a fast tempo in Chicago during the summer of 1923. Six months later he mailed a manuscript copy of *Cornet Chop Suey*, full of buglelike arpeggiations, to Washington, D.C., for copyright. Williams's *Bugle Blues* must have been an important precedent for this creative breakthrough.

*Cornet Chop Suey* begins with a strong set of solo arpeggiations around a single chord, just like the bugle calls. Faced with a challenge, Armstrong's instincts were to play faster (as Carmichael heard him do with *Bugle Call Rag* in 1923) and with greater elaboration (as he does with other arpeggiations in *Cornet Chop Suey*). Perhaps he remembered his own bugle playing at the Colored Waif's Home for Boys, where he blew *Reveille*, *Taps*, and *Mess* in 1912. The military-style gesture fits right in with the brash confidence and masculine assertion that were so much a part of jazz in New Orleans and now Chicago.

The title *Cornet Chop Suey* can be read as a reference to both *Bugle Blues* and *Clarinet Marmalade*. The latter had been going strong ever since the Original Dixieland Jazz Band's bestselling recording in 1918. Back in New Orleans, Armstrong had learned the clarinet solo on his cornet as a way to show off his quick fingering. That and the piccolo solo for *High Society* were measures of accomplishment that could be dished out in cutting contests. Alphonse Picou made a name for himself by transferring the piccolo solo of *High Society* to clarinet, and Armstrong did him one better by playing it on cornet, a harder assignment.

To call a piece *Clarinet Marmalade* meant that the featured instrument was delicious, and *Cornet Chop Suey* meant the same thing. The title promises music to savor like your favorite Chinese dish; there is a hint of exoticism, something new and fresh. Chop suey was immensely popular on the South Side. In January 1923, the *Defender* raved about the Dreamland Cabaret's new Chinese chef, whom Alberta Hunter remembered cooking the best chop suey in all of Chicago. (Coincidentally, it would be the Dreamland where Armstrong would first present *Cornet Chop Suey* to the public, with great success, several years later.) The Pekin Inn, another gathering spot for musicians, also served Chinese food, but chop suey places were all over the South Side. We know that Oliver, Jelly Roll Morton, and other New Orleanians loved Chinese food generally and chop suey in particular.[19] A musician who traveled with Armstrong in the 1950s claimed that he ate Chinese food every night of his life. The title *Cornet Chop Suey* was born out of a widely shared pleasure.

Armstrong gained a reputation for quick fingers in New Orleans in the late 1910s, and in Chicago he extended his technique further by signing up for formal lessons with a classical musician. We don't know the precise date, but it is possible that these lessons were part of the momentum that led to *Cornet Chop Suey*.

"Improving my position" was the slogan of immigrants from the Deep South, and formal study with classically trained teachers was how that aspiration manifested itself with musicians. The backgrounds of most New Orleanian musicians (that is, the ones Armstrong grew up with) in instrumental technique, music theory, and even the basics of notation were thin or nonexistent. Lessons made sense if they wanted to get ahead in Chicago. Bass player Ed "Montudie" Garland said that he "didn't take any kind of lessons 'til I got to Chicago. I didn't know nothing about no [written] music." Garland secured a studio slot with Professor James Jackson, at 31st and State Streets. Jackson also taught fellow New Orleanian Wellman Braud; "I was a faker until I went to Chicago," Braud remembered. Clarinetists Jimmie Noone from New Orleans and Buster Bailey from Memphis took lessons with German music teacher Franz Schoepp, first clarinetist with the Chicago Symphony; they were sometimes joined by the young Benny Goodman. Trumpeter Bob Shoffner and pianist Luis Russell, members of Oliver's band in early 1927, were both applauded publicly by Dave Peyton when they signed up for music theory lessons twice weekly. Trumpeter Reuben Reeves took lessons with another German teacher, Albert Cook, who also played in the Chicago Symphony. Kid Ory took a few lessons in Chicago with "some German guy" who played with the symphony, but the teacher was perplexed enough by Ory's tailgating ways to turn him away after a few attempts with the unlikely suggestion that the two should reverse roles, Ory as teacher and the German guy as student.

This kind of training had been within view but not within reach of Armstrong in New Orleans. He was able to pick up bits and pieces here and there, but he lacked access to a sustained program of Euro-centric pedagogy that Creole musicians, living on the other side of Canal Street in the Seventh Ward, were routinely brought up with. On the riverboat jobs he mingled with trained musicians who shared their knowledge with him; in fact, Fate Marable, the bandleader on the boats, had assembled the musicians with precisely this mix in mind. Now in Chicago he could advance further, urged on by his classically trained girlfriend.

New Orleans pianist Richard M. Jones, who was active in Chicago at this time, reported that Louis studied with a German teacher at Kimball Hall.[20] Kimball Hall was an impressive complex on Wabash Avenue, downtown "in the Loop," with a recital hall, 75 offices, and a warehouse for the W. W. Kimball Company, which manufactured pianos and organs. The *Defender* occasionally covered African-American participation there. It reported, for example, that lyric tenor William Hart gave a recital, in which he displayed excellent diction in Italian and Russian, and that Mrs. W. T. Gray, niece of "Mrs. and Mr. Jack Gray, the former cotton king of Candler, Arizona," took voice lessons at Kimball Hall. The March 26, 1921, issue reviewed a piano-vocal recital with "master" Hersal Thomas at the piano and his brother George Thomas singing his own composition, *Sweet Baby Doll*. Oliver's band recorded *Sweet Baby Doll* on October 26, 1923, and Hersal would record with Armstrong on several occasions in 1925 and 1926.

Jones did not say if the German teacher taught Armstrong cornet technique or music theory; it could easily have been both. (Jones did say that Oliver studied harmony in Chicago. We know that Armstrong knew solfège; here would have been his chance to learn it.) The method book of choice for cornet lessons was the "Arban" book, filled with tricky exercises in stages of increasing difficulty and designed to enhance facility with fingers, lips, and tongue through arpeggiations and ornaments—just the kind of thing that *Cornet Chop Suey* puts on dexterous display.

Armstrong said that he learned how to transpose music from a piano while playing his cornet and that this helped him in his practice sessions with Lil; that, too, is the kind of thing that was being taught by German music teachers at Kimball Hall. He and Lil liked to "wood shed," as he described it. "We bought classical trumpet music," he remembered. They performed the fruits of their labors in recitals at churches. He was nervous and, according to Lillian, got anxious before his solos. "He's a fellow who didn't have much confidence in himself to begin with," she said. "He didn't believe in himself." It is attractive to think of the confidence first documented in *Tears* as the product of lessons, practice, and recitals under the watchful eye of his fiancée.

There are stories of jazz musicians avoiding formal training because they were afraid it would make them sound "white." Partly defensive and partly assertive, we find signs of this attitude in sarcastic references to the "cute guys," musicians who could read music in New Orleans. Many years later, Miles Davis called that a "ghetto mentality." "Knowledge is freedom and ignorance is slavery, and I just couldn't believe someone could be that close to freedom and not take advantage of it," Davis insisted. "It's like a ghetto mentality telling people that they aren't supposed to do certain things, that those things are only reserved for white people." Armstrong and his self-improving friends in Chicago would have agreed. It is easy to imagine Hardin's pride in her boyfriend, who was definitely moving in the right direction with his nice clothes, music lessons, and picnics at St. Thomas Episcopal.

*Cornet Chop Suey* is a showpiece in the New Orleans tradition of *High Society* and *Clarinet Marmalade*, with the added precedent of *Bugle Call Rag* and the added ammunition of improved technique. In 1951, when Armstrong listened to his 1926 recording of the piece, it reminded him of cutting contests in early New Orleans with Buddy Petit, Joe Johnson, and Kid Rena. "We were all very fast on our cornets," he commented. When the recording came out, its purpose was clear back home. Kid Rena lost a cutting contest to Lee Collins, who scored the victory by playing *Cornet Chop Suey* note for note. When asked why he hadn't also played Armstrong's solos in the battle, Rena unleashed his scorn: "Because Louis was up North making records and running up and down like he's crazy don't mean that he's that great. He's not playing cornet on that horn; he's imitating a clarinet. He's showing off." Rena had heard Armstrong showing off in New Orleans by playing the clarinet parts of *High Society* and *Clarinet Marmalade*; now his old rival was upping the ante even higher. A more direct association for the challenging arpeggiations that provide the basic melodic material for *Cornet Chop Suey* would have been the lively rags of Scott Joplin (and virtually all other piano players). Can you top this one?—that was the message from the other end of the New Orleans–Chicago train line.

The fact that Armstrong created *Cornet Chop Suey* as a notated piece, and not just a solo that he memorized and played on stage, is important and part of the musical economy of the time. It also has a lot to do with the kind of creative musician he was becoming. We will watch this line of development play out during the next few years as he takes position as the leading figure of African-American jazz modernism in mid-1920s Chicago.

Lil and Louis had each been composing tunes before they even met. Lil had some success with *Sweet Lovin' Man*, which she copyrighted in September 1922 (the New Orleans Rhythm Kings recorded it in March 1923, Oliver's band in June 1923). Armstrong had been writing tunes with Oliver (*Canal Street Blues*, *Dipper Mouth Blues*), and before that on the riverboats, where he created *Weather Bird Rag*. Even before that he had composed a dirty little song called *Katie's Head* that was adapted and sanitized by Clarence Williams and Armand Piron, who published it as their own and entitled it *I Wish I Could Shimmy Like My Sister Kate*, a bestseller in 1919. It must have seemed like destiny that the two aspiring songwriters should hook up both musically and romantically.

Musicians in their circle were acutely aware of the cash potential of notated tunes, which they sent to Washington, D.C., for copyright. "Have you got any good blues?" Oliver wrote to his friend Bunk Johnson back in New Orleans. "If so send them to me and I will make them bring you some real money." Oliver put his name on a number of tunes during the early 1920s, and he probably wrote a few that were claimed by other people, too. Jimmy Noone insisted that he and Oliver cowrote *Royal Garden Blues*, one of the classic repertory pieces in early jazz, and that Clarence Williams stole it and published it under his own name. There are so many stories about Williams doing this sort of thing that there seems no reason to doubt Noone.

Armstrong once mused about occasions when musicians had done the same thing to him, but he was able to take the offenses in stride since, as he mused, "there will be other tunes. There's always another one coming along—like a streetcar." He and Oliver each had a knack for melodic invention. Armstrong praised his mentor's abilities on many occasions: "no one created as much as Joe," he wrote plainly. But what, precisely, did he mean by this? On recordings, Oliver occasionally plays a solo that is his own invention, but more often he simply paraphrases popular tunes.

My guess is that Armstrong was mainly praising Oliver as a composer who helped create *Canal Street Blues*, *Chimes Blues*, *Snake Rag*, *Camp Meeting Blues*, *West End Blues*, and many other tunes. How much he created and how much he shaped, arranged, abridged, combined, paraphrased, or simply notated is impossible to say. Composers everywhere routinely move through this same range of activity, which was standard procedure in the oral tradition from which jazz emerged. When the market for vernacular music opened up, the rush to copyright wasn't always pretty. Jelly Roll Morton was accused of claiming lots of pieces that were simply floating around, and Oliver undoubtedly participated in this kind of appropriation, too.

But what should not be missed is the status of composition as part of Oliver's musical identity. Armstrong admired Oliver's ability to make a phrase that stays with you. Oliver told his apprentice to avoid snakes—too many variations—and to state a clear lead. These were advanced lessons in composition for his promising student.

Oliver, Hardin, and Armstrong were interested in notating compositions because they held out the promise of big returns—"real money," as Oliver wrote to Johnson. Recordings for Gennett and OKeh did not generate much cash, but if a disc became popular and other musicians decided to record the piece, then the composer (that is, the holder of the copyright) might see a steady stream of royalties, based on sales of the new recordings. This, along with an expanded reputation, was the opportunity that race recordings—recordings aimed at the African-American market—opened up. Now there was an alternative to distributing notated pieces through sheet music.

Untrustworthy publishers could be avoided and the claim could be made simply by putting the notated melody in the mail.

This was the chain of economic logic that drove a great deal of composing, recording, and notating in the early 1920s. It was an unexpected, secondary effect of recording technology, which inadvertently brought this nexus into focus. Armstrong understood the incentive to think of composing, notating, and recording as a package rather than as separate activities. He remembered writing *Cornet Chop Suey* on the back steps of Lil's house at 3320 Giles Avenue. By January 18, 1924, the notated copy, which is clearly in Armstrong's hand, had reached Washington, D.C.[21] "We were all so ambitious," observed Baby Dodds as he mused about Lil's and Louis's compositions.

This economic situation—the financial incentive to create tunes that could be easily written down and copyrighted—shaped Armstrong's creative development. By finding his niche in melodies that could be notated, he was forced to think in those terms. Beginning with *Weather Bird Rag*, in April 1923, he relied on Lillian to write the lead sheets that were sent to Washington, but in December he started to notate them himself; perhaps this was a sign of progress in his studies.[22] All along he was training himself to channel his creativity so that it could be articulated in writing. *Cornet Chop Suey* marks an arrival in this regard. This is not to say that he does not bring his skills as a performer to the piece when he plays it, but the notation does capture something close to his full conception.

The proof of this is the recording of the piece made two years later, in February 1926. The fascinating thing is how close the recording is to the piece notated two years before. In his first run-through of the tune, there are a few improvements—that is the best way to think of them, and not simply as manifestations of a felt freedom to vary the material.[23] They illustrate the continued engagement of tinkering with a melody over time, little revisions of the kind that composers constantly make. Comparison between the lead sheet and the later recording documents the working method of someone who should be regarded as one of the twentieth century's great masters of melody.

The differences between recording and performance for the first run-through of the theme are not anything like what one would expect if one takes the view that jazz is a matter of adding vernacular performance traditions to received tunes, that what is written is simply a starting point for the performer's creativity. That model does not hold here. Instead, what we discover is that Armstrong conceived his piece so that it could be transmitted, completely and essentially, in writing. Nothing important is left out. The root cause of this situation was this: he was working in an environment where written transmission promised greater rewards than performance. The role of the written document in making a claim to copyright causes him to form his musical thought in terms of what can be inscribed.

There is no sense that his ideas have been awkwardly forced into notation. Jazz was born around the turn of the century in New Orleans, in an environment that favored unnotatable musical expression, and that kind of expression has been important for its entire history. Armstrong became one of the leading experts in it, but here he is pursuing a different creative model.

He was not good at freak music, so he searched for an alternative way to make his mark. There was no way to notate freak music anyway. To put Oliver's *Dipper Mouth Blues* solo on paper is to leave out most of what is important. Freak music had nothing to do with the economic nexus that surrounded the notation of tunes for copyright and came instead from the oral tradition that gave advantage to performers, not composers. The patrons who crowned Oliver at Royal Gardens were acknowledging him as a master in this tradition, which was expanding its territory through the Great Migration. In *Cornet Chop Suey* Armstrong was pursuing a musical idiom that was closer to ragtime (as Scott Joplin thought of that word) than to blues. He was thoroughly trained as a blues specialist and spent nearly two years in a late apprenticeship with Oliver at a venue that rewarded blues, but his creative breakthrough went in a different direction.

Taking a step away from Oliver, creating a showpiece for himself, thinking in terms of what can be notated and copyrighted—all of this shaped *Cornet Chop Suey*. So, perhaps, did another musical practice that is a bit surprising, a musical tradition that had a solid place in New Orleans, even though it seems trivial today: whistling.

Lillian said that she could hear Louis whistling from a couple of blocks away as he approached their apartment. His whistling was creative and unusual, "all the fancy runs that he later played," she said.

Whistling had been part of the musical scene in New Orleans. "They came up whistling and dancing and singing and it's born in them," said Baby Dodds about working-class Negroes in New Orleans. Cornetist Bunk Johnson learned to whistle Buddy Bolden's solos. The Ory–Oliver band in New Orleans in the mid-1910s actually worked out new pieces by whistling them. Lillian De Pass claimed that a certain style identified a whistler as a musician in New Orleans. And Preston Jackson described hanging out as a teenager, listening to a band and then having whistling contests among his friends the next day in an attempt to duplicate the event. "I could whistle anything anyone played," he bragged.

Armstrong whistled as a way to create ideas that he did not yet play on his cornet. "The thing that makes jazz so interesting is that each man is his own academy," said pianist Cecil Taylor. Whistling served as Armstrong's compositional laboratory, a way to sketch precursors to the fancy runs that eventually made him famous. There is no way to know how much that played out in *Cornet Chop Suey*, but it is certainly full of fancy runs, and it is the earliest of his famous solos.

Lillian urged him to break away from Oliver and develop his own style. "She didn't want me to copy Joe," Armstrong explained, "liked me to play the way I felt it." Experimental whistling combined with woodshedding the classics, with growing confidence acquired through recitals at church picnics and the composition and recording of *Tears*; with his competitive nature, developed through years of cutting contests; with technical lessons in the Eurocentric tradition; and with advanced lessons, sui generis, from Oliver, and his increased understanding of tune construction and how to notate. He put all of it together in his own academy, and the result was *Cornet Chop Suey*.

Lots of repetition helps a phrase stay with you; the recorded performance of *Cornet Chop Suey* from February 1926 offers more than usual. The piece is a hybrid of traditional strain form, used so often in the Oliver recordings from 1923, and verse and chorus form, associated with songs. Four distinct parts are marked in the notated lead sheet and two of them have labels—introduction (4 measures), a first strain or verse (16 measures), a section marked "chorus" (32 measures), and a section marked "patter" (16 measures).[24] Repeat signs for the chorus turn it into a 64-measure block that dominates the performance; the recorded version from 1926 includes one additional iteration, to make 96 bars.

The main melodic gesture, presented in the first two measures, is repeated a total of ten times in the first two choruses—perhaps a few too many (in the 1926 recording, Armstrong deliberately varies it in the third chorus). Yet it is a bouncy and attractive little phrase, with a little bit of swagger. It could be compared to the attractive melodic nuggets that open Scott Joplin's greatest rags, the first two measures of *Maple Leaf Rag*, for example, or the first two measures of *The Entertainer*. Armstrong is not quite at Joplin's level, perhaps just a notch below. But the gesture is certainly more distinctive and memorable than any other he had produced up until this point.

There may be too much repetition in *Cornet Chop Suey*, but there is also variety. The buglelike introduction announces the arrival of something special. It is followed by stepwise, continuous motion, in the manner of the first strain of *Weather Bird Rag*. Melodic contours are interesting, varied, and neatly organized, again resembling *Weather Bird*. Each section is different in this way, with the chorus featuring the swaggering, descending gesture that has a good bit of rhythmic energy and the patter section returning to the military assertion of the introduction, then taking that idea in a fresh direction. The chorus includes notated breaks; this may have been new. When Louis and Lillian composed *Tears* in October, they did not notate a single break, which we now see as the main point of the piece. In *Cornet Chop Suey* he notates four of his breaks for copyright. I see no obvious precedent for this in his Chicago circle.

One would like to know where he got the idea of calling the main section a "chorus," a word usually reserved for vocal music. The word highlights this section as a melodic statement that is memorable and repeatable, like a song lyric. "Patter" indicates "stop time," the technique of reducing the accompaniment to punched accents from the band, in this case on the first beat of each measure. There seem also to have been few precedents for copyrighting a stop-time chorus. In any event, stop-time choruses would, in just a few years, frame some of Armstrong's most important solos.

Compared with lead sheets filed by Oliver, Hardin, and Armstrong around this time, *Cornet Chop Suey* stands out for its melodic variety. Bugle fanfare, a taut two-bar gesture that stands up to repetition, continuous motion in the style of *Weather Bird Rag*, notated breaks, fragments of second playing, and a stop-time chorus that combines twisting arpeggiations (Oliver would have called them snakes) with step-by-step motion—that is a lot of melodic variety. He throws in harmonic variety, too, including notated blue notes and, once again, a diminished chord. It is clear that by January 1924 he had absorbed the stylistic principle of variety, which would dominate his mature style for the rest of the decade and beyond.

"Where's that lead?" Armstrong heard Oliver say in 1915, and that admonition was still ringing in his ears when he soloed on *Chimes Blues* in early 1923. By the end of the year he was redefining what a lead might be like. Why not bring some of the energy of the break, the rhythmic tension and melodic surprise, into a lead? This is the kind of question I imagine Armstrong responding to, unconsciously or consciously, during the 1920s and 1930s: *What kind of a melody will a jazz solo be?* That question would continue to animate the central innovators in jazz for decades to come, their solutions depending on training, audience, employers, notation, bandleaders, social justice, racial pride, and the searchings of creative minds. *Cornet Chop Suey* is Armstrong's first bold answer.

To see *Cornet Chop Suey* as a musical and psychological breakthrough is to connect it to a complex biographical moment that included his late apprenticeship, his marriage, and his reluctant but felt need to break away from Oliver. The reluctance is indicated by a fascinating detail: his bold assertion of independence was suppressed. The piece was notated, sent to Washington, D.C., and then tucked away in a drawer for two years. There is not a shred of evidence that it was ever performed beyond the back steps of Lillian's house until early 1926.

The most obvious explanation for the silence is that Armstrong was committed to staying under Oliver. Oliver was not interested in shining a spotlight on his apprentice's splendid piece of bravura; I find it highly unlikely that Armstrong even broached the idea. If *Cornet Chop Suey* reminded Louis of the cutting contests back home, there was only one other cornet player on the stage of Lincoln Gardens to challenge. The piece would have left Oliver in the dust. Even after he broke away from Oliver in the summer of 1924, Armstrong could not

*Newlyweds (Courtesy of Chris Albertson)*

find a way back into the creative channel opened up here for quite some time. There would be no outlet for it with Fletcher Henderson in New York City, and his chance didn't come until Lillian convinced a cabaret owner to feature him upon his return to Chicago.

Armstrong married his fiancée on February 5, 1924, at City Hall. The *Defender* noted the bride's "Parisian gown of white crepe elaborately beaded in rhinestones and silver beads." A reception was held at the Ideal Tea Room, 3218 South Michigan Avenue, on February 7, with music provided gratis by the Oscar Young band, including Preston Jackson on trombone. (Years later, Armstrong rewarded Jackson's generosity with a job in his big band, one of countless gestures of loyalty.) On their wedding night the happy couple made the rounds of after-hours spots, and at each one they were showered with rice, the door sills blanketed with white. In lieu of a honeymoon they decided to put money away for the purchase of a house. They moved into a rented apartment at 38th and Indiana.

If Oliver and the other musicians in the band were surprised by the marriage, it was even harder for Lillian's mother, Dempsey, to get used to the idea. Alberta Hunter said that Dempsey "had a fit when she heard that Lil was going to marry Louis." She thought Lil "was too good for Louis, you know." Lil later reported that her family "gave me hell for marrying Louis; they said he was almost ignorant." As a devout Christian who worked for whites as a cook, Dempsey raised Lillian with higher goals; a few church picnics would not have been enough to change her bias against a dance-band musician from New Orleans. Dempsey taught her daughter to pay attention to things like table manners, and the rough ways of the New Orleanian musicians were precisely what she was trying to hold at bay.

Today it might easy to sneer at Dempsey's dash of snootiness, but it must be noted that everybody else's initial reaction was that Lil was too good for Louis, too—that was the first thought even of the future bride and groom when they met back in late 1922. From his side there must have been at least a little bit of hesitation as well, rooted in more than just a sense of insecurity. His mother May Ann had taken him to the Sanctified Church, where the sisters used music for intense emotional release and communal bonding, and where they surrounded him with loving approval when he made his first attempt to sing in public. Dempsey would not have been shouting with the sisters; her place was in a forward-looking church focused on racial progress. The paradox for Louis was clear: May Ann taught him to disdain anyone who put on airs, but his betrothed and her mother offered a classic example of what dicty could look like.

Perhaps Louis's burgeoning success, combined with his good nature, finally won Dempsey over. "He was just as sweet and nice as he could be," said Hunter. From the other side of the match Lil offered savvy career sense and firm loyalty. What mattered in the end was not her credentials but Armstrong's confidence in her, and the confidence she in turn gave him. His sense of who this small, pretty, intelligent, and ambitious woman was exceeded reality, but his own reality turned out to be what counted. "If she hadn't run into the New Orleans Greats she probably would have married some big politician or maybe play the Classics for her livelihood," he believed. Though exaggerated, her education and refinement were immense in his eyes. She was a big, high-powered chick who gave him courage to plunge into their joint schemes for fame and fortune, which ended up being mostly about him.

"I remember someone told me that when a woman marries she should work for her husband," explained Lil. "So if I wanted to be someone, Louis had to be someone." Exaggerated claims have been made for Lil's role during these important musical years, but she herself did not play that game. She framed the matter well when she said that it was her job to stand "at the bottom of the ladder, holding it, and watching him climb." It is not so easy to carry the burden of working your own academy, and not easy at all for a dark-skinned, undereducated musician from New Orleans. Thanks to Lillian, there would be no more staying under. Neither one of them could have imagined how high his ladder would reach, but in February 1924 the world seemed full of possibilities, musical, financial, and romantic.

Opposites do not always attract. Certainly Armstrong's love interests in New Orleans had been nothing like Lil, and it would have been easier for him to hook up with someone like Alpha, his third wife, who was much less like Lil and more like him. The social dynamics of the Great Migration threw people from diverse backgrounds and aspirations together—a classically trained pianist and a blues specialist from a culture that ridiculed note-reading musicians as "cute boys." The two of them sat down to play in King Oliver's Creole Jazz Band, and the friction that marked their partnership was productive, at least for a while. Circumstances put them together, violent love fueled a romance, and their opposite qualities turned complementary. Eventually Armstrong grew tired of the friction, but for now it carried a creative edge. After his wedding he gradually gathered the courage to break away from Oliver. And then came an unexpected opportunity to play in New York City with the most successful African-American dance band of the time, another felicitous intervention in his rapidly unfolding march toward the big time.

# FOUR

# The Call from Broadway

*While Louis was playing more than anybody I ever heard before,
Joe Smith was doing what the people understood.*
—Clyde Bernhardt, on hearing Armstrong in 1925

**Shortly after Lillian and Louis were married, in February 1924, Oliver was approached** by a booking agency with a proposal to take his band on tour. The plan was to swing through the midwestern states, and the promised pay was attractive. A rift broke up the band, however, and replacements had to be found at the last minute.

The breakup had multiple causes. In one telling of the story, Armstrong said that the Dodds brothers and Dutrey did not want to travel, Dutrey especially, because of his asthma. Johnny Dodds noted a musical conflict: because of Oliver's failing abilities, the melody instruments covered him up, yet he was not willing to solve the problem by letting Armstrong play lead. There was also some bitterness about Oliver having used other musicians on a few recording sessions.

But the main problem seems to have been money. Gennett Records did not pay up front but instead distributed royalties dependent on sales; these were supposed to be shared with the entire band. When the checks came in, Oliver refused to show them to anybody, while the shares got smaller and smaller. "King Oliver's men were always talking about striking for something or other," Armstrong said, and in the heat of anger the Dodds brothers took that defiant attitude a step further, threatening to beat up their leader. Oliver answered that threat by purchasing a pistol, and the happy days were clearly gone. After the breakup, Dutrey led a band with the two Dodds brothers at Lincoln

*Oliver band, 1924: Charles Jackson, Snags Jones, Buster Bailey, Oliver, Zue Robertson, Lil Hardin Armstrong, Armstrong, Rudy Jackson (The Frank Driggs Collection)*

Gardens for a while, and then he took a job at Kelly's Stables; Johnny Dodds continued to play there for a number of years.

To rebuild the band, Oliver brought in Buster Bailey from Memphis on clarinet and Rudy Jackson on clarinet and tenor sax. Zue Robertson eventually joined on trombone, Charlie Jackson on bass sax, and Clifford "Snags" Jones on drums. Only Lil and Louis remained from the group of 1922–23. The reformed band rehearsed and launched their tour on February 22.

Armstrong believed that Oliver's was the first African-American band ever booked by the agency MCA. The band followed the Orpheum vaudeville circuit through Pennsylvania, Maryland, Illinois, Iowa, Wisconsin, and Michigan on a series of one-nighters. Bailey and Jackson were intrigued by the Oliver-Armstrong duet breaks and tried to do some of their own in Madison, Wisconsin, but couldn't pull it off.

Oliver started to loosen his hold on his protégé: "he decided to let me do everything and anything that I choosed," wrote Armstrong.

Feeling, perhaps, that Armstrong was less of a threat on the road, or perhaps needing more help to carry the show, Oliver let him sing and do a little comedy dance in which he pretended to fall and hurt himself. It was probably Louis's first appearance on a vaudeville stage since a talent contest in his early teens. He took some solos to "help the ol' man out," he said; "the customers really went for it in a big way." Oliver got in the habit of disappearing for a stretch during the middle of a performance.

Rudy Jackson remembered how word of Armstrong's appeal got around, with some managers insisting, to Oliver's great irritation, that Armstrong's featured participation be designated in advance. But Jackson also remembered how Armstrong was devoted to his mentor and credited Oliver with all of his own success. Oliver liked to pose as the star, making his entrance only after everyone else was seated, with the expectation of special applause. When he grew ill-tempered over the growing interest in Armstrong, his student toned things down. In Armstrong's memory the tour was a big success, with shorter hours, more money, and lots of fun. When the band returned to Lincoln Gardens, they were wildly popular once again.

The tour made it clear that Louis was no longer a second cornetist. Lil made a direct appeal: Oliver was holding him back, she said, and his "ego and wounded vanity may hurt you." He listened in shocked silence. "I told him I didn't want to be married to a second trumpet player," she remembered. "I wanted to be married to a first trumpet player. I told him he had to get out of Oliver's band."

Finally, on a train ride back to Chicago after one out-of-town gig, Lil and Rudy Jackson convinced him that it was time to leave. He agreed and asked Jackson to break the news to the King. Jackson expected Oliver to be furious, but he merely shrugged and said that he had been lucky that Louis had stayed with him this long. Armstrong left at the end of June without saying a word.

Oliver had invited Louis to join him because he desperately needed support, but for Armstrong the nearly two years of playing second were crucial in shaping his rapidly maturing talent. "Sitting by [Oliver] every night I *had* to pick up a lot of little tactics he made," he acknowledged. Those tactics would have included the most important aspects of Armstrong's mature style: blues phrasing, a vigorous initial attack that communicates vitality, vibrato that expresses passion, the ability to invent a phrase that stays with you, and various ways of creating rhythmic drive, including commitment to the fixed and variable model. It was a thorough and deep transmission of one man's vision to a worthy disciple, the kind of relationship all teachers hope for. The relationship produced the greatest representative of the New Orleans tradition, the musician who carried the uptown vernacular around the globe.

Oliver wrote to friends at home, asking who the best young cornetists were. Eventually Lee Collins was identified, brought to Chicago, and installed as second cornetist at Lincoln Gardens. Someone from the audience requested *High Society*, but Oliver said they couldn't play it since they didn't have a clarinet player from New Orleans. Collins stepped up and offered to play the part on his cornet, just as Armstrong used to do. At the end of the evening the bouncer turned to Oliver and said, "Joe, this is the first time I seen you smile since your boy Louis left the band." Lee was invited to the Oliver home for a late dinner prepared by Stella.

Lillian didn't want to make it obvious that she had prompted Louis to leave, so she stayed in Oliver's band. "One of us is gonna have to be working," she quipped. Oliver was skeptical about Louis's chances and predicted he would come back. Still a bit shy, Armstrong had trouble figuring out what to do. He heard that Sammy Stewart was putting together a band, so he approached him to see if he needed a cornet player. It turned out to be an unfortunate choice.

In the summer of 1924, Stewart, a classically trained pianist from Ohio, was beginning to make a place for himself in the musical networks of Chicago. He dazzled audiences by playing Gershwin's *Rhapsody in Blue* without missing a note. Featuring complex arrangements with a strong string section, the group's arrival was hailed by the *Defender* as a "group of ten young men . . . from the best families of Ohio, well educated and highly trained musicians." The writer predicted that it wouldn't be long before Stewart reached a level of popularity now enjoyed by Paul Whiteman. Stewart and his musicians stopped by Lincoln Gardens to see Oliver's band and laughed out loud; we "thought they were funny," one of them admitted.

Armstrong gathered his courage to ask for a job, but Stewart brushed him away with barely a word. He slinked back to Lil, his confidence crushed. Stewart looked at Armstrong and understood immediately that he was not a well-educated musician, and he probably even sensed that he was not from one of the best families. According to Earl Hines, Stewart's band was made up of light-skinned musicians, which presented a barrier that neither he nor Armstrong could hope to overcome. Armstrong was familiar with this kind of discrimination, which was common in New Orleans, but it must have felt like a real downer to be slapped by it on his first attempt to step out of his hometown circle in search of a position equal to his abilities. "I wasn't up to his society," Armstrong remembered about Stewart, bitterly.

Lil suggested Ollie Powers, the singer to whom she had introduced him at the Dreamland. A large person with a lovely tenor voice, Powers was warm, friendly, and well liked. He gave Armstrong a place in his new band at the Dreamland. It was a small band, with only one cornetist, so there were solo opportunities. "That's when Louis started playing and showing what he had in himself," Lillian reported (the comment reaffirms the likelihood that the solo opportunities he had with Oliver were limited). Now was his chance to shine.

Word of his ability reached Fletcher Henderson in New York City. Henderson first heard him while touring through New Orleans, in April 1922, and when he got back to New York he telegrammed an offer. Armstrong responded that he would only leave if Henderson hired his buddy, drummer Zutty Singleton, as well. Now, in 1924, Armstrong was more confident. Henderson offered $55 a week to come to join his orchestra at the Roseland Ballroom, on Broadway. Armstrong accepted, thus making a break with Chicago and putting the Oliver years behind.

Interestingly, Lillian stayed in Chicago. She apparently accompanied Louis on the initial trip in September, but did not stay long. Her mother needed help, but there was probably more to it than that. The mutual passion of the down-home hustler from New Orleans and the high-powered chick from Fisk University did not fully compensate for their imposing differences. As long as Lillian was dedicated to the task of holding a ladder for her husband to climb, they were working in synchrony, but that kind of energy can also be difficult to manage. She told him how to tip, how to dress, how to eat properly, how to manage his money, how to notate music, how to play the classics, where to go to church, when to leave Oliver, and what to do next. Musicians teased him about being henpecked, but Armstrong dismissed it as jealousy. "They were broke all the time and I always had a pocket full of money," he chortled.

The friction between Louis and Lillian was sparked by differences in class as well as personality. He disdained people who put on airs, while she had been taught to do precisely that. So it is easy to imagine that there was already, barely eight months after their wedding, a degree of discomfort that made the move attractive. Armstrong's experience with the stress of conflicting class positions in both New Orleans and Chicago prepared him for similar tensions with the Henderson Orchestra in New York. During the period 1918–21, he played with riverboat orchestras in the summers, learning a Eurocentric way of making music, while extending his command of the vernacular in New Orleans the rest of the year. In Chicago this balancing act played out in a different way as Louis navigated between performing with Oliver's band every night and hanging out with Lillian. His later career would be closely bound up with his ability to deal productively with social tensions like these.

His first rehearsal with Henderson is another landmark moment in the Armstrong biography, right up there with his first night at Lincoln Gardens. The differences between the Henderson and Oliver bands were dramatic. Henderson's orchestra worked in sections, with several instruments of the same kind playing written arrangements. Armstrong's main job was to play improvised solos, and when he wasn't doing that, to play the third cornet part. "I had just left Chicago," he remembered, "where the way we used to do it was just take the wind in, and take what's left of it and blow out—and now I got to watch this *part*." He had done that on the riverboat bands, too, but with Henderson it may have become clear that this would be the way of the future. Indeed, for the next two decades or so he would primarily make his living in an orchestra with sections, reading written arrangements, with important but limited excursions, almost exclusively in recording studios, into smaller, one-on-a part, ear-playing ensembles.

After arriving in New York, Armstrong found his way to the rehearsal at 143rd Street and Lenox Avenue in Harlem and introduced himself to the leader, who greeted the nervous twenty-three-year-old with a gruff "Your part's up there." He remembered the piece as *By the Waters of Minnetonka*, a light classical composition by Thurlow Lieurance from the mid-1910s. Paul Whiteman had recently made a big splash with *Minnetonka*, turning it into a fox trot arranged by Ferde Grofé. Whiteman's June 1924 recording was probably released in time for Henderson to get the piece ready for this October rehearsal. In his 1926 book *So This Is Jazz*, Henry Osgood touted Grofé's arrangement as a model worth imitating. The high-toned pedigree, combining light classic status with the glamour of Whiteman and Grofé, made *Minnetonka* an appealing number for Henderson.

Later in the rehearsal, Henderson called for a medley of Irish waltzes. The arrangement included dynamic markings for playing loud and soft. By this time, Armstrong had considerable experience reading music, but it is quite possible that he had never seen this range of dynamics before, from *fortissimo* to *pianissimo*. When the band came to a very soft passage, signaled by the standard abbreviation *pp*, everyone quieted down except him. "In this band we read the marks as well as the notes," Henderson scolded him. Armstrong quipped that he thought *pp* meant "pound plenty." (My guess is that this was not simply a joke on Armstrong's part. As trombonist Preston Jackson explained, "pound plenty" was musician slang: "When you was playing shows you had to, what we called pound plenty.")

For the most part it was a miserable day. Armstrong sat bent over, nervous and self-conscious, painfully aware that everyone was checking him out. He got frustrated reading the arrangements and yelled out impulsively, "Man, what is that thing?" The other players mostly ignored him, and he kept to himself. "I'm saying to myself," he remembered, "'This bunch of old stuck up . . .'" The fringes of his long underwear stuck out below his pants, he carried a cardboard suitcase, and his stomach protruded out of his poorly fitted clothes. Drummer Kaiser Marshall teased him about his clunky shoes.

Things would improve with the Henderson band, but he never really settled in completely, in spite of the professional success that came his way. In public statements he avoided negatives, but near the end of his life he sometimes cut loose, especially in the privacy of his home, getting things straight for his posterity, as he liked to say, via pen, typewriter, and tape recorder. On several occasions he lashed out bitterly at Henderson and his musicians, as if trying to heal a long-festering wound. "The fellas in Fletcher's band had such big heads," he grumbled. Henderson was condescending and told him he could be good if he would only take some lessons—"but in my head I'm saying, 'You can go fuck yourself.'" Above all, he couldn't stand the pretension. "Fletcher was so carried away with that society shit and his education," he wrote bluntly.

In the end, he successfully negotiated the social and musical challenges and moved up another step on the ladder of his career. New York was more challenging than Chicago, where it had been easy for him to adjust with the help of the large community of New Orleanians. Milt Hinton thought that people in New York were less friendly than those in Chicago. There were fewer black-owned businesses, and Harlem "was more high class and cold blooded" in his experience. Danny Barker, the candid banjo player from New Orleans, described New York City as "a *machine* town, like everything is in a hurry . . . very cold black people and very cold white people." The dancing was different, Barker insisted, less sensuous and with the partners not as close together. Issues like these undoubtedly affected Armstrong, but his main challenge with the job was Henderson. In place of the familiar ways of New Orleans, he found a scene where music was used relentlessly as a source of elite social distinction. The leader staring him down from the front of the band was an imposing personification of that.

## The Talented Tenth

In the spring of 1924, Armstrong received a more extensive introduction to the Harlem elite. Very few social occasions in Harlem attained the splendid heights—the "pinnacle of posh," as the journalist and novelist George Schuyler described it—of the annual NAACP ball, hosted by the Women's Auxiliary of the New York branch. The third ball, on March 27, 1925, was held at the spacious New Manhattan Casino, 155th Street and 8th Avenue, with music provided by Fletcher Henderson. The *Interstate Tattler* called it the "foremost social event of the year." General admission was $1, loges $3, and boxes $6. Music for dancing was provided first by Henderson's Rainbow Orchestra, which made its inaugural appearance at nine o'clock. Then at midnight followed the celebrated Roseland Orchestra, with Armstrong on third cornet.

Guests with reserved boxes were escorted by one of 12 beautiful sub-debs, carefully selected from their club of 50 supervised by Dr. Ardelle Mitchell Dabney. Interest was so strong that additional loges and boxes were constructed at the last minute. In spite of bad weather, society people arrived from as far away as Washington, D.C., Philadelphia, Baltimore, and Toledo, the gathering swelling to an estimated 4,000. The Green Room on the balcony floor, artistically decorated by Mrs. Le Tang, provided a quiet space for light dining, with salads and sandwiches.

On the main floor sat Mrs. Binga Desmond in a flame tulle over satin, trimmed with gold cloth. Prominent physicians, including Dr. Edward Best, Dr. Leo Fitz Nearon, podiatrist William J. Carter, and the well-known (and somewhat scandalized) surgeon Dr. U. Conrad Vincent, gathered with their wives, as did society musicians Ford Dabney; David Martin, a violinist, music educator, and president of the New York local chapter of the National Association of Negro Musicians; and Robert F. Douge, trustee of the Martin-Smith Music School. Mrs. Fletcher Henderson served on the reception committee that organized the event, as did Addie W. Hunton, a founding member of the National Association of Colored Women. Politicians included Charles W. Anderson, collector of Internal Revenue for the third district of New York City, State Assemblyman Pope Billups, and Dr. George F. Haynes, secretary of Race Relations to the Federal Council of the Churches of Christ in America, with his wife Elizabeth, the first Negro woman ever appointed to the national board of the YWCA. Everyone was delighted to see famed military veteran Capt. Alonzo Myers, as well as the successful real estate entrepreneur W. H. Roach and John Nail, president of the Association of Trade and Commerce.

From the NAACP there were Rev. Robert W. Bagnall, accomplished orator and director of branches for the organization; Walter White, author of *The Fire in the Flint* and assistant secretary; Augustus Granville Dill, business manager of the *Crisis* (he was also a musician who played pipe organ and "*piano forte*," as he liked to call it); and, of course, Mr. and Mrs. W. E. B. Du Bois. Alain Locke, the first African-American Rhodes scholar, sat near the legendary James Weldon Johnson, accompanied by his wife and Wilhelmina Adams, their goddaughter. The distinguished writer Jean Toomer and the vivacious poet Countee Cullen circulated pleasantly. The Baltimore *Afro-American* noted that there were so many illustrious names that it was impossible to mention them all, though one who couldn't be overlooked was A'Lelia Walker, heiress to an immense fortune built on hair-straightening products, whose every social move was the subject of intense interest.

In short, the box holders were a cross-section of the "talented tenth"—W. E. B. Du Bois's phrase for the top layer of African-American society. He argued that the race would advance most directly through the leadership of members possessing higher education and cultural refinement, in contrast to Booker T. Washington's vision of race progress through industrial education. In mid-1920s Harlem, Du Bois's position was ascendant.

Fletcher Henderson was drawn to this crowd like a cold hand to a kid glove. As Sy Oliver, the great swing-band arranger from the 1930s, observed, "Keep in mind that when I was born in 1910, the only salvation for a Negro was education and of course there were two societies in the black community: the educated on one side and the uneducated on the other. They led totally different lives." There was no doubt about where Henderson and Armstrong stood.

Henderson (b. 1897) grew up in Cuthbert, Georgia, a little town where his father, Fletcher Hamilton Henderson, was an administrator and teacher of Latin at the Howard Normal School for many years. Fletcher Sr. had attended Atlanta University, where he was mentored by the school's president, Edmund A. Ware. That connection led directly to the position of principal in Cuthbert, where he became a regional leader. He was the deacon and superintendent of Sunday school at the AME Church, which undoubtedly followed the vision of that denomination to eliminate the vernacular practices of ecstatic worship that had been so closely identified with slavery. Fletcher Sr. was eventually honored as "State Education Evangelist" by the state-wide AME.

In his classroom at the Howard Normal School, Fletcher Sr. liked to demonstrate his ability to speak Latin fluently. He made sure that all three of his children had extensive music lessons. One detail about Fletcher Jr.'s piano studies is telling and hardly surprising: at daily practice time, the six-year-old was locked in the living room with instructions to produce a steady flow of sound that could be monitored in other parts of the house. His childhood training resembled Lillian Hardin's in that vernacular music was simply out of the question. Even after Fletcher Jr. became famous as a jazz musician, his father continued to prohibit that kind of music in his home. Located at opposite ends of the African-American cultural spectrum in the early twentieth century, the childhoods of Fletcher Henderson and Louis Armstrong could not have been more dissimilar.

In 1916 Fletcher Jr. followed his father's example and matriculated at Atlanta University, majoring in chemistry and serving as university organist. An admiring classmate predicted that he was destined to be "classed with Rachmaninoff and other noted musicians." Atlanta University was in some ways the heart of the talented-tenth vision. Du Bois taught there from 1897 to 1910, while he was making a name for himself nationally. Walter White was a graduate of Atlanta and regarded by Du Bois as the perfect talented-tenth model. When Henderson took the train to New York in the summer of 1920, degree in hand and full of promise, he must have realized that his background and connections put him in a strong position. He was one of only around 2,000 African Americans attending higher-level colleges and universities in the entire country during the late 1910s, an elite group that deserved protection and encouragement. Nowhere was that protection stronger than in Harlem.

Henderson took the trip with the intention of studying at Columbia University, but he quickly dropped those plans and plugged into Harlem's expanding musical scene. One thing led to another, and before he knew it he was sitting in the offices of the Pace and Handy Music Company, run by W. C. Handy, the famous composer, and Harry Pace, who happened to be class of 1903 valedictorian of

*Fletcher Henderson Sr. and Jr., New York, ca. 1923 (Collection of Duncan Schiedt)*

Atlanta University, where he had studied with Du Bois and became proficient in Latin and Greek.

The great commercial explosion of blues sold through sheet music had brought Pace and Handy together fortuitously in the mid-1910s, but in January 1921 Pace broke away to form Black Swan Records. He positioned his new phonograph company in a market niche quite different from that of OKeh and the other race record catalogues. Backed by capital investment from his talented-tenth acquaintances, Pace's company veered toward highbrow classical recordings. Luminaries like Jack Nail and James Weldon Johnson served on the Black Swan board of directors, and the *Crisis*, the mouthpiece of Du Bois and the NAACP, invested its profits there. Henderson became "musical director" and "recording manager" of the new company.

Why were Du Bois and the talented tenth investing in phonograph records? Because they realized how powerfully the technology could define black identity and thus shape the future of the race. Their interest followed a cultural vision that Du Bois had articulated as early as 1903: "Was there ever a nation on God's fair earth civilized from the bottom upward?" he wrote. "Never; it is, ever was, and ever will be from the top downward that culture filters." The talented tenth were not inclined to think of the black vernacular as a positive resource. They simply could not imagine what we today, a century later, take for granted, after the breathtaking achievements in black vernacular music throughout the twentieth century, as the tradition intersected in so many different ways with commercial structures in the United States: it is precisely "bottom-up" motion that has produced the deepest and farthest-reaching results.

But for Du Bois and his powerful followers it had to be top-down, and Pace gave them a chance to put their money where their mouths were. The poet Langston Hughes, walking into this elite Harlem scene a couple of years after Henderson did, understood their motivations. In order to gain white acceptance, the talented tenth had to promote a black culture that whites would respect. "They wanted to put their best foot forward, their politely polished and cultural foot—and only that foot," Hughes wrote.

But of course there was more to it than that. The existence of a talented tenth depended on a distinctly untalented nine-tenths. It could be useful, on a personal level, to highlight the differences. Danny Barker arrived in Harlem a few years after Hughes did, and his assessment was harsher. "I had seen many of the important men and women [in the Harlem Renaissance] and I noticed the way they moved about with a straight-faced solemn attitude: an attitude of superior surveillance and a deep inside disgust—a defeat, or helplessness," he wrote. "They would smile at nothing . . . [like] defeated wounded soldiers trudging back from the battlefront."

When Henderson settled in and figured out what was going

on, he must have turned a slight, sheepish smile. The son of a Latin teacher who majored in chemistry at Atlanta University was in a good position to know about privileged leadership and its advantages. He proved to be a quick learner, and it would not be long before he was gathering praise for his *status*, not just for his musical achievement.

Pace quickly realized that, for purely practical reasons, it was best not to exclude blues and jazz from the Black Swan catalogue, and Henderson became the default piano man for accompanying blues singers on their recordings. It was not an obvious use of his abilities. Yet, as it turned out, he found a way to offer the right mix of reliability, professionalism, and adaptability. A young Ethel Waters walked into the company offices in 1921 and met Henderson, looking "very prissy and important." He asked her if she would rather record a popular song or a "cultural" song. Her *Down Home Blues* (May 1921) was the commercial success that "got Black Swan out of the red," according to Waters. She and Henderson later went on a tour that included a stop in New Orleans, where Henderson first heard Armstrong. Waters told a story that sums up Henderson's awkward transition from university organist to blues accompanist. In Chicago she purchased some piano rolls made by James P. Johnson and asked Henderson to study them. He listened closely and practiced placing his fingers in the depressed keys as the machine cranked along. "He began to be identified with that kind of music, which isn't his kind at all," Waters remembered.

In summer 1922 Henderson landed an opportunity to head up his own dance band, and with that he arrived at the position in which he would thrive for the next decade or so, one that made good use of his talented-tenth skill set of selecting repertory, shaping musical arrangements, managing employees, rehearsing, holding up standards, and dealing with white employers. It must have been a relief to no longer be chasing James P. Johnson's fingerings around the player piano. He continued to accompany blues singers in recording studios for a couple of years, since the easy and lucrative gigs empowered him with extra work to offer his employees. But his future success would unfold in a very different direction.

At a white Manhattan dance hall called Terrace Gardens, Henderson's group played opposite a white orchestra, the two taking turns throughout the evening. An excited write-up in the black press bragged how the dancers rested while the white orchestra played, only to jump up and dance when Henderson and his "masters of the art of playing modern dance rhythms" took the stage. By January 1924 he was heading a band hired for dancing and floor shows at Club Alabam, an upscale white cabaret on West 44th Street, near Times Square. Violinist Allie Ross conducted, but the musicians decided to make Henderson the leader, since he "made a nice appearance and was well-educated," as Don Redman put it. By February, "Fletcher Henderson and His Famous Club Alabam Orchestra" were being promoted weekly in prominent advertisements in the *New York Times*, and ads were soon trumpeting them as the "Greatest Colored Orchestra in the World." Vocalion recorded and promoted the band in white newspapers alongside Ben Selvin's Famous Moulin Rouge Orchestra; this set Henderson apart from black bands who recorded for race labels (though Vocalion did put "Colored" in parentheses under Henderson's name). The group took a step forward by signing with Columbia, which released its records on the company's general label, marketed to whites. The large number of recordings produced by this band indicates the success of this strategy. Just as Armstrong used his contacts from New Orleans to enter the preeminent band on the South Side of Chicago, so did Henderson use his talented-tenth connections to enter into good-paying recording contracts and venues in white Manhattan.

In July 1924 Henderson took his band into the whites-only Roseland Ballroom, on Broadway between 51st and 52nd Streets, described by *Variety* as the "'class' dance place on Broadway." As the *Amsterdam News* put it, the job itself was "proof of [the orchestra's] greatness." The Roseland would remain his home base for almost a decade. Like most large ballrooms, the Roseland hired two (and sometimes more) orchestras every night, alternating on separate bandstands to provide continuous music for dancing. Less typical was the Roseland's format of having a white orchestra going head to head with a black one. During his first year there, Henderson played opposite the Sam Lanin Orchestra, Phil Romano and His Rainbow Orchestra, and Vincent Lopez's orchestra. Music columnist Dave Peyton, writing in the *Defender*, insisted that the key to Henderson's success was polished ensemble work. "Each section of this band is molded into one player, it seemed," he wrote. "The rhythm of the band was perfect, the color and attack excellent. Continuity of playing with one another has made this organization a stand out." This kind of quality control—based on standards set by the elite white bands and, in the minds of many, set in clear opposition to collectively improvising bands from New Orleans—proved to be Henderson's strength.

In spite of the fact that the Roseland was a segregated dance hall, the job helped Henderson attract attention in the black community, partly through far-reaching radio broadcasts and recordings, but also simply because it put him in a class with elite white orchestras. With Henderson, Armstrong played opposite Lanin, Lopez, Isham Jones and His Orchestra, Ray Miller and His Orchestra, and the Benson Orchestra of Chicago ("le plus ultra of society dance music," according to cornetist Rex Stewart). In November 1924 the *Pittsburgh Courier* encouraged its black readership to vote for Henderson's band in a contest conducted by the *New York Daily Mirror* for most popular radio artist. "He ranks with the best white offerings of his kind," bragged the *Courier*; that statement could be supported by the fact that few other black bands could be heard on the radio. In winter 1925 Henderson purchased a house on "Striver's Row," the elite section of West 139th Street in Harlem. In May the *New York Age* reported that he was raking in $1,200 for a six-night work week. In September, Harlem papers announced a musical victory by the Henderson Orchestra over Lopez—no small claim since Lopez was about to play at the Metropolitan Opera House, giving jazz, according to the *Wall Street Journal*, "the most ceremonious recognition it has yet received in America or anywhere else."

Armstrong's leap from Oliver to Henderson could not have been more dramatic. One had come up through the shouting Baptist and rough blues traditions of the plantations to lead the most successful black band on the South Side of Chicago; the other was raised with classical music and talented-tenth grooming, which put him in a position to form the most successful black band playing for whites in midtown Manhattan. The key to Oliver's ascent was his cultivation of the bluesy vernacular; the key to Henderson's was his ability to mimic the likes of Lopez, Lanin, and Whiteman. The binary opposition—defined musically, racially, and in terms of social class—could not have been more firmly drawn. One thing is obvious: each audience got the kind of music it was looking for. Another thing was less obvious, and needs to be fleshed out: what each audience wanted was heavily shaped by attitudes about race.

## The Roseland Ballroom: "Jazz Bands Will Not Be Considered"

Jazz fans today may be surprised to learn that Fletcher Henderson's Orchestra, when Armstrong joined it in the fall of 1924, was actually not a jazz band. Henderson's band has a firm place in modern history as the prototypical jazz orchestra with multiple instruments forming sections. But to understand what was happening during Armstrong's year in New York, we need to put that point of view aside and think about the period's understanding of the word "jazz." The definition most people think of today is the result of intense effort over many decades to police the boundaries of what jazz is and what it is not. Usage in the mid-1920s was contentious, pluralistic, and unstable, and it was inevitably inflected with racial and social dynamics.

An advertisement in the *New York Clipper* for the job at the Roseland Ballroom that Henderson eventually landed included this:

> We have an opening for TWO VERSATILE BANDS. Two high grade Dance-Orchestras (five to seven men each) wanted by a high-class New York ballroom to play for the evening sessions. Jazz bands will not be considered. . . . Apply by letter only to . . . Roseland, Broadway at 51st Street, The Home of Refined Dancing.

The Roseland was not looking for jazz, and with Henderson it got what it wanted. The confusing thing is that Henderson's group was gradually and indirectly *becoming* a jazz band, simply by being swept up in the currents of the day. This movement had little to do with Armstrong, or even with any spark of inspiration from Henderson himself. Instead, what drove it was Henderson's keen sense of how to place his unit in competition with leading white bands.

*Roseland Ballroom interior, ca. 1926 (Collection of Duncan Schiedt)*

There were at least five different usages of "jazz" in broad circulation during the 1920s.[25] There was room for overlap, for ambiguity was part of the strength of this surprisingly durable little word. Some found it easy to throw up their hands and accept vague and inclusive definitions, but that does not mean that ideologically driven usage ever drifted completely out of play.

*Jazz was black music from New Orleans that featured bluesy effects and collective improvisation.* This was King Oliver's specialty at Lincoln Gardens and the 1920s definition that lines up best with modern understandings of "jazz." This is the social-musical configuration that Isham Jones, the white orchestra leader, was thinking of when he said, in 1924, that his own band did not play jazz, which was, instead, a "down South Negro type" of blues. The main audience base was African Americans in New Orleans and Chicago, but it was expanding through race recordings and tours. That the musicians did not use notation but played by ear was part of the music's identity. African-American associations with blues and church music were recognized and appreciated. Insiders heard the music as sophisticated and profound, outsiders as raucous, immoral, and primitive. Dave Peyton, the most prolific writer on African-American music during the mid-1920s, wrote scornfully about "New Orleans hokum" and "clown music."

*Jazz was a white version of that tradition.* The key intervention here was the Original Dixieland Jazz Band from New Orleans, which came to the world's attention in 1917 through phonograph recordings that spawned many imitators. For some years this must have been the music most people in the United States thought of when they heard the word "jazz." It is impossible to know how many understood the music's black origins. Some who did regarded this kind of jazz as cultural miscegenation on a dangerous level. Some may have suspected black origins but didn't know the details, others denied those origins (an attitude that is still current today, though in very small circles), and others simply found it useful to ignore the issue altogether.

This music was understood as either uncivilized and dangerous or uncivilized and refreshing, depending on one's point of view. But even whites who were aware of the music's black origins did not understand the connection between collective improvisation and African-American communal singing. They did not hear that practice as African Americans from the Deep South heard it: as a music of social balance and interconnectedness. To outsiders, collective improvisation could be cast as anarchy and the rule of base impulse, music that appealed "to the vile instincts in human beings," in the words of contemporary composer John Alden Carpenter, rather than the achievement of social harmony.

*Jazz was composed music, syncopated and/or bluesy.* This definition helped "jazz" enjoy open-ended success across the sprawling landscape of popular songs and dance music, from W. C. Handy's blues songs to catchy Broadway tunes. The key step was a shift in focus from music that embraced the impossibility of musical notation (collective improvisation and blues), signaling the black vernacular, to stylistic markers that could be easily captured in notation. For example, Irving Berlin's *Everybody Step*, the big song hit of 1921, has simple blue notes, an extended passage of additive rhythm, a simplified bass pattern associated with blues, and allusions to blues harmonies. It was all written out and it sounds like it was.

Music that could be captured in notation would automatically be less "black" than jazz as practiced in the first two positions described above. Notatable jazz featured syncopation and additive rhythm but not collective improvisation, and for blue notes it used specific flattened intervals rather than less definite bending of pitch. Again, from a white point of view these transformations could be either bad, meaning that civilization was under siege, or good, meaning that jazz was now in the hands of composers who knew what they were doing, as opposed to primitives who did not. A writer in *Etude* (March 1924) ranked *Everybody Step* among the ten greatest masterpieces in music history, right up there with Bach's B-Minor Mass and Stravinsky's *Petrouchka*. A 1925 biographer of Berlin half-lamented "the preposterous fashion of using the word 'jazz' and the word 'Berlin' as interchangeable terms."

The large Jewish presence in the popular-song industry—and the talents of Berlin and Gershwin—provided an opening for another dimension of American racial logic: Jews could be regarded as mediators between primitive Africa and advanced Europe. Some imagined that Jews had darker skin in the past. "The simple fact is that the Jew responds naturally to the deeper implications of jazz, and that as a Jewish-American he partakes of the impulse at both its Oriental and its Occidental end," wrote one observer.

*Jazz was "the free, frank, sometimes vulgar spirit of the bourgeoisie"*—as Henry Osgood defined it in *So This Is Jazz* (1926). White dance-bandleaders reproduced the style characteristics of composed jazz songs. It was their job, after all, to accompany not only the tango and waltz but also the fox trot, while the Charleston intensified this trend. This is what caused the label "jazz" to be hung on bandleaders like Jones and Whiteman, who futilely tried to shake it. "What we have played is 'syncopated rhythm,' quite another thing," insisted Whiteman. More than a few black musicians would have agreed with him. "We didn't accept Whiteman's as a great *jazz* band," explained saxophonist Benny Waters. "We just called it great music."

Yet the usage stuck, and it became attractive to think of jazz as something that naturally belonged to the bourgeoisie—and Osgood did not have to say that it was the white bourgeoisie he was thinking of. The more jazz belonged to whites, the less it had to do with blacks. Osgood nods briefly to the black vernacular in *So This Is Jazz*, but he quickly argues for its irrelevance, pointing out, for example, that musical improvisation was practiced in Europe all the way back to the Middle Ages. And since European composers sometimes created musical events resembling jazz, perhaps the African-American antecedents had no importance at all. Beethoven, for example, could write some pretty aggressive syncopations when he wanted to, and the most sublime blues chord ever heard was located in Wagner's *Tristan und Isolde*.

Henderson showed that by working hard to eliminate "vulgarities and crudities," blacks could be just as bourgeois as whites. Now we can see why he was a little concerned in that October 1924 rehearsal about just how vulgar and crude his new hot soloist actually was. And we can also see why many historians who have written about the Henderson band are at complete odds with talented-tenth critics who admired this unit in the mid-1920s. The common interest of these two groups in "jazz" is an illusion: they are working with completely different definitions of the word. Each scorned what the other treasured. Talented-tenth critics looked at Henderson's accomplishment as hope for the future of the race; Armstrong was not even on their radar screen. When, a half-century later, jazz historians looked at the great jazz tradition they loved and regarded Armstrong as its first great master, perhaps even the central figure, disdain for Henderson's early work, which was so out of sync with what they valued, was not unusual.

*Symphonic jazz brought the imagined sequence all the way to "pure art."* The February 12, 1924, premiere by Paul Whiteman's Palais Royal Orchestra of George Gershwin's *Rhapsody in Blue* at Aeolian Hall in New York City may have equaled the impact of the Original Dixieland Jazz Band recordings in 1917. Whiteman and Gershwin wanted to show that jazz could be a new kind of vibrant American art music. Their concert brought into high focus the phenomenon of "symphonic jazz," a phrase that was increasingly used to clarify not only this new artistic possibility but also the conceit that there was a continuum, an evolutionary progression of jazz with precise social-cultural markers along the way. The concert was designed to demonstrate this by opening with a condescending performance of the ODJB's *Livery Stable Blues*.

Some insisted that symphonic jazz required violins, while others dropped that condition and applied the phrase to bands like Hen-

*Fletcher Henderson Orchestra (Courtesy of the Louis Armstrong House Museum)*

derson's. "Symphonic" made clear the refined nature of this kind of jazz compared to all others, promising complex arrangements, strong ensemble work, and slick harmonies. And it communicated the complete separation of white jazz, created by and for the white bourgeoisie, from black jazz—with the occasional exception of an exceptional person like Henderson.

What was Armstrong's opinion? As a professional musician running for top dollar, he was willing to put up with a lot of "society shit," and he never flinched from that willingness for the rest of his life. But my guess is that if he took the time to reflect on jazz's alleged upward mobility, he was not impressed. The fiction of lining up these five definitions to form a narrative of cultural evolution was very much a white project, from which it became a matter of interest to the talented tenth. One thing we do know is that Armstrong was ambivalent about the word "jazz," as were many of his colleagues from New Orleans, who understood the term's commercial advantages but put little stock in it. The intensely racist ideologies that shaped so much thinking may be part of the reason why musicians from Armstrong to Ellington to Gillespie and beyond tried to avoid labels for their music altogether, as a general principle.

Henderson, on the other hand, made it his business to stay in close touch with what was jazz, what was becoming jazz, and what used to be jazz but was now symphonic jazz. During the first half of 1924, when the "Fletcher Henderson Club Alabam Orchestra" (aka "Fletcher Henderson and His Famous Recording Orchestra," and "The Greatest Colored Dance Orchestra in the World") was advertised heavily in the *New York Times*, the word "jazz" was nowhere in sight; it was also absent from most of the small press releases on Henderson in black newspapers. January 1924 advertisements for his Vocalion recordings do not mention jazz; a *Defender* ad on March 29, 1924, makes a fleeting reference to his "jazzy fox trots." An ad for Emerson Race Records in the *Baltimore Afro-American* on May 30 describes the band as "nightly performers on Broadway in a weird, wild mixture of jazz and soothing symphony." Thus, by the summer of 1924, Henderson had solidified an image that made his band attractive to the Roseland Ballroom.

Keeping up with the likes of Lopez, Lanin, and Whiteman meant playing a certain repertory. Henderson's orchestra recorded 36 different titles during Armstrong's year with them, and most are right in step with the elite white bands Henderson was emulating.

Ever since the dance craze of the mid-1910s, the popular-song industry and dance bands had been discovering symbiotic ways to make money. Publishers recognized the potential of a dance band to promote a song, and songs were conceived with dancing in mind. A bandleader who plugged a tune could get his picture on the cover of published sheet music. As Osgood wrote in 1926, "where one person knows a popular song from hearing it sung, a dozen will be familiar with its title and tune through its fox-trot orchestral version." It was with pride that the *Afro-American* called Henderson one of the "best of dance tune purveyors" in August 1925.

In October 1924, Armstrong's first month with the band, Henderson recorded numbers that were also recorded by the Benson Orchestra, Isham Jones and His Orchestra, Paul Whiteman and His Orchestra, and the California Ramblers, with lesser-known white orchestras represented, too. The pattern continued through Armstrong's 12 months with Fletcher Henderson and His Orchestra, with Henderson often recording the same title within weeks or days of rival white bands.[26] His choices indicate what the Roseland patrons were interested in hearing and also his sense of how to position himself. His was often the only black band to record these tunes, which is precisely what he wanted. He was competing with elite white bands on their terms in a splendid display of talented-tenth confidence.

Like many bandleaders, Henderson often relied on standard commercial arrangements—"stocks," as they were called—that could be personalized. The arrangements juxtapose different combinations of instruments, accompaniments, and textures in a colorful flow of variety. Each section contrasts with the one before and after. Lively introductions, interludes, breaks, and codas pop out of nowhere. "The new demand is for change and novelty," wrote Whiteman. Chicago bandleader Sig Meyer referred to this as the "stodgy New York ballroom style." To modern ears the style often seems cluttered and overblown.

Henderson hired Armstrong as "hot soloist," which meant playing brief solos, 15 to 30 seconds long, at designated spots in the arrangement, providing another bit of variety. This was how the distinct worlds of the talented-tenth bandleader, who shapes the arrangement and the ensemble to his liking, and the vernacular specialist, who brings to the moment a very different skill set, came together. The flow from ensemble to solo and back could be seamless, with no difference in style from one to the other, or it could be one of startling juxtaposition. It was a relatively new format, and it is no exaggeration to say that its potential would continue to be explored for the next two decades as a source of creative tension in the swing era.

Many years later Armstrong bristled at the limitations—"He'd give me 16 bars, the most, to get off with." It is easy to project on these performances a sense that he is bursting out of the tightly controlled arrangements, but at the time he seems to have accepted the assignment fully and did everything he could to make the best of his brief moment in the spotlight. His willingness to work with the situation made it an important moment in his development as a soloist.

Henderson got what he wanted when he decided to challenge the elite white bands, but at a price. It was not only Armstrong and Ethel Waters who thought he was dicty. Clarinetist Garvin Bushell insisted that he "was never accepted by blacks as much as Duke. I don't

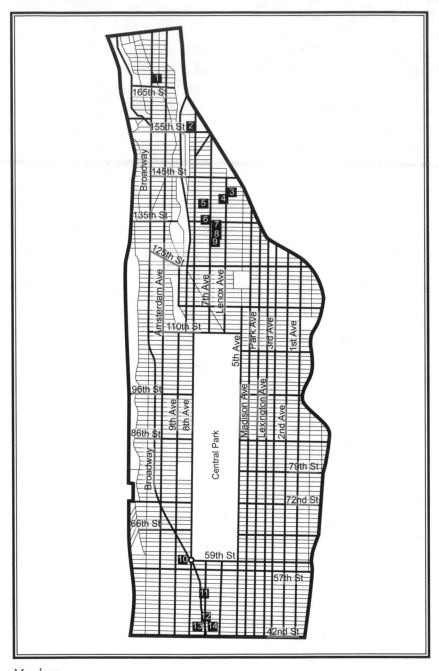

*Manhattan*

1. Audubon Theater
2. New Manhattan Casino
3. Cotton Club
4. Savoy Ballroom
5. Fletcher Henderson's house
6. Small's Paradise
7. Lafayette Theater
8. Rhythm Club
9. Connie's Inn
10. Columbia Recording Studio
11. Roseland Ballroom
12. Gaiety Theater
13. Club Alabam
14. Hudson Theater

think the blacks of Harlem bought many of his records: they were too sophisticated, not racy enough, and sounded like a white band." When Henderson toured in the spring of 1926 and played a big hall on the South Side of Chicago, attendance was slight; "our group is slow in supporting artistic organizations like this one," lamented Peyton in the *Defender*. High praise for Henderson in the black press creates an unbalanced impression. As always—and especially with the history of African-American music—we have to remind ourselves that voices in print are not necessarily representative. In this case, that means that the talented tenth did not speak for the entire black community.

The fascinating thing about the meeting of Armstrong and Henderson in October 1924 is that, though they were on very different social trajectories, they were converging by virtue of their drive to enter white markets. Armstrong was one of the leading young representatives of the black vernacular that smelled like garbage to the talented tenth, but with the help of his wife and some lessons at Kimball Hall, he had achieved more precision, more control over his instrument, more speed, and less funk. As he mimicked the elite white bands, Henderson followed their tendency to pick up on the energy of jazz.

## Hot Solos

Baby Dodds claimed that bandmates need to be relaxed and familiar with each other's ways, like husband and wife. "Your wife can look at you and you understand what she means," he explained, and "that's the way an organization of musicians should be." Armstrong enjoyed that kind of rapport in New Orleans and Chicago, and its absence for him in the Fletcher Henderson Orchestra was disconcerting. Fortunately, help was on the way. Henderson asked him to recommend a hot clarinet soloist, and he put forward Buster Bailey, his buddy from the Oliver band. Bailey arrived before opening night at the Roseland, October 13, 1924. "Then I had company in the band, and that made a difference," Armstrong remembered.

The difference emerged in a performance of *Tiger Rag*. After about two weeks at the Roseland, Henderson called for this old New Orleans standard, which he set up as a feature for Bailey and

Armstrong. Bailey used a growl technique, and his playing inspired Armstrong. "They gave me about four choruses," he said. "Following Buster made me really come on a little bit." The performance seems to have made a huge impression. "His faults and everything, his deficiencies, he made up in his playing," said Howard Scott, the second trumpeter. "He brought that New Orleans stuff here."

Armstrong could impress simply with his *sound*, his big, confident, imposing, authoritative sound, produced with razor-sharp precision, a bursting initial attack, a full, rounded tone, and lots of volume. "We were told that there were some people passing by that stopped, listening to him, he was so loud," said Scott. It was a sound born on the streets of New Orleans, "brassy, broad and aggressively dramatic," in the words of critic Amiri Baraka, and shaped by a cultural vision of sound production whose roots lay in West Africa. Today New York City is the undisputed capital of the jazz world, but in 1924 it was hardly on the map. It is easy to believe that Armstrong's four choruses on *Tiger Rag* stopped the Roseland dancers in their tracks.

Yet it is also true that his unrecorded solo on *Tiger Rag* was exceptional. His normal duties did not allow him to expand through four choruses, but instead required brief snippits of paraphrase. Armstrong's early solos with Henderson sound tentative and unconvincing, as if he doesn't quite know how to proceed. *Manda*, the first, has a lot of noodling; saxophonist Coleman Hawkins's offering on the same performance is more polished and effective. Armstrong's solos on *Tell Me Dreamy Eyes* and *My Rose Marie* are straightforward and slightly clumsy. For all the talk over the years about how he immediately changed the band, these solos are right in step with those from trombonist Charlie Green and Hawkins. In *Words* his embellishments are poorly integrated with the melody, creating the pronounced effect that they are two different things (CD 0:43–1:03); Hawkins immediately follows with a more sequential approach, a straight presentation of the tune followed by hot filigree. In many of these October solos Armstrong seems happiest when he gets to the break (or to the place in a phrase where it would be logical to insert a break), which was something he definitely knew how to play. These breaks have the feeling that he is putting his feet up in his Harlem apartment after a stuffy rehearsal, tired of flashy dressers sneering at his clunky shoes.

In paraphrase solos (*Go Long Mule* and *My Rose Marie*, for example), he sometimes takes one of his own embellishments and turns it into a little musical motive, a technique heard on *Chimes Blues* back in 1923. Repeating a small musical gesture was a simple way to create a "phrase that stays with you." To my ear, the solo that shows his debt to Joe Oliver most clearly comes in *Shanghai Shuffle*, where he cleverly recasts the written tune and produces a melody in the mold of *Dipper Mouth Blues*. The first four measures (CD 1:56–1:59) basically paraphrase the original tune and intensify its blues implications. That reworking becomes the basis for the whole solo, which expands in range upwards, in the manner of Oliver's three choruses, with the extra touch of a few exciting leaps. The strategy balances paraphrase and free invention.

Henderson's recording of *Copenhagen* (October 30) has been heralded as a landmark in jazz history, an unveiling of the arranging skills of the leader and Don Redman. The performance is indeed much jazzier than the other seven titles recorded in October. In a classic study, however, musicologist Jeffrey Magee has shown that, rather than leading the way with *Copenhagen*, Henderson and Redman were actually tracking the elite white bands. No other performance so vividly reveals the musical-social dynamics surrounding jazz in late 1924.

The story of *Copenhagen* begins with a white band, Charlie Davis and His Orchestra, performing their leader's new composition in Indianapolis in April 1924. Among Davis's admirers were members of the Wolverine Orchestra, seven musicians very much in the mold of the young alligators who were sitting at Oliver's feet in Lincoln Gardens and including, in fact, one of those alligators, cornetist Bix Beiderbecke. With Davis's blessing, the Wolverines made *Copenhagen* their own. Beiderbecke created a head arrangement, which the Wolverines recorded in May 1924.

The captivating opening section joins a neatly arranged chromatic passage of four measures, played in unison rhythm, to a four-measure phrase of comparatively wild collective improvisation. The effect is one of controlled, 1920s cool bursting into excitement. This is followed by two blues choruses, one for clarinet solo and the other for tenor sax. The performance continues with a series of calls and responses, sometimes with solo instruments in the call position and sometimes with an alternative refrain idea, also chromatic and also in unison; all the calls are answered by collective improvisation. A great deal of this Wolverine recording would be repeated verbatim by Henderson five months later.[27]

The transmission to Henderson occurred not through the recording, however, but through a published arrangement that carried full acknowledgment of both Davis and the Wolverines. The publication promised to capture the spirit of collective improvisation. "This arrangement is RED HOT as written," screamed the title page. "Play what you see and the horns will start smoking." *Copenhagen* got picked up by the Benson Orchestra of Chicago, the California Ramblers, and Al Turk's Princess Orchestra, all recording it in September and October along with nine other units plus Henderson's.

Collective improvisation, blues, call and response—*Copenhagen* documents the increasing reach of black New Orleans, first to young white musicians in the upper Midwest, then into a published arrangement, and from there to elite white bands. The piece neatly moved through the first four definitions of "jazz" outlined above, and it demonstrates how Henderson was following well-marked currents of fashion.[28]

The arrangement was dictated from afar, and so was Armstrong's famous solo, at least in part. The assignment must have pleased him greatly, for it was the first straight blues he had a chance to put on record with Henderson's band. He tried to tweak his solo for *Shanghai Shuffle* into a blues, but *Copenhagen* was a straightforward invitation to do what he did best.

To his paraphrase of the notated solo he adds bluesy gestures straight out of New Orleans. He only needed to tweak the notated lines slightly to turn them into the blues prototype of classic "sawtooth" design—a sharp initial leap upwards followed by twisting, gradual descent. Flatted thirds from the melody are intensified and repeated. His final phrase (CD 0:53–0:57) begins with a biting leap followed by descent through a blue tritone dissonance, a gesture that was bread and butter for Johnny Dodds in the Oliver band.

Perhaps, in a reflective moment, the whole scenario brought a smile to Armstrong's face: the music he and his friends had carried from New Orleans to Chicago was now sitting in front of him on his music stand in midtown Manhattan. The musical energy from dirt-floor dance halls had somehow come full circle to find him in the classiest ballroom on Broadway. Henderson's success with *Copenhagen* had nothing to do with his arranging skills. Rather, it was because he had the real thing in his pocket: Armstrong's driving blues solo and Bailey's obbligato, with Charlie Green's energetic outbursts jump-starting each section of collective improvisation.

When Henderson hired Armstrong and Bailey to expand his arsenal of hot soloists, he was certainly not looking for a vernacular touch that he could work into a sophisticated musical vision (the kind of Harlem Renaissance orientation that literary scholar Houston Baker has identified as "an artistic reformulation of black folkways"). Henderson was no Ellington. Rather, he recognized an opportunity that was open to him and very few others. White and black orchestras never competed on an even playing field, no matter how light-skinned the bandleader might be. But Henderson enjoyed an opportunity the white bands didn't have: he could hire black soloists. Enforced segregation took away with one hand, and sometimes it gave with the other. Armstrong's and Bailey's command of the black vernacular was something white musicians couldn't match. It was a classic demonstration of "taking advantage of the disadvantages." Back in Chicago, Sammy Stewart had been a step or two behind Henderson and turned Armstrong down.

Hot solos were relatively new in these circles. It was more typical for soloists to offer a straight rendition of a tune, which was livened up with syncopated accompaniment. Henderson and Redman sometimes frame solos by Green and Hawkins in this way, even though both could play hot. Armstrong, however, was not hired to play the tune straight. All of his solos with Henderson are supported by reduced accompaniment, which directs attention to what he could add to a tune.

As Armstrong thought about his creative challenges with Henderson, the central one was this: what would a hot solo be like?

With his strong, confident playing, his sure grasp of rhythm, and his commitment to a memorable phrase, he was already ahead of the game. Hot solos in the early 1920s often dissolve into aimless noodling, incoherent rhythm, or both. Since the solos were short, no one seemed to mind. Armstrong could afford to experiment, and that is what he did with Henderson. There are signs that people were puzzled by him. Trumpeter Louis Metcalf first heard the Henderson band during a rare appearance at a Harlem theater. Armstrong's solo on *Copenhagen* was "*so* good," he said, "but different, and the audience didn't know about how much to applaud." Clyde Bernhardt heard the band when it toured Harrisburg, Pennsylvania, in August 1925, and described Armstrong as "very ahead of his time, very advanced—at least for Harrisburg." Joe Smith, who had joined the band as an additional trumpet soloist in April, "wasn't as exciting, but whatever he played was so beautiful—had those curves in there and trills and triplets over a simple melody, it all sounded so soulful, so mournful." Bernhardt said that it was easier for the crowd, musicians included, to appreciate Smith. "While Louis was playing more than anybody I ever heard before, Joe Smith was doing what the people understood," he explained.

Tension between popular accessibility and creative exploration has long been fundamental to jazz history, and this may be the first documentation of it. Smith's solo on *Alone at Last* (CD 1:38–2:12), recorded with Henderson in August, is a lovely paraphrase of Ted Fiorito's tune, and it does not lack in rhythmic verve, either (though Smith's articulations are very different from Armstrong's hard-edged, percussive attack). What makes the solo easy to understand is how it conforms to the original melody. He firmly rounds off each four-bar grouping with a nice held note. Popular music of the time—and popular music before and after, not just in Harrisburg—thrives on this kind of obvious periodicity, which makes the flow of patterned sound easy to grasp.

But Armstrong was exploring alternative ways to construct phrases, and this was what made him challenging to listen to. Ultimately it made him modern, according to terms that he largely defined by himself. Smith and Armstrong presented two extremes, with Armstrong taking the riskier path, more demanding and more ambitious. One of the true delights in his recorded oeuvre is to go through his year with Henderson and follow his increasingly bold experiments.

It is no surprise that the creator of *Tears* felt most at home when he was playing breaks. Sometimes he sprinkles breaklike material

*Charlie Green, Elmer Chambers, and Armstrong, Harrisburg, August 14, 1925
(The Frank Driggs Collection)*

into solos as a way to make the solo hot, especially at phrase endings
(*Tell Me Dreamy Eyes*, October 1924, CD 1:38 and 1:48; *Bye and Bye*,
January 1925, CD 1:09). Even with the accompaniment still playing,
you can tell that he is thinking in terms of a break.

In *Words*, a break effectively launches his solo with a burst of
energy (October 1924, CD 0:43), and he often uses the same strategy
on a smaller scale in what musicians call "pick-ups," an unstressed
pitch (or syllable in poetry) that leads to a stressed one. His pick-
ups have so much force that the relationship seems to be turned on
its head: the main gesture is the one that comes first, in preparatory
position, rather than the one that falls in stressed position (*Words* is
again a good example). In *Go Long Mule*, pick-up figures form two-
bar groups packed with internal tension, with alternation between
syncopated figures and "straight" rhythms that reinforce the background beat. These two-bar groups stand one measure out of phase
with the patterned flow of the original tune. It is as if he is "filling
in" according to the strategies of collective improvisation, setting
his part as a second line against the regular flow of phrases in the
accompaniment.

Moving in and out of phase with the background beat and phrasing is the central feature of the fixed and variable model, which is now moving to the center of Armstrong's solo playing. In contrast with *Chimes Blues*, from the spring of 1923, his line dances on top of the fixed foundation, constantly changing in its relationship both to the fixed level and to the patterns he has previously defined. We saw in Chapter 3 how he sometimes joined Johnny Dodds and Honore Dutrey to fill in between four-bar and eight-bar phrases of the lead melody, complicating the texture. Now he creates this effect all by himself. In the second phrase of *I'll See You in My Dreams* (January 1925, CD 1:40), for example, he rides right over the articulation of the four-bar tune, just the kind of articulation that Joe Smith observes so faithfully in *Alone at Last*.

He extends this strategy in *Mandy Make Up Your Mind* (December 1924). Two-bar groups here resemble those of *Go Long Mule*. The extension comes in a daring touch at the solo's end (CD 1:27), a climactic leap emphasizing the out-of-phase construction, but with a twist: his solo outlines *not* the chord presently sounding in the accompaniment but the chord of the *next* measure. This is an emphatic display of the fixed and variable model, an imaginative expansion of the concept he has been experimenting with all along.

This gesture makes no sense according to the musical logic of Henderson's talented-tenth training. It only makes sense if we think of the fixed and variable model as being *primary in Armstrong's mind*. What made it possible was complete immersion in the musical values of uptown New Orleans. These connections to collective improvisation and the fixed and variable model have been largely ignored in most writings on Armstrong, but they form the foundation for the first phase of his musical modernity. To overlook them is like trying to explain a fifteenth-century Italian painting without mentioning fixed perspective: there might be a lot to say, but the basic organizing principle has been missed.

What has not been ignored is the superior sense of melodic coherence one gets from Armstrong's solos, compared with those of his contemporaries. In 1924–25, coherence often comes from his use of important pitches from the paraphrased tune. Virtually all of his solos with Henderson paraphrase the given tune to an extent.[29] *Ala-*

*bamy Bound* (February 1925) shows him picking out skeletal pitches and building around them. He extracts the main pitches of the tune and reconfigures them with new rhythm and new phrasing. Why not use the simple logic of the given melody to hold together his much more active creation?

What sets him apart from the other soloists in Henderson's band, then, is first, his training, which none of them could match, and second, his developing sense of melodic design. Musicians who played their paraphrase solos safe did not have to worry about melodic coherence. Players who "got off" ("get-off men" was another name for hot soloists) completely from the main melody usually weren't worried about coherence, either, for their assignment was to play hot, not to compete with Tin Pan Alley tunesmiths. Armstrong was confident enough to experiment with paraphrasing and playing hot at the same time. Precision, drive, a big sound, and cornet dexterity were what got him the job. His training in New Orleans, his ambition, and his searching creativity turned the job into an opportunity to explore fresh ways of designing hot solos.

Adding breaks, pick-ups, blue notes, fill-ins, radical harmonic anticipations—it all led to a dense and somewhat daunting level of activity. Listeners may not have fully understood him—did not know how much to applaud, as Louis Metcalf put it—but Armstrong was apparently a hit at the Roseland.

One milestone for the band was its recording of *Sugar Foot Stomp* (May 1925). Armstrong showed Don Redman "a little book of manuscripts, some melodies that he and the famous King Oliver had written in Chicago," and wondered if Redman might like to pick one out and make an arrangement.[30] Redman chose the celebrated *Dipper Mouth Blues*, the biggest seller among the 1923 recordings. The arrangement is playful, almost to the point of parody. Redman sets collective improvisation aside in favor of sustained chords, cool riffs, and irregular stop time. Near the end of the performance the bass makes a splendid foray into 4/4, as if to confirm the association of this texture with Oliver's band—like a muscle flexing regularly, four to the bar, as Eddie Condon described it. Redman said that *Sugar Foot Stomp* was "the recording that made Fletcher Henderson nationally known."

Armstrong's solo was a milestone of sorts, as well. He reproduces Oliver's famous solo, the very one that he had tried unsuccessfully to imitate in late 1923, but without the wah-wah effects that had frustrated him so much. He puts aside his recent stylistic experiments: there are no breaklike passages, no filling in, no picking out structural pitches and creating a new line around them. Instead, he follows Redman's playful lead and exaggerates the effects of floating across the beat and also backing off from the climax, while giving just enough intensity to make everyone aware that he knows how to do it. When Redman calls out, "Oh play that thing," quoting Bill Johnson from the 1923 recording, the phrase has a completely different meaning, one of lighthearted detachment rather than an urging on to greater heat.

If Armstrong's paraphrase solos show him imposing his will on the question of what a jazz solo could be like—imposing his will on the talented tenth and on Broadway, one could say—*Sugar Foot Stomp* shows him evolving with the 1920s. During the next few years he would become more multidimensional, as he followed jazz through a more complex emotional field. Parts of *Sugar Foot Stomp* remind me of his 1929 recording of *Mahogany Hall Stomp*, which has a wistful, evocative quality of New Orleans that includes both the 4/4 stomp bass and Armstrong's cool relaxation, though the comparison also makes clear how much happened during those four years.

*Sugar Foot Stomp* may have encouraged Henderson to lean harder into jazz, but that turn was hardly direct. In August 1925 the band was still producing dicty arrangements like *I Miss My Swiss*, recorded under the name the Southern Serenaders with white singer Billy Jones. (Presumably, the pseudonym was needed to disguise the racial integration.) It is hard not to laugh at the absurd juxtaposition of the flawless polka accompaniment and Armstrong's driving solo. But in the last two recordings Armstrong made with Henderson, *TNT* and *Carolina Stomp*, Redman followed a new tack, integrating Armstrong's solos into the flow of the arrangement rather than conceiving them as one hot moment in a series of strong contrasts. This was perhaps the clearest harbinger of the Henderson band's future.

His year with Henderson brought him greater exposure thanks to the band's long reach through radio broadcasts from the Roseland, recordings, and a summer tour. Trumpeter Bill Coleman, in Cincinnati, learned Armstrong's solos by heart. The band's arrival in Pittsburgh, in late August 1925, was promoted by the *Courier*. "Next Monday night, August 31st at Duquesne Garden, Pittsburghers will be permitted to hear and dance to the music of one of America's most famous orchestras," the *Courier* wrote, and it is worth noting the order of the terms of engagement—hearing first, dancing second. Jazz has always been a music that people listened to as they danced, or even instead of dancing. The year with Henderson also brought constant exposure to elite white bands, since they were playing in the same venue, face to face. He noticed first-chair trumpeter Vic d'Ippolito's impact on Sam Lanin's band, and in Vincent Lopez's band he heard trumpeter B. A. Rolfe show off his high range, playing tunes an octave higher than written, something Kid Rena also used to do in New Orleans.[31]

There were also a few occasions to sing. Thursdays were "vaudeville night" at the Roseland. When there was a shortage of entries one Thursday, his colleagues encouraged Louis to sing. He offered *Everybody Loves My Baby*, on voice and then on cornet, and won first prize. The event is barely documented in the band's commercial recording of this tune: at the conclusion, Armstrong "mugs"—playful verbal jives that create an atmosphere of spontaneity while conveying very little content—in dialogue with the band, in a series of three breaks. The mugging was dropped on the second take. The regular Thursday night crowd started calling for him, and he continued to appear now and then. Bing Crosby attended some of these contests, and it may have been the first time he heard Armstrong sing.

Henderson claimed that Armstrong sang with the band "with that big fish horn voice of his," but his appearances did not extend beyond these contests.[32] The lack of a regular opportunity to sing became one of his gripes. More fundamentally, he was irritated by the combination of arrogance and lack of commitment among some of the Henderson musicians. Henderson didn't think Armstrong had enough training, but still relied on him to play the high notes that the "big prima donna" first-chair trumpeter couldn't hit (this is probably a swipe at Joe Smith). He was unimpressed with Redman's arrangements—"too much airs and all that shit." And he felt stifled by the brief solo space. "I personally didn't think that Fletcher cared too much for me anyway," he concluded.

His year with Henderson was thus a mix of artistic success and frustration. Contrary to much talk over the years, his impact on the band was not all that obvious. In March 1925, the *New York Age* praised Henderson's "symphonic jazz," but the compliment didn't apply to Armstrong, who had little to do with Henderson's goal of matching standards set by Whiteman and the other elite white bands. An October 1925 report in *Variety* noted "considerable discussion among colored musicians as to who ranks the highest in the east as cornetists. It is claimed by many that the best two are Joe Smith and Louis Armstrong." That says as much as anything about how people were listening in the fall of 1925.

Armstrong was another quiver in Henderson's bow, a dose of hot playing that did not need accompaniment and could thus be inserted for contrast in the variety-packed arrangements. Perhaps his most direct impact was on the young trumpeter Rex Stewart, who idolized him and copied every move. A year or so after Armstrong left, Bud Freeman from Chicago was in New York on a visit and met Stewart. Stewart gave him a folded piece of paper and asked that he deliver it to Armstrong when he got back to Chicago. "Dear Rubber Lips, you are my idol," it read. "God bless you and keep on blowing. Your boy, Rex."

## "Harlem Saved My Life"

Henderson worked hard to expand his network of gigs, filling up the band's off-nights from the Roseland. Sometimes they played for private parties at lavish mansions on Fifth Avenue; they looked forward to being served the same fancy food offered to guests. There were also appearances at places like the Lafayette Theater, the main vaudeville house in Harlem. This was the only theater in Harlem, according to Garvin Bushell, where African Americans could sit downstairs and did not have to climb up to the balcony. It was here that musicians Louis Hooper and Benny Waters first heard Armstrong play. The band also played in Harlem at "after-hours" jobs that kicked in after the Roseland closed at 1:00, lasting until 2:00 or 3:00 in the morning.

A favorite hangout spot in Harlem was the Rhythm Club, a place for musicians to pick up jobs that featured long jam sessions and cutting contests. The Rhythm Club was a notch below the more prestigious Amsterdam Club. Rex Stewart was playing in the Amsterdam Club house band one night when he looked up from the bandstand and saw "a tall, distinguished man, closely followed by a short, heavy set widely smiling young man" being escorted in. When he realized it was Henderson and Armstrong, his distant idol whom he must have heard on records and radio, he was so nervous that he wanted to leave the building.

Armstrong seems to have had a girlfriend in Harlem, a dancer known as Fanny. The information comes from a source that is early but also, like so many writings on jazz, undocumented and sketchy in reliability. Given what we know about his romantic history, it is hard to believe that he gave up female companionship while Lillian was away for long stretches. Certainly he was not waiting patiently, "no one to talk with . . . just me and my radio," as he would humorously sing in *Ain't Misbehavin'* a few years later. Fanny may have been another reason for the prolonged stay in New York.

When Armstrong said, "Harlem saved my life," concerning his year with Henderson, he was probably thinking of a few musicians from New Orleans who lived there. He began making records with two of them, Clarence Williams and Sidney Bechet, almost immediately. He also did a lot of studio work with blues singers who stopped in the city on tours. These race-label recordings count out to some 33 issues. They present a musical world far removed from the Henderson band, a place to relax in a loose atmosphere of pick-up bands, no rehearsals, and a lot of blues. "I knew what I could do with my horn and I proved it when I played with Bessie Smith and them people," he later grumbled, recalling his dissatisfaction with Henderson.

If the recordings with Henderson stand at the talented-tenth nexus with upscale dance music on Broadway, these sessions document the commercial production of the vernacular as it was processed in New York City. The Henderson enterprise was conceived for whites, but these pick-up sessions were distinctly pitched to blacks, as marketed through the race labels.

Just a week or so after he arrived in town, Henderson hired him for a studio session with blues singer Ma Rainey (around October 16, 1924). Henderson had been putting together sessions like this since his days with Pace and Handy, as a way to make easy dollars for him and selected members of his orchestra. Coleman Hawkins, who grew up in a middle-class home taking cello and piano lessons, described these assignments as "playing the cotton mood." Henderson told Rainey's representative that his first trumpeter, Joe Smith, would not, unfortunately, be available for this particular session (Smith was not currently in the orchestra, but he had recorded with Henderson on pick-up gigs like this as recently as September), so he would have to bring along his second trumpeter. Bailey and Green were also invited, giving Rainey Henderson's three bluesiest players.

If Mamie Smith's singing on *Crazy Blues* was the prevailing style in Harlem in 1920, by 1924 the scene had expanded dramatically with the ascent of the southern style represented by Rainey and Bessie Smith; this featured extended blue notes, pronounced southern accent, and tempos so slow, quipped bandleader Sam Wooding, that you could scoot to the bathroom at the beginning of a verse and come back in time to catch its end. Tellingly, not everyone in the Henderson band enjoyed this kind of music. Howard Scott, who sat next to Armstrong in the trumpet section, candidly offered an opinion that must have been shared by others: "I had to make records of blues, and well, I got sick of them. Because you know when you get down to fundamentals, the blues are nothing but the blues. . . . I preferred to play popular music."

This view was definitely not shared by Armstrong. For him, the 1924–25 sessions with Rainey, Smith, Margaret Johnson, Maggie Jones, Alberta Hunter, Eva Taylor, Sippie Wallace, Clara Smith, and Trixie Smith recalled the music he was surrounded by for the first 21 years of his life. In turn, these sessions became the primary way that his playing first got known in the African-American community, beyond those who were able to hear him in person.

Trumpeter Bunny Berigan, a close follower of Armstrong, described his own practice of accompanying blues singers. "Your best bet is to keep your fill-ins rather simple. . . . By all means be careful to avoid playing anything that will conflict with the voice, or attract too much attention from it. In other words the voice must hold the spotlight." This describes well Armstrong's playing on the Rainey session, though it is startling how much more assertive he became in just a few months.

The session with Rainey left no room for instrumental solos, only brief moments to shine in introductions and conclusions. Things would be different the next day, in his first session with Clarence Williams. In July 1923, Williams had introduced a studio band he called "Clarence Williams's Blue Five," following the success of the King Oliver recordings in a low-budget effort to explore the market for blues-oriented instrumental music. Williams's concept, in turn, would be the direct model for Armstrong's celebrated Hot Five series. On his first date with Williams (October 17, 1924), Armstrong recorded *Texas Moaner Blues* alongside Sidney Bechet.

Williams had known Armstrong from the mid-1910s, when he and Armand Piron purchased (or stole, depending on how the story was told) a song Armstrong had written called *Take Your Feet off Katie's Head*, which they tweaked into the bestselling *I Wish I Could Shimmy Like My Sister Kate*. Williams's entrepreneurial ambitions led him into more and more contacts for recording, publishing, and managing African-American musicians. In the fall of 1924 he was leasing office space at 1547 Broadway, five blocks south of the Roseland, in the Gaiety Theater Building, a focal point for blacks in the music business, with Perry Bradford, Bill Robinson, Eubie Blake, Shelton Brooks, W. C. Handy, and others renting offices there. George M. Cohan wickedly nicknamed the building "Uncle Tom's Cabin."

Williams is credited as the composer of *Texas Moaner Blues*, which, as a composition, is nothing more than a simple succession of blues choruses, with an arranged one at the end. It is the kind of thing middlemen associated with race labels routinely cranked out. In this case the banality of the piece was an asset, since the simple blues form inspired stunning performances from the two principals, Armstrong and Bechet.

Trumpeter Mutt Carey remembered the first time he heard Armstrong, back in New Orleans around 1916 or so. Carey was a successful blues player, but the introduction shocked him. "He played more blues than I ever heard in my life," he said. "It never did strike my mind that blues could be interpreted in so many ways." Armstrong and Bechet grew up surrounded by the first generation of wind players who specialized in blues; as they reached maturity they followed the next generation, musicians like Buddy Petit, who were putting their own stamp on the idiom. Blues was expanding in New Orleans, becoming fancier and more creatively daring, and they took it all in.

The October session with Williams was the first chance Armstrong had to put this kind of playing on record. Bechet, however, had been recording blues like this since his July 1923 *Kansas City Man Blues*, his first session with Williams. We know nothing about the relationship at this time between Armstrong and Bechet, who had known each other slightly in New Orleans. Years later there was tension between them, but there is no reason to suspect it at this point. In *Texas Moaner Blues* the two of them produce vigorous collective improvisation and even share a break—not simultaneously, the way Armstrong and Oliver used to, but successively, with Bechet starting the break and Armstrong finishing it (CD 0:57). It is a touching detail, a rare collaborative event that may have been unprecedented.

Blues had always been relatively free of harmonic constraints, which encouraged melodic invention. Slow southern tempos invited the expressive power of blue notes, growls, ornaments, vibrato, rhythmic displacement, speechlike phrasing, and freak playing. Three chords defined the conventional blues pattern: the "one chord" built on the main pitch that organizes the performance; the "four chord," four steps up the scale from one; and the "five chord." The kind of popular music preferred by Howard Scott used a greater variety of chords and demanded precision in matching them, but with blues it has always been perfectly acceptable for soloists to disregard the chords and organize around the basic scale or even the basic pitch—we could speak of the "ubiquitous one." That is what made blues such a perfect training ground: aspiring musicians who had no understanding of chords were free to work on melodic invention and performer-centered means of expression.

The two solos that distinguish *Texas Moaner Blues* each show a mix of ubiquitous one and more meticulous reckoning of the chords. Most impressive, in each case, is the tremendous precision of the filigree, with leaps, rhythmic complexity, and blue notes all neatly placed in a melodic flow that is confident and varied. Armstrong and

Bechet both follow the archetypal sawtooth design of a vigorous leap up followed by irregular descent. Armstrong seems a little nervous: he rushes his double-time break. Bechet poignantly descends from his intense, vibrato-packed peaks with an air of complete control and perfect relaxation; these descents remind me of Armstrong's *West End Blues*, recorded four years later. The connection is obscured by the step forward in recording technology during those years, from acoustic to electronic, and also by the trend toward greater isolation of the soloist, which was standard practice by 1928. But the comparison makes you realize how jazz history might have been different had Bechet not moved to Europe for most of the 1920s but stayed in the United States. He might have continued to develop in tandem with Armstrong, and he certainly would have left a more substantial legacy of recordings.

But in late 1924, Bechet was tough to beat. A few years older than Armstrong, he was perhaps a step ahead, and that must have been a spur for the maturing cornetist, a challenge to set alongside the paraphrase project he was locked into with Henderson. Armstrong and Bechet "were two of a kind," said Pops Foster. "You didn't make any showing when you played with them." Suddenly the two best musicians New Orleans ever produced were joined in a recording studio in the capital of the entertainment industry.

Clarence Williams's Blue Five was not a working band and there were no rehearsals, so the nature of the whole enterprise was spontaneous. That was fine for blues, but for other songs the situation presented a challenge. Armstrong's solos with the Henderson band usually stay the same with repeated takes, indicating that he has worked on the solo in rehearsals and performances. Many writers have marveled at his ability to create beautiful melodies on the spot, but, as discussed in Chapter 2, the New Orleans approach was to work on a solo until it was the way you wanted it, then keep it. One limitation, then, of the race-label recordings Armstrong did in New York is that there was no opportunity to work out solos in advance. Sometimes he simply plays a straight lead and sometimes he embellishes lightly; both can be heard in *Of All the Wrongs You Done to Me* (November 6, 1924).

One piece he got to know very well, however, was *Everybody*

*Loves My Baby (but My Baby Don't Love Nobody but Me)*, the song that won a vaudeville contest for him at the Roseland. In early November he recorded the tune twice with Williams and with two different ensembles. (Lillian was in town to play on one of them.) The Henderson band recorded the tune by the end of the month, and the differences in tempo, rhythm, and prissiness compared with the Blue Five illustrate well the two worlds between which Armstrong was moving back and forth. Armstrong's solos on this tune are extended and well planned, indicating that he had time to work them out in advance. Clarinetist Paul Barnes, back in New Orleans, remembered listening to the Blue Five issue when it first came out.

The cotton-mood sessions continued with Armstrong backing up Margaret Johnson (November 25), Sippie Wallace (November 28), Maggie Jones (December 9, 10, and 17), and Josephine Beatty, aka Alberta Hunter (December 22). Highlights include a blistering break on *Changeable Daddy of Mine* (CD 2:12) that hints at his famous introduction to *West End Blues*. He has extended solos on the Maggie Jones sessions, which were done with reduced accompaniment, just him and Henderson. For Fats Waller's *Anybody Here Want to Try My Cabbage*, he produces a number of quality licks, including one borrowed from the patter section in *Cornet Chop Suey* (CD 1:07); he then makes a nice little answer to his own lick in his next fill-in. *Screamin' the Blues* inspires an overwhelming flood of musical invention, with varied and arabesque fill-ins.

One of his personal favorites was *Good Time Flat Blues*, where he offers a lovely solo, full of intricate twists, rhythmic displacements, and rapid, double-time figuration. The density of varied ideas may have been unprecedented for a 20-second solo. Oliver would have mumbled something about too many snakes, too much figuration, not enough lead, but, more to the point, the solo successfully distinguishes Armstrong from Bechet. When these recordings with blues singers in 1924–25 reached Texas, pianist Sammy Price felt that Armstrong had "emancipated the jazz musician."

The up-tempo *Cake Walking Babies from Home* is the most famous of the December recordings, and the most famous collaboration by Armstrong and Bechet. The vocal duet from Alberta Hunter and Clarence Todd is a token, barely 40 seconds of the three-minute performance; the rest is instrumental. Armstrong plays lead with tremendous drive, embellishing with rhythmic intensity while not getting too fancy and still anchoring the texture, very much in the New Orleans tradition. Bechet's obbligato is outstanding. Commentators have cast the performance as a competition, a studio version of the cutting contests from New Orleans, where two bands on horse-drawn wagons, wheels tied together, battled for the crowd's endorsement. But Bechet's domination is simply the result of engineering imbalance, no more indicative of competition than is Armstrong's second playing, close to the acoustic horn, on *Mabel's Dream* with Oliver, from October 1923. Williams brought Bechet and Armstrong into the OKeh studios in early January to record the piece again with much better balance. It is true that Bechet plays a lot of notes and with tremendous assertion, but that is simply how he liked to play.

January 14, 1925, was another momentous day in music history: in Columbia's recording studios on Columbus Circle (near the current home of Jazz at Lincoln Center), Armstrong joined Bessie Smith. With pianist and harmonium player Fred Longshaw they recorded five tunes, then another four in May. These legendary pairings, first with Bechet and then with Smith, are part of the magic of Armstrong's year in New York. They document the collaborations of the three greatest musicians in the African-American vernacular from the 1920s. In a very specific way, these meetings stand as markers in the city's history: they indicate the increasing entanglement of the African-American vernacular with the nationally organized music industry. New York had long been the industry center, but it would be several years before it became the center for jazz, while it never became a center for blues. Thus these collaborations do not follow from any changes in New York per se; rather, they show the increasing commercial organization of diva blues and African-American jazz, with the inevitable role of New York following from that.

Armstrong said that he didn't get to know Smith very well and never saw her outside of the studio. He knew her well enough to ask for change for a $100 bill, though, and he was astonished when she cheerfully lifted her dress and pulled a fistful of bills out of an apron tied around her waist, "like a carpenter carries his nails." "Louie, I'll give you change for a thousand dollars," she quipped. The two shared a distaste for people who put on airs. "There was never any-thing hoity-toity about Bessie," said her niece, Ruby Walker. "She never forgot where she came from, and she hated to see black people get all fancy and try to act white—she had no use for that." Those words apply perfectly to Armstrong, as well.

In 1925 Smith was at the top of the world of blues singers, a celebrity with her own train car for touring and huge record sales. The stylistic basis for her success was very different from Armstrong's. While Armstrong was expanding his range from high to low, Smith's strategy was to reduce melodies very narrowly. His lines were full of clever dips, dives, and variety, while she got rid of all melodic dis-tractions, leaving the listener with the sense of a deep, heartfelt core. He presented dexterity, she solidity. She was the ultimate example of the blues diva as preacher, commanding the attention of her audience with a theatrical presence and delivering the goods with emotional intensity that, if it did not duplicate church expression, somehow drew on the same energy.

The traditional fill-ins of the cotton-mood accompanists could be heard as something like a congregational response, though this equiv-alence was not straightforward. A preacher aims to incite congregants to more and more emotional involvement. Fill-ins around a blues singer cannot follow that model without the risk of overshadowing the diva preacher. Smith did not make her millions being overshad-owed by fill-ins.

Ruby Walker said that Smith's preferred cornetist was Joe Smith, whose name keeps popping up as Armstrong's rival during this year in New York City.[33] Smith's fill-ins are usually more reserved than Arm-strong's, which may explain the preference. It seems unlikely that she actually disliked Armstrong's playing, however, since she went back to him again in May, after their first session in January.

Generally, however, Armstrong is not too showy on the Janu-ary 14 date. The only extended solo he has comes in *Cold in Hand Blues*, and it is subdued compared to the flashy one on *Good Time Flat Blues*, recorded a month before with Maggie Jones. His solo on *Cold in Hand Blues* was one that trombonist Jack Teagarden and his musical friends listened to over and over again in Texas. (Armstrong would use the main ideas in the first session of the Hot Five record-

*Bessie Smith (Library of Congress, Prints & Photographs Division, Carl Van Vechten Collection, LC-DIG-ppmsca-09571)*

ings, in *Gut Bucket Blues*, which was quickly put together when the studio requested an extra number.) But as soon as he has finished his solo in *Cold in Hand Blues*, he turns to more active, even-note, and double-time filigree for his fill-ins (CD: 2:41), as a way to differentiate the last section of the tune. The effect is jarring, and shows his increasing attraction toward the principle of variety.

*St. Louis Blues*, on the other hand, was not one of the tunes thrown in front of him just before the recording light flashed on. Smith, Armstrong, and Longshaw lift the famous tune to a higher plane to create one of the most beloved performances from the period. Someone had the striking idea of using a harmonium, a folksy reed organ with foot pedals, instead of piano. (Longshaw also plays harmonium on *Reckless Blues*, in the same session.) The sustained organ chords automatically distinguish the performance and provide a lofty, almost contemplative atmosphere. Smith's tempos from this period usually clock in around a very slow 78–84 beats per minute; here the tempo is slowed down even further, to about 70, enhancing the sense that this is a singular statement. The recording begins not with the typical cornet flourish but with a simple held chord, played by Armstrong and Longshaw.

It is clear that Armstrong had already found ways to negotiate Handy's famous tune. His creative and ambitious fill-ins during 1924–25 sometimes feel highly localized, as he focuses on chords as they pass by and tries to be fresh and interesting with each one of them. Here his lines have more purpose and continuity. Smith reduces Handy's varied contours to the narrow span of a perfect fifth; everything she sings occurs within this small range. In the repeated first strain (through CD 1:30) the reduction draws attention to her subtle exploration of a range of blue notes (on the words "sun," "see," "tomorrow," "feel"). Armstrong's fill-ins sometimes sound like complementary answers to Smith's calls, slightly more active but not out of character; other times they feel more like extensions of her line. A third option is to integrate with the harmonic turns, landing on the next chord with a sense that he is making a presentation of both it and Smith's next vocal phrase.

In Chapter 2 we considered how Handy used formal variety to set his published blues songs apart from the oral tradition. Specialists in the African-American vernacular—the performer-centered tradition emphasizing unnotatable means of expression—may intensify or complement formal design with the right gesture at the right moment. The performer does not have to create a form; that is rarely where the expressive power of the vernacular lies. But there is always the possibility of interacting effectively with a form that already exists. (Misunderstandings of this practice are rampant in written commentaries, and they go in both directions, toward exaggerating the formal thinking of a soloist and asserting that such thinking does not exist.) Armstrong's interest in applying the fixed and variable model to the periodic forms of song repertories is a good example.

Smith's response to the three-part form of *St. Louis Blues* is to distinguish the second strain (1925, CD 1:30–2:24) with more forceful declamation, especially on the high note of her narrow range, and to put aside for the moment the heavy blue notes of part 1. Armstrong's fill-ins become more expansive, forceful but not flamboyant, with more bending of pitch (and on a fresh pitch, the lowered seventh of the scale) than she does in this section, as if to keep up the blue-note intensity. Smith then sets off the third strain with a growling "I got them St. Louis blues," rocking back and forth between the blue third and the main pitch with rhythmic force. She has made the piece her own, and Armstrong buys into her vision.

This *St. Louis Blues* gave young trumpeter Zilner Randolph his first exposure to Armstrong. "I had never heard such a thing," he remembered. "And I said, 'That's the kind of horn I want to play.'" Many years later, British trumpeter Humphrey Lyttelton memorized the two parts, Smith's calls and Armstrong's responses, and performed them as one continuous line, a lovely way to preserve this collaborative conception in a living tradition of performance.[34]

Armstrong's last recording session in New York before his return to Chicago was organized by Perry Bradford on November 2, 1925. Bradford assembled an eight-piece band that included pianist James P. Johnson to record his own composition *I Ain't Gonna Play No Second Fiddle*, with Charleston rhythms, collective improvisation, vibrant solos, and a few tightly arranged passages. It was a good situation for Armstrong: the tempo is a bit slower than typical of the Henderson band, and Armstrong knew the tune from his performance with Bessie Smith. After a fine solo by Buster Bailey, he enters with an energetic ascent to the high register. He varies phrase lengths and details of the melody almost continuously, confirming his commitment to the fixed and variable model with unwavering confidence and precision.

A few days later Armstrong attended a farewell party in his honor at Small's Paradise, 135th Street and Seventh Avenue. Years later he remembered the party as one of the few times in his life when he got thoroughly drunk. The festive moment was spoiled when, sitting next to the talented-tenth leader, he vomited all over Henderson's neatly pressed tuxedo shirt. The dignified Henderson turned to Bailey and mumbled, "Take him on home." It was an inglorious end to an eventful year, and the next morning he was on a train, hungover and headed for Chicago.

Like Armstrong, Sidney Bechet bristled at the restrictions of brief snippets of solos in tightly arranged music when he first arrived in New York City. One big difference between the two was Armstrong's ability to adapt, which helps account for their contrasting career trajectories, and perhaps also for the evolution of their styles. Armstrong met the challenges of playing with Henderson, which put him in a good position to climb another rung on the ladder of his career. Waiting for him in Chicago, besides his wife, was a situation that would be similar in some ways to the New York scene, with elite white standards in place, but very different in social context and musical possibility. These changes proved to be just what he needed, and they led him into his musical maturity, where he defined a fresh kind of African-American modernity.

# FIVE

# "This Is What Really Relates to Us": The Dreamland Café, the Vendome Theater, and the First Hot Five Records

His method of playing jazz, which causes controversy even among jazz musicians, was first worked out when he was playing in a cinema orchestra in Chicago.
— *Manchester Evening News*, England, summer 1932

**Armstrong's return to Chicago can be dated, like so much else in his adult life, by** recording sessions: on November 2, 1925, he was making a record in New York with Perry Bradford, and on November 9 he was in Chicago for a session organized by Richard Jones, backing up the singer Bertha Hill. He returned later the same day to accompany Blanche Calloway, Cab Calloway's older sister. Clearly, Chicago was waiting for him. Hill and Calloway sang blues songs composed by Jones, a studio pianist and middleman for OKeh Records, while Armstrong improvised garlands of second playing around them, just as he had done so many times in New York.

On November 11 he worked a longer session and, for the first time, got his name featured on a disc—"Hociel Thomas acc. By Louis Armstrong's Jazz Four." And on the very next day "Louis Armstrong and His Hot Five"—Armstrong, Kid Ory, Johnny Dodds, Johnny St. Cyr, and Lillian Hardin Armstrong—made their debut. The step from sideman with Clarence Williams's Blue Five in New York to headliner for Louis Armstrong and His Hot Five in Chicago was a little one, but sometimes a clean break is necessary to put the next phase of a career in motion.

His wife had been cooking up some deals to coax him back. She was now leading a band at the Dreamland Café, a "nice little swing band," he called it, and she convinced management to offer her husband $75 a week. That got his attention, since it was $20 more than Henderson was paying him. Lillian persuaded the Dreamland to hang up a sign promoting "The World's Greatest Cornetist, Louis Armstrong," and the café took out an ad in the November 14 issue of the *Defender* saying the same thing. The Dreamland started a banner campaign on advertising trucks, "Louis Armstrong's Coming Back to Chicago!" The splashy claim of being the world's greatest cornetist embarrassed him, probably because he still felt shy about upstaging Oliver.

"Louis Armstrong. Who is he?" wrote Dave Peyton in the *Defender*. "He is the jazz cornet king, and he just got in from old New York, where he left 'em sad on account of his departure. Louis is the feature man in Lil's jazz band at the Dreamland. I am surprised that he hasn't named himself 'King Louis.'"[35] That was quite a compliment from Peyton, who usually represented the old-settler, conservatory-trained wing of Chicago musicians. In the same column he praised the Harlem Symphony Orchestra, "the Race's pride," and railed against "our lax musicians" who "bang away on so-called jazz." Armstrong was now cast as a local rather than as an immigrant from New Orleans: an article in the *Defender* announcing his return was headed "Home at Last."

During the next five months he made his mark at the two premiere entertainment venues for African Americans in Chicago, the Dreamland and the Vendome Theater. He continued at the Vendome until April 1927, a healthy run of 16 consecutive months, with time off for a brief summer vacation and not much more. This was where Armstrong's mature solo style crystallized and flourished, where he achieved a status in black Chicago as one of the leading singers and cornet players on the scene—significantly, and for the first time, the priority between the two is not clear. It was at the Vendome, he later told a newspaper in Manchester, England, where he worked out his style. These were relatively elite venues, and the Vendome shared some cultural leanings with the talented tenth in Harlem. Yet the difference was that his Chicago audiences were fully receptive to what he had to offer, which could be understood as a new mix of the African-American vernacular with the flashy sophistication of northern show styles. His activities extended through a third venue of sorts, the Hot Five recording series.

Together, the three created a multidimensional field of African-American reception that allowed him to take center stage, no longer a dash of hot variety in a fancy arrangement or background support to blues singers.

## "Our Own Place of Amusement"

Among South Side cabarets the Dreamland Café stood apart, since it was owned and operated by an African American. A huge building, almost a block long, where customers discreetly brought bottles, the Dreamland benefited from the *Defender*'s "race pride" initiatives. "This is the only cabaret in the city operated exclusively by our Race," cheered the newspaper in 1923. An article from October 1924 laid out clearly what was often implied: "Residents and business men of the Race throughout the city could feel safe in taking their close friends and the members of their families there with the knowledge that nothing would be allowed, by word or act, to cause complaint."

The word "class" often comes up in discussions of the Dreamland. The decor was decorated "to the queen's taste." In the middle of the dance floor was a section of glass lit from below by colored lights. Tables were set with crisp white linens, and the Chinese chef's superb chop suey was a major draw, a notch or two above typical cabaret food. The entertainment was classy, too. There was no shortage of risqué songs or sexy female dancers, but the cruder language of downscale vaudeville and burlesque was avoided. Classy entertainment meant tempos leaning to strong, peppy jazz and not the "vulgar mush kind that invites immoral dancing," as the *Defender* noted in its praise of Lil's Dreamland Syncopators. Showbiz celebrities popped in from time to time, white actors and singers passing through Chicago who liked to check out the latest black entertainment, especially on Thursday matinees. Al Jolson once asked Alberta Hunter to sing his favorite song, *Mammy's Little Coal Black Rose*, a moment of decidedly mixed emotions for Hunter and probably everyone else that did not get recorded by the *Defender* but was preserved in her memory for decades.

The enterprising hero in all of this was the main owner and operator, "our own" Bill Bottoms. Bottoms did well for himself with the

Dreamland and various real estate ventures. One observer noted that only three people on the South Side drove Marmons, a prestigious automobile—the owner of a local insurance company, Jelly Roll Morton, and Bill Bottoms.

The Dreamland had classy aspirations, but its entertainment package was similar to cabarets all across the country. Singers and sexy dancers topped the bill. Entertainment was shaped by values of novelty, variety, speed, and humor. Armstrong fit right in, since he excelled in all four categories.

Singers were the main draw, just as they are in music today and just as they always have been in most musical cultures throughout the world, since they provide the easiest way for most people to relate to music. We have already mentioned Ollie Powers. Alberta Hunter was a big draw in extended engagements in the late 1910s and early 1920s. Women singers dominated the cabarets almost as much as they dominated the blues circuits, drawing subtly or not on sexual allure. "Alberta wore heavily beaded dresses that glittered and sparkled as she shimmied around the room and sang," remembered Lillian Armstrong. "Every now and then she'd make her breasts jump and then the cats really loosened up on their bankrolls." *Chicago That Toddlin' Town* was a featured number for Hunter.

The main presentation for each performer was known as an "up," as banjoist Danny Barker explained: "Some guy comes on and does his thing of singing like a soprano and then singing like a baritone—that's his 'up.'" The up was the singer or dancer's spotlit moment in the snappy flow of cabaret entertainment, presented in front of the band. Singers needed to fill up a large space with no assistance from a microphone (though megaphones were sometimes used), as they did in vaudeville houses, theaters, and tent shows. "Ollie Powers and I had the biggest voices," insisted Hunter. Armstrong's recordings reveal a vocal style that is right in step with these demands, which do not foster nuanced shadings of loud and soft; the more punch in the attack, the better. When he started to use microphones later in the decade, his vocal style changed dramatically, but the 1926 recordings with the Hot Five document a singer who has worked out his style in front of large audiences in large spaces.

After their ups, the singers circulated between tables, stopping wherever tips were offered, with continued accompaniment from the band. They took requests, but otherwise they sang the same song over and over again, in a softer voice so that just the people sitting in front of them (and tipping them) could hear. The singer could hear the band, but the band could not easily hear the singer, who threw up his or her hands as a signal when it was time to stop. Tips were supposed to be shared equally, though there are many stories about bills dropped on the floor for a waiter to pick up for storage or stuffed slyly into hidden parts of a dress.

In both the main presentation and the little table visits, the singer worked to convey intimacy and emotion. Singers were actors as much as vocalists. The great Sophie Tucker was a pioneer in this cabaret style. "You've got to give something of yourself across the footlights," Tucker explained. In cabarets, the entertainers were close to the audience and on the same horizontal plane, not distant and elevated as in a theater, giving patrons a sense that they were being admitted to a privileged and somewhat risqué space. Styles of visual expression typical of cabaret singing certainly shaped Armstrong's own style. He first saw Sophie Tucker at the Orpheum Theater in New Orleans, in the late 1910s, sitting in the balcony, or "buzzard roof," as he called it. A video of him singing from 1933 shows what seems today like a strange display of highly stylized facial expressions, which probably owed much to both minstrelsy and cabaret singing. At the Dreamland he had his first chance to work out his technique, night after night.

Singing and dancing were thoroughly intertwined, the two routinely mentioned together in newspapers, as in a reference to "the clean-cut principals with their singing and dancing specialties" at the Dreamland. "The entire cast dance the Charleston in a decidedly pleasing manner," was the opinion of a reviewer in November 1925. The principals may have been clean-cut, but minimal costumes were typical for women at every cabaret. "Restaurant audiences do not want men. They want women, the more the better and the less they wear also," wrote *Variety* bluntly. Like the lead singers, the dancing girls flirted with men in the audience. "They glance mischievously down at you," reported an observer, "and she swings her foot over the railing above you, smokes a cigarette and smiles." Florenz Ziegfeld's hiring priorities for cabaret dancers were beauty, personality, and talent, in that definite order. African-American dancers had to have light, café au lait skin. Couple-dancing teams demonstrated how to do various dance steps so the patrons could try them out during the open-dancing portion of the evening.

"Now ladies and gentlemen, we have a little novelty for you this evening"—that was Armstrong's promise to his invisible audience at the outset of a 1931 recording. Like sex appeal, novelty is a timeless commodity, but it had special resonance in the 1920s, a period of inventions. "In those crazy Twenties the sensation-hungry public was ready for a new fad every twenty-four hours," said clarinetist Mezz Mezzrow. In music, novelty ranged from animal imitations to all kinds of physical displays—playing three clarinets at once, playing the bass viol while lying down, shimmying the stomach muscles rapidly while playing the drums, playing a miniature piano that rolled through the room, trotting out a four-foot coach trumpet.

The words "eccentric" and "novelty" were close in meaning. "Eccentric" was especially flexible; the word was, in fact, applied to Armstrong's innovative playing. "Louis has promised to give the Chicago public some new figures in jazz," Dave Peyton wrote in August 1926, after Armstrong returned from vacationing with Lillian in Idlewild, Michigan, "as he has had ample time to figure out some eccentric ones." The following April, in a brief review of the publications *Louis Armstrong's 125 Jazz Breaks for Cornet* and *Louis Armstrong's 50 Hot Choruses for Cornet*, Peyton wrote that "Louis has penned in book form some of his eccentric styles of playing." Two other formulations were "trick figure" and "trick manipulation," as in a column "Vaudeville News" from *Heebie Jeebies* (September 4, 1926): "The orchestra rendered some classy numbers Sunday night that won thunderous applause from the patrons. Louis Armstrong and Earl Hines copped 'big hands' all week on their trick manipulations."

"Eccentric," "trick," and "novelty" were standard categories for the entertainment industry; "weird" and "crazy" were more informal ways of saying the same thing. It is easy to imagine that Armstrong's "up" at the Dreamland was introduced as an eccentric act. In 1924 and 1925, his solos with Henderson seemed challenging and unfamiliar to audiences from Harlem to Harrisburg; undoubtedly, many listeners in Chicago had the same response. Reminiscing about a saxophone player in Chicago who had his own distinctive way of playing, pianist Glover Compton explained how it was challenging for him to blend: "He was one of them fellas who everybody just stay down and let him play *his* style, like Louie was. . . . His [Armstrong's] style was so odd, so different from anything anyone had ever heard." "Eccentric," "trick," "weird," and "crazy" were familiar categories that helped make room for his innovative playing, which clearly stood outside of the range of normal jazz.

In their pathbreaking account of jazz dancing, Marshall and Jean Stearns concluded that "the term 'eccentric' is a catchall for dancers who have their own nonstandard movements and sell themselves on their individual styles." African-American eccentric acts typically exaggerated the distinguishing features of their own tradition. Freak music with plunger and wah-wah effects, for example, fell automatically into this category; it was not accidental that Joe Oliver chose the rag *Eccentric* as a vehicle for his specialty. The Stearnses mention contortionist dancer Jigsaw Jackson, the Human Corkscrew, who performed with his face on the floor, feet spiraling around in vigorous rhythm. "He did everything around the beat," remembered Charles "Honi" Coles, in a formulation often used to describe jazz musicians.

In an analysis of Earl Hines's style, the great swing pianist Teddy Wilson defined eccentric music with some precision. The analysis is worth quoting at length, since what he says applies well to Armstrong. Hines, explained Wilson,

> has a beautifully powerful rhythmic approach to the keyboard and his rhythms are more eccentric than those of Art Tatum or Fats Waller. When I say "eccentric" I mean getting away from straight 4/4 rhythm. He would play a lot of what we call accent on the "and" beat. This is the beat that comes *between* the 4/4 quarter note beats, and Hines accented it by starting a note between the 4/4 beats. He would do this with great authority and attack. It was a subtle use of syncopation, playing on the in-between beats or what I might call "and" beats: one–*and*-two-*and*-three-*and*-four-

*and* . . . Now Hines would come in on those "and" beats with the most eccentric patterns, that propelled the rhythm forward with such tremendous force that people felt an irresistible urge to dance or tap their feet, or otherwise react physically to the rhythm of the music. . . . He had such a beautiful approach to playing rhythmic piano that he could easily move an audience. . . . As I have said, Hines is very intricate in his rhythm patterns: very unusual and original and there is really nobody like him.

Nobody like him—except perhaps Louis Armstrong. Wilson is describing a way of working with the fixed and variable model, and in this Armstrong was leading the way during the 1920s. That is one reason why Hines is sometimes said to play "trumpet style" piano; the phrase is partly in recognition of Armstrong's influence. It is impossible to know how widely Wilson's understanding of "eccentric" circulated during the 1920s, but it is easy to believe that it was understood intuitively as a way to make sense of this kind of music.

Alongside novelty stood the principle of variety, another aesthetic principle that has enjoyed great favor in many kinds of art forms. Armstrong's first recorded solo, on *Chimes Blues*, reveals very little interest in variety, but six months later (October 1923) his series of breaks for *Tears* shows him firmly focused on this principle, which he then took to heart as he explored different ways of constructing solos with Henderson. In his embrace of variety, he is thoroughly in step with the period's tendencies, signaled by the title of the trade magazine for the entertainment industry—*Variety*. Virtually all programs in cabarets and theaters featured different kinds of performers following one another in rapid succession, and within each performance, too, there had to be a flow of continuously fresh detail. Performers who were good at generating a lot of ideas had an advantage, and no one was better at this than Armstrong.

Speed may have been more important than anything else. The entire decade embraced it through cultural and technological inventions. "Behold now the days of super-speed, of super-brilliance, of super-power," wrote the *Chicago Daily News*. A taste for quick dance tempos in Chicago required the New Orleanians at Lincoln Gardens to make some adjustments, and speed shaped entertainment of all kinds. The swiftness of shows was a frequent point of emphasis in reviews, as in this 1924 comment from New York: "the new show sped along without an interruption in its pace. . . . From the very first scene . . . the show traveled at breakneck pace." "'Speed' is the present day slogan," agreed a show columnist for the *Defender* in 1926. "'Step on it!' 'Give her the gas!' 'Jazz it up!' 'Snap into it!' are familiar exclamations that beat a tattoo upon one's eardrums from every direction." Performers entered on the previous act's exit or even before its finish, avoiding any lull in the snappy stream of variety. Armstrong was thoroughly caught up in the race. Nevertheless, the fastest tempos were not conducive to the dense flow of ideas that marked his creativity, and his greatest solos tend not to be his fastest ones.

Speed was a cutting-contest weapon in New Orleans, alongside freak playing and technical facility. *Cornet Chop Suey*, with its quickly moving arpeggiations and filigree, was designed with this in mind. Armstrong had been sitting on *Cornet Chop Suey* since January 1924: there was no way to use it with Oliver, where his assignment was to stay under, and no way to introduce it in New York, where he took short solos and accompanied blues singers. With his name now on the Dreamland marquee, he was finally in a position to perform this carefully crafted display piece. He remembered how the piece "turned out to be a very popular tune—especially among the musicians and actors and music lovers," which places it directly in the Dreamland. *Cornet Chop Suey* must have been his "up," the Chinese chef smiling broadly.[36] The piece found success not as an accompaniment to dancing but as a piece for listening, a context that would shape Armstrong's return to Chicago and his musical maturity.

Entertainers often integrated comedy into their routines, and specialists were in high demand. "A show without a comedian was no show at all," insisted trumpeter Doc Cheatham. Earl Hines agreed that "the Negro comedians were very successful. . . . Their funny comments on everyday life, and on what happened in the Southland, were all mixed up with references to segregation that were particularly funny to us Negroes who knew what it was all about. It was a relief to the distress and the turmoil and the obligations we always had, and that is where a lot of that great soul feeling came from." One of the oldest surviving documents associated with Armstrong is his copy of a comedy skit called "The Boy from Gaffney Alabama." It would be hard to overestimate the extent of humor in his vocal music. His two big hits of 1926, *Heebie Jeebies* and *Big Butter and Egg Man*, were primarily expressions of cabaret-style comedy.

Musicians were rarely the main attraction at a cabaret. Pianist Art Hodes explained how the other entertainers were far more important than the band, which "was at the bottom of the ladder." A newspaper review praised Lil's Dreamland band for its versatility, for following the entertainers well, and for playing good dance music; there was no mention of any musical solos, which was absolutely typical. Armstrong transcended these limitations. Though we have little detail about his performances at the Dreamland, we do know that his name was featured on the marquee and in the newspaper, that within a short time he was in position to demand more money, that, according to Lil, people lined up "ten deep" in front of the bandstand to hear him, that, according to Ory, people "lined up in the snow to get in to hear us," and that, according to Armstrong himself, he "became more popular every night and was the talk of Chicago." An undated newspaper clipping preserved in a scrapbook kept by Lil also frames the matter clearly: "Louis Armstrong, the greatest jazz cornet player in the country, is drawing many Ofay musicians in Dreamland nightly to hear him blast out those weird crazy figures. This boy is in a class by himself."

## Sunday Afternoon at the Symphony

Sociologists St. Clair Drake and Horace Cayton, writing in 1945, claimed that the "five years from 1924 to 1929 were the most prosperous ones the Negro community in Chicago had ever experienced." That relative prosperity happily coincided with Armstrong's coming of age as a soloist, the first period of his musical modernity. "Things were jumping so around Chicago at that time, there was more work than a cat could shake a stick at," he wrote. Steady patronage is always a great boon to artists, and support for Armstrong from the African-American community was now beginning to flow in unprecedented volumes. In return, he helped define and bring to artistic life a sense of what that community was all about.

*Vendome Theater (The William Russell Photographic Collection, MSS 520 F. 52, Williams Research Center, The Historic New Orleans Collection)*

Soon after his name lit up the Dreamland marquee, conductor Erskine Tate invited him to join the Vendome Theater Symphony Orchestra. The Vendome was a movie house on State Street at 31st; Armstrong worked there from December 1925 through April 17, 1927. Because of the length of his stay and the prominence of the venue, we know more about what he did there and what went on around him than we know about the Dreamland.

If Armstrong was embarrassed by being advertised as the world's greatest cornetist at the Dreamland, the prospect of playing with

Tate was terrifying. "I like to have fainted," he remembered. His wife scolded him: "Boy—if you don't get out of this house and go on down there to Erskine Tate's rehearsal, I'll skin you alive." He had good reason to be nervous. Henderson tolerated his unschooled ways with a touch of contempt, but Tate's outfit may have been the most sophisticated African-American orchestra in the country. He took the job, and it turned out to be a good decision. It "was my greatest experience of them all," he wrote much later. "I wouldn't take a million for that experience."

Entertainers often doubled up on jobs that fit two different time slots, and that is precisely what Armstrong started to do in December 1925. The Vendome opened at two o'clock every afternoon and closed at eleven.[37] (The organist probably played by himself for the early shows, with the orchestra arriving for the later ones.) The timing was perfect for Louis to trot over to the Dreamland, four blocks away, in time for the late show there. After that he might grab his horn and check out an after-hours club or two, retiring to bed around dawn. He occasionally extended his work day with a midmorning recording session. Routines like this, seven days a week, helped keep the music profession young.

Of all the venues Armstrong played in during the 1920s, movie theaters were most unlike what people expect today. To go to the Vendome meant that you were going to watch a movie, but that was not all, and it wasn't necessarily the main attraction. "We sell tickets to theaters, not movies," explained Marcus Loew, who made a lot of money with that point of view. From the beginning of the silent-picture era, movies were packaged with an astonishing range of live entertainment. Theaters explored different formats as they tried to hook into one market niche or another. There was always some kind of music to accompany the films, and the music itself could become a major draw.

Music could in fact be more important than anything else.[38] When the silent era ended, music receded into the background, where it remains today, but in 1925 many theaters used it to attract customers. There was, for example, the Pied Piper concept of a small performance outside the entrance to the building, luring customers in. There might be a player piano for atmosphere in the front lobby.

Music always accompanied the film, and there were often musical highlights before and after, such as the community sing-along, the "illustrated song," the orchestra overture, the featured singer, the instrumental soloist, and the organ solo. Every theater needed at least a pianist, larger halls at least an organist. Many had small combos of piano, violin, and drums. And the ones that relied on music the most had "symphony orchestras," a term that carried special resonance at the Vendome.[39]

African-American musicians felt that there was more theater work in Chicago than in New York City, which meant that there was more than anywhere. "They improved their ability that way, and so could read a little better than jazz musicians in the East," explained Garvin Bushell. In the spring of 1926 one writer counted around 100 African-American musicians, all of them unionized, working in South Side theaters. Theater work was coveted because it offered the best pay scale, reasonable hours, and steady work throughout the year. A feature in the *Defender* (August 1926) gave a list of "Chicago Orchestras and Where They Play," and it described the makeup of 29 ensembles. The list included seven theaters: the Monogram Theater had two musicians, the Pickford four, the Grand five (soon to be augmented to seven), the Twentieth Century and the Owl seven, the Metropolitan twelve, while the Vendome topped the list with fifteen.

Management had decided to distinguish the Vendome in this way in June 1924. To publicize the initiative, they scattered large posters around the neighborhood reading simply, "9 to 15," with no hint of explanation or even a mention of the Vendome. The *Defender* solved the mystery on June 28: on July 3, the Vendome would be expanding its orchestra from nine to fifteen players, which would make it "the sensation of the time." This move swung the balance of interest toward music to a degree unprecedented for South Side theaters.

There were plenty of models, though. Setting national standards were the Rialto and the Rivoli in New York City, both under the musical direction of Hugo Riesenfeld, a protégé of Gustav Mahler and former first violinist at the Imperial Opera House in Vienna. In the early 1920s the Rialto and Rivoli had orchestras of 45 players. Each week, Riesenfeld and his four assistant conductors perused their combined music library of some 32,000 pieces to assemble programs. Riesenfeld's aim was not simply to make excellent music to go with films; he wanted to have the finest orchestras in the city. Theaters across the country imitated his strategy, routinely raiding traditional symphony orchestras for the best musicians.

Riesenfeld popularized the practice of featuring the overture as a presentation completely independent of the main movie. A new one was selected every week, the title often advertised. This was followed by an orchestral segment of classics, both light and serious. Why pay for Carnegie Hall when you could hear Beethoven and Wagner performed at the movie house? "No concert schedule needed in New York," ran an advertisement in 1921, since "the best orchestral and vocal music is always available at the theaters under the direction of Hugo Riesenfeld." Venues like these stretched out the range of class positions associated with movie theaters, positions defined by shifting social, economic, and cultural packages.

By the standards of the Rialto and Rivoli, the Vendome was modest. What mattered was that it was good enough to be the best on the South Side of Chicago. The Vendome had full-dress orchestral music, played with distinction, with additional entertainment to fill out the program. The articulation of social class through cultural practice is always a relative thing, and the requirements for an elevated position in white Manhattan were different from those in black Chicago. What Riesenfeld did with 45 musicians, the Vendome could do with 15—increased to 20 when Armstrong joined.

If you wanted to hear African-American musicians playing the finest classical music at the highest technical level, you headed to the Vendome, no matter where you lived. "The Vendome theater . . . has one of the finest symphony orchestras to be found in any theater in the country regardless of size. The type of music offered the patrons of this house is equal to the best to be heard in the largest movie houses of the country." That is how Bill Potter, writing in the *Defender*, regarded the Vendome in September 1925, and that is why Armstrong was a bit nervous when Erskine Tate invited him to join his orchestra.

Tate was well suited to this job, which he supplemented with instrumental lessons at his studio in the Columbia Hotel, a half-

*"Erskine Tate's Vendome Theater Orchestra has new pictures of the gang, and they look like a million bucks, in modern grouping. This organization played over the radio last week from the Drake Hotel studio and created quite a sensation."* Defender, *December 5, 1925 (The Frank Driggs Collection)*

block from the Vendome, and sales from a little music store. Like most leaders of theater orchestras, he was a violinist. And like Lillian Hardin Armstrong and Fletcher Henderson, his background was strictly classical. In late 1925 he was at the top of his game. Though jazz in its various forms was gaining popularity on the South Side, he and other theater musicians with no background whatsoever in improvised music hardly felt threatened. They were secure in their niche. "See, music you fit in certain slots," explained drummer Red Saunders. "You're either a good theater man or you're a good cabaret band, at that time, or you're a good ballroom band, you know."

Musicians from New Orleans enjoyed advantages on most instruments in Chicago, but not the violin, as Johnny St. Cyr acknowledged when he counted off the names of six players who were all better than the best player from New Orleans. Good string playing carried tremendous symbolic value. A theater orchestra of 12 to 14 musicians usually had two violins, viola, and cello, which is apparently what the Vendome carried. When first violinist Joe McCutcheon was out for five days because of an injury, his absence and the name of his replacement were duly noted in the *Defender*, much as the sports page reported injuries of star players for the White Sox. Percussionist

Jimmy Bertrand was occasionally mentioned in the press for solos on tympani or xylophone. The orchestra included bassoon, oboe, flutes, clarinets, and trombone. Paul "Stump" Evans, alto saxophonist, took solos while sitting in a distinct way on the back of his chair. Tate hired Eddie Atkins from New Orleans to play trombone. The piano player was the great Teddy Weatherford, a model for Earl Hines. "So cruel is this man on the poor little ivories, so barbaric is this creator of eccentric jazz figures on the piano keyboard, I have decided to name him Terrible Teddy," wrote Peyton. "Teddy is wholly original in everything he does."

Erskine's brother, James, occupied the first trumpet chair; he was applauded in one review for a beautiful solo that was, "as usual," an "ear smacker." Shortly after Armstrong joined, Erskine took him aside and gently pointed out a little problem. With Louis playing the cornet and James sitting next to him with the longer trumpet—well, it just didn't look good. You look "funny there with [your] stubby little cornet," Tate joked. It took Louis a while to get used to the new horn, but such were the demands of a symphony orchestra.

"Never [before] played any classical music—*Cavalleria Rusticana*, reading music, turning sheets and all that," Armstrong observed as he tried to describe what a leap it was to join Tate.[40] In New York he learned the hard way what the abbreviation *pp* meant; at the Vendome he would be confronting classical terms like "segue" and "tacet." What theater musicians did better than musicians in dance halls and cabarets was to read notated music, precisely and quickly. They had to, since a lot of new music, written at considerable levels of difficulty, was thrown at them every week or even every few days. In 1918 Armstrong was motivated to take a job with Fate Marable's riverboat orchestra because he realized that it would develop his reading skills, which would in turn expand his job opportunities. Marable took him on fully aware of his limitations, and the situation at the Vendome was similar. "I really did sharpen up on my reading there, man, especially when we played for those silent pictures," he remembered. "I couldn't read music like a lot of them cats, but I never was embarrassed in music with bands 'cause I'd state my case. I'd say, 'Now I can *blow*—and you give me elbow room, you going to have a nice time. But don't put me to no tests.'"

At the Vendome he advanced to the point where he could read fluently. There was no room for faking. "Anyone that wasn't familiar with reading music, why there was no place for him," said Omer Simeon, who played with Tate later. "So if a musician couldn't read there he was lost. Didn't have any job."

In his later career Armstrong never flaunted his ability to read music, and he even kept it somewhat hidden, as did other African-American musicians who understood that white audiences liked to think of them as primitive and illiterate. Zilner Randolph performed with him in the early 1930s and recalled how word was going around that Armstrong could not read music. Randolph was astonished when he put a new and challenging arrangement in front of Armstrong, who promptly sang it, complete with solfège syllables, flawlessly and effortlessly.[41]

Theaters that tried to make their mark with fancy dress, lofty repertory, impressive orchestras, and classical overtures had gotten to a point by the late 1910s where their superior status was no longer in doubt. This allowed them to backtrack a little and factor popular music into their programs, with an eye toward even more robust competition against lower-cost theaters. The goal was to appeal to as many people as possible without compromising the toniness of the enterprise. Thus, in the late 1910s, theaters like the Rivoli and Rialto began to embrace the principle of variety while keeping a distinctly classical spin. Riesenfeld even featured "classical jazz," which meant syncopated versions of melodies by Chopin, Gounod, and Puccini, scored for his conservatory-trained musicians.

By the end of 1925, Tate likewise understood the potential of symphonic jazz to broaden his appeal and keep enough people happy to fill up the Vendome.[42] "Select a variety program, giving all classes of the patronage what they want," was Peyton's advice to Chicago conductors, and he cited Tate as the one who was getting it right. It seemed logical to add get-off men who could improvise solos. "That's what they hired me for, anyway, them hot numbers," said Armstrong. Saxophonist Ralph Brown explained that by hiring get-off men, Tate was trying to bring in younger people. Interested in producing jazz and popular songs in a classy way, Tate found the perfect solution in Armstrong. The Vendome was tailor-made for the cornet player turned trumpeter, who stepped in at the right time, with the right preparation, the right abilities, and the right ambition.

A typical program of live entertainment for a movie theater around this time included five to eight performing units; the movie and the program were repeated in alternation, four times a day. The best source for details about the Vendome is a rare South Side weekly called *Heebie Jeebies*, from which Lillian clipped articles, gluing them into scrapbooks to document Louis's career.[43] In one of these clippings the magazine boasts that Armstrong himself was a "pet writer" for *Heebie Jeebies*.

Three of Lillian's clippings describe programs at the Vendome, one with some precision in the sequence of events. After the movie, the orchestra played its overture. Then Walter Richardson, a regular in South Side cabarets and theaters, sang two songs, *Ten Commandments of Love* and *Say It Again*, in an "up-to-date manner." After Richardson came Armstrong singing *Little Ida*. "My how we wondered who little Ida was, as he seemed to have put the feeling of his soul in the music," joked the reviewer. This was followed with a cornet solo from James Tate and several numbers from the orchestra. Next up was Leroy Broomfield, a singer-dancer from Omaha, who started his rendition of *At Dawning* with the stage in darkness; after that he performed *Talking to the Moon* and *I Want to Be Happy*, concluding with a recap of *At Dawning*. The title of the entire program was *Mid-Summer Frolics*. A different program included Cole and Man, "two neat dancing chaps hardly out of the 'teens,'" offering "real hot steps of the terpsichore, including the Charleston, Waltz Clog, kneefalls, and everything imaginable." On another occasion the Vendome featured "Racehorse" Mamie Smith's dancing-comedy versions of *Where Did You Get Those Eyes* and *Baby Face*, both "riotously applauded."

It is easy to see how, in a theater like the Vendome, African-American entertainers had special value for the simple reason that the movies themselves were hardly made with African Americans in mind. Movies rarely included African-American actors, and when they did, the characters were usually treated with condescension and contempt. How much better to see a flashy dancer, a smooth singer, a fancy cornet solo, a great comedian, and the finest race orchestra in

the country—all of it black, all of it classy. Even if the movie was racist and degrading, the live program reassured the audience that the
race was doing just fine.

Tate's orchestra became, in Peyton's words, the "pride of the Race
and the pets of Chicago's music lovers." The Vendome was all about
status, but that didn't mean you had to be rich to buy a ticket. Prestigious theaters in New York City typically charged 10 to 50 cents for
admission, and the Vendome offered a similar range of prices. It only
took a little bit of money to enter a lovely theater where everyone was
dressed up and intent on enjoying first-rate music, comedy, and dancing, with a movie and newsreel to boot.

Milt Hinton, the bass player whose move from Mississippi we
tracked in Chapter 2, attended every Sunday afternoon with his
mother, the two of them dressed in their finest clothes. His mother
was buying violin lessons for him with the goal of turning him into a
classical musician, perhaps to play in a theater orchestra or to work as
a choir director at a nice church. "This was high class for us," Hinton
remembered. "We couldn't go downtown, but we could to go a high
class theater in our neighborhood. . . . People of any kind of stature
at all would try to get down to the Vendome Theater on a Sunday,
to see this marvelous show." The high culture, large size, and range
of ticket prices confirm an observation made by sociologists Drake
and Cayton: some symbols of respectability and success were available even to members of the working class, to people "of any kind of
stature at all," as Hinton put it.

There was apparently little overlap between the Vendome and
Dreamland audiences, the two venues drawing from different parts
of the African-American community. Trumpeter William Samuels
explained how his parents would never have entered one of the cabarets just a few steps from their front door, but they often went to
theaters. "Back in those days there were two sets of society," he said.
Doubling up at the Vendome and the Dreamland turned out to be
more than a way for Armstrong to earn more money: it extended the
range of his reputation. With 1,500 seats and multiple shows every
day, the Vendome brought in more people than he could reach anywhere else. And as classy as the Dreamland was, it was simply not
in the same musical league as the Vendome. It turned out to be the

Vendome, more than any other place, where he made his reputation in South Side Chicago.

## The Movie

Orchestras were obliged to enhance the featured presentation with music, but critics constantly complained that the musicians didn't take the job seriously. Some white musicians working in a Chicago theater in 1927, for example, joked about playing *Clarinet Marmalade* while a French general placed a wreath on the Tomb of the Unknown Soldier. "It became a regular gag with the band to tear into *Hold That Tiger* whenever a heart rending scene was in progress," one of them remembered.

It was a lot easier to have a single keyboardist accompany the movie, which is what many theaters did. A pianist or organist can improvise or spontaneously dish out any number of standard tricks without having to coordinate with anyone else. One reviewer enjoyed how an organist "shouts vengeance, frantically claws the enemy, wails with impassioned grief, screams with victory, sobs thickly with love, moans with remorse, cries like a baby, giggles like a young girl, does a Charleston, barks like a dog, and finally shoots itself with a bass drum." Fats Waller briefly played organ at the Vendome alongside Armstrong in April 1927, and he was praised for his witty cueing of the movie and his "eccentric stop coupling." His tenure was cut short when domestic troubles led to his arrest and forced return to New York City. "The old organ is dull at the Vendome since the strong arm of the law took 'Fats' away," wrote Peyton on May 14.

Tate's orchestra was praised for taking movie accompaniment seriously. "They characterize [the film]," wrote Peyton; "nothing is missed by the well trained Tate in the picture." Tate used cue sheets, the standard way to put together accompaniment. Cue sheets were published for every picture, with a series of visual cues (for example, "boy upsets glass of wine") indicating to the conductor each musical change, which he then cued to the musicians. It was probably the first time Armstrong had ever played for a conductor using a baton. "Watching [Tate] was how I learned to conduct an orchestra," said

Earl Hines. "His arm and finger movements, his concentration—he was terrific and it was beautiful to watch him."

Music matched to the changing emotions of the narrative—the funeral, the love scene, the rescue, and so on—was often drawn from the familiar repertory of overtures. The conductor could put a lot of effort into making good transitions from one mood to another, modulating between different levels of loud and soft and different tempos. There were no pauses: "had music in front for everything that happened," wrote Armstrong. A little collection of themes, one or two phrases long, was constantly used for scene changes and other transitions. Tate had a set of signals. His fourth finger, for example, meant music for a rough passage in the narrative, cued, perhaps, by ominous clouds on the screen. Crossed fingers meant turn back four pages, and so forth. The musicians had to be alert and in control of their reading. Armstrong liked to tell a story about playing for *The Sea Beast*, based on *Moby Dick* and starring John Barrymore as Captain Ahab (May 6, 7, and 8, 1926, at the Vendome). When the climactic scene came around, with the great white whale attacking the captain and biting off his leg, Armstrong couldn't take his eyes off the screen and lost his place in the score. "Erskine Tate was swinging his arms everywhere and he turned to me and said—'*Come on you.*'" But he was lost: "I had sixty measures to count—I missed my count."

The newsreel gave the improvisers in the group a chance to shine. Armstrong remembered improvising for a Pathé newsreel about an Indian reservation. When the Indians did a war dance, the band settled into a lively accompaniment that got everybody's attention. "The audience were *still* applauding for that same scene" five scenes later, he wrote.

Today we tend to think of silent pictures as lacking something essential, but audiences loved the Vendome productions. "You enjoyed looking at the fine pictures, those fine actors, and hearing that fine music," said Ralph Brown. "Nobody wants to go back to silent pictures, but I mean, in that day people enjoyed it much more than people do nowadays. I'm telling you. Beautiful music, soft music. You could close your eyes and hear that music playing, and this is a love scene, you could tell what was going on if you closed your eyes. I'm telling you, you could do it." For those eye-closing love scenes, Tate often relied on a little piece composed specifically for the purpose by one Minnie T. Wright. It was entitled simply *Love-Song*. Armstrong played it so many times that he was able to reproduce it, presumably from memory, in the goofy recording *Laughin' Louie* from 1933.

## The Overture

The overture was the orchestra's moment to shine. Though in some theaters the overture came before the featured film, in the manner of an opera overture, the Vendome played it after the movie, which suggests that at least one and probably two showings of the film were given before the orchestra even arrived.

The repertory had nothing whatsoever to do with the feature film; it was chosen to allow the high-class orchestra to play high-class music. Documented overtures at the Vendome included light classics that were popular everywhere, such as the overtures to *Poet and Peasant* by Franz von Suppé and *William Tell* by Gioachino Rossini. *Heebie Jeebies* praised a rendition of Léo Delibes's ballet *Naila*. The overture might be nothing more than an arrangement of the main melodies from a piece, casually strung together. The music was not necessarily difficult, for either the performers or the listeners, but it served the needs of South Side audiences. "Everybody's sitting there like we were at the opera," remembered Hinton.

Tate's interpretive abilities were praised. Theater conductors often made their own arrangements or tinkered with published versions. Special features would have required Tate's intervention, as indicated in this review from Peyton: "Jimmy Bertram, the hot little drummer in the Vendome orchestra, stopped the overture with his xylophone specialty." It seems to have been common to arrange overtures so that they featured a soloist. "When mine came around, mine was *Cavalleria Rusticana*," remembered Armstrong.

*Cavalleria rusticana*, the much-loved opera by Pietro Mascagni— Peyton called it a "soul stirring masterpiece"—was one of the true workhorses of theater orchestras. When the assignment was made, Armstrong was initially reluctant to leave his seat in the orchestra pit and mount the stage to play his solo. Management offered him more money, but he still resisted, and we can sense here the same hesita-

*Dave Peyton, from* The Light, *January 14, 1928 (Chicago History Museum, ICHi-67129)*

tion that surfaced in his embarrassment at seeing his name on the Dreamland marquee. Somehow he was persuaded, and his solo from *Cavalleria rusticana* contributed to his expanding reputation.

Melodies from the light classics were used in vaudeville, but the Vendome provided Armstrong with his first extended contact with the repertory. Constant exposure to a core repertory is part of any kind of musical training, as, for example, when Armstrong memorized Oliver's solos as a teenager. Eugene Ormandy, the conductor of the Philadelphia Orchestra, played in theater orchestras early in his career and credited the experience as an important part of his education. "Works were played by the week, and this meant that each one got performed twenty-eight times," Ormandy explained. "Tchaikovsky's Fourth, Beethoven's Fifth, or whatever. By the end of the last show on Saturday night you *knew* the music." Ralph Brown memorized the *William Tell* overture by playing it at the Vendome, and Armstrong memorized his solo from *Cavalleria rusticana*.[44] Years later he liked to run through it as part of his warm-up routine in dressing rooms. He also memorized a couple of other classical pieces that he undoubtedly learned at the Vendome.

The Vendome put musical figures from the middle-brow classics under his fingertips, though we should be careful about exaggerating the significance of that connection. Virtually any repertory he played, from trumpet exercise books to *Home Sweet Home*, was a source for his ongoing interest in ordering pitches logically. The light classics probably had no more impact on his emerging solo style than the dexterity exercises he was memorizing. (It is possible that he was continuing lessons at Kimball Hall during this period, or even just beginning them.)

We should take note of his first-rate work ethic. Around these years his former wife, Daisy, visited from New Orleans, and he brushed her off—"no more boisterous, barrel house stuff," he said, "am trying to cultivate myself." This was the classic immigrant attitude, which, in his case, matched up splendidly with talent, training, ambition, and patronage. The difference between Daisy and Lil was one measure of how far he had traveled in just a few years; *Cavalleria rusticana* was another. It would be fascinating to know what he sounded like, playing it from the stage. Did Tate flash a discreet wink at the oboe player while Armstrong belted it out with his percussive, driving attack?

It is easy to imagine that he did. It is true that opera had a long history in New Orleans, but it was located in a social realm far removed from the streets, store-front churches, honky tonks, and dirt-floor dance halls where Armstrong spent his time.[45] Listen to any performance of *Cavalleria rusticana* and the dramatic contrast of performing style, compared with the African-American vernacular, will be readily apparent. Armstrong's mature solo style of the mid-1920s is made up of short, irregular phrases that constantly dart in and out of synchrony with the fixed patterns of beats and chord changes. The flow of melody is very different from the expansive unfolding of long phrases of opera. In opera the accompaniment is a fluffy bed of feathers that supports a passionate melody in every possible way; Armstrong's solos depend on tension between melody and accompaniment. He regularly peppers his phrasing with the accents of a hard-edged initial attack, communicating vigor and assertiveness to produce an emotional undertone that is the opposite of the legato effortlessness of bel canto singing. His microscopic level of blues phrasing, with constant shadings of pitch and dynamics and quick flashes of irregular rhythmic patterning, belongs to a world quite different from the elegant swells of dramatic tension in opera.

Armstrong's late-life persona as Ambassador Satch includes the image of him as exceptionally open-minded; there is a temptation to regard his interest in opera and other kinds of music as a manifestation of that mindset. There is some truth to that transcendent, open-minded image, which suited the cultural position he occupied so well in the segregated America of the 1950s. But it must not be allowed to eclipse the Armstrong who was one of the greatest products of the African-American vernacular and one of its most modern representatives during the decade 1925–35. The idea of a transcendent Armstrong carries the subtext that his soaring solos represent a social transcendence that was waiting for the rest of the country to catch up with him, blossoming fully in the 1950s, when the dark-skinned and disadvantaged child from the slums of New Orleans won hearts around the world.

There is no doubt that Armstrong, like so many of his peers in Chicago during the 1920s, was interested in classical music, particularly when it could do something for him professionally. But with opera, especially, the connection is secondary and ultimately irrelevant if our goal is to understand the formation of his mature style, which would not have been one bit different had opera never existed. Far more important was the cabaret culture of speed, humor, novelty, and variety.

### Singing, Comedy, and Stunts

Another special part of Armstrong's Vendome experience was the fact that he made his name as a singer there. He liked to point out that he was a singer before he ever touched a cornet, first in church and then in a vocal quartet with his friends, where he imitated barbershop singing. There was no singing with the Ory band in New Orleans or the Marable band on the riverboats, and only an exceptional opportunity with Oliver and with Henderson. Now, at the Vendome (and probably the Dreamland, too), he sang with great success, using a megaphone. From now until the end of his career, his singing

and trumpet playing would stand alongside each other, one sometimes more important than the other, but both always present.

We know that at the Vendome he sang his two most famous vocal
numbers from 1926, *Heebie Jeebies* (not directly related to the weekly
rag) and *Big Butter and Egg Man* (both songs discussed later). There
are several reports of cross-dressing acts, one with Armstrong dressed
as a woman, bantering with another musician about exchanging his
"li'l old cornet" for a trumpet, and another with oboist Charles Harris dressed as the woman while Armstrong sang *My Baby Knows How*
to him. "The fans laughed themselves dizzy," wrote a reviewer in
*Heebie Jeebies*. In another comic number he staged an "instrument
argument" with saxophonist Stump Evans.

But his splashiest comic number was a preaching act. Later in
his career he performed a vocal act as a preacher, but this one was
done with his trumpet. Come and see him "'preach the gospel' with
his instrument," wrote *Heebie Jeebies*, which rated the number the
"fun of the week." His costume was a frock-tail coat with battered,
high-top silk hat and white-rimmed glasses, rims only. According
to one account, he "preached a sermon on his wicket trumpet"; in
another, he led the musicians in a "prayer" with his cornet, suggesting call and response with several of Tate's players. He was probably
using the plunger mute, something close to the talking cornet style
made famous by Oliver at Lincoln Gardens. It was, according to
*Heebie Jeebies*, the funniest act ever seen at the Vendome, repeatedly
requested by "a hundred or more patrons."

Another observer explained with precision that Armstrong was
imitating a preacher, not a minister in this act; the significance of the
distinction was that preachers were illiterate, while ministers glossed
readings from the Bible. The minister demonstrated his learning,
interpretive skills, and indeed literacy, while the preacher offered
something quite different. In other words, the act was loaded with
the social-cultural dynamics of the Great Migration.

It is easy to get the joke, even from such a distance. Chicago was
a town that witnessed daily negotiations between the old ways of the
South and the forward-looking ways of the South Side. Armstrong's
dressed-up audience at the Vendome looked at his beat-up, flamboy-
antly out-of-date costume and immediately understood that he was

marking distance from the oral tradition. Attending to the overture as if at an opera, many in this crowd had moved beyond the cornfield ditties and ecstatic shouting of lay preachers in the Sanctified Church. Although this was not the talented tenth of the NAACP, these were black people who were moving up; there were no head scarves at the Vendome. It must have been easy to laugh and be pleased about how far everyone had come in such a short time.

Armstrong had grown up with preachers, not ministers; with participatory singing rather than the tidy singing of a choir; with ecstatic shouting instead of polite smiles and nods; and this must have given him good sources for his skit. But what mattered at the Vendome was the distance he had traveled. He was no longer the uneducated rube snubbed by Sammy Stewart and dissed by the Henderson men. He was a modern, sophisticated, northern, well-paid musician. Whether he knew it or not, the task that lay before him was to help his audience understand themselves more deeply by providing them with a musical identity that was black and modern. This is the context of his mature style, the reception of which included social-cultural humor like the preacher act.

He also discovered at the Vendome a stunt that extended his reputation even more—high-note playing. The ability to control the extreme range of an instrument or voice may smack of empty virtuosity, but it is a universal way to attract attention. In New Orleans, high-note cornet playing had been part of cutting-contest weaponry, right up there with loud playing as a way to claim superiority. In New York City, Armstrong had seen what the high range was doing for trumpeter B. A. Rolfe. In Chicago, Lillian chided him for not being able to play as high as a classical trumpeter named Strombach, and he rose to the challenge, as she undoubtedly knew he would.

He started with high F at the end of a number and was favorably noticed. "They keep one picture three days, cats would come three days to see if I'm gonna miss that note," he remembered. He was nervous, afraid that he would miss the note, even though he kept delivering it flawlessly, so Lillian suggested practicing high G's at home, thus making it psychologically easier to hit the F's. Naturally he started performing high G's, followed by A's and C's. Tate began to feature him in "freakish high registered breaks," which, to Peyton's dismay, made the patrons "howl." And from there came the practice of repeating the high note again and again, like so many acrobatic flips. "Up there in the high register all the time," he remembered. "And if I had some more chops left, just use them some more—hit 40 or 50 high C's." Just two years earlier he had been locked into staying under Oliver. He continued to trot out this trick for more than a decade until he blew his lip out and simply could not do it anymore. He liked to point the trumpet up in the air and gaze at the ceiling as he ascended into the high range.

To see this as more than just a stunt would be to understand it as a gesture of personal power, superior status marked through the musical metaphor of height. The gesture has long been characteristic of trumpet playing, as critic and historian Krin Gabbard has described so vividly. Armstrong valued clean execution on an instrument, and he aimed for that in the high range, cultivating an ability to hit the notes with confidence and precision. The whole high-note project expanded his comfortable range for solo improvisation. His mature solo style is distinguished by use of a varied range, which was stabilized by this extended control.

## The Jazz Concert King

### The Hot Number

Armstrong was funny as a comedian and daunting as a high-note specialist, but both were secondary to his role as hot soloist. Tate had several options for this slot in the program—pianist Teddy Weatherford (and, after he left, pianists Walter Johnson and Earl Hines), saxophonist Stump Evans, and drummer Jimmy Bertrand, who played a blues called *My Daddy Rocks Me* on tympani. There could be several hot numbers on a program, but Armstrong's was always the one known as the "primary," taken from the stage, in front of the curtain. What Armstrong offered was perfect for the Vendome audiences, who rewarded him with standing-room-only attendance, week after week. "It was the biggest thing in the world," remembered Doc Cheatham. The program opened with the orchestral overture and finished with Armstrong's primary, another indicator of his popularity.

At his first rehearsal with Tate, in December 1925, the orchestra was working on *Spanish Shawl*, which he described as a "swing tune." A number of bands recorded *Spanish Shawl* in the fall of 1925, a sure sign that a stock arrangement had been recently released. Perhaps Tate's version was similar to recordings issued by Fletcher Henderson's band (under the name Dixie Stompers) and Ray Miller.

One of Tate's more imaginative hot numbers, performed in February 1926, was a version of Clarence Williams's *Royal Garden Blues*. Tate divided the orchestra into sections and positioned them in different parts of the auditorium. A drum roll signaled a march toward the pit, with each section taking turns playing the piece. This was followed with another surprise: oboist Charles Harris, left out of *Royal Garden Blues*, started his march down the aisle after the others were seated, playing a solo version of Irving Berlin's *All Alone* to everyone's amusement.

Along these same imaginative lines, Tate arranged an orchestral version of *Cornet Chop Suey*. The tune "could be played as a trumpet solo or with a symphony orchestra," Armstrong wrote in 1951, and the most likely place for the latter was the Vendome. In early 1926 the piece must have become the strongest articulation of his eccentric, crazy figures.

The primary hot number turned over every week, just like the overture. In March 1926, Tate brought out *Sugar Foot Stomp*, with Armstrong doing a takeoff on Oliver. "He fluttered, he cried, he raved, and the band raved with him," wrote Peyton. "Over in a corner I heard a brother say, 'Yes, yes.'" Sometime during the spring Tate offered *Static Strut* and *Stomp Off, Let's Go*, both well-known jazz numbers and the only two pieces Armstrong recorded with Tate's outfit. The tempos are very fast and Armstrong responds with verve and confidence, though neither solo is especially compelling. The frantic pace does not favor the density of ideas that was becoming his trademark. *Static Strut*, in the unfamiliar key of D-flat, presented a special challenge. His solo shows constant rhythmic variety, with two-bar modules always in flux. A nice rhyming touch anchors the busy line when he uses the same simple rhythm—*ta-ta-ta-rest*—at the beginning of phrases one and two, the first time descending from the third of the chord, the second time ascending from the lower fifth. The simplicity and rhyme of these two gestures help locate the melodic flow in the periodic form of successive eight-bar phrases. There is nothing particularly new in this; he had featured this kind of rhyming detail on his very first recorded solo, *Chimes Blues*. But in his mature style, devices like this helped provide balance and order to increasingly complex melodies.

Trumpeter Doc Cheatham, recently arrived from Nashville, sat in the cheap seats, high in the balcony, every single day and with only one purpose: "I wanted to be able to play like Louis Armstrong," he said. "I wanted to be able to understand how he played and why he played certain things at different times. In fact I was on his tail all the time, studying little clichés that he would do." Sometimes the audience was so boisterous during Armstrong's solos that Cheatham had trouble hearing him. One week Armstrong decided to sneak out of town and asked Cheatham to substitute. When Cheatham showed up, the other musicians stared at him, wondering what he was there for, since Armstrong hadn't told Tate he would be gone. The primary hot number was Tate's arrangement of *Poor Little Rich Girl*, a feature for Armstrong.[46] The band played the introduction, Tate cued Cheatham to stand up, the spotlight hit him, and the audience started screaming. But when they realized it wasn't Armstrong, a cold silence took over the hall. "It took me years to get over that," Cheatham remembered. Armstrong paid him $85 for the humiliation and Cheatham continued to sub for him now and then, even though Tate was not happy about it. There was little Tate could do; Armstrong was so popular that he could call the shots.

Willie "The Lion" Smith observed that wind instruments were more dominant in Chicago than in New York, and the only reason for that was the influx of musicians from New Orleans. In early 1926 Fred Keppard was taking solos at the Deluxe Café (across the street from the Dreamland), Jimmie Noone led a band at the Apex Club, Johnny Dodds did the same at Kelley's Stables, Joe Oliver headlined at the Plantation cabaret, and Armstrong soared at the Vendome and Dreamland. The South Side successes of his older colleagues made it easier for people to appreciate his eccentric innovations and paved the way for him. Drummer and vibraphonist Lionel Hampton saw Armstrong for the first time at the Vendome

*A movie theater in Chicago, 1940s (Library of Congress)*

as a teenager. "We were in the front row of the first balcony, and we could see the entire audience go crazy after his first, fifteen-minute solo," he remembered.

Milt Hinton saw the Vendome scene in a way that opens up a deeper understanding of Armstrong's accomplishment:

> The people would come on Sundays to the theater and they would be dressed, having on their tuxedoes with the roll collars, and it was like, you know, like white folks, like it was a big white theatre, you know. Because they thought that this was the way it was supposed to be, that you were white and you were right and this was the only way it could be. . . . This was a very conditioned thing that had been brought down to us, that this was the only way of life. . . . And we'd sit and listen to this orchestra play *Poet and Peasant*. . . . And Louis stood up and played one of his great solos, and you could see everybody letting their hair down, "Yeah that's the way it should be, this is it." So we were beginning to relate—"well, great to be like that, but this is what really relates to us."

To some, it must have seemed like destiny that music would carry the burden of defining a new African-American identity during these optimistic years. "Looking back at that, our black people had been so browbeaten that they were nothing, they believed that," insisted Hinton. "[My mother] accepted this inferiority which she was trying to get me not to accept." She chose music as the path to respect for her son—violin lessons at 50 cents a piece. She wanted him to be good enough to play professionally so she took him to the Vendome, where he could hear music at its best and "see some black people that are really doing and making a success of it."

The Vendome audience was looking ahead, moving up, bettering their condition, and receptive to change. They were less fixated on white standards than the talented tenth and more open to new possibilities, which were playing out most vividly in jazz. Langston Hughes described the alternative point of view: "The Philadelphia clubwoman is ashamed to say that her race created [jazz]," he wrote in June 1926. "The old subconscious 'white is best' runs through her mind." Armstrong at the Vendome appealed to a broad swath of the upwardly mobile working class, who found music that related to them in his modern transformation of the black vernacular. He demonstrated sophistication and technical excellence without a trace of talented-tenth condescension toward familiar values.

Even if they had not been looking for a modern black identity, Armstrong was now making that impossible to ignore. His music was brimming with the black vernacular. In Chapter 6 we will consider how that played out at the level of melodic detail; on a more general level, the connections are easy to see. As one of the two greatest masters (Bechet was the other) of the African-American vernacular as it had been transformed and professionalized in New Orleans, Armstrong was shaped by virtually all aspects of that tradition, the distinguishing and most prominent features of which carried forward a strong African legacy, which could be cultivated or suppressed according to various pressures on audiences and innovations from the most creative practitioners.[47] In New Orleans it flourished. One thing that marks his achievement—it is one of the central themes of this book—is that in the creative moment of his first modern phase this African legacy was strengthened.

That legacy included the idea that music is conceived as an event rather than as a "piece"; this is bound up with (though not identical to) music as an oral/aural practice rather than one fixed in writing. Armstrong was a great master of non-notated music, there was no question about that at the Vendome, with his blue notes and quicksilver, eccentric phrasing. It included high value placed on improvisation. Malcolm X noted how "white people danced as though somebody had trained them—left, one, two; right, three, four—the same steps and patterns over and over.... But those Negroes—nobody in the world could have choreographed the way they did whatever they felt." Improvisation—musical, kinetic, doing the dozens, preaching, signifying—was a marker of black sophistication and virtuosity, and at the Vendome Armstrong was exploring unknown territory. The African legacy included a strong, percussive attack, generating a sound that holds the confident energy of the life force. The Vendome audience delighted in the vocal qualities of his instrumental music and the instrumental qualities of his voice, mapping out a range of ambiguity that opened up creative potential. And they understood, at an intuitive and very precise level, his use of the fixed and variable model, which anchored their perception of music that was carefully crafted in complexity and depth.

Musical details were bound up with values that go beyond music; we can be sure of that, even though the connections are not always documented. Trombonist Preston Jackson was asked what he liked about Armstrong during these years: "Well, the thing that impressed me perhaps more than the music was his bearing. I had to be impressed in this manner, because he was outstanding; there was the way he carried himself, like somebody bragging and all, and saying 'look, I am good.'" This attitude was very much in the tradition of the great black musicians from New Orleans, where the musical utterance came from a place of power.

The people who grew up in Armstrong's New Orleanian neighborhood rarely had access to the kind of sustained training in the Eurocentric tradition that downtown Creoles had, with their skilled teachers and years of patient lessons. Instead, he was surrounded by the sisters in church who cheered him on as he sang and the rags-bottles-and-bones man who held him spellbound with talk of music and soul. He improvised harmonies with his buddies in a vocal quartet, followed parades all through the city, and enjoyed the attention of prostitutes urging him on to play blues. He flourished in a thriving culture that had a strong sense of its musical values. Who cared if whites thought this was primitive music that belonged in the basement of their mansion of the muses?

But to play at the New Orleans Country Club—that was another matter. In his late teens Armstrong understood what everyone else in his neighborhood who aspired to be a professional musician also understood—that white gigs paid more. Certain things had to be learned in order to get them. This could mean asking a pianist how a chord was formed, or it could mean tutorials in musical notation while working on the Mississippi riverboats. In Chicago it meant running the classics with his wife and lessons at Kimball Hall, and in New York City it meant learning on the job with Henderson. Once white musicians started learning the music and interacting with the black musicians, the whole exchange became more animated, with many possibilities of cross-social influence, often difficult to document.

Yet it is easy to overestimate this process (or ignore it completely, the usual alternative). Music is a slippery object, open to virtually any interpretation, but this slipperiness does not obviate the need for precise historical inquiry. The question addressed here is this: what is the best way to make sense of Armstrong's mature style, given what we know about him and the scene in which he formed it?

He worked to gain greater control of his instrument, faster fingering, an even tone through the entire range, speed, and high notes. He brought the techniques of the cornet virtuoso to the hot solo. As he mastered the complicated system of keys, his solos started to glow with precision. He clarified his "natural" sense of chords—the different types, the altered tones, the different ways of arpeggiating, ways of using nonchord tones—and increased his precision further. Fluency in scales, keys, exercises, and chords, playing through new pieces week after week, month after month, paraphrasing and finding ways to keep the original tune noticeable while imaginatively embellishing it—all of this made him more and more at ease. By 1926 he was reaching the creative facility that comes to all great artists after they have thoroughly internalized the technical and conceptual demands of their craft.

The trick was to find ways of adapting white technique *without losing an African-American vernacular identity*. There can be no doubt that Hinton was speaking for more than a few of the 1,500 screaming members of the Vendome audience when he said that Armstrong had discovered something that related to "us." He replaced the harmonic and textural funkiness of collective improvisation with learned precision in scales and chords, and he put aside the freak music of Oliver in favor of extended range, impressive dexterity, and speed. It turned out to be fortuitous that he stumbled over Oliver's plunger technique and turned in another direction.

The new black identity at the Vendome had to somehow match the white sophistication of a symphony orchestra. "You'll never be able to swing any better than you already know how until you learn to read," a musician told him in 1918, on the riverboat. "Then you will swing in ways you never thought of before." "And he was right," Armstrong recognized. That is one way to conceptualize the entire range of white practices that he was working on in the 1920s.

"To my mind it is the duty of the younger Negro artist . . . to change through the force of his art that old whispering 'I want to be white,'" wrote Langston Hughes, and that is precisely what Armstrong did. "I'm a Negro—and beautiful," Hughes insisted. Armstrong stifled the need to buy into white standards by selectively folding them into his vernacular-shaped vision. Jazz as Armstrong learned it in New Orleans had nothing to do with dicty refinement. It was all about the intensity and directness of blues-based sensitivity on the one hand, and a brash and aggressive street posture on the other. It was about masculine strength and dance-hall excitement, and those values did not directly transfer to the Vendome Theater. Armstrong's modern Negro beauty made manly excitement from New Orleans less rough, less on the level of street camaraderie and more precise and well designed, but with no trace of wanting to be white. He internalized white scales and chords so thoroughly that the values of the New Orleans style came through without compromise. "The common people will give to the world its truly great Negro artist, the one who is not afraid to be himself," predicted Hughes in

June 1926, not knowing that this was happening in Chicago at that very moment.

Armstrong's advantage was that African Americans had been relying on music for centuries to demonstrate their individual worth, to fashion a sense of self that was under no one else's control. Black culture in New Orleans during Armstrong's youth was collectively dedicated to this project. In 1926 he stepped forward as the most current creator of an uplifted intervention in the African-American vernacular. No one could have imagined how profoundly this intervention would radiate out, past the Vendome Theater, out of Chicago, across the country, and across oceans. His localized transformation of an African-American sense of who they were became a global regard for new musical possibilities.

One reason it has been easy to overlook the social dimensions of Armstrong's mature style is the strong integrationist theme in popular discourse on jazz, a view of jazz history as a happy social field that transcended racial tension long before the general public got around to doing so. (Jazz "corrects the fiction that America is racist," said broadcaster Willis Conover of the Voice of America, apparently with a straight face.) That view is at best dramatically incomplete; it should not be allowed to obscure the inevitable impact of racism on the history of this music, playing out in many forms, some crude and violent, some subtle and insidious. A second reason is that since Armstrong's accomplishment became the basis for jazz solo playing all over the world, his universality makes it seem like the idiom lacked social determinants, as if it was born fully grown as an emblem of world culture.

The 1920s was full of stimulating cross-currents, with influences leaping across boundaries of class and race to produce the success of Ira Gershwin's lyrics, with their mix of formal diction and colloquial speech; Paul Whiteman's Orchestra, with its dressing up of jazz to make a proper lady of it; and Duke Ellington's cosmopolitan black identity, with its framing of the black vernacular in elegance and sophistication. Armstrong belonged to this expansive mindset, but his engagement with these dynamics played out quite differently. His solo style was less the product of self-conscious conceptual manipulation than the result of an extended effort to become a better soloist, first according to black standards that he grew up with, and later according to white standards that promised more money. His success was not based on the self-conscious play of social signifiers. The source of his strength was that he internalized social-musical tensions and came up with a creative synthesis that cannot be broken down into binary oppositions.

Armstrong even impressed Dave Peyton, who "was completely anti-jazz, you know," as Milt Hinton put it, though that assertion needs to be qualified. "Polite syncopation during a comedy or newsreel picture dealing in the popular syncopated melodies is delightful to hear, but the awful, lowdown so called blues should be eliminated entirely from the pit," wrote Peyton in a typical rant. Yet he admired what Tate was doing at the Vendome. "They handle the heaviest kind of music, ranging from operatic suites, standard overtures, comic operas and great symphonies down to modern jazz," he wrote in April 1926. The condescending "down to" should not be missed. What allowed jazz to enter his lofty realm of approval at all was the qualifier "modern."

Peyton heard Armstrong's eccentric figures as a fresh alternative to discordant jazz; we may assume that he heard it as an alternative to symphonic jazz, as well. Armstrong gained the approval of this old-settler spokesman for Eurocentric standards by expanding the range of what jazz could be. Peyton may have been the first aspiring member of the talented tenth to recognize that Armstrong was broadening the concept of jazz with a race offering that was neither primitive nor vulgar (like discordant jazz), but also had no need for white legitimation (like symphonic jazz).

Novelist Richard Wright wrote that he could "never really leave the South, for my feelings had already been formed by the South, for there had been slowly instilled into my personality and consciousness, black though I was, the culture of the South." "Southern" music—meaning, in this case, the black vernacular as it had been professionalized in New Orleans—and its feelings had that kind of hold on the South Side immigrants. At Lincoln Gardens in 1922, Oliver helped them measure their distance from the cotton fields through music that was both professional and down home, solos sometimes inspired by the dockworkers, rags-bottles-and-bones men, and railroad crews of New Orleans that in a sense belonged to everyone, including the man who liked to play them in the streets of Chicago on a comb covered with wax paper. Three years later, at the Vendome, Armstrong was offering something new. The distance from Lincoln Gardens to the Vendome was measured by proper attire, classical overtures, and Armstrong's innovations. The connection to the Deep South could still be heard, but there was also a step up and forward into a more sophisticated professional world. No one was playing Armstrong's solos on wax-papered combs.

Part of the difference was that people went to Lincoln Gardens mainly to dance, to the Vendome to listen. This difference in audience position became another important dimension of his Chicago success. The great historian Eric Hobsbawm (writing as Francis Newton) once claimed that there are "three ways of listening to jazz: in a dancehall or club, on record, or at a concert. By far the worst of these is the last. In fact, if we tried to think of the worst possible setting for living jazz . . . we could hardly envisage a more disastrous one than the typical concert." Armstrong's concert hall glory at the Vendome turns this late-1950s view on its head. The dignity and attentiveness of the hall provided the perfect environment for his solo ambitions, which turned out to splendidly represent the ambitions of his fans, just as the relaxed atmosphere of uptown streets, marked by interaction and accommodation, was the perfect nurture for the participatory music making he grew up with.

Listening to jazz instead of dancing to it was not new, but this form of appreciation was gathering a special aura in the mid-1920s. In New Orleans it was always possible to stop moving, stop interacting with everyone else, and simply listen to what was going on. But as the mercurial concept of jazz touched different kinds of music in the early 1920s, it found a firm place in institutions for listening. Paul Whiteman's concert entitled *Experiment in Modern Music*, at New York's Aeolian Hall on February 12, 1924, was in some ways the natural culmination of a trajectory. For the 1922 opening of the luxurious Trianon Ballroom in Chicago, the owner paid Whiteman the unprecedented sum of $25,000 for six nights. To his astonishment, the event flopped. "My God, they just wouldn't dance to our music," explained one of Whiteman's musicians. Whiteman was staking out a musical territory that appealed more to listeners than to dancers.

"Those who like his music refuse to patronize a dance hall and mingle with the masses; while dance hall patrons won't pay $2 to get into a Whiteman concert," explained the *New York Clipper.*

It was in theaters and cabarets, not dance halls, where Armstrong first made his mark as an innovative soloist. Whiteman and his followers (including Henderson) were the reference for Peyton's praise of modern jazz at the Vendome, but now Armstrong was unveiling an alternative that came from a very different direction. He was thoroughly trained as a musician who played for dancing, and until this moment that was how he had spent most of his time. He remained grounded in the stylistic principles of black vernacular dance music, while exploring new approaches to melodic design. Whites established one set of evaluative terms with symphonic jazz, and now, just as Langston Hughes predicted, the "common people" of New Orleans had given to the world a young African-American artist who challenged white cultural supremacy, not so much by beating whites at their own game—that was Henderson's project—but by creating new terms of expression and accomplishment that were every bit as sophisticated and also related to "us."

As if by magic, *Cornet Chop Suey* was waiting for him on his return to Chicago. A display piece that reminded him of cutting contests in New Orleans, it perfectly fit the listening context of the Vendome. The Dreamland Café, too, put a premium on listening when his "up" came around. Sure, people danced, but the bigger draw was to hear the creative accomplishments of the world's greatest cornet player. The hierarchy of venues on the South Side of Chicago was weighted toward listening, with theaters being most prestigious and the Vendome the most prestigious of all.

Armstrong was regarded as eccentric, as modern, and as the "jazz concert king," which is what Peyton called him in December 1927. At a Halloween Ball organized by Tate for Saturday, October 30, 1926, with 5,000 in attendance at the Eighth Regiment Armory, on South Giles Avenue near 35th Street, just around the corner from the Sunset Café, Armstrong stole the show. The celebrated team of Brown and McGraw was on hand to dance the "famous 'Heebie Jeebies,'" with Armstrong ready to "play it on his cornet." But when Tate and his orchestra started to play, "the people refused to dance" and "crowded close to the bandstand," reported *Heebie Jeebies*. "It was impossible to clear out space for Brown and McGraw so they withdrew; still, it was a 'righteous party' that lasted until dawn." Brown and McGraw must have been miffed, but for many it seemed just the right thing to do—to refuse to dance while listening to the jazz concert king.

## *Heebie Jeebies* and the Hot Five

In the winter of 1925–26, while making a name for himself at classy venues like the Dreamland Café and the Vendome Theater, Armstrong was also extending his reputation thanks to the Hot Five series on OKeh Records. The recordings sold in Chicago, but the main target audience was African Americans in the Deep South, where race records were immensely popular.

Three Hot Five sides recorded on November 12, 1925, launched the most famous series of recordings in jazz history, though no one was thinking that grandly at the time. "The musicians didn't know this music was going to be important," explained Lillian. "Sometimes you'd have a date and you wouldn't bother to write the songs you were going to play until you got to the studio." *Yes! I'm in the Barrel* was composed by Louis, *My Heart* by Lillian. *Yes! I'm in the Barrel* had been tucked away since December 1923, around the time when he was working on *Cornet Chop Suey*. That the latter piece was not brought out for this session is probably a reflection of the urgency of the situation: there was simply no time to work up *Cornet Chop Suey*, which is more demanding than the other pieces.

"Pops, I don't need no rehearsal if it's the blues," explained Armstrong to Richard Jones. "All you got to do is knock it off." The third piece recorded on November 12 was *Gut Bucket Blues*, made up on the spot with composer credit given to Armstrong. The title was an allusion to fish waste that poor people in the South relied on for nourishment; it signaled that the music would be a relaxed celebration of low-class culture, the unpretentious and nonassimilative world of honky tonks and dirt-floor dance halls. Each player takes a solo, and Armstrong introduces them as they do, urging them on, "Oh play that thing, Mr. St. Cyr, Lord you know you can really do it,

*The Hot Five (The William Russell Jazz Files, MSS 536, F. Louis Armstrong 325, Williams Research Center, The Historic New Orleans Collection)*

everybody from New Orleans can really do that thing—Hey! Hey!" "That thing" was the blues, the staple of race recordings in the early and mid-1920s.

When the take was over, someone from OKeh came out of the control room and quipped, in response to Armstrong's friendly bantering, "What are you doing, writing a letter home?" The reference was to the intended market, the southern down-home population, people who bought records before bread and who were in fact buying anywhere between five and ten million discs in 1925. If the preacher routine and *Sugar Foot Stomp* highlighted the cultural distance between South and North, the Hot Five series was aimed straight at southern taste. This marketing strategy explains why the Hot Five was so unlike all the other groups Armstrong was working with in 1925 and 1926—Fletcher Henderson's Orchestra, Erskine Tate's Vendome Orchestra, Lillian Hardin's Dreamland Orchestra, and Carroll Dickerson's Sunset Café Orchestra. It was a five-piece pick-up band, with four of the musicians from New Orleans.

The arrangements for the first three tunes recorded were very slender, the rehearsals brief or nonexistent. The recording company had very few opinions about the repertory. What mattered, mainly, was that the copyright holders, Louis and Lillian in this case, agreed to cut a deal in OKeh's favor in exchange for a flat fee and the possibility that the tune might catch on and get recorded by someone else, which would generate royalties. No one at OKeh cared if the compositions *My Heart* and *Yes! I'm in the Barrel* were any good, or if there was a well-planned and well-rehearsed arrangement, such as was mandatory at the Roseland Ballroom, Dreamland Café, and Vendome Theater.

Instead, the band was encouraged to click into collective improvisation, which they could produce at the drop of a dime; certainly this group was assembled with precisely that goal. The four New Orleanians had perfected that texture when they played together in the late 1910s, in a band led by Ory. With unfamiliar pieces being brought in and little or no preparation, the finished result did not have a chance to sound like "it was all mixed together as if someone had planned it with a set of micrometer calipers," as Eddie Condon said about the Oliver band at Lincoln Gardens. That kind of ensemble playing depended on performing the same tunes for many months. In truth, the November 12 performances are a bit sloppy. Armstrong's playing is fine, but it is certainly not the kind of thing that made people line up around the block at the Vendome Theater. His lead is confident, and Ory and Dodds produce a vigorous texture.

The format is close to that of the 1923 Oliver recordings except that collective improvisation is generally reserved for beginning and end, with reduced accompaniment for solos in the middle. Armstrong plays the lead with crisp ornamentation, usually in the context of collective improvisation, and contributes some strong breaks. Dodds and Lillian get more exposed solos. There are no "special choruses" of the kind that would later make Armstrong the central figure in the history of jazz solo playing. Ory contributes a few hot breaks, and the atmosphere is relaxed and buoyant, though not distinguished. It must have been a lot of fun to rejoin his old friends and relax into collective improvisation, where everything flowed and nobody worried about *pianissimo* or anything else.

"The records I made with the Hot Fives were the easiest I ever made," Ory remembered. Just two weeks earlier Armstrong was throwing up into Fletcher Henderson's lap, and now he was surrounded by his home boy buddies. "The important part about playing music is the idea of having a happy heart and a happy mind. We had it then," said Baby Dodds about the Oliver band from 1922 to 1923, and the Hot Five recordings transmit the same spirit. It was not just a New Orleans ensemble but an *uptown* New Orleans ensemble that Armstrong had assembled—not Jimmy Noone with his smooth, flowing clarinet lines but Johnny Dodds with his biting blues licks; not Honoré Dutrey with his command of cello parts but Kid Ory with his simple and effective tailgate style. "Mellow moments, I assure you," was how Armstrong remembered the Ory band in the late teens, and in the fall of 1926 he was revisiting that atmosphere.

After the modest November session, the group did not record again until February 22, 1926, with another mediocre tune, *Come Back Sweet Papa*, composed by friends and fellow New Orleanians Paul Barbarin and Luis Russell. The 14-week gap established a loose pattern that would hold for Armstrong's "Hot" units through 1926, 1927, and 1928, with visits to the OKeh studio spaced in clusters of three per year. These recordings document Armstrong's artistic growth, and it is important to try to analyze what they tell us about what he performed outside the studio, even though such correlations are not straightforward. One obvious problem was built into the differing business plans: the recording companies wanted from their "race" artists original material that the performer signed away to the company, while cabarets and theaters wanted well-known hits. These strategies made the repertories largely, though not completely, incongruent.

Nevertheless, the Hot Five series had three things in common with what Armstrong was doing at the Dreamland and Vendome. First, it was designed to feature him. His abilities as a cornet soloist, and soon as a singer, were now recognized as something people were willing to pay for. Second, this was music conceived for a black audience. Ironically, at the very moment Armstrong became headliner at the Vendome, the classiest theater on the South Side, OKeh began marketing him to the down-home rural South. None of these enterprises had incentive to turn white dollars away, but there was absolutely no sense of designing the musical product so that it appealed to white audiences.[48]

Third, the recordings, too, were for listening. It is true that people danced to them, but it was just as easy to simply listen. Virtually everything Armstrong played—and for virtually his entire life—could support dancing. But now he was stepping into a different and parallel role of playing for an audience that listened, and doing it from three different directions.

On February 26, 1926, the band returned to the studio to record six tunes—*Oriental Strut, Georgia Grind, Cornet Chop Suey, Muskrat Ramble, Heebie Jeebies,* and *You're Next.* The session produced two major hits and a much-loved standard of New Orleans jazz. Perhaps these successes were due to familiarity with the tunes from the Dreamland, where Lillian was in charge of the band, choosing repertory, and where all five musicians worked.

*Oriental Strut* was composed by banjo player Johnny St. Cyr. Both the title and the extended stop time solo for Armstrong suggest that it was conceived as a follow-up to *Cornet Chop Suey.* The twisting and unpredictable turns of his solo are just the kind of eccentric figures that were catching attention at the Dreamland and Vendome. The differences between this stop-time solo and the one created two years earlier for *Cornet Chop Suey* are notable and indicate his developing sense of style. Though not one of his classic solos, *Oriental Strut* is nevertheless a historical gem that shows him reaching toward his mature approach.

The solo in fact begins with a very strong reference to (almost a quotation of) the stop-time solo from *Cornet Chop Suey.* After that the new solo is much more adventuresome. The earlier solo conforms to the flow of two-bar groups, as defined by the harmonic rhythm, while the solo for *Oriental Strut* is highly irregular. Listen to the highest notes as the line unfolds. They pop out of the texture on different beats, sometimes in between beats, spinning out figures that constantly change in length and are in tension with the fixed levels of sub-beats, beats, measures, and two-bar groupings, as well as with the previous patterns of the solo. Armstrong uses the main pitches of St. Cyr's simple tune to hold the otherwise unpredictable line together, a technique he had been exploring with Henderson.

This is eccentric playing according to Teddy Wilson's definition, the kind of melodic flow that characterizes some of his most famous solos from the next few years. Here it is slightly out of control; one can hear him feeling his way toward something that he imagines and has not quite found. He was fond of *Oriental Strut* and continued to play it after he moved in April to the Sunset Café, where Cab Calloway remembered hearing it. It was also another piece (*Good Time Flat Blues* was the first) that impressed Jack Teagarden, listening in faraway Albuquerque. "When I played that for Jack he thought it was the end," said Wingy Manone. The two of them decided to honor *Oriental Strut* by burying the phonograph disc in the desert sand, hoping that this treatment would preserve the artifact for all time, like petrified wood.

From the first Hot Five session in November 1925 though November 1926, the band recorded 24 different tunes. *Georgia Grind*, by Spencer Williams, was the only one composed by someone who did not have an obvious local connection. The easiest explanation for its appearance is the enterprising energy of Clarence Williams, who published Spencer's tunes and probably had an arrangement with OKeh; Richard M. Jones, who worked for OKeh, also started working as the Chicago representative for Williams's publishing firm in 1926. Perhaps the piece was featured at the Dreamland, but the only musical detail hinting at this—that is, the only distinction of the performance—is Armstrong's vocal solo. Here is his first extended singing on record. Lillian also sings two choruses, and it is easy to imagine her part being covered by one of the professional singers at the Dreamland. Armstrong offers attractive speechlike music. He completely ignores the composed melody, and if he did perform this at the Dreamland, perhaps that success gave him confidence for the daring scat vocal on *Heebie Jeebies*.

*Cornet Chop Suey*, discussed in Chapter 3, was certainly performed at both the Dreamland and the Vendome. It was probably the number that made people line up around the block, waiting to get in. Released in June 1926, the recording was a "biggie" in New Orleans according to Barney Bigard. Josiah Frazier talked about learning it there from the record and bringing it into his band's repertory. "When we played that number the house just screamed and hollered and right now if it was left to them people we'd still be play-ing," remembered Frazier. Trumpeter Henry "Red" Allen memo-rized it, and Wild Bill Davison said it changed the way he played. Kid Rena complained that Armstrong was showing off, and it was clear to everyone that he was no longer the home boy they once knew.

Kid Ory is listed as the composer of *Muskrat Ramble*, but Arm-strong claimed that they wrote it together; Ory named it, so Arm-strong "gave it to him." This probably means that Armstrong composed the first strain, a theme of riff-based arpeggiations charac-teristic of him and not of Ory, and that Ory added the second strain, which features the trombone. The two strains combine well, the sec-ond one providing the basis for the solos and the first one return-ing at the end with nice variations from Armstrong. *Muskrat Ramble* flows with the relaxed swing of New Orleans. Ory is at his best. A musician of limited technique, with weak reading skills, Ory had clear strengths—a strong and crisp attack and also great timing, both valuable for collective improvisation. The piece has long been a New Orleans standard, and it is difficult to spend more than a few days in the Crescent City without hearing it played somewhere.

The relaxed environment of *Muskrat Ramble* inspired one of Armstrong's most accomplished solos to date, one thoroughly shaped by the fixed and variable model and at the same time beautifully designed. The tempo here, and also the tempo for *Oriental Strut*, favors the density of ideas that he was continuing to work with; com-parison with the much faster *Static Strut* and *Stomp Off Let's Go* will make this clear. Speedy northern tempos during the year with Hen-derson may have inhibited Armstrong's growth as a soloist: a frantic pace simply did not accommodate his explorations of constant shifts in rhythmic patterning and microelements of melodic design. A ten-dency toward more moderate tempos may have been an unexpected benefit of the Hot Five series, with its southern orientation.[49]

Notable in *Muskrat Ramble* is a harmonic anticipation near the beginning of Armstrong's solo. This is the device observed already in *Go Long Mule*, where it was analyzed as a creative extension of the fixed and variable model. The foundational harmonies are clearly directed toward the arrival of the main chord in the third measure, and so is Armstrong's opening melodic gesture. But he arrives one beat early. When the main chord falls into place at the proper time in the accompaniment, at the downbeat of the third measure, his solo melody has already collapsed from its high-note arrival (CD 1:07) into an effortless downward sweep. It is this ease of motion, in and out of phase with the fixed and periodic foundation, that makes the event so attractive.

The relaxed flow of melody continues for the rest of the solo. There are several more harmonic anticipations of the main chord, suggesting the blues technique of "ubiquitous one," and they are always well integrated in the line. What I hear in examples like this is Armstrong using pitch to dislodge his melody from the harmonic foundation without severing the connection. This is another way to capture the effect more typically achieved through rhythm in the fixed and variable model. In these examples, we find him using pitch both to enhance rhythm and to reproduce the same effect in a different musical parameter. Notable also is his use of ninths, sevenths (especially the joyous leap up to the major seventh in measure 8; CD 1:15), and sixths for the same purpose. These nonharmonic tones create the effect of dangling above the harmony, a middle ground that is not dissonant yet not fully consonant with the foundation. In this way, they, too, distance his variable line from the fixed foundation without severing the connection. Again, they are well integrated into the design.

*Muskrat Ramble* was paired on the flip side with the big hit of the session and probably Armstrong's biggest hit until *Ain't Misbehavin'* in 1929. *Heebie Jeebies* made him a local celebrity. It was at the Vendome, Armstrong remembered, that he really began to sing; *Heebie Jeebies* became the song with which he was most associated. Armstrong said that the record reached sales of 40,000. Barely a month after it was released, OKeh was advertising it as "the biggest selling record ever known." Armstrong later quipped how composer Boyd Atkins "must have made a nice little 'taste' (meaning) the tune made a quite a bit of 'loot' (meaning) they sold lots of records and made lots of 'dough' (meaning) 'money.'"

The success of *Heebie Jeebies* had nothing to do with Atkins's skill as a songwriter, for Armstrong's scat chorus was the sole reason for its popularity. The huge impact of the recording caused many people to believe that it documented the origins of scat, a myth that was later promoted by an unscrupulous publicity agent. Preceding him on recordings were Ukulele Ike, Don Redman, and, all the way back to 1911, Gene Greene's *King of the Bungaloos*. But since *Heebie Jeebies* gave many listeners their first exposure to scat, associations with Armstrong remained strong, especially after he began to incorporate the technique into his new singing style of the early 1930s.

In one of several late-life tirades, Jelly Roll Morton insisted that the originator of scat was not Armstrong but a comedian named Joe Sims from Vicksburg, Mississippi. But clearly Armstrong grew up with strong local exposure to the practice, which probably came from West Africa. Trumpeter Punch Miller said that scat was popular "up and down the street [in New Orleans] but they didn't know what they were doing. Louis went up there and made something out of it." As a child, Armstrong and his buddies imitated marching band instruments—"did you hear that riff, son, Bum Bum Da De, Da De Da DA DA . . . that was the way we went on for years," he remembered. His street-corner vocal quartet included scat as part of their routine. Armstrong's friend and fellow quartet singer James "Red Happy" Bolton turned out to be an important model for Armstrong in his teenage years. When the two of them became old enough to sit in with bands, Red Happy entertained the crowd with a scat number as a comic interlude, giving the paid musicians a little break. A fantastic drummer and also a good buck dancer, Bolton shaped Armstrong's own singing style, according to one observer.

Many signs—from comedian Joe Sims to Red Happy's interludes and from Gene Greene's *King of the Bungaloos* to Ukulele Ike—indicate that scat was mainly received as humor. Asked about *Heebie Jeebies*, Lillian said, "I don't know if he planned to scat or not. I know that ever since Louis started working alone he would always add little extra touches and things, and little comical things to his work." Kid Ory remembered Armstrong making funny faces while he scatted *Heebie Jeebies* in the OKeh studio. Violinist and trumpeter Peter Bocage said that people in New Orleans laughed when they first heard the recording back home. It must have been funny indeed to buy the recording at a store, open up the fancy package, and encounter local street jive, shipped down from Chicago. Whenever music is presented without words, it is possible to spin virtually any interpretation, and scat is no different. Such are the terms of musical expression that people can hear abstract utterances in highly imaginative ways that have nothing, necessarily, to do with the conception of the creator and his or her immediate audience. But if listeners regarded scat as a serious enterprise with covert meaning in 1926, there is not a shred of evidence from the period to indicate it.

Humor aside, scat had a solid place in African-American vernacular culture. It was a special example of blurring boundaries between speaking, singing, and playing an instrument, an orientation that gave rise to a rich array of creative possibilities, including Joe Oliver's virtuoso freak music, African-American preaching styles, West African talking drums, blues phrasing and inflections, and "talking blues" by the comedian Stringbeans (of Stringbeans and Sweetie May) and others. Bass player Bill Johnson with the Oliver band sometimes mixed talking and scatting at Lincoln Gardens. "Well my singing's nothing," said Armstrong in 1931. "I just try to put the rhythm of instrumental playing into my voice."

What distinguishes Armstrong's scat from examples recorded earlier is his unabashed vigor. It is as if he is strutting down the dirt streets of New Orleans in a crowded, funky parade, doing what he can to draw attention to himself. *Heebie Jeebies* is an assertive celebration of an unrefined, everyday African-American voice, the opposite of dicty snootiness. Percussive consonants explode from his gravelly throat, and his curt melodic utterances are so vivid that you can almost see them. Atkins's song is named after a dance. Armstrong first sings about the joys of the dance before he slips into the scat chorus. The sharp jabs and sudden dips of his lines—he has abandoned Atkins's melody completely—dislodge the song from any narrative function and turn it into a sonic representation of bodily motion. The effect further saturates the performance with markers of vernacular culture. "The Heebie Jeebies is rich in haunch movements," was one description of the dance from 1927, and it is easy to hear Armstrong's lines in that way. He defines the dance as having little in common with polite fox trotting at the Roseland Ballroom. Singing like this had not been heard before at the Vendome or the Dreamland Café, and it is significant that Armstrong did not introduce it in those places. The place to do it turned out to be a recording studio, hiding behind a supposed mistake.

The phrase "heebie jeebies" (or "hibby jibby," "heebie geebies," "hebe-jibies," and so on) had wide currency in the 1920s. In the late 1910s a band in Atlantic City assumed this very name. By 1925, the phrase was popping up all over, in the comic strip *Barney Google*, as the title of a song recorded by Lovie Austin and Her Blues Serenaders, as the title of the South Side magazine, and as the title of a movie. The phrase implied eccentric movement and vague associations with mental disturbance. It was a perfect name for a dance that aimed to satisfy the mid-1920s fascination with cutting loose and stepping out of convention for a couple of happy minutes.

Like drummer Paul Barbarin, who composed *Don't Forget to Mess Around* at the very same time (February 1926), Atkins wrote an instrumental tune, not a song with words. Both composers were aiming to hook their tunes up with dances, a common strategy that held the potential for great economic reward: if the dance took off, your song might ride on its coattails. James P. Johnson's *Charleston Rag* was a famous example, but there were many other attempts, including *Georgia Grind*, *Irish Black Bottom*, and *Sunset Cafe Stomp*, all recorded by the Hot Five.

Atkins and Barbarin had something else in common: each asked his prestigious friend to promote his new song. Atkins knew Armstrong from a Mississippi riverboat band, where he played violin alongside Armstrong's cornet from 1920 through 1922. Armstrong agreed to place *Heebie Jeebies* on the February 26 OKeh session, and we may assume that Atkins was delighted to cut a deal with the company. OKeh was now encouraging Armstrong to sing, so Atkins's tune needed some words, which Armstrong supplied himself. It is easy to read between the lines here: as co-composer, he would be in a position to receive royalties if the song got recorded by others. This, too, was a common strategy, a way to increase the commitment of a person or publishing house who held powers of promotion. Armstrong wrote out some words and brought them to the studio.[50]

What happened next is another famous moment in jazz history. Armstrong brought along his sheet of paper, but in the middle of the recording he accidentally dropped it. Not wanting to spoil the wax, he continued the performance with scat. The story later was used to support the idea that he had invented scat on the spot. There seems to be no doubt that he dropped a piece of paper; Armstrong, Ory, and St. Cyr all included this detail in their independent accounts. Whether or not he planned to scat is interesting to speculate about, though difficult to get very far with.

It is clear that the scat version did not exist, except perhaps in Armstrong's mind, before February 26, 1926. He was surprised that OKeh released the recording, but the studio turned out to be the place to take a risk like this. It would have been too unnerving to introduce scat at the Vendome. The impersonal recording machine enabled innovation; spoiled wax could be melted down and reused, so why not try something new? Usually we think of recordings during this period as providing a restricted glimpse of what was going on in live performance. Here may be a case of the studio prompting an innovation that was less likely on stage.

OKeh took a chance and was handsomely rewarded. Perhaps the studio was emboldened by institutional memory of its 1920 success with Mamie Smith's *Crazy Blues*. "There's fourteen million Negroes in our great country and they will buy records if recorded by one of their own, because we are the only folks that can sing and interpret hot jazz songs just off the griddle correctly"—that was Perry Bradford's plea to OKeh executives in 1920. Perhaps Bradford's lesson was still ringing in some executive's ears when Armstrong unleashed his startling romp through an unfamiliar range of the black vernacular voice. The combination of low overhead and the intended market—the "letter back home"—encouraged OKeh to take a chance.

If the scatted *Heebie Jeebies* was created in the recording studio, then when was it first performed in public? That may well have happened on the very next day. On Friday, February 26, the Hot Five was in the OKeh studio, and on Saturday they were featured in "OKeh Race Record Artists' Night" at the Chicago Coliseum. It was only the second time that blacks had been admitted to this venue; clarinetist Bud Jacobson attended with Floyd O'Brien, and they felt like they were the only two whites in the entire building. OKeh took out ads in the *Defender* highlighting the participation of the celebrated Broadway team Miller and Lyles, but another ad, now unidentifiable, included pictures of Armstrong and blues guitarist Lonnie Johnson—and only them. OKeh promised to select three beautiful Chicago girls from the audience to dance in the chorus line. The event included a demonstration of how "OKeh records are made, finished and played—all within 15 minutes." The Hot Five were among the demonstrators. Three thousand people attended and the show was heard on radio.

If Armstrong did demonstrate *Heebie Jeebies* with scat at the Coliseum, it would help explain both the increased demand for his services in the spring of 1926 and the tremendously quick sales of the record after it was released around May 1. Sometime during the spring, and probably not too long after the February breakthrough, he was singing *Heebie Jeebies* through a megaphone at the Vendome. The name of the piece connected well with the radical nature of his singing and his eccentric cornet. In mid-April the Sunset Café lured him away from the Dreamland with a substantial boost in salary.

On May 1 the *Defender* advertised the recording. Peyton described Armstrong as the "big feature in Carroll Dickerson's Sunset Orchestra." OKeh soon signed him to a five-year contract, and on Saturday, June 12, OKeh rented out the Coliseum for another big blast, promoted as the OKeh Cabaret and Style Show. "Nothing of this kind has ever happened in the world before," wrote Peyton. This time there was no doubt about who the headliner was. "LISTEN!" shouted a *Defender* ad. "At the Big Main Coliseum . . . You Are Going to Have an Opportunity to See How It Was Done: Louis Armstrong and His Hot Five Will Actually Make an OKeh Record Right on the Stage of *Heebie Jeebies Dance*. . . . The biggest selling record ever known." Ads promised the estimated 20,000 who attended that all 21 orchestras present would join together to play not only *Heebie Jeebies* but also *Cornet Chop Suey*, *Muskrat Ramble*, *Oriental Strut*, and *Come Back, Sweet Papa*, along with a few other tunes. Armstrong stole the show. "Never has any record artist received such an ovation as the one that greeted him on that memorable night," crowed an OKeh ad.

To capitalize on Armstrong's spiking popularity, OKeh rushed the Hot Five back into the recording studios on June 16 and 23. The group scraped together four tunes by Hardin, two by Richard Jones, one by Ory, and one cowritten by Barbarin and Armstrong. Ory gave this account of the general approach to Hot Five preparations: "We didn't rehearse much on those records with Louis. We rehearsed right in the studio before we started. If we were going to do eight numbers we'd start about 45 minutes or an hour at the most with the whole numbers." That level of casualness would certainly explain the undistinguished performances from these June dates; there is no reason to believe that any of the pieces were worked up ahead of time. The tunes were not designed to showcase Armstrong's ability to create a special trumpet chorus; the only solo that even hints at such at thing comes in *King of the Zulus*. OKeh had a trumpet king/singer on their hands, but in June 1926 it was the singer who was selling records.[51] He sings on five of the eight tunes recorded.

*King of the Zulus* seems to have had the most impact, perhaps due to its title, a reference to Armstrong's favorite New Orleans parade, the parody of the famous Mardi Gras Rex that originated in his neighborhood. The Zulu theme was perfect for the large Halloween Ball on October 30, held at the Eighth Regiment Armory: a Zulu King was crowned at 2:00 a.m. and a Zulu King's feast of free chit'lins offered. Interestingly, the featured vocals in the June sessions did not include scat. Armstrong had not yet developed his technique of mixing in scat with a more or less straightforward presentation of a song's lyrics, the kind of blend that would become so important to his new vocal style in the early 1930s. *Heebie Jeebies* must have seemed like such a novelty that to produce another scat chorus would have been too obviously derivative. A scat follow-up to *Heebie Jeebies* had to wait until November to get recorded: the lovely *Skid Dat De Dat* does not have a chorus, but features multiple scat breaks. This slow, poignant performance, with its brief phrases of scat presented in dialogue with instruments, is actually less connected to *Heebie Jeebies* than to the later *West End Blues*. The simplicity of *Skid Dat De Dat* made it easy for the others to contribute without feeling like they had to keep up with Armstrong's flash.

In July, Percy Venable staged and produced *Jazzmania*, a new revue at the Sunset Café. The magazine *Heebie Jeebies* described *Jazzmania* as "the fastest and most colorful show ever staged at this popular night club."[52] For the finale of the revue the entire cast supported Armstrong singing *Heebie Jeebies*, in coordination with five-foot-tall dancer Kid Lips, who had, the year before, originated "the backward, skating, knee drop and other improvements of the Charleston." At some point (it could well have been later) Blanche Calloway, a popular singer on cabaret circuits, asked the musicians if they could find a place on stage for her brother Cabell, who had dropped out of school. Cab hung around, heard Armstrong play *Muskrat Ramble, Gut Bucket Blues, You're Next*, and *Oriental Strut*, and heard him scat. "All of the songs he did were full of fire and rhythm, and he was scat singing even then," said the future singer of *Hi De Ho*. "Louis first got me freed up from straight lyrics to try scatting." White clarinetist Mezz Mezzrow and his Chicago friends bought Armstrong's *Heebie Jeebies* and played it over and over until saxophonist Frank Teschemacher insisted that they drive 53 miles to Hudson Lake, Indiana, to play it for Bix Beiderbecke. "All the way there we kept chanting Louis' weird riffs," remembered Mezzrow, who "kept the car zigzagging like a roller coaster to make the explosions," in a reckless representation of Armstrong's scatted dance.

Summer contracts were drawn up for an "orchestral roll" and a piano roll, and in the fall OKeh's parent company published sheet music. Boyd Atkins was credited as composer, new lyrics were added, and a new "eccentric" dance was created by Floyd DuPont ("America's fastest dance producer," according to the *Washington Post*) and introduced by Tinah Tweedie. A photograph of bandleader Paul Ash was placed on the cover of the sheet music. Armstrong's name was nowhere to be found, even though the printed music included a transcription of his "skat chorus." There followed a batch of fall recordings by Alberta Hunter, the Red Heads, Ethel Waters, the Original Indiana Five, and the Goofus Five; some included Armstrong's solo, played by instruments, and the Goofus Five did it in scat.

OKeh's coordinated strategies lifted *Heebie Jeebies* into a more lucrative market—that is, into a white market. The dance was heavily promoted in Chicago, where, in the fall of 1926, white ballrooms placed printed directions for the dance on every table. Advertisements featured photographs of (white) Miss Tweedie posing in the various steps—the get-off, the stomp-off, the fling-off, the heebie-off, the jeebie-off, and the blow-off. By February 1928 the dance had reached

*The Heebie Jeebies Dance (The William Russell Archive at the Historic New Orleans Collection, accession no. 92-48-L.109)*

England, where it was protested by a missionary who had "spent a lifetime teaching the natives of darkest Africa to abandon suggestive dances" and was shocked "beyond words" to "find his people doing the same dances which he had attempted to stop in Africa."

As it positioned the piece to sell to whites, OKeh shamelessly dropped all mention of Armstrong, without whom nobody would have heard of it, even while they kept his version of Atkins's melody (whose original tune was closely derived from Joplin and Chauvin) at the heart of the piece's identity. This is important for our understanding of the demographic trajectories of Armstrong's career: it is likely that very few whites outside the Sunset Café heard his scat breakthrough, or even heard of him at all during these productive years in Chicago. The Boswell Sisters made a hit out of the piece in 1932; they recorded it in video and audio and opened their programs with it. Their neatly arranged performance, complete with minstrel-style black dialect, was based on Armstrong's scat chorus. I see no reason to believe that white audiences who enjoyed the Sisters made any association with Armstrong, even though by that time he was well known.

But the tune continued to be strongly associated with him among blacks. In January 1927 Bill "Bojangles" Robinson was in Chicago and stopped by the Sunset to check out the scene. He was so impressed that he decided to immediately build *Heebie Jeebies* into his own act. "Music is now being prepared for Bill, who ordered it 'Rush,'" wrote an unidentified source. There is another report of Armstrong performing the song in Chicago in October 1927. In December Dave Peyton stopped by a "chop suey cafe" and encountered for the first time an early version of the jukebox; it was playing Armstrong's *Heebie Jeebies*. Peyton was impressed by the machine's sound, but he viewed it as another threat to the livelihood of musicians, along with the vitaphone (the sound system used in movie theaters) and radio: "Orchestras, beware!" he wrote. A revue at the Alhambra in Harlem in the summer of 1929 included Manda Randolph leading the Alhambra Girls "in Lewis [*sic*] Armstrong's favorite number, the lively *Heebee Jeebees* [*sic*]."

Late in life, Armstrong explained why he didn't mind satisfying the public's insistence that he sing *Hello Dolly* so often—"How many times? Six jillion?" he quipped. "Aw, I am paid to *entertain* the people." During his long career, there would be quite a few pieces that the public demanded again and again. *Heebie Jeebies* was the first.

Ultimately, scat would open up a new style for Armstrong, but that came slowly; it didn't really take off until he changed his way of singing under the influence of the microphone. His huge success with *Heebie Jeebies* put him on the map as a singer in the entertainment world of Chicago, and his next big hit was *Big Butter and Egg Man*, which he sang as a duet at the Sunset Café in the summer and fall of 1926. But there was one big difference: *Big Butter* also featured him in an extended trumpet chorus, a deliberate attempt to combine his two-sided abilities in a single performance. During 1927, while he continued to sing both pieces at the Vendome and the Sunset Café, the trend would be more to the instrumental side, both quantitatively and qualitatively. It was a magical combination, singing and playing trumpet, that would continue to lift him higher and higher in the South Side world of entertainment.

# SIX

# Melody Man at the Sunset Café

I'm just an old melody man.

—Louis Armstrong

Armstrong's wife had a lot of opinions about his dress and much else, but as his boss at the Dreamland—well, the potential conflicts were many. Musicians teased him: "Look out there, Louie, your wife will fire you," they taunted. He was embarrassed and grew harder to get along with, both at home and at work. "I would get ready to start the band off and he'd have all the musicians on one side, telling them a damn joke," Lillian remembered. "I got after him about it, and he said, 'Well if you don't like it fire me.'"

In early April an offer came from none other than Joe Oliver, who was running a band at the Plantation Café, across the street from the Sunset Café. Armstrong said yes, and the move was announced in the *Defender*. He was on his way to a rehearsal one day when he bumped into Earl Hines on the street. They had gotten to know one another at the musicians' union; Hines remembered the first piece they read through there together, *The One I Love (Belongs to Somebody Else)*, composed by Isham Jones and Gus Kahn in 1924. Hines was on his way to a rehearsal, too, though not with Oliver. He was employed by Carroll Dickerson at the Sunset, and he decided to go to work on his friend: "Why don't you come on over with us young fellows?"

Here is another special moment in the Armstrong biography, a choice between the greatest influence of his formative teenage years and the musician (Hines) who was best able to keep up with him in mid-1920s Chicago. "I loved Joe Oliver, and here I was back in

Chicago with all these Chicago boys, and I thought I'd be more at home with Papa Joe, sitting by his side," he remembered. But Lillian convinced him to go to the Sunset, which sweetened the deal with $10 more per week than Oliver was offering. Of course Oliver was offended, though he got over the bad behavior eventually.

Armstrong started at the Sunset on April 17, 1926, and Oliver ended up convincing Ory to leave the Dreamland and join him at the Plantation. Seating around 500 people at 100 square tables, each covered with a white tablecloth, the Sunset offered a "new departure in ventilation" of a "refrigerator character" that cooled the place down to 70 degrees on summer nights. It stayed open past the closing times of other cabarets, usually until 3:30 or 4:00 in the morning. Musicians worked seven nights every week, as usual.

Armstrong stayed at the Sunset for the some 18 months, until fall 1927, doubling up after the Vendome gig. His friends Buster Bailey, Rudy Jackson, Honoré Dutrey, and Andre Hillare were all working there, and Bobby Williams of *Bugle Blues* fame was first-chair trumpet. He believed that Dickerson's 12-to-14-piece unit, with two violins, was the best cabaret band on the South Side.

## "Stir the Savage in Us with a Pleasant Tickle"

Armstrong's arrival was part of a change in musical strategy for the Sunset. Before Dickerson was hired in March, music was supplied by none other than Sammy Stewart, the blue-veined, conservatory-trained pianist from Ohio who had snubbed Armstrong in the summer of 1924. By hiring Dickerson—and then Hines and Armstrong—the Sunset was responding to increased interest in jazz. The Plantation, across the street, was leading the way. Before Oliver took over, Dave Peyton, the *Defender* columnist, had been directing a band with considerable success. With their strong Eurocentric orientations, the rivalry between Peyton and Stewart must have been a good one. Peyton brought in Oliver as a featured soloist in late 1924, perhaps under pressure from management, and by early 1925 Oliver had taken over, apparently through a bit of deception; his power move recalls similar takeovers of Ory's band in 1916 and of Duhé's band in 1919.

*Sunset Café, transformed to the Grand Terrace, 1937 (The William Russell Photographic Collection, MSS 520 F. 54, Williams Research Center, The Historic New Orleans Collection)*

Oliver transformed the Plantation into a place known for jazz. "The mammoth King Oliver and his 10 musicians provide the music," wrote *Variety*. "If you haven't heard Oliver and his boys you haven't heard real jazz. It is loud, wailing and pulsating. You dance calmly for a while, trying to fight it, and then you succumb completely, as King makes his trumpet talk personally to you—and the trumpet doesn't usually say nice things." The contrast with Sammy Stewart's college-educated musicians at the Sunset must have been dramatic.

Since both venues catered heavily to whites, the success of Oliver and then Armstrong at 35th and Calumet is an important indicator of the growing reach of African-American jazz. This is the same trend that Fletcher Henderson was tracking in late 1924 and 1925, now moved several steps forward as it was playing out on the South Side of Chicago. Oliver's popularity is indicated by the 30-minute radio broadcasts he made from the Plantation each evening. The irony must have been evident to both the King and his successful student: their dark skin and their commitment to the African-American vernacular of the Deep South had been a liability at these locations just a few years earlier; now both markers were assets.

Management at the Plantation produced an atmosphere worthy of the venue's name, with trailing vines rising up from picket fences and blossoming on the ceiling into tissue-paper watermelons. The entire staff was black. When you handed your hat to the check girl, she kept time with the music as she found a place for the garment. The waiters did the same thing as they swung their trays. The cashier hit the register with a little ring that punctuated the flow of Oliver's pulsating jazz, and even the bathroom attendant brushed guests down with a rhythmically precise whisk broom, jingling the change in his pants pocket with a little flourish, as if tapping a cymbal.

Jazz around 35th and Calumet spread to the Nest Club (later called the Apex), an after-hours spot where clarinetist Jimmy Noone played for many years beginning at 1:00 a.m. every night, right next door to the Plantation. The density of activity was part of the attraction, with customers wandering back and forth between the venues as the evening unfolded. Preston Jackson said it reminded him of latter-day Bourbon Street in New Orleans. In springtime the cabaret windows opened wide and the musical competition became more direct. Oliver sent a playful note over to Armstrong: "Close your windows or I'll blow you off 35th Street." "The fire department is thinking of lining 35th Street with asbestos to keep these bands from scorching passersby with their red hot jazz music," quipped Peyton in the *Defender*.

In 1922 and 1923 Lincoln Gardens had tried to lure whites with a midnight ramble on Wednesdays, but the effort failed. Now, in the spring of 1926, the Sunset, Plantation, and Nest were hitting paydirt at 35th and Calumet. "All the white people, all the night lifers, the rich people from Sheridan Road and the big hotels would come out there on the South Side," Armstrong remembered. The period's term for this social phenomenon was "slumming."[53]

The white draw depended on a felt sense of safety. The fact that the clubs were large and right next to each other was a plus since large numbers of patrons made the location feel secure, though problems are hinted at in a few reports. An unidentified article from November 1925 mentioned "undesirable characters" at the Plantation "whose actions have driven off practically all the white trade this café once enjoyed." The writer counted four white couples and twenty African

Americans on the night of his visit. An April 1926 article in *Variety* complained that white women and entertainers did not feel safe. "Although the Plantation Café makes a great play for the white trade and the performers, the performer is laying himself open to unpleasant publicity and trouble by being in attendance," the writer asserted ("performers" meaning white professionals who were in town for a different job and stopped by on their days off).

African-American men acted as guides, taking whites for a stroll down to the corner of 35th and State, the main hangout for local blacks with round-the-clock buzz, to buffet flats, and to places of prostitution. The reputation of organized crime also helped make the area feel safe, ironically enough. Many accounts report that the Plantation and the Sunset were thickly bound up with organized crime, if they were not in fact run by it totally. The Sunset may have provided Armstrong's first sustained exposure to gangsters and their ways, a world he would remain connected to for years to come, dealing with life-threatening situations along the way.

This was the era of prohibition, of course, and alcohol, the life-blood of organized crime, was a big part of cabaret entertainment. "Outside the cabaret Negroes loiter in doorways, eager to supply you with any variety of liquor," advised *Variety* in a review of the Sunset and the Plantation. "They ask $3 a pint for gin, but will consent to a lower price after bargaining." A New Year's Eve raid of both cabarets in December 1926 exposed a scene of 500 merrymaking men and women, "white and colored," drinking heavily and dancing wildly. A quick investigation uncovered an alcohol storage depot at 338 East 35th Street, two doors down from the Plantation.

Kingpin Al Capone enlisted local blacks into his operation and had a reputation for treating them fairly. Milt Hinton and Lionel Hampton each had uncles who worked with Capone; Hinton described him as a "Robin Hood" type figure admired by the locals. "He had all the black guys, he'd sit down and talk to them, 'I'm the boss, I'm running it, but you're going to run the South Side,'" explained Hinton. "'You're going to make money as long as you buy your alcohol from me.'" Police were paid off and little intrusions like the New Year's raid cleared up quickly.

Rivalries for turf control produced outbreaks of violence now and then, but the victims were usually other criminals; as one owner joked to a musician: "Buddy, don't ever worry about anybody in this here joint because *nobody* in this here joint will hurt you unless he gets paid for it." Ory told a story of hiding under the kitchen stove at the Plantation, smothered by the smell of fried potatoes, and Hines remembered hiding under the piano at the Sunset. "You had to have a certain amount of courage to work in those clubs," said Hines.

But it was also possible to regard gangsters as a benign element, especially as a source for huge tips. Armstrong described Capone as a "nice little cute fat boy, young, like some professor who had just come out of college to teach or something." On a slow night the gangsters might walk into a cabaret, instruct the manager to lock the doors, hand over $1,000, and announce that "this is our night." They enjoyed mixing with the musicians and showgirls, everyone having a good time. Drummer Sonny Greer said that he could always rely on the gangsters to keep their word, an uncommon virtue in the music business.

Armstrong developed a special relationship with Capone, which is startling but not surprising given the dynamics of the situation. "Louis was very, very in with Al Capone," said Cheatham, who claimed that he once got a job when Armstrong asked Capone to intervene. Capone was very fond of music. In one story he requested a number from Johnny Dodds, but Dodds didn't know the tune. Capone took out a $100 bill, tore it in half, put one half in his pocket, and poked the other half into Dodds's pocket, saying, "Nigger, you better learn it for next time." That must have humiliated the dignified Dodds, who had refused to play in certain venues in New Orleans because of similarly offensive behavior. Most of the musicians were willing to overlook the occasional crude remark, and they remembered Capone fondly. Capone once sent two bodyguards to accompany Hines on a road trip, which Hines regarded as a favor. "They protected us because we kept their clubs open," insisted Hines, but he probably also understood the implication that he "belonged" to the gangsters and that they would do what they had to do to secure their property.

Some jazz histories claim that the Sunset and Plantation were exclusively white, but it is clear that both places were integrated. It is often difficult to pin down in detail the social makeup of venues during this period. Policies changed over time, and one person's experience could be different from someone else's. But integration was one of the things that made Chicago's South Side cabarets different from the elite cabarets in Harlem. The Cotton Club in New York City, the most famous black and tan of all, was rigidly segregated, with all staff black and virtually all patrons white, with the exception of a famous celebrity now and then. A different history and dynamic were in place in Chicago.

Evidence of black patronage at the Sunset and Plantation comes from various sources. There are a few interviews with blacks who went there. And the frequent mentions of both venues not only in the *Defender* and *Heebie Jeebies* but also in black newspapers from Pittsburgh, Baltimore, and New York suggest an integrated policy; any whiff of exclusion would have been quickly condemned, just as the Cotton Club was condemned. *Defender* columnist Salem Tutt Whitney made the rounds of South Side cabarets in July 1926 and was impressed by the Sunset and Plantation. Cabarets did not deserve their bad reputations, he insisted, for they were places where "one can be one's self for a time; lay aside superficialities, traditions, customs and conventions. . . . Class lines and color lines are temporarily obliterated and democracy holds sway while the lights scintillate, the band plays and the dancers frolic."

Buster Bailey explained that "all the places then were black and tan . . . in terms of race, everything on the South Side was all right." Black society clubs occasionally rented out the Sunset for their gatherings. Armstrong even told a joke once about integration at the Sunset Café. An older couple is visiting from "way down in Galilee" (that is, the South). The gentleman wants to request *Old Black Joe*, so he stands up and calls out to the band, "Hey fellas, can you play . . ." But as he speaks he turns around and notices the integrated audience, which causes him to adjust: "Can you play *Old Colored Joe* up there?"

It was not segregation but high prices that discouraged black attendance. That was how upscale cabarets tried to create an elite atmosphere, and the Sunset and Plantation were aiming for the top of Chicago. Patrons wanted to appear rich and glamorous, and the steep prices helped them do that. Even though an integrated experience was an attraction at these two venues, their success was based on the patronage of high-rolling whites. Fundamentally, they were places of white privilege. Whites arrived from distant neighborhoods—the rich people from Sheridan Road and the big hotels, as Armstrong remembered—so we need to raise the question: why did they come? It was certainly more than a thirst for peppy entertainment and bootleg booze.

So much was packed into white views about African-American culture that it is difficult to imagine a neutral observer, someone whose interest in black entertainment had nothing to do with race. White attitudes in the early twentieth century were conditioned by a system of thought known as "primitivism." Primitivist thinking could be engaged as a highly developed ideology with a long history of extended reflection dating back to the eighteenth century and before, or it could operate more casually, as a cluster of vaguely defined attitudes. Either way, it was difficult to escape. It flourished as a way to articulate what whites regarded as racial differences of far-reaching importance.[54]

First of all, the primitivist view sustained a vivid sense of social-racial hierarchy. African Americans were inferior; that belief was a given. Even the most informed and sympathetic observers had

*Dancers at a Chicago cabaret, 1941 (Library of Congress)*

trouble giving up the notion that African-derived cultures were lacking the fundamental qualities that made white society so obviously advanced; those less informed and less sympathetic noticed signs of inferiority everywhere they looked. These assumptions justified the meticulously controlled system of economic exploitation, with inferior schools and jobs, lack of voting rights, and so forth. Since we are dealing with expensive nightclubs in a city that bustled with economic growth, this attitude was not marginal. It is safe to assume that none of the big spenders at the Sunset experienced even a flash of doubt that every single African American working there was an inferior person, even if he or she did happen to be good at stepping fast, playing high, or singing with a lot of heart.

Specifically, they were deficient in reason, civilization, self-reflectivity, critical capacity, and control over emotions. These shortfalls were the cause of their apparent lack of progress, culturally, socially, politically, and intellectually. The only way for primitive people to break out of their simple and childish ways was to imitate Western models, which they did somewhat pathetically. Spirituals and ragtime were understood as classic examples of this primitive black imitation of white models.

But the alleged differences also included a mysterious set of advantages. Lacking reason, primitives had access to creativity; lacking the ability to calculate, they were spontaneous; lacking analytical skills, they were intuitive; lacking civilization, they were unrepressed; lacking cities, they lived in harmony with nature; and lacking the filter of the superego, they were sexy. In an enthusiastic review, written in 1926 for the *Nation*, novelist Mary Austin explained how Bill Bojangles Robinson's splendid dancing could restore with its "primal freshness their [the audience's] own lost rhythmic powers." Robinson was able to accomplish this "only by the sincere unconsciousness of his genius," his dance moves coming to him in dreams, Austin explained, "as inspiration has always come to tribal man."

Even an observer as astute as Marshall Stearns, who made strong contributions to jazz history and was as sympathetic as anyone to the accomplishments of black musicians, could fall into this trap. Looking back in 1936, Stearns viewed the (white) Friars Society Orchestra of the early 1920s as having introduced "a new genre, characterized by an improvement in technique, less glissando to cover unsure attack, less vibrato to hide errors in pitch, less forcing, and inevitably less emotional fervor and intensity. It has always been the white man's gain and loss, that with improved technique, less of the primitive emotion exists." Stearns does what he can to soften the word, but "primitive" still jumps off the page. Primitive emotions went along with primitive thinking, primitive music, and primitive culture. If the concept is taken seriously, there is only one way to go from primitive: toward the supposedly more sophisticated emotions, music, and culture achieved in the West.

Due to what Austin called their "accumulated cultural rubbish," advanced Westerners had trouble in some of the areas where primitive people excelled. African-American music and dance offered "release and return"—release from the burdens of civilization and return, however temporary, to primal freshness, or, as George Tichenor put it in a 1930 review of cabarets in Harlem, "a sort of primitive abandon which rises in the blood under pale skins and which centuries of expert tailoring and fashionable table manners have not quite dried out." Thus formed a taut mixture of condescension and desire around this set of projections, a potent emotional mix that was available even to people who never read a book and didn't spend much time thinking about cultural evolution or psychology. Condescension and desire went hand in hand: the cause of inferiority was also the cause of the attractive attributes. Lifted from the philosopher's desk and placed in the texture of everyday American experience, primitivism produced both an absolutely unquestioned stance of dominance and a circumscribed opening for appreciation and imitation.

The dominating side of the equation was well tended by organizations like the U.S. Supreme Court, which monitored practices of "separate but equal," and the Ku Klux Klan, which organized a steady stream of violence as a way to keep everyone alert to the consequences of violating the established social order. The Sunset was also designed to bring the social hierarchy of white supremacism to life, and it did this night after night. Every employee understood his or her place of inferiority. One night at the Sunset Armstrong encouraged the young white trumpeter Muggsy Spanier to play his (Armstrong's) own solo for the tune *Big Butter and Egg Man from the West*.

He knew that Spanier had memorized it, note for note, and Spanier was thrilled by his hero's approval. But when Armstrong's friend and bandmate Natty Dominique later did the same thing, he was scolded for copying: "Listen Nique, don't do that. That's a bad idea you have playing like I play," Armstrong said. The difference in attitude is a small demonstration of the social dynamics of the Sunset.

The Sunset provided its guests with a reassuring enactment of white dominance, but what made it special was the mysterious and alluring side of primitivism. The cabaret charged high prices for the opportunity to witness and even participate in an impassioned display of African-American dance, music, comedy, and sexuality. What cultural historian Lewis Erenberg has called "vicarious bohemianism" was a strong part of postwar cabarets generally. Entering a cabaret was supposed to feel like walking into the living quarters of glamorous and risqué entertainers. A host or hostess welcomed the guests to their table. One of the entertainers themselves might be seated nearby and from there casually make an entrance onto the stage, which was at the same level as the seats, rather than elevated. The performers wandered around the room, greeted customers, sang for them, and flirted. Dancers, comedians, and chorus girls had skits that were designed to break down barriers between performer and audience. Cabarets offered their bourgeois guests a taste of leisure-time liberation, a "certain delicious wickedness," as one writer put it, that was intensified by the thrill of bootleg booze. How much more intense that thrill could be when merged with the racial dynamics of the black and tans. "Black men with white girls, white men with yellow girls, old, young, all filled with the abandon brought about by illicit whisky and liquor music," ran one breathless account from a white newspaper of a South Side venue.

In a sense, the Sunset and Plantation offered a magical collapse of distance. The clubs were located far away on the South Side where Negroes lived apart, thus intensifying the illusion that you were actually entering the living quarters of black entertainers. The coveted tables were right next to the stage, putting patrons close enough to reach out and touch the performers. Cabarets were intimate spaces of safety and protection. Physical distance collapsed and so did cultural distance. An elite transformation of the African-American vernacular was on display, yet one could still jump up and join the Charleston contest. And if so inclined, there was no reason to stop the distance-collapsing magic short of sexual intimacy. Thirty-fifth and Calumet was primitivist heaven, Gauguin's Tahitian paradise in the City of Big Shoulders. There was perhaps no other space quite so perfect as this one, with its combination of white hegemony and the skillful channeling of black primitivism into cultural forms like the Charleston, café au lait dancing girls, and Armstrong's stunning solos.

"A whole race going hedonistic, deciding on pleasure," wrote F. Scott Fitzgerald in his analysis of the "jazz age," and he didn't have to say which race he was talking about. Sexual liberation was a major theme for the 1920s, with its short skirts, lipstick, and petting parties. "Jazz didn't change the morals of the early twenties," explained composer Hoagy Carmichael, "but it furnished the music, I noticed, to a change in manners and sexual ideas. Women wore less and wore it in a slipping, careless way on the dance floors." Healthy sexuality meant full and responsive attention to the libido, and blacks were understood to be more in touch with their libidos than whites were. Thus sex was a huge part of primitivist pleasure at the black and tans, with black dance and music defining in a very public way what sexual liberation was all about.

Light-skinned female singers and chorines tapped into legendary fantasies of the octoroon. Singer Mae Alix, a mainstay at the Sunset who sang duets with Armstrong, was described as a rare beauty with a shapely body who looked white; given her limited vocal ability, as revealed in recordings, it is easy to believe those reports. Alix sang, flirted, and did running splits, picking up bills as she slid across the floor and stuffing them down the front of her dress. "Margaret Simms, a New Yorker, is hitting 'em up at the Sunset Café these breezy days with her little 'Wrigley' dance," ran one write-up. "Mae Alex [sic] in 'Hello Aloha' wriggles also, so the argument around the house is who is the wriggliest."

Twenty-four chorus girls worked at the Sunset, many looking "almost white" and dividing into two sets of twelve each, the "parade girls" and the "ponies." Hines explained that the parade girls were used for "picture numbers," which implies some kind of *tableau vivant*; picture numbers were accompanied by light classics like *Poet*

*Cotton Club program, New York City (Collection of Duncan Schiedt)*

*and Peasant Overture* and *Rhapsody in Blue.* The ponies, smaller in height than the parade girls, were the dancers. "Sometimes the chorus would steal the show at the Sunset and Louis used to get a great kick out of backing them up," remembered Hines. Moralists routinely complained about the "nudity" of chorines, whose costumes exposed a lot of skin.

The first option for customers interested in more than passive gazing was to get up and dance. The ponies and the headlining dance teams demonstrated the latest hip-shaking dances, and descriptions of new steps were written up on little cards placed on tables. In 1926 the Heebie Jeebies, the Mess Around, the Charleston, and the Black Bottom, each with firm origins in the black vernacular, were in full, vigorous motion at 35th and Calumet. "Hip dancing is carried out wholesaledly between the customers," wrote *Variety* in April. "Native jazz has no conscience." The pretense employed by the Castle dance team during the 1910s that black-derived dances were good for your health was irrelevant in this environment, and the Juvenile Protective Association complained constantly about the new "supremacy of the extreme 'Jazz Dances.'"

The Mess Around had been popular for a long time in the black community and was just now breaking through. The dance was said to have come from Louisiana. Paul Barbarin wrote a tune with the title *Don't Forget to Mess Around* in February 1926, and Armstrong added lyrics that included the line, "Don't forget to mess around when you're doing the Charleston."[55] The strategy is clear: having hooked a song to a dance, why not hook it also to the most popular dance of the day?

By early summer the Brown Brothers had introduced the Mess Around to the Plantation, while Valaida Snow and Brown and McGraw did the same thing at the Sunset.[56] In early July W. E. B. Du Bois visited Chicago and the weekly magazine *Heebie Jeebies* scored an interview at a breakfast gathering. In a light moment, Du Bois danced the Charleston, right there at breakfast, demonstrating how he was still keeping up with things at age fifty-eight; he had to admit that he didn't know the Mess Around.[57]

"Black Bottom" was slang for an area inhabited by poor blacks. This dance, too, had been around the black vernacular for some time. One description alludes to crouching, a position of power in African dances: "You clap your hands on your rear end. Then you bend your legs and go down, down to the floor, twisting and turning, close to your partner. Then you come back up and move away from your partner and give him the come-on with your fingers down here."[58]

In the summer of 1926, the Black Bottom drew white attention when Ann Pennington featured it in the Broadway show *Scandals*. It quickly became a multidimensional success with dedicated songs, singers, bands, and film.[59] The *Defender* responded with an amusing little feature (July 24, 1926) entitled "Aristocracy," which aligned cultural taste with social class according to four categories: "Low-Brow," "High Low-Brow," Low High-Brow," and "High-Brow."

Gold, W. E. B. Du Bois, and slumming forums defined High-Brow; Episcopalians, the NAACP, operetta, and phrases like "I shahn't because I can't" belonged to Low High-Brow; spirituals, the Charleston, Marcus Garvey, and cabarets were High Low-Brow; and craps, poor grammar, Holy Roller churches, and the Black Bottom were Low-Brow.

One can only guess if such ridicule weakened or heightened white enthusiasm. In September, the (white) Dancing Masters of America declared the Charleston out of date; it had been replaced by the Black Bottom, described by the Masters as a "combination of the hula-hula, the Charleston, and the shuffle." That same month the *Los Angeles Times* reminded its readers that "we always told you no good could come from these gallivanting dances" and gleefully reported an injury to an actress who had been stepped on while dancing the Black Bottom at a cabaret. In October the prince and princess of Romania announced that they were looking forward to visiting the United States so that they could learn the dance. This momentum inspired Percy Venable to compose for the Sunset a humorous number entitled *Irish Black Bottom*, which Armstrong sang with enthusiasm for a Hot Five recording session on November 27.

Several videos show whites dancing the Black Bottom, one featuring a gyrating Joan Crawford. The dances were so popular that some venues were forced to prohibit them. Guyon's Paradise in Chicago, accommodating 4,000 dancers, banned the Charleston, which must have made it all the more thrilling to trek south to 35th and Calumet for the real thing. Like all African-American dances, the Charleston was basically open-ended and improvisatory; as often happened, whites then codified the steps. The black and white versions inevitably differed. We may assume that the *Defender* was not thinking of Joan Crawford when it grouped the Black Bottom with craps and Holy Roller churches. Yet it appears that white dancers at the Sunset were exploring some of the more provocative possibilities—according to police reports, anyway.

In December 1926 the Juvenile Protective Association teamed up with the Chicago police to simultaneously raid the Sunset and the Plantation. "The so called 'Black Bottom,' as danced in these places, has ceased to be a dance at all and is merely an immoral exhibition," the association explained to Chief Collins, who agreed, adding that the dance is "particularly vicious in [its] effect upon young men and women." Collins noted the great number of college students in attendance, even some intoxicated seventeen-year-old girls, dancing wildly. Joe Glaser, manager of the Sunset (and Armstrong's future manager), was arrested, and so was Ed Fox, manager of the Plantation (and Hines's future manager). Judge John F. Haas declared the Sunset a public nuisance.

But that was hardly enough to stop either the Black Bottom or the Sunset. In early February Percy Venable designed a new show featuring Eddie Rector, "the world's greatest buck dancer"; Armstrong, a "prime attraction," singing *Big Butter and Egg Man*; Lillian Westmoreland, the "double voiced marvel"; and soubrettes Mae Alix and Mae Fanning. By March (and probably before that), the Black Bottom and Charleston contest nights were in place again.[60]

Armstrong himself was one of the demonstrating dancers at the Sunset. "Four of us would close the show doing the Charleston," he remembered, "and I was as fat as ever." The act was designed for him and based on Noel Coward's song *Poor Little Rich Girl*; we know that it was performed in February 1927, with a "mixed" quartet of fat and thin musicians (the characterizations of body types come from Armstrong): Armstrong (fat), Hines (thin), drummer Tubby Hall (fat), and trumpeter Bobby Williams (thin).

I know of no video footage that shows Armstrong dancing, but James P. Johnson praised him as the "finest dancer among the musicians." He had grown up in an environment where dancing was highly valued. Two of his childhood buddies, Red Happy Bolton and Nicodeemus, were known for their dancing skill, and there are several reports of Armstrong's own dance activity during his youth, one describing how he "used to dance, shadow box, everything." He himself said that he had a "jive routine" with tap dancing. At the Sunset he became, at least for a moment, a quadruple threat—song, comedy, dance, and trumpet. Versatility like this had big advantages, as Willie "The Lion" Smith explained: "It was the Lion's policy to give the yearlings tips on how to make it in show business. I used to tell them to learn to sing and dance. They could starve if they depended too much on just being a good instrumentalist."

"If you've been in vaudeville, you have a knowledge of every type, every nook and corner of show business," explained singer and comedian Billy Glason—"dramatics, comedy, timing, pacing." The dance team Butterbeans and Susie, who made a phonograph recording with Armstrong and the Hot Five in the summer of 1926, learned how to mix in a little comic bantering between their stepping numbers. Gradually the banter became the main attraction, the dancing a supplement; Susie then added a few blues songs. Armstrong turned out to be good at this kind of category hopping. If nothing else, the dance routine gave him additional training in how to hold a stage. The demands on jazz musicians in 1926 were very different than they would be in the late 1940s, when the expectation was single-minded focus on solo improvisation. A purist view of jazz took over and Armstrong fell victim to it, though it certainly must have comforted him to know that in terms of sheer popularity he towered above almost all other jazz musicians even during the last, impure decades of his career.

The thrill for slumming whites of hooking up with black women and black men must have been one of the reasons that the Chicago black and tans maintained integrated policies—and one of the reasons that moralists were so outraged. "Slumming parties ... are apparently pleased with the atmosphere of sensuality and find delight in seeing the intermingling of the races," complained the Juvenile Protective Association. When the Plantation burned to the ground in the spring of 1927, the *Defender* pointed its finger at "white reform organizations which were bitterly opposed to seeing the two races mix." "The audience, the dancers [i.e., social dancing] were 'mixed,'" explained trumpeter Reuben Reeves, and then he added: "Do not pass over that term lightly." "Even the mixing of white girls and colored pimps seemed to be an attraction" at the Sunset, acknowledged Hines. A tradition of flirting via notes delivered by waiters was called passing "grenades" because of the occasional blowups the practice generated. Prostitutes solicited by winking from the tables. "Stags are abundant," wrote *Variety*.

The list of white musicians known to have patronized the Sunset is long: Bix Beiderbecke, Frank Teschemacher, Paul Whiteman, Mildred Bailey, Hoagy Carmichael, Benny Goodman, Mezz Mezzrow, Eddie Condon, Wild Bill Davison, Jess Stacey, George Wettling, Muggsy Spanier, James Rosy McHargue, Bud Freeman, Art Hodes, Jimmy Dorsey, Tommy Dorsey, Tut Soper, Joe Sullivan, Whitey Berquist, Red Nichols, Miff Mole, Wingy Manone, Bing Crosby—that's a start. "It was a ritual that every Friday night after work we'd all pile into the Sunset," remembered Benny Goodman's brother, Freddy. They frequently sat in with the band, giving Armstrong and his colleagues a welcome break. For white musicians to sit in with black musicians—the reverse was not allowed by white clubs—was considered a natural thing to do, part of the mix of condescension and admiration that drove primitivist attitudes. Hines made clear the need to be deferential: "Whatever section they wanted to sit in, why a musician would step out from his chair." "I had a lot of nerve doing it but we were nervier when we were kids," admitted Freeman. Armstrong was flattered by the attention. "I just came up from the South, I was just thrilled with the closeness and warmth of these great musicians, performers, etc.," he wrote 30 years later. "In fact, it gave me such a lift until, the Leader could see the beam all over my face. . . ."

How did a dark-skinned cornetist working in black neighborhoods become the dominating influence in jazz in the mid-1920s? The Hot Five recordings are one answer, and alligators hanging out at the Sunset Café are another. "It has been the custom for many years for the white musicians to come around our orchestras, spending a few dollars for drinks, getting our players to feeling good and then having them (our players) to show them the different jazz tricks that they make on their instruments," wrote Dave Peyton in October 1926. "Hold on to your ideas. Don't show them a thing," he warned. Peyton even insisted that anyone who violated this principle was an Uncle Tom.

But his words had no measurable impact. There was too much momentum in the other direction. "We had most of their tunes memorized and could really swing out on them," admitted Spanier. Wild Bill Davison kept his own table at the Sunset and was there every night at 11:00. "In 1928 I made an OKeh recording of *Can't Help Lovin' Dat Man* and *Craze-O-Logy*," said Freeman, "and to my ear today it's ALL Armstrong. I put in everything I could remember that he played." (The connection is clearest in *Can't Help Lovin' Dat Man*.) "Ain't a trumpet player alive that don't play a little something I used to play," said Armstrong 40 years later. "Makes them feel like they're getting hot or something. Real Negroid. That's all right. Makes me feel good."

The involvement of the alligators with African-American jazz ranged through different levels of engagement, from adolescent rebellion to preprofessional study, from postwar revolt against Victorian mores to full-scale primitivist embrace. Clarinetist Mezz Mezzrow staked out the extreme end of the spectrum. Mezzrow craved as much of the primitive as he could get. "To me there's more natural suggestion in the snap of a colored singer's fingers than you get from all the acrobatic routines of these so-called 'hot' [white] singers," he wrote. His autobiographical account of deep and thorough attraction to black music, black culture, and black people may be an unprecedented document. (It is also fun to read, self-aggrandizing, intelligent, and insightful.) By 1926, he remembered, "I'd started to use so many of the phrases and intonations of the Negro, I must have sounded like I was trying to pass for colored." In 1928 he moved to Harlem, and when he was later arrested for drug possession he insisted on being housed in the black section of the segregated prison. "My education was completed on The Stroll [in Harlem], and I became a Negro," he wrote.

Mezzrow's extreme position makes clear what the rest of the patrons were and what they were not. The black and tans were not processing the "negroization" of the 1920s. Those who leaped into the Charleston contest at the Sunset were no more interested in becoming Negroes than Marie Antoinette was interested in becoming a cow-milking peasant. Theirs was a bracketed fun—temporary, expensive, protected, and therapeutic. The primitive energy put at their disposal served two goals simultaneously: it helped the customers cut loose and it confirmed their superiority over blacks. Perhaps they recognized the desire to "stir the savage in us with a pleasant tickle," as one writer in the 1910s described the effects of black music. To paraphrase Erenberg, the embrace of liberating black culture at the Sunset did not represent a rejection of white values; rather, it was a reward for having arrived at a point so secure that a little loosening up did not threaten the established order. It was an "emotional holiday," as George Tichenor put it in 1930.

The challenge was to locate a balance between control and liberation, and the 1920s had to find its own way. White interest in black dance, which had been growing for many years, experienced a fresh rush of enthusiasm in the postwar revolt against Victorian conventions. The black and tans in Chicago—and the Sunset and Plantation were probably the most famous black and tans in the country in 1926—put this enterprise into high relief. On a personal level the typical Sunset patron might purchase the services of a black prostitute, but he did not advocate cross-racial marriage; on a cultural level, he enjoyed the Black Bottom but understood its place. In his celebrated book *The Seven Lively Arts*, Gilbert Seldes showed respect for African Americans and for jazz while keeping both at arm's length: "I say the Negro is not our salvation because with all my feelings for what he instinctively offers, for his desirable indifference to our set of conventions about emotional decency, I am on the side of civilization." Mezzrow, on the side of the Negroes, shows what had become possible on the radical fringe.

Across the turn of the twentieth century, black music moved from its traditional primitivist location, on the minstrel stage, to vaudeville, to black Broadway productions, and to cabarets. This movement involved as much discontinuity as continuity. On the minstrel stage the emphasis was on ridicule, farce, and parody, iconically defined by blackface makeup. The minstrel mask shifted the balance to the side of social control; personal liberation of the Freudian libido was less clearly in play, and we must force our imaginations in an effort to tease it out. In contrast, the business of the black and tans was to offer the correct dosage, individually defined according to the taste of each patron, of interior-savage tickling. It is not simply that the venues and audiences changed: the music now moved into a position where it could function more fully in a culture of risk taking, losing inhibition, slumming.

The 1920s black and tans document a transition to white attitudes about black entertainment that are still in place today. They were based on a vision, however contorted, of a shared humanity that made black culture not only fun but therapeutic. The case can be made that this same balance between control and liberation remained at the center of most white interest in jazz, continuing through the 1930s and hanging around until the advent of rock and roll, which then took over that function. Armstrong was a witness to the expansion of this phenomenon as he watched the young white alligators riding their bikes to Lincoln Gardens, and then the larger numbers of slumming whites at the Sunset.

And what primitive role (beyond demonstrating the Charleston) did he play at the Sunset? Certainly his scat vocal in *Heebie Jeebies* slaked primitivist thirst in a novel way during the summer of 1926; as we have seen, this performance pushed him into the center of a revue finale for the first time. More fundamental were blues gestures that indexed orality, the vitality of percussive attack, eccentric phrasing, improvisation, and the integration of music with movement. His year or so doubling at the Vendome Theater and the Sunset Café was based on a strange musical-social mixture: the qualities that made him a cutting-edge African-American modernist at the Vendome, playing for black audiences, were framed as fresh primitivist energy by wealthy whites at the Sunset. That contradiction was thoroughly part of the times. One of the main arguments of this book is that his most important asset at both venues was the one that often goes unremarked, even though it is absolutely foundational—his ability to invent a new melodic idiom that was, at its core, identified as black.

Sometime in the fall of 1926, Percy Venable wrote a comic tune for a new Sunset review, and he gave it the title *Big Butter and Egg Man from the West*. The song featured Armstrong as singer and trumpeter. Armstrong recorded it with the Hot Five on November 16. Though the other Hot Five musicians were not working at the Sunset, the two principals in the recording, Armstrong and vocalist Mae Alix, were the two for whom the piece was written. In the case of *Cornet Chop Suey*, Armstrong composed a display piece for himself that later found a home in the Dreamland Café and the Vendome Theater. With *Heebie Jeebies*, the local success of the Hot Five recording caused the Dreamland, Vendome, and Sunset to find a place for an established hit. With *Big Butter and Egg Man from the West* we can be certain, for the first time, of a sequence in which a piece found its way onto a Hot Five recording after it was worked out in a cabaret.

That sequence helps explain the success of Armstrong's famous and beloved trumpet solo.

Revues helped cabarets like the Sunset and Plantation distinguish themselves from less elite venues. Instead of a stream of unrelated performances, vaudeville style, a revue tied together the various acts with a little theme, the various performers appearing and reappearing in different roles. The organization of choreography and music was very loose, with everything coming to a climax in the finale, performed by the entire cast. A master of ceremonies told jokes and moved things along. Trumpeter Natty Dominique remembered the Sunset having four shows per night, with three shorter periods of social dancing in between the shows and one intermission per evening. "Jobs like the Plantation and the Sunset wore a trumpet player out," explained Preston Jackson. Oliver prolonged the use of his steadily deteriorating chops by having Bob Shoffner play the shows at the Plantation, while he came in only for the featured part of the social dance segment.

Light classics were often worked into revues, and since there was a new show every four weeks or so, the musicians had to be able to read. Stock arrangements were used, but musical arrangers were sometimes hired, too; Dave Peyton arranged for the Plantation, for example, and he wrote difficult music. The reading demands tripped up more than a few of the New Orleanians. Drummer Paul Barbarin played for social dancing at the Plantation, but he couldn't keep up with the revue, so George Smith was brought in. At the Sunset Dickerson was meticulous and issued penalties for wrong notes. "What are you carrying that union card for if you can't read music?" he'd bark at an erring musician. "Get rid of it!"

The Sunset hired Venable to run their revues in early 1925 and he stayed on until March 1927. It was Venable's job to select the music, teach the chorus girls their routines, and coordinate everything with the music director. Rehearsals were squeezed into the busy seven-day-a-week performing schedule. "Opening night could be a real madhouse, the scariest thing you could want to see," remembered Hines. Venable was greatly admired. "One of the greatest producers I've ever seen," remembered Budd Johnson, "just like Ziegfeld would put on something, you know."

The best source for details of what a revue at the Sunset was like is the magazine *Heebie Jeebies* (and its continuation as the *Light and Heebie Jeebies*). The February 19, 1927, issue described a new revue called *Sunset Gaieties*, a "series of variety sketches with single numbers supported by a chorus of ten 'Dancing Dimpled Darlings.'" From the moment conductor Earl Hines's baton "is first lifted until he wearily lets it drop four hours later, a fast pace is maintained which is contagious to both performers and patrons." The reviewer felt this was the Sunset's best show in two years, and he listed the goodies in this order: pretty girls, Class A dancing, good singing, striking and novel costumes. Carmen Lopez, "pretty and naïve," opened the show and introduced the entertainers. She was followed by Dotty McClendon, "a beautiful long-haired girl," singing *I'd Love to Have Somebody to Love Me*. Singer Slick White was well received, and so were dancers Chick Johnson, Sammy Vanderhurst, and Georgie Staten, the latter a "midget dancer." But the true stars of the evening were Buck and Bubbles and the "pachydermatous mistress of the splits," Mae Alix, with her gorgeous gowns. Buck and Bubbles performed for 45 minutes. The band, Louis Armstrong and His Stompers, got a mention at the end of the review, which drew attention not to Armstrong's stunning solos but to a number that they danced by themselves "in a spot which is probably the most humorous of the entire production." (This was probably the fat-thin-fat-thin Charleston routine mentioned earlier.)

In spite of this lack of musical notice, it is clear that the surge of interest in jazz at 35th and Calumet was lifting Dickerson's band and Armstrong into a spotlight not customarily directed at musicians. Peyton, whose job it was to write about music, confirmed this in July 1926: "the cause of the large nightly crowds [at the Sunset] is Carroll Dickerson's orchestra." Another (unidentified) reviewer explained that there was no doubt about who the star of the orchestra was: "With all due respect to Carroll and his ability, personality, etc., it must be stated as a fact that Louie is a million dollar asset to the band and many patrons who come there from all over town just to watch and listen to this marvel 'toot his tooter.'" When Venable decided to feature him in *Big Butter and Egg Man from the West* in the fall of 1926, he was responding to a six-month run of success that had begun the previous April.

*Big Butter and Egg Man* became Armstrong's next big hit, and he continued to perform it as late as 1933. The trumpet solo stands today as one of his most admired achievements of the 1920s. Its canonic status in jazz history is very high. Martin Williams included it on his important anthology *Smithsonian Collection of Classic Jazz*, and jazz scholar Gunther Schuller believed that "no composer, not even a Mozart or a Schubert, composed anything more natural and simply inspired" than the first eight-bar phrase.

My hunch is that Venable wrote *Big Butter and Egg Man* to fill the finale spot in his new revue. In July 1927 (as noted in Chapter 5) he placed *Heebie Jeebies* in that position for a revue called *Jazzmania*, with dancer Kid Lips and the entire cast complementing Armstrong. *Big Butter and Egg Man* features a duet for two singers, a woman and a man, who banter back and forth through their megaphones about the woman's need for a big butter and egg man (a more familiar term today would be sugar daddy) and the man's interest in meeting that need. To the comic duet Venable added Armstrong's trumpet and perhaps also the dance team Brown and McGraw. The natural place for such a full flush of cabaret variety would be the spectacle of the finale. The combined effect, delivered with humor, pep, variety, and a stunning density of eccentric tricks, must have been impressive. *Big Butter and Egg Man* was performed every night, seven days a week, for the duration of the revue. These are the conditions that led to the creation of Armstrong's famous solo, which musicians flocked to hear, memorizing every note.

The phrase "big butter and egg man" was one of those slang terms that help define an era. The concept was all about reckless spending and conspicuous consumption as a means to define personal success. The phrase was made famous by legendary nightclub hostess Texas Guinan at the El Fey Club in Manhattan, just a few blocks from the Roseland Ballroom, where Armstrong had worked with Henderson. Guinan liked to single out wealthy men in the audience and taunt them into spending sprees. After one man gave out $50 bills to the dancers and bought everyone in the house a drink, she called him to center stage and introduced him: "Folks, here's a live one, a buyer, a good guy, a sport of the old school—encourage him!" In the logic of the roaring twenties, everybody won in this scenario: the big man benefited from the attention and enhancement of his status, his date benefited from the riches wasted on her, and the cabaret and its employees skipped away with a pile of money. A genuine big butter and egg man could put out as much as $1,000 in a single night.

Venable's clever idea, then, was to write a comic finale that celebrated cabaret culture. Tex Guinan invited the big butter and egg man to center stage because he was indeed at the center of the whole cabaret enterprise. He was a model for other cabaret patrons. More than a few who walked through the Sunset's front door were buying a little piece of this concept, even if they couldn't match the standards of the biggest spender in their midst. This was the scene Venable playfully invoked in his new song.

Danny Barker said that Mae Alix was a "superstar" in Chicago. She certainly performed a lot in the most expensive venues, not just in Chicago but in New York City, too. Earl Hines remembered Armstrong being smitten by her and choking on his lines during the first performance of their duet. According to Hines, Alix "used to put her arms around him, look at him, and sing, 'I need a big butter and egg man,' he would stand there and almost melt, and everybody in the band would get up and shout, 'Hold it Louis! Hold it!'"

On the recording, Armstrong boasts about his high-note playing, which had become an easily identifiable marker of his greatness. He jokes that he will buy "all the pretty things" she thinks she needs, "as long as I can keep this cornet up to my mouth." The skit includes an unspoken racial dimension, for part of the humor came from having the dark-skinned cornetist acting the part of a big butter and egg man, who was, unquestionably, white in the popular imagination. It was a cross-racial role that derived instant humor from the dramatic play of opposites, just like his cross-dressing skit at the Vendome and just like his performance at the Sunset, also in the fall of 1926, of Venable's song *Irish Black Bottom Stomp*—"Well I was born in Ireland," he sang with a little chuckle. Having the white-looking Alix and the dark-skinned Armstrong act out courtship roles took the racial fun to a more risqué level.

Kid Lips, five-foot master of the backward, skating knee drop, helped fill out the *Heebie Jeebies* finale in Venable's July revue, and the husband-and-wife dance team known as Brown and McGraw was called upon to put *Big Butter and Egg Man from the West* into rapid motion. This was at least the second appearance for Herbert Brown and Naomi McGraw at the Sunset. Hines described this couple from New Orleans: "she was very cute and he was a handsome little fellow . . . they were both short but he had sharp uniforms and she was well developed and always wore a pretty dress." Like virtually all cabaret dancers, they spiced up their act with comedy and singing.

The problem with researching dance in the 1920s is severe lack of documentation. Imagine how crippled our understanding of music would be if we did not have the vast legacy of commercial recordings: that is precisely the situation we face in studying African-American cabaret dancers. There is no video footage that would reveal with precision what the dancing of Buck and Bubbles, Kid Lips, and Brown and McGraw was actually like. Verbal descriptions are helpful, and so is later video, but style was changing rapidly, with as much competitive innovation in professional dancing as there was in jazz.

In spite of these obstacles, musicologist Brian Harker has demonstrated how thoroughly mixed dance and music were at the cabarets, and he has done so with special focus on Armstrong, Brown and McGraw, and *Big Butter*. Brown was an innovative tap dancer who worked on rhythmic variety and flash as a way to distinguish himself from traditional tap, exemplified by the famous Bill Bojangles Robinson. Like Armstrong and other entertainers, he was pushing the limits of speed. Brown and McGraw packed their routines with an impressive density of activity. *Variety* described "a million twists and turns, grimaces and floor fol-de-rol plus the time step, which clicks all the way." The duo was promoted as the world's greatest eccentric dancers, with emphasis on rhythmic complexity.[61] All of this suggests compatibility with the trumpet style Armstrong was working out in 1926.

The background for kinetic-sonic synergy in the cabarets was the African-American vernacular tradition of the Deep South. Little is known about the early experience of Brown and McGraw in New Orleans, but we know that Armstrong was raised in an environment that took for granted the complete synthesis of music with movement of the body. It was almost impossible to conceive of one without the other. That was how he was taught in church, where bodies swayed in synchrony with congregational singing, on the streets, where the second line performed a kind of ring shout behind funky marching bands, and in dance halls. Even when people gathered close to the bandstand in Chicago to listen to the jazz concert king, they must have articulated their engagement with at least some slight movement of the body.

It's not surprising, then, to discover musical-kinetic synergy at the highest professional levels. Of course, professional dancing was always accompanied by music, typically by drummers who made creative use of various accessories. The task demanded perfect timing and strong concentration. "Shows are the hardest thing to play, especially for toe dances," explained Pops Foster. "They're counting beats all the time, and the musicians got to be following the music very close. . . . If he misses, the whole thing looks silly." The dancers set the tempo and the musicians followed, playing softly enough that the taps could be heard.

In the mid-1920s a tradition of trumpet players accompanying professional dance acts was gaining a little bit of momentum. The key event happened on Broadway in the fall of 1924, with the great dancer-comedian Johnny Hudgins accompanied by none other than Joe Smith, Armstrong's New York rival. Hudgins pantomimed a song, moving his lips but not making a sound, while Smith played wah-wah trumpet. The pantomime was followed straight away by a coordinated dance, Smith matching a note to every one of Hudgins's steps. At the Sunset, Armstrong stepped off the bandstand to do something similar with Brown and McGraw, and he used Venable's *Big Butter and Egg Man from the West.*

Earl Hines said that Brown and McGraw "had a riff they used that later became very popular with big bands. It used to go *bomp-bomp-bomp-bu-bomp, bomp-bomp-bomp-bu-bomp,* and Louis used to take his trumpet and do it right with them." "Every step they made I put the notes to it," explained Armstrong. His quick mind and nimble fingers had found a new outlet, the effect similar to the surprisingly synchronized cornet breaks with Oliver at Lincoln Gardens. Armstrong "made Brown and McGraw one of the most famous dance acts in Chicago at that time," according to Doc Cheatham. The act was so successful that when the two dancers left the Sunset

*Bubber Miley and Roger Pryor Dodge, 1931 (Roger Pryor Dodge Collection, courtesy of Pryor Dodge)*

to tour, they had an arranger write out what Armstrong was playing so that another trumpet player could take his place, wherever they went.[62] "Louis gained a lot of popularity from doing that thing with Brown and McGraw," remembered Hines, and then he added, "of course that was his heart," making it clear that Armstrong's professional standard at this time, as later, was to pour everything he had into every performance.

Like *Heebie Jeebies* before and like *Ain't Misbehavin'* a few years later, *Big Butter* was a comic vocal. These were his three biggest hits of the 1920s. Today we value his eccentric trumpet solos much more than his singing from this period, but for mainstream taste of the time jazz instrumentalists were small potatoes compared with singers.[63] Nevertheless, it is also clear that the trumpet chorus on *Big Butter* played a role in his growing popularity. From now on, choruses like this would become more and more central to his identity as an entertainer. *Big Butter and Egg Man from the West* was the first recording he made that features him in a vocal and also includes a trumpet solo that he performed regularly—indeed, it was probably the first time this happened for any musician during this period. Venable combined the two in his revue, and this must have seemed like a fairly obvious thing to try in the fall of 1926.

One clear inference from this set of circumstances bears emphasis: the famous trumpet solo from the November recording was not improvised. Commentators have marveled at the miracle of Armstrong improvising melodic gems that rival the best of Mozart and Schubert, but in fact he was just as much a planning composer as those two were.

The first phase of Armstrong's modern achievement, which reaches a crystallized moment of excellence with this solo, is all about the insertion of a composed chorus into a preexistent piece. *Cornet Chop Suey* was conceived differently: it was written out on paper in a reach for the rewards of sheet-music publication. Nevertheless, it was an important step along the way, for it shows him working out carefully made choruses, which is precisely what he did with *Big Butter*. Now the final product is simply kept in his head, with no intention of notation. The strong advantage to that was the ability to make performer-centered details of melodic nuance, including eccentric rhythm and blues phrasing, part of the conception. His expanding sense of melodic style could now be based even more directly on the orally based vernacular of New Orleans.

In New Orleans, too, solos and collective improvisation were planned, rehearsed, and improved over time, while no one thought of notation.[64] "Even back in the old days it was like that," Armstrong said in a 1966 interview, "when everybody was supposed to be improvising. Who knows who's improvising?"

His solo for *Chimes Blues* conforms to current notions of a melodic lead, with none of the excitement and richness of the fixed and variable model. *Cornet Chop Suey* represents a step in that direction within the limitation of what can be notated; the challenge he faced is evident in the mistakes in rhythmic notation in the lead sheet that was mailed to Washington, D.C., for copyright. In the second half of the 1920s, he inserted non-notated choruses into composed pieces. Notating them for copyright was no longer part of the plan. They simply had too much of the dense and varied complexity that he had been experimenting with since his departure from Oliver and was now bringing under control. If notating *Cornet Chop Suey* was a struggle, he just would have chuckled at the idea of notating his solo for *Big Butter and Egg Man.*

In New York City Armstrong had been finding ways to bring rhythmic complexity into his solos. He refined his approach with greater clarity in *Muskrat Ramble* and *Oriental Strut.* By the fall of 1926 the idea of composing melodies by ear and keeping them in his head, rather than thinking about what he could wrestle into notation, must have seemed like the obvious way to go. Besides, the copyright project wasn't going anywhere. It must have been clear by now that he was not going to publish the next *St. Louis Blues* or *Alexander's Ragtime Band.* Meanwhile, Venable was giving him a bigger spotlight. Armstrong did not stop writing tunes for copyright, but from now that would no longer be his creative priority. His special choruses could not harvest the rewards of a notated tune that hit the jackpot, but between the Sunset, the Vendome, and the Hot Five series he was being rewarded handsomely enough.

The chiseled perfection of *Big Butter and Egg Man* came from working on it night after night, like a sculptor fussing over a chunk of marble. Armstrong changed the history of jazz solos by composing rather than improvising. He knew the difference, and so did his New Orleanian colleagues, who relentlessly heaped scorn on bebop improvisation in the 1940s, calling it Chinese music, playing routines, music that musicians play for themselves and not for the public, modern slop, catcalls, and a gang of hogs crying for corn. The idea of putting a jam session before the public was simply incomprehensible to them.

As for the relationship of Armstrong's breakthrough solo to Brown and McGraw's dance steps, I find it difficult to imagine him learning much about rhythm from anyone in 1926. The lack of documented detail makes it hard to say anything with certainty, but dance rhythms seem to have been simpler than the rhythms of this solo. Earl Hines described the relationship as one of Armstrong adding a melody to the dancers' simple riffs, and Cheatham said plainly that "their act was nothing without a trumpet." His famous solo probably had little to do with the music he played for their dance: these were independent creations, made for different purposes, performed at different times and with different results. Nevertheless, the idea that he was inspired by and in competition with dancers brings us closer to the internal dynamics of the cabarets. Given the integration of body movement with music in the African-American vernacular, it is not surprising to see parallels at the highest professional levels, with Armstrong and the Brown and McGraw duo both experimenting with density, variety, and rhythmically vigorous activity at the Sunset Café. It is easy to believe that if dancers were going to dazzle the audience with eccentric figures, one after the other, he was prepared to do them one better.

What about the first phrase of Armstrong's solo, which reminded Schuller of Mozart and Schubert? Critic André Hodeir found it "impossible to imagine anything more sober and balanced." The phrase is beautifully conceived, but instead of relating it to standards outside the tradition, I find it more revealing to locate it in the stream of melodic exploration Armstrong had been pursuing during the previous two years. This phrase is actually a paraphrase of Venable's melody, which we can identify from Mae Alix's vocal rendition in the opening chorus, as shown in Example 6.1.

From Venable's tune Armstrong extracts a single pitch, which he places at the top of three upwards arpeggiations of the "one" chord (or something close to that; there are subtle and important adjustments). In Chapter 4 we noted his experiments with this kind of radical reduction, a technique Bessie Smith often used, for example, in *St. Louis Blues*. Oliver's *Dipper Mouth Blues* solo is not a paraphrase, but it is close to this phrase from *Big Butter* in its simplicity and use of repetition. The benefit Smith and Oliver get from this kind of simplification is this: it is a way to shift emphasis away from melodic

Example 6.1   Big Butter and Egg Man (*After Anderson 2007, 122*)

Example 6.2    Chimes Blues (*After Anderson 2007, 184*)

contour and toward the nuances of blues phrasing. Armstrong uses melodic reduction for a different purpose.

The most telling comparison of the first phrase of *Big Butter* may be with the first phrase of his solo for *Chimes Blues* (Example 6.2).

The phrases are of different lengths, but the similarities are striking.[65] In each case Armstrong finds a way to hold a little melodic idea—let's call it a riff—steady through three chord changes, with only slight alterations. The riffs are based on chordal arpeggiations. He is thinking carefully about the chords, yet he is not obsessed with harmonic accuracy: continuity of the riff through the chord changes is more important to him than complete harmonic precision. In each solo, a contrasting idea follows the triple statements.

The conceptions are similar, yet *Chimes Blues* has never inspired comparisons with Mozart and Schubert. Why is the first phrase of *Big Butter and Egg Man* so superior? The answer leads us directly into the heart of Armstrong's mature style.

First, notice the subtle changes in rhythm that mark the three statements of the riff in *Big Butter and Egg Man*. Pushes and pulls against the regular pulse keep the line from settling into synchrony with the fixed foundation. Armstrong has things both ways: it is easy to hear the repetition and easy to hear the variety. This had not been part of his thinking in the spring of 1923, but by the fall of 1926 variety had become central to his concept of a solo. The principle conditions the entire chorus for *Big Butter and Egg Man*.

Second, consider Armstrong's deepening interest in musical logic. Thanks to the triple repetition of the rising riff in *Big Butter and Egg Man*, the arrival of the high F in measure 6 sounds like a completion of the upward trajectory; the arrival is then answered by a balancing descent. The high F is the main pitch of the piece, making it stronger still, and it initiates yet another (now descending) arpeggiation of the main chord of the piece. The "one" chord is the basis for the entire phrase. This is strong musical logic indeed—

strong to the point of being overdone. A phrase like this could easily flop into banality.

What saves it is the fact that the high-note climax and the subsequent arpeggiation come too early. Doubly early, in fact. The chordal accompaniment—that is, the "fixed" level of harmonic rhythm in regular groupings of four beats, eight beats, and eight-measure phrases—arrives in predictable, periodic fashion on the F chord at measure 7. But the solo arrives on this chord a measure ahead of time, creating a harmonic clash against the foundation. The other thing that makes the high note feel like it has come too early is that each of the triple riffs begin on beat three, creating a pattern that is broken by the sudden leap to high F on the second half of beat one. Now we can understand the utility of his overdone musical logic: it draws attention to the out-of-phase early arrival and helps justify the radical clash of harmonies. Harmony, melodic design, and rhythm work together toward the same end.

Armstrong used harmony in the same anticipatory way in *Mandy* (December 1924) and *Muskrat Ramble* (February 1926); now he strengthens the conception with melodic design that governs the entire phrase. Harmonic dislocations like this account for some of the most distinguishing features of jazz. During the 1930s the practice got extended through substitute chords, and in bebop it was intensified further still. These harmonic dislocations rest on the fixed and variable model. They simultaneously provide a connection to the ground harmony while also stretching that connection, pulling the variable line away from its foundation without severing the tie. It is the same process that happens all the time on a purely rhythmic level.

The third detail that contributes to the success of the first phrase of *Big Butter and Egg Man* is the use of two intervals, specifically the ninth and sixth. Paraphrasing Venable's melody, Armstrong discovers the pitch A, which Venable treated (in measures 3–5) as a nonchordal tone that must resolve. Armstrong's solo features the A *without* the resolution: in measure 3 the pitch hovers on top of a G7 chord, forming an unstable ninth above the root of the chord, and in measure 5 it's on top of a C7 chord, forming the sixth. He is drawn to ninths and sixths because they occupy an uncertain middle ground that is neither fully consonant nor fully dissonant. Seizing this in-between status, he finds a way to extend the fixed and variable model. The sixth and the ninth float above the foundational harmony, detached from it but not fully severed, adding richness to the phrase. His clever strategy integrates melodic design, rhythm, and harmony, all working toward the same effect—the effect of the fixed and variable model.[66]

The phrase succeeds on three levels that were most important to his evolving conception of style in the fall of 1926: it is memorable; it highlights variety; and it offers a fresh, compelling version of the fixed and variable model. With Schubert and Mozart he shares the first concern; the second was a staple of cabaret culture; the third was part of the vernacular splendor he had been immersed in since childhood. The coordination of all three put him in a class by himself. Armstrong could only have developed this stylistic model by ear. *Chimes Blues* was compatible with notatable visions of the melodic lead, but no one would have given the slightest thought to notating this solo. His admirers understood that they were witness to an ear-playing virtuoso who was taking the African-American musical vernacular to a completely new place.

## *Potato Head Blues* and Stop Time: "Strictly Negro"

While Armstrong may have benefited from competition with dancers at the Sunset, an even greater spur came from his former mentor, who was working across the street. In most narratives of Armstrong's life Oliver tends to drop out after 1924, but that is a mistake. From March 1926 through March 1927, Oliver was producing thriving and vigorous jazz, even while he struggled with serious gum problems that limited his performance. Oliver's achievement during these 12 months undoubtedly stimulated this wonderfully productive period of Armstrong's career.

The Plantation Café staged elaborate revues, just as the Sunset did. Yet there are signs that the Plantation may have conceded a sliver of superiority in this area to its neighbor. Dickerson's orchestra had 12 musicians, Joe Oliver's Dixieland Syncopators only 10. At the Sunset Venable was a well-publicized force running revues, but there is less information about those at the Plantation, where Paul Barbarin played for the dance segments of the evening only, with a different drummer brought in for the revue; Oliver apparently did the same thing.

The Plantation's emphasis on the dance segments may have been part of a strategy to craft an image on the far edge of the uncivilized wing of the spectrum of African-American entertainment. "People preferred dancing to seeing shows," remembered trumpeter Bob Shoffner, and Oliver's hard-driving cornet was the key. Oliver's band used written music for the revues, but head arrangements and collective improvisation for the social dancing. "Dixieland is a style of music that makes people happy and want to dance," said Shoffner, explaining the choice of styles. The throbbing primitive heat at the Plantation—"loud, wailing and pulsating," as *Variety* described it— was a draw: "Whites from everywhere crowd this place to hear Joe do his stuff, as only he can do," wrote Peyton in October 1926.

During social dancing Oliver could keep a single number going 30 or 40 minutes, opening up a leisurely stretch of improvisatory creativity. Shoffner said that expansions like this helped him and the other band members generate musical ideas that were later turned into compositions. Armstrong and many other musicians admired Oliver's ability to invent, which was steadily documented through a series of recording sessions: two numbers in March 1926, two in April, three in May, three in July, and four in September; another five came in April 1927, before he quit Chicago for New York City. This run included *Snag It* and *Doctor Jazz*, two of his best-known pieces.

The two cabarets were so close to one another, and the two New Orleanian principals had each internalized the tradition of cutting contests so deeply, that it would have been impossible to avoid direct competition. The musicians regularly walked across the street to visit each other's bandstands. Oliver popped in one night and dashed off a phrase from *Snag It*; as he turned around and headed for the door, he called out over his shoulder, daring the Sunset trumpeters to try and play it. "I can play it alright, but I run out of gas," Armstrong confessed to Natty Dominique. We know that Oliver and Armstrong both featured slow drags in the dance segments, which gave them a chance to demonstrate their skill with slow blues. Armstrong performed Jelly Roll Morton's *Wild Man Blues* (recorded with Johnny

*Louis Armstrong's Sunset Stompers (University of Chicago)*

Dodd's Black Bottom Stompers in April 1927 and then, at a slower tempo, with the Hot Seven in May) at the Sunset in this way. He played it so slowly that Earl Hines made a show of going out to the kitchen to eat a steak, returning before the solo was finished.

*Wild Man Blues* is something of a throwback with its many breaks, recalling the good old days with the Oliver band. Armstrong devours the breaks with so much enthusiasm that it is easy to imagine him hurling them across 35th Street as answers to Oliver's challenge. The performance may also be taken as a measure of how far Armstrong had come with his melodic experiments. In Chapter 4 we noticed him adding breaklike material to his solos, mixed with simpler embellishments and straight presentations of a tune. *Wild Man Blues* is marked by an effortless flow between melody, embellishment, fill-ins, and breaks.

The solo also documents a breathtaking breakthrough. There is a sense of drama here that, if not unprecedented, is very fresh. Perhaps the slower tempo for the Hot Seven recording (relative to the Dodds ensemble's tempo a month before) inspired him, or perhaps he had simply grown more relaxed with the tune. His emotional intensity is right in step with New Orleans tradition, and the principle of variety is also evident. But what is new is how those two values put together lead him to a loud and sudden, vibrato-filled and stretched-out high note around two-thirds of the way into his chorus (CD 1:13). After this anything can happen. The usual variety in filigree, blue-note figurations, pace, and range unfolds in a more highly charged atmosphere. This is not the drama of opera, certainly, and it is only partly related to the "colored folks' opera" of Ma Rainey and Bessie Smith. It is really a matter of Armstrong's own sense of drama as it is now emerging from well-developed principles of how to construct a solo, which in this case stretches out for two minutes.

An even more magnificent outpouring, apparently, was crafted to go along with Noel Coward's *Poor Little Rich Girl*, which became a feature for Armstrong during the dance sets. He never recorded the piece, no doubt because of OKeh's policy of avoiding royalty payments whenever possible and selecting repertory accordingly. But we know that it was one of his outstanding numbers. Several reports describe him extending his solo for 20 or 25 choruses. The band supplied minor theatrics by walking off the stand, leaving him in the spotlight for his choruses and returning as his solo swelled to an exciting climax. "I have *never* heard anything like it," insisted Bud Freeman. Venable worked the tune into a revue and used it as the basis for the fat-thin-fat-thin Charleston routine. Cross-fertilization between dance set and revue must have been much more common than we know.

A hapless Johnny Dunn, whom Perry Bradford identified as "the first hot cornet man in the recording field," naïvely wandered into this glorious atmosphere one evening. Four years older than Armstrong, Dunn, from Memphis, had established a solid career with W. C. Handy and Mamie Smith before forming his own band. Known for double-time effects and wah-wah, the well-dressed Dunn had a huge and commanding presence; he liked to flash around large wads of bills. One night he entered the Sunset with his entourage and demanded that Armstrong yield his horn. In one version of the story, Dunn stumbled embarrassingly while trying to negotiate an unfamiliar key. In another, the two of them took turns dueling with set solos, Armstrong dishing out *Poor Little Rich Girl*. "Every time he played a new one [chorus]," said Hines, "he just kept going higher and higher." Dunn slithered away in shame.

If Armstrong was focused on keeping up with Oliver during 1926, by early 1927 he seems to have arrived at a place where he could relax. By this time it seems that Oliver's lip was rapidly declining. A cryptic report in the *Light and Heebie Jeebies* implies serious dissatisfaction with Oliver's playing.[67] On tour that spring and eventually in New York City, it was clear to his musicians that he was crippled by the gum disease known as pyorrhea. Armstrong's comment that he started to "take Joe Oliver's crowds away" may refer to the first months of 1927. He gently asked Oliver if there was anything he could do for him. The Sunset erected a billboard describing Armstrong as the "World's Greatest Trumpet Player," which must have embarrassed him, at least slightly. In April the Plantation burned to the ground, and Oliver was in New York by May. He apparently tried to get Armstrong to come with him, but Armstrong declined, citing the lack of a firm job offer.

His growing success must have made the idea of leaving seem ridiculous. "Luis [*sic*] Armstrong and his hot Recording Rhythmasters are keeping patrons on their toes [at the Sunset]," wrote the *Light* on January 8, 1927. This notice is the earliest documentation of him taking over the Sunset band, which would be known more commonly as "Louis Armstrong's Sunset Stompers." Dickerson was fired sometime between October 1926 and January 1927. He was a good musician, though crippled by stage fright and a problem with alcohol. He was resilient enough to quickly organize another band, which he called Carroll Dickerson's Syncopators. He got the idea of hiring out Warwick Hall every Sunday afternoon and charging admission for dances. The arrangement must have been profitable since it continued for many months; it established a precedent that Armstrong himself would follow a year later.

Also in January the Sunset came up with a promotion night, handing out a free recording of *Big Butter and Egg Man from the West* to all ladies. Bill Bojangles Robinson stopped by and heard Armstrong perform *Heebie Jeebies*, which inspired him to incorporate the piece into his own act. Armstrong recognized that leading a band was not for him, and even though he was nominally the leader, Hines did the conducting and rehearsing and worked with Venable. "Earl Hines smiles continuously while directing," reported a reviewer.[68]

Against Oliver's hard-driving freak music Armstrong put his dense, flashy, and increasingly well-organized solos, the two of them standing in dueling spotlights across the street from one another. In the spring of 1927 Armstrong was clearly the winner. High-rolling slumming at 35th and Calumet turned out to be a strong stimulus for him. He was riding a swelling wave of interest in his kind of music, a moment when white Chicago was leading the rest of white America in its patronage of jazz that was strongly connected to the African-American vernacular. The combination of good patronage and high-level competition helped lift him into a creative phase that produced a series of remarkable solos that are documented in six different recording sessions yielding performances of 14 pieces during the week of May 7–14, 1927.

These recordings were made by a new formation called the Hot Seven. The expansion was spurred by a new technology: OKeh now made electronic recording available to him for the first time, which made it easy to add tuba (Pete Briggs) and drums (Baby Dodds). Ory must have had something else going on, for he was replaced by Honoré Dutrey, who had no trouble keeping up with the core of Armstrong, Lillian, Johnny St. Cyr, and Johnny Dodds. The important exception to this list was the May 9 recording of Jelly Roll Morton's *Chicago Breakdown*, which was credited to "Louis Armstrong and His Hot Seven Featuring Earl Hines," but was actually performed by a ten-member band drawn straight from the Sunset and excluding the Dodds brothers, Lillian, and St. Cyr.

*Chicago Breakdown* is the first sonic documentation of the Sunset bands Armstrong played with. For *Big Butter and Egg Man from the West*, he and Mae Alix sang and played as they did at the Sunset, but there is no reason to believe that any other part of the recorded performance was connected to the cabaret. *Chicago Breakdown* is a full-blown arrangement, carefully worked out and played by the musicians who were performing it every night. The piece was a vehicle for Hines, who almost certainly put the arrangement together. The relaxed tempo and the four-beat emphasis inspire attractive ensemble work and well-designed solos, especially from Hines and Armstrong, the latter with two

*Earl Hines, Grand Terrace Café, Chicago 1928 (The Frank Driggs Collection at Jazz at Lincoln Center)*

lovely solos that include some of the same gestures and strategies that shaped his solo for *Potato Head Blues*, recorded the following day.

*Alligator Crawl*, recorded on May 10, was composed by Fats Waller, who had been kicking around town for a couple of months, making guest appearances on organ at the Metropolitan Theater and taking on a regular position at the Vendome before he was chased down by the police for domestic problems and sent back to New York City. Waller stopped by the Sunset one evening and was invited to sit in. Punch Miller, a trumpeter from New Orleans, happened to be there and asked to sit in also. "Man you can't play this music," Armstrong told him. "Everybody is reading in this band." But Miller insisted. His fumbling over his part inspired a quip from Waller at piano that musicians were still quoting years later: "What key are you struggling in? Turn the page!"

There is nothing to suggest that the arrangement for *Alligator Crawl*—or the arrangements for any of the other recordings from May—had the kind of direct connection to the Sunset that is evident in *Chicago Breakdown*. The opposite seems to have been the case, first, because the Hot Seven sidemen were not employed there; second, because there is really nothing about the arrangements that indicates that kind of planning and familiarity; and third, because these performances are right in step with previous Hot Five recordings. In other words, most of the musical product was generated in the studio, by studio musicians hired for the day. "All we needed was a lead sheet and everybody would figure out his own part," said Kid Ory about the OKeh sessions generally, and it is easy to believe that this is what happened with *Alligator Crawl*, *Gully Low Blues*, and most of the other May recordings. Commentators often project too much on these performances, exaggerating their overall importance or putting too much attention on the sidemen. The sidemen need no apologies for work that does not match Armstrong's lofty standards. They were simply picking up a little lagniappe on a sleepy morning after a long night at work.

But Armstrong's solos are a different matter. It seems likely that some, though not all, were well planned out. For example, he recorded two takes of *Gully Low Blues* (one given the title *S.O.L. Blues*), and the solos are close enough to one another and also interesting enough to suggest that they were made in advance. The main solo is confidently delivered and nicely designed (it anticipates in some details the central solo for *West End Blues*). Thus, even if, as seems likely, the arrangement was created in the recording studio, Armstrong's solo was not. Armstrong's solos on *Gully Low Blues* and *Wild Man Blues* made a big impression on sixteen-year-old Roy Eldridge, who would become one of the great trumpet soloists of the swing era.

*Willie the Weeper* is another good candidate for thorough planning. A number of bands recorded the tune in spring and summer 1927, suggesting that a stock arrangement had recently been published. This was probably a repertory piece at both the Plantation (Oliver recorded *Willie the Weeper* in April) and the Sunset; it is easy to believe that the solo Armstrong played for the Hot Seven recording reflected what he was playing at the cabaret (and/or at the Vendome, lest we forget that he continued to perform there through mid-April 1927). Similar arguments could be made about *Weary Blues*, *Wild Man Blues* (already documented at the Sunset), and *Mel-*

*ancholy Blues*, all recorded by Johnny Dodds's Black Bottom Stompers in April, with Armstrong and Hines sitting in.[69]

In other words, it seems to me that the reason we get so many superior solos from May 1927 is that they were shaped by many nights of planning and refinement at the Sunset and the Vendome. The solos were lifted out of those settings and placed in a funkier, lower-paid, underrehearsed, and more southern-sounding musical context. The OKeh series was still conceived for the race market in the Deep South and still made on the cheap, with no expectation of rehearsals and with reliance on Armstrong to carry sales.

It is notable that Armstrong sings on only four of the twelve titles from May. This is a huge change. In the Hot Five recordings from the previous November he sang on four of six titles, in June 1926 five of eight. Moreover, the May 1927 singing all took place in the final two (of six) sessions; it is as if OKeh suddenly realized that he had recorded a week of instrumental tunes and they intervened, insisting that the group patch together a few vocal numbers.

This suggests an increased emphasis at the Sunset, and perhaps the Vendome, too, on Armstrong's special choruses for trumpet. The development of his special choruses was distinctly marked with *Cornet Chop Suey* in early 1926 and with *Big Butter and Egg Man from the West* that fall. It is possible that, by the spring of 1927, his creative efforts in this form became the main draw. Sure, he still sang *Heebie Jeebies* and *Big Butter*. But the implication of the May sessions is that he was now recognized as a trumpeter with extraordinary creative gifts. His promotion to leader of the Sunset Orchestra may have been tied to this. His trumpet playing had been admired from the moment he arrived in Chicago in late 1925, but without the expectation that a specially designed chorus would be the centerpiece of his performance, the thing that drew people in the door. Now that was precisely what customers were looking for.

Since January, Armstrong had been leading the band and calling the tunes, so why not include his own compositions that featured his special choruses? Though we can only speculate, it seems likely that this was the case with the gem of the May sessions, the much-loved *Potato Head Blues*. Ralph Ellison considered the central solo to be a classic demonstration of African-American elegance, and virtually all commentators rank it among the most important solos in jazz history.

This is a stop-time solo, with reduced accompaniment. We have already seen stop time used in *Cornet Chop Suey*, *Oriental Strut*, and some of the 1923 Oliver performances. Earlier documentation of stop time includes two rags by Scott Joplin, *The Ragtime Dance* (1906) and *Stoptime Rag* (1910). In *Potato Head Blues* the stop-time accompaniment is more sparse than usual, with a chord sounding on the first beat of every other measure (that is, one chord sounding every eight beats). The format gave rise to one of Armstrong's most stunning achievements, so it is worth thinking about its historical and cultural associations. The place to start is with the tradition of using stop time to accompany dance displays.

Composer and political activist James Weldon Johnson wrote in 1926 that "for generations, 'buck and wing' and 'stop time' dances, which are strictly Negro, have been familiar to American theatre audiences."[70] The reduced accompaniment of stop time did more than simply place a spotlight on the dancer: it opened up a space for rhythmic complexity, since the dance rhythms now stood alone. That is certainly how the practice was used in professional dancing. In this way, stop-time format and rhythmically complex dancing became strongly associated with African-American vernacular culture.

Those who knew this "strictly Negro" tradition would have automatically made the association when they heard a stop-time jazz solo. And there could not have been many situations where the connection was more obvious than the Sunset Café in 1927. Stop time undoubtedly helped define the Sunset as a place for the full and vigorous flow of African-American vernacular dance, taken to a high professional level. Reviews make it clear that this kind of entertainment was just as popular as jazz was.

The first few months of 1927 brought an especially rich stretch of professional dancing to the Sunset. Brown and McGraw were there in early May or a bit before. The dance team of Eddie Rector and Ralph Cooper started in January. And the team known as Buck (Ford L. Washington) and Bubbles (John William Sublett) started a successful run in mid-February in a new show called *Sunset Gaieties*. They were "the stars of the evening," along with Mae Alix, wrote the *Light and Heebie Jeebies*. "For forty-five minutes Mr. Buck and Mr. Bubbles were compelled to respond to their wild admirers," the reviewer reported. A display ad for the Sunset saved the biggest typeface for the two of them. "They did things with their feet that looked impossible," remembered Hines.

Armstrong shared much with this sparkling pair. Bubbles's specialty was tap dancing, but he could do a lot more than that. "I would do more or less a song when dancing, the melody," he remembered. "I could do *Ole Man River* dancing and you could almost tell the words, the way I danced it. . . . The personality for singing, the personality for acting, the personality for dancing, that's three of them." And then he added this broader social reflection: "Do you understand what a Negro has to do to be recognized? You've got to be twice as great, twice as good." Armstrong and Buck, the pianist, became close friends, often hanging out together when Buck was in town during Armstrong's last couple of years in Chicago and later in New York City.

Bubbles was good at inventing steps, just as Oliver and Armstrong were good at inventing tunes and breaks. He avoided repetition in his routines, thinking that this made it difficult for others to copy him. He developed a strategy of identifying his best steps, based on audience reaction, and stringing them together, one after the other, to create a dense and varied presentation. Stop time, with its regular punctuations, may have encouraged this approach. In *Potato Head Blues* one hears breaks and figures that Armstrong used earlier (in *Tears*, for example), suggesting something similar, though certainly not so deliberate. It's unlikely that the relationship of Armstrong's solo to Bubbles's taps was one of rhythmic equivalence, but he certainly could have been engaged in good-natured competition with Bubbles and the other dancers, noting their successes and responding in his own way, with observable similarities between the two art forms in variety, density, rhythmic complexity, and originality.

With Armstrong performing a spectacular stop-time solo just after or before Bubbles performed a spectacular stop-time dance, the connection would have been hard to miss. It is a connection that would have come naturally at 35th and Calumet, which appealed to white interest in black vernacular culture taken to the highest professional level. Armstrong's solo for *Potato Head Blues* is his musical answer to a stop-time dance. The association may even have been so obvious that virtually all jazz solos in stop time were heard in this way—strictly Negro, even when played by a white musician.

Comparison between his stop-time solos for *Cornet Chop Suey* and *Potato Head Blues* highlights how far he had traveled in three years. The earlier solo, written on the back steps of Lillian's apartment, has the feeling of a melody conceived for notation, unfolding in two-bar units with variety in melodic contour but less in rhythm. The melody is not too far from Scott Joplin's style; compare the first four measures of the A strain of *The Entertainer*, for example, with the first four measures of Armstrong's stop-time solo.

But the stop-time solo for *Potato Head Blues* is hardly a melody that would have been worked out in (or for) notation. Two-bar modules are much less predictable. The dazzling melodic flow is in constant motion with its vigorous twists and turns, varied in contour and rhythmic profile. It is full of the weird, crazy, and eccentric figures that were now Armstrong's bread and butter.

*Potato Head Blues* is, on one level, a demonstration of how to work with varied figures of syncopation and additive rhythm, each module completely different from the previous one. At times the melody breaks out of the two-bar box to soar across the regular signposts and take variable tension to a higher level. Armstrong manipulates harmony in ways similar to *Mandy, Muskrat Ramble*, and *Big Butter and Egg Man*; the stop-time format encouraged him to go further with this technique.

Breaks, snakes, and fill-ins provide the basic musical material for the solo, the kind of playing he was good at in his teenage years and that Oliver encouraged him to put aside in favor of a solid lead. As we know from *Wild Man Blues*, he had not lost interest in breaks, and in the spring of 1927 he published two books, *125 Jazz Breaks for Trumpet* and *Fifty Hot Choruses for Cornet*. These were commercial efforts that might also be taken as creative exercises focused on a small and versatile unit of melody. Armstrong "penned in book form some of his eccentric styles of playing," wrote Peyton. "The Melrose Music Company is publishing both books for Louis, who is all smiles nowadays riding around in his brand new Hupmobile Eight." Melrose cut him a check to the tune of $600. *Potato Head Blues* demonstrates perfection of a musical idiom that was not beholden to the normative features of popular song and instead emerged directly from the vernacular vigor of New Orleans, pushed forward by the strictly Negro tradition of stop time and dancers like Herbert Brown, Eddie Rector, and John Bubbles.

Yet this stop-time solo is not simply a series of breaks and fill-ins strung together. Its appeal also comes from melodic design. "Louie [and other great jazz soloists] played and sang . . . with melodic continuity," explained trumpeter Jimmy Maxwell. "If you look at their solos, although they're playing a lot of notes and there is a melodic line, there is a continuity in the direction." White musicians Esten Spurrier and Bix Beiderbecke, admiring Armstrong from ringside seats at the Sunset, came up with the phrase "correlated chorus" to describe his practice of relating phrases one to the other. Armstrong's solo is full of goal-directed details, which are sometimes interrupted before coming to late arrivals and sometimes redirected through coy misses. Bud Freeman referred to a "conversation of notes" that Armstrong and Lester Young were both good at. *Potato Head Blues* is so well known that it is easy to forget how radical it must have sounded in 1927, with absence of familiar markers of popular-song coherence and with intensification of the fixed and variable model. ("Telling a story" was another way of speaking about this, though it is easy to be misled by this metaphor.)[71] Fleeting patterns, correlations, and conversations of notes helped bridge the gap and added to the solo's complexity and appeal. Like a Bach partita or a Brahms intermezzo, one can listen again and again and still get satisfaction from hearing the line unfold.

The solo is full of surprises that somehow seem to fit, including one of the bluest notes ever heard, a D-flat resolving to the seventh of a D7 chord. Trumpeter Humphrey Lyttleton admired how, in the second two-bar module, the line "stalks majestically across the beat." The playfulness of the varied modules, the brilliant tone—now transmitted through electronic recording—and Armstrong's superb precision give the solo a shining aura. If the sudden high note in *Wild Man Blues* was a dramatic charge, the high-note excursions in *Potato Head Blues* are outbursts of joy. In the first half of the solo G is the high note, yielding to A in the second part and finally C at the end, each ripping leap upwards carrying more emotional impact. He has figured out how to make the stratospheric stunts of the Vendome serve an artistic purpose.

The high value placed on invention was part of the reception of this solo. Armstrong "is always trying to create some form and style in jazz playing that will bring him distinction," wrote Peyton in June 1927. "This he has accomplished." At 35th and Calumet Oliver was spinning out new tunes and solos, Bubbles was stringing together new steps, and Armstrong was also responding to the demand to make it new. Much later, *Esquire* magazine solicited his comments on *Potato Head Blues*, and his thoughts quickly turned to his mentor: "There never was a creator of cornet any greater than Joe Oliver." Oliver's understanding of composition may have been among the last lessons he imparted to the only student he ever took on.

Armstrong's creative solos were now featured at the Sunset, and for some they must have been the main draw. Certainly they were for the alligators. Beiderbecke studied his solos and formed his own style; he may be considered Armstrong's first great disciple. One of the two-bar modules from *Potato Head Blues* provided Hoagy Carmichael with a distinctive melodic turn for *Star Dust* (measures 3–4 of Carmichael's chorus; the tune was first recorded in October 1927 and demonstrated at the Sunset while Armstrong and Hines were there). "I'm going out tonight," Carmichael wrote to his wife Dorothy in the early 1930s. "Louis Armstrong is in town. He's going to show me purty notes. And so I'll learn some more about composing."

The significance of the Sunset for Armstrong was, first, that it was a center of primitivist interest in jazz, and, second, that it put him in the middle of an intensely competitive and creative environment. He responded as he always did to a good job: he gave everything he had. The slumming white subculture made its demands, but a lot of the details were left to him. His first modern style was nurtured by the dual patronage of upwardly mobile blacks and slumming whites, a contradiction that was thoroughly part of the times. It is hard to imagine that he hesitated even for a second to simply accept it.

## Modern Melody

"I'm just an old melody man," Armstrong once quipped. That is a good way to think about both his creative achievement and his historical importance. The melody man composed some 80 tunes that he sent to Washington, D.C., for copyright, but those melodies (with the stunning exception of *Cornet Chop Suey*) were largely inconsequential. Instead, his genius found a better outlet in the "special choruses" that he created by ear and inserted into performances. The goal was not to chase after financial reward through copyright but to hold his place in the spotlight that was shining on him ever more brightly and yielding bigger and bigger financial rewards. If we focus on the special chorus as a *melodic* achievement, we can begin to think of him not only as a great jazz musician and a great entertainer but as one of the great melodists in American music. "All them beautiful notes," he once said. "My livin' and my life."

Several semantic and conceptual obstacles stand in the way of thinking about Armstrong as a great melodist. First, a long history in writings about jazz sets rhythm in opposition to melody. This way of speaking misses the point that melody always includes rhythm—you cannot have melody without it. It is true that his solos are often rhythmically sophisticated, but there are advantages to reframing the discussion in terms of melody. A similar problem arises with harmony. Did he think harmonically when he was improvising, or does it even matter? The fact is that his solo lines are always shaped by harmony, even when he contradicts the given chord of the accompaniment. Without an analytical approach that views melody as including both rhythm and harmony, we will always come up short in assessing his creative achievement, left to fall back on the old quip, "If you have to ask what jazz is, you'll never know."

It's not that being a great melodist is the only thing that matters in jazz. Driving energy, lovely tone quality, and stunning virtuosity were all as important in the 1920s as they are today. The solo as melody isn't the only thing, but Armstrong made it one of the main things. Furthermore, he did so in response to racial dynamics of the time. To think of what makes his melodies special is to examine on a deep level the impact of race on his music.

As we have seen, Armstrong's creativity is primarily shaped by the workings of the fixed and variable model. It is this that distinguishes his first modern phase, that made it the basis for developments in jazz solo playing for the next two decades, and that infuses it with a vernacular sensibility that was audibly indebted to Africa. We have had plenty of chances to note the importance of variety and density, which many soloists cultivated without folding them into a coherent vision of the fixed and variable model, at least not in the same way that Armstrong did. This priority made him the central figure in the history of the jazz solo and connected his style to an African way of organizing music.

Dave Peyton wrote, in February 1926, that the "style of jazz the public has gone wild about is that which Paul Whiteman, Vincent Lopez, the late James Reese Europe, Leroy Smith and Fletcher Henderson's orchestras are putting out—beautiful melodies, garnished with eccentric figurations propelled by strict rhythm." That is a felicitous description and surely an accurate gauge of taste for at least one segment of the population. Armstrong's melodic achievement was very different. It was built from the stuff of breaks, fill-ins, and obbligatos, with eccentric figuration in the foreground, no longer the garnish but the main dish. This was how he created an alternative standard of melodic beauty.

What made his breakthrough possible was the nearly universal sense of periodicity that shaped popular songs and dance of the period, the absolutely predictable flow of time through symmetries of beats, half-measures (two beats), measures (four beats), two-measure groups (eight beats), four-measure half-phrases (16 beats), and eight-measure phrases (32 beats). Harmonic rhythm (the rate of change of chords) contributed in a fundamental way. The ear naturally follows this ground level of fixed activity and uses it to understand events on the variable level. In West African music, periodicity is achieved through ostinato patterns that can reach considerable complexity all by themselves. Though the patterns in 1920s popular songs are simpler, periodicity can be achieved on the different levels of temporal organization just described. This rigid layering is what allowed Armstrong to bring the fixed and variable model, ubiquitous as it must have been throughout the Deep South when he was growing up, to the theaters and cabarets of Chicago.

The periodic organization is obvious, but the implications of thinking about Armstrong's solos in these terms are less so: the solo, the variable level of activity, is *completely dependent on the fixed foundation for its meaning*. On one level this is easy to accept. After all, popular songs of the day also depend on the easily perceivable and completely regular plan of the typical eight-bar phrase. But Armstrong's solos have a very different relationship to this foundation. The regular unfolding of the ground level allows him to build a variable line that moves in and out of phase. Interest comes from the rich relationship between the two levels of activity.

Without agreement, the variable line sounds chaotic. Agreement comes from precise synchronization with the beat (Miles Davis on Armstrong: "He plays on the beat and you can't miss when you play on the beat") and precise control of chords (Willie "The Lion" Smith: "[Armstrong] works like a horse, knows how to pace himself, and knows his chord construction"). The variable line creates tension against the foundation by moving in conflict at the local level of the beat (syncopations, delayed phrasing), at the level of the measure (additive rhythm, irregular, "eccentric" accents), and at the broader level of two-measure groups (fill-ins across the bar and phrase, harmonic anticipation).

Armstrong does all of this more extensively than others do it, with greater melodic clarity and greater intensity, and he extends the model to include harmony, thus duplicating in pitch relations what others articulated only through rhythm. His solos unfold with confidence and with various features of design in a continuous pas de deux with the foundation. His terms of expression insist on having things both ways: the variable line moves in and out of phase against, is connected to and detached from, is synchronized with and in tension with the fixed level. This is what it means to say that the meaning of his solo is determined by its relationship to the ground.

His melody is in *dialogue* with the fixed level. There was tremendous emphasis on musical dialogue in the music of his youth. Music as a form of dialogue is a fundamental feature of traditional West African music, and it was a primary feature of collective improvisation from New Orleans, with the lead musician in conversation with the rhythm section and with the musicians playing second. This conception is very different from the relationship of a popular tune to its harmonic plan. It must have seemed natural to Armstrong to think in terms of musical dialogue.

Less predictable, perhaps, was his move toward greater abstraction. The terms of expression for his first modern style insist that social interaction is less important than the wit and compositional skill of the soloist. Dialogue in church was open-ended and radically egalitarian, with everyone invited to contribute to the creative event. In the professional dance bands of uptown New Orleans, roles for collective improvisation were more firmly predetermined yet there was still a group dynamic involved. Appreciative audiences at the Vendome must have recognized that Armstrong was now shifting the balance in an abstract direction. Indeed, this became part of his virtuosity. The stop-time solo for *Potato Head Blues* is as one-sided as it can be: Armstrong is overwhelmingly active, while the accompaniment is reduced to one beat out of every eight. One might be tempted to diminish the importance of the fixed level or dismiss the dialogic model altogether, but that would be a mistake. Even when it is as slender as it is here, the fixed level still anchors perception by providing a consistent marker in the time line and the basic harmonies. Without it, the listener would lack these organizing references and the musical event would become something completely different.

In Chapter 2 we looked at Armstrong's interest in harmony and his mastery of it by the time he composed *Weatherbird Rag* and recorded *Chimes Blues*. Western-style "common practice" tonality, a system of organizing chords in a logical way, had little relevance for music made by slaves on the plantations of the Deep South. The ecstatic styles of congregational singing and the funky street bands in Armstrong's neighborhood put much more value on dialogue, texture, and expressive markers than chords. This music was rough, untutored, and primitive from a Western point of view, and the two musical systems appeared completely at odds with one another.

Taking a global view, we could locate Armstrong's achievement in a long-lasting, multidimensional encounter between two great musical systems, one based on the fixed and variable model of the African diaspora, and the other on common-practice tonality from Europe. A degree of simplification was necessary to combine them, getting rid of some details while reassessing the basic functions of others. It is an understatement to say that this encounter opened up many possibilities. It largely accounts for the tremendous explosion of twentieth-century creativity in the vernacular traditions of African American music, each inevitably touched by various social and musical trajectories.

As argued in Chapter 5, Armstrong could not have achieved high status at places like the Vendome Theater and with critics like Dave Peyton if he had not mastered harmony so thoroughly—and, by extension, he would not have ultimately reached white audiences to the degree that he did in the early 1930s. Harmony was important, but even more important was how he subordinated it to the fixed and variable model. This was what made possible the audacious—at least by the standards of popular songs in the 1920s—gesture at the end of the first phrase of *Big Butter and Egg Man* (measures 6–7 in Example 6.1), and it is how critical assessment of Armstrong's solos should be guided.

With harmony subordinated, further innovations were possible, including the use of "extended" tones (dangling sixths and ninths), anticipations, and substitute chords (which became important for the next generation, led by players like Art Tatum and Coleman Hawkins). Armstrong was precise enough about harmony to satisfy the ears of Peyton, who disdained "discordant jazz," but also loose enough to be innovative. The unspoken balance alluded to here would remain active in jazz solo playing through bebop and beyond, as musicians discovered ways of using harmony that were very different from its use in the popular songs they performed every day. By using harmony, first, to establish a connection between fixed and variable, and, second, to find ways of detaching variable from fixed, they transformed common-practice tonality in ways that had never been imagined before. An educated observer might have believed, in the early twentieth century, that common-practice tonality was a dead system, with nowhere left to develop. Armstrong and his followers proved that wrong.

It is the priority of the fixed and variable model that defines Armstrong's creative breakthrough in the mid-1920s as an intensification of West African musical values, and it is important to note that things did not have to turn out this way. It was hardly inevitable that the future of jazz would be shaped by someone so thoroughly tutored in the vernacular from New Orleans. Joe Smith, Armstrong's rival in New York, was content to lay his phrases down in neat modules of two and four and deck them out with eccentric garnishes, chasing after the style of beautiful melody that was working so well for Whiteman, Lopez, and Henderson. So were many white players; Frank Teschemacher, for example, a prominent saxophonist in the 1920s, developed an influential style that was similar in this regard. What Armstrong accomplished was modern in the mid-1920s, and it still sounds modern today, in spite of the many redefinitions of jazz that have come and gone over the decades. The reason is the integrity of his commitment to the fixed and variable model, which commands the attention of many musicians still working at the highest creative levels. When this is no longer the case, Armstrong will no longer sound modern.

*What will jazz melody be like?* Joplin showed how vigorous the fixed and variable model could be through written composition, with the scope of conflict between the two levels limited to the measure. Based on that, he contributed a highly influential model for ragtime. Armstrong took the material of breaks, fill-ins, and obbligatos, derived from the ear-playing tradition of New Orleans, combined that with creative manipulation of harmony, and offered an equally influential model for jazz—to be more precise, he offered a modern, African-American melodic model for jazz.

Like virtually all jazz models during the 1920s, his was inevitably touched by concepts about race. It is often difficult to work with the ideological impact of race at the level of musical detail, but in this case the broad outlines are clear enough. Armstrong's embrace of the fixed and variable model had something to do with confidence in his own heritage, just as Joplin's more conservative position, 20 years earlier, had something to do with his interest in matching the Eurocentric classics at their own game. What seemed right for Armstrong in the 1920s needed adjusting a few years later, in the early 1930s, when he moved into white markets on a national level. Indeed, one amazing thing about him was his ability to adapt. *Hello Dolly* has little to do with the fixed and variable model, and that is no accident.

His modern jazz was rewarded handsomely at the Vendome and the Sunset, for different but connected reasons. Both audiences were interested in black music. Both would have understood what Duke Ellington meant when he said that the only definition of jazz he could come up with was "music with an African foundation which came out of an American environment."[72] The intensity of Armstrong's commitment to the fixed and variable model, and the obvious location of his creativity in the realm of the ear-playing vernacular, set off his music from white styles and made it perfect for serving a modern black identity. He did not simply *sustain* a connection to the African past, he *intensified* that connection. He offered at an unspoken, musical level a new way of being black that was assertive, intelligent, and accomplished. He offered more than simple "heat," and he clearly distinguished his modern black identity from similar identities formed through blues, ragtime, and the beautiful melody of Henderson and his peers.

This is one of the reasons why analysis of musical style matters. A precise investigation of musical style can demonstrate how music accomplishes cultural work at a very deep level, deep enough for long-lasting results. In the present case, stylistic analysis helps expose the inadequacy of talk about jazz as a mongrelized, multicultural, Creole hybrid, the kind of lame analysis that is so common nowadays and so dramatically at odds with the experience of someone like Armstrong, who grew up during a time and at a place where it was dangerous to be intelligent, assertive, and black, where to be called mongrel was no compliment. Music probably mattered more than we will ever know.

Armstrong's daunting mix of imaginative variety, ear-catching conversations of notes, and forbidding density was unified by his rigorous commitment to the fixed and variable model. "How high a goal can an artist set himself and get agreement on from people?" asked pianist Chick Corea many decades later. "That's a broad question and defines a very high purpose for the artist." In the mid-1920s Armstrong was leading the way, in spite of the fact that people didn't initially understand what he was doing. His drive toward a new and modern musical invention made him the greatest master of melody in the African-American tradition since Joplin. And it made him the central figure in the history of jazz solo playing.

# SEVEN

# "Some Kind of a God"

A musician in Chicago in the early twenties were treated
and respected just like some kind of a God.

—Louis Armstrong

The summer of 1927 was busy and fruitful. On June 4, Armstrong and his orchestra appeared at the Vincennes Hotel, East 36th Street, and on June 9 they played for a victory celebration for mayor "Big Bill" Thompson at the Café de Paris (in the former Lincoln Gardens). Also in June a young Cab Calloway, described as a "juvenile tenor," joined the Sunset regulars as a singer alongside Adelaide Hall, Jazz Lips Richardson, Brown and McGraw, and Mae Alix. On July 4 Armstrong took his orchestra out again, this time for a breakfast dance at the venue known as Alvin Dansant.

But that performance was done under duress. About three months earlier Lillian had traveled to New Orleans to bring Armstrong's mother back to Chicago, so that they could care for her in what would be her final illness. May Ann died on July 6, 1927, at the house her son and his wife owned, at 421 East 44th Street.[73] She was forty-four years old. The funeral was conducted by Rev. Prentice A. Bryson, pastor of Carter Temple CME church, and she was buried in Lincoln Cemetery.

Armstrong did not record for posterity the thoughts that went through his mind at this moment. Perhaps he remembered May Ann's vigilance in looking out for him from the moment he reunited with her, around age five, until she saw him off at the train station in August 1922. Perhaps he remembered attending church and learning to sing there, or his first parade with the Waif's Home band, when

276

## Mrs. Mary Armstrong
### (Mother of Louis Armstrong)

Mrs. Mary Armstrong, mother of Louis Armstrong the famed jazz cornetist, died Wednesday morning at the home of her son, 421 E. 44th Street, Chicago.

Mrs. Armstrong was born in New Orleans, Louisanna, 44 years ago. She had been ill for more than six months and had been in Chicago with her son for the past three months. Besides her son and daughter-in-law, Mr. and Mrs. Louis Armstrong, she leaves a daughter in Florida, and a divorced husband, Willie Armstrong, in New Orleans.

The funeral of Mrs. Armstrong was held Friday from the chapel of Kersey, McGowan and Morsell, undertakers. Rev. Bryson officiated. Interment in Lincoln Cemetery.

Death notice for May Ann (Courtesy of the Louis Armstrong House Museum)

somebody ran to wake her so she could witness his triumphant debut on lead cornet. She had taught him tricks for keeping good health, how to hold his liquor, how to stay out of trouble, how to defend himself. She advised him to be himself, not put on airs, not envy others, be comfortable with how he looked, and stay true to the culture he grew up with. "Oh what a sweet and helpful girl May Ann was," he remembered 40 years later. "Only tears I ever shed was when I saw 'em lower her into that ground."

But the show must go on. In July he scored another triumph when he took his orchestra for a two-week engagement into the Black Hawk Grill in downtown Chicago, an establishment for whites inside the Loop. The initial offer paid for only six musicians, but Armstrong insisted that all twelve members of his orchestra be hired or no deal.

In the summer of 1927 Percy Venable returned to the Sunset, having left the previous March. Several rich descriptions of revues put together by Venable for the fall enhance our sense of what the entertainment was like. The September show was called *Sunset Affairs*. Cab Calloway had moved into the emcee position and was singing solos with chorus backing. Gorgeous gowns were supplied by Juliette Costumers. The opening number was based on the popular song *Hallelujah* (composed by Leo Robin and Vincent Youmans, 1927), performed by the trio Three Classy Misses, consisting of soubrette Eloise Bennett, pianist Irene Edie, and violinist Katherine Perry, who had become Earl Hines's girlfriend. They were joined by the "boy Caruso," Slick White; the "world's greatest freak clarinetist," Wilton Crawley; and blackface comedian and pantomimist Jimmy Ferguson. Blanche Calloway, with "personality a plenty," sang *I Need Lovin'* (Henry Creamer and Jimmy Johnson, 1926).

The finale earned high praise. "Some weeks ago, a musical critic stated that Louis Armstrong's Sunset Stompers could not play classics," explained a reviewer, "but now this statement can be refuted." The orchestra did well with *Poet and Peasant* and *A Hunt in a Black Forest* by George Voelker Jr., for which Venable choreographed challenging steps for the eight chorines, followed by the principals. The reviewer admired how "the two numbers are used in their straight composition forms, and the dance steps have been arranged to fit the variated tempo. . . . The principals are appreciated in their diversified presentations, but without the chorines and Louis Armstrong's orchestra, they would be blanks." Armstrong was still singing and playing *Heebie Jeebies* and *Big Butter and Egg Man*. He also contributed a version of *Underneath the Moon* (Vincent Plunkett and Jeff Branen, 1920), which, according to the *Courier*, was "a scream."

In late August Fletcher Henderson's Orchestra came to town for a six-week gig at the Congress Hotel. Peyton devoted several columns to the significance of a race orchestra cracking this "aristocratic hotel," commenting only indirectly on the sadness of African Americans not being able to enter the venue: "I only hope that opportunity will allow one night for our group in Chicago to hear this wonderful orchestra before they leave," he wrote. His wish came true and a concert was given on September 17 at the Coliseum, complete with a "battle" between Henderson and Armstrong's Sunset Stompers. Tommy Ladnier—"a good blues man, good shout man, but he didn't have no range," according to Armstrong—from New Orleans was now Henderson's featured hot trumpet soloist. An unmarked clipping quipped that Armstrong and Jimmy Harris, trombonist for Henderson, were seen "stopping the milkman, then drinking milk and eating doughnuts while sitting on Louis's front steps" one morning. Armstrong hosted a party for the Henderson men and their "choice chicks" at his house, and 30 years later he still remembered how someone walked off with his personal copy of the OKeh *Chicago Breakdown.*

In September Armstrong doubled up again with a theater job, now at the newly built Metropolitan Theater at 4644 South Parkway, directly across the street from the Savoy Ballroom, under construction and scheduled to open in late November. The Metropolitan was in vigorous competition with the Vendome and doing very well. Clarence Jones's Orchestra took over the pit band in mid-September. Jones had a reputation as a fine pianist who was often heard on radio broadcasts, and his eleven-member group now placed him in the lead of theater orchestras. The Vendome was in rapid decline; by the following April, Peyton would lament the new low of four musicians in the orchestra.

Even though Armstrong was now a star musician, receiving more attention than ever, he still performed comedy. He described a skit he did at the Metropolitan during intermission with Zutty Singleton, an old friend from New Orleans who was now playing drums with Jones. Singleton dressed up as "one of those real loud and rough gals," in a short skirt with a pillow tied to his back, while Armstrong wore rags with his hat askew. Armstrong started the act singing *I Ain't Goin' to Play No Second Fiddle* from the stage, while Singleton, as his gal, walked down the center aisle, loudly interrupting the song and eliciting tremendous laughter from the audience.

The band performed its nightly feature from the stage. The lights went out and an image was flashed on the lowered screen, introducing the band director and conductor. For their Metropolitan debut conductor Jimmy Bell announced a new number called *Butterfly Fantasy* that Jones had arranged, a medley of tunes based on the popular song *Just Like a Butterfly That's Caught in the Rain* (Harry MacGregor Woods and Mort Dixon, 1927). The medley began with a theme from Puccini's *Madama Butterfly* and then flowed into a violin solo followed by a trombone solo; the trombonist then put his instrument down and sang *Just Like a Butterfly* with his lyric tenor voice. Then Armstrong stood up and was applauded wildly before he even played a note. "Well now comes the big punch," wrote Peyton. "Louis Armstrong delivered the knockout wallop with that famous jazz version of his on the butterfly song. After this rendition the applause was deafening for at least 5 minutes." Flowers were strewn over the musicians. The band's hot specialty was an arrangement of *The Joker*, featuring Jones; as an encore the band repeated the tune, now adding Armstrong and "one of his freakish, high register breaks that brought the patrons to a howl." The key to this unit's winning combination, explained another reviewer, was the "nice, sweet arranging and playing of Clarence Jones, the 'freak' cornet playing of Louis Armstrong, and the 'Paul Ash' directing of Jimmy Bell."

In early November, the Paul Whiteman Orchestra arrived for a gig at the Chicago Theater, downtown in the Loop. Armstrong finished up late after the Sunset and then stayed up in order to see the morning show on Whiteman's first day. He enjoyed the performance of *From Monday On* and purchased the recording by Paul Whiteman and the Rhythm Boys. The program highlight at the Chicago Theater was Tchaikovsky's *1812 Overture*, with gun blasts, church bells, and sirens. This was the first time he heard Bix Beiderbecke playing in a large group, and he was impressed by how Beiderbecke's cornet projected through the noisy spectacle. "You take a man with a pure tone like Bix's and no matter how loud the other fellows may be blowing, that pure cornet or trumpet tone will cut through it all," he explained. He went backstage afterwards to greet Beiderbecke and a few of the other musicians, whom he knew from the Sunset Café.

Beiderbecke stopped by the Sunset every chance he had. Most jobs in the Loop and on the North Side usually finished at 1:00 a.m. or so, after which Beiderbecke and his colleagues headed for the South Side, took a seat, sat in with the band, and hung around after closing. "Bix used to start his journey to the end of the night after the places closed and he'd latch on to anybody who felt they could keep up with him—the brothers Dorsey, Ben Pollack, Joe Sullivan," remembered Hoagy Carmichael, who also said that Armstrong was Beiderbecke's idol. Several participants described late-night jam sessions after the doors were locked. Oliver might stop by and teasingly put a handkerchief over the valves of his cornet, disguising his fingering. "We sat around waiting to see if these guys were actually going to come up with something new or different," admitted Hines candidly. Armstrong, whose position could not have been more secure, was relaxed and jovial: "Bring in that load of coal," he used to say to drummer George Wettling when he saw him. Wingy Manone remembered how the "best jamming was on the blues."

In jazz histories, Beiderbecke and Armstrong are sometimes presented as a pair of binary opposites, each defining what the other wasn't. That representation is ultimately based on race, but the language used sometimes moves around a contrast between introvert and extrovert, even drifting close to a feminine-masculine polarity.[74] Beiderbecke doesn't play as high as Armstrong or as loudly, and he plays with less vibrato and smoother articulation. His melodic activity is not as dense or rhythmically vigorous. The atmosphere is reserved, laid back, lyrical, cool, by comparison.

But it is clear that Beiderbecke had absorbed some important lessons from the New Orleanians. References to Armstrong's style include occasional blue notes, upward rips, and eccentric patterning through irregularly placed accents. Especially important was the correlated chorus, though Beiderbecke had an independent sense of strong melodic design. "His intervals were so orderly, so indescribably right, like a line of poetry," said Max Kaminsky, but he could have easily been talking about Armstrong. His solo on *Singin' the Blues*, recorded in February 1927 with Frankie Trumbauer and His Orchestra, is one of his best known. There is something historically poetic about the recording of it midway between Armstrong's *Big Butter and Egg Man*, from the fall of 1926, and *Potato Head Blues* in the spring of 1927. The three creations, very different from each other in mood and design, stand as distinguished examples of what jazz solos could be at this time.

Beiderbecke owed something to Armstrong, but he also found his own way to become one of the great solo stylists. At the Sunset jam sessions he liked to play piano, too, and on one occasion he demonstrated on solo piano a new composition, *In a Mist*. He enjoyed classical music, especially the suave and harmonically sophisticated French impressionists. The extended harmonic palette of these composers had already been making its way into various types of American music; it found a direct path of entry into the Sunset Café through Beiderbecke. Mezzrow remembered him going on and on about classical music, "needling these kids with his skull busting classical jive." Beiderbecke became one of the truly tragic figures in jazz history. Severe alcoholism and shadowy sexual deviance, including pederasty and masochism, indicate a deeply troubled mind that he tried to deal with through alcohol and an overwhelming dedication to music. He died at age twenty-eight, in 1931.

In September 1927 and again in December, the Hot Five gathered for five separate recording sessions. The original five were now in place again, with the addition, in December, of guitarist Lonnie Johnson. The sessions generated nine different sides, three of which now stand among Armstrong's most famous performances.

From the September sessions came *Put 'Em Down Blues*, *Ory's Creole Trombone*, and *The Last Time*. *Ory's Creole Trombone* dated from the early days in New Orleans and features some splendid collective improvisation; the performance was almost certainly slapped together at the last minute. All of the September recordings—and, indeed, all of the December ones as well—conform to the repertorial policy that dominates the OKeh series: they were composed by local musicians who undoubtedly made a special deal with the company, signing away any claim to royalties.[75] Only one trumpet solo from September, from *Put 'Em Down Blues*, sounds to me like it could have been a special chorus, worked out for the Sunset and played many times, though *The Last Time* could easily have been a vocal feature for Armstrong at the cabaret.

The treasures came in December. Armstrong's playing on *Struttin' with Some Barbecue* is so superb—and so obviously planned, with density and variety, bluesyness and showiness—that we must assume it was regularly featured at the Sunset in the fall of 1927.[76] *Hotter Than That* was probably generated for the studio, but the magical synergy of Armstrong and Lonnie Johnson made the performance very special. *Savoy Blues* was composed by Ory, who had a job at the

Savoy Ballroom, two days before the recording session on December 13. Ory's piece inspired one of Armstrong's most delicate and poignant blues solos.

*Cornet Chop Suey, Potato Head Blues, Struttin' with Some Barbecue*—there was no shortage of food titles in the Hot Five series, as if Armstrong was rejoicing in a lifestyle where he no longer had to worry about where his next hot meal was going to come from. The title *Struttin' with Some Barbecue* is rich in implications. There are a number of stories about him and his friends going out for barbecue; Big Fat Mammy from Alabama was the name of one of their favorite places. Like *Gut Bucket Blues*, the title of this tune invokes an iconic dish from the plantation South, but "barbecue" was also slang for a woman. That usage was certainly in play here, since advertisements for the recording provocatively depict a black chef holding a knife in one hand and placing the other hand around the waist of a white woman, the two of them obviously enjoying the "juicy bit of fox trot HEAT!" provided by the recording. The word "struttin'" should not be overlooked, either. Cakewalk specialists were said to strut, and musicians spoke of "struttin' time" to indicate a tempo and/or rhythmic figure, as referenced in a number of other titles (for example, *Bogalousa Strut*, recorded by Sam Morgan's Jazz Band in October 1927). "Barbecue" and "struttin'" are thus in-group references to be picked up by southern blacks and their friends and relatives who had moved north.

Armstrong's brilliance shines in a well-coordinated performance that carries some hints of a preexisting arrangement, suggesting usage at the Sunset Cafe. To be sure, his trumpet carries all of these performances, but that is especially true here. The stunning stop-time solo is flawlessly executed and full of little eccentric conversations and correlated phrases that dart in and out of synchrony with the ground, while bluesy gestures come and go in a continuous sweep of melody. The climactic passage (around CD 2:02) shows off dexterity exercises he had learned at Kimball Hall and practiced with his wife. Bud Freeman held up this performance as an example of the "beautiful, graceful, powerful line" that set Armstrong apart.[77] The last chorus, with vigorous collective improvisation, is one of the true joys in music. Armstrong rises through the texture and then sails high above, slightly out of phase as if floating, effortlessly and confidently, like some kind of god sitting on top of a cloud.

Guitarist Lonnie Johnson was added to the regular group for December 10 and 13. If frequency of recordings and intensity of advertising are reliable indicators, Johnson, singing blues and accompanying himself on guitar, was an even bigger hit for OKeh than Armstrong. In the 1910s, Johnson made a living playing on the streets of New Orleans. He turned into a flashy guitarist; "Lonnie was the only guy we had around New Orleans who could play jazz guitar," said Pops Foster. His presence accounts for some lovely moments in *I'm Not Rough, Hotter Than That,* and *Savoy Blues.*

Armstrong said that it was OKeh's idea to add Johnson to the Hot Five mix. On Johnson's first day in the studio, the Hot Five greeted him with the familiar *I'm Not Rough,* another tune from the old days in New Orleans with lots of ensemble work. Johnson's impromptu collaboration was facilitated by the new electronic technology that OKeh had been using for the group since May: the microphone carried his dancing and bluesy single-string lines through the thick texture.

Armstrong immediately asked Ory to compose a piece for this group, and Ory responded with *Savoy Blues,* which the band recorded three days later. Armstrong said that he himself composed *Hotter Than That* (phonograph discs credit his wife). My guess is that this also took place during those interim days. Or perhaps he took a piece that was already made and thought about how to arrange it to feature Johnson. *Hotter Than That* was also grounded in New Orleans practice, since it was based on the harmonies of the widely known *Tiger Rag.*

In recent decades *Hotter Than That* has become one of the best-known recordings of the Hot Five series. One reason for that is the overflowing abundance of African-American vernacular practices. It is as if the New Orleanians decided to turn the piece into a vehicle for their hometown bag of heartfelt musical tricks—a stunning passage of polymetric tension, rigorous commitment to the fixed and variable model, microphone-aided scat, vehement attack, vocal inflections on the guitar, plaintive dialogue, timbral diversity, and, of course, the Crescent City specialty, collective improvisation. At the climactic center (CD 1:55) stands an out-of-tempo exchange between Armstrong and Johnson. The lengthy polymetric passage (CD 1:40) is shocking, with Johnson running his obbligato through the entire stretch of Armstrong's scat solo. Armstrong stunningly concludes the piece with a rocketing liftoff (CD 2:35), his trumpet rising magically out of a mushy trombone solo. In the final chorus he sits on top of the texture like a king on his throne, ripping off a dozen high C's.

*Hotter Than That* is justly famous today, but it was the flip side, *Savoy Blues*, that became the hit of these sessions after its release in late February 1928. In April, when Armstrong began working at the Savoy Ballroom, the piece became a featured number for him, often talked about in the press. The melody that Ory wrote for the first strain is in a style the New Orleanians sometimes described as "rinky dink," with a seesaw feeling intensified by the accompaniment. Usually, when I listen to the Hot Fives I am not bothered by the accompaniment, which is discreet enough to let Armstrong's splendor shine through. But on this recording I find myself imagining what the performance could have been without the oompah rhythms; there is also a problem of balance, with the guitar louder than Armstrong. The intrusive accompaniment makes clear the importance of the flat 4/4 that is more typical in the Hot Fives: the oompah fights with Armstrong's eccentric and unpredictable phrasing, rather than laying down a neutral platform for him to interact with freely.

The solo is lovely, nonetheless, softer and more delicate than most of his trumpet solos, and many listeners have heard great poignancy in it. The filigree is very traditional in some ways, with descending lines following the sawtooth archetype. Armstrong's solo dances gracefully through a mix of pastel added tones (sixths, sevenths, ninths), harmonic anticipations, and the ubiquitous one chord, all of it detaching the line from the fixed foundation. The rhythmic fluency of the line alternately presses forward and hesitates in subtly shifting patterns.

The melody is elusive yet orderly, detached yet controlled. It belongs to a tradition of blues playing that was delicate and subtle rather than powerful and showy. Until this point, Armstrong was not typically associated with this side of black experience—relaxed, reflective, and lyrical. I doubt that he ever played like this in cabarets.

Perhaps Lonnie Johnson was the inspiration, or, more prosaically, the possibilities were opened up by the microphone. Like *Struttin'* and *Hotter Than That*, the final chorus features an inspiring ascent into the high range.

On December 24, 1927, pianist Glover Compton wrote a letter from Paris to Dave Peyton, in care of the *Defender*, saying that he had just had a nice chat with the famous bandleader Paul Ash, also in Paris. The main topics of their conversation were Chicago, Peyton, and "Louie" Armstrong. With Armstrong, OKeh had an unmatchable soloist. But in 1927 there was an impressive amount of sophisticated jazz being recorded, not just by the leading black bands but also by white musicians whose music lessons at the Sunset Café and elsewhere were paying off. OKeh's decision to bring in Lonnie Johnson may reflect an awareness of the expanding field of competition. The Hot Five was designed to be funky and down home, but after two full years of recording there may have been a feeling that the regular formula was wearing thin. In any event, there were changes for the next go-around in June.

By December 3, 1927, Armstrong had left his job at the Metropolitan Theater, and he apparently had already left the Sunset as well. His only words on that were that "the old boss man [Joe Glaser, the manager] got tired of looking at us." Hines said that the Sunset closed down in 1927, putting them out of a job. In any event, they were both unemployed, except for the studio sessions with OKeh.

Initially, being out of work seems not to have bothered Armstrong. He was riding high as one of the most famous musicians on the South Side. Zutty Singleton was working at a place called Club Baghdad, at Cottage Grove and 64th Street, an area Peyton called the "highbrow district." Two large bands, one white and one black, alternated sets every evening. Armstrong took to stopping by every night to sit in with the black band for one number, performing *Big Butter and Egg Man* to great applause, then driving his friend Singleton home.

With brimming confidence, he, Hines, and Singleton decided to form what they called a "little corporation." Why not cut out the middlemen and reach for bigger paychecks? Lillian would be their manager. They booked a place called Warwick Hall, at 543 East 47th

Street, diagonally opposite the brand-new Savoy Ballroom. They brought in three other musicians and called themselves Louis Armstrong and His Hot Six. Carroll Dickerson had been doing something similar at Warwick Hall, playing on Sundays. Armstrong boldly signed a lease for one year.

"Man we didn't do nothing!" lamented Singleton. "It was a floperoo." The Savoy Ballroom, a beautiful and sparkling facility, was pouring lots of money into advertising, with full-page ads week after week in the *Light and Heebie Jeebies*.[78] The little corporation didn't

*Warwick Hall (Jelly Roll Morton Book Photographic Collection, MSS 508, F. 127, Williams Research Center, The Historic New Orleans Collection)*

stand a chance. By late December failure was obvious. Finally, the owners of the hall offered Armstrong a settlement on his one-year lease and he agreed to pay it off. "He was a long time paying," Singleton admitted.

Armstrong reasoned that the Hot Five series had made him popular, so the corporation planned a tour through eastern states organized by the Ike Dixon Amusement Company for the first week in January, with stops in Harrisburg, Martinsburg (West Virginia), Richmond, Norfolk, Newport News, and Wilmington; it is hard to know whether or not the tour actually came off.[79] They tooled around Chicago in a yellow Ford roadster they called "the covered wagon," but they couldn't afford to have it repaired. Not having enough money to fill the tank, they bought one gallon of gas at a time. They took gigs that paid as little as three dollars per person. "Things gotten so tough with us until fifteen cents looked like fifteen dollars," Armstrong remembered. They took comfort in their shared misery. "We were starving to death," insisted Hines. "I'll never forget, old Louis and I and Zutty Singleton were sticking together. If you wanted to hire one of us you had to hire all three of us."

Finally, a decent offer came in. Clarence Jones was now back at the Metropolitan Theater, and in mid-February Armstrong and Singleton joined his band. In mid-March, Jones took the entire unit over to the Vendome, the place that had provided Armstrong with such tremendous support for 18 months or so, ending in the spring of 1927. He was now the star once again. Jones worked up an arrangement of some "haunting melodies" that he called *A Trip Through Southland*, including a featured number for Armstrong on a tune called *Mississippi Mud* (James Cavanaugh and Harry Barris, 1927). But the Vendome was struggling, facing steep competition from the beautiful, 3,000-seat Regal Theater, which had opened in January right across the street from the Savoy. Four large venues, the Regal, the Savoy, the Metropolitan Theater, and Warwick Hall, now formed a cluster of entertainment around the corner of 47th Street and Vincennes, drawing crowds away from the old hubs at 31st and 35th Streets. On April 7, Peyton lamented the reduction of Clarence Jones's Orchestra at the Vendome to four pieces. "Our leaders should stop and think how long it takes to build a reputation and defend the

*Savoy Ballroom, Chicago, 1938 (The William Russell Photographic Collection, MSS 520 F. 59, Williams Research Center, The Historic New Orleans Collection)*

fruits of their labor by refusing to satisfy promoters who will not gamble a while," he grumbled.[80]

Carroll Dickerson, scheduled to begin work at the Savoy on Wednesday, April 11, approached Singleton and cleverly offered him a job if he could bring Armstrong along with him. There may have been bad feelings between Dickerson and Armstrong, as there certainly were between him and Hines, who said that Dickerson blamed him for the Sunset dismissal a year earlier. Hines apparently was in New York City at this moment, and when he got back to Chicago he was upset to find that Armstrong and Singleton had accepted a job without him, thus breaking their pact. "It's rough out here," Armstrong pleaded, "and I gotta make them payments on the house." On April 11, Armstrong started work at the Savoy, where he would enjoy tremendous success during the next ten months or so. As Red Saunders put it, "Armstrong at that time really took over."

The heavily funded Savoy had been going strong since opening the previous November. Its size was unprecedented for the South Side, and so was the elaborate decor, with high-polish maple floors with mahogany inserts and a triple subfloor to support the dancers. The checkroom accommodated 6,000 hats and coats. From the entrance on South Parkway it was 400 feet to the bandstand on the other side of the dance floor. The building housed a barbershop, beauty parlor, shoeshine stands, and an outdoor pavilion for dancing during warm weather. Boxing matches, basketball games, and various kinds of contests were hosted there. The payroll included chaperones, dance "hostesses," a house doctor, and a registered nurse. Ethel Waters performed during the inaugural week (though the *Defender* complained that it was difficult to hear her), Percy Venable was brought in to stage a revue, and Brown and McGraw stopped the show with eccentric dancing.

Like many large dance halls, the Savoy employed two bands every night. When Armstrong and Singleton joined Dickerson, they were complemented by Clarence Black's band. Dickerson's band was "more on the high spirit, peppy plan," reported a reviewer, and Black's "more of a subdued sweet music atmosphere, which gives the Savoy patrons all that they could expect in a ballroom." Armstrong immediately tilted public opinion toward Dickerson. Peyton praised his "cyclonic figures" that "stopped the ball"—given the image of Armstrong as a jazz concert king who inspired people to listen, this may have literally happened. Radio broadcasts streamed out nightly from 11:00 p.m. to midnight (extending until 1:00 a.m. on Saturdays and Sundays) over WCFL, "The Voice of Labor," reaching as far as Baltimore. In April 1928 the ballroom claimed attendance of 15,000 customers per week; patronage was overwhelmingly (and perhaps completely, most of the time) black.

One promotional article explained that it was Armstrong's renditions of *Some of These Days*, *Irish Fantasy*, and *Savoy Blues* that made him the "radio fan's delight." In a battle with McKinney's Cotton Pickers, guest artists from Detroit, Armstrong earned victory with the help of Dickerson's arrangement of Franz Liszt's *Liebestraum*. On another occasion Erskine Tate's band made a guest appearance. The climax of the evening was a performance by all three orchestras—Dickerson's, Black's, and Tate's—of *Savoy Blues*. Armstrong was featured, of course. "The crowd gathered around him and wildly cheered for more and more," Peyton reported. Perhaps this was the night pianist Arthur Hodes witnessed Armstrong being carried across the dance floor on the crowd's shoulders.

Thrills were put on pause in late April with the sudden death of Ollie Powers, age forty-one, whom Armstrong had first met in 1923, when Lillian trotted him around to the cabarets and showed him how to request a song from the very large tenor. Services were held at Liberty Congregational Church, with people standing in the aisles and spilling onto the sidewalk. Armstrong played a trumpet solo (unaccompanied, I assume)—Dvořák's melody from the slow movement of the *New World* Symphony, widely known as *Going Home*. This may have been done in the manner of a New Orleans funeral with music, such as Armstrong witnessed on a nearly daily basis throughout his youth: playing the melody straight, with no embellishments, bold and clear and confidant. Powers could not have asked for more.[81]

In early May some entrepreneurs lured Armstrong to St. Louis for a visit with the promise of $100 per night for two nights, plus expenses, to play with Floyd Campbell's Orchestra, "an unheard of figure to pay a colored musician for a gig in those days," according to Campbell. Local interest was undoubtedly fueled by radio broadcasts from Chicago. In June and July, Peyton started calling him "King Menelik," the late-nineteenth-century Ethiopian king who drove the Italians from his country, thereby becoming a hero to African Americans. It was a powerful analogy, made in the context of increasingly frequent white claims to jazz superiority. H. L. Mencken, for example, had argued a year before that "the best jazz of today is not composed by black men but by Jews: and I mean best in every sense. Why did the Negro composers wait for George Gershwin to do his 'Rhapsody in Blue'? Why, indeed, did they wait for Paul Whiteman to make jazz a serious matter?"

If jazz was going to be a contested area of racial supremacy, Peyton knew where to turn. He was not the most obvious candidate to defend Armstrong's music, being firmly placed in the note-reading camp; a defense of Fletcher Henderson along these lines would have come much more naturally to him. But Peyton must have understood that it was King Menelik, and not Henderson or Sammy Stewart or even Duke Ellington, who had redefined the terms of competition. Armstrong "slaughtered all of the ofay jazz demons appearing at the Savoy recently," he wrote in July ("ofay" being familiar African-American slang for whites, pig Latin for "foe"), fully aware that there were no white rivals to his kind of jazz anywhere in sight.

If we are wondering what Armstrong's weapon of choice for

the Savoy slaughter was, there is no better candidate than *West End Blues*, which was recorded on June 28, 1928.

Louis Armstrong and His Hot Five recorded eight new numbers in late June, with one more to follow on July 5. In spite of the band's name, there were now six musicians: Armstrong, Singleton, Mancy "Peck" Carr on banjo, Fred Robinson on trombone, and Jimmy Strong on clarinet and tenor sax were all drawn from Dickerson's Savoy unit, with Hines, apparently having reconciled with Armstrong and Singleton, joining on piano. Of the nine titles, *West End Blues* is the only one for which we have testimony confirming performance at the Savoy Ballroom.[82]

The slaughtering starts right away. Armstrong's opening state-ment—it has been called both a cadenza and a fanfare—is one of the most famous introductions in all of jazz, right alongside Duke Elling-ton's *Mood Indigo* and John Coltrane's *A Love Supreme*. Though there were several mild precedents in the Hot Five series, it is safe to say that no one had ever heard music quite like this before.

The introduction is analogous to a break (in fact, the last part of it closely resembles one of Armstrong's breaks from 1924), the brief musical eruptions that had long provided opportunity for African-American performers to assert an individual identity. Putting such a statement at the beginning and expanding it to 15 seconds makes the effect very different from a break, however. Armstrong's display of individual power reaches the level of a proclamation of military vic-tory, with a buglelike ascent, a bravura hold at the lofty peak, speed and extended range to communicate technical strength, precise and intricate passage work, brilliance of tone—it all comes across as a heraldic flourish appropriate to a battlefield, which is precisely what ancestors of the trumpet were invented to do.

Here is fresh articulation of the cultural distance Armstrong had traveled since his arrival in Chicago; by their identification with him, the dancers who carried him on their shoulders at the Savoy Ballroom came along with him. The 15-second introduction demonstrates mastery over both worlds—black and white. Few trumpeters could match his technical brilliance. Lillian said that the basic material for the introduction came from trumpet exercise books she and Louis had been drilling, a spectacular application of his lessons at Kimball

Hall in his efforts to improve himself and advance his position.[83] He has mastered white technique and made it his own.

The title of the piece alerted all New Orleanians in attendance to expect music that "really relates to us," as Milt Hinton put it. The West End was the last stop on the trolley line that transported people from downtown New Orleans out to Lake Ponchartrain. The location hosted a popular resort, a place to escape the summer heat. The music of African-American New Orleans is immediately recognizable in the fantastic bravura, the attitude Amiri Baraka called "brassy, broad and aggressively dramatic" that had been a central part of jazz all the way back to the famous Buddy Bolden. This begins with the percussive articulation of the startling first three notes.

That much, however, is not qualitatively different from the flashy bugle call that opens *Cornet Chop Suey*, the most direct antecedent. The wonder of the *West End Blues* introduction is that its character is so different from a straightforward military call or a display of finger-busting runs. Armstrong has infused this fanfare with the kind of musical expression he explored in *Savoy Blues*, that delicate, reflective energy now taking shape as a gesture designed to fill the Savoy Ballroom with breathtaking, majestic splendor.

As with *Savoy Blues*, he skillfully mixes hesitation, metric changes, acceleration, and rhythmic patterns that easily move in and out of an elastic flow of melody. The elasticity is not only rhythmic but harmonic: the phrase never settles into a single direction but is peppered with a series of small twists and turns that constantly shift direction. Rhythm and harmony thus work together to keep the sense of musical order in constant motion.

Traditional fanfares are not like this. They are designed to communicate stability and political strength, a position of social control that is seemingly eternal and beyond challenge. Armstrong aims instead for the supple quality of throbbing life itself, a feeling of movement where nothing is fixed and everything is dissolving into something else. His fanfare is all about the pliancy of blues, about a cultural attitude of relaxed detachment, a transcendence of the pain of any worldly situation that is beyond one's control.

Virtuosity, precision, strength, and Eurocentric credentials combined with fluidity of motion, elegance, and blues-based detachment—

*Carroll Dickerson Orchestra, Savoy Ballroom (The Frank Driggs Collection)*

all of it, put together, makes Armstrong one of a kind. There was, literally, no one else on the planet who could play like this. There was no room for doubting that it was the African-American vernacular that was being represented. The introduction could not have been created through musical notation. It is a flamboyant assertion of the ear-playing tradition that was so relentlessly and caustically belittled and that the black New Orleanians cultivated so proudly. It was easy for Armstrong to notate the introduction to *Cornet Chop Suey* because the rhythms were straightforward. No one in the 1920s ever would have thought to notate the introduction to *West End Blues*.[84] The ofay demons were slaughtered, as Peyton and everyone else in the Savoy Ballroom must have understood, because the music could only have come from deep immersion in the African-American vernacular, from a world where performer-centered means of expression reigned supreme. A lot can happen in 15 seconds.

We know that Oliver was in Chicago in June, so perhaps this was the moment he witnessed from the sidelines, dressed in his best clothes, tears streaming down his cheeks, reflecting on his similar glory, perhaps, at Royal Gardens ten years earlier. Oliver was the composer of the tune and then song called *West End Blues*, with assistance from Clarence Williams, who added lyrics for the published sheet music. King Oliver's Dixie Syncopators recorded the piece as an instrumental number in Chicago on June 11, 1928; they were followed by Armstrong's Hot Five on June 28. Then came song versions by Ethel Waters (August 21), Hazel Smith (August 29), and Katherine Henderson (November). The five performances make it clear that Oliver wanted the piece performed in a very slow tempo; Armstrong's performance is right in the middle, at 90 beats per minute. Only a few of his recordings before this move so slowly (*Lonesome Blues*, *Wild Man Blues*), and one is even reminded of the extremely slow pace of *St. Louis Blues* with Bessie Smith, from 1925. The song that would emerge from Oliver's tune is about a wronged woman, full of gin, who grabs a gun to hunt down her man, who had gone off with her best friend down to the West End. The tempo puts the performance in a world far removed from the fast, bright, and slick moves of the high-rolling 1920s.

"When Louis started blowing the introduction to *West End Blues* (man was it mellifluous) everybody in the ballroom started screaming and whistling," remembered George Wettling. "And then Louis lowered the boom and everybody got real groovy when he went into the first strains of *West End*." In the first chorus, Armstrong's trumpet delivers Oliver's opening phrases with boldness and panache. As the strain unfolds, his filigree becomes increasingly animated, leading naturally into a restatement of the vigorous ascent from the introduction. The second chorus features a subdued trombone solo, with Hines playing tremolo figures in the background.

Chorus three introduces an equally subdued and very effective series of calls and responses between clarinet and Armstrong, now scatting. The richness of the clarinet in low register, combined with the simplicity of the lines (was this played by the clarinet section in the Savoy Ballroom?), inspires vocalizing that is surprisingly tender and delicate. Again Armstrong becomes more animated as the chorus progresses, eventually releasing delicate and carefully sculpted blues filigree with a quality that is perhaps unprecedented in his recordings. It is essentially a new vocal style for him.

So the question needs to be raised: assuming that the recording reflects the Savoy Ballroom, what was Armstrong doing singing delicate phrases like this in such a massive hall? The answer directs us not only to the special qualities of *West End Blues*, but to the impact of technology on the new vocal style that would play a huge role in his stunning innovations during the next few years, carrying him to national fame with audiences black and white: the microphone.

Armstrong "had to stand back from the mike to avoid blowing the roof off the Savoy Ballroom," reported Art Hodes, confirming that there was, in fact, a microphone on the stage. His trumpet did not need it, but the new electronic gadget became his voice's best friend. The vocal style that we are familiar with through recordings up to this point was designed to fill up large spaces, sometimes with the assistance of a megaphone. Musical expression was conditioned by the need to self-amplify. *Heebie Jeebies* was not about nuance and tenderness but vigor and surprise, his voice transmitting danceable energy with forceful attack, rough delivery, and only slight ornamentation.

*The microphone (Courtesy of the Louis Armstrong House Museum)*

"There was none of this whispering jive," said Buster Bailey about singing in the premicrophone era. Armstrong began singing into microphones in recording studios in May 1927, when OKeh first used them for the Hot Five series, but he probably did not use a microphone in public performance until he entered the Savoy Ballroom. Thus, the large-venue style carried through into the studio, in spite of the presence of an electronic microphone there, until June 1928.[85]

*Sugar Foot Strut* and *A Monday Date* are both excellent and fully texted examples of the new vocal style.[86] *A Monday Date* features nuanced shadings of loud and soft and varied styles of initial attack, some very soft and gradual; gone are the relentless explosions of *Heebie Jeebies*. Each of the first two vocal phrases ends with a light and effective vibrato ("date," "Tuesday,") that quickly fades until the syllable melts into silence. The touch is all light and mellow. The scat break at the end of the vocal chorus (CD 1:35) begins as a burst of energy, like the scat of old, but quickly relaxes into a more casual and softer delivery. There are few flubs from the musicians and a lot of brilliant playing from Armstrong and Hines.

*A Monday Date* may be a direct reference to Whiteman's *From Monday On*, which Armstrong heard performed in Chicago and which must have been released on disc during the spring of 1928. *From Monday On* features playful scat dialogue combined with crooner-style solo singing, backed by close male harmonies; the latter appear for the first time in the Hot Five series in *Squeeze Me*, recorded two days after *A Monday Date*.[87] This little cycle of scat dialogue and barbershop-style harmonies moved from the African-American vernacular in New Orleans into white popular music and then back into Armstrong's performances, closing the same circle that we tracked in *Copenhagen* from 1924 (see Chapter 4).

In late December 1929, the *Harlem Tattler* praised "Louis Armstrong, whose cornet and individual style of crooning a ballad have made him a Broadway and recording sensation." Today the word "crooning" is heavily associated with white vocals from this period and later, but racial connotations were more complicated in the 1920s. In 1925, twenty-three-year-old Langston Hughes won a poetry contest with *The Weary Blues*, which describes a musician on Lenox Avenue performing a "drowsy syncopated tune" and "rocking back and forth to a mellow croon." Perhaps the primary association of the word was with lullabies sung by southern "mammies"; from there it could be applied to any soft singing. Gene Austin, a white southerner who in a sense launched the crooning period with his extremely popular recording of *My Blue Heaven* in 1927, said that he patterned his style after black cotton pickers he heard during his youth.[88]

The early history of what could be called "crooning blues" is poorly documented on recordings, which drew on star performers with big voices who filled big venues and could project into acoustic horns in the recordings studios. White crooning gave Armstrong a model for his own more bluesy microphone style, but it would be a mistake to assume that this was the only, or even the most important, antecedent. The microphone was the technological innovation that brought crooning into all three of the major communication technologies for transmitting music—movies, radio, and phonograph records. As a reviewer of a new movie called *Four Sons*, from February 1928, observed: "For a picture of some pretensions its defects are singularly noticeable. In the scene where Joan Crawford sounds the Indian love call several close-ups show her in the act of crooning in a drawing-room manner whereas, in order to have made her voice carry to the distant mountain where her lover awaited the signal, the vocal force of a Wagnerian prima donna would have been in order." The microphone changed other instruments, too, but it would change singing most dramatically.[89] It became an essential component of Armstrong's second modern style.

*West End Blues* had immediate and far-reaching impact. It made a huge impression on thirteen-year-old Billie Holiday in Baltimore, who was running errands for a prostitution madam in exchange for access to her record collection. *West End Blues* was Holiday's first exposure to scat. "Ba-ba-ba-ba-ba-ba-ba and the rest had plenty of meaning for me—just as much meaning as some of the other words that I didn't always understand," she remembered. "But the meaning used to change, depending on how I felt." Five years later Holiday made her first recording in a New York studio where, just three days before, Bessie Smith had made her last recording. Thus it was that the greatest blues singer of what we might call the megaphone era (though I know of no evidence that Smith used megaphones) symbolically yielded to the greatest jazz singer of the microphone era. Holiday's style is unthinkable without a microphone, and the fact that *West End Blues* was one of her first inspirations adds sparkle to the reception history of Armstrong's performance.

After the vocal-clarinet duet comes a beautifully crafted piano chorus for Hines, which a reviewer in the British magazine *Melody Maker* praised for being "as rhythmical, as clever in construction, as perfect an example of originality in harmony, phrases and general style" as Armstrong's own solo playing. Sixteen-year-old pianist Teddy Wilson learned this solo note for note. "I had never heard that style of piano before—the melodic improvisation, the off-beat bass, the eccentric rhythm, and the ideas in the right hand like a trumpet would play," remembered Wilson.

Finally comes the climactic trumpet chorus. The rapid and complex introduction creates a dramatic atmosphere in which anything can happen; this chorus is now the fourth and final answer filling that space of possibility. There is nothing particularly flashy about it, yet it is full of dramatic intensity. The long high note is held for a full 15 beats, the simplicity seeming to balance the flashy fanfare of the introduction. Spinning out from its peak, the line communicates an effortless sense of pliancy, as five bluesy descents move through the same set of pitches, each one subtly different from the others. Armstrong's allegiance to the principle of variety has led him to a new standard of blues resilience. The bluesy trumpet chorus caps off this masterful demonstration of a rich range of the African-American vernacular.

The eclecticism of *West End Blues*, its many points of discontinuity and surprise, expose the fallacy of thinking in terms of a "total unified conception" better than any other performance by Armstrong does for the simple reason that it was so successful.[90] Jazz solos in the 1920s are much more about variety and discontinuity than unity and coherence. The explosive introduction, the inscrutable and tender scat-clarinet dialogue, the spritely piano chorus, and the majestic trumpet chorus—contrast is far more important than unity. (A better place to find unity would be in Oliver's June recording or Ethel Waters's from August.) Armstrong's *West End Blues* resembles a "fantasy" or "rhapsody," a type of piece that makes no pretense of integrating the parts into a coherent whole but, rather, offers delight in the unpredictable unfolding of different sound images, one after the other.

Gershwin's *Rhapsody in Blue* was the reference for all rhapsodies in the 1920s, but *Black and Tan Fantasy* by Duke Ellington and Bubber Miley, first recorded in April 1927 (and again in October and November), became the main reference in Armstrong's circles for fantasies. *Black and Tan Fantasy* frames the vernacular with sophistication but without a trace of condescension, putting it at the center of expression rather than holding it back as ancillary spice. Ellington took the move of jazz from dance music to music that rewards listening a step further and encouraged reflection. He brought to the task the skills of a composer who understood contrast and emotional complexity. Like *West End Blues*, *Black and Tan Fantasy* is a succession of relatively slow choruses, most of them in blues form, one after the other. The piece includes a passage with trumpeter Bubber Miley holding a long high note (16 beats on the October recording, compared with Armstrong's 15), followed by very bluesy, speechlike phrases.

If Armstrong had been more interested in crafting an image for himself as a composer, he might have called his recording *West End Fantasy*. There is no direct evidence that he and his colleagues were thinking of Ellington when they put together *West End Blues*, but we do know how important Ellington was to them. Zutty Singleton remembered going over to Carroll Dickerson's house to listen to Ellington on the radio, with Armstrong and the whole band, and hearing Bubber Miley play *East St. Louis Toodle-Oo*. "It was sort of a special deal," Singleton remembered. Ellington was expanding everyone's sense of what was possible in jazz, and it would not be surprising if his impact on the Hot Five's *West End Blues* was direct. Radio and phonograph recordings were now fully imbedded in the unfolding of jazz history, with influences crisscrossing the country quickly through radio and repeatable through recordings. Whatever trappings of primitivist degradation were attached to *Black and Tan Fantasy* at its point of origin, in a venue not too different from the Sunset Café, these were sprung free by radio and records, which allowed the music to work its magic in unprescribed social settings.[91]

The mood of *West End Blues* has often been described as deeply pensive, but perhaps things are not quite that straightforward. This is true of Armstrong's playing generally. He mixes in emotional signs—blue notes, dramatic gestures, fierce and complex licks, forceful attacks—but the mood is not simple or uniform. Billie Holiday said it well when she described how, with *West End Blues*, "the meaning used to change, depending on how I felt." This can be true of any music, yet some musicians deliberately exploit the possibility. The emotional climate of Armstrong's solos during this period is quite different from popular songs, for example, which wear feelings on the sleeve and make it easy for the listener to align with them. Armstrong's intellectual-musical play with the materials of sound does not necessarily forbid that kind of simplistic engagement, but it definitely suggests alternatives.

Oliver and Bessie Smith specialized in blues of unmistakable emotional weight; Armstrong uses the same markers of expression and places them in a stream of melody that directs attention elsewhere, toward intellectual complexity. So many writers have classified Armstrong as a nonintellectual, intuitive musician, but what I hear instead is a formidable musical intelligence that is very much in the foreground. In the case of *West End Blues*, the terms of expression have more to do with blues pliancy, made possible by extended technique (and by the microphone), than with blues weight. When Armstrong was growing up, blues in New Orleans was already diversified; in Chicago he carried that tradition forward. Hoagy Carmichael insisted that "*West End Blues* was his real beginning as an artist."

Quite a few musicians learned from, imitated, reproduced, and responded to the recording. Even King Oliver got into the action. His band's playful recording from January 1929 is essentially a parody, with references to Armstrong (and Hines) from beginning to end; the tone of the performance resembles the Henderson band's parody of *Dipper Mouth Blues*, recorded as *Sugar Foot Stomp* in 1925. Jabbo Smith, an explosive player who specialized in quickness and high notes, memorized a lot of Armstrong's solos, including *West End Blues*. His *Take Me to the River*, recorded in March 1929, is very much a response to Armstrong's celebrated performance. Smith was not always able to match Armstrong's standards: "he had a tendency to play one degree above his capabilities as if he was seeking to prove

something," explained a fellow trumpeter. Punch Miller's contribution to *Down by the Levee* with Wynn's Creole Jazz Band in October
1928 was another response to *West End Blues*, though Miller wisely
stayed away from the introductory fanfare. Violinist Stuff Smith said
that *West End Blues* first sparked his interest in jazz. Critic Leonard
Feather, in England, heard *West End Blues* at age fifteen, and the performance gave him "a sense of direction, a lifestyle, an obsessive concern with every aspect of jazz, as nothing had before."

## Birds of a Feather

When he first arrived in Chicago, in 1923, Earl Hines had already
worked out a way of playing melodies with his right hand that he
himself referred to as "trumpet style" piano. His large hands made it
easy for him to play octaves in his right hand, doubling the melody,
and, with a punching attack, help the piano cut through the texture
of a band. He was two years younger than Armstrong. Armstrong
said that the first time he heard Hines play, at the musician's union
on the South Side, he was "speechless." Their musical partnership
during the 1920s, amply preserved on recordings, is one of the great
treasures of jazz history.

Hines convinced Armstrong to join him at the Sunset Café in
the spring of 1926, and by September Hines was also playing at the
Vendome, the two of them doubling up there before going over to
the Sunset. Like Armstrong, though perhaps not to the same degree,
Hines was a draw with his eccentric solos, which stood out in a piano
environment that, for the most part, leaned more toward notebound
playing.

Together they endured the strains of a musician's life—the long
hours, seven days a week, with a completely inverted schedule, sleep-
ing during the day and working all night. Hines remembered how
Armstrong would sometimes lie down on the floor and take a quick
nap when they were out carousing. One day he noticed Armstrong
picking at a scab on his lip, and he asked him how his lips felt. "Well,
they're *rare*!" Armstrong quipped. "He was always a trouper," Hines
remembered. "He knew how to get by, but many times I knew he
must have been playing in pain. He never showed it. He was all

smiles." One day Armstrong went out shopping for a new instrument at Lyon and Healy's music store, at Wabash Avenue and Jackson Boulevard, with Hines tagging along. Hines sat down and started playing piano, so Armstrong joined him, testing out the trumpet. In short order, a crowd gathered outside, listening to the two of them jam.

When Singleton arrived in the fall of 1927, they became the "unholy three." Singleton had an odd sense of humor. Walking home from work, early in the morning, Singleton would approach men carrying lunch pails on their way to work and ask them, "Where's the picnic?" Or he might walk up to a girl and say, "You look beautiful today, but where did you get those pimples?" Armstrong was the celebrity, but he was three years younger than Singleton and deferential to his friend. "Whenever at night Zutty and I would walk into those nightclubs, he was the star and I'd walk behind him," he remembered, adding bitterly, "but I always paid the bills."

The three friends rented an apartment two blocks away from the Savoy that they called "The Ranch," a place for trysts with women, parties with friends and visiting musicians, and poker, black jack, and craps. The wife of Gene Anderson, pianist at the Savoy, was hired to "run" the place, which must have meant cleaning and stocking it with food and liquor. Zutty cooked big pots of gumbo. A woman named Mrs. Circha supplied them with homemade gin, which was commemorated for eternity in the opening banter for the June 1928 recording of *A Monday Date*. As the musicians tune up, Hines says, "That sounds pretty good," and Armstrong comes back, sarcastically, "That sounds pretty good. I'll bet if you had half a pint of Mrs. Circha's gin you wouldn't say 'that sounds pretty good.'"

Their social world included mainly the people they worked with—chorus girls, dancers, singers. Some musicians, Jelly Roll Morton, for example, were drawn to faster crowds of prostitutes, pimps, and gamblers, and Fred Keppard liked to hang out with a group of professional athletes, including baseball players from the Negro Leagues and prizefighters. Armstrong was a local celebrity, but he stuck to being a "regular guy." "That was the difference with musicians," said Howard Scott. "You were either regular or you weren't."

There is no reason to believe that the Hot Five recordings reached many white listeners at all, but Armstrong's reputation among white musicians on the dance-band scene had by now spread widely. "Every professional musician admired and was greatly influenced by the blacks," said white arranger Archie Bleyer. "As a white musician developed, he incorporated more and more of the black idiom into his arranging and playing." No one was more closely studied than Armstrong, but Hines got his share of attention, too.

White musicians flocked to hear him at the Savoy Ballroom, even though, unlike at the Sunset Café, they were a tiny minority amidst the huge gathering of black dancers. "We'd stand there with the colored folks and listen to those bands play," remembered Wild Bill Davison. They made sure to visit Armstrong in the dressing room before and after the show and during intermission. Art Hodes remembered hanging out there with Armstrong, King Oliver, and a couple of Hodes's friends, Armstrong keeping everyone relaxed with warmth and good humor. Hodes and Wingy Manone took turns wearing a warm bear coat the two of them had purchased. Every evening Armstrong greeted them with, "Who's the bear tonight?"

Spanier, Stacy, Teschemacher, O'Brien, and Wettling put together a (white) cover band at the Triangle Café, in Forest Park, for six months in 1928, playing his solos and arrangements note for note. "Yeah, Muggsy, rip it out!" Armstrong would shout from the sidelines, flattered by the imitation. Davison had the experience of playing his solos only to have Armstrong respond by bursting out in laughter, Davison not quite figuring out if the great man was laughing at him or with him.

It must have been a heady experience for Armstrong, for Hines, and perhaps for a few of the other black musicians. Never before in the history of this country, it is safe to say, had so many white musicians shown such enthusiasm and indeed respect for black music. Nevertheless, we must resist the temptation to think of the scene as an idyllic postracial lovefest. The off-stage integration of black and white musicians in Chicago in the mid-1920s was a phenomenon of complex emotions. Not all musicians experienced it in the same way. It can be difficult from such a distance to identify the nuances of race relations, which were not regularly spoken about—especially by Armstrong.

For one thing, it is easy to exaggerate how much integration there actually was. Scoville Brown was asked how close black and white musicians were and answered, "Well not too close then, not too close. We fraternized a little bit." Brown had particularly harsh words for the white musicians' union, which treated the black union "like master and slave." Even Muggsy Spanier, one of the more aggressive of the white musicians who inserted themselves into the black scene, said that "White and Negro musicians kept to themselves pretty much."

But they sought out Armstrong; as Hodes put it, "it was just a bunch of people wanting to be around the fire." Lillian remembered how they made afternoon stops at the house she and Louis owned, and Armstrong remembered them visiting the apartment he was renting with Hines and Singleton. In turn, he visited the white musicians at least once. Davison invited him to a party at his apartment on the North Side, at 6970 North Sheridan Road. Armstrong apparently made the trip by himself, and he turned out to be the only black person there. As much as Davison tried to make him feel comfortable, he could not persuade Armstrong to leave the kitchen. Caution about mixing with whites had been so thoroughly drilled into him since childhood that he could not let go, even among whites who idolized him.[92] The gesture sadly links the experience of one of the greatest musicians America has ever produced to the history of slavery. "Though I had fled the pressure of the South, my outward conduct had not changed," wrote novelist Richard Wright in *Black Boy*. "I had been schooled to present an unalteringly smiling face and I continued to do so despite the fact that my environment allowed more open expression. I hid my feelings and avoided all relationships with whites that might cause me to reveal them."

Robert Moton, principal of Tuskegee Institute and author of the 1929 book *What the Negro Thinks*, explained how, "other things being equal, the Negro prefers to retain his self-esteem in a restricted sphere rather than accept a larger freedom of movement under the implication of being tolerated. So widespread is this feeling that it is very difficult to get Negroes in any numbers to accept even specific invitations from white people to join them in mixed gatherings. . . . If the truth were known it would be discovered that there is far greater tendency on the part of white people to seek the association of Negroes than there is on the part of Negroes to seek the association of whites." Clarinetist Garvin Bushell put an even finer point on that: "As a matter of fact, we had no *desire* to integrate then. Our culture was something else. We didn't talk the same language, and we didn't eat the same kind of food, and what was funny to whites wasn't funny to us. We were thankful of the fact that they enjoyed what we did on stage. They'd applaud, stop the show, and all that. But when we'd come off the stage we'd go our way. Because we knew it was a precarious thing. Some drunk might come along and call you a nigger, and you'd either cut him or shoot him and have a fight with him. So we tried to avoid that. Living then as a black man you were too uncertain about what could happen from day to day. That's why you were happy to get in your neighborhood and stay there."

Certainly Armstrong enjoyed the attention, and, being the gregarious person that he was, he found ways to relate to his new white friends. It was all so radically different from his experience in New Orleans, and, indeed, radically different from the normative experience in Chicago. It is no surprise that his attitudes toward whites, during this and other periods, are very hard to uncover. A lot of his commentary on this period comes from the 1950s, a time when he assumed the identity of Ambassador Satch and when he occasionally liked to articulate visions of universal brotherhood. Stories about staying in the kitchen on North Sheridan Road were not the ones that first came to mind.

Did he and the other black musicians resent the alligators studying their music and then turning around and making a lot of money with it? "Well it's human nature," said drummer Red Saunders, "if someone takes a product of yours, any kind of a product, and takes it and does well, does better than you do, and you have the original and can't do as well, and you don't have not only the resources but you can't reach the right people to even sell your product—naturally there would be some resentment." What seems clear is that while the small number of black musicians at the top—Armstrong, Hines, and a few others—were flattered by white attention, the experience was very different for the wide swath of second-tier musicians, those less rewarded and more vulnerable, who didn't have quite so much inventive power or dazzling technique. It is not surprising that, for them, the fact that whites were taking black music and making money off it in places where blacks could not perform stuck in their craw. "Save our stuff . . . don't show them a thing," wrote Peyton in the *Defender*, and he surely understood the challenges his readership was facing.

Armstrong's experience of integration was exceptional because he was exceptional—and the white musicians treated him that way. "There's always another one coming along, like a streetcar," he said in reference to his own ability to generate fresh music and in response to a thought about musicians having ripped him off.[93] That was a position few could afford to take. "So if you learn how to maneuver with that, you can survive," said Danny Barker. "But a lot of musicians died, you know, at the bar, you know, right next to the spittoon and the sawdust on the floor, drank themselves to death because they couldn't stand up under the pressure." Of all the Jim Crow injustices, with whites stacking the deck against black achievement and doing their best to ensure disadvantage and low wages at every turn, the sight of white success built on the imitation of black music was particularly tough to deal with. "It's a hard thing for a man to sit around and play in a smoke-filled room, in a cellar, and play his heart out, and have some white guy come in there, and listen to him play, and go out there and half play what he's playing and become famous . . . and you still in that hole," insisted Milt Hinton. "That's the reason you've got to give a guy like Louis Armstrong so much credit. . . . You got to have a really tough skin."

The alligators got a lot by warming themselves at Armstrong's fire. One thing they gave in return was marijuana. All that backstage laughing during intermission at the Savoy was enriched by "gage"—otherwise known as "weed," "tea," "mezz," "muta," or "muggles." Hines and Armstrong were both very fond of marijuana.

Marijuana usage among musicians has often been associated with New Orleans, but it is clear that Armstrong's first exposure took place in Chicago, courtesy of white musicians. The liberated Mezz Mezzrow was such a strong user and seller that his nickname became another name for pot. An amusing letter from 1932, written by Armstrong while touring in England, to Mezzrow, his supplier, is full of barely coded directions about where and how Mezzrow should send the next batch. Mezzrow had been introduced to the drug by Leon Roppolo, a white clarinetist from New Orleans, and his supplier was a Mexican named Pasquale. A tobacco can of golden leaf without any sticks or seeds cost two dollars.

The recording by Louis Armstrong and His Orchestra of *Muggles* (December 7, 1928) is a lasting testament to those mellow days. Composer credit went to Armstrong and Hines jointly, and they play beautifully. Though "muggles" was a well-established nickname for marijuana, there is no obvious reference to the drug in the music. *Muggles* is a slow blues (about the same tempo as *West End Blues*), fancied up with interpolated and embellished chords in the beginning and merging into a splendid double-time solo by Armstrong (CD 1:38). He energetically dances through many repetitions of a single note, an old New Orleanian trick that both Oliver and Keppard were known to pull out, before stretching out with simple but effective blues licks. Apparently, the recording was a big hit at house parties, no doubt with a chuckle over the title.

Armstrong spent most of his free time with Hines, Singleton, and his fellow black musicians. The summer of 1928 was full of camaraderie and even sports such as baseball and golf. He started a team called "Louis Armstrong's Nine," with Zutty as catcher, Boyd Atkins, composer of *Heebie Jeebies*, at second base, Hines at shortstop, tuba player Peter Briggs on third base, drummer Tubby Hall in left field, pianist Walter Johnson as umpire, tenor saxophonist Albert Washington in right field, and Armstrong himself in center field. Cab Calloway occasionally pitched. Hines shied away from hard grounders, protecting his hands, and Armstrong avoided catching pop-ups, afraid that he would miss the ball and injure his mouth. The team played visiting bands at Washington Park, the winner taking two barrels of beer. Crowds gathered to watch. Louis, full of beer and ribs and weighing 230 pounds, once hit a long fly ball, stumbled going around second base, missed third, and, with his teammates yelling for him to go back and touch the base, fell flat on his belly 20 feet from home plate. He just lay there, grinning.

Basketball was a popular feature at the Savoy. The hall had its own semiprofessional team that was covered in the *Light and Heebie Jeebies* even more than the dances and music were. The games were scheduled before dances. Dickerson's musicians became friendly with the players, and eventually the manager of the Savoy thought up a publicity stunt: make up two teams, drawn from the two dance bands, to play a little exhibition game before the real teams take the floor. Armstrong's girth made it difficult to find a suit to fit him, so he wore a bathing suit. Tremendous applause greeted the players as they ran out onto the floor, but it quickly became clear that they had no idea what to do. As frustration mounted, Armstrong finally grabbed the ball and ran toward the basket without dribbling, the audience roaring with laughter. He assumed position under the basket and ceremoniously took his shot, missing wildly, while the other players fell to the floor, howling in delight. Clarence Black's team won the game 2–0. Armstrong was so exhausted that he got pneumonia and spent the next week at home in bed.

In September, Fletcher Henderson came to town and played the Savoy. He immediately offered Armstrong $200 a week to join him, but bad memories of New York interfered; he used the offer to increase his salary at the Savoy. One day the unholy trio met Jelly Roll Morton, wearing a pale pink silk shirt and a Panama hat, on the street after a rehearsal at the Savoy. They invited Morton over to Armstrong's house to check out the Kimball grand piano he had just purchased for Lillian. Morton held them spellbound with his mix of playing and storytelling—where *St. Louis Blues* had come from and so on. The radio broadcasts from the Savoy on WCFL, were probably heard in St. Louis, for in December, Armstrong and the band were there for a featured dance, 75 cents in advance, $1 at the door.

Armstrong said that musicians "were treated and respected just like some kind of a God" in the 1920s, and Milt Hinton concurred: "The early '20s to the '30s was the most glamorous era in Chicago for jazz, for black musicians. I can't possibly . . . I wish I had the words to explain to you what tremendous glamour." Armstrong strutted around town, chauffeured by his valet, living the life of a celebrity who worked seven days a week until the break of dawn. "Oh you were like Mr. Sousa," explained Scoville Brown. "You were something . . . you were quite a boy." Yet Armstrong remained, for the most part, a regular guy, or, as Doc Cheatham described him, "just an ordinary-extraordinary man," joking around and dishing out nicknames left and right, usually with the suffix "face," as in "Zuttyface."

In 1928 Armstrong and Hines made 29 recordings together, when

*Crowd at Savoy Ballroom, 1941 (Library of Congress)*

they weren't working or roaming around the South Side, picking up women, enjoying the adulation of fans and fellow musicians, finding themselves sought after by white musicians who wanted to befriend them, and having a great time. One wants to say that the joy of their friendship is sonically evident in the commercial recordings.[94] Their musical synergy is delightful to listen to, and it is a fascinating part of Armstrong's musical production around this time, even if it was largely limited to the recording studio.

Hines's musical upbringing was quite different from Armstrong's. He was not really trained in blues, for example, and the idiom never really interested him. Instead, what he cultivated was an eccentric style, with rhythmic and harmonic daring taken to an extreme. The term "trumpet style" fit his piano playing not just because of the strong octave doublings and clear lines: there was something cocky and brassy about his music, a confidence and assertiveness that were right in step with the brass players from New Orleans.

Rhythmically, Hines was very good at taking his melodic lines further and further away from the fixed foundation, creating a radical sense of detachment for a few beats or measures, only to land back in time with great aplomb when finished with his foray. The left hand sometimes joins in the action. Drummers and bass players testified to how hard it was to keep up with him. "Earl is a very difficult person to play with," said drummer Oliver Jackson. "His sense of timing is uncanny; he's got practically perfect time on that piano and that means that *you've* got to do everything perfectly." Hines and Armstrong were, unquestionably, among the leading exponents of eccentric phrasing in 1928.

What is especially distinctive about Hines are the startling effects he creates by harmonically enhancing these rhythmic departures. Like Armstrong, he thought about chords creatively and with great precision. But he was a step ahead of his colleague in his willingness to experiment. He became fond of radical dislocations, sudden turns of directions with dim or nonexistent connection to the ground harmony. "Poor old Hines mess you up," confessed bassist Montudie Garland. "Liable to be playing in A-flat and he jump way down to D-flat, jump back to C." "He would show me chords I didn't know existed and how you could fit so many different chords together," added Pops Foster. By pulling away from the ground, temporarily but to an extreme, Hines was pushing the fixed and variable model in fresh directions. This put him right in step with Armstrong's own creative exploration, coming from another direction.

But with Hines—in contrast to Armstrong—the listener can be thrown into an atmosphere of reckless abandon. Musically speaking, he was a supreme risk taker. In early December 1928, in the midst of a busy stretch of recordings made with Armstrong in Chicago, he traveled to New York City to record a series of piano solos for a company named QRS. The chance to stretch out beyond the special chorus inspired a smattering of daring episodes in almost every performance. For example, the first take of *A Monday Date* includes a disorienting ten-second stretch (around CD 0:46) that seems to have no ground whatsoever. It is possible that he actually lost control here. But when he emerges from the chaos with complete confidence and locks his line back into a firm relationship with the regular periodicity of the tune, the whole thing sounds like it was planned. We realize that he has stayed connected to the fixed layer, even while seeming not to be.

Risk-taking displays like this were well beyond Armstrong and virtu-ally everyone else, and they make the eight QRS performances one of the true joys in early jazz.

The two of them shared a strong work ethic, and not just in the sense of showing up every night. Lillian said that the introductory fanfare for *West End Blues* came from the classical exercises she and Louis were running through together, and it is clear from a piece like *Chicago Breakdown*, recorded in May 1927, that Hines was doing (or had done) something similar. Hines was also drawn toward the princi-ples of musical density and variety, just like Armstrong and their col-leagues Buck and Bubbles. And like Armstrong he was tremendously inventive. There were more than a few superb African-American pianists in the 1920s, but perhaps none of the others matched Arm-strong so well, in all of these ways. Each was taking his instrument and his personal style into unknown territory, each was challenged and stimulated by the other; together they basked in the glory of their shared success. "We were very close and when we were playing we would steal ideas from each other," explained Hines. Singer Anita O'Day articulated the nature of deep musical relationships in a way that rings true for the two of them: "I can tell you now that musical intimacy is on a completely different plane—deeper, longer-lasting, better than the steamiest sexual liaison. Passion wears out, but the closer you work with a really rhythmical, inventive swinging musi-cian, the closer you become."

Their shared musical intimacy is captured frequently in the 1928 recordings. Musical dialogue had been a fundamental fact of Armstrong's life since childhood, in church and in the collective improvisation of street bands and dance bands: sounds interacting with sounds, sounds with movement, and movement with move-ment. Musical dialogue was professionalized and standardized in the texture of collective improvisation, the New Orleanian specialty. *Hotter Than That*, from December 1927, provided a fresh articula-tion of direct exchange with the plaintive, out-of-tempo dialogue between Armstrong and Lonnie Johnson, and something similar happens in the second chorus of *West End Blues*. The recordings with Hines in 1928 also take this procedure to a level not previously documented on commercial recordings.

There are many examples, some brief, some buried, and two fore-grounded. The June 1928 recording of *Skip the Gutter* was arranged to give Armstrong and Hines a full chorus of direct exchange, all by themselves, with no ensemble accompaniment. Beiderbecke and Trumbauer had played similar choruses, for example, in *Borneo*, recorded in April 1928 for OKeh. But in *Skip the Gutter* Hines and Armstrong elevate the format to a kind of musical "doing the dozens," the public display of dueling wits that was so popular in the African-American community and that Oliver, for one, was very good at.

Hines gets to go first. One has the feeling for the rest of the cho-rus that Armstrong is reacting to him, figuring out how it will be possible for a trumpet to compete with Hines's wide-spanning and nimble hands. Hines begins with two bars of double-time passage work, laced with light chromaticism, and Armstrong answers in kind. Aiming for variety, Hines then slows down; Armstrong again follows in step. After this, the arrangement calls for six full measures from Hines. He fills them with a brilliant descending run from the top of the piano, followed by a sweeping and tricky ascent before breaking into trumpet-style bounce, only to back away from that with a mys-terious dissolution before firming up the harmonic direction just in time to pass the challenge back to Armstrong. It is a lot of variety—textural, harmonic, rhythmic—in a brief period of time. Armstrong's response this time is a smart one: he shifts the terms of exchange to a play of opposites, countering Hines's stunning variety with half-valve slurs, idiomatic for the trumpet, understated and bluesy.

Their best-known collaboration is *Weather Bird*, recorded Decem-ber 5, 1928. Here it is just the two of them from beginning to end. Armstrong wrote the piece some seven years earlier, during his time on the Mississippi riverboats, and after he joined Oliver's band in Chicago his mentor agreed to include it in an April 1923 record-ing session as *Weather Bird Rag*. We hear nothing about it again until this performance in December 1928; Hines made it clear that he had never heard of the piece before he walked into the studio to record it. Here is yet another indication of OKeh's contractual expec-tations that their performers play their own compositions and sign away rights to the company. Running out of product, Armstrong dug into his "little book of manuscripts" (probably the same one that he showed to Don Redman in New York City in 1925) and dusted off *Weather Bird Rag*. The recorded performance, in spite of its reputation in recent decades, does indeed suggest that Armstrong had not looked at the piece for quite some time.

In other words, *Weather Bird* should be put in the category of studio-generated performances that made good, along with *Gut Bucket Blues* in 1925 and *Heebie Jeebies* in 1926. In this case, however, success was considerably delayed. The recording was not released until around the middle of 1930, suggesting that the admiration it enjoys today was not shared by OKeh decision makers. Certainly, it would have surprised everyone involved to see a transcription of the performance included in a 1975 anthology of classical repertory entitled *The Virtuoso*, rubbing shoulders with one of Liszt's *Hungarian Rhapsodies*.

The first two minutes of the performance (which lasts two minutes and 42 seconds) are conventional—strikingly so. Armstrong plays the melody he composed seven years earlier with only slight ornamentation and no departures. Certainly, he was reading from a lead sheet, which must have looked a lot like the one Lillian wrote out for him in April 1923.[95] They both play with the easy swing, full of confidence, precision, and verve, that marks virtually all of their recordings in 1928. Hines's skill as an accompanist is on display as he "stays under" the lead, keeping the beat in a light and steady way, not dwelling on a relentless stride and adding just enough eccentric phrasing to keep things lively.

"Louis had some ideas and I soon grasped the chord structure," remembered Hines. In fact, Hines makes virtually no reference to the original melody throughout the performance. Armstrong was looking at a lead sheet that included melody and a formal plan of repetitions, while Hines had probably written out a simple sequence of chords; it would have been a waste of time to write out the melody for him. The arrangement called for Hines to take the second statement of the second strain by himself, so he improvises on the chords, producing a fresh departure from the notated tune. His playing is full of dazzling little touches. Especially effective is a driving chordal passage (CD 0:50) that segues into a burst of trumpet style in the right hand (CD 0:56). Armstrong then reenters for a conventional restatement of the first strain, with slight but effective ornamentation. A brief interlude sets up the third strain, which is again given over to Hines.

Hines said late in life (after *Weather Bird* had been elevated), "When we were playing together, it was like a continuous jam session, like when we made that record of *Weather Bird Rag.*" Among the charms of virtually all their 1928 recordings are the fleeting musical conversations that flicker in and out of the texture, in a more informal way than the organized dialogue of *Skip the Gutter. Weather Bird* has this, but really no more than many of the other recordings. Hines was a sensitive accompanist, just as good as Armstrong was at filling in. Since Armstrong carries the lead, it falls on Hines to contribute sparkling commentary and exchange.

But the mutual jamming does not really begin until the second statement of the third strain (CD 1:42). Now there will be organized dialogue in the manner of *Skip the Gutter*; this was perhaps one of Louis's "ideas," mentioned by Hines. Again Hines livens up the texture with his driving chords (CD 1:45). The C strains have been prearranged to feature a two-bar solo break plus six-bar ensemble. But Hines creates an effective moment with what we might call a "false break" (CD 1:49): he stops, as if framing another break for Armstrong, but then, as Armstrong plays, adds a little countermelody. This is the kind of moment that makes *Weather Bird* more interesting than *Skip the Gutter*, where the two of them simply take turns. For his next break, Armstrong ascends into the high register, arriving at his peak on an off-beat, a gesture that recalls the great final choruses from December 1927 (*Struttin' with Some Barbecue, Hotter Than That*, and *Savoy Blues*). But now the effect is completely different: instead of riding above a thick final chorus of collective improvisation, his glorious peak is totally exposed. Whether planned or not, it is a beautiful moment. Still, in this strain Armstrong does not seem to have found his bearings fully; to close it off, he falls back on conventional figuration.

The real fun begins in the third statement of the third strain, with Hines as protagonist once again. Out of the blue, he pounces on a rhythmic-harmonic dislocation of the kind that had been his fond focus in the QRS sessions. He suddenly plays (CD 2:11) two full measures of wide and jarring leaps, all over the piano, an aug-

mented octave leap harmonized by an augmented chord, dissonance piled on dissonance. Without missing a beat, he then blithely
and smoothly returns to trumpet-style texture and the harmonies
of the tune. There is enough harmonic logic here to make this hold
together, and enough strangeness to make the entire event seem like
a high-level magic trick. Armstrong holds tight, offering a lightly
paraphrased lead and carrying the show forward as if he were the
magician's assistant. It is this little passage, I believe, that largely
accounts for the recent fame of this recording. The whole thing is
handled flawlessly, almost as if it were planned, but the only thing
planned was the space of a two-bar break for Hines. He is able to fill
it with such splendor because he had, in recent weeks, been carrying
out an extended exploration of gestures like this in the December
recordings—and, one might assume, in live performances around
this time as well.

Hines's 3-second, dislocating splash suggests that anything can
happen, and the 23-second coda does not disappoint. The passage
may have been unprecedented in recorded jazz. Now they take turns
with two-bar breaks, followed by a quickened exchange of one-bar
breaks. But the breaks are nothing but jagged fragments of melody,
full of tension and unpredictability and making a strong effect after
the stability of Armstrong's lead. It is all held together by the periodicity of the exchange and the harmonic logic. An assertive diminished-
seventh chord from Hines immediately electrifies the texture, and
Armstrong follows with a simple arpeggiation. Hines does it again,
this time in ascent, and Armstrong's response is to sit on a single note;
this is essentially a complementary gesture, recalling *Skip the Gutter*.
The time of exchange is now quickened and the entries overlap, to
exciting effect. Armstrong caps everything with a slow rubato ascent
to his final high note, which is embellished harmonically and rhythmically by his buddy, who, while still staying under, has nevertheless
found a way to shine.

*Weather Bird* is fun and exceptional, a worthy document of a
unique musical friendship. Perhaps because of that, it has been easy
to overstate its excellence. Armstrong composed the piece and carries the lead; in this case, that was an invitation to Hines to carry the
creative work, which he did splendidly. The performance is a special

testament to their collaboration and also something of a farewell. At the end of December Hines took a job at the Grand Terrace, where he stayed for a long time. A few months after that Armstrong had his sights set on New York City. The two of them made a few more recordings together in December, but after that they would not record together again until February 22, 1948.

## *Tight Like This:* It's All About Sex

That musicians hold powers of sexual attraction exceeding those of normal people is a cliché. Willie "The Lion" Smith described a formula for picking up women: "You had to be real sharp in the way you dressed, the manner in which you approached the piano, and in the originality of your ideas." Women indicated interest by standing alongside the piano or sometimes in cruder ways. Billy Eckstine remembered singing *Sophisticated Lady* with the Basie band at Carnegie Hall, and "some bitch way up in the gallery hollered, 'Billy you're making me come!' 'Maybe the lady isn't so sophisticated,'" Eckstine quipped. A mix of musical-sexual attraction was undoubtedly an important part of Armstrong's music, both in a general sense during the 1920s and in particular with his extraordinary performance, recorded with His Savoy Ballroom Five on December 12, 1928, of a piece entitled *Tight Like This*.

James Baldwin insisted in 1961 that "there is probably no greater (or more misleading) body of sexual myths in the world today than those which have proliferated around the figure of the American Negro." In fact, the phenomenon we are discussing here was certainly not limited to African-American musicians or to jazz. Yet it appears to have been a prominent feature of the social landscape Armstrong was moving through in the mid- and late 1920s. There has been some reluctance to talk about this dimension of his music, partly because the dominant discourse about him has been hagiographic and partly, perhaps, because of the lingering resonance of Norman Mailer's notorious equation of jazz with orgasm. But Mailer's crude generalization doesn't mean that the topic of jazz and sex is irrelevant.

In fact, the relationship between music and sex was strong for much of Armstrong's life. It began in New Orleans, where the musicians he knew often stretched their earning power by working as pimps. Armstrong gave that a try, and he used his emerging powers as a blues soloist to draw women to a local hotel, where he had ongoing arrangements with a clerk. The masculine world that he was stepping into during his teenage years included exploitive views of women. "Ever since I was a little boy in New Orleans hanging around those ol' hustlers and pimps down there," he remembered, "and they used to tell me, 'Never worry over no one woman—no matter how pretty or sweet she may be. Any time she gets down wrong, and ain't playing the part of a wife—get yourself somebody else, also.'" Serial monogamy and promiscuity were not unusual in New Orleans and also in Chicago, where womanizing was part of the social world he shared with Hines, Singleton, and the other musicians.

What got the ladies so interested? Certainly, the musicians were making good money. Earl Hines believed that it was the luster of the stage spotlight that did the trick. James P. Johnson said that an ability to dance was helpful, and he claimed that Armstrong was one of the better dancers among the musicians. But Willie "The Lion" Smith probably summed up the core of the matter best: "The women always wondered if the piano man was as good in bed as he was on the keyboard. Playing music, fighting and loving have all got to be done the same way to be any good. The way you feel while doing these things is what counts. You've got to put a lot of feeling into these activities to get favorable results." For Cootie Williams, the energy flowed fruitfully in both directions: "All great jazz musicians, every one of them, have had many loves and girls in their lives. People don't read about these things in books, but a girl *is* jazz music. They throw something into the mind that makes you produce jazz."

Percussionist Art Lewis explained how "sometimes you might play *to* a woman. You might see a certain woman in the audience and you do try to project to her." Something like that happened to Armstrong at the Vendome. A nineteen-year-old girl named Alpha Smith got in the habit of attending twice a week, following the change of movies, and she placed herself in the front row, right in his line of sight. "And she had big pretty eyes, anyway, I couldn't keep from *diggin'* her," he remembered. "There were times when Lil would be in the Vendome at the same time as Alpha. Well, on those nights we couldn't flirt so much." Alpha eventually became his third wife, in 1938.

Apparently, things weren't going so well with Lillian anyway. The tension created by their dissimilar backgrounds and social aspirations was relentless. Armstrong held a special disdain, all of his life, for pretentious people, and Lillian had her share of pretentions—"a certain spoon for this and a certain fork for that," he complained. "I think you an educated fool," he told her. "'Your ego making an ass out of you chick, 'cause my schooling was down there in New Orleans, playing cards, laying around and always eat, sleep and stay clean. I was taught things like that, and my mother, Mary Ann, was the same. She didn't give a damn what you had; didn't make no difference to her. . . . And that's my life."

His nephew Clarence was an additional source of conflict. Back in New Orleans, when Clarence was a baby, Armstrong was taking care of him one day when Clarence fell from a second-floor balcony, injuring his head. He needed special attention for the rest of his life. Armstrong made arrangements for Clarence to be sent to Chicago to stay with him and Lillian. Lillian and her mother sometimes lost their tempers and yelled at the child, infuriating Armstrong. The situation must have been hard on everyone.

"Well you can knock me down, knock me up and even kick me, or black both my eyes but Daddy, please don't quit me"—that's what Lillian sang to Louis in May 1927, in a recorded performance of *That's When I'll Come Back to You*. It was a comic number, Armstrong explained, but the reality is that he did in fact hit her during the summer of 1926.

The direct cause of their fight was money. After his success in the spring of 1926 with *Heebie Jeebies*, OKeh arranged an exclusive contract for him. Meanwhile, Tommy Rockwell of Columbia Records asked Lillian to put together a couple of sessions in July under the names "New Orleans Wanderers" and "New Orleans Bootblacks." George Mitchell played cornet and Armstrong did not participate, but Rockwell wanted Armstrong's name to appear as composer for three of the tunes. When the records were released, Armstrong was credited as composer on all four of the numbers, even though (according to Lillian) she had written them all. Since the method of

*Louis and Alpha (Courtesy of the Louis Armstrong House Museum)*

identifying composers was simply to put the name in parentheses, directly under the title and above the name of the performing group, the precise nature of his participation was ambiguous. In this way Columbia manipulated Lillian and her husband, using his name to boost sales and enraging him so much that he slapped her after OKeh confronted him. He had already been reprimanded for playing on a Vocalion session organized by Lillian in May, so he must have felt that the situation jeopardized his favorable arrangement with OKeh.[96]

As a child he grew up in an atmosphere where violence between friends and lovers was not unusual. He had violent spats with his girlfriend, Nootsy, and his first wife, Daisy. When his mother noticed blood on the back of his shirt and found out that Nootsy had taken a knife to him, she chased the girl down and throttled her mercilessly.

"That taught me a lesson," Armstrong remembered. His memoirs of his childhood include plenty of violence between women and men, women and women, men and men. It is perhaps notable, as historian Bruce Boyd Raeburn has observed, that he only slapped Lillian once. Unsurprisingly, Lillian, too, was straying from the marital bed during these years, "running around with one of the Chicago pimps while I was at work," according to Armstrong.

Nineteen-year-old Alpha must have looked pretty good as she flirted with him from her front-row seat at the Vendome. Armstrong described her as a "poor girl, not near as fortunate as Lil was when I first met her." She did domestic work for a couple named Mr. and Mrs. Taylor in Hyde Park. At first, she invited him over to the Taylor home and cooked meals for him while her employers were out. One evening the Taylors unexpectedly dropped in on them, sitting in the parlor, tapping into the whiskey and dancing to phonograph records. But the Taylors grew to like him, as did Alpha's mother, Florence. He soon realized that he was happier at the Smith apartment at 33rd Street and Cottage Grove Avenue, humble as it was with a wooden bathtub and cramped quarters, than at the nice home he owned with Lillian. He brought Clarence over to visit and the child was so happy that it seemed to make sense for both of them to move in. He bought an expensive blue coat with a lamb collar for Alpha and some diamonds.

"I became quite a figure at the Vendome," he explained, "especially with the gals." It is in this context or something like it that we might think about his extraordinary solo on *Tight Like This*. The title was a direct reference to *It's Tight Like That*, a song composed by pianist Thomas Dorsey and Hudson Woodbridge. "The suggestive songs always sold well," remembered Dorsey. There were a lot of pieces like this with titillating double entendres. *It's Tight Like That* was first recorded in September 1928 and did extremely well. McKinney's Cotton Pickers recorded an instrumental version in November, and a few weeks later their arranger and clarinetist-saxophonist, Don Redman, Armstrong's friend from the Henderson band, was in Chicago, working with Armstrong for the OKeh sessions on December 11 and 12. Redman brought with him a takeoff composed by Cotton Picker trumpeter Langston Curl called *Tight Like This*.

When the Cotton Pickers recorded Dorsey's *It's Tight Like That*, they dropped the words and substituted a vigorous scat chorus. In place of the suggestive lyrics, they came up with an idea that was just as titillating, if not more. In dialogue with the scat, sung by a male lead, another male voice enters in falsetto voice: "Oh it's tight like that," the female impersonator shouts out. The effect is obviously sexual and comic. A pleased female, played by a "cross-dressing" man, urges on her male lover, whose inarticulate scat, in this context, depicts the aroused vocalizations of the sex act. The band had first worked out this concept in its performance of another suggestive tune, *Four or Five Times*, recorded the previous July.

The Cotton Pickers' arrangement of *It's Tight Like That* inspired trumpeter Langston Curl to replace scat with his own trumpet in his knockoff, *Tight Like This*. My guess is that Armstrong's solo had little or nothing to do with Curl's original solo; in any event, the results are magnificent. Some writers have been reluctant to discuss the obvious sexual connections. Putting scat eroticism to the side gave Armstrong a chance to demonstrate what he could do with his trumpet—which must also be taken as a suggestion of what he could do in bed.

These erotic markers are obviously pertinent, but it is important not to be seduced by them, so to speak. The necessary response to Norman Mailer and anyone else who overemphasizes the relation-ship between jazz and sex is to insist that superior jazz always carries the workings of superior musical intelligence. White observers in the 1920s were hardly thinking in this way: "It is only within the last two or three years that intelligence has been brought to bear upon [jazz's] musical development," wrote Henry Osgood in 1926, and he was clearly not giving the credit to ear-playing African Americans. Even today one often reads how Armstrong was a nonintellectual musician, an intuitive improviser who preferred not to think too much.[97]

In *Tight Like This* his intelligence manifests itself as a dazzling display of blues figuration, splendidly varied and nicely framed over three choruses according to a pattern of increasing intensity. His solo starts (CD 1:31) with bare and simple gestures, but quickly grows more animated. By the end of chorus one he is showing his stuff, with elaborate sawtooth descents and double-time syncopations. A falsetto voice urges him on, "Oh it's tight like that, Louie." Chorus two (CD 2:06) features a simple but assertive rhythmic figure in the accompaniment, almost identical to the accompaniment used in his famous chorus, three years later, on *Star Dust*, which musicians at one time referred to as the "fucking rhythm."

The blues were what did it for him in New Orleans, and they do it for him here, with a strong role for rhythmic pliancy. The piece is in the minor mode, which takes away the impact of the blue third and leads him instead to a poignant lowered fifth (CD 2:37). Chorus three (CD 2:40) amounts to a sustained climax. Again and again the trumpet pounds on its high note, finally collapsing into a lowered fifth (CD 3:12) and then the home pitch. There is nothing subtle about this sexual metaphor. Storytelling in Armstrong's music is rarely as explicit as it is here. One can only wonder why the falsetto voice descends to the normal male register for its final two interjections; maybe the performer was simply distracted by the magnificence of Armstrong's trumpet, or perhaps there was a decision to soften the sexualized context for the OKeh businessmen.

Can the solo stand on its own, without a sexualized narrative? Of course it can. But this context certainly stimulated and shaped his creativity. We may prefer a pure and "classic" Armstrong, but for him, musical and sexual power were probably conflated more than we can possibly know.

It was his old friend Don Redman who delivered *Tight Like This* from Detroit, along with several arrangements for the December sessions. The group recorded on December 5 and 12 as "Louis Armstrong and His Savoy Ballroom Five," then on December 4 and 7, with only slight changes in personnel, as "Louis Armstrong and His Orchestra." Armstrong was probably leading one of the Savoy bands himself and needed some fresh arrangements; all six of the numbers recorded by Louis Armstrong and His Savoy Ballroom Five were probably arranged by Redman.[98]

*Beau Koo Jack* (an amusingly frenchified way of saying "lots of money") is a spritely arrangement that would have been at home with many modern jazz orchestras. Armstrong and pianist Alex Hill share credit as co-composers. Hill had arrived in Chicago in early October and was playing "eccentric piano" (according to the *Defender*) at the Dreamland with Jimmy Wade's band. A copyright deposit for *Beau Koo Jack* reached Washington, D.C., on November 23, with Redman listed as the arranger.[99] The piece is full of breaks and moves at a very fast tempo. Armstrong's contribution to the composition was almost certainly limited to his solo, which is written out in the arrangement and played note for note by the trumpet section of Earl Hines and His Orchestra in a recording made two months later. The solo itself features five two-bar breaks. *Beau Koo Jack* is a rare example (along with *Cornet Chop Suey*) of one of Armstrong's mature solos that seems to have been conceived with notation, copyright, and publication in mind.

Alex Hill bounced into town and talked Armstrong into cowriting a piece with him, dangling the possibility of good returns from copyright and sales of a stock arrangement. The result was a notationally conceived solo that has a nice shape but it is out of sync with the bluesy pliancy of *Savoy Blues*, *West End Blues*, and *Tight Like This*. With its fast tempo, emphasis on two-bar, breaklike modules, and relatively stiff rhythmic profile, it is a somewhat of a throwback to the Henderson days, four years before.

The Redman sessions also included an Armstrong composition entitled *Heah Me Talkin' to Ya?*[100] At the beginning of the performance he speaks those very words; the rest of the recording is purely instrumental. "Hear me talking to you" has been associated with him ever since, as a dash of his inventive jive talk. But in 1928 the phrase firmly referenced a comedian named Marshall "Garbage" Rogers, who was popular on the South Side that summer. Rogers made it the centerpiece of a comedy routine for which he became well known. Rogers and his partner called themselves "The Savoy Twins," and they performed nightly in the spring of 1928 with the Savoy Ballroom Orchestra. On June 23, 1928, Garbage married Gladys Mike in a "syncopated wedding" at the Savoy Ballroom. The *Light* announced the wedding on its front page with the huge headline "Oh, Heah Me Talkin' ta Ya." Armstrong obviously conceived his piece for the Savoy, where he could connect to Marshall's humor by simply speaking the phrase. It is easy to believe that the piece was even created for the Savoy ceremony on June 23—who else would the successful Garbage have turned to in order to create a syncopated wedding?

The "non-Redman" December recordings feature bluesy work from Armstrong in loose arrangements, a sign of hasty assembly. Nevertheless, there is some stunning music here. His filigree on *No* and *Basin Street Blues* is beautifully crafted, bold, and multidimensional, with shadings of dynamics, varied range, and a heightened sense of drama. The relaxed cool-blues-crooning style first documented in *West End Blues* comes to the fore in these sessions. *No One Else but You* gives Hines a chance to stretch out with his eccentric harmonies, and Armstrong negotiates Redman's changes with a strong trumpet solo. Armstrong's vocal solo for *Save It Pretty Mamma*, another Redman composition, elicits lovely accompaniment from Hines.

When Armstrong finished the December 1928 recordings, he probably did not know that he would soon be leaving his own personal "second city." Chicago, after New Orleans, is inseparable from his musical achievement. In each place his accomplishments were built around a strong African-American identity, Chicago's being somewhat dependent on New Orleans, with the transformative power of the Great Migration accounting for much of the difference. His career for the next few years would be more peripatetic—a year in New York City, a little less in California, a summer in New Orleans, some time in England, and so forth. No other place would have the impact of Chicago, where he apprenticed with Oliver, broke away and married, stepped into the spotlight as a great soloist at premiere venues, and generated a long and rewarding series of recordings. Most of the places he knew in New Orleans are now gone forever, and even less survives as material witness to these glorious years in Chicago. The surviving witnesses are mainly the discs, cheaply made products that provide priceless access to a monumental musical achievement now recognized as one of the world's great flourishings of artistic production.

# EIGHT

# The White Turn

In October 1928, Armstrong enjoyed an extraordinary moment of recognition in a white nightclub, courtesy of bandleader Guy Lombardo. Lombardo and His Royal Canadians were seated for an extended gig at the Granada Inn, 6800 Cottage Grove Avenue, "one of the swellest white night clubs in the country," as the *Defender* put it, the band billed as "the sweetest jazz band this side of heaven." The popular Lombardo invited Armstrong and Singleton to attend the Granada as his special guests. He went so far as to cue their entrance into the club with a special chord from the band, then have them escorted to a ringside table near the bandstand. Later in the program Armstrong was asked to stand up and sing a number with the band. "Louis says he was never lauded and treated any better anywhere in his life as he was by this famous orchestral group," reported the *Defender*.

As impressive as Armstrong's rise was during the second half of the 1920s, he was still small potatoes compared with the big-name white bandleaders. There was Paul Whiteman, of course, who is best known today. Paul Ash enjoyed tremendous success in Chicago, with an estimated four million people walking through the doors to hear him during a 17-month run. Lombardo was beginning to accumulate that kind of momentum, and Armstrong liked to listen to him with his Savoy Ballroom colleagues, huddled around a radio set late at night in their shared apartment.

It was even possible, under quirky circumstances, for a few of the elite black musicians to perform with white bands. Ash made a single-night appearance at the Savoy in April 1928, and when he invited Armstrong on stage to sing, "the effect was just simply too obstreperous," according to the *Light and Heebie Jeebies*. Ash wanted to feature Armstrong with his band at the Roosevelt Theater, downtown, but the white musicians' union blocked him. During an extended stay at the Hotel Sherman, a singer with the Whiteman Orchestra had worked up a specialty number with violin obbligato. When the violinist, Joe Venuti, suddenly quit the gig, the singer insisted on bringing in Eddie South to replace him. South was hired, but management insisted that he stand behind a portable screen, making it impossible for the audience to see who was playing. "If only you were white . . . ," Whiteman used to say to Hines.

Lombardo was a specialist in "sweet" jazz, with little or no syncopation, emphasis on elegant and legato melody, and polished ensemble playing. Armstrong's interest in Lombardo's music—which remained strong throughout his life—has seemed incongruous to jazz purists, but he was not alone among black jazz musicians in admiring high standards of musicianship, no matter who was playing and in what style. Respect for expert control of the instrument became one of the distinguishing markers of jazz early on, and it remains so to the present day.

It is especially easy to understand his interest given the combination of polished musicianship and tremendous financial reward. Armstrong wanted what Lombardo had—big-time success, beyond the South Side of Chicago. Capturing the Lombardo sound would become part of his white turn in the second half of 1929. "When I had my first big band I always tried to get my sax section to sound like theirs," he explained, and he mentioned, in particular, choruses from *When You're Smiling* (recorded September 1929) and *Sweethearts on Parade* (December 1930).[101] When he was a teenager, Oliver had given him a recipe for commercial success: avoid too much variation and stick to the lead. In the late 1920s he understood that a path to greater (white) success would be careful study of this latest master of the melodic lead.

The appreciation was happily mutual. Though they were experts in the sweet style, at least some of the Lombardo men were also passionate about the kind of jazz Armstrong specialized in. They enjoyed jamming with black musicians on the South Side, telling them how sick they were of playing what they called "surfing" music. "I come down here to be reborn," Lombardo told Earl Hines. Thus it was that Lombardo went out of his way to honor a black musician in a place that Armstrong would not normally have been allowed to enter. Armstrong made a point of never forgetting personal favors (or slights, for that matter), and his moment at the Granada Inn clearly meant a lot to him. He put up with racist bigotry for virtually his entire life—stopped entry through the front door of a hotel, not receiving invitations that everyone else on a movie set got, announcers refusing to introduce him on the radio, bombs exploding outside of a venue where his integrated band was playing, and so forth. Lombardo from Canada made up for some of that in October 1928.

In the spring of 1929 Armstrong was continuing his gig at the Savoy, and he also appeared occasionally as a guest at the Regal Theater, across the street. Dave Peyton was leading the house band there, the Regal Symphonists, and his featured hot soloist was the twenty-four-year-old trumpeter Reuben Reeves, who had arrived in Chicago a year or so earlier, just in time to take Armstrong's place at the Vendome.

When the Regal opened in January 1928, it quickly upstaged the Vendome as the primary place to hear classy music, enjoy great entertainment, and see a movie to top it off. As the *Light* explained to its readers, the opening of this enterprise was "fraught with a definite racial significance." Fess Williams was lured from New York City to direct the orchestra. "For a performer or musician who appreciates class, this was what you could call a dream engagement," explained Williams, who waved his arms in such a way while conducting that people started calling him the black Ted Lewis, another popular white bandleader. The Regalettes, the house dancers, were choreographed by none other than Percy Venable. The orchestra accompanied the movie from the pit, but moved onto the stage for its featured segment of the program. Reeves was the leading hot soloist from virtually opening day. Peyton, who was initially in charge of hiring at the Regal, greatly admired Reeves, whom he identified in April 1928 as "now the cornet jazz king of America." Peyton knew that Armstrong was about to begin a stint four days later at the Savoy, right across the street, and the hyperbole would certainly have been taken by Armstrong as a direct challenge. Reeves was probably as much of a spur to Armstrong's accomplishments in the spring and summer of 1928 as Oliver had been the year before, when the two of them were battling across the street from one another at the Plantation and Sunset.

In late April 1929, Armstrong appeared at the Regal for a week as guest artist. The visit gave Peyton a chance to put his theory of Reeve's superiority to a test.[102] Instead of the typical light classic overture, he put together an arrangement designed to show off Reeves's various strengths. Since Armstrong was the featured guest, highlighting Reeves like this was a blatantly aggressive gesture; in Danny Barker's opinion, it was "vicious." Peyton waved his arms, urging Reeves into a frenzy with the kind of playing generally reserved for a finale, not the opening of a program.

The number that won the day for Armstrong was *I Can't Give You Anything but Love*. A review of his performance at the Regal called this tune his "favorite," which suggests that it was a regular repertory piece for him at the Savoy and Regal. He sang it with his "great big jovial smile" and "characteristic style." The last chorus was given to a cornet solo, and the audience demanded five encores.

It is no surprise that he was performing *I Can't Give You Anything but Love*, for the song ranked among the big hits of 1928 and 1929, having emerged from the very popular *Blackbirds of 1928*, a show produced by Lew Leslie for the Liberty Theater on Broadway, where it hung around for an unprecedented (for an all-black production) run of 518 performances. Lots of musicians, white and black, were performing and recording *I Can't Give You Anything but Love*; one advertisement touted it as "the song success of the Nation." We have seen on a number of occasions how Armstrong, like everyone else, sang and played current hits at the cabarets and theaters on the South Side, and this is simply one more example. Those current hits didn't get recorded because they didn't fit OKeh's business plan—until now.

For in March 1929 Armstrong made a brief trip to New York City. The visit was organized by OKeh executive Tommy Rockwell, who was stationed there. Perhaps Rockwell recognized that Armstrong had been selling well enough on OKeh's "popular" series (as I will soon explain, OKeh had been issuing his records on both the race series and the popular series) that it was worth trying out tunes that had genuine national status. *I Can't Give You Anything but Love* was recorded on March 5.

What is most distinctive about the performance is how Armstrong harnesses the breathy, silky quality of voice he had been cultivating, with the assistance of the microphone at the Savoy Ballroom, in service of the tender sentiments of the song. The sexuality communicated by his voice is rather different than the full-throttled aggressiveness of his trumpet in *Tight Like This*. His imaginary lover is treated to the sensual caresses of mellow ornamentation and delivery, which verge on gestural (in the first phrase, the words "love, baby"). Exaggerated articulation (in the second phrase, "of") is followed by slurs ("guess") and then effortless movement between words and scat ("all those things you've always pined for"). The latter combination is a new technique, one he had not previously put on record. It would now become standard for him.

*I Can't Give You Anything but Love* is another example of a piece for which he had time to work up his own distinctive version, leading to an achievement that defines him as a great melodist. The opening chorus, rendered by saxophones in the low register and by Armstrong on muted trumpet (the trombonist completes the chorus for him), serves as an indirect reminder of the connections of early jazz to heterophonic practices of the black vernacular: the saxophones play the melody straight while he simultaneously ornaments it and adds fill-ins. But the dialogue doesn't sound like heterophony, since he usually delays a beat or two behind the saxes and sometimes paraphrases the tune to form a counterstatement.

In the vocal chorus that follows he uses the same strategy, but now his version of the tune is completely recast. The saxes play the melody straight, and what he sings is an obbligato, not a paraphrase. The formula allows him to have things both ways: it relieves him of the burden of carrying the lead while simultaneously providing that lead in the background, where it can still serve as an organizing principle. He can move between a feeling of being in synchrony with the sentiments of the words and playful, dancing detachment. The fluid style of verbal articulation contributes to the same feeling. The line "gee I'd like to see you looking swell, baby" is arranged in a way that is almost comic; perhaps the idea came from Chicago.

The trick of this performance is the inversion of the "second" part—the kind of ensemble line that he used to play with Oliver and that was the heart of collective improvisation—and the lead: the unadorned lead is put in secondary position, played by subdued saxophones, while the sung second part grabs your attention. Since virtually his first vocal on record Armstrong had been singing similar transformations of the given tune; *Heebie Jeebies* is an excellent example. What is new for him (at least on recordings) is the straight lead in the background. The same format had been used for many years with hot instrumental solos, but there cannot have been many precedents for doing it with a vocal. Perhaps this was Rockwell's attempt to make his singing more accessible to white audiences unprepared for his radical transformation of the melody.

The performance ends with a beautifully conceived trumpet solo that was probably worked out at the Savoy and Regal.[103] It is full of the design details that we have seen him experimenting with during the past few years—double-time figuration, a phrase of bluesy pliancy moving through the same set of pitches, sudden and dramatic gestures, and varied phrase lengths. The principle of varying phrase lengths is extended more than ever, with short and subdued phrases followed by longer and unpredictable ones, irregular placement of phrase beginnings and endings, and constant variety of rhythmic-melodic detail. The solo is one more magisterial realization of the fixed and variable model as he conceived it in the late 1920s. We could regard this entire performance of *I Can't Give You Anything but Love* as a farewell song of appreciation to his adoring African-American fan base in Chicago, a way of recognizing that what mattered most for his musical development was this: the loving dialogue between his creative engagement with the black vernacular and the rousing, sustained endorsement of the results from his African-American audiences.[104]

The recording was noticed by Hoagy Carmichael in California, by Doc Cheatham in Europe, and by Bud Freeman in Chicago. Ethel Waters parodied him in her 1932 recording of the same tune.

"When we were bored we could always listen to Louis Armstrong recordings," remembered Carmichael. "They were lifters and gave life meaning again."

Coincidentally, this foray into the national distribution of current hits happened alongside what may have been the last studio-generated piece Armstrong ever recorded. *Knockin' a Jug*, with composer credit to Armstrong and banjoist Eddie Condon, is a simple blues. (Kaiser Marshall remembered that the name came from a gallon jug of whisky the musicians had brought along to the studio.) Armstrong plays a bluesy solo and Jack Teagarden, who had admired him ever since the release of *Cold in Hand Blues* in 1925, plays a trombone solo. It was Armstrong's first interracial recording session and an appropriate welcome to New York City, since his stay there for the next 12 months would involve whites to unprecedented degrees and in various ways.

For *I Can't Give You Anything but Love* and the third tune recorded on March 5, *Mahogany Hall Stomp*, Rockwell used the Luis Russell Orchestra, which he was currently managing. Russell, the pianist and leader, was born in Panama but started work in New Orleans in 1919. The studio was full of New Orleanians. There was guitarist Lonnie Johnson, with whom Armstrong had so much fun recording *Hotter Than That*; Paul Barbarin, with whom he coauthored *Don't Forget to Mess Around When You're Doing the Charleston* in 1926; Albert Nicholas and Luis Russell, with whom he had played in New Orleans; and Pops Foster, his buddy from the coal-cart days. *Mahogany Hall Stomp*, composed by Spencer Williams (who literally grew up in the famed house of prostitution on Basin Street), is a joyous celebration of music from home, made new in New York City.

The rhythm section is especially effective. Beginning with Armstrong's solo (CD 1:32) it is all flat 4/4, a groove led by Foster's prominently plucked bass. To this Armstrong responds with relaxed playing, full of charm and economy. Foster claimed that the recording made a big impression in New York. "I thought it wasn't anything, but *Mahogany Hall*, that's the number that made the string bass famous. Louis just holds that note and I'm just walking behind it. Then everybody started buying string basses." "Jazz is happier music than any other," said Foster on another occasion, "the beat and

*Savoy Ballroom, New York City, 1936 (The William Russell Photographic Collection, MSS 520 F. 241, Williams Research Center, The Historic New Orleans Collection)*

the tempo make it," and he could have cited *Mahogany Hall Stomp* as a classic manifestation of those qualities.

This brief visit to New York included two appearances at the Savoy Ballroom in Harlem on Saturday and Sunday, March 9 and 10, accompanied by the Russell band. People lined up on Lenox Avenue to enter the 5,000-capacity hall and many were turned away. The Savoy management honored Armstrong with a banquet, with Fletcher Henderson as master of ceremonies and speeches from Rockwell, Jimmie Harris, Chick Webb, and Bennie Carter. When he got back to Chicago, he assured everyone that he was happier there, that New York was too fast for him and dangerous with cars rushing through the streets. He rejoined Dickerson at the Savoy and made appearances at the Regal in early May alongside comedian Marshall "Garbage" Rogers of *Heah Me Talkin' to Ya?* fame. Both venues were experiencing a downturn. The owner was persuasive but kept stringing the musicians along. "Every time pay day come around, oh, oh, another hard luck story," Armstrong remembered. His mortgage payments were past due. He and Zutty talked it over: if there's no money this week, we quit, they agreed, several weeks in a row.

In fact, the glory years of jazz on the South Side were coming to an end. Oliver had left a year before, when the Plantation was shut down. Federal agents were now stepping in aggressively. Raids became so frequent that Earl Hines got in the habit of racing to the paddy wagon so that he could get a seat and didn't have to stand. Theater orchestras were hit hard by the introduction of talkies, known by the commercial name for the sound system, "Vitaphone." Unemployed musicians joked to one another, "Could I have a cigarette until the Vitaphone blows over?" String players took the heaviest blows, but all the musicians suffered; Loew's announced that it would not even be hiring organists anymore. On top of all of this radio was picking up, with more options for listening and more radios purchased every year. It is not surprising that more than a few Chicago musicians headed for New York City.

Meanwhile, Tommy Rockwell had his mind set on bigger things than just a couple of recording sessions. What he really wanted was to manage Armstrong in New York. His next move was to lure him back with the offer of a movie as well as a new show by Vincent Youmans called *Great Day*. Armstrong thought about it and talked it over with his friends.

They decided to take the trip together, the whole Dickerson band. He divided up the advance from Rockwell and they patched up their cars. Armstrong got his Hupmobile repaired, Dickerson bought a used Marmon, Gene Anderson had his Essex, and Fred Robinson bought something new and relatively lightweight. Lillian borrowed some money through a pawn. Zutty gave his wife, Marge, half of his share and told her that he would send for her in a month. Lillian planned on staying in Chicago. (Alpha's activity at this time is not known.) She did eventually go to New York, at least for a bit, but for now her place was here. While Armstrong was in transit, she performed a piano recital on May 27 in celebration of her studies with Louis Victor Saar at the Chicago College of Music, with Mozart, Weber, Chopin, Saar, Debussy, and Scriabin on the program. "I always did feel more at home with the longhair stuff, anyway," she once admitted.

With Singleton's vibraphones strapped to the roof of a car, the musicians wound their way across the country. They were astonished to hear Armstrong's records being played in some of the towns they stopped in—Toledo, Cleveland, Detroit, Buffalo. People knew him thanks to his records and also the radio broadcasts from Chicago. When Dickerson's car broke down, they all squeezed into the remaining three cars. They wanted to see Niagara Falls and got lost, driving 200 miles in the wrong direction. When they finally straggled into New York, the radiator cap on Armstrong's Hupmobile blew up at 42nd Street and Broadway, steam spraying out in all directions. A policeman noticed their Chicago license plates and asked them with a grin if they had any shotguns in the cars. "No Suh, Boss," they replied. Tired, hungry, and broke, with a rusty set of vibraphones, they plopped themselves down in Rockwell's office.

An irritated Rockwell insisted that he had invited only Armstrong, not the whole band. Armstrong kept his composure and simply answered, "Just the same, my boys are here in New York, so find something for us to do." *Great Day*, with a pit orchestra built around none other than Fletcher Henderson's Orchestra, turned out to be not for him. At the rehearsal, run by the composer and arranger of the show, Armstrong was asked to change chairs from first trumpet to second. They rehearsed the number again and the results were still unsatisfactory, so "the decision was made that Armstrong was not adapted to the show business," as the *New York Age* delicately put it. It was not the first time he was deemed lacking in "legitimate" abilities, and the event might have reminded him of his first rehearsal with Henderson in the fall of 1924.[105]

He and his friends stopped by the Rhythm Club, which was run by one Bert Hall. Hall had recently reopened the club in a lovely new building at 163 West 132nd Street, working with painter Aaron Douglas on the interior decorations. Hall was from Chicago, and Armstrong and his bandmates certainly knew him already. The Rhythm Club was the natural place for them to socialize and find gigs.

Trumpeter Rex Stewart described a "caste system" of black professional musicians in New York that dated back to the 1910s and the heyday of James Reese Europe. Europe was a major figure in society orchestras and one of the founders of the Clef Club, which assumed an exclusive position servicing musicians suited to the talented-tenth vision. The name itself indicated the kind of place it was—a place for note-reading, legitimate musicians. Armstrong was hardly a Clef Club

*Niagara Falls with Homer Hobson (Courtesy of the Louis Armstrong House Museum)*

musician. His place was the Rhythm Club, which catered to newcomers; he probably could have figured it all out just from the names.

Several musicians left rich descriptions of the Rhythm Club, its jam sessions, and its social atmosphere. With bookers stopping by regularly to see who was available, musicians were eager to sit in with the house band and show what they could do. Danny Barker remembered them standing in line, waiting for a turn to improvise a chorus on Gershwin's *Liza*, with Pops Foster slapping his string bass. The main activity was very late; the regular slot for the house band was 3:30 to 7:30 a.m. Jelly Roll Morton, dressed in candy-striped silk shirts, liked to give "lessons" to anyone who would listen, predicting what music would be like in 20 or 30 years and explaining how he had created jazz. When no house band was scheduled, the pianists took over. Willie "The Lion" Smith liked to provoke competitions: "'Lead me to a piano my fingers are itchin', I'm rearing to go. I'm the Lion." Morton retorted from across the room: "'Man let the kid go and *practice*. Let him go and practice man, he don't know what he's doing." Hot dogs and hamburgers were sold for 25 cents. Gambling was in the rear, with five pool tables. Morton and Bill Robinson liked to play pool together, bantering back and forth.

The first job Armstrong and the Dickerson band landed was at the Audubon Theater, 3950 Broadway, as a substitute for Ellington's band, which had to pull out at the last minute. Their assignment was to accompany Letha Hill, who kept turning around to glance at the band, distracted by Armstrong's fancy playing. He was not in the mood, apparently, to stay under. The band's featured number, performed from the stage, was *St. Louis Blues*, and Armstrong laid on the high notes, astonishing everyone. Even the pit band, with its large violin section and classical players, stood up and joined the applause when he finished, something Zutty Singleton had never seen before. A glimpse of this moment must have been captured on the December 13, 1929, recordings of *St. Louis Blues* by Louis Armstrong and His Orchestra.

Next the band opened for a week at the Savoy Ballroom, between 140th and 141st Streets on Lenox Avenue. They tried out for a Ziegfeld production called *Show Girl*, with Florenz Ziegfeld himself sitting in the front row, checking them out, but the job went to Ellington. Within a few weeks Rockwell placed them at a premier, long-term spot, Connie's Inn, which would become Armstrong's stepping-stone to Broadway. Working at Connie's and on Broadway placed him in the central axis of black entertainment for white audiences in New York City. For the most part, the expectations were nothing new: these venues thrived on exploitive white primitivism, a conception that simultaneously glamorized and demeaned black music. But the scene was very different from South Side Chicago in the extent to which it was organized, with a lot of money pouring into a diverse and highly controlled industry. The exposure ultimately opened up huge white audiences for him.

## Hot Chocolates

Trombonist Clyde Bernhardt, from Harrisburg, Pennsylvania, was astonished when he got off the train at 125th Street in 1928 and opened his eyes to Harlem for the first time. His family had advised him to wear his Sunday suit, but that did not prepare him for the upscale dressing on Seventh Avenue. Tall women who worked as chorus girls strolled around in furs, pulling little dogs on long chains. Others wore small hats and semi-flapper dresses with the belt low in the back. Men favored form-fitting Oxford gray suits with pinstripe pants, short jackets, vests, spats, shiny black patent leather shoes, buttonhole flowers, breast-pocket handkerchiefs, derby hats, and homburg hats. There was clearly some money in Harlem.

A good chunk of it was coming from wealthy whites who streamed in for evening entertainment. Since 1925, especially, white tourism had become big business; pianist and composer Eubie Blake called it a "heat wave." The Negro was in vogue, as Langston Hughes put it.

Armstrong had plenty of experience with white slumming, but he had never seen anything quite like this. Black entertainment in Harlem was so popular and fueled by so much money that some clubs found it profitable to become whites-only. Others were not exclusively white but predominantly so. In 1927 writer Rudolf Fisher returned to Harlem after being away for five years, and he was shocked by the demographic changes in his favorite clubs. He wrote an article for the *American Mercury* and called it "The Caucasian Storms Harlem." Whites had become "spellbound" by Negro music and "that endemic Negroism, the Charleston dance," he wrote.

The Cotton Club was the elite black and tan that notoriously prohibited black admission. As at all of the Harlem clubs, everyone working there was black. Someone like Bill Robinson or Ethel Waters could get in, but such exceptions were few. "Nobody wants razors, blackjacks, or fists flying," explained entertainer Jimmy Durante, in defense of segregated policies, "and the chances of a war are less if there's no mixing."

Danny Barker wrote about the "crafty night people" who made a living producing the racial fantasies of the black and tans. "Harlem could be a farce," he wrote. "It was a place of wretched poor black people making believe they were happy, putting on an act, dancing and singing on the outside but all tangled up with misfortunes and degradation on the inside." Slumming whites called out, "Come on, monkey! Entertain me!" Barker thought of these places as "special slave quarters."

The familiar primitivist package was decked out with unprecedented glamour and excitement. James Weldon Johnson wrote about whites "attempting to throw off the crusts and layers of inhibitions laid on by sophisticated civilization; striving to yield to the feel and experience of abandon; seeking to recapture a state of primitive joy in life and living; trying to work their way back into that jungle which was the original Garden of Eden; in a word, doing their best to pass for colored." "You go sort of primitive up there," acknowledged Durante, "with bands moaning blues like nobody's business, slim, bare-thighed brown-skin gals tossing their torsos, and the Negro melody artists bearing down something terrible on the minor notes. The average colored man you see along the streets in Harlem doesn't know any more about these dumps than the old maid in North Forks, South Dakota." Those bare-thighed gals were light brown, of course, café au lait, close to white standards of beauty, but slightly dark and exotic.

It was the familiar mix of controlling black people and desiring them at the same time. Relative to Chicago the whole scene was cranked up a couple of notches, with more money, more patronage, more competition, more hired creativity, more business savvy. "The whole set was like a sleepy-time down South during slavery," remembered Cab Calloway, who was at the Cotton Club for many years, "and the idea was to make whites who came feel like they were being catered to and entertained by black slaves." Black music was heard as a natural sonic production coming from a place of no inhibition. It was for putting aside restraints, sinking into the body, getting in touch with the primordial id. Everything happened late at night, after the Broadway stages emptied out, when less adventurous New Yorkers were asleep.

Connie's Inn was a basement club on Seventh Avenue at 131st Street, second in prestige only to the Cotton Club. In June 1929 the owner needed the regular house band, led by Leroy Smith, for a new Broadway show that he was sponsoring downtown, so he hired Armstrong and his friends to replace them. In front of the club grew the Tree of Hope, a talisman that entertainers touched to improve their chances of landing gigs, and next door was the Lafayette Theater.

With its steep cover charge ($2.50) and intimate atmosphere, Connie's had something special. It went after the best entertainers and paid them well. It usually ran two shows per evening, one at midnight and the other at 2:00 a.m. Policies were not always consistent, but few African Americans were able to make it through the door.[106] Locals gathered in the alley behind the building to lis-

*Connie's Inn (Photographs and Prints Division, Schomburg Center for Research in Black Culture, The New York Public Library, Astor, Lenox, and Tilden Foundations)*

ten through a window and in the rib joint above to feel vibrations through the floor.

The assignment for the Dickerson group was to play for the floor show and for social dancing, the format familiar from the Chicago cabarets. Dancer Louise Cook stood out in Armstrong's memories of summer 1929. One reviewer described Cook as "a lady made entirely of rubber" who performed the kind of dance that "grandfather used to sneak off and see at the county fair"; Mezzrow said her dance was a "Salome routine." Immerman purchased a set of tunable tom-toms to help drummer Zutty Singleton accompany her sinuous moves. Cook's act always elicited demands for encores.[107] Italian-American sculptor Antonio Salemme, who produced renowned busts of Ethel Waters and Paul Robeson in the 1920s, asked Cook to pose for him in September, claiming that hers was "the most perfect form he has seen among Negro women."

One number for the social dance period of the evening was *Indian Cradle Song*, which Armstrong characterized as a slow fox trot. Singleton's tom-toms were featured in the introduction. The recording Armstrong made in May 1930 preserves a beautifully designed trumpet solo, intricate and rich, confirming that this was a solo he played often and improved over time, getting it just right in the tradition of the special chorus. The solo is not particularly well known, but it can easily stand alongside his great solos from the late 1920s.

The crowds of slumming whites included a good number of musicians who studied the riffs, warmed themselves by the fire, and asked to sit in. On a Sunday night in late July some of them rented out Connie's for a banquet in Armstrong's honor, presenting him with a gold wristwatch inscribed "To Louis Armstrong, the World's Greatest Cornetist, from the Musicians of New York."

Connie Immerman and his brother George took an active role running their club. Connie, described by one musician as "a little fat guy," had designed his latest revue, *Tan Town Topics*, with Broadway in mind. After a trial run, he took the show to the Hudson Theater on West 44th Street and changed its name to *Hot Chocolates*. Direct connections to Broadway were another thing that distinguished the elite black and tans in New York City from those in Chicago. The Cotton Club and Connie's each put together two floor shows a year with the goal of transforming them into successful Broadway hits in a chase after big financial rewards. Armstrong walked right into this fully developed scene like a champion and made his mark.

"All-colored" shows on Broadway did not pay performers as much as the elite cabarets or big-time vaudeville, but the potential boost in reputation was enough to entice the performers to sign up anyway. Black composers James P. Johnson, Fats Waller, and Eubie Blake went back and forth between the cabarets and Broadway, as did white composers like Jimmy McHugh. The mutually reinforcing publicity of the cabarets and theaters generated one big swell of "Nubian" excitement, as white marketing liked to put it.

When Rudolf Fisher lamented the rush of whites that had ruined his favorite places of African-American sociability in Harlem, he blamed the whole mess on the 1921 Broadway success of *Shuffle Along*. "*Shuffle Along* was a honey of a show," remembered Langston Hughes, "swift, bright, funny, rollicking, and gay, with a dozen danceable, singable tunes." The show was conceived by a fortuitous combination of two sets of partners, the song-writing team Eubie Blake and Noble Sissle, and the comedy team Flournoy Miller and Aubrey Lyles. At the 63rd Street Music Hall (22 West 63rd Street), *Shuffle*

*Along* revived the tradition of all-black casts on Broadway that had started decades earlier but since faded. The talent-filled cast included blackface comedians Miller and Lyles; singers Florence Mills, Adelaide Hall, and Paul Robeson; the future choir director Hall Johnson (playing viola in the orchestra); and the future composer William Grant Still (oboe). Sixteen-year-old Josephine Baker made the most out of her place as "end girl" in the dancing chorus, taking advantage of the little solo spot allotted to this position in exits and, as Blake remembered, "doing all the steps the rest were doing, but funnier." The narrative was very loose, like all Broadway shows at this time, with lots of room for specialty acts, one after the other, in a dazzling flow of variety and exciting ensembles. "Just enough plot," according to *Billboard*, "to be easily remembered and afford some good comedy."

*Shuffle Along*'s combination of low ticket prices, low salaries, recycled costumes, and first-rate entertainment produced profits. The show ran for 504 performances in New York City, followed by three years of national tours. The musical hit was *I'm Just Wild About Harry*. Blake claimed that his melodies helped usher in a new style on Broadway, replacing "mushy, sobby, sentimental love songs" with "lively, jazzy" tunes. From now on the typical song mix on Broadway would include uptempo jazz-ragtime alongside ballads and comedy songs. Musicians in the orchestra memorized their parts, since white audiences expected black musicians to be illiterate.

*Shuffle Along* was packed with stereotypical black stage humor, much of it derived from minstrelsy, even including two minor characters named Uncle Tom and Old Black Joe. One highlight was a choreographed comic fight, with Miller and Lyles portraying two mayoral candidates; this scene became a favorite of Fiorello LaGuardia. Representations of black humor and black music were both important, but what made *Shuffle* sizzle with heated blackness was the dancing. The prominence of dance was signaled by the very title of the show, a nod to minstrel stereotypes and also a point of humor: any onstage shuffling was of the parody type. Most of the dancing was fast, peppy, versatile, eccentric, and varied. Tommy Woods twisted acrobatically across the stage in perfect rhythm, tap dancer Charlie Davis astonished audiences with his speed, and the lovely chorus girls were amazing. Blake explained how traditional white offerings on Broadway had beautiful girls in beautiful clothes who would "just walk around and kick a little"; in contrast, "our girls were beautiful and they *danced*! There had never been anything like it." Dancing was usually mentioned first and most often in white reviews of not just *Shuffle Along* but virtually all "Colored Broadway" productions during the 1920s.

Black patrons were admitted but not encouraged. Theater critics for black newspapers found it difficult to get complementary tickets so that they could write reviews.[108] A reviewer for the *Interstate Tattler* called all-black shows on Broadway "o'fay revues"; they "leave me flat, peeved and irritable," she confessed. *Shuffle Along* launched so many imitations that a song was composed to make fun of the situation. *It's Getting Dark on Old Broadway* (1922) was based on a pun that was just too good to pass up, as the sudden popularity of all-black casts threw a different set of meanings into the nickname the "Great White Way": "Pretty choc'late babies / Shake and shimmie ev'rywhere / Real dark-town entertainers hold the stage." More than a few white performers must have felt a touch of the same anxiety that was driving the white musicians' union in Chicago toward exclusionary practices.

The primitivist conventions of the cabarets were represented on black Broadway, but with considerable modification. Theaters had elevated stages, of course, with distance between stage and seats and with less expensive admission, thus opening the event to a broader swath of the public. In contrast to a place like the Sunset or Connie's, whites did not go to theaters to try out the Charleston with one of the chorines or flirt with sexual transgression. The entertainment was pitched for a mainstream audience, and representation of the African-American vernacular varied. The contrast between dancing and music makes this clear.

For while the music was designed to be catchy and danceable, its contribution to the effect of "real dark-town" entertainment was limited. An interviewer once asked Sissle and Blake if they made concessions to white taste when they wrote and performed for Broadway. Blake's answer was decisive and perhaps unexpected: "You see, Sissle went to white schools," he said, "and he had a different slant on a lyric than the average Negro person. I wrote waltzes. The reason I did that is because I was exposed to them; these were great writers, Victor Herbert, Franz Lehár, Leslie Stuart." Sissle and Blake did not have to adapt to white taste because that was how they had been trained. The majority of white patrons at the 63rd Street Music Hall must have felt that the music was black enough, though dissenting voices occasionally popped up. *In Bamville*, a 1924 follow-up to *Shuffle Along*, was attacked by a white critic who complained of "too much 'art' and not enough Africa . . . even in the music of that gifted melodist, Eubie Blake. He might now be a Professor Blake, Doctor of Music Blake, for all the real Blakiness of his music in the first act. . . . No feeling within you that Victor Herbert couldn't have composed it on a bet."

This concession to white musical style was a key element of all-black productions on Broadway. The burden of carrying the energy of the black vernacular was assigned to dancing, which, compared to black vernacular music, was much easier for mainstream whites to relate to. Eubie Blake, James P. Johnson, and Fats Waller all understood that. Broadway audiences—and by extension audiences throughout the country—were pleased to have a doctor of music setting the tunes that sprang the light-brown-thighed bodies into vigorous, seductive motion across the stage.

Following the success of *Shuffle Along*, *Liza* brought the Charleston dance to Broadway in 1922. *Runnin' Wild*, with music by James P. Johnson and lyrics by Cecil Mack, carried the Charleston to greater popularity in 1923, aided by Johnson's tune of the same name. "Jimmy Johnson had the band lay out while he, the bass, and the drums went along with the whole chorus singing and patting 'Charleston—Charleston—that dance from Carolina,'" remembered Perry Bradford, "as Josephine Baker was twirling her sexy body and twisting those gorgeous legs to that African beat." The year 1923 also welcomed *Dinah*, with tunes (only one survives) composed by Tim Brymn and Sidney Bechet. "Too much attention has been paid to the feet and not enough to the head," complained a reviewer of *Dinah* in the *Defender*.

Lew Leslie was the central figure who connected cabaret floor shows to Broadway. He became so closely associated with all-black shows that many people were shocked when they first heard he was white. Black entertainers like Florence Mills were loyal to him, and in turn he made Mills famous. But he preferred to use whites behind the scenes, including composers J. Russell Robinson and the team of Dorothy Fields and Jimmy McHugh. "The two greatest Negro songs now sung were written by white men—*Ol' Man River* and *That's Why Darkies Were Born*," explained Leslie, in defense of his hiring practices.

With *Blackbirds of 1928* Leslie hit it big, to the tune of 518 performances at the Liberty Theater. The whole country got to know *I Can't Give You Anything but Love* by Fields and McHugh. Earl "Snakehips" Tucker, weaving his undulating pelvis across the stage, was a dance sensation. But the true standout was Bill Bojangles Robinson in his Broadway debut. After *Blackbirds of 1928* had gathered only lukewarm reception for three weeks, Leslie hired Robinson as an "extra attraction" inserted late in the show. Praise for Robinson's stair dance was instant, universal, and dramatic, with at least seven newspapers heralding him as the greatest of all dancers. If Leslie's earlier productions had established Florence Mills as the queen of black female entertainers—when she died suddenly in 1927, an estimated 150,000 people lined the streets for her funeral—*Blackbirds of 1928* did something similar for Robinson. *Blackbirds of 1928* had been developed at the Cotton Club, where Fields and McHugh were regularly employed, and it was the model for Immerman's *Hot Chocolates*.

Immerman hired Andy Razaf and Fats Waller to write the music and Leonard Harper, who had worked on *Shuffle Along*, to stage and produce his new revue. *Hot Chocolates* started as *Tan Town Topics* at Connie's in late February 1929, and by June 3 it was ready for the Windsor Theater in the Bronx. Immerman tried unsuccessfully to lure Bojangles Robinson, Snakehips Tucker, and Ethel Waters. On June 20 the production opened at the Hudson Theater with a cast of 85.

"It is distinctly a dancing show," wrote *Variety* in its review of the Hudson premiere. The male chorus line, named the "Bon Bon Buddies," eclipsed the female line, a rare feat.[109] The girls nevertheless used "every muscle of their bodies as well as their hands, ears and heads in wild flurries of maddening dance routines." Louise Cook did her "phallic dance" in a set piece called the *Goddess of Rain* with a specially made backdrop, leaving "her audience either speechless or hysterical, depending upon its temperament." (This was one of the songs that Cab Calloway sang when he joined the show in September.) Baby Cox, described by the *Defender* as a "little dark-skinned girl with remarkable talent," pleased the crowd with her cross-dressing routine, hooking up with the petite Madeline Belt. In *Hot Chocolates*, Cox, who is known to jazz fans today for her performances with the Ellington Orchestra, "not only dances but sings and tosses across the footlights a personality that makes her a wow," reported the *Interstate Tattler*. The handsome Paul Meers, stripped to the waist, led his equally beautiful and slender wife, Thelma, in a graceful adagio routine.

"The dancing does it," insisted the *Tattler*, which agreed with most other newpapers that the eccentric Jazzlips Richardson, "tap dancer, adagio dancer, contortionist, and capable of making his lips do incredible things," stood out above all others. "Blacker than a rent collectors' heart," Richardson performed his "unbelievably acrobatic dance." "I don't believe yet that he did everything I saw him do with that one pair of rather large feet," wrote a reviewer. Like so many of these performers, Richardson combined comedy with dance. "Jazzlips Richardson and his demented feet and old frock coat throw themselves about with such abandon as to quiver the chair beneath you," reported the *Evening Graphic*.

Humor was also prominent in the risqué skits and songs assigned to Edith Wilson, who did her job a bit too well for Broadway taste. The lewd double entendres of her first number, *Pool Room Papa*, caused it to be scratched after the Hudson Theater debut. Her second number, *Traffic in Harlem*, featured her as an automobile. Her third comic number was *(What Did I Do to Be So) Black and Blue*, which she sang from a bed; the bed was removed after the first night, judged to be too suggestive.

"The show in the Hudson does not go in for music very heavily," complained the *Amsterdam News*. "There is a song called *Ain't Misbehavin'* on which much reliance is placed." Mezz Mezzrow said that Waller taught *Ain't Misbehavin'* to Armstrong at Waller's apartment, before it was performed on stage. This is plausible, since, seven years later, Armstrong wrote about first hearing the song, being impressed by it, "woodshedding it until I could play all around it," cherishing it because it was "one of those songs you could cut loose and swing with," and being ready to go when he first offered it to the public. *Ain't Misbehavin'* was sung by so many performers in *Hot Chocolates* that *Variety* called it "virtually the theme number of the show." Armstrong's woodshedding paid off: Connie Immerman sent him downtown to the Hudson in time for the premiere, while the rest of the Dickerson musicians stayed behind at 135th Street. Unable to snag Bojangles Robinson, Snakehips Tucker, or Ethel Waters, Immerman must have been hoping for a boost from the magnetizing newcomer, the kind that Robinson had given Lew Leslie as a late addition to *Blackbirds of 1928*.

At the Hudson Armstrong sang *Ain't Misbehavin'* from the pit at the end of intermission, just before the beginning of the second act.[110] We know about a few similar offerings from earlier Broadway productions. In 1924–25, his rival Joe Smith came out of the pit to play wah-wah effects with a coconut in the Sissle-Blake show *In Bamville* as patrons were leaving the theater. People hung around so long, listening and jamming up the exits, that Smith's act had to be canceled. Another one of Armstrong's rivals, Johnny Dunn, did something similar with *Blackbirds of 1928* when it toured Europe. Bessie Smith was brought in for one week of *How Come* in Philadelphia, in 1923, before the show went to Broadway, also to sing between acts.

These few examples suggest that while music closer to the black vernacular—talking cornet music with mutes and the blues of Bessie Smith—was not suited to the normative musical flow of a Broadway show, it could occasionally be worked in as a supplement. Music like this was best presented to white audiences as a novelty, set off to the side of the main musical production. This must have been the logic that guided Immerman when he asked Armstrong to sing *Ain't Misbehavin'* from the pit before the start of Act 2. Immerman's hunch was right: Armstrong turned out to be a "decided sensation," as the *Interstate Tattler* reported on June 28.

We can only imagine how loudly he had to sing to get everyone's attention and be heard. There was certainly no microphone, and the first thing one notices from the recording made on July 19 is that he is using not his mellow crooning voice, developed with the assistance of the microphone at the Chicago Savoy and the Regal, but the barking, explosive voice that went over big in Chicago with *Heebie Jeebies*

*Fats Waller (Library of Congress)*

and *Big Butter and Egg Man*. All signs suggest that this July recording substantially preserves his performance from the Hudson. It even includes Carroll Dickerson's violin, an echo of the string section that was seated in the pit orchestra.

Armstrong once described a formal approach that he liked of moving further and further away from a tune: "On the first chorus I plays the melody, on the second chorus I plays the melody around the melody, and on the third chorus I routines." That is a pretty accurate description of *Ain't Misbehavin'*. The performance opens with a fairly straight rendition of the tune, followed by his vocal chorus, where he reconceives the melody without straying too far. Waller constructed his riff-based tune out of bright bursts of melody that circulate through different chords and different pitch levels, all nicely balanced and appealingly rich; he also came up with a terrific bridge (about which Dizzy Gillespie said, "I haven't heard anything in music since that's more hip, harmonically and logically"). Armstrong punches out the riffs with the vigor that worked so well in *Heebie Jeebies* and *Big Butter and Egg Man*. His adjustments "around the melody" are largely reductive, limiting its contours, just like *Heebie Jeebies*, and, indeed, like blues singers in the tradition of Bessie Smith.

In the vocal chorus, his "play around the melody" is a dancing commentary on the tune, again like *Heebie Jeebies* and also *I Can't Give You Anything but Love*, and a world apart from the preaching aura of Bessie Smith. He dances and he jokes. Waller and Razaf created a funny song, and Armstrong figured out what to do with it. His first witticism is to take the descending line in the fourth measure and exaggerate it (CD 1:05), as if he is filling in between phrases rather than carrying the lead. This is but a warm-up for the shocking outburst of scat at the end of the phrase, taken as a double-time break. Few people in the Hudson audience would have heard anything like it before.[111] The next break is simpler, but no less effective, with bluesy strokes. His diction throughout is clear, with scat and blurred syllables mixed in at the breaks.

The trumpet solo that follows is free of the tune, another excellent "special chorus" filled with bluesy filigree, eccentric phrasing, and double-time breaks. Highlights include a dramatic ascent for the bridge (CD 2:33), a lovely, relaxed riff (CD 2:49) for the last phrase, and a nice series of fancy breaks for the ending. It is one of his great solos from 1929, right there with *I Can't Give You Anything but Love*, *Indian Cradle Song* (not recorded until 1930, but probably developed in the summer of 1929), and *St. Louis Blues*.

Humor erupts again in the break at the end of phrase one (CD 2:14), which is a quotation of Gershwin's *Rhapsody in Blue*. *Rhapsody* was the most famous piece of music from the 1920s, at least for the Hudson audience; it had its premiere five years before at Aeolian Hall, some 20 blocks away, on West 43rd Street. This is Armstrong's first documented musical quotation, which comes, appropriately enough, at a break, adding wit to the usual element of surprise. You can almost hear the murmurs and chuckles from the audience: "Clever boy . . . It's Gershwin!"

The quote departs from his supposedly extemporized (that is how it would have been regarded) trumpet solo to form a musical pun. The listener is not sure, for a moment, how to parse the gesture: is it part of the stream of improvisation, or does it belong to a different musical discourse? Is it a verbal pun, too?—by which I mean, is there some significance in the title, in Gershwin, in race relations, class relations, and so forth? As always, the listener is free to provide such an interpretation, though there is no evidence that Armstrong thought in that way. At the minimum, the quotation carried the message that Armstrong might be a hick from down South, but he knew what was going on in midtown Manhattan.

In an insightful and elegant study, Gary Giddins suggests that what I am calling Armstrong's first modern style made entertainers like Bojangles Robinson old-fashioned. There may be something to that, but in 1929, in New York City, the ranking was clearly set up in exactly the opposite direction. At age fifty, Robinson was neither the flashiest nor the fastest dancer around, but it didn't matter. In *Blackbirds of 1928* he hit the right combination for white success. This was basically a matter of three things: first, a style that was clearly black, with vivid connections to the vernacular; second, superior stage presence and professionalism; and third, a sense of how to make it easy for white audiences to appreciate him. Armstrong was now in command of a similar formula. In New York, "I got to be around actors like Bill Robinson," he remembered. "So I found out the main thing is live for that audience, live for the public."

"Bo's face was about 40% of his appeal," said dancer Honi Coles, in a testament to his strong stage presence. The details of how he made his act appealing to white audiences are more elusive, but we can clearly sense this in statements from the white press, for example, a review from *The New Yorker*, which was not atypical: "Bill Robinson just goes right ahead—one-two-three-four-one-two-three-four—in the regulation beat, slow measured, and indescribably liquid, like a brook flowing over pebbles, and . . . satisfies every craving for rhythm. . . . It is very simple, once you realize that it isn't speed and that it isn't complexity and that it isn't acrobatics that make a satisfying tap. All you have to have is a God-given genius and take your time." From the platform of *Blackbirds of 1928*, Robinson jumped into films and fortune.

"He always did things in eight bars, and he loved those breaks"—

that is another analysis of Robinson that could be applied to the Armstrong of *Ain't Misbehavin'*. Armstrong could be as blisteringly acrobatic as any trumpeter (or dancer), but what did it for him at the Hudson was his vocal paraphrase, with black touches mixed in—double-time breaks for fun and surprise, bluesy gestures for the down-home touch, a dash of scat for something really exotic. Plus musical wit. It was all coherently delivered according to the formula of increasing distance from the tune that almost everybody in the cast had a crack at that evening, making it easy for the audience to appreciate his originality.

What I am imagining, for the black Broadway productions of the 1920s, is a steady and not always obvious process of negotiating and renegotiating the details and the degree of cultural (and even physical) blackness.[112] This was happening elsewhere in the country, too, but in Manhattan, with its extensive press commentary and high monetary stakes, the process was especially vivid, the results widely influential. Armstrong complained that it took Broadway five years to accept him. Mainstream tastes in midtown Manhattan had indeed changed between 1924 and 1929, and so had he. Henderson wouldn't let him sing in 1924, and Henderson knew what he was doing. The success of *Copenhagen* in late 1924 was a marker of changing attitudes, as the black vernacular from New Orleans started to leave its stamp on civilized dance music. Five years later, Armstrong did something similar with *Ain't Misbehavin'* with a voice that was as different from the normative style of Broadway show singing as black from white.

The musical negotiations were not exactly the same as those for dance or humor. Pit musicians in *Shuffle Along* memorized their parts because white audiences liked to think that they were unable to read. Eubie Blake had to find the balance of enough but not too much blackness in his tunes; he got it right and set a model for others to follow. "The best scenes are those of darktown extraction," wrote one white reviewer of the 1927 show *Africana*, and by 1929 Armstrong had arrived at a singing style that could satisfy that expectation, mixing scat, blues, double time, and witty paraphrase, keeping things black, humorous, and accessible, just like Bojangles Robinson. I doubt that he could have made the same splash at the Hudson singing *Heebie Jeebies*. What made *Ain't Misbehavin'* work was the paraphrase of the (overly) familiar tune; his own musical invention was spice, sprinkled into the main dish. The concept was not all that different from the Henderson–Redman arrangements of 1924 and 1925, with their polished ensemble playing and hot solos.

As much as we value today the special choruses of Armstrong's trumpet solos from the mid- and late 1920s—*Potato Head Blues, Savoy Blues, Hotter Than That, Struttin' with Some Barbecue*, and so on—it was the vocals that gathered the most attention. And of the vocals, the funny ones were the blockbusters. The humor of *Heebie Jeebies* put him on the map in Chicago, and the humor of *Ain't Misbehavin'* did it for him on Broadway. For more than a century humor had been making it easy for whites to relate to black culture on the minstrel stage. These two songs, along with *Big Butter and Egg Man*, were his biggest hits of the decade, by far. Much later, there would be tension in jazz over humor, with younger musicians disdaining it and demanding respect; Miles Davis criticized Dizzy Gillespie in this way, for example. But that was a debate for the future. In 1929, Armstrong's humor made it easy for white audiences to accept his transformations of familiar melodies, his raspy voice, and his scat. "When you get people relaxed [with laughter], they're more receptive to what you're trying to get them to do," explained Gillespie. "Sometimes, when you're laying on something over their heads, they'll go along with it if they're relaxed." Armstrong understood this fully.

There was one more comic number from *Hot Chocolates* that turned out well for him. *(What Did I Do to Be So) Black and Blue* belonged to a robust tradition of making fun of dark skin. Lyricist Andy Razaf provided what was called for, but he simultaneously made the song a poignant lament on the plight of African Americans. *Pool Room Papa, Traffic in Harlem*, and *Black and Blue* were Edith Wilson's comic numbers. *Black and Blue* is about the obvious difficulties—obvious to both whites and blacks at this time, apparently—confronting a dark-skinned woman in her efforts to lure a man. (Wallace Thurman's *The Blacker the Berry*, a novel about the sorrows of a female protagonist with dark skin, was published at the beginning of 1929.) The Hudson Theater audience laughed openly at the first lines of the verse, which describe the protagonist, left alone because of her complexion.

It was a cruel but commonplace kind of humor.[113] Making fun

*A scene from* Hot Chocolates *(Photo by White Studio © Billy Rose Theatre Division, The New York Public Library for the Performing Arts)*

of dark skin was the foundation of black-faced minstrelsy. "Give me a light my color," Bojangles Robinson liked to quip, and the house lights shut off instantly, leaving the audience in darkness and laughing uproariously. "Lokka here, my Man Tan's coming off!" joked Armstrong in later years as he wiped perspiration from his face with a handkerchief. Wilson originally delivered *Black and Blue* from a breathtaking stage set, sitting on a bed with pilings of white sheets, surrounded by white stage props including a white carpet, and dressed in a white satin negligee, her dark skin glowing out in stark contrast.[114] She jokingly pleaded that, even though she was white inside, the situation was hopeless, and sang the break with an over-the-top, melodramatic flair (CD 2:25).

Armstrong performed *Black and Blue* with a touch of humor until the end of his life. "Way I sing it now with a little chuckle, get a *big* reaction," he said in 1966. It is easy to imagine him delivering the lines with exaggerated grimaces and facial muggings, gestures Edith Wilson must have used, too, to make people laugh at her dark skin, which, according to the caste system of the United States, placed her inescapably beneath everyone else. But he also struck a note of sincerity with the lamenting, less funny lines of the chorus.

When stripped from the Broadway context and from all visual

cues, delivered with Armstrong's bluesy touches, the song sounds like a powerful indictment of color prejudice, which is how Ralph Ellison framed it in *Invisible Man*, where the novel's protagonist smokes a reefer, turns on 1,369 light bulbs in the basement where he lives, puts on a recording of Armstrong singing this song, and contemplates the horrors of slavery.

The reception history of *Black and Blue* testifies to the power of the phonograph, which dislodges the performance from the racist trappings of 1920s Broadway, from the "aura" (as Walter Benjamin famously put it) of a century of minstrel savagery. Armstrong simplifies the melodic contour and sits on a plaintive blue third, dropping down to the main pitch only occasionally. He slows and stretches the title phrase (CD 1:50) until it is out of phase with the beat, a statement of pronounced sorrow. The break (CD 2:37) is more like a brief cadenza, with the meter suspended. He acknowledges the impossibility of hiding his face with just the right touch of complexity while keeping sincerity of tone (the contrast here with Wilson's melodramatic perfomance is pronounced). For Armstrong everything is understated and declamatory; the phonograph produces a lament, absent the comic.

Ultimately, *Hot Chocolates* did for Armstrong what *Blackbirds of 1928* did for Robinson. His triumph signaled the increasing reach of the black vernacular into the white mainstream. It put him in a position where he could experiment with techniques of paraphrasing popular songs, sometimes radically, and in the process create another fresh musical modernism, riding that energy into an expanding range of white success, against all odds.

## Crooning a Ballad

One critic found it hard to imagine how the cast of *Hot Chocolates* was able to run uptown to Connie's Inn every evening and ramp up for another performance. The show was simply too draining. "If they always pour as much energy into their work in the theatre as they did last night, I cannot for the life of me see how they can do anything more uptown [at Connie's] than stagger across the floor," warned the *Amsterdam News*. In fact, a number of the performers refused to double up: Immerman was eventually forced to find substitutes for the chorines, Paul and Thelma Meeres, Baby Cox, Edith Wilson, and a few others. It is unlikely that he heard any complaints from Armstrong, who was used to long hours and doublings from his days in Chicago. "Had to get my sleep coming through the park in a cab," he quipped. "Didn't exactly feel I had the world at my feet, but it was very nice that everyone was picking up on the things I was doing."

At Connie's the band was called Louis Armstrong's Chocolate Drop Orchestra, with Dickerson conducting. He and his friends kept the gig going through November. Meanwhile, at the Hudson, his act was expanded and moved up on the stage. In the summer of 1929 the *Amsterdam News* carried display ads dedicated to his recordings only, without the typical mix of other entertainers. Reporting on a June performance from the Lafayette Theater, the *News* applauded his "rousing snappy jazz and sweet, tender melody," and the writer described him as a "genius," probably the first time that had happened in print.

The Lafayette gig turned his doubling into a formidable tripling. In Chapter 4 we noticed the twofold nature of his earlier year in New York City: Henderson paid him well to play in the premier African-American dance orchestra performing for whites, yet he also settled into an extended series of race records organized by Clarence Williams, which called for funky collective improvisation and blues. The Lafayette Theater became his main point of contact with black audiences in 1929. He tripled up there for significant stretches from June through November, somehow sandwiching the job between the Hudson and Connie's, facilitated by the proximity of the cabaret and the theater.

The Lafayette had long established itself at the center of vaudeville entertainment for African Americans in Harlem. It had some history of African-American management, and it was one of the first theaters in Harlem to desegregate its seating. The black press showered it with attention. Talented-tenth critics complained about crude humor and seminudity, but overwhelmingly black audiences regularly filled the 2,000 seats. The Lafayette was a rowdy place that made special demands on performers and, in turn, compensated them with special rewards.

John Bubbles, Armstrong's tap-dancing friend from Buck and Bubbles, talked about doubling from the Lafayette to the Ziegfeld Theater downtown. "It was like going from the ridiculous to the sublime," he remembered. Downtown everyone sat attentively, while at the Lafayette it could be hard to hear yourself. "In Harlem the audience practically dared you to dance, and you had to swing," Bubbles remembered. "I danced loose and rhythmic uptown." "When you appeared in the all-colored theaters of those days you had to grab 'em fast," added Willie "The Lion" Smith.

In early October Armstrong's new manager, Tommy Rockwell, helped put together a show at the Lafayette called *Louisiana*, with Armstrong as the headliner. The *Amsterdam News* applauded the "sweet musical score, some hilariously funny comedy situations and really splendid chorus and specialty dancing." The audience broke into ecstatic applause as soon as the orchestra started *Ain't Misbehavin'*, even before Armstrong walked onto the stage. He sang, played his trumpet, and also danced to this tune. At a performance on October 8 he presented six numbers altogether, going strong until the curtain mercifully refused to raise for another encore.

The Lafayette was the favored place for musicians to go and hear him. Natty Dominique believed that all New Orleans musicians were entertainers first; they were artists only for other musicians. That was very much the dynamic that trapped Armstrong at the Lafayette. He felt like he was "standing on my head, blowing my brains out, to please the musicians," who clustered in the first three rows, a cloud of marijuana smoke hovering over their heads. Eventually, he turned himself in the direction of the audience. At the Lafayette he started introducing numbers from the microphone, to "tell the people what we're going to play and what's happening." In attendance was fourteen-year-old Billie Holiday, recently arrived in the city and eager to hear him sing *West End Blues*; to her disappointment, he didn't.

In September he performed five numbers for a Harlem fundraiser—*Ain't Misbehavin'*, *St. Louis Blues*, *Tight Like That*, *Heebie Jeebies*, and *I Can't Give You Anything but Love*. If he had any time for reflection in his crazy schedule, he might have simply shaken his head in disbelief at the staying power of *Heebie Jeebies*, the studio throwaway from February 1926 that had set him on a path to fame as a singer. "Louis's orchestra was all dressed in flannel trousers and the men wore beautiful brown double-breasted coats with large pearl buttons," reported the *Defender*.

"I believe that great song, and the chance I got to play it, did a lot to make me better known all over the country," he remarked about *Ain't Misbehavin'* seven years later. On September 10, OKeh called him back into the studio to record *Some of These Days*, an old cabaret standby that had been recorded some 22 times before this and was Sophie Tucker's theme song. On September 11 came a recent Broadway hit, *When You're Smiling (the Whole World Smiles with You)*, and then on November 26 *After You've Gone*, another older repertory piece, having been recorded some 16 times previously.

Rockwell was clearly trying to extend the success of *I Can't Give You Anything but Love* and *Ain't Misbehavin'* with some well-known songs. There were no more concerns about cutting cheap deals with local composers in order to avoid royalty payments. Yet he was still hedging his bets. What is interesting about these sessions from a marketing point of view is that two different versions of each song were made, one with Armstrong singing and the other purely instrumental. The vocal versions of *Some of These Days* and *When You're Smiling* were immediately released on the OKeh "popular" series, marketed for whites, the instrumental versions on the race series that Armstrong had been associated with for years. *After You've Gone* was then released only as a vocal version.

What was going on in Rockwell's head? Blacks had been gobbling up Armstrong's vocal recordings ever since *Heebie Jeebies*, and there is no reason to believe that they had lost interest now. To the contrary, all signs suggest that his singing was just as popular as ever. Why then have two versions, and why market them in this way? The answer, it seems to me, is indicated by the low quality of the vocals.

The instrumental performances are strong, and it seems clear that the band had played these arrangements a lot, either at Connie's or perhaps in the show *Louisiana* at the Lafayette. And Armstrong's trumpet solos are well done. We know that his familiarity with *Some of These Days* went back to his days at the Savoy Ballroom in Chicago; his solo here skillfully builds in dramatic intensity over two choruses. *When You're Smiling* gives us another glimpse of Dickerson's violin (CD 0:26), mixed in with the Lombardo-style saxophone chorus. For the final chorus Armstrong plays the melody an octave higher, showing off his range; he remembered hearing trumpeter B. A. Rolfe first perform this trick with the song *In Shadowland* at the Roseland, back in 1925. The whole package for *When You're Smiling* was conceived for white audiences, with Armstrong's riff-based trumpet solo (CD 0:51) added as the hot spice.

But the vocal solos are generally uninteresting and sometimes sloppy. They make clear the importance of the woodshedding he put into *Ain't Misbehavin'*, which was apparently absent here. *Some of These Days* sputters along without any clear definition or recasting of the tune. *After You've Gone* opens with a splendid trumpet solo, a carefully worked-out paraphrase of the tune with lots of beautiful detail, but the vocal is less well conceived; the break (CD 1:56) is uninteresting and the second half (beginning at CD 2:00) dissolves into incoherence. The vocal for *When You're Smiling* is not flawed by clinkers like this, but neither is it especially interesting.

Most likely the band had three instrumental arrangements ready to go. Realizing the white marketing appeal of his singing, Rockwell asked for vocal versions, too. The vocal versions were then issued in the series that was heavily represented by Seger Ellis, the lily-white crooner and one of OKeh's bestsellers. The integrity of the instrumental versions encouraged OKeh to issue them on the traditional race series as a way to cover all bases.

In fact, OKeh had been experimenting with how to market Armstrong for over a year. The company made a fresh move with *West End Blues*, recorded in June 1928 as part of the first batch of recordings that document Armstrong's new microphone-based style of singing. The recording was quickly released on the race series, and just as quickly—judging, at least, from the catalogue number assigned to it—it was released in the popular series, as well.[115]

The experiment must have paid off, for OKeh immediately started to think about other possibilities. Here is a list of recordings that were issued as both race and popular numbers; recording dates are in parentheses, but the order of the list follows the numerical sequences assigned to phonograph records in the catalogues.

> *West End Blues* (6/28/1928) and *Fireworks* (6/27/1928)
> *Knee Drops* (7/5/1928) and *Skip the Gutter* (6/27/1928)
> *St. James Infirmary* (12/12/1928) and *Save It Pretty Momma* (12/5/1928)
> *I Can't Give You Anything but Love* (3/5/1929) and *No One Else but You* (12/5/1928)

*Basin Street Blues* (12/4/1928) and *No* (12/4/1928)
*Ain't Misbehavin'* (7/19/1929) and *Black and Blue* (7/22/1929)
*That Rhythm Man* (7/22/1929) and *Sweet Savannah Sue* (7/22/1929)

What is clear, first, is a degree of caution. In 1928 Armstrong was the headliner for nineteen recorded tunes; all but two (*Don't Jive Me* and *Weather Bird*) were soon released on the race series. Of those seventeen, six were issued in the popular series in a timely way. *I Can't Give You Anything but Love*, recorded in March 1929, inspired the rerelease of three more (*No One Else, Basin Street,* and *No,* from December 1928). OKeh was feeling its way ahead with Armstrong as a cross-over artist, the more recent label for this phenomenon.

*Ain't Misbehavin'* was then issued in the same double way, as both a race record and a popular record marketed for whites. It must have been even more successful, for it caused Rockwell to reassess the strategy. What he came up with was the curious plan of producing two versions on each session, one vocal and one instrumental, the former issued on the popular series, the latter in the race series:

*Some of These Days* (9/10/1929)
*When You're Smiling* (9/11/1929)
*After You've Gone* (11/26/1929): two versions recorded, but only the
    vocal issued right away

In December OKeh adjusted once again. They continued to produce two versions, one vocal and the other instrumental, but the pattern of release was flexible:

*I Ain't Got Nobody (and Nobody Cares for Me)* (12/10/1929): vocal
    released in race series only, instrumental not released
*Dallas Blues* (12/10/1929): vocal released in race series only, instrumen-
    tal not released
*St. Louis Blues* (12/13/1929): vocal released in popular series only,
    instrumental not released

The double versions stop with *Rockin' Chair,* also recorded on December 13. From now on there would be no more instrumental versions; Armstrong sings on every record. But the experimenting continued as the executives divided up the tunes, placing some in the race series and some in the popular series:

> *Rockin' Chair* (12/13/1929): released in race series only
> *Song of the Islands* (1/24/1930): popular series only
> *Bessie Couldn't Help It* (2/1/1930): race series only
> *Blue, Turning Grey Over You* (2/1/1930): popular series only
> *My Sweet* (4/5/1930) and *I Can't Believe That You're in Love with Me*: popular series only
> *Indian Cradle Song* (5/4/1930) and *Exactly Like You*: popular series only
> *Dinah* (5/4/1930) and *Tiger Rag*: race series only

The four tunes recorded on May 4, 1930, were split down the middle, two for the race series and two for the popular. And that was the end of the experiment. Armstrong soon left New York City, headed for California, greeted with the decision to release all recordings in the popular series, the race records that had been such a prominent part of his artistic life since the moment he arrived in Chicago a thing of the past.

It is hard to imagine what the discussions were like when OKeh decided, for example, to put *Rockin' Chair*, a new song by Hoagy Carmichael, in the race series and *St. Louis Blues* in the popular series. Maybe they were guided by good data about marketing trends, or maybe they were simply shooting in the dark. But what is clear from this nearly two-year process is that Armstrong's place in the white market was not automatically obvious. OKeh was testing the market with various probes. The milestones in this long transition are clear: *West End Blues* inspired the double-release strategy; *I Can't Give You Anything but Love* put an end to the penny-pinching limitations of repertory and matched him up with well-known hits;[116] *Ain't Misbehavin'* led to a process of dividing up the performances, one for the race series and the other for the popular series. It took white record buyers a while to get used to Armstrong. His debut at the Hudson Theater marked Broadway's acceptance of his voice, and in recordings he was gradually catching up with Henderson, who had been selling records to whites since 1924.

He had, of course, been singing prominently for three years, at the Vendome, the Sunset, and the Savoy Ballroom in Chicago. His singing was featured on the Hot Five series, where the number of vocal performances runs very close to the number of purely instrumental performances, and there is every reason to suspect that similar proportions were at work in the Chicago venues. The success of his singing was not new for him in 1929; new was the acceptance of his voice by mainstream white America—not the relatively small group of admiring alligators and slumming whites who liked to flaunt bourgeois conventions at the Sunset and Connie's, but theatergoers who filled up Broadway houses like the Hudson. These were the people who now made him a singing celebrity on recordings, not just in the minority market of race records but as a primary presence across the nation. His vocals carried him forward in his white turn, and it was in his vocals that he put his main creative energy during his second modern phase.

At some point in late fall 1929 the Dickerson band broke up. The gig at Connie's ended; Armstrong attributed that to poor behavior from several members of the band. Most of them went back to Chicago, with Zutty Singleton staying on at Connie's with the new band there, having made himself indispensable with his tunable tom-toms. "All the show girls and principals wanted me to stay," Singleton remembered.

Rockwell started booking Armstrong as a single act. He hooked him up again with Luis Russell's group and told him to "just stand in front of the band." Around 1928 the jazz industry had turned its attention to college campuses as a source of revenue for concerts and recordings, and Armstrong was now in a position to come along. One of his admirers at Princeton in the fall of 1929 was the actor José Ferrer, then a student there. Excursions were made to Boston and Philadelphia, the latter for New Year's Eve.

The Russell band included his buddies Barbarin and Foster from the old days, and also the young Henry "Red" Allen, a trumpeter who was closely modeling his style on Armstrong's. Armstrong remembered this band fondly: "the warmth, the feeling, the swing, the beat, the everything were there," he said.

The December 10 recording session with the Russell band

*With the Russell band, Saratoga Club, New York, 1930, Teddy Hill, Paul Barbarin, Otis Johnson, Charlie Holmes, Pops Foster, Red Allen, Armstrong, Bill Johnson, Luis Russell, J. C. Higginbotham, Albert Nicholas (The Frank Driggs Collection)*

appears to have been an impromptu affair, with weak vocals, especially *I Ain't Got Nobody (and Nobody Cares for Me)*, in which exaggerated dragging behind the beat doesn't hang together. But on December 13 there was no holding back for *St. Louis Blues*. The band was obviously familiar with this driving, riff-based arrangement. Foster's slapping 4/4 bass is prominent here and elsewhere through these sessions. Trombonist J. C. Higgenbotham tosses off some nice licks (urged on by a wailing, sustained blue note from Allen at [1929] CD 0:57), and Allen leads the band in riffs behind Armstrong's vocal. With its rousing momentum of chorus after chorus, the recording seems to capture better than any other the excitement of a live performance around this time. It is one of the great performances of New Orleans jazz.

*Rockin' Chair*, a tune composed by Hoagy Carmichael that later became a repertory piece for Armstrong (he performed and recorded it often and as late as January 1971), was a completely different story. It sounds like the band is sightreading an arrangement, with Foster missing some changes; according to saxophonist Charlie Holmes, that was precisely what happened. Carmichael found his way into the studio carrying a lead sheet and directly approached Armstrong about doing the number. Armstrong had a hard time saying no. "Poor Russell had to get up the ideas for the arrangement," remembered Holmes, and the band turned around and cut the record.

*Rockin' Chair* was one of countless songs from this period that lightly touched the stereotypes of minstrelsy. The songwriter could buy into the ideology of racism without having to do the dirty work himself or herself. One antecedent for the song's "Aunt Harriet" was the legendary anti–Uncle Tom song *Aunt Harriet Becha Stowe* (1853), a blatant and successful southern effort to counteract Stowe's celebrated novel.[117] Armstrong delivers a solid rendition of the melody on his trumpet, but in general the results are uninspired, even if they are historic, with Carmichael himself bantering a vocal duet with Armstrong. The performance anticipates a practice he would use a lot during the 1950s, when, in more prepared contexts, his fill-ins around the leads of Bing Crosby, Frank Sinatra, and other white singers were often brilliant and effective at the same time that the arrangement made clear that it was the white celebrity who was in charge; the effect was integration without a challenge to the established social order. Some of the duets with Sinatra (*Lonesome Blues*, *Birth of the Blues*) are particularly interesting, with Sinatra becoming more and more uncomfortable, while Armstrong, with his dazzling, emotive, and playful commentary, seems to be making love to the great man.

Armstrong's march into the white market actually played out over several years, and the musical details also played out gradually. As usual, we are forced to rely heavily on recordings, but must also realize that the story they tell can be misleading.

Collective improvisation had been going out of fashion on race recordings for some time, which makes it seem unlikely that the transition to written arrangements had anything to do with an attempt to reach white markets. The Hot Five series was originally conceived for the record-buying public in the Deep South—poor people who bought record players before cutlery—and it went over big at Lincoln Gardens; those are the reasons why collective improvisation was prominent on the early Hot Fives. But the texture drops away from Armstrong's recordings during the second half of 1928. It is well represented in the summer, usually at the beginning and end of each performance (*A Monday Date*, *Fireworks*, *Skip the Gutter*, and *Knee Drops*), but in the December recordings it is nowhere to be found. Coordinated with this disappearance was a change in names, from the Hot Five (and Hot Seven) moniker to "Louis Armstrong and His Orchestra" and "Louis Armstrong and His Savoy Ballroom Five." In the second half of 1928, OKeh's marketing strategy for Armstrong more closely reflected what was happening at the Savoy Ballroom in Chicago, where collective improvisation was not part of the scene.

In the years around 1930, "sweet" jazz was far more popular than "hot" jazz; this balance would not shift until the middle of the 1930s, marking the beginning of the swing era. Somewhere between the two was a style that may be thought of as "cool," based on later use of that word. As jazz became more diverse, a bohemian stance, laid back and detached, found expression in Bix Beiderbecke's lyrical, introspective trumpet and Frankie Trumbauer's saxophone, with softer attack, lighter tone and vibrato, subdued phrasing, and diminished intensity of the fixed and variable model, especially with Trumbauer. "Compared with the Hot Five, this music sounds almost lethargic," complained trumpeter and critic Humphrey Lyttleton.

This white bohemian stance was all about turning away from bourgeois values; unsurprisingly, the utility of that was not immediately obvious to upwardly mobile black musicians in the 1920s. The difference between the two groups shows up in tune titles. Trumbauer and Beiderbecke named one of their compositions *For No Reason at All in C*, while Armstrong and his friends stated the reasons very plainly in titles like *Struttin' with Some Barbecue* and *Beau Koo Jack*. Yet many black musicians were eventually influenced by the white bohemians, especially Trumbauer, who was an important model for Lester Young and others.

The interesting thing for Armstrong is that while he was in step with white crooning styles during the early 1930s, his trumpet solos did not depart very much from the style he had created during the

1920s. His vocals felt like they belonged to the private reflections of the front porch or drawing room, but his trumpet, for the most part, continued the "brassy, broad and aggressively dramatic" (Amiri Baraka) vein of communal music making from the streets of New Orleans. The breathy whispering of a Miles Davis trumpet, if it had been an option, would not have made sense to him. The only signs of the cool aesthetic in this New York period come with his use of a mute, which pops in and out on the recordings, usually in an early chorus and yielding to open playing at the end (*After You've Gone, Blue, Turning Grey Over You, Exactly Like You*). But there is no discernible change in his melodic style in these muted passages, which mainly serve to add another dash of variety to the arrangement.

Breaking into the white market meant heavy emphasis on popular tunes, and Armstrong figured out how to do that while offering something distinctive, something identifiably black yet accessible, just like his own successful performance of *Ain't Misbehavin'* at the Hudson. Vocal paraphrase of popular tunes turned out to be the main vehicle for reaching whites, his trumpet in secondary position. There was financial incentive for black musicians during this period to develop multiple styles, especially when white audiences were the target. "We played our jazz numbers but we also played tunes of the day and even waltzes," reflected Earl Hines. "We did a little bit of everything and became very popular." The *Defender* praised Ellington's orchestra in late 1931: "They can play 'sweet' and discreet jazz in the manner of Paul Whiteman, then turn about and twist their music into weird and primitive strains, with all the barbaric rhythm of the jungle."

It was a get-ahead decade, and Armstrong was the get-ahead soloist. Nobody got ahead of *him*—the competitive drive that was so much a part of the music scene he grew up with served him well. By the end of 1929 he was on a course toward nationwide white success. In December white trumpeter Jack Purvis, one of the alligators who liked to sit in with black bands, recorded a number called *Copyin' Louis.* The February 8, 1930, issue (p. 67) of *The New Yorker* included brief mention in a section on (otherwise all-white) "popular records" of the OKeh release of *St. Louis Blues/After You've Gone*: "New conceptions of familiar Senegambiana, and there is nothing quite so smoky as Mr. Armstrong's singing of vocal choruses." In December

1930 he was written up in *Time* magazine's monthly record review, with paragraph one dedicated to opera, paragraph two to Schumann and Ravel, paragraph three to Bach, and paragraph four to Beethoven before a brief turn to four dance records, headed up by Armstrong's *Memories of You*, "for those who like hot jazz and husky singing"; again he was the only African American mentioned. The publisher of sheet music for *After You've Gone* bragged about all the artists who had recorded the song, with tiny photographs of "The World's Greatest Musical Directors" decorating the cover, pictures of 45 different men including Whiteman, Vallée, B. A. Rolfe, Lombardo, Lopez, and Armstrong, who was, once again, the only African American.

Ironically, his ascent to the top of jazz-age entertainment coincided with the collapse of the jazz age. Fletcher Henderson's Orchestra helped define the jazz age, while Armstrong's position was much more peripheral; his main orientation was toward the aspirations of African Americans, and his music followed suit. Whites grew more familiar with the sounds of African-American jazz as it had developed from the southern vernacular, and they eventually caught up with him. The tremendous white appreciation he would enjoy in the early 1930s coincided with the bottoming out of the Great Depression. It is sometimes possible to identify how, at deep levels of style and expression, music precisely coordinates with social structures and events. In this case, the stylistic features central to Armstrong's white appeal during the Depression were pretty much in place before the crash of 1929. He made some adjustments in his reach for large white audiences, but they actually changed more than he did.

Rockwell took note of Armstrong's expanding reputation and booked him at various locations in late 1929 and the first half of 1930, joined mostly by local bands.[118] Black venues and white venues were both represented, though the balance seems to have tilted white. In December he was in Chicago for triumphant returns at the Regal and the Savoy. In January he played Philadelphia, Baltimore, and Washington, D.C. According to a report from Baltimore, "so enchanting was the music produced by the combination and so crowded was the hall, that hundreds of persons stood in front of the orchestra stand and in the balcony the entire period without taking a dance. In front of the orchestra stand the crowd was fourteen persons thick."

A week-long performance at Loew's State Theater, a vaudeville house at Broadway and 45th Street, gathered mixed reviews. The show was headlined by white entertainers George Price and Irene Bordoni, with Armstrong and the Russell musicians replacing Ellington's band at the last minute. His act included a "peg leg dancer" (Peg Bates) and a "dusky beauty" (Bobbie De Leon), along with a "peppy offering packed with delicious rhythm in the Harlem manner." Another reviewer found Armstrong's band inferior to Ellington's and admitted that, while he may have been popular at Connie's Inn, "Mr. and Mrs. State were rather cool to him in this show." His conducting style was "peculiar," his voice "far from a Rudy Vallée." *St. Louis Blues* brought the 18-minute act to a rousing conclusion. In late February he returned to Loew's with much the same act expanded to 23 minutes, with elaborate scenery, costumes, and lighting. "Arranged in a semicircle, the orchestra opens with an introductory paraphrase, following with a peppy number. . . . To the strains of *Ain't Misbehavin'* Armstrong makes his entrance." *When You're Smiling, Some of These Days*, and *St. Louis Blues* were performed.

On January 24 he recorded *Song of the Islands* in New York City, with an attractive scat chorus obbligato around the main tune as hummed by several of the musicians. Walter Winchell described the performance as "pashy platter . . . simply swelegant" in the *Daily Mirror*. On February 1 came *Bessie Couldn't Help It* and *Blue Turning Grey Over You*, his last recordings with the Russell band until October 1935. A week later he made another splashy return to Chicago to share the Regal stage with Marshall "Garbage" Rogers, of *Heah Me Talkin' to Ya?* fame. Armstrong featured a "new stunt," playing an "octave higher than the orchestra."

April 5 brought another visit to the OKeh studio in New York City, which produced a one-off duet with Buck Washington and band versions, with a new set of sidemen, of Hoagy Carmichael's *My Sweet* and Jimmy McHugh's *I Can't Believe That You're in Love with Me*. The band arrangements are riff-based, slightly up-tempo, and fresh, relative to the plodding February performances of the Russell group. *My Sweet* is one of my personal favorites. In the opening chorus Armstrong's soaring trumpet is the perfect foil to the syncopated riffs, with Washington making nice fill-ins on piano. There is a wonderful moment in the vocal that was just the kind of thing Billie Holiday was paying close attention to: after several dreamy phrases, he bounces (CD 1:50) into trumpet-like inflections with sprightly articulation. "I just try to put the rhythm of instrumental playing into my voice," he said in 1932.

In mid-April he traveled to Detroit for a week, in time to make an appearance at the Monday night "colored ball" at the Graystone Ballroom. And later in the month he appeared at the African-American Pearl Theater, 21st Street and Ridge Avenue in Philadelphia, where he offered $5,000 cash to anyone who could match his high-note playing. In May came another New York recording session, his last until 1935. This session produced *Indian Cradle Love Song*, already cited for its splendid trumpet solo, and a fine version of *Exactly Like You*, by Jimmy McHugh and Dorothy Fields, a brand-new song from another Lew Leslie production on Broadway.[119] Given the importance of *I Can't Give You Anything but Love*, one of the key tunes in his white turn, there is a bit of historical poetry in the fact that this last New York session included another McHugh–Fields song. As with *I Can't Give You*, he sings a heavily reconceived version of the tune while the instruments play it straight, in the background.

*Indian Cradle* and *Exactly Like You* were issued on OKeh's popular series, but it seems like the race series got the two standouts from this session—*Dinah* and *Tiger Rag*. The band is largely the same as in the April session, though without Washington, and the arrangements are up-tempo, riff-based, and driving. *Dinah* was one of the most frequently recorded tunes from the 1920s. The simple arrangement here is made up of six choruses, one after the other, with nothing of the fancy introductions, interludes, and arrangement details that fill most of the 20-odd pieces Armstrong had recorded during the past ten months. It was not just the lack of a fancy arrangement that made this an unlikely candidate for OKeh's popular series; even more of an issue, perhaps, was Armstrong's stunning vocal transformation of the tune, which is more radical than anything he had ever put on record. His delivery is more distorted, with distinct lyrics, fragments of words, and slurred words blending in and out of scat. The final three choruses feature his trumpet riffing across the static harmonies and throwing in smart quotations as he dances on top of the steady groove.

*Tiger Rag* was recorded during the 1920s even more often than *Dinah*. Armstrong once called *Tiger Rag* and *St. Louis Blues* "studies in rhythm." "I get new ideas about them each time I play them," he said in 1932, adding that he learned them both in 1917. Again the arrangement is simple, just the kind of thing that local bands accompanying him in Baltimore, Chicago, and elsewhere could easily pick up as soon as he arrived in town for a gig. He must have performed these pieces constantly on tour during the spring of 1930. After the first two strains, the third strain is played five times, the last three given to Armstrong.

Again musical quotations are thrown around liberally. *Tiger Rag* was based on an old quadrille, with melodies drawn from various places, and in fact this kind of quotational collage was built into the early history of this genre. As a scholar of early American music put it, "quadrilles consumed melodies at a fearful rate, and it was common practice to make the music up out of bits of popular songs or snatches of opera airs." In three choruses Armstrong quotes *Singing in the Rain*, *Irish Washerwoman*, and *Vesti la giubba* from Leoncavallo's *Pagliacci*. In the final chorus the band rocks along in call-and-response riffs while Armstrong pumps out a series of high B-flats, relaxed and confident, now on the beat, now a little behind it, now falling away, now leaping higher—22 B-flats in all, by my count, followed by a pop up to high F at the end. *Tiger Rag*, like *St. Louis Blues*, was a piece that went way back and then way forward, hanging around until very late in his career, with dozens and dozens of recorded performances.

Armstrong did not know it then, but *Tiger Rag* and *Dinah* were his spectacular farewell to race records, the inexpensive letters back home that played a central role in the career of this eminently modern artist.

## The Modernity of Phonograph Recordings

The only way we have to connect directly with the sounds of this period is through phonograph recordings, and we train ourselves to overcome their limitations. One theme of this book has been to relate the recordings to what was going on nightly, in Armstrong's working gigs. Their apparent uniformity is deceptive in this regard: some of them document solos that made him famous at the Vendome, Dreamland, Sunset, Savoy, and Hudson, but many more were ad hoc products of the studio, created on the spot or a day or two in advance. It is important to also think about the phenomenon of the disc itself, for, as a representation of 1920s modernity, recordings had a huge impact not just on Armstrong's career but on all of jazz. As others have argued, recordings shaped jazz history in fundamental ways. They were as much a part of the texture of modernity as the Great Migration was in Armstrong's circles, and like that complex social movement they had multiple effects on his music.

On the production side there was the record company and its hired musicians, brought in for a one-time gig—though in Armstrong's case this arrangement was, significantly, extended in the spring of 1926 for a full five years. The company knew what it wanted. Above all, it wanted Armstrong's name. Second, it wanted music that would appeal to the masses of southern blacks (intense blues and collective improvisation), and, third, it did not want to pay royalties. Those were the basics of a low-budget enterprise. They played out in the various ways we have described, shaping ensemble, repertory, and style while leaving many details up to the performers.

As the musicians entered the studio midmorning, they prepared to make a set of adjustments relative to last night's theater and cabaret jobs. Instead of facing an audience, they pointed their horns at the cold, impersonal equipment, run by the calculating, penny-counting businessmen who flashed a red light as each performance neared its three-minute limit. "Mike fright" was common in the beginning. The engineer positioned the musicians around the room in unfamiliar configurations. They struggled to hear each other, and the diminished rhythm section made things even harder. The enterprise was not designed to produce epoch-making statements, though sometimes that happened anyway.

It would be a mistake to conceive this setting as uniformly negative. The experiment of *Heebie Jeebies* was more likely to be launched in the OKeh studio than at the Vendome Theater; in this case, the impersonal setting emboldened Armstrong. Having been raised with the practice of working out solos and arrangements over time, getting them right and then sticking with them, he regarded a recording as a place to put forward his best work. Keppard and Oliver were suspicious, afraid of theft. But Armstrong relaxed into his five-year contract with the confidence of a musician who knew that the density, quickness, and range of his solos made them difficult to copy, and that there would always be more ideas coming along, like streetcars.

Few hot soloists were suited to the demands of a five-year contract, with the necessity to create new product every few months. OKeh's insistence on tunes that came cheaply actually played to Armstrong's strength. It didn't matter that the compositions themselves were worthless; he was expected to carry the performance on his own, and that is what he did. The repeatability of the recording gave his audience a chance to get to know the solos very well, which in turn required him to come up with new ones. It was a special dimension of the phonograph, unlike live performance and unlike radio.

Whether or not Armstrong actually did put his best material on record depended on the OKeh executives. *Poor Little Rich Girl* got everybody's attention at the Vendome and Sunset, but he did not record it, since OKeh was not interested in paying royalties to Noel Coward. With Venable's *Big Butter and Egg Man from the West* and Oliver's *West End Blues*, we can assume that the composers, each on the spot in Chicago and each hoping for the lift that Armstrong's performance and OKeh's distribution could give them, cut a deal. Within these limitations OKeh welcomed Armstrong's best. The three-minute scope of the commercial product encouraged cutting out showy fluff—200 high C's ripped off one after the other. We may assume that recordings attracted a good percentage of his best work, with the obvious exception of multiple-chorus performances, though flashes of that kind of energy emerged in *St. Louis Blues*, *Dinah*, and *Tiger Rag*.

The two magical facts of the phonograph were, first, its ability to capture unnotatable techniques of expression in the African-American musical vernacular, and, second, its ability to repeat the performance. Twenty-five years earlier, Joplin's creative energy was matched to the technologies of sheet music and piano rolls. Armstrong tried to follow that model, writing lead sheets on the back steps of Lillian's apartment and sending them to Washington, D.C., for copyright, but by 1926 it was clear that the phonograph record suited his creative talents much better. *Cornet Chop Suey* was a strong accomplishment, but there was no way that the intricacies of *Big Butter and Egg Man*, full of the unnotatable power of blues and eccentric melody, were going to be jotted down on paper and sold for profit. Once race record companies realized that they could make money selling music from the African-American vernacular, a new kind of history of recorded blues and jazz unfolded, giving prominence to the intensity of blue notes and the detachment of blues phrasing, to the wild richness of collective improvisation that nevertheless seemed like it had been made with micrometer calipers, and to the workings of eccentric melody conditioned by the fixed and variable model.

Recordings preserved all of that, and they preserved the designs of Armstrong's solos, allowing the purchaser to repeat the performance and get familiar with his modern music at her leisure. The cyclonic density of his special choruses made them challenging to listen to, and people didn't know how to respond at first, as Clyde Bernhardt and Louis Metcalf tell us. As he upped the ante with greater density, wilder eccentricity, and overwhelming variety, repeated listening became proportionately more rewarding. White alligators could sit ringside at the Sunset, listen to his solos night after night, and memorize them, and anyone with a record player could do something similar.

Repeated listening to recordings offered the possibility to absorb the full force of his innovative creations after the initial shock of radical novelty subsided. Our familiarity with the Hot Five corpus today is the same familiarity that was available in the 1920s. The impact of recording technology on jazz was thus fundamentally different than it was on classical music. In jazz, recordings preserved and distributed musical expression that could not be captured through notation; in classical music, they cheapened the highbrow artistic aura. Aspiring jazz musicians studied recordings just as aspiring classical composers studied scores. This was how the power of Armstrong's new melodic idiom extended through several generations of jazz solo playing. Without recordings, it would not have happened in this way.

Richard Wright wrote about reading novels as a teenager in

Jackson, Mississippi, after an Irish coworker lent him a library card. "It would have been impossible for me to have told anyone what I derived from these novels, for it was nothing less than a sense of life itself," Wright remembered. How often did something like that play out with race recordings during the 1920s? The recordings must have had far greater impact on working-class African Americans than novels, plays, paintings, speeches, dancing, and poetry—greater in the sense of sheer numbers of people who were involved and how much the experience mattered. Culturally, one has the sense that only religion counted more.

Recordings did not take the place of live music making, but became an entwined supplement. They could not carry the strong physical presence of the performer—Bessie Smith with head bowed, presiding over a hushed audience who waited for her to unleash her power; or Armstrong's bearing, "the way he carried himself, like somebody bragging and all, and saying 'look, I am good.'" And they could not fulfill one of the central goals of the African-American musical vernacular—a musical and kinetic dialogue among those present. The centrality of musically charged social interaction was actually being challenged by the formidable skill of great practitioners like these. One thing is certain: the normal condition of musical life today, with technological mediation as standard, would have seemed bizarre to these record buyers. Recordings did not have everything, but with vigorous music making opportunities around, that wasn't a problem.

The status of a recording in this environment was very different than it is today. Being relatively new and relatively (to today) expensive, the recording was special and less taken for granted. The machine and the disc were both objects of value, something to show off. They brought the owner into the modern technological age. The disc indicated commercial success for the artist, who had emerged out of the pack to take position in the top tier of the entertainment world.

And it was, in important ways, a northern world. It was not simply coincidence that jazz from New Orleans did not get recorded until the musicians left the city for Chicago, New York, and Los Angeles. There was something nonindustrial about New Orleans—

decidedly, there still is today—and there was something industrial, forward-looking, and legitimizing about the northern places from which phonograph records emerged. In this way the discs were symbols of the Great Migration no less than the *Defender*, and they picked up some of the aura of that social movement.[120] It was a perfect match, Armstrong's modern jazz carried through the sprawling territories of race record–buying African America by little discs that were, themselves, emblems of modernity and of the Great Migration. A three-minute record supplied emotional texture for one's imagined place in a vast community of black people.

The recordings lost the aura of their original performing context, and that was not necessarily a bad thing. A stunning solo like *Big Butter and Egg Man from the West* lost the primitivist trappings of the Sunset Café; instead, the disc carried the shiny glow of modern technology and high-level commercial success. At home the listener was invited to create a private context in her imagination. We have practically no documentation about this kind of listening experience, aside from the testimony of dozens of musicians who were interviewed precisely because they were established musicians who had been active during this period. In New Orleans, trumpeter Bob Watts took lessons with Henry "Red" Allen twice a week, learning by ear, the two of them playing along with Armstrong's solos. Watts became known as "Little Louis Armstrong, Junior," a phrase he had embossed in gold letters on his trumpet case. When twenty-year-old Texan Oran "Hot Lips" Page arrived in Kansas City from Dallas in 1930, he could play all of Armstrong's solos note for note. "If you put one in one room and one in another, you could hardly tell them apart," remembered Budd Johnson. "I thought he was the greatest thing I ever heard," said Cootie Williams from Alabama. "Nearly everyone had an idol, and he was my idol." In Texas, Sammy Price believed that Armstrong had "emancipated the jazz musician."

Because the Hot Five series was directed toward African Americans in the Deep South (and their relatives who had moved north), it highlighted blues and collective improvisation. The recordings yielded little of the tonal beauty of Armstrong's cornet and nothing of his charismatic presence, but they captured his modern melodic idiom in splendid detail, melody that included blues features and dia-

Big Butter and Egg Man *(Courtesy of Ron L'Herault)*

logic principles in abstract designs on a new level of sophistication. Thus, the nature of Armstrong's phonographic supplement to the mainstream values of African-American participatory music making becomes clear: it was primarily a *melodic* supplement. The recordings were good at preserving melodies, and he was good at creating them. They demonstrated that there were no limits to African-American achievement. The solos matched the terms of sophistication of white achievement while belonging entirely to the black vernacular. They must have resonated in this way in the fields where people worked and the streets where they scatted and patted Juba. Shoeshine boys on Royal Street in New Orleans tapped out the rhythms of his solos as they serviced their customers. What began, in November 1925, as a letter home turned into something like a declaration of racial progress.

The recordings focused attention on Armstrong's new melodic idiom, they captured the vernacular qualities of that idiom, they offered repeatable exposure to its challenging complexity, they confirmed the northern, legitimizing status of his invention, and they put his achievement into historical play, a way to let the staying power of his music go to work. This was how recordings helped make him modern and also the central figure in the history of jazz solo playing.

Race records came to an end for Armstrong, an ominous sign that there would be less and less place for his African-American fans during the next few years, as he played mostly in white venues. A trip to Paris was announced in April 1930. It did not materialize, at least not immediately, but instead Rockwell hooked an even bigger fish: the chance to make a movie in California. Previous biographers have wondered what drove him out to the West Coast, but there is really no doubt. It was the talkies, which were now giving African-American dance bands the chance to extend their reputations beyond what records and radio could do; Ellington's band, for example, took the same trip in the summer of 1930. *Ex-Flame* would become the first of many films for Armstrong. Yet this part of his career would truly be a mixed blessing, as movies helped lift him more fully into white stardom while simultaneously dragging him down with the worst racial stereotyping America had to offer.

# NINE

# The Rosetta Stone

[Armstrong] found the Rosetta stone. He could translate everything.
He could find the good in the worst material.

—Sonny Rollins

**Armstrong left Chicago for Los Angeles in early July 1930.** "To go to California was like going to Tibet now," explained Milt Hinton. "It was all trains, a two or three day trip by train from Chicago to Los Angeles." He arrived at the Dunbar Hotel (4025 South Central Avenue), a nerve center for African-American entertainers and his home for the next ten months, with a wallet full of cash. Lillian lived there with him, although their relationship was fitfully fluid. She had a boyfriend with whom she spent a bit of time during the California year, and at some point Alpha showed up, unannounced, saying that she had been missing Louis in Chicago, so she quit her job as a chorus girl and hopped on a train. Please don't be mad, she begged him. To the contrary, he was delighted and promptly found her an apartment. "The Lord Must have sent her out there to me," he quipped.

The Dunbar was the only hotel west of the Mississippi servicing African Americans, and in 1930 it was going strong. It had an elegant lobby with tapestries and murals, an attractive dining room seating 100, a nice bar, barbershop, flower shop, and 100 guest rooms. To W. E. B. Du Bois, the Dunbar was "an extraordinary surprise to people fed on ugliness—ugly schools, ugly churches, ugly streets, ugly insults. We were prepared for—well, something that didn't leak, that was hastily clean and too new for vermin. And we entered a beautiful new inn with a soul." Armstrong got a kick out of the miniature golf course, toking on marijuana cigarettes while he putted around with

377

his friends. Guests at the Dunbar while he was there included Stepin Fetchit, Walter Richardson, Jazz Lips Richardson, and eighteen-year-old Nina Mae McKinney, fresh from a starring role in King Vidor's *Hallelujah*. Duke Ellington was there in July and August, while his band worked for RKO Pictures, which had apparently done well with the movie *Black and Tan* from December 1929. Ellington's 1930 assignment was *Check and Double Check*, starring Amos 'n' Andy.

On the day of his arrival, Armstrong checked into the Dunbar and quickly buddied up with a soldier who showed him around town. They stopped by a barbershop where Curtis Mosby, a bandleader who was running a nightclub adjacent to the Dunbar called the Apex, happened to be getting a haircut. When the soldier introduced Armstrong, Mosby was obviously flustered. Mosby had been running an act where he imitated Louis's singing, and now the real thing was standing in front of him. He mumbled something about giving Armstrong a free meal at the Apex, which both the soldier and Armstrong found insulting. Armstrong implied that he would have started working at Mosby's club, if Mosby had been interested.

What lured him to Los Angeles was the movies—a "special featured part in a new picture at one of the largest studios," as one article described it. He also settled into a nightly gig at Frank Sebastian's Cotton Club, in Culver City, a 30-minute drive from the Dunbar. Beginning July 10, the *Evening Herald* covered his forthcoming debut with nine articles in 19 days, all of them dutifully clipped by Lillian and pasted into her scrapbook. Rockwell trotted out his new publicity slogan: "Louis Armstrong, hailed as one of the world's great cornet players, 'king of the trumpet,' master of modernism and creator of his own song style."

Sebastian's Cotton Club was run as a West Coast imitation of the legendary Harlem venue, with first-rate floor shows and whites-only admission. When Frankye Marilyn Whitlock and Harry Levette filed their regular columns for African-American newspapers back east, their comments on the Cotton Club were based on what they could gather from the radio. Trumpeter Cootie Williams, in town with the Ellington band, remembered dropping his miniature golf clubs at the Dunbar and racing to the radio when it was time for Armstrong to play, and Lillian listened on the radio, too. In spite of the segregation, musicians remembered the 1,200-seat Cotton Club fondly, especially for the generous helpings of excellent food. Sebastian, a gregarious Italian, liked to stand in the doorway to greet people, framed by a spotlight so that you could see his tall figure as you approached.

Local policemen ate for free, a strategic move that helped protect a secret gambling room for high-rollers, where Howard Hughes was a regular. Hughes liked to have some fun with Dudley Dickerson, a comedian-dancer who weighed 260 pounds and performed in ballet shoes. Hughes and his entourage sat at their table and heated up silver dollars with a candle until they glowed. Then they threw them on the floor for Dickerson to pick up between his toes. Dickerson was supposed to yell out, "Oh, that's a hot one!," causing everyone at Hughes's table to burst into laughter.

Forty entertainers ran a revue that changed every two to four weeks. The entertainers were identified as "Creole," a little nod toward New Orleans that may have had something to do with the train lines that ran directly from the Crescent City to Los Angeles. Rehearsals for new shows began at 3:00 in the morning, after the night's work was finished, and carried on until midmorning; this went on for three days before each new show. Aurora Greely was in charge of the dancing, with lovely chorines selected from the school she ran. Headliners while Armstrong was there included Baby Mack (a singer married to musician Les Hite), Evelyn Preer (a blues singer), Dick Campbell (a youthful tenor), Rutledge and Taylor, Martha Richie, and Connie and Eddie Anderson. LeRoy Broomfield produced the revues and served as master of ceremonies. Three shows ran every night. Armstrong was the star and got paid $500 per week—"the highest salary ever paid to a musician on the Pacific coast," according to one clipping.

He brought along a "plot" for the revue that began on July 17, which must mean that he also brought parts for the musicians. On opening night he "took over affairs, musical and otherwise," with *When You're Smiling, Exactly Like You, Song of the Islands*, and *St. Louis Blues*. Social dancing was timed for 11:00 p.m. hookups with radio broadcasts. By July 26 he had "taken Southern California by storm," advertised as "The Last Word in Heat" in 300 cards placed in Red Top taxis.

The Cotton Club was positioned across Washington Boulevard from the MGM studios, with studios for RKO right down the road. It was patronized by "the newly found rich of Beverly Hills and Holly-wood and the motion picture industry," as saxophonist Marshall Royal described them. Actor George Graham liked to approach Armstrong on the bandstand and demand 40 choruses. Armstrong remembered first meeting Bing Crosby at the Cotton Club. "Patrons have registered with Mr. Sebastian from practically every state in the Union and a num-ber of foreign countries, who state that 'Louie' was the magnet who attracted them," claimed one of Lillian's clipped articles.

This audience was certainly more open-minded than "Mr. and Mrs. State" who had been cool to his act at Loew's in Manhattan a few months before, more interested in the radical transformations he was experimenting with. There were, of course, limits to their open-mindedness. White celebrities loved his entertainment, but few were willing to socialize with him. Director James Cruze (*The Covered Wagon*, *I Cover the Waterfront*) was one of the few who invited him to his home. "The few [white] parties I did go to left a sour taste in my mouth," Armstrong remembered. "Somebody would always come up with a few drinks in him and say, 'Y'know, I once had a Colored Mammy.'" "You felt they wouldn't want you in their kitchens, or in their pools."

The band included two young players destined for top-tier careers. Trombonist Lawrence Brown, who played for a long time in Duke Ellington's orchestra, and drummer/vibraphonist Lionel Hampton were each twenty-two years old when Armstrong arrived.[121] "I discovered the greatness of those two youngsters the very first day I went to rehearsal," Armstrong remembered. Born in Birmingham, Alabama, in 1908, Hampton moved with his family to the South Side of Chicago when he was eleven, and came to musical maturity under Armstrong's spell at the Vendome Theater. In Los Angeles, during rehearsal for *Song of the Islands*, Hampton started playing a vibra-phone, reproducing Armstrong's solo from the recording. Impressed, Armstrong told him, "When I sing, you play behind me like that." Cootie Williams considered this unit to be the very best of Arm-strong's many backup bands over the years. Armstrong liked the band's phrasing, tone, endurance, and "willingness and the spirit that the eastern musicians or the southern musicians used to have before they got to Broadway and became stinkers, looking for power and egotisms, the desire to do practically anything but enjoy their first love, which is their instrument."

In August 1922 Armstrong had been introduced to the patrons of Lincoln Gardens with a featured blues solo. In late 1925, when he returned to Chicago after his year with Henderson, he stepped into the OKeh studio and explained to Richard Jones that he didn't need any rehearsal for the blues numbers they would be recording that day. On his return visit to New York in March 1929, he again knocked off a blues right there in the studio. Something similar was waiting for him with his first California recording, on July 16, 1930: a one-off blues with white singer and songwriter Jimmie Rodgers and Lillian on piano. The three of them recorded *Blue Yodel Number 9 (Standin' on the Corner)*. Armstrong was under contract with OKeh Records, and this session was for Victor; hence his name was not listed on the disc.

Rodgers, a hot commodity in 1930, must have found out that Armstrong was in town and requested his participation. The moment was heavily laden with racist ideologies. Two southern musicians found themselves in a recording studio in exotic Los Angeles. The white one was stretching out with his "Blue Yodel" series as a creative extension of black-faced minstrelsy; the black one was making a comfortable berth for himself by blues-crooning pop hits for white America, the latest musician to benefit from a long history of white fascination with "real Negroes." In *Blue Yodel Number 9* Rodgers impersonates a black man standing on the corner of Beale and Main Streets in Memphis. It is a famous recording, but Armstrong is hardly distinguished. Rodgers's song is full of irregular phrases, and Lillian is able to follow them pretty well; she was undoubtedly using a lead sheet. But Armstrong, either inattentive to the notation or declining access to it and preferring to play by ear, is frequently thrown off. You can almost hear him breathe a sigh of relief when he settles into his solo chorus in the middle—the only regular 12-bar chorus in the entire performance.

The next recording session was a proper OKeh introduction of the new band on July 21. Armstrong would record 12 titles with the

Sebastian New Cotton Club Orchestra between July 1930 and March 1931, each released, it seems, very soon after recording. The July 21 offerings were *I'm a Ding Dong Daddy (from Dumas)* and *I'm in the Market for You. Ding Dong* was probably a piece from his spring tours; the Cotton Club band was certainly using charts that he knew already. *I'm in the Market for You* had just been introduced through the film *High Society Blues.* On *Ding Dong* he sings "I done forgot the words" after a sprightly scat interlude, putting onto record what may have already become the explanation for how he supposedly invented scat on the *Heebie Jeebies* recording of 1926.[122] It is an explicit play to the assumptions of his audience, who might have grown up with colored mammies and were now fascinated by his seemingly spontaneous outpourings of musical primitivism. ("He rarely has more than a rough idea of the words," *Time* magazine assured its readers in June 1932.) You can almost hear the chortlings from Howard Hughes's table, though it is easy to imagine some awareness at the Cotton Club that it was all an act, a gesture of recognition from one performer to another.

This scat solo was certainly not spontaneous. The vocal has some lovely stretches of additive rhythm (CD 1:22), recalling a similar passage in *Hotter Than That* from 1928. Lawrence Brown gets a chance to show off his trombone (he has an even better solo on *I'm in the Market for You*), and Armstrong ends the performance with a trumpet solo that builds through four continuous choruses, with plenty of eccentric patterning and elegant dips and dives. My favorite chorus is the second one (CD 2:14), but what is most impressive is the cumulative effect, crafted through sustained familiarity. This solo made a big impression on eighteen-year-old trumpeter Buck Clayton. *Ding Dong* also became a favorite of Lionel Hampton, who liked to call out from his drums, "One more chorus," urging Armstrong on with cowbells. Armstrong remembered playing 40 choruses of *Ding Dong* one evening in Culver City.

The new show in August was called *Hitting the High Spots with Louis Armstrong.* True to form, he was marking his turf with his miraculously high range. The $5,000 he offered in April to anyone in Philadelphia who could match his high range was not collected, and it is unlikely that there were any challengers in Los Angeles. Lillian remembered hearing *Tiger Rag* on the radio and being astonished when he made his usual high note and then just kept going, higher still.

In August, Sebastian hired Charles Lawrence to be the new musical director, and we can assume that his work is preserved in the band's recordings from that month. The arrangements didn't have to be complicated or even interesting; expectations were very different than they had been for the Henderson band in the mid-1920s, where there was a need to individualize each arrangement. Armstrong was now the main point of every performance, and a creative arrangement would only get in the way. Featured soloists were wary of "overloading the arrangement," and for good reason: attention grabbed by the arrangement was attention taken away from the soloist. "If he'd wanted [fancier arrangements] he'd have brought them," explained saxophonist George James. Armstrong wanted his accompanists to stay under, just as he himself had done with such loyal perfection so many times in the past. When Lionel Hampton got a little too excited with a vibraphone obbligato for the October 1930 recording of *Memories of You*, Armstrong told him to hold back. Years later he regretted the decision and wished he had let the youngster play out.[123]

In addition to presenting Armstrong properly, the job of the arranger was to emphasize the tune that was the basis for the entire performance. The formula for mainstream white success that worked so well with *I Can't Give You Anything but Love*, in March 1929, was simple but effective: play the chorus of the song, in the foreground or the background, straight or embellished, again and again. The performance could be dressed up with introductions, interludes, and codas, but none of these should be very long. Armstrong sings a vocal chorus on every one of the California recordings, paraphrasing the song, and he plays plenty of paraphrase of the same tunes with his trumpet.

It was now mainstream popular songs, all the time. In this regard the situation was not that different from the old days with Henderson. The Henderson band had more emphasis on distinctive arrangements and on variety, and the biggest difference of all was tempo. With the wind knocked out of the roaring twenties by the Great Depression, the music slowed down. The "off-time fox trot" or "slow fox trot" was popular around 1930; there is no evidence that the celebrated Lindy Hop, the latest thing in Harlem, was known at Sebastian's.[124]

The crooners led the move to moderate tempos. "The old-style jazz singer, the speed-manic of St. Vitus movements, has passed on to a better world," wrote Martha Gellhorn in 1929. "It is a relief to have a man sing like a human being and not like an hydraulic drill." From Armstrong's California year, the most successful performances, by popular acclaim and in his own opinion, are delivered in slow to moderate tempos. It was in ballads like *Confessin' That I Love You, If I Could Be with You (One Hour Tonight), Memories of You,* and *Sweethearts on Parade* that his distinctive way of crooning came through most powerfully. In 1930 he had arrived at a place where few African-American musicians could go. For most, the possibility of recording this side of their book of arrangements simply did not exist.

*Confessin' That I Love You,* from August, was the first Armstrong recording Buck Clayton ever heard, walking down Central Avenue as he passed by a shop window. "I just stopped still and stood listening to that golden tone," he remembered. "I had never heard anyone play with such soul." The entire performance impressed him, from Ceele Burke's guitar introduction through Armstrong's vocal chorus and the trumpet solos.

African Americans got a chance to see him in August at the Appomattox Country Club, promoted as "the finest colored recreational club resort in the world," and at Los Angeles's Loew's State Theater, where the featured film was *Way Out West.* A reviewer from the *Evening Herald* described his technique of sound production: "He not only expands his cheeks to produce his silver notes, but his neck, also. He can give a perfect imitation of the bullfrog's throat swelling out and in as he hits notes unbelievably high and pleasing. In addition, he is one of the best showmen I have seen at the head of an orchestra. He has only a husky voice to supplement his trumpet in his musical offering. But he has a sure-fire personality and a native instinct for blues in addition."

Life was good in southern California. Curtis Mosby drove around town showing off his new automobile radio, a rare thing. In August Armstrong played a round of miniature golf at the Dunbar in a five-some filled out with his wife, Ellington, May "Miss Snakehips" Diggs, and Myrner Rosseau. White musicians in the Cotton Club audience scooped up his discarded handkerchiefs as souvenirs.

The primary reason that both Ellington and Armstrong were drawn to California was to make movies; secondary were the excellent rewards for live performance. Ambitious musicians usually follow the big bucks, and these two were no exception. Hollywood was the perfect antidote to the financial gloom smothering the country. When Armstrong arrived, Bill "Bojangles" Robinson had just finished his debut film, *Dixiana*. Dozens of black entertainers came and went for movie work during his California year: Stepin Fetchit, Earl "Snakehips" Tucker, Nina Mae McKinney, Clarence Muse ("paving the way for the Race in the motion picture industry," as the *Defender* put it), Walter Richardson, John Hall's 41-voice choir, the Four Covans, Baby Mack, Miller and Lyles, and Little Farina (Allen Hoskins of *Our Gang*).

Armstrong began making movies in early September 1930. Dave Peyton liked to dish out uplifting advice to aspiring musicians in the *Defender*, and Harry Levette was now doing something similar for aspiring actors. "Blessings: Actors who quietly mind their own business and wait for order on the movie lots," Levette wrote in the *Afro-American*. "Pests: Actors who loudly tell their own and everyone else's business, 'hog' the camera, play, attempt flirtations with white extras, etc." In the wake of *Hearts in Dixie* and *Hallelujah*, both made with largely black casts in 1929, film optimism was high in the African-American community. The Ellington Orchestra pulled in $27,500 for four weeks of work on *Check and Double Check*, which included an effective ballroom segment featuring the band playing *Old Man Blues*. With stars Amos 'n' Andy, the film surely boosted Ellington's reputation.

Disappointingly, *Ex-Flame* did not do the same for Armstrong. He received no mention in the credits, and a review in *Variety* included barely a nod to a "colored orchestra." The *Los Angeles Times* did applaud "some merry moments from Louis Armstrong and his jazz band." A publicity still shows an animated group of musicians with Armstrong standing at the center, but the group is identified as "Les Hite and His Orchestra," with no mention of Armstrong. Advertised as "Adults Only, Censor's Orders," the RKO film previewed in Los Angeles in late October, to poor reviews. Sadly, no copies of the film survive today.

In October, Louis Armstrong and his Sebastian New Cotton Club Orchestra recorded *Body and Soul, Memories of You,* and *You're Lucky to Me. Body and Soul* was new and popular, with at least eight recordings released already. Most, including Armstrong's, were done in moderately up-tempo fox trot time. In the first chorus, the sax section plays the melody straight while Armstrong paraphrases it in the heterophonic style used for *I Can't Give You Anything but Love* from the previous year. At the end of the phrase (CD 0:23) he dashes off double-time fill before moving into lively second playing against the continued melody from the saxophones; heterophony then returns by the end of the phrase (CD 0:34). At the bridge the band slips into a chordal background, yielding the melody to him, and for the return of the main theme it is only saxophones as he puts down his trumpet and prepares to sing. It is somewhat amazing that the texture of heterophony, so closely associated with African-American congregational practices and so inherently funky, was holding strong at the Sebastian's slick new Cotton Club in 1930. In Armstrong's vocal chorus for *Body and Soul,* the same format is used: George Orendorff plays the melody straight on solo trumpet while Armstrong inventively and dynamically rags the tune. *Body and Soul* was another of Buck Clayton's favorites from the California year, and he especially admired this combination of Orendorff and Armstrong. In his trumpet solo Armstrong stays very close to the tune; he probably felt constricted by the unusual and challenging harmonies of the original.

In the up-tempo *You're Lucky to Me,* Armstrong is understated and clever. His final solo ends with a big, rising glissando, one continuous blur of pitches, like a trombone. Earlier in 1930 the *Baltimore Afro-American* casually mentioned how trumpeters Sidney De Paris (Charlie Johnson's Paradise Ten) and Obie Austin (Bill Brownie's Boys) were giving Armstrong a run for his money on the high end of the instrument, and doing so with a particular flair. "They have a new and original minor slur to those same high notes that is fast becoming popular with all professionals who can master them."

Trombones are built for glissandos; trumpets are not. Buck Clayton was convinced that his hero must have been using a special instrument equipped with a slide. He decided to try and meet him, to ask how he did it. He managed to get to know one of the Cotton Club performers, who told him to show up at six o'clock; he would introduce him to Armstrong in his dressing room. "How do you make your trumpet sound like a soprano trombone?" Clayton asked. Armstrong gave him an autographed picture and told him he would explain—"but if we were down in New Orleans, I wouldn't," he cautioned. "In New Orleans whenever I did it, I'd put a handkerchief over my valves so nobody could see how I did it." The two of them casually trotted down to the restroom and Armstrong entered a stall, beckoning his young admirer to follow. There he lit up a joint and insisted that Clayton share some of it. Sufficiently relaxed, he demonstrated his technique of pushing the valves halfway down while tightening his lips. Clayton was so upset when he got home that he dropped down on his knees and prayed that the marijuana would not set him on a path to drug addiction.

## "This Whole Second Book Might Be About Nothing but Gage"

On the evening of November 13, during intermission at the Cotton Club, Armstrong and a white drummer named Vic Berton strolled over to the parking lot to smoke a joint. As soon as they lit up, two detectives popped out from behind a car and arrested them for possession of marijuana. Armstrong was allowed to finish out his night of work before they hauled him off to jail around 3:00 a.m.

On the drive downtown he politely asked the detective not to hit him in the mouth, since, he explained, this could destroy his career. The detective took a protective stance and told him that the only reason this whole thing happened was that a rival bandleader, hurting for business, had set him up. Armstrong spent the night in jail and was released on $500 bail, charged with a felony punishable by "not less than six months and no more than six years in the penitentiary," as the *Defender* noted, for having in his possession the "flowering tops and leaves of Indian Hemp." A trumpeter named Red Mack, who had developed an act imitating Armstrong's voice and trumpet, filled in for him on the radio broadcast that night.

As noted in Chapter 7, Armstrong had started using marijuana regularly in 1928 at the Savoy Ballroom in Chicago. He became a

*Frank Sebastien's Cotton Club (The Frank Driggs Collection)*

lifelong, daily user. "[Louis] smoked pot just like you smoke regular cigarettes," reported Pops Foster. In 1953, after he finished his autobiography *Satchmo: My Life in New Orleans*, he began working on a sequel. "This whole second book might be about nothing but gage," he wrote, "gage" being one of many names for marijuana. But his manager, Joe Glaser, was not going to allow that. Armstrong had the example of Mezz Mezzrow's autobiography in front of him, and he was impressed by Mezzrow's candor: why couldn't he be just as honest? Neither Glaser nor Armstrong would give in, and the book was held hostage to gage. "Joe keeps asking about the book but it won't be done until he lets that part stay in," he told an interviewer. In a tape recording made barely a year before he died and clearly intended for public disclosure, he spoke candidly about his fondness for pot.[125] "The respect for gage will stay with me forever," he says. "My life has always been an open book, so I have nothing to hide. And well Mary Wana honey, you sure was good and I enjoyed you berry, berry, very much."

When he joined King Oliver's Creole Jazz Band in 1922, none of his colleagues was smoking marijuana. Contrary to often-repeated claims, the musicians in his New Orleanian circles simply did not use it. "Some of the white musicians wanted me to use it," remembered Baby Dodds, speaking of his time in Chicago. White musicians from New Orleans like Leon Roppolo were into pot ("Roppolo was probably higher than a kite when he made *Tin Roof*," suggested bandleader Sig Meyer, "invention seems weak"), but as a rule they kept their distance from the black New Orleanians. The whites who were eager to share their fondness for gage with Baby Dodds and Armstrong were the young alligators from the North—Mezz Mezzrow, Hoagy Carmichael, Bud Jacobson, Jess Stacey, Gene Krupa, and others. Mezzrow eventually became Armstrong's supplier, sending discreet packages by mail when Armstrong toured.[126]

By the time of the California arrest, tension had been building nationally over marijuana. The Federal Bureau of Narcotics was established in summer 1930, with Harry Anslinger appointed commissioner by President Hoover. A few years later Anslinger would write an article entitled "Marijuana: Assassin of Youth." In October 1930, a newspaper article in distant Norfolk, Virginia, painted lurid pictures of "weird, bizarre, reckless and freakish parties that have been going on among certain members of the colored screen and stage colony" in Los Angeles. The report ended with an informational briefing on marijuana, "the most prevalent form of dope using here on the border." The *Defender* ran an article in September describing "orgies of perversion" fueled by marijuana, placing them at a "leading hotel," which could only have been the Dunbar, where a "young girl whose face has been seen a great deal here of late on the screen" (Nina Mae McKinney?) dropped her pajama pants "for the entertainment of other guests." On November 2 the *California Eagle* approvingly wrote about the first local raid on suppliers of the "dope evil," which, according to the article, was being grown by Mexicans in their backyards and distributed by whites.

Armstrong's trial was scheduled for January and then postponed until March 10. Sebastian had been trying to secure an extended contract with Armstrong from the beginning, and now he finally got at least some of what he wanted, with Armstrong bound to remain in Los Angeles until the case was resolved. Armstrong remembered how he occasionally encountered the detectives who arrested him: "They'd give me a beautiful smile and ask me, 'Armstrong are you being a good boy?' I said to them, 'You know I'm being a good boy,' and they'd drive away smiling."

Transcripts from the March 1931 trial have recently been uncovered and they include advice from the judge: "If you have a nice home and a good wife, and you are getting along all right, don't be cultivating evil habits. . . . Some people mix marijuana with bootleg whiskey and they go around here with the most exorbitant ideas, and would walk up to this building here, at the corner of it, and try to lift the whole building up with one hand," the judge warned. "You leave marijuana alone." He was sentenced to thirty days in jail, of which he served nine. In jail he buddied up with two of the inmates and stayed in touch with them for the rest of his life. When he walked through the cell blocks to leave, some of the prisoners asked him to sing. He retrieved his suit, which had been torn apart at the linings in a search for drugs, packed up, and immediately moved to Chicago.

As the decades passed and Armstrong continued smoking pot, the steady hassling and the increasing severity of punishment enraged him. He compared pot laws with the casualness in the United States toward racial violence: "Why I'd much rather shoot a nigger in his ass than to be caught with a stick of *shit*," he wrote. "The Judge would honestly respect you better." On file in the Library of Congress is a questionnaire about narcotic use by jazz musicians, complete with Armstrong's handwritten, indignant responses, such as, "The music that comes of a man's horn is good enough for me—his personal habit, I don't care." "Telling kids that gage is the same as heroin and morphine is wrong," he told interviewer Bill Russell in 1953.

He thought of marijuana as an herb similar to the peppergrass and dandelions his mother used to collect around the railroad tracks for him and his sister to consume as a laxative. That was her recipe for good health, and he stayed true to "physics" for his entire life. "Where other cats make their main ambition money or fame, I've made mine health," he insisted, and the main tools available to him were physics and pot. Marijuana purged the stresses of his mind just as laxatives purged the germs that accumulated in his bowels.

"It relaxes you, makes you forget all the bad things that happen to a Negro," he explained.

Marijuana was "a thousand times better than whiskey," and he surely said that with the authority of someone who had seen the damage alcohol could inflict. "As a youngster, I witnessed a lot of the old time musicians who were fading out of the scenes, had turned to drinking on and off their jobs, trying to prove to themselves that they were still as good as they once were," he wrote. Fred Keppard ("slipped out of the scene . . . a heavy drinker"), Carroll Dickerson ("whisky killed him, babe"), Jack Teagarden ("a sad case"), Bix Beiderbecke, Dave Tough, George Wettling, Eddie Condon, Tommy Ladnier—the list is long and tragic. Marijuana was clearly safer. "Bottle babies," as Mezzrow called them, were inclined to brawling and loutish behavior; gage kept things "mellow and mild." Armstrong found drinkers sloppy and dirty, pot smokers neat and clean and full of better thoughts. He did not shun alcohol completely, as Oliver did ("will power personified," as he put it), but his preferences were clear.

The legal status of marijuana was unstable, even more than liquor, with varied laws from state to state. "The law [i.e., police] didn't give a damn" about pot smoking, insisted pianist Jess Stacey. Budd Johnson, who played saxophone with Armstrong beginning in 1933, said that musicians smoked pot from the bandstand and were not harassed but rather protected by police. Cartoonist E. Simms Campbell's beguiling 1932 *Night-Club Map of Harlem*, designed to lure white slummers to the cabaret scene, noted the open sale of marijuana. The movie *Murder at the Vanities* from 1934 featured a song called *Sweet Marijuana*, sung by the tragic lead and accompanied by smiling Mexican musicians strumming guitars and wearing sombreros. "Sooth me with your caress, sweet marijuana," Gertrude Michael sang.

Armstrong wasn't the only one who thought marijuana was a thousand times better than whiskey. During this period "viper clubs" were forming around the country. Armstrong defined a viper as "anybody from all walks of life that smoked and respected gage." "When you're with another tea smoker it makes you feel a special kinship," he explained, and he seems to have had plenty of friends. Vipers were waiting for him on his tours. At a gig in St. Louis, in 1933 or so, the musicians were surprised to discover joints on their music stands. Six identically dressed men gently walked up to Armstrong, who greeted them warmly. "We want to present you with this," they said and handed him a giant joint, one foot long, inscribed "To the king of the vipers, from the vipers club of St. Louis, Missouri." As the decade wore on, he and Billie Holiday became the reigning monarchs of a loosely knit, national society of vipers, affectionately known as Queen Billie and King Louis.

This society may have been built on marijuana, but music gave it a sense of national coherence. There were dozens of viper songs, including Stuff Smith's *If You're a Viper*, Don Redman's *Chant of the Weed*, Leon Roppolo's *Golden Leaf Strut*, J. Russell Robinson's *Reefer Man*, Richard M. Jones's *Blue Reefer Blues*, Mezz Mezzrow's *Sendin' the Vipers*, Pha Terrell's *All the Jive Is Gone*, and Armstrong's *Muggles* (discussed in Chapter 7). In November 1931 Louis Armstrong and His Orchestra recorded a comic number, *The Lonesome Road*; at the end of it Zilner Randolph says, in a high voice, "Bye bye, all you vipers." In 1933 Budd Johnson had the idea of doing a recorded performance of *Sweet Sue—Just You* in viper's language, identified as such by Armstrong for the audience just before he "translates" Johnson's gibberish.

Cab Calloway's famous *Minnie the Moocher* was designed to titillate white slummers while Calloway worked hard to police pot smoking in his band, firmly wishing to avoid scandal and keep songs like that in the realm of fantasy. On the other hand, one has the feeling that for Armstrong the primary role of viper music was to invite vipers to join his club.

He was adamant that musicians should not drink on the job—"it makes it too hard for him to keep that beat going," he observed. It is hard to know exactly how extensively he coordinated pot with his stage work. It certainly could have been something that he enjoyed before and after performances and at intermission, as the arrest at the Cotton Club demonstrates. The lifestyles of professional entertainers, who travel constantly and are separated from the stability of family and home, often involve psychoactive crutches, some mild and some crippling. Coping strategies become normalized among one's peers, the group that sustains the entertainer's life. The degree of emotional fragility and instability that can accompany addiction is probably no greater among professional entertainers than it is among the general population, but the pressures to deal with a challenging lifestyle through psychoactive substances are many times greater, hence the association.[127]

John Hammond, the record producer and critic, thought that marijuana had a negative impact on Armstrong's music, that it was the primary cause of an exhibitionist streak that Hammond detested. That causal relationship seems highly unlikely. Using the instrument in exhibitionist ways was built into jazz from the beginning, and it was completely compatible with 1920s expectations of entertainment. Armstrong played for the crowds as well as those in the know. What is worth pondering, however, is the impact marijuana might have had on his creativity and stylistic choices during the late 1920s and early 1930s.

Hoagy Carmichael believed that marijuana fostered a state of mind in which time stands still, where "everything seems easy to do," with inhibitions thrown to the side and creative urges given a wide berth. Mezzrow was even more adamant: "Tea puts a musician in a real masterly sphere," he wrote. "You hear everything at once and you hear it right. When you get that feeling of power and sureness, you're in a solid groove." Armstrong pushed marijuana on the young Charlie Carpenter, who remembered him recommending it as a creative aid. "Puff it, puff it!" he told Carpenter. "You want to write those songs?"

Artists of many kinds, from many times and places, have used psychoactive substances as creative aids, from Samuel Taylor Coleridge and Hector Berlioz with opium to Sigmund Freud and Igor Stravinsky with cocaine to John Lennon and Paul McCartney with LSD. The drugs are not the cause of creativity; they are simply one way to open up the possibility. It is easy to believe that Armstrong experienced something similar with marijuana.

What is harder to assess is the impact of pot on his second modern style. The first modern style is bold and aggressively dramatic, while the second is cooler, more detached, floating. It is too facile to attribute the change to marijuana, which, after all, is associated with many different kinds of music (Willie Nelson comes to mind). Armstrong's new style was shaped by a thickly interwoven set of conditions—his training in blues and ragging the tune, the microphone, crooning, the turn toward slower tempos in the early years of the

Depression, his reach for the largest white audience possible, and his ambition to present himself as an innovative African-American entertainer. Marijuana was not an essential part of this set of conditions.

What can definitely be said is that Armstrong was a tremendously disciplined performer. If he had a pot-smoking habit, he had it under control. His work ethic was second to none. "Bill Robinson used to tell me, 'it don't matter whether there's four people out there or four thousand, you got to give them your best show,'" he remembered. He mastered every skill required, not only musical technique but also reading, memorizing, rehearsing, and concentrating, and performed flawlessly, night after night, year after year. He was the consummate professional. His ideal death would have been similar to James Baldwin's, the latter's in the middle of a sentence, the former's on stage. Dizzy Gillespie said about Earl Hines (another marijuana smoker) that he was "a true bandleader. He doesn't let anything come between him and what he calls a certain level of perfect. Leaders like him are real classy *every* time you see them, ready to act, to perform, right then." The same was true of Armstrong. Marijuana was his "assistant" in bringing great music to the public. It is no wonder that lumping pot together with narcotics infuriated him. "A man such as myself who've played nothing but good music for his public all over the world. . . . Never has let them down during the whole forty-five years," he grumbled.

## Creator of a Song Style

In Armstrong's first modern style the primary unit of expression is the special chorus for trumpet inserted into the performance of a song. The standard features of popular songs—regular periodicity, strongly determined points of arrival, the unmistakability of their forms—these are what he needs to anchor his fiercely original inventions, with their variety and density and little conversations of notes that come and go. Since his solo is *primarily* shaped by the workings of the fixed and variable model, its nature is radically different from the melodic idiom of popular songs. The first style was both "strictly Negro" and very modern, and it represents a major intervention in the history of American music.

The second modern style is very different. Its point of departure is not the fixed and variable model but the African-American tradition of ragging the tune. This was an accommodating practice that allowed room for everything from the first modern style. Nevertheless, the allegiance to ragging the tune creates a fundamentally different outlook.

An early description of this venerable practice comes from a northerner who happened upon the African Baptist Church in Port Royal, South Carolina, in 1863 and found himself stunned by the congregation's performance of William Tansur's hymn *St. Martin's* with "crooks, turns, slurs, and appoggiaturas, not to be found in any printed copy." Early jazz from New Orleans was closely aligned with this tradition. Lawrence Duhé, a clarinetist born in 1887 on a plantation near LaPlace, Louisiana, moved to New Orleans in 1913 and subsequently to Chicago, where he played with Lillian Hardin at Royal Gardens. Duhé explained how, on the plantation, "we'd rag all pieces . . . *Turkey in the Straw* I can remember." In New Orleans Armstrong heard ragging in church, in marching bands, in bars where men sang barbershop harmonies, and in dance halls. Along with blues and the fixed and variable model, it was one of the foundational practices in his community.

Ragging the tune gave the black musician several advantages when called to perform white music for white people. Asked to play a familiar tune, the musician applied the techniques of the black vernacular. The performance became an opportunity to display not just a beautiful voice and quick fingers, but creative transformation. The player could trump white claims of composition and copyright, adding his or her own identity to form a distinctive rendition. It was another way to "take advantage of the disadvantages." This is the tradition Armstrong was given free rein to explore in California, and he did so with all the energy and skill he had dedicated to his first modern style.

Because it had been around so long and was practiced in so many places, ragging the tune carried a strong African-American identity. Armstrong delivered songs "in typical Negro fashion," as one 1931 reviewer put it, but he also did much more than that. Essentially, he created a second modern style through an expansive set of techniques that included "crooks, turns, slurs, and appoggiaturas, not to be found in any printed copy," as well as conversational blues, scat, eccentric dashes, a surprising mix of dense variety and more spacious gestures, a blend of passionate intensity with detached cool, and a dazzlingly inventive relationship to popular songs.

The basic assumption of ragging—that the listener knows the tune and can identify what the performer has added and subtracted—must have been Armstrong's assumption, too. That was why *I Can't Give You Anything but Love*, the song success of the nation in 1928 and 1929, and *Ain't Misbehavin'*, virtually the theme number of *Hot Chocolates*, had such big impact. People knew the tunes and they could follow his radical transformations. This was how the boldest innovator in the African-American vernacular during the 1920s found a way to make his searching creativity acceptable to white Americans. He took what he wanted from the crooner phenomenon, just as he took what he wanted from popular songs in his determined and sustained effort to create a new kind of distinctly African-American music.

Ragging the tune in jazz is often called "paraphrase." It can be hard to put your finger on what makes a paraphrase solo so attractive, as flickering details come and go.[128] Fractional adjustments in timing and phrasing can make a big difference, as all great singers know. With the first modern style our task was to identify the workings of a coherent system for organizing music; the second is less systematic and more quirky, with each tune offering a different set of possibilities. Gestures pop out of nowhere: "She loves me body and soul," Armstrong interjects at the end of a chorus, one of many glittering outbursts of joy that help make the early 1930s so special.

In *Lazy River* (recorded November 1931), he sings two choruses. In the first he sits on a single pitch, radically reducing the contour of Hoagy Carmichael's tune while keeping the lyrics intact. This serves as a foil for the second chorus, where he is all over the place, up and down through imaginative arpeggiations, with a torrent of trumpet-like scat. Chorus two is interrupted with a self-congratulatory aside, one of several commentaries sprinkled into this performance: "Oh you dog! Boy am I riffin' this evening, I hope something!"

"Riffing" was the word he and his friends in New Orleans used to identify scat. He does, indeed, do a lot of riffing in the early 1930s. The first thing scat did for his white audiences was to identify him as very black, culturally speaking, a firm association that it is easy to lose sight of today. Carmichael described Armstrong's "blubbering, cannibalistic sounds" that "tickled me to the marrow"—and Carmichael was one of his biggest fans.

Often he integrates scat into a more or less "normal" rendition of the lyrics, the procedure we first heard in *I Can't Give You Anything but Love*. In *Confessin' That I Love You*, scat is saved for little outbursts that mimic breaks at phrase endings. Verbal and musical departures are often synchronized: scat signals his melodic invention, while straight lyrics coincide with more or less straight versions of the tune; there is even a sort of middle ground of partial lyrics, partial scat, and partial melodic invention.

Clearly, Armstrong does not consider his duty to be direct conveyance of the original song. Scat combines with melodic invention, with smeared and dropped lyrics, with spoken asides—the performances overflow with a dizzying array of indirection, a nearly constant subversion of any reasonable interest a listener might have in hearing a straightforward presentation of the original. It all begs the question: when Armstrong sings these songs, what is his relationship to them?

Songs like these usually trade in the conventions of love lost, love desired, love in jeopardy, love under attack, and love leading to bliss. They are user-friendly vehicles that carry the listener into a light emotional fantasy. Richard Wright wrote about white waitresses at a restaurant where he worked in Chicago in the late 1920s. Observing them helped him understand the psychological gap separating whites and blacks. He noticed a superficiality that was foreign to his black community, though he found himself wishing that "Negroes, too, could live as thoughtlessly, serenely as they." Wright understood that the psychological texture of the waitresses' lives differed as much from his as blues differed from the popular songs they were drawn to and which he equated with "radios, cars and a thousand other trinkets." As Wright saw it, the popular songs provided "the words of their souls." It is a harsh view, perhaps, but it says something about how these songs could function.

It is the job of the melody to lift the lyrics into a flow of sonic emotion, with the chords enhancing that emotional texture. As Wright suggests, the terms of emotional engagement should not go very far or very deep. Quality arises from some creative twist in melody or chords, or from an interesting interplay between words, tune, and chords. *Body and Soul* is a good example, with unusual harmonies that toss around the words and tune, hither and thither, imparting a melancholy feeling.

White crooners delivered these musical trinkets with blushing sentimentality. When Rudy Vallée sang *You're Driving Me Crazy* and *Confessin' That I Love You*, for example, he did his best to paint an image of humility and submission by falling off the ends of phrases with fluttering vibrato, landing on high notes with a distinct retreat in volume and a light and delicate tone, hesitating just a little in his rhythm, now and then, and phrasing with a gentle legato throughout. "Tenderly, coaxingly he sings love-songs to every romance-silly female in these U.S.A," wrote one commentator. Armstrong obviously could not enter the white market in the same way. When he performed *You're Driving Me Crazy*, he sped up the tempo, injected a humorous exchange with his bandmates, replaced the lyrics at the bridge with cannibalistic scat, and finished his vocal chorus with a series of trumpet-like outbursts of joy. As one reviewer put it, "he picks music to pieces and reconstructs it at his own pleasure."

If popular songs belonged to what James Baldwin called the "sunlit playpen" of mass culture, then Armstrong was finding a way to refract that comforting light into a strange and radiant display. "Whatever the Negro does of his own volition he embellishes," wrote Zora Neale Hurston, and in the early 1930s Armstrong was leading that tradition into uncharted territory. As Rudy Vallée put it, "In so many ways Louis and I are direct opposites."

Armstrong sang some good songs in the early 1930s, but the quality of the originals did not really matter. The strength of Eubie Blake's *Memories of You*, for example, lies in the melodic arc of its first phrase, which the harmonies enrich unconventionally.[129] The line ascends and sounds more urgent, which sets up a descent into the relaxed, warm glow of the memories. (To hear what can happen when a great singer completely embraces this melodic logic, listen to Frank

*Inside the Cotton Club, October 1930, Charlie Jones, Henry Prince, Marvin Johnson, Les Hite (kneeling), Lionel Hampton, Joe Bailey (bass), Armstrong, George Orendorff, Bill Perkins, Harold Scott, Harvey Brooks, Luther "Sonny" Craven (The Frank Driggs Collection)*

Sinatra's recording from 1961.) Armstrong's response to this line is the classic one of flattening it out, the technique perfected by Bessie Smith before him and Billie Holiday after.

More important than carefully crafted details of the original was the song's popularity, which gave him the chance to pick apart and reconstruct without bewildering the audience completely.[130] Sonny Rollins's image of Armstrong finding the Rosetta Stone for interpreting popular songs is felicitous, but the standard idea of "interpretation" does not precisely fit. In truth, we are never quite sure what his relationship to the original actually is. Is he embracing the sentiments or ridiculing them? When his own invention takes over, how does that affect meaning? The questions are, themselves, the answer: in his second modern style, expressive ambiguity is part of his conception.

Armstrong has often been praised for his ability to sing with emotion, but in this period he never settles into a one-dimensional rendition. Again consider Baldwin, who could have been thinking about Armstrong and the crooners when he wrote, a bit harshly, how "white Americans seem to feel that happy songs are *happy* and sad songs are *sad* and that, God help us, is exactly the way most white Americans sing them—sounding, in both cases, so helplessly, defenselessly fatuous that one dare not speculate on the temperature of the deep freeze from which issue their brave and sexless little voices." Bluesy touches, the kind of plaintive delicacy that impressed Billie Holiday in *West End Blues*, paint the tender side of his emotional range. But when Armstrong sings *Sweethearts on Parade*, no one imagines him standing distraught and isolated on the sidelines, as they well might imagine Carmen Lombardo singing it with the Royal Canadians. Armstrong is simply having too much fun.

Gene Austin, Rudy Vallée, Seger Ellis, and Bing Crosby used the microphone to create the illusion of direct access to a vulnerable and sensuous interior, a conjured intimacy carrying over the radio waves and into the listener's bedroom. Armstrong also exposes his inner world, but never for very long and never with fixed meaning. The set of familiars on which his success is built—microphone whispering, repertory, and big-band accompaniment—now function as a bridge to a world where the laws of a comforting emotional surface no longer apply. It is less an interpretation that he offers than a slapping, twisting, caressing, and totally unpredictable manipulation of the song, which becomes a found object subjected to his relentless, ragging creativity.[131]

Ragging the tune had always been a way of dissociating singer from song, African-American performer from white copyright holder. The ragging musician is not bound by rules dictated by a composer. We have seen how dialogue was a bedrock principle of music making in Armstrong's community of origin, and dialogue is a felicitous way to think about his music from the early 1930s. In his first modern style, his solo is in dialogue with the harmonic foundation, the two working together according to the fixed and variable grid. In his second modern style, his ragging rendition is *in dialogue with the song itself.*

By this I mean that Armstrong is in dialogue with the tune as well as its sentiments. He had never belonged to the heart-baring, fully cathartic blues tradition. He knew how to arouse emotions, but where he really excelled was in the inventive practices of ragging the tune and all that went along with it, including second playing, obbligato, and paraphrase. He was a ragtime virtuoso, not in the sense of Joplin but in the sense of how the word "ragtime" was used before Joplin in the poorly documented history of the plantation vernacular. In the early 1930s this orientation led him to a vision of cool detachment mixed with straightforward sentiments.

His play with melody and emotion launched a tradition that includes Thelonious Monk and Miles Davis. With Armstrong, cool detachment never comes across as disaffection, the outsider attacking with sarcasm and irony. Irony is a slippery quality in music, and it depends on explicit cues to put it in motion. Armstrong does not give much to work with, and it would be surprising if he did, given his ambition to reach the largest white audience possible. What one hears instead is a quicksilver playfulness that puts familiar materials into a new realm of design and expression that is hard to pin down. Melody and words flicker through the performance like novelist Vladimir Nabokov's butterflies—colorful, precise, and evanescent, "divine details" that never quite settle into a fixed meaning.

In the early 1930s there are some wonderful up-tempo solos, but it is the slow to moderate tempos, around 100 to 140 beats per minute, that inspire Armstrong's greatest accomplishments. With the exception of *Confessin' That I Love You* (84 beats per minute), these are not the *very* slow tempos sometimes used by Vallée (or by Bessie Smith, for that matter). They are dance tempos for the medium fox trot. A slow to moderate pace gives him plenty of room to combine a recognizable rendition of the song with carefully crafted interjections.

In the vocals he often introduces breathing room in which anything can happen next (again one thinks of Monk and Davis). This can happen in the trumpet solos, too, but they usually incline toward heavy ornamentation. *If I Could Be with You* is a great example. He constantly plays variations on the simple metrical pattern of James P. Johnson's melody, while connecting to the original through phrasing. Even though the solo carries an overwhelming flood of ornamental details that have little to do with the contours of the tune, we clearly hear him playing a version of *If I Could Be with You*. A key to this is his strong connection to the phrasing of the chords, which carry the rhetorical shape of the original tune, its main points of emphasis, arrival, confirmation, surprise, detour, and originality; these are supported by the band arrangement, as well.

The emphasis is quite different than it had been in his hot solos from the 1920s, where the chords function as little more than an abstract grid. Slower tempos in the early 1930s allow him to achieve tremendous rhythmic variety through double time, with his line moving twice as fast as the original tune, while keeping the phrasing in touch with important points of arrival, as implied by the sequence of chords. His new approach also makes it easy to hear vocal solo and trumpet solo as cut from the same cloth, likewise a new effect for him. In this way, his paraphrasing technique of the early 1930s can lead to a sense of integration and extended expression.

*Sweethearts on Parade* is a magnificent example. Armstrong dominates the performance from start to finish with three full choruses, muted trumpet, vocal, and open trumpet. The tune offers virtually nothing: everything valuable about this performance arises from his interventions. In the first trumpet chorus he lays out some of the paraphrasing details he will use in the choruses that follow, in a gentle and reflective mood, with some lovely effects (CD 0:17–0:21) that float away from the tune and then drift back. Ornamentation increases as the chorus progresses, a fairly standard procedure for him, with the bridge (0:36–0:51) bringing a bit more decoration without challenging the identity of the tune.

His very first vocal utterance ("two by two"), a simple gesture saturated with swing, puts the listener in a world far removed from the Lombardo original. With a little effort you can "see through" the music, as Armstrong liked to say, to a parade marshal's strut, minus New Orleans exuberance. The concluding trumpet solo begins with the swinging gesture, which quickly turns into an agitated rhythmic figure, urged on by Lionel Hampton, that explodes into a double-time break, making it clear that the parade has now entered a new phase. The break references New Orleans explicitly: it is from the piccolo solo for the march *High Society* that Armstrong learned as a teenager. The musical pun probably went unnoticed at Sebastian's Cotton Club, though the audience had a better chance of catching the bugle call *Assembly* at the end of the performance (used also in Guy Lombardo's 1927 recording).

A lovely effect rises out of the bridge, when straight delivery of the tune suddenly swells to an intense climax (CD 2:38–2:43), supported by the accompaniment. Surging figurations take over, a stunning waterfall of varied and cascading decoration, with only brief glimpses of the tune, reaching high and then higher still before Armstrong releases into a glowing descent in which you can almost feel the California sunshine (CD 2:49–3:00). The phrase cuts across the periodicity of the eight-bar phrasing, a classic manifestation of the fixed and variable model. The parading sweethearts have witnessed a magical marriage of ragging splendor with the song's rhetoric, as articulated through melody, chords, and accompaniment.

Detached ragging created an opening for intellectual-emotional complexity, for creative exuberance, for virtuosity, and for independent melodic design. Slower tempos made it easier for Armstrong to do all of this while staying connected to the melody and harmony of the song. The glorious apotheosis of this approach came a year later, in November 1931, in his legendary recording of *Star Dust*.

Hoagy Carmichael conceived this celebrated tune in 1927 as a medium-tempo, instrumental dance piece; the first recording, by Hoagy Carmichael and His Pals, clocks in at 138 beats per minute. Words were added in 1929 to launch one of the most popular songs of the twentieth century. By 1931, crooners had slowed down the tempo—Bing Crosby, for example, to 108 and Cab Calloway to 102. Armstrong's performance in the same year bumps the tempo back up to 132, which was probably the preferred dance tempo.

In this case, we can say that the crooners slowed down the tempo for more reasons than conjuring a bedroom atmosphere. Carmichael's challenging tune is made up of constant twists, turns, and leaps through varied and chromatic harmonies. It moves more like a trumpet solo by Armstrong or Beiderbecke than a traditional croon, and the resemblance is no coincidence, since Carmichael was influenced by both. Like his peers in 1927, he was a huge fan of Beiderbecke. On Carmichael's 1927 recording, trumpeter Byron Smart does a pretty good Beiderbecke imitation, as if to make that connection clear. We have already heard from Carmichael several times about his passion for Armstrong's music, including the confession that listening to Armstrong helped him with his own composing. The likelihood that a key melodic gesture in *Star Dust* was lifted from *Potato Head Blues* has often been noted.

*Sweethearts on Parade* was pure hack work, but the beauty of *Star Dust* comes through almost any performance, with words or without, and at virtually any tempo. Nevertheless, Armstrong's *Star Dust* cannot be regarded as simply one more possible interpretation. Like *If I Could Be with You* and *Sweethearts*, its success emerges from a dialogue between his vigorous ragging and the listener's perception of the original. Again he dominates the entire performance with three choruses, and again there is strong continuity between them.

Armstrong's *Star Dust* conveys a tremendous sense of breadth and power. To see how this is accomplished, let's start with the rhythm section and the chords. Around 1930 the two-beat style of the roaring twenties was gradually yielding to the more spacious flat 4/4 of the swing era. This performance is built on the relatively expansive foundation of four-beat accompaniment, and that quality is reinforced with a simplified harmonic plan. In Carmichael's song, elegantly chromatic passing chords guide the drifty melody along, but in the arrangement Armstrong is using, the harmonies have been simplified to usually only one chord per measure, with chords sometimes extended to two measures. When the complete set of chords as Carmichael wrote them is played with two-beat accompaniment—you can hear this in parts of the 1931 recording by Bing Crosby with the Victor Young Orchestra, for example—the results feel relatively fussy. The simpler harmonic rhythm and the regular four-beat pulse provide relaxed support for Armstrong's pliant rhythms and phrases, qualities that are evident from the very beginning.

The simple gestures of the first four measures (Example 9.1) reveal the touch of a great melodist aiming for excitement and modernity. The two ideas are simple, with the rise of the first balanced by the descending thrust of the second. What is surprising is how different the two are in character, the first halting and stark, the second legato, dense, rapid, and confident. The space between them, longer than it should be by normal standards of phrase construction in popular songs, defines this as a moment of unpredictability, out of which

Example 9.1   Star Dust, *opening (after Schuller 1989)*

burst the rapid arpeggiations. Even a detail like the abrupt end of the phrase, on the very last fraction of the measure before the downbeat of measure 5, a conventional point of arrival, points toward the decidedly modern nature of Armstrong's *Star Dust*; phrasing like this would later become a cliché in bebop.

The first trumpet chorus, a paraphrase of elegance and imagination, is saturated with the kind of bluesy pliancy we first encountered in *Savoy Blues*. Delayed notes blend into triplet figures, blue notes merge with glissandos. The chromatic arpeggiations of Carmichael's melody, so challenging for the crooners, have returned home to King Menelick's agile trumpet. Armstrong introduces a different kind of energy midway through the chorus (CD 0:30) with a double-time figure in midrange. Subdued yet agitated, the figure is packed with tension, which only increases when he expands it in the third statement through dazzling arabesque. At the end of the chorus Armstrong puts down his trumpet, prepares to sing, and releases a low postcoital moan, as if to demonstrate how deeply he is relaxing into *Star Dust*.

Then comes the famous vocal chorus with its extended opening gambit on a single note, sung 15 times, in complete negation of the up-and-down flow of Carmichael's line. The delivery is conversational, slightly out of phase with the foundation. Patches of euphoric invention ("Now that Baby you know, long ago") blend effortlessly with descending ornaments, some derived from the song ("nightingale tells his fairy tale"), and others sounding like that even when they aren't ("in my heart it will remain").

The astonishing final chorus for trumpet includes enough references to Carmichael's melody to remind us of its course, but even when free invention takes over, the solo follows the two-bar segments of the eight-bar phrases. There is a deliberate quality in this approach, which might have surprised a fan from the 1927 Vendome Theater who was prepared to hear Armstrong darting in and out of agreement with the fixed harmonic background. But this is now a standard procedure that helps him discover what can be gained by working *with* the phrasing and hence the rhetoric of the song.

He uses the regular harmonic rhythm and the four sectional divisions of Carmichael's chorus to craft a nice arc to the entire solo. Carmichael has written an intricate maze of balancing rise and fall; Armstrong strips away the rise and runs with the fall: his first eight-bar section (CD 2:23–2:39) is built entirely on descending arpeggiations derived from the original tune. That is basically all it takes for him to transform *Star Dust* into the blues archetype of descending sawtooth lines that we first identified in Chapter 2. The second eight-bar section (CD 2:40) rises with swelling emotion, leading to an inevitable descent (CD 2:55–2:58) that spills across the boundary of phrase three, a moment much like the third break of *Sweethearts*, except that now the descent can be tied directly to Carmichael's tune.

And that is how it goes in this gorgeous variety of bluesy, powerful, and infinitely plastic phrases. The powers of invention that distinguish Armstrong from virtually every other soloist are stronger than ever. His dialogue between composed tune and ragging invention is fluid and effortless, not only in the crafted sense of apparent relaxation and spontaneity, but also in terms of the listener's ease of comprehension. Certainly, the recording reflects careful planning and repeated performances, getting it right and sticking with it, just as soloists in New Orleans had always done.

*Star Dust* is the masterpiece of his second modern style less because Carmichael created such a terrific song than because that song suited so well Armstrong's interest in ragging dialogue. The two aspects that were particularly useful to him were, first, the arpeggiating melody, with its point of origin in the stylistic arena that he himself was leading in 1927; and, second, the rich harmonic foundation, simplified slightly so that it is just a touch more deliberate and less fanciful. The chords carry a narrative arc that is interesting and varied, thus giving shape to Armstrong's series of cascading descents. The true soul mate for Armstrong's *Star Dust* is Coleman Hawkins's equally legendary *Body and Soul* (1939). The slower tempo of Hawkins's performance and his relatively homogeneous rhythmic figuration should not obscure the fundamental similarities in procedure—double-time ragging, made successful by a perfect match of style and tune, with a harmonic foundation of rich variety helping to give shape to a rhapsodic effusion of eccentric melody. Had Armstrong slowed the tempo down this much when he worked out his own *Body and Soul* in 1930 (Hawkins is at 102, Armstrong at 120), he might have stolen Hawkins's thunder by nine years.

Standards of musical expression derived from popular songs simply do not apply. Armstrong's was the most modern jazz going in 1931, and it was completely African-American, coming from somewhere far away—culturally, socially, racially, psychologically—yet delivered safely and with a dash of adventure and perhaps even transgression, a small taste of the forbidden thrill that slumming primitivists were so fond of.

His play with sentiment in *Sweethearts on Parade* and *Star Dust* was something like the play of humor in *Heebie Jeebies* and *Ain't Misbehavin'*: it helped whites relax with the musical intensity of a sophisticated black musician who treated "a beautiful romantic song . . . as a madman would treat it," as Rudy Vallée, a genuine admirer, put it. Easy melodic memorability was trumped by overwhelming virtuosity, cozy sentiment by cool blues detachment and untamed outbursts of joy, immediate accessibility by complex design and unpredictability, first-person sincerity by deflection, asides, and scat jive.

This music is almost antipopular. Armstrong leans toward abstraction, which is one way to relate both of his modern styles to high modernism from Europe. During the 1920s there was an uneasy dynamic between American middle-brow modernism, which was based on extensions of vernacular idioms, and high modernism, with its ruthless attack on bourgeois conventions. Lack of sentimentality provided a bit of common ground between the two. Vernacular modernism was firmly positioned against traditional Victorian values. Gilbert Seldes, the most prominent critical champion of vaudeville, jazz, and the other "lively arts," thought of ragtime as the important first musical step that "literally [tore] to rags the sentimentality of the song[s] which preceded" them. It would have been easy to speak of Armstrong's fractured ballads in the same way.

But ragging the tune was more traditionally conceived as a manifestation of African primitivism, a weak and incoherent distortion of white hymns, marches, and songs. That was why the talented tenth looked elsewhere for signs of cultural advancement. The advantages of putting trite white songs "into spade's life" (to borrow Armstrong's words from a different context) were not immediately obvious to them. Nor would it have been obvious from the tables of Sebastian's New Cotton Club how Armstrong's transformation of popular songs into bizarre little dramas shared goals and methods with the forbidding formations of high modernism from Europe. The case for a connection has been argued by Alfred Appel, who also offers sustained commentary on Armstrong and Fats Waller, a musician who is even more difficult to come to grips with. Appel's book *Jazz Modernism: From Ellington and Armstrong to Matisse and Joyce* is beautifully illustrated and fun to read, though one might hesitate to align with its main thesis.

While it is valuable to observe commonalities—lack of sentiment, a turn toward abstraction, techniques of assemblage, shifting point of view—a deeper comparison would take account of very different social positions. Picasso looked down on primitive inspiration from a secure place as master of an elite lineage of European artists, but Armstrong was singing his ballads looking up at the next rung on the ladder of his career. Each was a master in his culture of origin. Armstrong's early training included tips on how to enter the white market in a place where African-American musicians stood only a very slight step above domestic servants. In 1929 this kind of outreach became a full-time occupation for him.

It is unlikely that anyone at Sebastian's thought of Matisse when they shuffled to the medium fox trot tempo of *Sweethearts on Parade*, but the analogy came more easily to Europeans. The paper record of Armstrong's first trip to England in the summer of 1932 shows British critics articulating the primitive-modern contradiction with special flare. His innovations were "ultra modern," yet he was said to have received them through dreams and played them with "natural ability." One Hannen Swaffer, writing for the *Daily Herald* of London on July 25, 1932, gleefully complained about Armstrong's perspiration and, under the heading "Mr. Ugly," compared him to a gorilla: "He might have come straight from some African jungle and then after being taken to a tailor's for a ready made dress suit been put straight on the stage and told to 'sing.'" Swaffer counted the "young Jewish element at the back" of the Palladium among the few enthusiasts. But Swaffer also thought the trumpet playing was as revolutionary as Richard Strauss's opera *Elektra* had been in 1909. Comparisons like this turn up in several British reviews, one mentioning James Joyce and insisting that Armstrong's "is the only kind of music being written today that has any importance at all," while another reminded readers that Matisse, Wagner, and van Gogh each had their detractors, too.

Back in the United States, it must have been clearer than ever how the African-American musical vernacular was providing the charge that helped middle-brow American modernism break free of Victorian sentiment, as Seldes observed. The more African the product, the stronger the dose of the modern. Controversy over the word "jazz," discussed in Chapter 4, was on one level a debate over just how far white America could go in this direction. In the early 1930s Armstrong emerged as one of the winners as he carried jazz and a considerable market share of the country along with him into uncharted territory.[132]

His was advertised as the "highest paid colored band in the world," and that may not have been an exaggeration. In November 1931 the *Defender* listed bands led by Ellington, Henderson, Armstrong, and McKinney as the outstanding African-American units, with Ellington and Armstrong making the most money. His record sales were soaring. In the spring of 1932 OKeh sued to stop his move to RCA Victor, which planned to "replace Ruddy [*sic*] Vallée with the colored troupe." *Time* magazine explained what all the fuss was about: Armstrong had sold more than 100,000 records in the past year. It had been barely three years since Rockwell decided to market him with current hits, in the spring of 1929, and now he was being courted as a replacement for Vallée, one of the biggest names in the business.

Records had become huge for him, but radio may have been even bigger. Radio was the medium of choice for the crooners, with Vallée leading the way, and it was now doing its work for Armstrong. Radio was alive and personal, yet powerful through its extraordinary reach, and it carried a modern glow. "Are your new neighbors modern people?" rang a little quip in a 1922 edition of the *Buffalo Express*. "Modern? Say, they sent in last night to borrow our Radio set!" was the answer, which immediately located both neighbors on the modern scale.

When Armstrong arrived in California in 1930, the African-American newspaper *California Eagle* mentioned how his local reputation had been established through records. By the time he left a year later, radio may have been more important. In Los Angeles he was heard nightly on stations KMIC and KPVD, with broadcasts distributed nationally to Chicago, New York, Baltimore, and Detroit. "Everybody in California for miles and miles around catching our programs, which were the *last words*," he wrote, with emphasis. Radio certainly extended his reputation within the African-American community, but it worked even more dramatically with whites. The black vernacular had become an increasingly familiar presence in white living rooms and bedrooms, which made it easier for whites to accept his stunning modernity.

Did Armstrong have more impact on musicians in the early 1930s than in the mid- and late 1920s? Some observers have speculated that he did, given his far greater exposure. Yet a quantitative surge for the influence of his trumpet playing seems unlikely, simply because so many musicians had been tracking him for quite some time. Bud Freeman was exaggerating when he said that every musician in the world knew of him by 1929, but by how much? In the early 1930s younger players encountered his solos for the first time, while older players struggled to catch up. Bunny Berigan regularly stopped by his local music store looking to buy new Armstrong records, memorize them, and play them on his next job. Jimmy Maxwell spent hours one summer figuring out the solo from *When You're Smiling*, and twenty-year-old Roy Eldridge was stunned when he first heard Armstrong in 1931 at the Lafayette Theater in New York City. Nat Gonella freely acknowledged his debt to the recordings he was able to find in England, explaining that "short of being a musical genius . . . the next best thing is to model oneself on the lines of someone who is." In New York City, Ward Pinkett was noticed sitting next to a jukebox with his horn in his lap, listening to Armstrong, tears of admiration in his eyes. Secure and confident in his ability to adapt, imitation never bothered Armstrong. "Pops, a lotta cats has copied the Mona Lisa, but they still line up to dig the original," he once quipped.

With his voice, however, the trajectory of his impact was, without question, very different, as he was now much more widely imitated. Cab Calloway's *Dinah* from 1932 is almost a compendium of Armstrong's techniques. Whites could come that close to his vocal style only as parody, as one Norman Selby did in blackface makeup. More important than wholesale imitation was the gradual absorption of the various components of his style—scat, sudden outbursts of unscripted melodic joy, rhythmic punch in effervescent service of the fixed and variable model, tendencies toward melodic reduction, bluesy phrasing, and swinging detachment from the beat. The popular Boswell Sisters told the press that they modeled their style on his. Bing Crosby, who liked to stop by Sebastian's after work at Cocoanut Grove in Hollywood, was catching on. And so was Billie Holiday, whose first recordings, at age eighteen in 1933, make clear her debt to Armstrong, especially the behind-the-beat phrasing of *Riffin' the Scotch*.

There has also been much discussion through the years about whether or not Armstrong's step into the white market was a sellout of tragic proportions, a surrender to the "creepy tentacles of commercialism," as Gunther Schuller vividly phrased it.[133] John Hammond insisted that Armstrong "made his greatest recordings, the Hot Fives and Hot Sevens, in the mid twenties," after which came deterioration. This was a deeply ingrained way of thinking for one small but influential swath of jazz fandom during the swing era, and it has played out in writings about jazz history for many decades.

In the swing era, the main ingredient of selling out was too much emphasis on popular songs and not enough on hot solos. Armstrong's embrace of popular tunes put him on the wrong side of jazz authenticity, conceived in this way, and for many years the value of his second modern style was downplayed as a result. Needless to say, he did not think this way, and there were few in the early 1930s who did. It would have baffled him to elevate the scrambling and funky Hot Five recordings, most of them impromptu versions of hack tunes made and sold cheaply, above the big-band recordings of the early 1930s that were selling more than 100,000 copies in a single year. Today it is easy to see that his turn to big bands and mainstream popular hits was no tragedy but rather a step that presented a new set of limitations and possibilities, to which he responded beautifully. The whole point for him was dynamic dialogue between his radical, ragging invention and the popular tune.

The real tragedy came next, when he climbed another rung on the ladder of his career: it came with movies, which were loaded with a Faustian bargain.

## A Manager's Fit

Released from jail on March 19, 1931, and wary of further skirmishes with the California justice system, Armstrong turned down a lucrative offer from Sebastian. He may also have had the first inklings of a serious managerial problem that would follow him to Chicago and come to fruition there. McKinney's Cotton Pickers stepped in at Sebastian's, followed by Les Hite's new orchestra, who billed themselves as "Louie Armstrong's boys."

On Sunday, March 22, he arrived in Chicago, greeted at the house he and Lillian still owned by five young men with guitars and ukuleles who had come to serenade him. They played some music and then pulled out a huge joint. "That moment alone helped me to forget a lot of ungodly, unnecessary, you know, all that shit that happened on the coast," he remembered. Lillian stayed in California.

The South Side of Chicago was now very different from the glory years of the mid-1920s, when people were spending money left and right on his compelling music. Banks had closed, work was scarce, and evictions were commonplace. The *Defender* was advising its southern readers to stay home and forget the northern promise. This dramatic decline had little effect on Armstrong's return, for he immediately stepped into a one-week gig at the Regal Theater, which sold out every night. After that he took a nine-day break, "having a little fun, etc.," as he put it later. His strong memory of a nine-day vacation is notable, and we should remind ourselves how special a break like that was in a working world where even a celebrated musician hesitated to put his horn down for more than a few hours. He bought a two-door, yellow Model A with rumble seat for cruising around town and hired young Charlie Carpenter as his valet, plus a friend from New Orleans as his chef.

Meanwhile, a visit to the OKeh studios was arranged. He put together a band of local musicians and the first person he hired was trombonist Preston Jackson, to whom he was still grateful for playing at his wedding reception seven years earlier. Tubby Hall, Mike McKendrick, and Charlie Alexander, all from New Orleans, were brought in. He brought parts with him, and the band learned the tunes he already knew, rehearsing for two weeks and recording eight new sides in late April. *I Surrender Dear*, another of his majestic ballads, was later singled out by Rudy Vallée for special praise. *When It's Sleepy Time Down South* would soon become his theme song. The sessions included a wonderful transformation from Armstrong (and also a fine arrangement) of the up-tempo *Them There Eyes*, another performance that Billie Holiday surely knew well. Being back in Chicago may have inspired his introduction for *Blue Again*, a fond—though not nearly as successful and probably extemporized, or nearly so—nod to the introductory fanfare for *West End Blues*. *I'll Be Glad When You're Dead You Rascal You*, which Armstrong had first tackled back in January, was also included. "It has some pretty risqué lines, but the censors are not kicking," noted the *Defender*.

On April 8 he opened at an after-hours, whites-only walk-down called Show Boat (formerly My Cellar) at Lake and Clark Streets, inside the Loop. He and the band were hooked to a live broadcast, every night, on WIBO beginning 12:15 a.m. and ending sometime around 3:00, with a network that reached New Orleans. "The best musical minds of the city" attended the premiere, reported the *Defender*, to hear him play *Confessin'*, *Rockin' Chair*, *If I Could Be with You*, *Peanut Vendor*, and multiple choruses of *Dinah* and *Tiger Rag*, ten of the latter, "each in a different style," the aesthetic principle of variety still reigning supreme. Each chorus of *Tiger Rag* was greeted with applause on the magnitude of "a victory cheer at a football game," the next chorus then treated as an encore. Johnny Naitland jumped up and said that he was going to give up trumpet playing. Louis Panico was moved to tears. Bud Freeman was impressed with his playing "at the top of the horn, not just for an effect, but as a regular thing," along with a new sense of economy in the design of his solos.

Johnny Collins, a booking agent Armstrong had met in California, was now making arrangements and claiming to be his manager.

*With Johnny Collins (Courtesy of the Louis Armstrong House Museum)*

Armstrong was told that Collins had made a deal with Tommy Rock-well to take over management, but it would soon become clear that those two were in volatile disagreement. "Come to think of it, I sure had a manager's fit," Armstrong wrote later, with understatement.

The Show Boat, "all glitter and glass," as saxophonist George James described it, was controlled by criminals and doubled as a major bookie operation during the day, a cabaret at night. Milt Hinton said that the place scared him, even though the gangsters tended to be good tippers. Preston Jackson never saw so many guns in his life as the evening when a gangster insulted the girl-friend of a rival. Armstrong continued playing through the inci-dent, while most of the musicians ducked for cover. According to Jackson, Louis Panico leapt up from his table to stand in front of Armstrong, guarding him during the ensuing fight in a heroic ges-ture. This was the environment in which, a week or so after the gig began, Armstrong's life was threatened with the aim of returning him to Rockwell's management and to Connie's Inn in Harlem. "I knew that it was [Rockwell] that did it," Armstrong confided to friends years later.

Frankie Foster, a notorious gangster associated with Al Capone, helped deliver the threat. Armstrong and Collins were defiant. They hired bodyguards to protect Armstrong, solicited help from any underworld connection they could think of, brought in the police, and blitzed the media. "The more they scare him, the better he plays the cornet, gets those shivery, shakery, tremolo effects like the girls love," Collins quipped in one newspaper.

But the pressure did not relent, and Collins soon realized that the best strategy would be to get out of town. He and Armstrong left Chicago in mid-May, accompanied by two bodyguards who would continue to stay by his side for many months. Collins put a tour together, complete with chorus girls. They stayed in Detroit for a full week (May 24–30), playing opposite McKinney's Cotton Pickers, led by his old friend Don Redman, at the Graystone Ballroom. At Ohio State University in Columbus, they played an extravaganza opposite Fletcher Henderson, Cab Calloway, and two other bands. In Louisville, a white woman called from the dance floor, "Louis, oh sweet Louis." Armstrong wisely hid in his dressing room at intermission. Disappointed by his retreat, she scolded him, pointing out that Paul Whiteman did not act that way. The next day they were able to watch the Kentucky Derby. After a series of one-nighters in Minneapolis, Milwaukee, Cleveland, Cincinnati, Lexington, Indianapolis, and West Virginia, they returned to Louisville, where they caught a train for New Orleans.

Plans were to go to New Orleans for two weeks, followed by a return to California and some more movie making. Those two locations were about as far from Chicago and New York City as Collins and Armstrong could get and still stay in the United States. A year later they dropped that limitation and escaped to England. The Show Boat replaced him with Jabbo Smith, who could play the introduction to *West End Blues* note for note, along with strong versions of *Beau Koo Jack* and *St. Louis Blues*. Armstrong took at least one firm lesson from his manager's fit and his brush with gangsters: "You needed a white man to get along." It was a principle he had long understood. "Always have a white man who likes you and can and will put his hand on your shoulder and say 'this is my nigger,' and can't nobody harm you"—that was the advice that his older friend Black Benny

Williams had given him before he left New Orleans. The problem was getting the right white man, which was not easy.

The irony was that in order to escape the manager's fit he would have to return to the "disgustingly segregated and prejudiced" city of his birth, where the structures of white supremacy played out in vivid ways. The high rungs on the ladder of his career put him in a position where he could blow his horn and cultivate his unusual singing style on his own terms, and that was a rare and treasured luxury. But this new position did not help him escape the traps of racism, which were magnified rather than reduced. When he eventually returned to the North, there were even more traps waiting for him. They were not quite as deadly as the gangster threats in Chicago, but they were insidiously powerful, in a different way. The next ladder on the climb of his career brought him fully into the twisted imagery favored by the most modern media in their treatments of African Americans, disguised in humor and glamour but requiring him to apply his intelligence, charisma, and musical power to an especially degrading set of conditions.

# TEN

# Sleepy Time Down South

*Music is such a tremendous proposition that it probably needs government supervision.*
*There does not seem to be any proper protection for anything in this line.*
—Jelly Roll Morton

**The cultural impact of the Great Depression included drastic consolidation of the music** industry. Phonograph recordings and vaudeville, two dominant institutions in the 1920s, fell into steep decline, yielding to the cheaper mediums of radio and movies. Around 100 million records were sold in 1921, 2 million in 1933. Ironically, this decline coincided with Armstrong's triumph in the national market, as he became the bestseller in a sinking field. The fancy orchestras of the movie houses became, in most places, a distant memory, and so did the glitzy blues divas. Black musicals on Broadway folded often and quickly. As F. Scott Fitzgerald famously put it, "Somebody had blundered and the most expensive orgy in history was over."

The Depression was especially hard on musicians from New Orleans who had been enjoying so much splashing success outside of their home city for some 15 years. Armstrong was one of the few who successfully transitioned into the swing era. The early 1930s were scrambling years for Jelly Roll Morton, Sidney Bechet, Kid Ory, and, most tragically, King Oliver, who lost a lot of money in failed banks. Like Morton, Oliver was reluctant to hire a manager, which put him at even greater disadvantage. "King was no business man," lamented one of his sidemen, who saw him turn down good offers and get stuck with inferior ones. Armstrong apparently approached Oliver with an offer to colead a band, but his proud teacher turned him down.

On a street corner in Harlem, Morton explained to anyone who would listen how he had invented jazz. Bechet opened up a tailor shop, Ory raised chickens in Los Angeles, and Johnny Dodds was rewarded for his cautious investments in real estate. Touring Savannah, Georgia, in September 1937, Armstrong discovered Oliver sweeping floors in a poolroom; seven months later the King was dead. "I watched all that and I profit by those people's mistakes," Armstrong said. (He was speaking of the benefits of good dentistry, but the remark could be extended in any number of directions.) His ability to adapt was far greater than most men's, and not just the musicians from New Orleans.

It was under these distressed economic conditions—and also under threats of gangster violence—that Armstrong headed south in 1931 for the first time since he left home nine years earlier. Collins booked him into a large and pricey whites-only venue called Suburban Gardens, just outside the city limits of New Orleans, in Jefferson Parish, near the river. He performed there six nights per week for nearly three months.

He and his band arrived on June 5 at the Louisville–Nashville Railway Station in a private railroad car. Sherman Cook, a home boy who was now Armstrong's personal attendant, had been sent in advance along with Lillian to orchestrate a triumphal entrance. Eight bands, including one sponsored by the Zulu Social Aid and Pleasure Club, escorted this "magnet of dark town adulation" (as a white newspaper put it) on a parade through South Rampart Street. A crowd numbering in the thousands carried him while he comically kicked his legs into the air. He was taken to Astoria Gardens, the ballroom of the (colored) Astoria Hotel, on Rampart Street. Capt. Joseph Jones and Peter Davis from the Colored Waif's Home for Boys were waiting for him, and so was Dave Jones, who had taught him to read music on the riverboats. A band led by Kid Rena, a childhood friend and competitor, played his tunes as they had learned them from recordings. After that the crowd followed him to the Patterson Hotel, 759 South Rampart Street, at Julia Street, where he lodged for his three-month stay.

Collins and Armstrong were hoping that the long train ride would put some distance between them and the manager's mess they now found themselves in, but the intimidation continued. On their

*Rampart Street (The Frank Driggs Collection)*

midwestern tour they had been tracked by three thugs, and now they were getting the same treatment in New Orleans. While Armstrong was playing Detroit at the end of May, the president of the American Federation of Musicians union telegrammed from New York City to demand that he fulfill his prior contract with Connie's Inn, and Rockwell was now working the New Orleans scene in a similar way. This didn't take much prodding, since the white musicians' union was painfully aware that Armstrong's immense popularity would drain business from their own members. Cornetist and union president Johnny De Droit called a meeting of the local board of directors, and the decision was made to take up the matter of Suburban Gardens hiring a Negro orchestra with Governor Huey Long.

But Suburban Gardens fought back. They hired bodyguards and the band opened on June 8. As was now normal for Armstrong's extended gigs, a radio broadcast was set up, on station WSMB. Opening night was marred by a bracing insult. The announcer walked up to the microphone, hesitated, explained to his audience,

"I can't announce that nigger man," and left the building. Armstrong was alerted behind the curtain, and he immediately walked out to the mike, asked the band for an introductory chord, and introduced himself. He did that for the rest of the gig and believed that it was the first time an African American even spoke on the radio in New Orleans.

The band was the only entertainment, six hours per night, with 40-minute sets and 20-minute breaks. The place was routinely full. On the first night they played *High Society*, a number strongly associated with his hometown, three clarinets playing the famous piccolo solo in unison. For another feature Armstrong stepped out to the center of the dance floor for 20 choruses of *Tiger Rag*, another piece with strong local connections.

"Virtually all of New Orleans was represented," claimed a white newspaper, and in a twisted way there was some truth to that. The newspaper was not thinking of African Americans, who could not enter the door. But thousands gathered outside the building on opening night, perched on the levee that kept the Mississippi River from overflowing its banks. They spread out picnic suppers and settled in for the evening, hoping to hear the music through the open windows. Accustomed to "nosebleed" balcony seats in segregated theaters, they satisfied themselves with a patch of dirt along the riverbank. "I'll never forget that sight," Armstrong confessed.

Did he play over and beyond the crowded white ballroom to the community he had grown up with, now assembled on the levee? Perhaps the scene reminded him of Lincoln Gardens, where the little white boys sat at ringside tables around the bandstand, while hundreds of African-American dancers filled the hall behind them—except now white enthusiasm for his music had multiplied a thousand times, pushing his African-American fans out of the building completely.

Radio was a much easier way for African Americans to hear him, and his visit caused a huge upsurge in unit sales during the summer of 1931. Networks carried the nightly broadcasts as far as Minneapolis. Telephone lines were set up so that people could call Suburban Gardens with requests. In response to one, Armstrong eagerly announced that the band was going to "take that baby like Grant

*Colored Waif's Home for Boys (The William Russell Photographic Collection, MSS 520 F. 2531, Williams Research Center, The Historic New Orleans Collection)*

took Richmond!" It's hard to know if he was being mischievous, but contemporary Confederates were so insulted that they clogged up the phone lines with complaints. He quickly issued an apology in the same set.

In late June he visited the Colored Waif's Home for Boys, where he was greeted by the boys' band playing their version of *Auld Lang Syne*. He sat in with them for one number and also played a solo version, "hot and high," of *When You're Smiling*. His first cornet was brought out for display and he fondly looked it over. He bought a radio for the home so the boys could listen to him that evening, when he dedicated a tune to them from the bandstand.

Zilner Randolph, a trumpeter who admired Armstrong greatly, had been hired in Detroit to rehearse the band and create their arrangements. During an intermission Armstrong turned to him and said, "Randy, pick out a set and take it down, this is your band." What he meant was for Randolph to select a group of numbers he would like to conduct, which he would be doing from now on while

Armstrong took breaks for part of a set or even an entire set, in which case Randolph would also take his solos. This development shocked the other musicians but they accepted it.

One night at Suburban Gardens, the club put on a southern theme, with the women all dressed in white lace and the men in white linen suits. "All you could see was white on white," remembered Preston Jackson. This was traditional summer style, but the racial implications must have been obvious. Randolph was conducting a waltz when an intoxicated young woman brushed up against him in the middle of her dance step; suddenly she grabbed his baton and drawled, "Aw I love you black man, I love you." She held on to him for what seemed like a full minute, until the band stopped playing. Tubby Hall, the drummer (and a New Orleanian native), was so unnerved that he lost track of timekeeping, but the crowd laughed heartily. All Jackson could think about were the thousands of African Americans standing on the levee and the potential for a riot. The musicians quickly filed off the bandstand and scurried back to Armstrong's dressing room. A few minutes later the club owner came to get them, told them not to worry, that the crowd felt sorry for the musicians and was taking up a collection of tips as a gesture of goodwill.

Armstrong was certainly not interested in managing and disciplining his sidemen in the way that, say, Cab Calloway or Duke Ellington did. He had a hard time disconnecting personal from business matters; what he wanted was the freedom to concentrate on music without worry. Bud Freeman talked about Jack Teagarden's troubles managing musicians: "the headaches of an artist like that trying to keep a band going are just too much," he insisted. "I was always amazed that people like Benny Goodman, especially, who is a great artist, and Tommy Dorsey could have a band and still play as well as they did. But they were hard men. They had to be. . . . I realized it was not for me. . . . If the players in the band didn't like me, I couldn't play, where Benny Goodman and Tommy Dorsey didn't give a damn what anybody thought of them."

Managing a band was not for Armstrong, either; he was happy to have Collins call the shots, though he intervened in special situations. Guitarist Mike McKendrick was Collins's straw boss, and one day McKendrick approached Preston Jackson with the news that Collins

*Suburban Gardens (The William Russell Jazz Files, MSS 536, F. Louis Armstrong 331a, Williams Research Center, The Historic New Orleans Collection)*

had decided to fire him. Jackson had lumbago and was taking time off work for a few days to rest. He quickly made his way to the Patterson Hotel to tell his friend the story. Armstrong exploded, "This is *my* band, not Johnny Collins's band!" and set out to argue with Collins until the situation was straightened out.

Loyal to his friend, who had played for his wedding to Lillian many years before, Armstrong started having Jackson sing a number in their standard set. Jackson became well known over the radio and gathered lots of lunch invitations, especially from ladies. Newspapers ran stories about the local musicians in Armstrong's band and how they had made good. Jackson noted how people who wouldn't have anything to do with him when he was young, because of his dark skin, were now very friendly. This was Armstrong's experience as well, multiplied to an incalculable degree.

In New Orleans began the ritual (if it hadn't already begun in Chicago) of people queuing up to greet him and ask for handouts. A line formed outside his hotel room every night in anticipation of the door opening at 6:00 p.m. Word got around that he was passing out dollar bills. "That happened the whole three months we were there," remembered Jackson.

On August 23 the Zulu Social Aid and Pleasure Club invited Armstrong to visit headquarters at 1125 Perdido Street and made him an honorary lifetime member. He sponsored a local baseball team, the "Secret Nine," buying them equipment and uniforms with his last name written across the fronts of their shirts. On August 16 the Secret Nine played the New Orleans Black Pelicans at Heinemann Park, at the corner of Tulane and Carrollton Avenues—2:00 p.m., admission 50 cents, with "special accommodations" for whites. On Sunday the 23rd his own participation was announced and 1,500 fans came to St. Raymond Park to watch him pitch. In between games he threw three pitches to Sherman Cook, catcher, with drummer Joe Lindsey, a friend from childhood, batting. After a comically exaggerated exchange of signals, Armstrong, cap turned backwards, wound up, ran down the mound, and hurled a "slow, tantalizing gumdrop." Lindsey, with the brim of his cap pulled down over his eyes, flailed away violently and missed, while Cook desperately tried to catch the ball in his catcher's mask. After strike three, the crowd urged Lindsey to run while Armstrong simply chuckled and walked off the mound.

The summer of 1931 was also marred by a tragedy—the death of cornetist Buddy Petit (ca. 1897–July 4, 1931). Four years older than Armstrong, Petit was one of the players he had imitated during his teenage years. Petit played in a narrow range but with an expanded command of harmony, fast fingering, a gift for variations, and imaginative counterpoint to the lead; he was an example for Armstrong in all four areas. At the end he was heavily alcoholic, living by himself in a one-room cabin on the north shore of Lake Pontchartrain. Armstrong served as a pallbearer, his presence attracting huge numbers to the funeral. What were his feelings, looking down at the sad end of an important musician in his life? Ten years before it would have been impossible for anyone to predict the dramatic differences in the trajectories of the two young musicians.

Efforts were made to schedule three performances for blacks. On Saturday, June 6, he was booked for an evening at Astoria Gardens, the venue on South Rampart Street that had hosted him on the day of his arrival. Thirteen hundred people showed up only to be told that his contract with Suburban Gardens prohibited him from playing. He tried to appease them by singing three lines of *Peanut Vendor*. Twenty-nine people were arrested. Another futile attempt was made July 8 at Pythian Temple Roof Garden, and finally a big "colored-only" event was scheduled for Monday, August 31, at the U.S. Army Supply Base, Poland Avenue and Dauphine Street in the Bywater neighborhood, right next to the Industrial Canal, price 75 cents. Thousands came from all over in Model T Fords and found the place padlocked. Someone decided that the Army base could not host dancing, after all, though Preston Jackson suspected that nearby club owners had intervened.

The only public performance Armstrong gave for black people during his three-month stay was a benefit for the Waif's Home at an African-American theater (probably the Lincoln Theater; a performance of some kind was scheduled there for Saturday, June 13). He and Lillian took the stage as a duet. "I had never seen such a superb act," said Randolph. "They looked like they could just breath together. They knew what one another was doing . . . just the witty little things that she and Louis would do."

The band left town on September 1, immediately after the fiasco at the Army base. Jackson implied that there was an element of escape in their departure, but it is clear that Collins had already arranged a tour through the South. He had been entertaining various offers from Europe, but decided to do this instead. The three months in New Orleans must have been immensely satisfying for Armstrong, except for the glaring fact that the people who had nurtured him, musically and otherwise, during the first 21 years of his life were not allowed to hear him play. The visit brought into high relief where he now stood on the ladder of his career—a step beyond the reach of the community he had grown up with.

Collins's southern tour was a grueling six-week run of one-nighters, some white, some black, and some precariously mixed. The band crisscrossed through Texas, Oklahoma, Louisiana, Mississippi, and Arkansas, counting on the buzz from the first program in a city to generate return visits. Armstrong remembered how tough it could be to find food. A reliable method was to go around to the back of a restaurant and plead with the African-American chef to feed them in the kitchen. "Many are the times I've eaten off those big wooden chopping blocks," he remembered. Sherman Cook and Joe Lindsey became part of his entourage, Cook as master of ceremonies and Lindsey to help book rooms and carry luggage. Armstrong subsidized Lindsey's salary in a gesture of gratitude for the favor Lindsey had shown him some 16 years earlier when he hired him for his very first musical job, a little trio of teenage novices.

First stop was Sam Houston Hall in Houston. The performance was a smashing success, with an estimated 8,000 in attendance and another 1,000 standing outside, hoping to hear something. A special dance floor was installed in anticipation of the "greatest ballroom event ever held in Texas." Special railroad rates were arranged for towns within a radius of 100 miles. "For the first time in the writer's recollection," wrote a reviewer, "the high and the low, the rich and poor, white and black, learned and unlearned all, all turned out under one roof to such an occasion in Houston." A return visit to Houston was sponsored by a group of African-American businessmen. Jackson remembered how Armstrong took Collins's word on attendance without bothering to ask for documentation. "It was foolish of him not to check," insisted Jackson. A December notice in the *Afro-American* gave some attendance counts for the tour: Galveston, 4,000; San Antonio, 2,700; Austin, 1,900; Wichita Falls, 2,200; Ft. Worth, 5,000; return trip to Houston, 3,000.

From Houston they went to Oklahoma City; this was probably when Ralph Ellison heard him play. Ellison was impressed by the appearance of white women at the segregated dance hall: "They were wild for his music and nothing like that had ever happened in our town before. His music was our music but they saw it as theirs too, and were willing to break the law to get to it."

In Wichita Falls there was a glitch with housing. Arrangements had been made with a woman who owned a 15-room house, but when her husband came home he told his wife to get the dirty musicians out immediately, then turned around and threatened to shoot them. Adventures like this were routine on southern tours in the 1930s.

They gave two performances in Dallas at the Fair Park Automobile Building, with a special section reserved for whites. For the return visit Paul and His Pals, a local black band, played while the

Armstrong band took breaks to produce continuous dancing from nine until midnight. From Dallas they went to Tyler, Texas, but couldn't find a bus, so they hunkered down for 95 miles in the back of a truck. In Tyler a rope was strung down the middle of the dance floor to separate the races. Someone from the black side snuck under the rope, according to Jackson, and the "Texas Rangers [state police] came down on him and beat the living shit out of him and they made the promoter give the white people all their money back." The dance folded quickly and the musicians bolted. As pianist Willie "The Lion" Smith once wryly observed, "Anything can happen where a lot of people can't read or write."

In attendance for the Austin dance, October 12, at the (still-standing) Driskell Hotel was sixteen-year-old Charles L. Black Jr., who would go on to teach law at Columbia and Yale and contribute to the Supreme Court case *Brown v. Board of Education* in 1954. Black said that Armstrong seemed possessed by some spiritual force, playing with his eyes closed. "Steam whistle power, lyric grace, alternated at will, even blended," wrote Black years later. It was the first time Black had ever seen an African American in any role but servant, and he considered his encounter with this evident genius to be part of what turned him toward civil rights law. "One never entirely knows the ways of the power of art," he observed.

After Tyler came Waco and then San Antonio, where they met up with Don Albert's band from New Orleans. Saxophonist Budd Johnson remembered a performance in San Antonio with Armstrong's band in 1933. The band had lodgings in a black neighborhood, but a white man walked up to them while they were sitting on the front porch in the middle of the afternoon. "I found out where you guys live," the man told them. "I just wanted to come and talk with you and say hello. . . . I heard the band last night, but I didn't get a chance to say anything to you, so you guys were great. But you don't mind if I say something, do you?" The musicians invited him to say what was on his mind. "Well you know one thing?" the white man said. "In talking with you fellows, you're not niggers. You're different from what we've got down here. These are niggers down here. They're not as intelligent as you guys are. You know, you are not niggers." It took a moment for the musicians to realize that he was sincere. They didn't reveal that they had all come from the South. "I got used to people asking me all sorts of, well, crude questions," remembered Armstrong in an unrelated discussion. "Maybe I was the first of my kind that they'd ever talked to."

Next came Galveston, where they hung out with King Oliver's band. Oliver had been touring, sometimes following in Armstrong's footsteps, and he was irritated that admission for Armstrong was $1.25, 25 cents more than for his band. From Galveston they traveled to Shreveport, Louisiana, where they spent some time with guitarist Snoozer Quinn, and from Shreveport they headed for Jackson, Mississippi, where Armstrong boarded overnight with blues pianist Little Brother Montgomery. The temperature in Jackson was 100 degrees in the shade.

The next day they set out on a chartered Dixie-Greyhound bus to Little Rock, via Memphis. What they didn't know was that the driver had been instructed to stop in Memphis and change busses; apparently, someone else had requested this particular vehicle, which had reclining seats. Manager Collins had returned to New York and left his wife, Mary, to travel along and supervise the arrangements. They arrived in Memphis at 1:00 p.m., and Mary Collins refused to accept the inferior vehicle. The bus company called the police, who were outraged to see Armstrong chatting with a white woman in the front seats and surrounded the bus.

The scene was tense, since it had become known that several band members were carrying guns. They were hauled to jail with the police talking loudly about a need for cotton pickers in the area. In jail Armstrong passed marijuana cigarettes around for the inmates. "Man, Louis could make the best of a bad situation," quipped George James. The *Commercial Appeal* of Memphis reported smugly in its October 7 issue about what a pity it was for the Negro population of Little Rock that the musicians, decked out in "fancy plus fours, bright hued golf socks and just below vari-colored berets, worn in the latest Jimmy Walker style," could not "perform for their edification." But in fact the manager of the Little Rock theater had arrived on the evening of the arrest and put up bail. The musicians were released on condition that they return the next day to play a benefit concert. When they pulled in to the gig at Little Rock at 11:00 p.m., the audience was still waiting for them.

Back in Memphis the next day, for the benefit matinee at the Peabody Hotel, Armstrong decided to dedicate his performance of *I'll Be Glad When You're Dead You Rascal You* to the Memphis police force. "It was then that I really thought that Louis had lost his marbles," remembered Jackson. "When it came to my solo I was all confused because all I could think of was cotton." But the policemen did not understand the words and were flattered by the gesture. Mezz Mezzrow, listening to the radio broadcast from New York, got the message clearly. Mezzrow had been sending packages of marijuana to Armstrong through the mail, and he dialed in his hero whenever he could. He was delighted to hear Armstrong call out, while the band played the introduction to *I'll Be Glad When You're Dead*, "Dig this Mezzeerola!"

Meanwhile, Collins had booked the band for a tour on the RKO vaudeville-movie circuit through St. Louis, Ohio, Kentucky, and Chicago; this would be followed by TOBA time in Philadelphia, Washington, Baltimore, and New York.[134] These gigs were often booked for a full week, with one-nighters mixed in here and there. This made the tour less enjoyable than the lengthy stay at Suburban Gardens, but far more relaxed than the relentless one-nighters through the Deep South. The *Defender* reported that Armstrong's unit was pulling in $2,250 per week from the Keith Vaudeville Circuit. In between movie showings the band accompanied other featured acts, while lesser acts supplied their own music; they were also a featured act themselves, with a coveted position in the program. They played four to six shows a day, with one day per week off for travel. George James remembered the RKO tour as "first class work though it was a hard grind."

The start of the RKO tour on October 17 in St. Louis, at the St. Louis Theater (today known as Powell Hall), did not begin smoothly. Vigorous and relentless booing streamed down from one section of the theater each and every time the band played. Apparently, Rockwell and Immerman had hired someone to sabotage the act. A vice president of RKO was called in to solve the problem. In St. Louis the band also played the Chauffeur's Club, where Charlie Creath directed the house band.

The next stop was Cincinnati and the 3,500-seat Albee Theater, opposite a band led by Zack Whyte. "There isn't the shadow of a symphonic touch, a legitimate musical approach in a bar of the band's music," snorted the *Enquirer*. "It's pure and strictly jazz." In Cincinnati Armstrong occupied the headliner position, which put him at the top of vaudeville's classiest circuit. Nevertheless, their hotel rooms at 6th and Mound Streets were blighted with rats as big as cats.

The rats, however, were not his main problem. Louis and Lillian had parted bitterly when the band left New Orleans on September 1. It was, by now, a familiar story: he left for New York City without her in 1924, then left for New York City without her again in 1929, then left Los Angeles without her in 1930. Alpha was now traveling with him, and Lillian had been following them in a small yellow Ford, accompanied by a man. Somehow she enticed the local police to raid his hotel room in Cincinnati, where they caught him in flagrante delicto with Alpha.

Whatever the flaws in their relationship, Lillian had been good to him. In 1923 she helped him notate his pieces for copyright, co-composed the breakthrough of *Tears*, and urged him to the breakthrough of *Cornet Chop Suey*; in 1924 she convinced him that it was time to leave Oliver and accept Fletcher Henderson's offer in New York City; on his return to Chicago she had his name put up in lights, helped co-compose for the Hot Five series, and wood-shedded the classical exercises that made his trumpet solos glow so brilliantly. But those are only the obvious musical results: it is impossible to gauge the psychological role Lillian played as Louis climbed higher and higher on the ladder of his career. She did not give up and file for divorce until 1938. In 1935, Lee Collins saw them at a club in Chicago and thought that they were getting back together, they looked so happy. Natty Dominique always expected them to end their lives together, back on 44th Street at the house they bought together, where she lived until the end. Lillian died on August 27, 1971, after collapsing at the piano during a performance in memory of Louis, who had died on July 6.

After Cincinnati came Chicago and the Palace Theater (151 West Randolph Street, today called Cadillac Palace) in late October. A review in the *Tribune* (November 2) singled out a "musical rampage that included the jungle fantasia called *Tiger Rag*."[135] Four months later Armstrong and many of the same musicians recorded *New Tiger*

*Lillian Hardin Armstrong (Courtesy of the Louis Armstrong House Museum)*

*Rag* for his last OKeh session. An even more important artifact is a video recording made in Copenhagen in October 1933. The video, which also includes *Dinah* and *I Covered the Waterfront*, presents him directly in front of the camera with a band of European musicians in a concert setting. It is the closest we can get to the visual side of his performances from the early 1930s.

During the introduction, while the clarinetist solos, Armstrong moves around unpredictably, schmoozing with the audience and acknowledging each break with a rhythmic bow. Hilda See wrote up a description of his performing style around this time, a taste of which can be sampled in the video: "When his orchestra is playing, no man works harder than Louis Armstrong himself. He is in there, all motion and rhythm, from start to finish. When in the execution of a number he fairly hypnotizes his audience by his motions of the body and with his interpretations of the numbers being played. It seems as though harmony oozes from him in visible waves of contagious energy."[136]

This is the visual counterpart to the steady stream of sonic indirection—the asides to band members, to himself, and to the audience, the puzzling shifts of mood, the blurred, smeared, and broken lyrics, the weaving between original tune and its narrative and imaginative forays. When most people first see this footage from Copenhagen, they are stunned by the strangeness of the visual performance, which was unquestionably the point. "One feels that a Negro's expression is not quite free from the matrix of the earth from which he is extricating himself," wrote George Tichenor in 1930. "His to-be subconscious self is not yet out of sight." It took a lot of work to conform to expectations like that, years of experiment, imitation, and practice.

Then, in the Copenhagen video, he talks to the audience: "Now ladies and gentlemen we're going to take a little trip through the jungle at this time, and we want you all to travel with us. That tiger's running so fast, it's going to take a few choruses to catch him. So I want you all to come with me, yes sir, seeing that this Selmer trumpet's going to get away for you in time. Get out there boys, I'm ready." He is all business as he and his trumpet take on the tiger, his trim body positioned diagonally to the audience now, in full concentration. The choruses build from simple repetition to more complicated obbligato playing, spliced with musical quotations, glissandos, bends, rips, held high notes, extended eccentric patterning, ending inevitably and explosively in the high range.

It was indeed a little novelty, as he says on the OKeh recording from March 1932, a jungle fantasia that carried little offense. This is vaudeville-minstrelsy soft and lite. *Tiger Rag* was the finale for his act at the Palace in Chicago, which opened with *When It's Sleepy Time Down South*, followed by *Dinah, I'm Confessin' That I Love You*, and *Shine*. All of these songs had been issued on record, suggesting that the phenomenon of audiences wanting to hear what they knew from recordings was in play.

In Chicago (Thursday, November 5) he also made a sold-out

appearance at the Savoy Ballroom, with 5,000 in attendance. The hall was too crowded for dancing so everybody rocked from side to side. "According to the crowd there is no such a thing as depression among dancers at least," snapped a reviewer. The Chicago visit revived the gangster threats, and Armstrong was routinely accompanied by police protection, continuing on to Cleveland.

The RKO tour was more than just another string of gigs sandwiched between a long series of dance halls and the TOBA circuit. RKO theaters were huge and classy venues with sophisticated entertainment, and many are still standing today. Positioning Armstrong as headliner was a big step for RKO. Reviewers bluntly admitted that they were not used to this kind of music. "If you like lowdown, dirty-hot jazz, you'll go nuts over this outfit; if you don't you'll wonder how they ever got into vaudeville"—that comment from Cincinnati was not isolated. A "fast and loud session of what has come to be expected from colored bands," wrote another, who also lamented the "forget-it-as-soon-as-possible singing." Not all the reviewers from the RKO tour were negative, but many were clearly perplexed. "Apparently this reporter was the only person in the theater not particularly entertained by Armstrong's trick solos, so I bow to an overwhelming majority," was the word from Columbus.

None of that bothered Armstrong, who was absolutely thrilled. In his scrapbooks he uniquely sprinkled little prideful commentaries over the mixed RKO notices. "Look! Do you still see me topping the bill?" he scribbled in the margins of a clipping from Cincinnati, with an arrow pointing to his name, "last day and still heading the bill!" next to a clipping from St. Louis. "Very good for a cabaret at 3 o'clock in the morning but not much entertainment on a vaudeville bill," wrote a reviewer in Cleveland, and for Armstrong that was exactly the point: headlining the Keith Circuit probably meant more to him than his unqualified successes at Suburban Gardens or Show Boat, and much more than the one-night stands in Texas. It meant that he had arrived at the top of the entertainment world.

Today that hierarchy seems very alien. The situation reminds us how jazz regularly moved through many kinds of venues. Sometimes people danced in huge auditoriums, and sometimes they listened in dance halls; sometimes they dressed as nicely as they could for the

Vendome Theater, and sometimes they went slumming at the Sun-set Cabaret; sometimes they wanted to be seen alongside the likes of Howard Hughes or with the best of New Orleans, turned out in white linens, and sometimes they went wild at TOBA theaters. That Armstrong's music was difficult to pin down had something to do with his ability to move around through these different social niches.

His ascent to the RKO headliner position paralleled his ascent to the top of the recording industry. OKeh sued to keep him from moving to RCA Victor, which wanted him to fill the gap left by the departing Rudy Vallée; RCA finally got him in December 1932. Legal wrangling between Collins and Rockwell led to court depositions, taken in September 1931, to decide whether he was a unique enter-tainer who could not be replaced. Paul Whiteman testified that, in his opinion, Armstrong was indeed unique, "not only by reason of the fact that his singing is on a par with his trumpet playing, which is superlative, but by reason of the fact that he is definitely a creator in the field of music . . . his style is individualistic, almost impossible of duplication." Ed Sullivan chuckled in the *New York Evening Graphic* that Rockwell had solicited testimony to use against Armstrong, which Collins then used to promote him. In a deposition taken March 1, 1932, Eli Oberstein, artist-and-repertory man for RCA Victor, tes-tified that "Armstrong is the largest selling artist on records today, bar none." "Of all classes?" he was asked. "Yes sir."

After the RKO tour came the Theater Owners Booking Associ-ation, the black vaudeville circuit. Playing TOBA in Philadelphia, Washington, Baltimore, and New York City was known as "going around the world," and that's precisely what the Armstrong band did in late November, December, and January.

The RKO reviews were mixed, but TOBA reviews were uniformly enthusiastic, even complimenting his conducting. He was hoarse in Philadelphia, at the Pearl Theater, but he still delivered, and the show was held over for a second week, with *I'll Be Glad When You're Dead You Rascal You* singled out as a highlight. Minta Cato was on the bill with him in Philadelphia, and Collins opened up discussions with her husband, Andy Razaf, Fats Waller's collaborator for *Hot Choco-lates*, to write a show that would feature Armstrong and Cato, though nothing came of it.

After that they went to the Howard Theater (still standing at 620 T Street NW) in Washington, D.C., where he was billed as the "greatest sensation in the theatrical history of Washington." Then it was off to the Royal Theater in Baltimore, where he personally handed out 100 bags of coal to anyone in need (no children, women preferred), as a Christmas gift. Prices at the Royal Theater ranged from 15 cents for a matinee to one dollar for a box. After Baltimore came Jersey City, where he shared a bill with dancer Peg Leg Bates.

Then came the Lafayette Theater in New York City, where they started at 10:30 in the morning and played until 11:00 p.m. Trumpeter Roy Eldridge had heard some of the Hot Seven recordings, but he wasn't truly influenced by Armstrong until he saw him at the Lafayette in early 1932. "Well I sat through the first show and I didn't think Louis was so extraordinary," Eldridge remembered. "But in the second show he played *Chinatown, My Chinatown*. He started out like a new book, building and building, chorus after chorus, and finally reaching a full climax, ending on his high F. It was a real climax, right, clean, clear. The rhythm was rocking and he had that sound going along with it. Everybody was standing up including me. He was building the thing all the time instead of just playing in a straight line." Teddy Wilson later had Armstrong's *Chinatown* solo transcribed and arranged for three trumpets in his big band.

Armstrong's recording of *Chinatown* from November 1931 preserves some of the excitement and momentum that got Eldridge's attention. Multiple-chorus numbers like this, going back to Oliver's performance of *High Society* and further still to New Orleans, pleased everyone. Zilner Randolph worked into his arrangement of *Chinatown* the conceit of a battle between the saxophone section and Armstrong's trumpet (which he calls "that little devil"). He challenges the band with humor: "Oh get your chops together boys, while we mug lightly, slightly and politely." The commentary continues even while he sings, interrupting one flashy riff with a spoken aside in the lower range, "Oh you rascal you," then slipping back into singing without missing a beat. His trumpet solo is integrated with the accompaniment in a way that is unusual for Armstrong's bands, though right in step with others who relied on complex arrangements. Charlie Carpenter remembered how Armstrong played the solo in the recording studio sitting on a table, swinging his legs back and forth.

Then the band settles into riffs as the solo builds higher in range and grows more majestic. It is a simple and effective formula. "He wanted simple riffs, hot but simple, behind his solos," said George James. Another great riff-based, driving flat 4/4 performance is *I Got Rhythm*, also recorded in November, with more light humorous banter and with a series of solos from the band members, each of them introduced by Armstrong, recalling the format of *Gut Bucket Blues* from the very first Hot Five session six years before. Danny Barker explained that there was a handful of standard repertory songs in the 1930s that everyone memorized and played in simple head arrangements, such as *Lady Be Good*, *Honeysuckle Rose*, and *Liza*. That status turned them into basic material for jam sessions and later for bebop. *I Got Rhythm* had probably been established in this way by the time of this performance.

Two Chicago sessions in January 1932 produced more recordings. *Between the Devil and the Deep Blue Sea* has a superb trumpet solo that constantly moves in and out of connection with the tune, while offering some phrases that are out of sync with the binary flow of measures, others in double time, gliding and sliding, all of it elegant, fluid, and impressively quick. *Home* and *All of Me* were released without delay; the *Courier* called them (April 9) "the greatest hits of the season." *All of Me* starts with a terrific introductory solo on muted trumpet, followed by a clever and attractive vocal, then a soaring solo on open trumpet, the familiar sequence that was working so well for Armstrong during these years.

Back on the East Coast, the band scooted up to New Haven to share a bill with film actress Ruth Roland, who headlined. The headliner always came on last, which meant, in this case, that Armstrong immediately preceded her. The crowd's response to Armstrong was so overwhelming that Roland sat crying in her dressing room when it came time for her to take the stage. The order was eventually switched, with Armstrong assuming final position. "Louis stopped the show every time," remembered Jackson.

In Boston, at the Metropolitan Theater (still standing at 252 Tremont Street and called the Wang Theater), they battled the Casa

Loma Orchestra and Fletcher Henderson's Orchestra, two formidable bands, with Armstrong trotting out two of his most reliable tricks for the contest: 260 high C's, ending on high F, along with dozens and dozens of choruses of *Tiger Rag*. "When he finished there wasn't nothing for the other fellow to do," observed Jackson. From there they moved (February 15, 1932) to Paul Revere Hall, with a reported fee of $6,000.

Nevertheless, the band dissolved that spring after problems getting paid. Jackson had to ask his mother to send some food to keep him going. There was talk of Europe, or perhaps California, or even a return to Suburban Gardens, but none of it came off. "The reason, I believe, is that Louis was an easy going fellow who left everything up to his manager, accounting and everything, and I don't think that was right," Jackson complained.

Part of what they were owed was a chunk of change for making two short films in Astoria, Long Island, probably in January 1932, for Paramount. *I'll Be Glad When You're Dead You Rascal You*, a Betty Boop cartoon, and *Rhapsody in Black and Blue* surrounded Armstrong with truly crippling racist imagery. It must have been bracing to go from the elegant lobbies of the Palace Theaters and the status of heading up the RKO tour to imitating cannibals.

## Cultural Racism

One reason Louis Armstrong was so important is the extremely high quality of his music; another is the complexity of the social environments in which his music was performed. His experiences reveal much about how African-American music functioned and evolved in the first half of the twentieth century. Put the two together—the greatness of the music and the complexity of the social context—and he becomes the ultimate representative of African-American musical history.

First came the rich array of music making in his community of origin, former slaves who had made the post-Reconstruction move to New Orleans. Sisters shouted in Sanctified churches, three-chord piano players pounded blues in honky tonks, men sat around bars and improvised "barbershop" harmonies, rags-bottles-and-bones men played blues on tin horns, dance bands inspired grinding hips at Funky Butt Hall, and ear-playing marching bands blasted back beats and obbligatos. The thrill of growing up in New Orleans was the easy accessibility and agreed-upon importance of these musical practices. We can trace that kind of experience—music by us, for us—all the way through Armstrong's great triumphs in Chicago, from Lincoln Gardens, where he played his rendition of the blues on his first night of work; through the Hot Five series conceived for the race market; into the Vendome Theater, where he worked out his modern method of playing solos; and on to the Savoy Ballroom, where thousands cheered as he slayed the ofay demons with *West End Blues.*

Simultaneously, their music—his music—entered the white world according to very different terms of reception. African-American jazz was cloaked in minstrelsy as soon as it left New Orleans: the Creole Jazz Band posed as "authentic plantation darkies" on their tours, Jelly Roll Morton put on blackface makeup, and King Oliver's band wore plantation clothes in San Francisco. Armstrong admired Bill "Bojangles" Robinson because of his sophistication and because he did not wear blackface. His own career in the 1920s largely kept him safe from such compromises. At Lincoln Gardens he patched his tuxedo, at the Roseland he got new clothes and looked sharp, at the Vendome he was coaxed to stand up and play tunes from *Cavalleria rusticana* from the stage, and at the Savoy Ballroom he emerged as the musical King Menelik. Minstrelsy was the last thing on anyone's mind in these celebratory settings. Trappings of minstrelsy were undoubtedly mixed into skits at the Sunset Café, subtly or not. Stereotypes of black sexuality were also in play, and he sang comic numbers like *Irish Black Bottom* and *Big Butter and Egg Man*, which relied on the play of opposites, a black man posing as an Irishman or as a rich white man.

Minstrel-derived humor surfaced more powerfully when Armstrong stepped into all-colored musicals on Broadway, with songs like *(What Did I Do to Be So) Black and Blue*. He sang several comic tunes like this in the early 1930s. In California these included *Little Joe* (recorded on his return to Chicago, with an arrangement that he brought from California). "Though your color isn't white, you're more than mighty like a rose to me," he sings to his "kinky-headed baby," and then personalizes the song: "Little Satchelmouth Joe . . .

though your eyes are black as coal, your little soul is white as snow to me." He obviously knew the tune and the arrangement, and delivered beautifully and inventively.

Sometimes he adds his own dash of racial comedy. The most famous example is *Just a Gigolo*, also from the California days, into which he drops a slight, punning transformation, changing the lines "When the end comes I know they'll say, 'Just a gigolo,' as life goes on without me" to "When the end comes I know they'll say 'Just a jig, I know'. . ." Buck Clayton remembered how "it kind of stirred up some people, especially the NAACP," but the crowd at Sebastian's Cotton Club surely loved it.

Even more upsetting to the NAACP would have been his *Shine*. He recorded this older song at the same Los Angeles session and performed it often on his 1931 tours. It was issued on the flip side of *Gigolo*, as if to deliberately construct a package of regressive minstrelsy. He was closely associated with *Shine* during this period, as it became one of the numbers that other musicians used to imitate him.

We have lost the offensive connotations of the word "shine," but they were very active in 1931. Robert Moten explained in 1929 that "shine" and "darky" were "only slightly less offensive" than "nigger"; the *Defender* modified his analysis and put all three words in the same class.[137] Originally published in 1910 as *That's Why They Call Me Shine*, the song as Armstrong performed it was simply called *Shine*. The original lists offensive names the speaker has been called, but now he is known simply as "Shine" because he "takes troubles smiling."

Armstrong's *Shine* opens with a rhythmic outburst—"Chocolate Drop, that's me!"—that would have been hard to recover from, no matter what the motive. The trend in recent writings has been to try and rescue him from the racist material of these years; Alfred Appel, for example, hears in this performance a "scat attack" on the offensive lyrics, a "deconstruction and destruction" of them. It is safe to assume that white critics who admired the "heat" Armstrong put in his performance of *Shine* (and also admired the flip side, *Gigolo*, which shows "what he can do when it comes to sweet stuff") did not hear that—and there is no evidence that anyone else in the 1930s did, either. Anyone who regarded scat as an attack probably did so in the context of African cannibalism, which is not quite the same.

Black critics were reluctant to condemn performers who crossed over the racial divide, no matter what they did. Salem Tutt Whitney surely spoke for most: "the jokes and the shows may disgust the manager and also the actor, but they are thinking of their meals, and not their ideals."[138] Any comments would have been along the lines of the African-American review of a performance by the Creole Band in 1917, quoted in Chapter 1: "It is an act that shows very clearly what the white theatre patrons like the colored performer to do." Armstrong was hitting the big time on all cylinders and satisfying expectations, even if they disgusted him.

*When It's Sleepy Time Down South*, also introduced in California, belongs to a massive song tradition of romanticized southern plantations, where African Americans knew their place and enjoyed it, a utopian charade that goes back a long way. The songs are happy and everything is relaxed; there are no fat-bellied, stinking white folks with shotguns, no tree stumps painted red. "When I was coming along, a black man had hell," Armstrong once observed, but plantation songs portray only a perverse version of heaven.

In *Sleepy Time* the whole range of stress, insult, and attack yields to blissful images of happy darkies crooning songs, dancing, and strumming banjos, living a life of ease. The derivative lyrics are closely connected to songs like *Carolina Sunshine* (1919) and *In the Evening by the Moonlight in Dear Old Tennessee* (1914). An African-American speaker yearning for the South in 1931 could be perceived as reversing the momentum of the Great Migration. *Sleepy Time* was in fact written in California by two brothers from Louisiana, Leon and Otis René, with help from actor Clarence Muse. Armstrong liked the song the first time the René brothers sang it for him, at a gumbo dinner with red beans and rice in Pasadena, at the René family home. He decided to feature it at Sebastian's.

In sunny Pasadena the composing trio captured a relaxed atmosphere in a simple, brilliant stroke, in the first phrase of the chorus. The vocalist sings, "Pale moon shining on the fields below" as a delicious major seventh sitting on top of the texture, a sonic full moon that actually does feel like it is shining down on the fields of the subdominant chord underneath—lush richness blended with timeless relaxation. The pale-moon melody note stays where it is while the chord underneath shifts mysteriously, as if to magically put into motion a fairyland of crooning darkies. A review of his recorded performance headed "Louis Armstrong Scores Again with a Sweet Southern Melody" gushed over "one of the sweetest tunes in a long time."

With his bluesy, black authenticity, Armstrong brought tremendous authority to *Sleepy Time*. Witness, from box seats at the Palace Theater in Cincinnati, the most modern Negro musician of the day happily defining his place as a second-class citizen. With his dark skin and watermelon smile he creates a world of perfect social harmony on the stage. There is no playful ambiguity here: you are convinced that Armstrong, who had a gift for acting that would emerge with more and more brilliance in the 1930s, identifies with the song completely.

And not just at the Palace Theater—also on phonograph records (Jos Willems's discography lists 161 recorded performances over 40 years), across national radio networks, and at the top of countless stage performances and dances. It is almost as if the modern master *had* to sing *Sleepy Time*, and it is easy to understand why. If he was going to advance further on the ladder of his career—and he definitely was—he had to assure white audiences on a deep level that he had no designs on social progress. In the mid-1950s he sang this song at the beginning of his program and then again at the end. But by then, politically engaged African Americans did not hesitate to condemn him. Thurgood Marshall, chief legal counsel for the NAACP, labeled him "Number 1 Uncle Tom, the worst in the U.S.," and Dizzy Gillespie "violently disagreed" with him "because of his Uncle Tom–like subservience." Marshall and Gillespie were not willing to accept how the song served to protect him, its function not so different from gage, laxatives, and tough gangster managers. Disgusting side effects simply had to be tolerated. Life is like that. Armstrong's life was like that.

"With one or two remarkable exceptions the American public does not want to hear a Negro singer in anything other than plantation melodies," lamented Robert Moten in 1929. That was the environment that conditioned Armstrong's rise to prominence in white markets, and he accepted it; it would have been extraordinary if he had not. The hell he had to deal with when coming up included very few, if any, possibilities for constructive political engagement. "I don't dive into politics," he admitted in 1971. "Haven't voted since I've lived in New York, ain't no use messing with something you don't know anything about." The potential of refusing to sing a plantation song as an oblique political gesture would never have occurred to him.

It's hard to tell if there was a quantifiable uptick in songs like this in the early 1930s, but *Sleepy Time* belongs firmly with cultural artifacts of the Great Depression. On one level it is an assertion of idealized southern agrarianism, defiantly staring down the collapse of industrial capitalism; it was created a year after the publication of *I'll Take My Stand: The South and the Agrarian Tradition*, a collection of essays by a group of white writers romanticizing southern culture. It would be impossible to overestimate the cultural work accomplished by songs like this in establishing the national image of the South.

But of course, the myth of crooning darkies relaxing in a mellow Dixie was not simply the product of a few essayists and songwriters. It was deeply ingrained in the entertainment industry of New York City and Hollywood. Songs like this were vigorously cultivated over and over with tremendous success in radio, sheet music, Broadway shows, and now, with the invention of the talkie, films. The *Sleepy Time* fantasy was not just for southerners, not even primarily so. Reconciliation of North and South was a project everyone (white) could buy into, and if the cost of reassembling a white national whole was black exclusion, it seemed a small price to pay. To buy into the fantasy of *Sleepy Time* was to confirm the legitimacy of white supremacy and all the attendant horrors, legalities, and daily insults that went along with it. With its luscious surface, *Sleepy Time* softened the harshness of the legal and social dirty work.

The fun of plantation imagery spilled out in all directions. In the second decade of the century, for example, the makers of Aunt Jemima's pancake flour realized how much more attractive their product had become thanks to a big picture of a southern mammy on the box, as depicted by Arthur Burdette Frost, best known for illustrating Joel Chandler Harris's Uncle Remus tales. The "appeal and glamour of the old South" conveyed by Frost's painting was credited with considerable increase in sales. It is easy to lose sight of how close Armstrong, the great and timeless jazz innovator, was to this set of icons in the white mind. Ed Sullivan usually concluded his columns for the *Washington Post* with a little gossip, but on September 13, 1935, he cracked a joke, writing, "Louis Armstrong and Aunt Jemima go into the Park Avenue Hotel. . . ." He didn't have to say anything more.

Armstrong's ascent to the top of the white market inevitably surrounded him with specialty numbers like *Sleepy Time*, and that must have been a cause for regret for African Americans who regarded him as the ultimate musical hero. What really did him in, however, were the movies. We have no idea what his role was in the lost movie *Ex-Flame* from 1930. But in two short films made by Paramount in early 1932, soft racism is thrown to the winds while Armstrong is assigned crippling roles in stories of explicit barbarism.

Plantation songs flourished as a kind of soft racism, perfuming the argument for African-American inferiority in a haze of happy images, verbal and musical. Movies could do that, too, of course, but many movies welcomed the chance to represent racist ideology much more explicitly. We need only think of D. W. Griffith's infamous and immensely popular *Birth of a Nation* (1915), with its presentation of the Ku Klux Klan as the necessary force fending off African-American savagery. Less virulent pictures highlighted African Americans' second-class status. Racism in the movies sold well, and it was waiting for Armstrong in January 1932 in Astoria, New York.

He was thrilled, no doubt, that these two brief films would be featuring him. *Rhapsody in Black and Blue* belonged to a series of ten-minute "shorts" launched by Paramount in 1929. Shorts were warm-ups for the regular feature; this one was the first in the Paramount series to feature an African-American performer. The breakthrough came at a price: Armstrong would perform two of his hits, the risqué *I'll Be Glad When You're Dead You Rascal You* ("you gave my wife a coca cola so you could play on her victrola") and the regressive *Shine*, dressed as an African savage in a sparsely cut leopard skin, his bandmates dressed similarly.

Armstrong sings the songs with his standard mix of full articulation, half articulation, blurred speech, and scat, the "blubbering, cannibalistic sounds" that delighted Hoagy Carmichael and so many others now finding their visual complement in the leopard skin and African headdress. Watching him sing *Sleepy Time Down South* from

box seats at the Palace Theater in Cincinnati would have been a cat-
egorically different experience from watching this barbaric framing
on the movie screen. Needless to say, far more people witnessed the
latter than the former.

His bearing changes when he picks up his trumpet and stands
fully erect, expands his chest, closes his eyes, flexes his exposed muscles, and plays with dazzling virtuosity and complete confidence. If,
in your imagination, you swap the leopard skin for a tuxedo, you can
understand that, in *Rhapsody*, Armstrong is performing just as he
always did. Vocally he offers his standard blend of verbal distortion
and melodic reinvention, and visually he is full of the mugging, grimacing, smiling, and general strangeness documented in the Copenhagen video, the hypnotizing motion of eyes and face and body.

The effect of these techniques is familiar to us from Chapter 9:
they suggest that Armstrong's relationship to the song is not straightforward, that he is distancing himself from its meaning. One might
even feel that he is distancing himself from the racism of the movie.
This has been an attractive line of interpretation for sympathetic
observers striving to rescue him from these (and other) degrading
films. Critics have seen his muscular posture and confident trumpet
in *Rhapsody* as standing above the context, a triumph over the primitive theme.

But since this was the way he always played, it is hard to attach
any special message to his technique. In Memphis, he sang out, "I'll
be glad when you're dead, you rascal you" to the police who had
arrested him. Who knows what was going through his mind when
he sang the same song in *Rhapsody in Black and Blue*? What comes
across on screen is someone who is in tune with the demands of comic
acting rather than trickster subterfuge.[139] As much as we might like to
imagine the two seamlessly overlapping, it is important to avoid the
temptation to project a point of view for which there is no evidence.

*I'll Be Glad When You're Dead You Rascal You*, the title of the
other film made in January 1932, leaves no opening for a rescue
opportunity (though that has not stopped people from trying). This
cartoon short was part of a series produced by Fleischer brothers
Max, Joe, Lou, and Dave for Paramount, based on the character Betty
Boop. The Fleischers liked to mix jazz musicians into stories about

their heroine, who, at this point in her career, was a fun-loving, sexualized flapper. They invented a technique of filming performers and then drawing cartoons over the photography to magically mix "real life" with Betty's cartoon life. When they filmed Cab Calloway dancing and scatting, for example, audiences were so delighted that they demanded that the short be replayed. Armstrong's mastery of *You Rascal You*, which he had been featuring for over a year now, inspired the Fleischers to what would become their most notorious effort in the integration of jazz photography with cartoon imagination.

The film opens with straight footage of Armstrong and his orchestra playing *High Society*.[140] As the music continues, the visual of the band yields to a close-up of Betty herself, twisting rhythmically at her hips and displaying her flapper body. This introductory sequence sets up in a pithy way the subtext of the entire cartoon—the lure of African-American jazz and its dangerous potential to seduce white women and, with that, the threat to the purity of the white race.

Then the story begins, with Betty and her friends KoKo the clown and Bimbo the dog enjoying a leisurely jungle safari. Suddenly, Betty is surrounded by an African tribe and abducted. As the hapless KoKo and Bimbo consider a rescue plan, KoKo, in a comically aggressive move, shouts, "Wait'll I get those babies"—shorthand for "jungle babies," a racial slur. The two sidekicks are caught and dumped in a boiling pot, though they escape quickly. As the song *I'll Be Glad When You're Dead* starts up, one of the tribesmen, in hot pursuit, turns into a disembodied head that resembles Armstrong, while Armstrong sings the song as the head mouths the words. Inspired by their new technology, the Fleischer brothers took the equation one step further by seamlessly morphing the floating head of the cannibal into photography of Armstrong singing; before the chase scene ends, the photo of Armstrong changes back to the cannibal, rounding out the equation. We could say that this visual blending of photography and cartoon is synesthetically matched by Armstrong's blending of words and scat, all of it fusing in perfect racist fun the bestselling recording artist of the day with cannibalism, the ultimate marker of African primitivism.

The band performs *Chinatown*, up-tempo, for the finale of this little story, while the cartoon cannibals chant rhythmically in a swell-

*Movie still from* I'll Be Glad When You're Dead You Rascal You

ing orgiastic frenzy as they prepare to toss Betty into the boiling pot. One of the pot stirrers morphs into Armstrong's smiling drummer, Alfred "Tubby" Hall. The classic fantasy of black male rape of a white woman is very close at hand. If Armstrong knew how to use laughter to create an opening for his modern jazz, the Fleischers knew how to use it to stir up the most damning racial stereotypes of the day.

King Menelik had met his match. One hopes that he was able to put the whole thing behind him in a private chuckle, as Robert Moton recommended in 1929: "Sometimes it is all a huge joke to [the Negro], and his richest humour, indulged only in private, surrounds his musings on the average white man's pretensions of superiority, the inconsistencies in his application of standards, and the hypocrisy of his professions in the face of the undisguised, unabashed, and often unrestrained humanity of his natural impulses and desires." Armstrong did not have to read *What the Negro Thinks* to figure that out.

It would be nice to blame the Paramount films on Johnny Collins, who seems to have had few scruples. But there is no reason to believe that Armstrong was reluctant to do them. It is easy to imagine that he simply chalked it up to the price of doing business in the white man's world. After all, jungle imagery was commonly associated with jazz. As African-American historian J. A. Rogers wrote in *The New Negro*, jazz "is a thing of the jungles—modern, man-made jungles."[141] What was received at the Vendome as the everyday made modern was, to the talented tenth and to most whites, a raw and contradictory mix of primitive and modern. The Paramount movie makers were simply taking familiar images to a humorous extreme.

What made Armstrong such a powerful presence in these movies was what also made him such a powerful singer of *Sleepy Time Down South*. He was no "musical octoroon," as Zora Neale Hurston vividly described concert arrangements of spirituals, but the real thing, a genuine primitive, strictly Negro. He fell harder than most into these racist traps because he foregrounded black authenticity in such a compelling way. He was the most likely candidate for jungle treatment. Cab Calloway and Duke Ellington also made Betty Boop cartoons and Paramount shorts, but with very different results. Armstrong's was hardly the only use of racist stereotypes in shorts and cartoons from this period (a number of them are so offensive that they have recently been expurgated), but none of the other jazz musicians was presented as a savage African.

What Paramount wanted was no *pretending* to be an African, no musical octoroon, but the greatest exponent of "familiar Senegambiana," as *The New Yorker* described his music in February 8, 1930, in a review of *St. Louis Blues* and *After You've Gone*. In the Paramount shorts, the full power of his musical creativity does not transcend the racist imagery but rather brings it to vivid life in a way that no other performer could. The best and most modern master of the black vernacular is successfully diminished with arrows of arrogant and derisive laughter.

These savage depictions had everything to do with the intensity of the African legacy in Armstrong's modern art. This was what the New Orleanians offered the country—"barbaric indigo dance tunes played with gusto and much ado that leaves very little doubt as to their African origin," as the *New York Clipper* (September 14, 1923) described recordings by Oliver's band—and Armstrong was the greatest New Orleanian of all, the one who soaked up everything his culture of origin had to offer and transformed it into a modern and thoroughly black art form. The fixed and variable model, blue notes, musical dialogue, ragging the tune, conversational phrasing, scat, something that "relates to us," as Milt Hinton put it—all of it could be identified with and diminished by savage imagery. The black success of Armstrong's first modern phase and the white success of his second were both built on "authentic" black expression. In one arena he was crowned King Menelik, slayer of ofay demons, in the other a savage buffoon. Primitivism was the key ingredient in white reception of his music, and movies turned out to be the most powerful modern medium for delivering the goods.

Movies produced unmatchable exposure while they locked him into degrading stereotypes. In *Pennies from Heaven* (1936) he played the role of a chicken thief, in *Every Day's a Holiday* (1937) he cleaned streets, and in a short video from 1942 he sang *Sleepy Time Down South* sitting on a bale of cotton, dressed as a hired hand. Rather than search desperately for subtle signs of subversion, it is more honest to simply acknowledge how he was damaged by one of the sweeping ideological battles of the twentieth century.

Armstrong was hardly the only great artist to suffer such a fate. To mention only two of the most famous musical examples: in the mid-1930s, in Russia, Dmitri Shostakovich came under attack for composing music that did not fit official Soviet expectations; his efforts to make up for "errors" in artistic judgment lay at the root of a tortured life. Richard Strauss's German-themed compositions were easily appropriated by the Nazis, boxing him into an image that he wanted nothing to do with; desperate to protect his Jewish daughter-in-law, Strauss made collaborative gestures and suffered the consequences in international condemnation.

Americans like to think of the United States as immune to this kind of crushing intrusion of politics into the minds of artists, but here it is. One of the greatest musicians our country has ever produced, by anyone's standards, was trapped by racist ideology that was imposed not only through official government channels, but also through the marketplace. Shostakovich and Strauss were crippled by government intrusion, while Jelly Roll Morton desperately yearned for it: "Music is such a tremendous proposition that it probably needs government supervision," he complained. "There does not seem to be any proper protection for anything in this line." There was hell to pay, either way.

What is amazing, as scholar Gerald Early has pointed out, is how resilient Armstrong was in response to a "culture that both psychologically and physically abused him as a person, misunderstood his art, and depreciated his real worth."He survived the ascent to the next rung on the ladder of his career with gage, with toughness developed through the hard knocks of his childhood, and with a single-minded dedication to music.

## The Making of a Great Melodist

What made Louis Armstrong so remarkably great? Put generally, his greatness emerged from a unique combination of where he came from, who he was, and the conditions that shaped his career. The inspired melodic results of this configuration still hold a powerful attraction, many generations later.

He came from a place where African cultural legacies were very strong, thanks largely to post-Reconstruction migration from plantations in the Deep South. This migration may be conceived as one more step along the way of an African diaspora that began with the Middle Passage. From the word "diaspora" we get the sense of a group of people scattered across political boundaries and holding on to an identity of origin. New Orleans, as the major port joining the Mississippi River with the Gulf of Mexico, was a place to which people of African descent came and from which they were dispersed, again and again, over many generations. It was a place where these patterns of social movement received musical articulation, and this may be the chief reason why the city has been so important in the history of African-American music. That is a different way of analyzing the special nature of New Orleans—different than emphasizing its connections to France, Spain, and the Caribbean, or its laissez-faire approach to racial mixing, or its population of *gens de couleur libres*, or its Big Easy thirst for entertainment. Those things played a role. But as a place where the musical side of the African diaspora was organized and shaped, New Orleans really has no equivalent in the United States.

Before the Civil War, slaves were forcibly distributed from New Orleans on the auction block; in the post-Reconstruction period the city magnetized the children and grandchildren of those slaves into uptown neighborhoods described by one observer as the "hotbed of dark, uneducated cornfield Negroes." Music was important all around. Churches, dance halls, and street parades functioned just as Place Congo had functioned some 70 years earlier: they were places where people of African descent came together to check each other out, discover reassuring points of common practice and stimulating points of difference, and invent cultural identities that were now urban rather than rural, and yet still distinctly African-American.

By moving in a way that was both individual and collective— "huddling for protection," as Du Bois described it—they reaffirmed the sense that they were, as African Americans, a people in motion, a people whose resilience included an ability to adapt to new social circumstances. The role of music in this resilience cannot be over-estimated. The phenomenon must rank among the most compelling social-cultural events in history. It is the story of how people who carried a culture shaped in Africa adapted that culture under extremely harsh conditions. Music for them was a collective enterprise with strong social purposes. It included an understanding that musical gesture must be fused with physical gesture in a way that instantly creates a sense of community. It explored an area of ambiguity between speaking and singing, and it took delight in flashing back and forth between the two while extending the principle of speech-like music to instruments. It manifested a conception of time that is cyclical rather than linear and arranged musical information with this in mind. It featured, sometimes simply and other times in ways that are highly complex, a model of two levels of musical activity, one fixed and foundational and the other variable and interactive, with the two levels moving between synthesis and tension. And it favored improvisation as an expressive value that was part of a lifestyle, an ability to respond creatively to dynamic social situations with markers of power and skill.

In New Orleans the plantation traditions were urbanized and professionalized, with many points of easy amateur entry into a diverse and low-paying market. The situation fostered innovation, diversity, and upward mobility, and it was perfect for a budding young talent. Musically nurtured from multiple directions, Armstrong mastered much of what his community had to offer. Especially important to him were the fixed and variable model and the embellishments of ragging the tune, with blues covering everything.

I doubt that his training in New Orleans was exceptional. Others had the same kinds of exposure and probably reached similar levels of mastery. He made more out of it than anyone else because of his tremendous drive and work ethic, his ability to negotiate changing and complicated environments, and an unbeatable skill set, including what we might call high musical intelligence.

"Musicians don't talk about music much, very few, very few musicians," said trombonist J. C. Higgenbotham, who played with Armstrong in the 1930s. Armstrong rarely gave much specific detail about his or anyone else's music. Great music is easy to listen to and difficult to talk about—why bother? In taking this position he had a lot of company, not just in his circles but among great musicians throughout history.

But the intensity of primitivist assumptions—and Armstrong's willingness to accommodate that kind of image—has made it easy to read his lack of detailed verbal commentary as the representation of an intuitive musician who understands little about what he does. Even the great conductor Leonard Bernstein, who admired Armstrong and featured him in a concert with the New York Philharmonic in 1956, rattled off a list of attributes in his introduction of Armstrong that included "simple"—and he meant it as a compliment. With concepts like "emotional intelligence" so familiar today, it is much easier than it used to be to think of Armstrong as having superior musical intelligence.

You can see the signs everywhere you look. He was a favorite in recording studios because the sessions were so effortless. "He can pick up an orchestral routine in quicker time than it takes to rehearse it," said a colleague. "In fact, there are virtually no rehearsals at all." His mind was precise, sure, and quick. Earl Hines said that the hot soloist was one "who had a fast mind, could think far ahead in regard to the chords coming up, and was good on his instrument." Hines and Armstrong set the standard for musicians of their generation.

Clearly, Armstrong had a fertile musical creativity and strong gifts in melodic design.

And he was skillful in adapting to changing expectations as he advanced in his career. He is often talked about as a musician who turned entertainment music into art. For anyone who recognizes the formal rigor and creative brilliance of his achievement, that must seem like a natural way to acknowledge his accomplishment. But I doubt that the concept of art ever occurred to him in any meaningful way, or that the distinction had any bearing on his musical development during this period.

White musicians during this period, especially those who thought of themselves as bohemian outsiders, thought about art much more than the black musicians in Armstrong's circles. Mezz Mezzrow and his friends scoffed at "commercial" players. "The rest of us, we were the artists, the boys with their heads in the clouds, scornful of keeping books and negotiating deals and adding up the give and take," wrote Mezzrow. "Bud Freeman . . . would rather starve than play commercial," remembered another musician. This was simply not how the New Orleanians thought about music and their place in the world. They recognized differences of quality and of sophistication, but the binary opposition between art and entertainment was remote to them, culturally and socially.

What really mattered to Armstrong, and what made things complicated as he tried to advance his career, was race. To the skeptical listener who values music for its beauty, values jazz for its happy role in social integration, and simply says, "What does race have to do with it?" the answer has to be—quite a bit.

The New Orleanians who carried a professionalized version of the black vernacular to the chilly urban North found themselves in an enviable position. Oliver was crowned King at Royal Gardens by people who had grown up on music from the plantations (or one generation removed) and still held close to that culture. People from New Orleans regarded the Oliver band at Lincoln Gardens as an exhilarating blessing from home, while those from other places in the Deep South connected easily.

The forced movement of slaves created special conditions and demanded special responses, as did the move to the North, spurred on, as many explained, by an urge to "better my condition." The Great Migration also brought people of diverse backgrounds together into an increasingly organized music industry. In the fall of 1924 Armstrong took up with Fletcher Henderson, despite their differences in social background, training, ability, and aesthetic preference. Increasing demand by whites for hot dance music gave them common ground. A year of experimenting with hot solos gave him confidence. His solos were fast, precise, bluesy, eccentric, and wildly creative—the combination turned out to be perfect for the Vendome Theater on his return to Chicago. As he intensified the fixed and variable model and foregrounded his African heritage, his new solo style became an emblem of a black modernity that was an extension rather than a denial of the vernacular. It was also sophisticated enough—precise with scales and chords, flashy with high notes, fast with fingering, beautiful in tone—to compete with white standards. The victory of his African-American modernism can be measured by the Savoy Ballroom patrons carrying him around the hall on their shoulders; by trumpeter Ward Pinkett, sitting quietly next to a jukebox, tears of joy in his eyes; and by the thousands lined up on the levee outside Suburban Gardens, hoping to hear him through the windows.

Armstrong's flexibility of mind, his musical and social intelligence, his matchless skill set and thorough training—all of it helped him negotiate complex formations of race and modernity. He studied what Oliver meant to recent immigrants at Lincoln Gardens, what Henderson meant to middle-class whites at the Roseland Ballroom, what OKeh's race records meant to people back home, what the Dreamland Cabaret and Vendome Theater meant to blacks who were moving up and thrilled to have upscale places of their own, what the Sunset Café meant to slumming whites, what the Savoy Ballroom meant when he slayed the ofay demons, what black Broadway meant to white Manhattan, what a blues crooner meant to the nation, and what a modern black artist meant for the most current imagery in racist minstrelsy.

Few if any people at these venues cared about differences between entertainment and art, but all of them cared about the racial implications of his music. His music was forged through steady negotiation between black modernity and cultural racism. Vernacular music meant orally based music and all of the African-American markers of expression that went with it. The same package could represent forward-moving modernity at one venue and laughable primitivism at another. For a creative musician, this was how the "problem of the color line," as W. E. B. Du Bois put it, played out. A reviewer (November 8, 1931) of his performance at the Palace, in Cleveland, wrote simply: "It isn't music." "Whites were not as hip to hot music [in 1931] as they are today," explained trombonist Clyde Bernhardt; "the average layman does not understand his type of work," agreed recording executive Eli Oberstein. White reception of his music can be measured on one extreme by Charles Black, so inspired by this evident genius that he became a civil rights attorney, and on the other by derisive laughter at a "chunky, coal-black boy" (October 18, 1931, Columbus, Ohio) cast as a cannibal and hopelessly chasing Betty Boop, jazz flapper.

His hard-earned white success stands as a landmark in the entry of the African-American vernacular into the marketplace of popular music. Scott Joplin's music was perhaps the strongest precedent, but the differences between the two men say everything. Joplin wanted to lift Negro music out of its vernacular limitations through notation. Armstrong created modern Negro music that unapologetically highlighted the vernacular.

The spread of white interest in Armstrong's music began with a handful of musicians hanging around Lincoln Gardens. Eventually, they based their emerging styles on his and thus prepared white audiences for his later acceptance, while the black vernacular gradually made its impact on white jazz with pieces like *Copenhagen*. The time was right when OKeh decided to market his second modern style, based on dialogue between a popular melody, well known and easily understood, and his inventive ragging—dynamic, unpredictable, and thoroughly black—combined with scat, blues, and eccentric patterning, producing an "an endless succession of beautiful and bizarre effects." That and a strong mixture of primitive fun was the formula that did it for him. His music was so thoroughly based on the non-notatable vernacular that it could not be turned into symphonic jazz and elevated to pure art; there was no possibility of reframing it as the "free, frank and vulgar spirit of the American bourgeoisie." Thanks to him, genuine Negro music rose to the top of white markets in radio, phonograph, and RKO palaces.

Both races heard Armstrong's music as black, as modern, and as beautiful. With such drastically different understandings of the first two attributes, how could there be agreement on the third? The answer is that his skills as a great melodist were strong enough to overcome ideological bias. Not only were his solos innovative and socially meaningful, they were crafted with melodic excellence. Of all the qualities of his greatness—tone, speed, high notes, comedy, precision, confidence, charisma, originality—this one best explains his broad and enduring success.

This book has covered many aspects of Armstrong's musical development; in conclusion, I would like to extend and summarize that coverage from a slightly different perspective. His musical world revolved around four different types of melody—blues, lead, hot solo, and paraphrase. These had different functions, different shapes, different economies, and different histories. All four were important in the world he grew up in, in New Orleans, and also through the 1920s and 1930s, but with different points of emphasis as his career unfolded. Thinking about these four styles will help us understand how he became such an expert in melodic craft, and it will further clarify the entanglement of music and race as he experienced it.

Blues came first and stayed strong until the end. There is no question about the priority of blues in Armstrong's musical development, or, as we have seen in Chapter 2, about its priority for the South Side immigrants in Chicago. His first musical job in New Orleans was playing blues for tips, blues all the time, hour after hour, week after week, and at a very slow tempo. There could have been no better training for a great melodist. With blues he could concentrate on melodic details and melodic sweep without having to worry much about ensemble or harmony. The job was essentially an opportunity to practice building the expressive gestures of blues into a coherent stream. The experience must have been something like that of young Mozart's, around the same age, writing dozens and dozens of Italian arias, internalizing a melodic discourse of simplicity and grace.

He came to the attention of Joe Oliver, who advised him to stick to the lead and avoid elaborate variations. The lead melody and the person who played it in New Orleans had special status. It had to be delivered with confidence, strength, and attractive tone. Blues playing was full of heart and second playing full of complexity, but to advance a musical career you had to be able to play a solid lead.

Armstrong's first recorded solo, for *Chimes Blues* in April 1923, shows his eagerness to please his mentor with a strong lead, a phrase that stays with you. It is a special moment, but it has always seemed a little unsatisfying as a marker in the historical record. There are no signs of the exciting, expansive energy of the great solos from a few years later. To compare *Chimes Blues* with *Big Butter and Egg Man*, which shows his first modern style in full bloom, is to move between two different melodic worlds.

The discontinuity is not simply due to a sudden leap into maturity. The problem is that we are comparing apples and oranges. His solo for *Chimes Blues* is a lead melody, while the famous solos from a few years later would have been called "hot solos." This is one key to understanding the development of his first modern style and, indeed, his development as a great melodist: he shifted his creative attention from one type of solo to another.

Standards for a lead melody were derived from mainstream popular tunes, with easy comprehension and memorability, a phrase that stays with you. The hot solo was a completely different conception. One could even say that the point of it was *not* to sound like a lead. Hot solos were fast and brief. When Armstrong was hired as featured hot soloist with the Fletcher Henderson Orchestra, his job was to provide a flash of variety, 20 seconds or so, in a densely packed and varied arrangement. The function was made clear by the name: hot solos were supposed to generate emotional heat with fast rhythmic energy, blue notes, and growling timbre. Since they were so short and since they were supposed to contrast with the lead melodies featured elsewhere in the arrangement, nobody cared how well designed they were. Whether or not a lead like his solo for *Chimes Blues* was notated, it sounded like it was. A hot solo, in contrast, had to have plenty of non-notatable features, since these were what made it hot. It had to sound like it was improvised, even if it wasn't.

In other words, the hot solo, like the blues solo, was heavily marked as an African-American cultural production. This was true even when the soloist was white. Eccentric rhythms defined the hot solo as an outpouring of spontaneous, libidinal energy, uncivilized and raw. If we are not used to thinking of Armstrong as a great melodist, the main reason is this emphasis on rhythm in the hot solo and the lingering biases of primitivist thought. In the 1920s and still today, a strong binary opposition between rhythm and melody was built into the way people thought about jazz. As noted in Chapter 4, jazz was conceived as a spectrum of possibilities, a range of musical expression so diverse that anyone who generalizes about all of jazz during this period—and people do this all the time—is bound to stumble into a tangle of contradictions. One end of the spectrum was defined by vigorous, African-influenced rhythm, the other by lightly syncopated orchestral arrangements with straight popular melodies in the foreground. Inevitably, this spectrum was wrapped up in racist ideology.

We have managed to outgrow most of the blatant assumptions of racism from this period, but thinking about jazz in terms of a binary opposition between melody and rhythm still creates a lot of confusion. As argued in Chapter 6, the simple facts are that you can have rhythm without melody, but you cannot have melody without rhythm. Rhythm and melody are not opposites. The questions to ask are: What kind of rhythm? What kind of melody? To say that Armstrong was a great melodist is to insist that he was creatively absorbed in a complete melodic conception. So was Joplin, and so was Gershwin. It was his commitment to melody that made him so distinctive in the 1920s and 1930s, and a proper assessment of his achievement must proceed along these lines.

Musicians in Armstrong's Chicago circle were vigorously creating lead melodies, and not just for performances and recordings. They were keenly aware of the cash potential from writing out their tunes and sending them to Washington, D.C., for copyright. Armstrong and Oliver composed *Dipper Mouth Blues* and *Canal Street Blues* together; the band recorded Armstrong's earlier composition *Weather Bird Rag*; Lillian and Louis composed *Where Did You Stay Last Night?*, *When You Leave Me Alone to Pine*, and *Tears*; and Lillian helped Oliver and Armstrong notate these efforts with this economic system in mind. In order to copyright a melody, it had to be written down. That legal fact created an economic logic that channeled a major part of Armstrong's creative energy in 1923 and early 1924 into leads that could be notated.

The culmination of these efforts was his breakthrough piece, *Cornet Chop Suey*, a notated tune that, years later, reminded him of cutting contests in New Orleans. It combined the reach for the next big copyrightable hit with a display of his formidable chops. He could not coordinate his hands to imitate Oliver's solo for *Dipper Mouth Blues*, and freak music turned out not to be his thing. Instead, he placed his bets on notatable melodies. Since the notated tune could not depend on the techniques of the performer-centered vernacular, the calling card of the uptown New Orleanians, the only way to succeed was with strong melody. It never would have crossed Oliver's mind to notate his famous solo for *Dipper Mouth Blues*, but *Cornet Chop Suey* was conceived for notation from the start, as an expanded and imposing lead.

This product of Armstrong's creative ambition got shelved for almost two years, since there was no chance to play it while he was with Oliver, and it wasn't what Henderson was looking for. Henderson wanted a hot soloist, a southern hot soloist, not a rough singer and not a fancy display piece like *Cornet Chop Suey*. He wanted a strong dose of heat when an arrangement called for it. And thus it was that Armstrong's focus turned from the creation of leads to the creation of hot solos. He sounded so good, so confident and strong, and he was so much better than most of the other (nonsouthern or non-African-American) soloists, that he could take risks and experiment. He could challenge listeners with his daring ideas. He used some paraphrase but did not feel overly bound to feature popular tunes. The main expectation was flamboyant heat, which he delivered with dividends.

Upon his return to Chicago, his ability to play a hot solo had risen to such a level that people lined up around the block to hear him at the Vendome; "that's what they hired me for, anyway, them hot numbers," he explained. The sophistication and excitement of his new modern style turned out to be just what African-American patrons at the classy Vendome Theater, with its symphony orchestra, and the

Dreamland Café, with its lit-from-below glass floor, were looking for. He gave them *Cornet Chop Suey*, which turned out to be both an ending point and a starting point. He continued to write songs for copyright, but his future success would lie elsewhere. He supplemented his hot solos for *Oriental Strut, Static Strut, Stomp Off Let's Go*, and *Muskrat Ramble* with the stunning novelty of *Heebie Jeebies*. Then in the fall, at the Sunset Café, his two strengths—voice and the special chorus of hot trumpet playing—merged in a number designed to feature him, *Big Butter and Egg Man*.

His expanded hot solos were now a main attraction, not just a sprinkling of spice. He did not stop writing leads, but his main creative focus would now be hot solos and blues. His melodic brilliance emerged most fully through non-notated but well-designed hot solos, which could be captured, transmitted, and preserved for repeated listening on a phonograph recording just as well as piano rolls and sheet music captured Joplin's differently conceived melodic brilliance.

Nevertheless, Armstrong's sustained focus on written melody was important for his development. It is easy to imagine that it took him just as long to compose his solo for *Big Butter and Egg Man* as it did to compose *Cornet Chop Suey*. He had learned the discipline of composing. Before the lead sheet sent to Washington, D.C., in January 1924 for copyright was discovered, *Cornet Chop Suey* was regarded by historians as an "improvisation." It was close enough to the solos generated by ear that it seemed to belong in that category. That resemblance indicates how his emerging sense of melodic style for hot solos was conditioned by thinking in terms of melody that could be notated. Yet the eccentric patterning and infusion of blues made it clear that the new modern style did *not* belong to the world of written music. His new conception blended melodic clarity, continuity, little conversations of notes, driving energy, blues touches, harmonic precision, technical brilliance, variety, density, and, especially, the fixed and variable model. This cyclonic mix made Armstrong an untouchable hot soloist who was opening up new possibilities of musical expression that he would continue to explore for years.

In Chicago he was singing popular tunes but not recording them, since OKeh was not interested in paying royalties. The company experimented with marketing some of his vocals to whites, and in March 1929 the New York branch took a risk and let him record *I Can't Give You Anything but Love*. A shift in emphasis from hot solo to paraphrase marks his second modern style. In fact, it was easy for him to blend the two. His trumpet solo for *Big Butter and Egg Man* has paraphrasing touches, for example, as does even *Potato Head Blues*. No one objected if a hot soloist paraphrased a tune, though they would certainly object if he sacrificed heat to do so. Paraphrasing touches in the trumpet solos of his first modern style are secondary, bits and pieces of the original tune that enhance the little conversations of notes. His main concern in constructing the flow of energy is darting and diving through the contours of the chords in the service of the fixed and variable model.

His modern versions of mainstream popular songs put much more emphasis on the tune, especially in the vocals, of course, but not only there. Intensification of the fixed and variable model was just right for the Vendome, radical ragging of the crooner repertory just right for broad white appeal. Ragging the tune, the preferred technique for African-American musicians when they wanted to reach white audiences, was now taking a modern form. And it was easy for Armstrong to bring in much of what he had already perfected—eccentric phrasing, scat, blues effects, density that now alternates with spacious textures, all of it mixed into a lush flow of ragging filigree around the recognizable contours of established hits. The combination must have sounded bizarre to many whites, who heard Negro authenticity, technical expertise, compelling melody of power, and brilliance. "Modern" was an easy way to sum it all up. John Philip Sousa complained about people listening to jazz through their feet rather than through their brains. By shifting the energy upwards, Armstrong gave the white brain pause. "Louis has achieved through natural ability what will probably never be achieved again by any trumpeter," wrote an admiring British critic in 1932. "I confess I do not understand him but at the same time I defy anyone to define his music, its purpose and its effect."

Great melody carried him through. There were other experts in blues, lead, hot solos, and paraphrase; what made Armstrong differ-

*(The William Russell Photographic Collection, MSS 520 F. 2056, Williams Research Center, The Historic New Orleans Collection)*

ent was the flexibility of his mind and his ability to use his experience as the basis for melodic innovation and excellence. He transferred lessons gained from one style over to the others, and he adapted his musical creativity to the conditions at hand. During the 1920s and early 1930s, the period of his finest musical achievement, he was occupied at a deep level with the task of creating melodic responses to varied social formations. He shaped the times and the times shaped him, which is why his value is not only artistic but also historical. Ralph Ellison wrote that "being a Negro means a *willed* (who wills to be a Negro? I do!) affirmation of self as against all outside pressures." Armstrong's willed affirmation took many forms during his long and much-loved career, but the most lasting and far-reaching were his great melodic accomplishments of the 1920s and 1930s.

# DISCOGRAPHY

Recordings referenced in the book are listed in alphabetical order and keyed to albums listed below.

*After You've Gone* (*Armstrong*, Vol. 5)
*Ain't Misbehavin'* (*Armstrong*, Vol. 5)
*Alone at Last* (*Timeless Historical*)
*Anybody Here Want to Try My Cabbage* (*Complete Louis Armstrong*)
*Body and Soul* (*Armstrong*, Vol. 6)
*Bye and Bye* (*Timeless Historical*)
*Canal Street Blues* (*Off the Record*)
*Changeable Daddy of Mine* (*Complete Louis Armstrong*)
*Chimes Blues* (*Off the Record*)
*Cold in Hand Blues* (*Complete Louis Armstrong*)
*Copenhagen* (*Timeless Historical*)
*Dipper Mouth Blues* (*Off the Record*)
*Hotter Than That* (*Complete Hot Five*)
*I'll See You in My Dreams* (*Timeless Historical*)
*I'm a Ding Dong Daddy (from Dumas)* (*Armstrong*, Vol. 6)
*Mabel's Dream* (*Off the Record*)
*Mahogany Hall Stomp* (*Armstrong*, Vol. 5)
*Mandy Make Up Your Mind* (*Timeless Historical*)
*A Monday Date* (*Complete Hot Five*)
*Muggles* (*Complete Hot Five*)
*Musrat Ramble* (*Complete Hop Five*)
*My Sweet* (*Armstrong*, Vol. 6)
*Riverside Blues* (*Off the Record*)
*St. Louis Blues* (1925) (*Jazz*)
*St. Louis Blues* (1929) (*Armstrong*, Vol. 6)

*Shanghai Shuffle (Timeless Historical)*
*Star Dust (Armstrong, Vol. 7)*
*Struttin' with Some Barbeque (Complete Hot Five)*
*Sweethearts on Parade (Armstrong, Vol. 7)*
*Tears (Off the Record)*
*Tell Me Dreamy Eyes (Timeless Historical)*
*Texas Moaner Blues (Young Sidney Bechet)*
*Tight Like This (Complete Hot Five)*
*Weather Bird (Complete Hot Five)*
*(What Did I Do to Be So) Black and Blue (Armstrong, Vol. 5)*
*When You're Smiling (Armstrong, Vol. 5)*
*Wild Man Blues (Complete Hot Five)*
*Words (Timeless Historical)*

## Albums

*The Complete Hot Five and Hot Seven Recordings.* New York: Columbia Legacy, 2000.

*The Complete Louis Armstrong and the Singers 1924/30.* Switzerland: King Jazz, 1993.

*Jazz: The Smithsonian Anthology.* Washington, DC: Smithsonian Folkways, 2010.

*Louis Armstrong, Vol. 5: Louis in New York.* New York: Columbia, 1990.

*Louis Armstrong, Vol. 6: St. Louis Blues.* New York: Columbia/Sony, 1991.

*Louis Armstrong, Vol. 7: You're Drivin' Me Crazy.* New York: Columbia/ Sony, 1993.

*Off the Record: The Complete 1923 Jazz Band Recordings, King Oliver's Creole Jazz Band.* Thurmont: Off the Record, 2006.

*Timeless Historical Presents Fletcher Henderson and Louis Armstrong: 1924, 1925.* Wageningen: Timeless, 1991.

*Young Sidney Bechet, 1923–1925: Featuring Louis Armstrong, Clarence Williams, Sara Martin.* Wageningen: Timeless, 1998.

# BIBLIOGRAPHY

## Archival Sources

CJA  Chicago Jazz Archive of the Regenstein Library, University of Chicago
COHP  Columbia Oral History Project. Columbia University, New York
FDC  Frank Driggs Collection, private
HJA  Hogan Jazz Archive, Tulane University, New Orleans
IJS  Institute for Jazz Studies, Rutgers University, Newark, NJ
LAHM  Louis Armstrong House Museum, Queens, New York
LC  Library of Congress, Washington, DC
UMKC  Marr Sound Archives, Miller Nichols Library, University of
    Missouri–Kansas City
WRC  Williams Research Center, New Orleans

Allen, Shep. WRC 1962, May 24, mss 519, folder 1.

Armstrong, Beatrice. WRC 1943, mss 519 Louis Armstrong, folder 30.

Armstrong, Lillian Hardin. WRC 1969, mss 519, folder 3 (transcript of interview conducted Jan. 19).

———. CJA 1960, Aug. 15 and Nov. 11 (interviews with Ray Dowell).

———. HJA 1959, July 1.

———. WRC 1938, mss 519, folder 14 (interview for *Jazzmen*).

———. CJA n.d. (interview with John Steiner, box 87, folder "W"; also folder "Lillian Hardin Armstrong"; also box 78).

———. IJS n.d.

Armstrong, Louis. LAHM 1970, Tape 426 (Armstrong reading a letter that is dated Aug. 15, 1970, and glossing it).

———. WRC 1970, mss 506, folder 14 (interview May 5).

———. LAHM ca. 1969, letter box 1, folder 8 (unknown recipient, on Bing Crosby; this may well be a memoir and not a letter).

———. LAHM 1967, Inv. 1997–25 ("Dear Slim," Sept. 31).

———. IJS 1965 (interview May 22, with Dan Morgenstern and Jack Brady).

————. LAHM 1960, Tape 564 (dubbing of interview from July 2, 1960).

————. IJS 1954 (Armstrong's typescript for *Satchmo: My Life in New Orleans*).

————. WRC 1954, mss 536 Louis Armstrong, folder 32 (transcript of interview with Armstrong, conducted by William Russell, Feb. 16, 23, 25, and March 4).

————. LAHM 1953, June 29 (letter to Leonard Feather).

————. WRC 1953b, mss 519 Louis Armstrong, folder 31 (transcript of interview with William Russell, Chicago, Nov. 29).

————. LAHM 1946, Dec. 21 (letter to *Melody Maker*, Dec. 21).

————. LAHM 1946a (letter to Miss Madeleine Berard).

————. IJS 1941 (letter to Leonard Feather, Oct. 1).

————. WRC 1939, Jan. 18, mss 519, folder 16 (interview for *Jazzmen*).

————. LAHM 1933, Inv. 2006–018 Jan. 21, 1933 (sent from 3529 South Parkway. Chicago, IL; folder identifies recipients as Renee and Sadie Gerther).

————. LAHM 1932, Inv. 2002–32 (transcript of 19-page letter, Sept. 17, 1932, "Dear Mabel").

————. LAHM Tape 17.

————. LAHM Tape 96.

————. LAHM Tape 173.

————. LAHM Tape 202.

————. LAHM Tape 239.

————. LAHM Tape 295.

————. LAHM Tape 495.

————. WRC n.d. mss 519 Louis Armstrong, folder 366.

————. WRC n.d., mss 519 Louis Armstrong, folder 6.

Barefield, Eddie. IJS 1978, Nov. 20.

Barker, Danny. IJS, Jazz Oral History Project, n.d.

Barker, Danny, with Milt Hinton. IJS, Jazz Oral History Project.

Barnes, Paul. WRC 1968, Oct. 15, mss 519, folder 2.

Barnes, Paul and Emile. HJA 1959, Oct. 1.

Bechet, Sidney. WRC ca. 1938, mss 519, folder 20.

Bernhardt, Clyde. FDC 1974, March 24 (interview with Frank Driggs).

Bertrand, Jimmy. HJA 1959, Sept. 9.

Bigard, Barney. IJS 1976.

————. HJA 1969–72.

Bocage, Charlie and Peter. HJA 1960, July 18.

Brown, Ralph. COHP 1971 (interview with John Lax).

Browne, Scoville. COHP 1971, Dec. 14 (interview with John Lax).

————. FDC n.d.

Brunis, George. HJA 1958, June 3.

Bubbles, John. IJS, Jazz Oral History Project, n.d.

Burton, Buddie. HJA 1959, Sept. 7.

Bushell, Garvin. IJS 1977, August.

Carew, Roy. HJA 191, June 21.

Cheatham, Doc. IJS 1976, April.

———. UMKC. (Interview with Frank Driggs).

Christian, Buddy. WRC ca. 1938, mss 519, folder 21.

Christian, Lillie Delk. WRC n.d., mss 519, folder 1.

Clayton, Buck. 1979. IJS, Jazz Oral History Project.

Cole, Cozie. 1980. IJS, Jazz Oral History Project.

Collins, Lee. HJA 1958, June 2.

Compton, Glover. HJA 1959, June 30.

———. CJA 1958 (interview with Francis Squibb).

Davison, Bill. CJA 1981, Sept. 10 (interview with Wayne Jones).

———. IJS 1980, Jan. 2–4.

De Faut, Voltaire. WRC 1970, Nov. 21, mss 519, folder 2.

De Pass, Lillian. HJA 1960, June 20.

Dickerson, Killis. CJA 1967, Nov. 27, John Steiner Collection, box 82, folder "Carroll Dickerson" (letter to Charles Sengstock and John Steiner).

Diggs, Laura, with Carrie Boote. HJA 1959, May 25.

Dixon, George. CJA 1990, Aug. 15 and 17 (interview with Richard Wang).

Dodds, John. WRC ca. 1938, mss 515, folders 15 and 28 (notes from interview with William Russell).

———. WRC mss 513, folder 32.

Dodds, John, Jr. CJA 1969, Aug. 21 (interview with John Steiner).

Dodds, Warren. HJA 1958, May 31.

———. WRC n.d., mss 515, folder 27.

Dominique, Natty. CJA 1981, Oct. 24 (interview with John McDonough).

———. HJA 1958 (interview May 31).

———. WRC 1952, mss 519, folder 88.

———. CJA 1952. John Steiner Collection, box 82, folder "Natty Dominique."

Dorsey, Thomas, with Mayo Williams. CJA 1971, Oct. 23 (interview with John Steiner).

———. CJA ca. 1960 (interview with John Steiner).

———. CJA n.d. (interview with John Steiner; notes in folder "Thomas Dorsey," box 96).

Duhé, Lawrence. HJA 1960.

Elgar, Charles. WRC 1970, Nov. 20, mss 519, folder 1.

———. HJA 1958, May 27.

———. CJA n.d., John Steiner Collection, box 82, folder "Charles Elgar."

Frazier, Josiah. HJA 1972, Jan. 19.

Freeman, Bud. CJA 1980 (interview, George Spink Collection).

———. IJS 1965, 1975.

Garland, Ed "Montudie." WRC 1969, July 30, mss 519, folder 13.

———. HJA 1958, Aug. 8.

———. WRC 1958, Aug. 16, mss 519, folders 11 and 12.

———. HJA 1957, April 16.

———. IJS n.d., Jazz Oral History Project.

Hall, Minor "Ram." HJA 1958, Sept. 2.

Henry, Charles "Sunny." HJA 1959, Jan. 8.

Higgenbotham, J. C. IJS, Jazz Oral History Project, n.d.

Hightower, Willie. HJA 1958, June 3.

Hines, Earl, with George "Pops" Foster and Louis Deppe. COHP 1971 (interview with John Lax).

———. CJA 1961, Jan. 30 (interview with John Steiner, box 83).

Hinton, Milton. IJS 1992 (interview by Billy Taylor).

———. IJS 1976 (interview with David Berger).

———. IJS 1974, July (interview by Tom Piazza).

———. COHP 1971 (interview by John Lax).

Hodes, Art.CJA 1988, Oct. 9 (interview with Don Phillips).

———. CJA n.d., box 83, folder "Art Hodes" (interview with John Steiner).

Holmes, Charles. FDC n.d.

———. IJS n.d., Jazz Oral History Project.

Howard, Darnell. HJA 1957, April 21.

———. CJA n.d. John Steiner Collection, box 83.

Howard, Paul. WRC 1969, July 31, mss 519, folder 1.

———. CJA n.d., box 83, folder "Darnell Howard" (interview with John Steiner).

Hug, Armand. HJA 1974, July 8.

Humphrey, Willie, Jr. HJA 1959, March 15.

Hunter, Alberta. IJS 1976–77.

Jackson, Preston. FDC 1973, April 13.

———. FDC 1973a, April 19.

———. CJA 1972, May 20, John Steiner Collection, box 96.

———. HJA 1958, June 2.

———. WRC 1938, mss 519, folder 15 (interview for *Jazzmen*).

———. WRC n.d., mss 519, folders 6, 9, and 13.

———. CJA n.d., John Steiner Collection, box 96, folder "Baby Dodds," and box 78, folder "Louis Armstrong."

Jackson, Quentin. IJS 1976.

Johnson, Bill. WRC ca. 1938, mss 519, folder 28 (interview for *Jazzmen*).

Johnson, Budd. IJS 1975.

Johnson, Manzie (Isham). WRC 1969, April 21, mss 519, folder 2.

Jones, Richard. WRC ca. 1938.

Lewis, Steve. WRC ca. 1938, mss 519, folder 34 (interview for *Jazzmen*).

Mares, Paul. WRC ca. 1938, mss 519, folder 31 (interview for *Jazzmen*).

Marsala, Joe. WRC ca. 1938, mss 519, folder 32.

Mason, Norman. HJA 1960, Feb. 6.

Matthews, Bill. HJA 1959, March 10.

Maxwell, Jimmy. IJS 1979, March 20.

McBride, Mary and Billy. HJA 1959, July 1.

McConnell, Charles. CJA, John Steiner Collection, box 87, folder "Trumbauer."

McHargue, Rosy. HJA 1991.

Meyer, Sig. CJA 1975, box 97, folder "King Oliver" (interview with John Steiner).

———. CJA 1966, July 1, box 86, folder "Dave Peyton" (interview with John Steiner).

———. CJA 1965, 1971, 1974, boxes 83 and 84, folders "Sig Meyer" (interviews with John Steiner).

Miles, Lizzie. HJA 1951, Jan. 18.

Miller, Punch. HJA 1960, April 4.

———. IJS 1960.

———. HJA 1959, Aug. 20 and Sept. 1, 25.

———. HJA 1957, April 9.

Millstein, Gilbert. IIJA n.d., vertical file for Louis Armstrong (article entitled "Africa Harks to Satch's Horn").

Mitchell, George. CJA 1969, April 18 (interview with John Steiner and Karl Dallas).

———. HJA 1959, July 1.

Moore, Fred. HJA 1959, June 19.

Morand, Herb. HJA 1950, March 12.

Morton, Jelly Roll. LC ca. 1938 (transcript of interviews conducted at the Library of Congress; circulating photocopy with no transcriber named).

Nelson, Louis. WRC ca. 1938, mss 519, folder 34 (interview for *Jazzmen*).

Nicholas, Albert. HJA 1972, June 26.

———. WRC 1970, mss 519, folder 10.

Noone, Jimmy. WRC 1938, November, mss 519, folder 24 (interview for *Jazzmen*; also in Dodds, John, WRC ca. 1938, mss 515, folder 28).

Oliver, Francis. WRC n.d.

Oliver, Joseph. WRC 1930, Feb. 15, mss 510, folder 507 (letter to Bunk Johnson).

Oliver, Stella. HJA 1959, April 22.

Ory, Kid. HJA 1958, Aug. 26 (interview with Manuel Manetta).

———. HJA 1957, April 20.

———. CJA n.d., John Steiner Collection, box 83, folder "Ory."

Palmer, Roy. HJA 1955, Sept. 22.

Perez, Manuel. WRC ca. 1938, mss 519, folder 34 (interview for *Jazzmen*).

Phillips, Babe. WRC n.d., mss 519, folder 1.

Picou, Alphonse. WRC ca. 1938, mss 519, folder 34 (interview for *Jazzmen*).

Randall, Willie. COHP 1971, Dec. 28 (interview with John Lax).

Randolph, Zilner. IJS 1977, Feb. 20.

———. FDC 1973, April 19.

Reeves, Reuben. FDC 1956, August.

———. IJS, Jazz Oral History Project, n.d.

Reich, Howard. HJA 2001 ("The Louis Armstrong Tapes: The Thoroughly Human Side of a Jazz Virtuoso." Typescript filed in vertical file "Armstrong" and dated Sept. 4).

Robinson, Ike. CJA 1988, July 17 and 25 (interview with Paige Van Vorst).

———. WRC 1969, April 23, mss 519, folder 1.

———. CJA 1961, Feb. 2 (interview with John Steiner).

St. Cyr, John. WRC 1969, Jan. 31, mss 519, folders 53 and 55.

———. HJA 1958, Aug. 27.

———. WRC 1944, August, mss 519, folder 71.

Samuels, William. COHP 1971 (interview with John Lax).

Saunders, Red. COHP 1971, Dec. 24 (interview with John Lax).

Sayles, Emanuel. HJA 1959, Jan. 17.

Scott, Howard. IJS 1979, March 8.

Scrapbooks 5, 6, and 83. LAHM (including newspaper clippings and publicity items).

Shoffner, Bob. CJA 1973, Jan. 22, box 86, folder "Bob Shoffner" (interview with John Steiner).

———. HJA 1959, Sept. 8.

———. CJA 1958, September, box 86, folder "Bob Shoffner" (interview with John Steiner).

Simeon, Omer. HJA 1955, Aug. 18.

Singleton, Zutty. IJS 1975, May, Tapes 1–6, Jazz Oral History Project (with Mrs. Zutty Singleton).

————. HJA 1969, Feb. 2.

————. WRC ca. 1938, mss 519, folder 37 (interview for *Jazzmen*).

————. CJA n.d., box 78, folder "Louis Armstrong" (interview with John Steiner).

Smith, Jabbo. IJS 1979, March 26.

————. HJA 1961, Oct. 15.

Smith, Willie "The Lion." WRC 1970, Dec. 23, mss 19, folder 2.

Soper, Tut. CJA 1983, July 19 (interview with Wayne Jones and Warren Platt).

Spanier, Muggsy. HJA 1961, Feb. 2.

Tate, Erskine. CJA n.d., box 78, folder "Louis Armstrong" (interview with Charles Sengstock, notes taken by John Steiner).

Valentine, Kid Thomas. HJA 1959, Nov. 8.

Washington, Leon. COHP 1971 (interview with John Lax).

————. CJA 1965, March 28, box 87, folder "Leon Washington" (interview with John Steiner).

Watts, Bob. HJA 1963, Feb. 28.

Wettling, George. WRC ca. 1938, mss 519, folder 40 (interview for *Jazzmen*).

Wiggs, Johnny. HJA 1962, Aug. 26.

Williams, Alfred. HJA 1961, Feb. 3.

Williams, Cootie. IJS 1976.

Williams, Mayo. WRC 1970, Nov. 21, mss 519, folder 1.

## General Sources

Abbott, Lynn. 2005. "Butterbeans and Susie." *Jazzbeat* 16, nos. 3–4: 3–5.

Abbott, Lynn, and Doug Seroff. 1996. "'They Cert'ly Sound Good to Me': Sheet Music, Southern Vaudeville, and the Commercial Ascendancy of the Blues." *American Music* 14, no. 4 (Winter): 402–54.

Albertson, Chris. 2003. *Bessie.* Revised and expanded edition. New Haven: Yale University Press.

Allen, Frederick Lewis. 1931. *Only Yesterday: An Informal History of the Nineteen-Twenties.* New York: Harper.

Allen, Walter C. 1973. *Hendersonia: The Music of Fletcher Henderson and His Musicians.* Highland Park, IL: published by the author.

Altman, Rick. 2004. *Silent Film Sound.* New York: Columbia University Press.

Anderson, Gene. 2007. *The Original Hot Five Recordings of Louis Armstrong.* CMS Sourcebooks in American Music, no. 3. New York: Pendragon.

————. 1994. "The Genesis of King Oliver's Creole Jazz Band." *American Music* 12: 283–303.

————. 1990. "Johnny Dodds in New Orleans." *American Music* 8: 405–40.

Anderson, Gillian B. 1988. *Music for Silent Films: 1894–1929.* Washington, DC: Library of Congress.

Appel, Alfred, Jr.. 2002. *Jazz Modernism: From Ellington and Armstrong to Matisse and Joyce*. New York: Knopf.

Armstrong, Lillian Hardin. 2005. "Lil Armstrong." 1957 interview published in Studs Terkel, ed., *And They All Sang: Adventures of an Eclectic Disc Jockey*. New York: New Press. Pp. 139–44.

———. 1963. *Satchmo and Me*. Recorded interview accessed through www .redhotjazz.com/lil.html.

———. 1950. "Lil Tells of 1st Time She Met Louis." *Down Beat* (July 14): 18.

Armstrong, Louis. 2008. *Fleischmann's Yeast Show; and Louis' Home-Recorded Tapes*. Audio CD. Oakhurst, NJ: Jazz Heritage Society.

———. 2005. "1962." Interview conducted by Studs Terkel in Terkel, ed., *And They All Sang: Adventures of an Eclectic Disc Jockey*. New York: New Press. Pp. 145–48.

———. 2003. *The Louis Armstrong Collection*. Transcriptions by Forrest Mankowski. Milwaukee: Hal Leonard.

———. 1999. *Louis Armstrong in His Own Words*. Ed. Thomas Brothers. Oxford: Oxford University Press.

———. 1971. "Satchmo Says." Letter published in Max Jones and John Chilton, *Louis: The Louis Armstrong Story, 1900–1971*. Boston: Little, Brown. Pp. 208–20.

———. 1966. *Louis Armstrong—A Self-Portrait: The Interview by Richard Merryman*. New York: Eakins.

———. 1961. "Daddy, How the Country Has Changed!" *Ebony* (May): 81.

———. 1955. "They Cross the Iron Curtain to Hear American Jazz." Interview in *U.S. News and World Report* (Dec. 2): 40–54.

———. 1954. *Satchmo: My Life in New Orleans*. New York: Prentice Hall.

———. 1950. "Louis on the Spot." *Record Changer* 9, nos. 6–7 (July–August): 24.

———. 1950a. "The Sweetest Music." *Record Changer* 9, nos. 6–7 (July–August): 26.

———. 1950b. "Care of the Lip." *Record Changer* 9, nos. 6–7 (July–August): 30.

———. 1946. "Chicago, Chicago, That Toddlin' Town: How King and Ol' Satch Dug It in the Twenties." *Esquire's 1947 Jazz Book*: 40–43.

———. 1945. "Mr. Armstrong and Mr. Robbins: An Interview Between Fred Robbins and Louis Armstrong, Over Station WHN, January 26, 1944." *Jazz Record* 3 (December): 7–13.

———. 1938. *Swing That Music*. London: Longmans, Green.

Austin, Mary. "Buck and Wing and Bill Robinson." 1926. *Nation* 122 (April 28): 476.

Baldwin, James. 1984. *Notes of a Native Son*. Boston: Beacon.

———. 1963. *The Fire Next Time*. New York: Dial.

———. 1961. *Nobody Knows My Name: More Notes of a Native Son*. New York: Dial.

————. 1959. "Mass Culture and the Creative Artist." In Norman Jacobs, ed., *Culture for the Millions? Mass Media in Modern Society.* Toronto: Van Nostrand. Pp. 120–23.

Balliet, Whitney. 1977. "Let It Be Classy." *The New Yorker* (Oct. 31): 100–114.

————. 1966. "Jazz Records: Hide and Seek." In Balliet, *Such Sweet Thunder: 49 Pieces on Jazz.* Indianapolis: Bobbs-Merrill. Pp. 293–97.

Banes, Sally, and John Szwed. 2002. "Dance Instruction Songs." In Thomas F. DeFrantz, ed., *Dancing Many Drums: Excavations in African American Dance.* Madison: University of Wisconsin Press. Pp. 169–204.

Banks, Ann, ed. 1980. *First-Person America.* New York: Knopf.

Baraka, Amiri [Leroi Jones]. 1963. *Blues People: Negro Music in White America.* New York: Morrow Quill Paperbacks.

Barker, Danny. 1986. *A Life in Jazz.* New York: Oxford University Press.

Barlow, William. 1989. *Looking Up at Down: The Emergence of Blues Culture.* Philadelphia: Temple University Press.

Barnett, Anthony, ed. 2002. *Stuff Smith, Pure at Heart: Anecdotes and Interviews.* 2nd ed. East Sussex: Allardyce, Barnett.

Bechet, Sidney. 1960. *Treat It Gentle: An Autobiography.* New York: Twayne.

Berlin, Ira. 2010. *The Making of African America: The Four Great Migrations.* New York: Viking.

Berliner, Louise. 1993. *Texas Guinan: Queen of the Night Clubs.* Austin: University of Texas Press.

Bernhardt, Clyde. 1986. *I Remember: Eighty Years of Black Entertainment, Big Bands, and the Blues.* As told to Sheldon Harris. Philadelphia: University of Pennsylvania Press.

Berrett, Joshua. 2004. *Louis Armstrong and Paul Whiteman: Two Kings of Jazz.* New Haven: Yale University Press.

————. 1992. "Louis Armstrong and Opera." *Musical Quarterly* 76, no. 2 (Summer): 216–41.

Berrett, Joshua, ed. 1999. *The Louis Armstrong Companion: Eight Decades of Commentary.* New York: Schirmer Books.

Bethel, Tom. 1977. *George Lewis: A Jazzman from New Orleans.* Berkeley: University of California Press.

Bigard, Barney. 1986. *With Louis and the Duke.* New York: Oxford University Press.

Black, Charles L., Jr. 1979. "My World with Louis Armstrong." *Yale Review* 69: 145–51.

Blesh, Rudi. 1946. *Shining Trumpets: A History of Jazz.* New York: Knopf.

Bogle, Donald. 2005. *Bright Boulevards, Bold Dreams: The Story of Black Hollywood.* New York: Ballantine.

————. 1994. "Louis Armstrong: The Films." In Marc H. Miller, ed., *Louis*

*Armstrong: A Cultural Legacy.* Seattle: University of Washington Press. Pp. 147–79.

Bourdieu, Pierre. 1984. *Distinctions: A Social Critique of the Judgment of Taste.* Trans. Richard Nice. Cambridge: Harvard University Press.

Bradford, Perry. 1965. *Born with the Blues: Perry Bradford's Own Story, the True Story of the Pioneering Blues Singers and the Musicians in the Early Days of Jazz.* New York: Oak.

Brooks, Edward. 2002. *The Young Louis Armstrong on Records: A Critical Survey of the Early Recordings, 1923–1928.* Studies in Jazz, no. 39. Lanham, MD: Scarecrow.

———. 2000. *Influence and Assimilation in Louis Armstrong's Cornet and Trumpet Work (1923–1928).* Studies in the History and Interpretation of Music, vol. 70. Lewiston, NY: Edwin Mellen.

Brothers, Thomas. 2009. "Who's on First, What's Second, and Where Did They Come From: The Social and Musical Textures of Early Jazz." In Howard T. Weiner, ed., *Early Twentieth-Century Brass Idioms: Art, Jazz and Popular Traditions: Proceedings of the International Conference.* Lanham, MD: Scarecrow. Pp. 14–34.

———. 2006. *Louis Armstrong's New Orleans.* New York: W. W. Norton.

———. 1997. "Ideology and Aurality in the Vernacular Traditions of African-American Music." *Black Music Research Journal* (Fall): 169–209.

———. 1994. "Solo and Cycle in African-American Jazz." *Musical Quarterly* 78: 479–509.

Brothers, Thomas, ed. 1999. *Louis Armstrong in His Own Words.* New York: Oxford University Press.

Bryant, Cora, et al., eds. 1998. *Central Avenue Sounds: Jazz in Los Angeles.* Berkeley: University of California Press.

Bushell, Garvin. 1988. *Jazz from the Beginning.* As told to Mark Tucker. Ann Arbor: University of Michigan Press.

Calloway, Cab. 1976. *Of Minnie the Moocher and Me.* New York: Crowell.

Carbine, Mary. 1996. "'The Finest Outside the Loop': Motion Picture Exhibition in Chicago's Black Metropolis, 1905–1928." *Camera Obscura* 23 (May): 8–41.

Carmichael, Hoagy. 1999. *The Stardust Road.* Published as *The Stardust Road and Sometimes I Wonder: The Autobiographies of Hoagy Carmichael.* New York: Da Capo.

———. 1999a. With Stephen Longstreet. *Sometimes I Wonder.* Published as *The Stardust Road and Sometimes I Wonder: The Autobiographies of Hoagy Carmichael.* New York: Da Capo.

Chamberlain, Charles. 2000. "Searching for 'The Gulf Coast Circuit': Mobility and Cultural Diffusion in the Age of Jim Crow, 1900–1930." *Jazz Archivist* 14:1–18.

Chernoff, John. 1979. *African Rhythm and African Sensibility: Aesthetics and Social Action in African Musical Idioms.* Chicago: University of Chicago Press.

Chevan, David. 1997. "Written Music in Early Jazz." Ph.D. diss., City University of New York.

Chilton, Charles. 1947. "Jackson and the Oliver Band." *Jazz Music* 6: 5–6.

Chilton, John. 1987. *Sidney Bechet*. New York: Oxford University Press.

Clark, Andrew. 2001. *Riffs and Choruses: A New Jazz Anthology*. London: Continuum.

Clarke, Donald. 1994. *Wishing on the Moon: The Life and Times of Billie Holiday*. New York: Viking.

Clayton, Buck, and Nancy Miller Elliot. 1987. *Buck Clayton's Jazz World*. New York: Oxford University Press.

Clifford, James. 1988. *The Predicament of Culture: Twentieth-Century Ethnography, Literature and Art*. Cambridge: Harvard University Press.

Cohen, Lizabeth. 1989. "Encountering Mass Culture at the Grassroots: The Experience of Chicago Workers in the 1920s." *American Quarterly* 41, no. 1 (March 1989): 6–33.

Collier, James Lincoln. 1988. *The Reception of Jazz in America: A New View*. ISAM Monographs, no. 27. Brooklyn: Institute for Studies in American Music.

———. 1983. *Louis Armstrong: An American Genius*. New York: Oxford University Press.

Collins, Lee. 1974. *Didn't He Ramble: The Life Story of Lee Collins as Told to Mary Collins*. Ed. Frank Gillis and John Miner. Urbana: University of Illinois Press.

Compton, Glover. 1956. *Meet Glover Compton*. Audio interview with Birch Smith. Palo Alto, CA: Windin' Ball Recordings.

Condon, Eddie. 1947. *We Called It Music: A Generation of Jazz*. Westport, CT: Greenwood.

Conway, Michael M. 1971. "A Genius . . . Didn't Have to Be Taught." *Chicago Sun-Times* (July 7): 7.

Cox, Karen. 2011. *Dreaming of Dixie: How the South Was Created in American Popular Culture*. Chapel Hill: University of North Carolina Press.

Crawford, Richard, and Jeffrey Magee. 1992. *Jazz Standards on Record, 1900–1942: A Core Repertory*. Chicago: Center for Black Music Research.

Crowder, Henry, with Hugo Speck. 1987. *As Wonderful as All That? Henry Crowder's Memoir of His Affair with Nancy Cunard, 1928–1935*. Navarro, CA: Wild Trees.

Dance, Stanley. 1983. "Earl Hines: A Musician Whose Genius Is Universally Recognized." *Stereo Review* (Aug. 23): 70.

———. 1977. *The World of Earl Hines*. New York: Da Capo.

———. 1974. *The World of Swing*. New York: Scribner's.

———. 1969. "Duke Ellington." *Stereo Review* (December).

Dapogney, James, ed. 1982. *Ferdinand "Jelly Roll" Morton: The Collected Piano Music*. Washington, DC: Smithsonian Institution Press.

Davin, Tom. 1995. "Conversation with James P. Johnson." In Nathan Irvin Huggins, ed., *Voices from the Harlem Renaissance*. New York: Oxford University Press. Pp. 324–36.

Davis, Miles, with Quincy Troupe. 1990. *Miles, the Autobiography*. New York: Simon and Schuster.

Deffaa, Chip. 1990a. *Voices of the Jazz Age: Profiles of Eight Vintage Jazzmen*. Urbana: University of Illinois Press.

———. 1990b. "Doc Cheatham, Part II: Chicago Memories." *Mississippi Rag* (July): 18.

DeVeaux, Scott. 1997. *The Birth of Bebop*. Berkeley: University of California Press.

———. 1989. "Emergence of the Jazz Concert, 1935–1945." *American Music* 7, no. 1 (Spring): 6–29.

Dickerson, James. 2002. *Just for a Thrill: Lil Harden Armstrong, First Lady of Jazz*. New York: Cooper Square.

Dixon Gottschild, Brenda. 2000. *Waltzing in the Dark: African American Vaudeville and Race Politics in the Swing Era*. New York: St. Martin's.

Dodds, John, II. Ca. 1969. Liner notes for *Johnny Dodds: Chicago Mess Around*. Mileston MLP-2011.

Dodds, Warren "Baby." 1992. *The Baby Dodds Story*. As told to Larry Gara. Baton Rouge: Louisiana State University Press.

Dodge, Roger Pryor, ed. 1995. *Hot Jazz and Jazz Dance: Roger Pryor Dodge: Collected Writings, 1929–1964*. New York: Oxford University Press.

Donder, Jempi de. 1983. "My Buddy: An Attempt to Find Buddy Petit." *Footnote* 14, no. 3: 24–34, and 14, no. 4: 4–13.

Douglas, Ann. 1995.*Terrible Honesty: Mongrel Manhattan in the 1920s*. New York: Noonday.

Drake, St. Clair, and Horace R. Cayton. 1970. *Black Metropolis: A Study of Negro Life in a Northern City*. New York: Harcourt.

Drew, Peter. 1950. "The Professional Viewpoint." *Record Changer* 9, nos. 6–7 (July–August): 26.

Du Bois, W. E. B. 1903. "The Talented Tenth." In Booker T. Washington, ed., *The Negro Problem*. New York: James Pott. Pp. 31–76.

Dupuis, Robert. 1993. *Bunny Berigan: Elusive Legend of Jazz*. Baton Rouge: Louisiana State University Press.

Early, Gerald. 1984. "'And I Will Sing of Joy and Pain for You': Louis Armstrong and the Great Jazz Traditions: A Review-Essay." Review of *Louis Armstrong: An American Genius*, by James Lincoln Collier. *Callaloo* 21 (Spring–Summer 1984): 90–100.

Ecklund, Peter, transcriber and editor. 1995. *Louis Armstrong: Great Trumpet Solos*. New York: Charles Colin.

Edwards, Brent Hayes. 2002. "Louis Armstrong and the Syntax of Scat." *Critical Inquiry* 28: 618–49.

Eisenberg, Evan. 1987. *The Recording Angel: Explorations in Phonography*. New York: McGraw-Hill.

Ellison, Ralph. 2000. *Trading Twelves: The Selected Letters of Ralph Ellison and Albert Murray*. Ed. Albert Murray and John Callahan. New York: Modern Library.

———. 1995. *Conversations with Ralph Ellison.* Jackson: University of Mississippi Press.

———. 1964. *Shadow and Act*. New York: Random House.

Ellison, Ralph, and Albert Murray. 2002. *Invisible Man*. New York: Random House.

Epstein, Dena. 1977. *Sinful Tunes and Spirituals: Black Folk Music to the Civil War*. Urbana: University of Illinois Press.

Erenberg, Lewis. 1981. *Steppin' Out*. Westport, CT: Greenwood.

Fass, Paula. 1977. *The Damned and the Beautiful: American Youth in the 1920s*. New York: Oxford University Press.

Feather, Leonard. 1976. *The Pleasures of Jazz: Leading Performers on Their Lives, Their Music, Their Contemporaries*. New York: Delta.

———. 1970. "Louis Armstrong: The Cat with Nine Lives Hits 70." *Los Angeles Times Calendar*, June 28: 35–37.

Fitzgerald, F. Scott. 1993. "Echoes of the Jazz Age." In Wesley Brown and Amy Ling, eds., *Visions of America: Personal Narratives from the Promised Land*. New York: Persea. Pp. 54–61.

Floyd, Samuel A. 1995. *The Power of Black Music: Interpreting Its History from Africa to the United States*. New York: Oxford University Press.

Foreman, Ronald C. 1968. "Jazz and Race Records, 1920–32: Their Origins and Their Significance for the Record Industry and Society." Ph.D. diss., University of Illinois.

Foster, Pops. 2005. *Pops Foster: The Autobiography of a Jazzman*. As told to Tom Stoddard. San Francisco: Backbeat.

Fox, Jack. 1960. "Ambassador Armstrong." *Saga* (October): 49.

Freeman, Bud. 1994. "Louis Armstrong: A Reminiscence." In Ralph de Toledano, ed., *Frontiers of Jazz*, 3rd ed. Gretna, LA: Pelican. Pp. 119–22.

———. 1974. *You Don't Look Like a Musician*. Detroit: Balamp.

Freeman, Bud, with Irving Kolodin. 1970. "The Father and His Flock." *Saturday Review* (July 4): 15–17.

Gabbard, Krin. 2008. *Hotter Than That: The Trumpet, Jazz, and American Culture*. New York: Faber and Faber.

———. 1996. *Jammin' at the Margins: Jazz and the American Cinema*. Chicago: University of Chicago Press.

———. 1995. "Signifyin(g) the Phallus: Mo' Better Blues and Representations of Jazz Trumpet." In Gabbard, ed., *Representing Jazz*. Durham, NC: Duke University Press. Pp. 104–30.

Garrett, Charles Hiroshi. 2008. *Struggling to Define a Nation: American Music and the Twentieth Century*. Berkeley: University of California Press.

Gellhorn, Martha. 1929. "Rudy Vallée: God's Gift to Us Girls." *New Republic* (Aug. 7): 310–11.

Gennari, John. 1991. "Jazz Criticism: Its Development and Ideologies." *Black American Literature Forum* 25: 449–523.

Giddins, Gary. 2001. *Satchmo*. New York: Da Capo.

———. 1998. *Visions of Jazz*. New York: Oxford University Press.

Gillespie, Dizzy, with Al Frazer. 1979. *To Be or Not to Bop*. Minneapolis: University of Minnesota Press.

Gillespie, Dizzy, with Ralph Ginzburg. 1957. "Jazz Is Too Good for Americans." *Esquire* (June): 55.

Gilroy, Paul. 1993. *The Black Atlantic: Modernity and Double Consciousness*. Cambridge: Harvard University Press.

Gitler, Ira. 1985. *Swing to Bop: An Oral History of the Tradition of Jazz in the 1940s*. New York: Oxford University Press.

Gleason, Ralph. 1961. *Jam Session: An Anthology of Jazz*. London: Jazz Book Club.

Gleason, Ralph, ed. 1974. Liner notes for *Louis Armstrong/King Oliver*. Mileston M-47017.

Goddard, Chris. 1979. *Jazz Away from Home*. New York: Paddington.

Goffin, Robert. 1977. *Horn of Plenty: The Story of Louis Armstrong*. Trans. James Bezou. New York: Da Capo.

Green, Benny. 1970. "Satchmo." *London Observer* (July 5): 2–4.

Grossman, James R. 1989. *Land of Hope: Chicago, Black Southerners and the Great Migration*. Chicago: University of Chicago Press.

Gushee, Lawrence. 2005. *Pioneers of Jazz: The Story of the Creole Band*. New York: Oxford University Press.

———. 1998. "The Improvisation of Louis Armstrong." In Bruno Nettl, ed., with Melinda Russell, *In the Course of Performance: Studies in the World of Musical Improvisation*. Chicago: University of Chicago Press. Pp. 291–334.

———. 1979. "King Oliver." In Martin Williams, ed., *Jazz Panorama: From the Pages of the Jazz Review*. New York: Da Capo. Pp. 39–43.

Hadlock, Richard. 1965. *Jazz Masters of the Twenties*. New York: Macmillan.

Hamm, Charles. 1979. *Yesterdays: Popular Song in America*. New York: W. W. Norton.

Hammond, John, with Irving Townsend. 1977. *John Hammond on Record*. New York: Summit.

Hampton, Lionel, with James Haskins. 1993. *Hamp: An Autobiography*. New York: Amistad.

Hansen, Chadwick. 1960. "Social Influences on Jazz Style: Chicago, 1920–30." *American Quarterly* 12, no. 4: 493–507.

Harker, Brian. 2011. *Louis Armstrong's Hot Five and Hot Seven Recordings*. New York: Oxford University Press.

———. 2008. "Louis Armstrong, Eccentric Dance, and the Evolution of Jazz on the Eve of Swing." *Journal of the American Musicological Society* 61, no. 1: 67–121.

———. 2003. "Louis Armstrong and the Clarinet." *American Music* 21, no. 3: 137–58.

———. 1999. "'Telling a Story': Louis Armstrong and Coherence in Early Jazz." *Current Musicology* 63: 46–83.

———. 1997. "The Early Musical Development of Louis Armstrong, 1901–1928." Ph.D. diss., Columbia University.

Harris, Michael W. 1992. *The Rise of Gospel Blues: The Music of Thomas Andrew Dorsey in the Urban Church*. New York: Oxford University Press.

Hasse, John. 1999. "Introduction" to Hoagy Carmichael, *The Stardust Road and Sometimes I Wonder: The Autobiographies of Hoagy Carmichael*. New York: Da Capo. Pp. v–xv.

Havens, Dan. 1992. "A Year with Satchmo: George James Talks to Dan Havens." *Jazz Journal International* (January): 6–9.

Henderson, Fletcher. 1950. "Henderson 'Had to Get Louis' for Roseland Ork." *Down Beat* (July 14): 4.

———. 1950a. "He Made the Band Swing." *Record Changer* 9, nos. 6–7: 15–16.

Hennessey, Thomas. 1994. *From Jazz to Swing: African-American Jazz Musicians and Their Music, 1890–1935*. Detroit: Wayne State University Press.

———. 1974. "The Black Chicago Establishment, 1919–1930." *Journal of Jazz Studies* 2, no. 1: 15–45.

———. 1973. "From Jazz to Swing: Black Jazz Musicians and Their Music, 1917–1935." Ph.D. diss., Northwestern University.

Hentoff, Nat. 1962. *Jazz Panorama*. New York: Crowell-Collier.

Herndon, Booton. 1964. *The Sweetest Music This Side of Heaven: The Guy Lombardo Story*. New York: McGraw-Hill.

Hewitt, Roger. 1983. "Black Through White: Hoagy Carmichael and the Cultural Reproduction of Racism." *Popular Music* 3: 33–50.

Hillman, Chris, and Roy Middleton, with Hennie van Veelo. 1997. *Richard M. Jones: Forgotten Man of Jazz*. Tavistock, UK: Cygnet.

Hines, Earl. 2005. Interview conducted by Studs Terkel (1976) in Terkel, ed., *And They All Sang: Adventures of an Eclectic Disc Jockey*. New York: New Press. Pp. 148–52.

Hinton, Milt, and David G. Berger. 1988. *Bass Line: The Stories and Photographs of Milt Hinton*. Philadelphia: Temple University Press.

Hodeir, André. 1956. *Jazz: Its Evolution and Essence*. Trans. David Noakes. New York: Grove.

Hodes, Art. 1988. "Stomping My Foot Was a Habit I Never Got Rid Of." *New York Times* (July 17, 1988): 30.

———. 1944. "Wingie, Louie and Me." *Jazz Record* 2 (January): 6–7.

———. 1943. "Everybody's in the Union." *Jazz Record* 1 (November): 4–5, 11.

Hodes, Art, and Chadwick Hansen. 1977. *Selections from the Gutter: Jazz Portraits from "The Jazz Record."* Berkeley: University of California Press.

Hoefer, George. 1950. "Will the Louis Sides on Cylinder Ever Turn Up?" *Down Beat* (July 14): 11.

Holiday, Billie, with William Dufty. 2006. *Lady Sings the Blues*. New York: Broadway Books.

Howland, John. 2009. *Ellington Uptown: Duke Ellington, James P. Johnson, and the Birth of Concert Jazz*. Ann Arbor: University of Michigan Press.

Hubner, Alma. 1946. "Kid Ory." *Jazz Record* 4 (April): 9–10.

———. 1944. "Muggsy Spanier." *Jazz Record* 2 (August): 4–7, 11; (September): 7–8.

Huggins, Nathan Irvin. 1995. "Interview with Eubie Blake, October 16, 1973." In Huggins, ed., *Voices from the Harlem Renaissance*. New York: Oxford University Press. Pp. 336–40.

Hughes, Langston. 1986. *The Big Sea: An Autobiography*. Foreword by Amiri Baraka. New York: Thunder's Mouth.

Hurston, Zora Neale. 2006. "Concert." Appendix to *Dust Tracks on a Road*. New York: Harper Perennial. Pp. 279–86.

———. 1995. "Characteristics of Negro Expression." In Nathan Irvin Huggins, ed., *Voices from the Harlem Renaissance*. New York: Oxford University Press. Pp. 224–36.

Hurwitt, Elliott S. 2000. "W. C. Handy as Music Publisher: Career and Reputation." Ph.D. diss., City University of New York.

Jablonski, Edward. 1961. *Harold Arlen: Happy with the Blues*. New York: Doubleday.

Jackson, Mahalia, with Evan Wylie. 1967. *Movin' on Up*. New York: Hawthorn.

Jackson, Preston. 2005. *Trombone Man: Preston Jackson's Story as Told to Laurie Wright*. Chigwell, UK: published by Laurie Wright.

———. 1994. "King Oliver." In Ralph de Toledano, ed., *Frontiers of Jazz*, 3rd ed. Gretna, LA: Pelican. Pp. 71–77.

———. 1974. "Reminisce Is the Word: My Years with Louis." *Mississippi Rag* (August): 5–8.

Jackson, Rudy. 1947. "My Story." *Jazz Music* 6, no. 3: 3–4.

Jasen, David A., and Gene Jones. 1998. *Spreadin' Rhythm Around: Black Popular Songwriters, 1880–1930*. New York: Schirmer Books.

Jenkins, Henry. 1992. *What Made Pistachio Nuts? Early Sound Comedy and the Vaudeville Aesthetic*. New York: Columbia University Press.

Jones, Max. 1988. *Talking Jazz*. New York: W. W. Norton.

Jones, Max, and John Chilton. 1971. *Louis: The Louis Armstrong Story, 1900–1971*. Boston: Little, Brown.

Katz, Mark. 2004. *Capturing Sound: How Technology Has Changed Music*. Berkeley: University of California Press.

Keepnews, Orin. 1950. "The Big Band Period." *Record Changer* 9, nos. 6–7 (July–August): 25–26.

Keller, J. R. Keith. 1989. *Oh Jess! A Jazz Life: The Jess Stacy Story*. New York: Mayan Music.

Kennedy, Rick. 1994. *Jelly Roll, Bix and Hoagy: Gennett Studios and the Birth of Recorded Jazz*. Bloomington: Indiana University Press.

Kenney, William Howland. 1999. *Recorded Music in American Life: The Phonograph and Popular Memory, 1890–1945*. New York: Oxford University Press.

———. 1993. *Chicago Jazz: A Cultural History, 1904–1930*. New York: Oxford University Press.

Kimball, Robert, and William Bolcom. 1973. *Reminiscing with Sissle and Blake*. New York: Viking.

King, Larry L. 1967. "Everybody's Louie." *Harper's* (November): 61–69.

Kleinhout, Henk, and Wim van Eyle. 1981. *The Wallace Bishop Story*. The Netherlands: Micrography.

Koszarski, Richard. 1990. *An Evening's Entertainment: The Age of the Silent Feature Picture, 1915–1928*. New York: Scribner's.

Kubik, Gerard. 1999. *Africa and the Blues*. Jackson: University of Mississippi Press.

Laird, Ross, and Brian Rust. 2004. *Discography of OKeh Records, 1918–1934*. Westport, CT: Praeger.

Lambert, G. E. 1978. "Johnny Dodds." In Stanley Green, ed., *Kings of Jazz*. New York: A. S. Barnes. Pp. 109–39.

Lange, Arthur. 1926. *Arranging for the Modern Dance Orchestra*. New York: Arthur Lange.

Laplace, Michel. 1988. *Jabbo Smith: The Misunderstood and the "Modernistic."* Menden, Germany: Jazzfreund.

Leonard, Neil. 1987. *Jazz, Myth and Religion*. Oxford: Oxford University Press.

———. 1986. "The Jazzman's Verbal Usage." *Black American Literature Forum* 20 (Spring–Summer): 151–60.

———. 1962. *Jazz and the White Americans: The Acceptance of a New Art Form*. Chicago: University of Chicago Press.

Levin, Michael David. 1985. "Louise de Koven Bowen: A Case History of the American Response to Jazz." Ph.D. diss., University of Illinois.

Levine, Lawrence W. 1993. *The Unpredictable Past: Explorations in American Cultural History*. New York: Oxford University Press.

―――. 1988. *Highbrow/Lowbrow: The Emergence of Cultural Hierarchy in America*. Cambridge: Harvard University Press.

Levinson, Peter J. 2005. *Tommy Dorsey: Livin' in a Great Big Way*. New York: Da Capo.

Lewis, David Levering. 2000. *W.E.B. Du Bois: The Fight for Equality and the American Century, 1919–1963*. New York: Holt.

―――. 1993. *W.E.B. Du Bois: Biography of a Race, 1868–1919*. New York: Holt.

―――. 1979. *When Harlem Was in Vogue*. New York: Knopf.

Lieb, Sandra. 1981. *Mother of the Blues: A Study of Ma Rainey*. Amherst: University of Massachusetts Press.

Locke, Alain. 1968. *The New Negro: An Interpretation*. New York: Arno.

Lomax, Alan. 1993. *Mister Jelly Roll: The Fortunes of Jelly Roll Morton, New Orleans Creole and "Inventor of Jazz."* Berkeley: University of California Press.

Lord, Tom. 1992. *The Jazz Discography*. West Vancouver: Lord Music Reference.

―――. 1976. *Clarence Williams*. Chigwell, UK: Storyville.

Lyons, Leonard. 1983. *The Great Jazz Pianists: Speaking of Their Lives and Music*. New York: Da Capo.

Lyttleton, Humphrey. 1978. *The Best of Jazz: Basin Street to Harlem*. New York: Taplinger.

Magee, Jeff. 2006. "'Everybody Step': Irving Berlin, Jazz, and Broadway in the 1920s." *Journal of the American Musicological Society* 59: 698–715.

―――. 2005. *The Uncrowned King of Swing: Fletcher Henderson and Big Band Jazz*. New York: Oxford University Press.

―――. 1995. "Revisiting Fletcher Henderson's 'Copenhagen.'" *Journal of the American Musicological Society* 48: 42–66.

―――. 1992. "The Music of Fletcher Henderson and His Orchestra in the 1920s." Ph.D. diss., University of Michigan.

Mailer, Norman. 1970. *The White Negro*. San Francisco: City Lights Books.

Major, Clarence. 1994. *Juba to Jive: The Dictionary of African-American Slang*. New York: Viking.

Manone, Wingy, and Paul Vandervoort II. 1948. *Trumpet on the Wing*. Garden City, NY: Doubleday.

Marshall, Kaiser. 1977. "When Armstrong Came to New York" (originally published 1943). In Art Hodes and Chadwick Hansen, *Selections from the Gutter: Jazz Portraits from "The Jazz Record."* Berkeley: University of California Press. Pp. 83–85.

McCarthy, Albert. 1978. "Louis Armstrong." In Stanley Green, ed., *Kings of Jazz*. New York: A. S. Barnes. Pp. 9–39.

McCracken, Allison. 2000. "Real Men Don't Sing: Crooning and American Culture, 1928–1933." Ph.D. diss., University of Iowa.

———. 1999. "'God's Gift to Us Girls': Crooning, Gender, and the Re-creation of American Popular Song, 1928–1933. *American Music* 17: 365–95.

Mezzrow, Milton "Mezz," and Bernard Wolfe. 1946. *Really the Blues*. New York: Random House.

Miller, Mark. 2007. *High Hat, Trumpet and Rhythm: The Life and Music of Valaida Snow*. Toronto: Mercury.

———. 2005. *Some Hustling This! Taking Jazz to the World, 1914–1929*. Toronto: Mercury.

Miller, Paul Eduard. 1946. "Thirty Years of Chicago Jazz." In Miller, ed., *Esquire's 1946 Jazz Book*. New York: A. S. Barnes. Pp. 1–13.

Millstein, Gilbert. N.d. "Africa Harks to Satch's Horn." Hogan Jazz Archive, vertical file.

Moore, Fred. 1945. "King Oliver's Last Tour." *Jazz Record* 3 (April): 10–12.

Moore, MacDonald Smith. 1985. *Yankee Blues: Musical Culture and American Identity*. Bloomington: Indiana University Press.

Morgenstern, Dan. 2006. Preface to liner notes for *King Oliver Off the Record: The Complete 1923 Jazz Band Recordings*. Champaign, IL: Archeophone Records.

———. 2004. *Living with Jazz*. New York: Pantheon.

———. 1985. "The Big Band Years." *Village Voice* (Aug. 27): 70.

———. 1978. Liner notes for *Souvenirs of Hot Chocolates*. Washington, DC: Smithsonian Institution.

———. 1965. "Yesterday, Today, and Tomorrow: An Interview with Louis Armstrong." *Down Beat* (July 15): 15–18.

Morton, Jelly Roll. 2005. *Jelly Roll Morton: The Complete Library of Congress Recordings by Alan Lomax*. John Szwed, ed. Cambridge: Rounder Records.

———. 1994. "I Discovered Jazz in 1902." In Ralph de Toledano, ed., *Frontiers of Jazz*, 3rd ed. Gretna, LA: Pelican. Pp. 100–103.

Moton, Robert Russa. 1929. *What the Negro Thinks*. Garden City, NY: Doubleday.

Murray, Albert. 1981. "Speaking Out on Armstrong." *Notes* (July–August): 2–5.

———. 1976. *Stompin' the Blues*. New York: McGraw-Hill.

Oliver, Paul. 1970. *Savannah Syncopators: African Retentions in the Blues*. New York: Stein and Day.

O'Meally, Robert G. 2004. "Checking Our Balances: Louis Armstrong, Ralph Ellison, and Betty Boop." In Robert G. O'Meally, Brent Hayes Edward, and Farah Jasmine Griffin, eds., *Uptown Conversation: The New Jazz Studies*. New York: Columbia University Press. Pp. 278–96.

———. 2003. "Checking Our Balances: Ellison on Armstrong's Humor." *Boundary 2* (30.2): 115–36.

Ory, Kid. 1950a. "Louis Was Just a Little Kid in Knee Pants; Ory." As told to Nesuhi Ertegun. *Down Beat* (July 14): pagination cut off.

———. 1950b. "The Hot Five Sessions." As told to Lester Koenig. *Record Changer* 9, nos. 6–7 (July–August): 17, 45.

Osgood, Henry O. 1926. *So This Is Jazz*. Boston: Little, Brown.

Pepper, Art, and Laurie Pepper. 1979. *Straight Life*. New York: Schirmer Books.

Peretti, Burton. 1992. *The Creation of Jazz: Music, Race, and Culture in Urban America*. Urbana: University of Illinois Press.

Peterson, Bernard L., Jr. 1993. *A Century of Musicals in Black and White: An Encyclopedia of Musical Stage Works by, About, or Involving African Amerians*. Westport, CT: Greenwood.

Pleasants, Henry. 1974. *The Great American Popular Singers*. New York: Simon and Schuster.

Pond, Steven. 2005. *Head Hunters: The Making of Jazz's First Platinum Album*. Ann Arbor: University of Michigan Press.

Raeburn, Bruce Boyd, Jr. 2004. "Louis and Women." *Gambit Weekly* 25 (Sept. 7): 9–12, 14.

Ramsey, Frederic, Jr. 1946. "Going Down State Street: Lincoln Gardens and Friar's Inn Set the Stage for Chicago Jazz." In George S. Rosenthal and Frank Zachary, eds., *Jazzways*. New York: Greenberg. Pp. 22–34.

———. 1939. *Jazzmen*. New York: Harcourt.

Randle, William, Jr. 1977. "Black Entertainers on Radio, 1920–1930." *Black Perspective in Music* 5, no. 1: 67–74.

Reeves, Edward. 1961. "Chicago in the Twenties (II)." *Jazz Journal* 14, no. 5 (May): 8–10.

Rogers, J. A. 1968. "Jazz at Home." In Alain Locke, ed., *The New Negro: An Interpretation*. With a new introduction by Allan H. Spear. New York: Johnson. Pp. 216–25.

Royal, Marshal, with Claire Gordon. 1996. *Jazz Survivor*. New York: Cassell.

Russell, William. 1999. *"Oh, Mister Jelly": A Jelly Roll Morton Scrapbook*. Copenhagen: JazzMedia.

———. 1994. *New Orleans Style*. Compiled and edited by Barry Martyn and Mike Hazeldine. New Orleans: Jazzology.

Sager, David. 2009. "Louis Armstrong, Bunk Johnson, and Jules Levy: The Art of 'Tonation.'" In Howard T. Weiner, ed., *Early Twentieth-Century Brass Idioms: Art, Jazz, and Other Popular Traditions*. Lanham, MD: Scarecrow. Pp. 143–54.

———. 2006. Liner notes for *King Oliver Off the Record: The Complete 1923 Jazz Band Recordings*. Champaign, IL: Archeophone Records.

Sandke, Randy, et al. 2000. *Tight Like This*. Composed by Langston Curl, edited by David N. Baker, transcribed by Randy Sandke. *Essential Jazz Editions,* Set 2*: Louis Armstrong, 1926–1929.* Miami: Warner Brothers.

Sanjek, Russell. 1983. *From Print to Plastic: Publishing and Promoting America's Popular Music (1900–1980).* ISAM Monographs, no. 20. Brooklyn: Institute for Studies in American Music.

Saul, Scott. 2003. *Freedom Is and Freedom Ain't.* Cambridge: Harvard University Press.

Savran, David. 2009. *Highbrow-Lowdown: Theater, Jazz, and the Making of the New Middle Class.* Ann Arbor: University of Michigan Press.

Schuller, Gunther. 1989. *The Swing Era: The Development of Jazz, 1930–1945.* New York: Oxford University Press.

———. 1968. *Early Jazz: Its Roots and Musical Development.* New York: Oxford University Press.

Seldes, Gilbert. 1957. *The Seven Lively Arts.* New York: Sagamore.

Sengstock, Charles. 2000. *Jazz Music in Chicago's Early South-Side Theaters.* Northbrook: Canterbury.

Shapiro, Nat, and Nat Hentoff. 1979. *The Jazz Makers: Essays on the Greats of Jazz.* New York: Da Capo.

———. 1955. *Hear Me Talkin' to Ya: The Story of Jazz as Told by the Men Who Made It.* New York: Dover.

Shaw, Charles Green. 1931. *Nightlife.* New York: John Day.

Shih, Hsio Wen. 1959. "The Spread of Jazz and the Big Bands." In Nat Hentoff and Albert J. McCarthy, eds., *Jazz.* New York: Rinehart. Pp. 178–210.

Singer, Barry. 1992. *Black and Blue: The Life and Lyrics of Andy Razaf.* New York: Schirmer Books.

Singleton, Zutty. 1950. "Zutty First Saw Louis in Amateur Tent Show." *Down Beat* (July 14): 6.

Smith, (Ducongé) Ada, with James Haskins. 1983. *Bricktop.* New York: Atheneum.

Smith, Jeremy. 2008. "Sound, Mediation, and Meaning in Miles Davis's *A Tribute to Jack Johnson.*" Ph.D. diss., Duke University.

Smith, Willie "The Lion," with George Hoefer. 1964. *Music on My Mind: The Memoirs of an American Pianist.* New York: Doubleday.

Snyder, Robert W. 1989. *Voice of the City: Vaudeville and Popular Culture in New York.* New York: Oxford University Press.

Souchon, Edmond. 1964. "King Oliver: A Very Personal Memoir." In Martin Williams, ed., *Jazz Panorama: From the Pages of the Jazz Review.* New York: Macmillan. Pp. 21–30. Repr. in Robert Gottlieb, ed., *Reading Jazz: A Gathering of Autobiography, Reportage, and Criticism from 1919 to Now.* New York: Pantheon, 1996. Pp. 339–46.

Spivey, Donald. 1984. *Union and the Black Musician: The Narrative of William*

*Everett Samuels and Chicago Local 208.* Lanham, MD: University Press of America.

Stearns, Marshall, and Jean Stearns. 1994. *Jazz Dance: The Story of American Vernacular Dance.* New York: Da Capo.

Stein, Charles W. 1984. *American Vaudeville as Seen by Its Contemporaries.* New York: Knopf.

Steiner, John. 1959. "Chicago." In Nat Hentoff and Albert J. McCarthy, eds., *Jazz.* New York: Rinehart. Pp. 139–69.

Stewart, Rex. 1991. *Boy Meets Horn.* Ann Arbor: University of Michigan Press.

———. 1972. *Jazz Masters of the Thirties.* New York: Macmillan.

Stratemann, Klaus. 1996. *Louis Armstrong on the Screen.* Copenhagen: JazzMedia.

Sudhalter, Richard M. 2002. *Stardust Melody: The Life and Music of Hoagy Carmichael.* New York: Oxford University Press.

———. 1999. *Lost Chords: White Musicians and Their Contribution to Jazz, 1915–1945.* New York: Oxford University Press.

Sudhalter, Richard M., and Philip R. Evans, with William Dean-Myatt. 1974. *Bix: Man and Legend.* New Rochelle, NY: Arlington House.

Sylvester, Robert. 1956. *No Cover Charge: A Backward Look at the Night Clubs.* New York: Dial.

Szwed, John. 2005. Booklet accompanying *Jelly Roll Morton: The Complete Library of Congress Recordings by Alan Lomax.* Cambridge: Rounder Records.

Taylor, Frank C., with Gerald Cool. 1987. *Alberta Hunter: A Celebration in Blues.* New York: McGraw-Hill.

Taylor, Jeffrey James. 1998. "Louis Armstrong, Earl Hines, and 'Weather Bird.'" *Musical Quarterly* 82, no. 1: 1–40.

———. 1993. "Earl Hines and Black Jazz Piano in Chicago, 1923–1928." Ph.D. diss., University of Michigan.

———. 1992. "Earl Hines's Piano Style in the 1920s: A Historical and Analytical Perspective." *Black Music Research Journal* 12: 57–77.

Taylor, Timothy D. 2002. "Music and the Rise of Radio in 1920s America: Technological Imperialism, Socialization, and the Transformation of Intimacy." *Historical Journal of Film, Radio and Television* 22, no. 4: 425–44.

Teachout, Terry. 2009. *Pops: A Life of Louis Armstrong.* Boston: Houghton Mifflin Harcourt.

Thompson, Kay C. 1950. "Louis and the Waif's Home." *Record Changer* 9, nos. 6–7 (July–August): 8, 43.

Thompson, Robert Farris. 1983. *Flash of the Spirit: African and Afro-American Art and Philosophy.* New York: Random House.

Tichenor. George. 1930. "Colored Lines." *Theatre Arts Monthly* (June 14): 485–90.

Torgovnick, Marianna. 1990. *Gone Primitive: Savage Intellects, Modern Lives.* Chicago: University of Chicago Press.

Trail, Sinclair. 1971. "Earl Hines and Marva Josie: An Informal Chat with Sinclair Trail." *Jazz Journal* (May): 3.

Travis, Dempsey. 1981. *An Autobiography of Black Chicago.* Chicago: Urban Research Institute.

Tucker, Mark. 1991. *Ellington: The Early Years.* Urbana: University of Illinois Press.

Tucker, Sherri. 2000. *Swing Shift: All-Girl Bands of the 1940s.* Durham, NC: Duke University Press.

Villetard, Jean François. 1984. *Coleman Hawkins.* The Netherlands: Micrography.

Vincent, Ted. 1995. *Keep Cool: The Black Activists Who Built the Jazz Age.* London: Pluto.

Von Eschen, Penny. 2004. *Satchmo Blows Up the World: Jazz Ambassadors Play the Cold War.* Cambridge: Harvard University Press.

Wald, Elijah. 2007. "Louis Armstrong Loves Guy Lombardo." *Jazz Research Journal* 1, no. 1: 129–45.

Waller, Irle. 1965. *Chicago Uncensored: Firsthand Stories About the Al Capone Era.* New York: Exposition.

Walser, Rob. 1999. *Keeping Time: Readings in Jazz History.* New York: Oxford University Press.

Wang, Richard. 1988. "Researching the New Orleans–Chicago Jazz Connection: Tools and Methods." *Black Music Research Journal* 8, no. 1: 101–12.

Washington, Booker T. 1907. *Up from Slavery: An Autobiography.* New York: Doubleday.

Waters, Benny. 1985. *The Key to a Jazzy Life.* Toulouse: Imprimerie des arts graphiques.

Waters, Ethel, with Charles Samuels. 1951. *His Eye Is on the Sparrow: An Autobiography.* New York: Doubleday.

Wettling, George. 1945. "Baby Dodds Knew How." *Jazz Record* 3 (February): 5.

Willems, Jos. 2006. *All of Me: The Complete Discography of Louis Armstrong. Studies in Jazz*, no. 51. Lanham, MD: Scarecrow.

Williams, Martin. 1961. *King Oliver.* New York: A. S. Barnes.

Williams, Martin, ed. 1979. *Jazz Panorama: From the Pages of the Jazz Review.* New York: Da Capo.

Williamson, Ken. 1960. *This Is Jazz.* London: Newnes.

Wills, Gary. 1971. "Black and Beautiful: Homage to 'Satchmo.'" *Virginian-Pilot*, n.d., n.p. (Summer; photocopy on file at Hogan Jazz Archive, Louis Armstrong vertical file).

Wilmer, Valerie. 1977. *As Serious as Your Life: The Story of the New Jazz.* London: Allison and Busby.

Wilson, Edmund. 1958. *The American Earthquake: A Documentary of the Twenties and Thirties*. Garden City, NY: Doubleday.

Wilson, John. 1968. "Miss Lil Armstrong Reminisces." *New York Times* (Dec. 10): 54.

Wilson, Olly. 1978. "The Significance of the Relationship Between Afro-American Music and West African Music." *Black Perspective in Music* 1: 1–21.

Wilson, Teddy. 2001. With Arie Ligthart and Humphrey van Loo. *Teddy Wilson Talks Jazz*. New York: Continuum.

Winer, Deborah Grace. 1997. *On the Sunny Side of the Street: The Life and Lyrics of Dorothy Fields*. New York: Schirmer Books.

Woll, Allen. 1989. *Black Musical Theatre: From* Coontown *to* Dreamgirls. Baton Rouge: Louisiana State University Press.

Wood, Junius B. 1916. *The Negro in Chicago*. Chicago: Chicago Daily News.

Wright, Laurie, with Walter C. Allen and Brian A. L. Rust. 1987. *King Oliver.* Chigwell, UK: Storyville.

Wright, Richard. 1998. *Black Boy (American Hunger): A Record of Childhood and Youth*. Introduction by Jerry W. Ward Jr. N.p.: HarperCollins Perennial Classics.

Zwicky, Theo. 1970. "Louis and Some West Coast Friends." *Storyville* (June–July): 176–84.

# ENDNOTES

[1] The impact of Armstrong's physical appearance should never be underestimated. Charlie Holmes, an African-American saxophonist who first played with him in 1929, first heard him in Boston in 1925, when the Fletcher Henderson Orchestra visited. Holmes remembered (Holmes IJS) that at that time (he was fifteen years old) he couldn't appreciate Armstrong because "he didn't look nice." The teenage Lionel Hampton had a similar impression (Hampton 1993, 24): "I forgot all about how he looked when I heard him play."

[2] The notoriously slippery designation "black and tan" meant different things in different cities and venues at different times. What is often missed in historical accounts is the fact that, from a white point of view, it was easy to turn a black venue into a black and tan just by showing up.

[3] Garvin Bushell (1988, 36): "I never saw a white person in a TOBA theater."

[4] Taylor 1987, 36. Hunter (Hunter IJS 1976–77) also gave this account: "He played that thing, 'Jerusalem, Jerusalem, sing for the night is over.' He played the lead and somebody else would play the other part of it you know. It would be three or four of them playing. And what a beautiful thing it would be . . . when Louie was there, then just he and Louie would play and it would be the most beautiful thing you ever heard in your life." Ed Garland (WRC 1958) played *Jerusalem* on his bass. Humphrey Lyttelton (Lyttelton 1978, 150) observed another important usage of *Holy City* in the 1920s: Bubber Miley's minor-mode transformation of the theme in Ellington's *Black and Tan Fantasy*.

[5] When Dodds was asked to fill out a questionnaire (Dodds, Johnny WRC n.d.) that included the question, "What musician influenced you the most?" he answered simply, "Sidney Bechet."

[6] Armstrong's solo on *Chimes Blues*, however, was on Richard M. Jones's mind when he entered the OKeh recording studios on Nov. 6, 1925, with clarinetist Albert Nicholas and banjoist Johnny St. Cyr. Jones's *29th and Dearborn* takes Armstrong's melody as a point of departure; and, as if to make the connection crystal clear, Jones follows it with a spin on the theme from *Holy City*. It cannot have been mere coincidence that Armstrong was in transit from New York City to Chicago at this very moment, having been away for a little over a year; he recorded with Jones three days later, on Nov. 9. A recording for "Hociel

489

Thomas, accompanied by Louis Armstrong's Jazz Four" followed on Nov. 11, and the inaugural recording of Louis Armstrong and His Hot Five on Nov. 12.

[7] Armstrong composed the tune *Weather Bird Rag* on the boats, and it includes a diminished chord, which deviates from the standard chordal formations of major and minor. Clearly he understood advanced chords like this before his arrival in Chicago. On Petit's use of diminished chords and his influence on Armstrong, see Brothers 2006, 266; on *Weather Bird Rag*, see also Armstrong LAHA 1960; Brothers 2006, 254. *Weather Bird Rag* is transcribed with some errors in Gushee 1998, 296, with useful analytical observations. A facsimile of the lead sheet is in Chevan 1997, 486. The diminished chord is placed on the second staff from the bottom, page 1; it is difficult to see in this photograph, but it reads C-sharp, B-flat, G, E-natural. I am grateful to David Sager for supplying me with a photocopy of the lead sheet. *Dipper Mouth Blues* includes prominent diminished chords, harmonized by Armstrong and Oliver, in the introduction; see the transcription by Harker 2003, 145. Gushee suggests that the lead sheet was notated by Armstrong, but my own analysis of handwriting in many lead sheets from this period leads me to conclude that Hardin notated it.

[8] The nexus of sheet music and phonograph record for *Dipper Mouth Blues*, both generated in April 1923, is particularly rich. Oliver's recorded solo for this piece quickly became his most famous one, and it remains so today. Lillian copied the lead sheet—which did not include Oliver's solo—that was sent in for copyright, and Oliver added his name in the upper-right-hand corner. That it was Armstrong and not Oliver who composed the music documented by the lead sheet is suggested by three pieces of evidence: first, Dipper Mouth was his nickname at this time; second, Bill Johnson, the bass player in Oliver's band, reported (Johnson WRC ca. 1938) that Armstrong was the composer; third, in 1925, in New York City, Armstrong pulled out a "little book" of music manuscripts and suggested that Fletcher Henderson's arranger, Don Redman, work one of them up. Redman chose *Dipper Mouth Blues*; it makes sense for him to be carrying a book of tunes he had composed. Does the lead sheet document "his rendition of the blues" that he played on his first night in Chicago, in August 1922? There is no way to know, of course, but a piece entitled *Dipper Mouth Blues* must be a likely candidate. Armstrong's notated tune and Oliver's famous solo are two different types of melody: one is a lead, the other a blues. Neither was an improvisation, both were composed by ear, but one was conceived for and documented by a lead sheet, while the other could only be documented on a recording. It would never have crossed Oliver's mind to notate his famous solo. It belongs to the performer-centered tradition of New Orleans, the highest goal of which was not copyright but the crown of king at places like Lincoln Gardens.

[9] Integration was not, of course, widely appreciated, and there are indications that authorities found excuses to close places like this down. The *Chicago Daily Tribune* reported (May 9, 1923, p. 11) that six black-and-tan cafés, including the Fiume, were being closed down for, among other things, "soul kisses between colored men and white women."

[10] *Tears*, as recorded in October 1923 by OKeh, is a classic case of the lead being too faint and not dominating the performance. This leads Brooks (2002, 59) to parse the form with trombone playing lead in the verse. But the lead sheet makes it clear that Oliver has the lead for the entire performance. Armstrong's

breaks are transcribed in Harker (2011, 30). A touching moment, late in life, is documented in Armstrong 2008, a CD that preserves Armstrong playing, in his home, the lead for *Tears* while the 1923 recording plays on his phonograph. He pauses for his twenty-two-year-old self to play the breaks, an homage to the creativity of that moment, and perhaps also a gesture of pride in having been the composer of the tune.

[11] See, for an example of the confusion, Howard Spring's analysis (Spring 1997) of trends in the 1920s. There are some useful observations here about the relationship between musical styles and dance styles, but Spring exaggerates the impact of recording technology when he says (p. 184) that "the appearance of electrical recording in the mid-1920s provided the conditions for the instrumentation and playing techniques that led to swing." He also misses the significance of the flat 4/4 in New Orleans (except for bass playing), maintained to various degrees by bass, piano, guitar/banjo, and sometimes drums. For me, the trend toward "more drive and forward propulsion" over the course of the 1920s, in both white and black dance-band music, is the result of spreading impact of the New Orleanians in specific and the African-American vernacular in general; "more drive and forward propulsion" could be a focus for analysis of so much of what happened in New Orleans, from sharp initial attack to swing triplets to collective improvisation to flat 4/4. Spring also exaggerates the role of the Lindy Hop. I prefer the analysis, suggested but not fully developed in the article, that the impact of horizontally oriented African-American vernacular dancing (in contrast with vertically oriented Euro-American dancing) grew over the course of the decade, in a development parallel to music, with the Lindy Hop being one point of focus in this long-term trend. But of course the problem with advancing this inquiry is the same problem we have for studying dance throughout the period covered in this book: there is very little video documentation. On New Orleans use of flat 4/4, see Brothers 2005, 43, 227, 245, and 285–86; also Lawrence Gushee 1979, 41. An undated and unidentified report on the Dickerson band playing at the Sunset Café (Scrapbook 83, LAHM), references "Louis (Rubberlip) Armstrong" playing there after his gig at the Vendome. The writer then makes an interesting observation about 4/4 time: "And just to check up, so to speak, I have made it a point to notice the increase in popularity recently of the 4/4 time with that peculiar staccato beat right on the nose. You can find the intent, if not the real thing, in nearly every place around town now and due to nothing else than the style that Carroll Dickerson and his Orchestra have originated."

[12] Condon 1947, 111; Bushell 1988, 26. Some recordings from the mid- and late 1920s document flat 4/4 slap-picking on the bass, and there is also some indirect evidence: for example, when Bill Johnson picks up his banjo to accompany a hot chorus by Johnny Dodds in *Canal Street Blues*, he seems to reproduce the muscular effect of his bass at Lincoln Gardens on the smaller instrument. One observer claimed that flat 4/4 drumming entered New Orleans dance bands during the late 1910s through the initiative of James "Red Happy" Bolton, a childhood friend of Armstrong's. Bolton, like Louis, grew up immersed in the African-American vernacular; he was good at scat singing, for example, and he probably influenced Armstrong in this. Described as a "sensational" drummer, Red Happy is said to have first brought the flat 4/4 into a dance hall during a

blues piece. Another friend of Armstrong's, "Black Benny" Williams, may have been the first to play four-beat drumming in street bands. Guitarist Bud Scott, inspired by hand clapping in church, claimed to have been the first to use flat 4/4 on his instrument in dance bands. Russell 1994, 51, 58, 67, 164; Paul Barbarin HJA 1957; Russell 1994, 58; Moore HJA 1959; Shapiro and Hentoff 1955, 37.

13 According to Michael Harris (1992, 79 and 84), Dorsey registered *Riverside Blues* for copyright on July 27, 1923; the March 1, 1924 (pt. 1, p. 7), edition of the *Defender* reports that he "made the special arrangement of 'Riverside Blues' for King Oliver's Creole Jazz Band when that organization recorded that number for the Paramount people." Since the two recorded versions of the piece, one made for OKeh on Oct. 26 and the other made for Paramount on Dec. 24, are very similar, it seems unlikely that Dorsey's arrangement was made specifically for the Paramount recording.

14 It seems that Oliver plays this solo in December (with Armstrong staying under with precision and strength), while Armstrong took the solo on the Oct. 26 recording. According to Chevan (1997, 500) a copyright deposit for this piece was filed on July 27, 1923, listing only Dorsey as composer.

15 At different places in this book I will draw attention to what is known as "harmonic rhythm," which brings the discussion to a technical level that is, nevertheless, of vital importance for understanding Armstrong's music. Harmonic rhythm is the rate of change of chords, and it forms a layer of the fixed foundation. In this repertory chords usually change at one- or two-measure intervals. Phrase lengths usually flow in four- and eight-measure groups, defined by harmonic arrivals. Popular music in 1923 almost always meant this kind of rigidly binary pattern, which made it easy to follow and dance to. Melodies unfold in eight-bar phrases, commonly built out of two four-bar subphrases, which are commonly built out of two-bar units, which are, in turn, built out of one-plus-one combinations. Rigid patterns like this, designed for instant comprehension, made further exploration of the fixed and variable model possible for musicians like Armstrong.

16 Could "frog-mouthed" have been a reference to the piece entitled *Froggie Moore*, which the band recorded in mid-June, featuring a solo by Armstrong?

17 The current clerk of the Circuit Court, Cook County, Illinois, has featured Armstrong's application for a divorce and the resultant hearings as a celebrity item on the website www.cookcountyclerkofcourt.org. At the November 1923 hearing, Armstrong stated his address as 508 East 42nd Street. He overstated his time in Chicago, claiming he had been living there three years, and laughably stated his occupation as machine mechanic. On Feb. 11, 1924, Daisy filed a complaint against the divorce and challenged that statement, asserting that Armstrong was actually earning "large sums of money" as a musician employed by the Sunset Cabaret. That early date for a connection with the Sunset Cabaret would be an addition to the Armstrong biography, but it seems more likely that she or her attorney confused the venue with Lincoln Gardens.

18 According to Preston Jackson (Jackson 2005, 78), Bobby Williams "was playing a lot of horn and many people were of the opinion that he was going to catch up with Louis Armstrong, but he died young—it was said that he was poisoned by his wife."

19 Cheatham IJS 1976; Vincent 1995, 74; McHargue HJA n.d. An interesting (and

pejorative) juxtaposition of chop suey with jazz is offered by a writer for the *Amsterdam News* in the Oct. 13, 1926, issue (p. 11): "[Jazz] is probably here to stay, in order to appease the exotic period which recreation seems to demand nowadays. It is the 'chop suey' of the musical world—but the world seems to want more and more of it, sad though that fact be."

[20] Jones WRC 1938. This source is part of a collection of notes made by William Russell, who was interviewing for his book *Jazzmen*. Hoagy Carmichael's report that Louis took "lessons from a German down at Kimball Hall, who showed Louis all the European cornet clutches" (1999a, 203) is often cited, along with the colorful assertion that "Lil worked the fat off Louis." But Carmichael is clearly dependent on *Jazzmen* for this and other content in *Sometimes I Wonder*; he is also acquainted, it is clear, with Lil Hardin's *Satchmo and Me*, issued on Riverside Records (1963). This is a common problem for historians: what looks like independent verification is actually derivative from a published source. In any event, Russell's notes from the 1938 interview with Richard M. Jones identify a German teacher at Kimball Hall, and there is no good reason to doubt Jones as a witness.

[21] The lead sheet for *Cornet Chop Suey* demonstrates that Armstrong does not yet control rhythmic notation fully. Measure 1 of the chorus has an extra beat notated, and the mistake is repeated every time this gesture comes around. The likely solution is that the first quarter-note should not be dotted and the last rest should be an eighth-rest. On several occasions Armstrong uses a V-shaped rest uncertainly, sometimes as an eighth-rest and sometimes as a quarter-rest. The first strain of the piece also shows mistakes in dotted half-notes.

[22] Here is the sequence of tunes that were created at least partially by Armstrong and filed for copyright in 1923 and January 1924 (this information derived from Chevan 1997, 495–97), along with identification of the handwriting, based on my own analysis of these documents and others. The most telltale sign is the treble clef, but there are a set of scribal patterns that are consistently presented (this analysis differs from that offered by Gushee 1998, 297): *Weather Bird Rag*, April 14, 1923, notated by Lillian; *Dipper Mouth Blues*, May 21, 1923, notated by Lillian; *When You Leave Me Alone to Pine*, Aug. 6, 1923, notated by Lillian; *Tears*, Oct. 20, 1923, notated by Lillian; *Coal Cart Blues*, Nov. 3, 1923, notated by Lillian; *Drop That Sack*, Dec. 8, 1923, notated by Louis; *I Am in the Barrel, Who Don't Like It?*, Dec. 8, 1923, notated by Louis; *Papa What You Are Trying to Do to Me I've Been Doing It for Years*, Dec. 13, 1923, notated by Louis; *Cornet Chop Suey*, Jan. 18, 1923, notated by Louis. It is significant that three of the last four pieces, all notated by Louis, were co-composed with people other than Lillian, with the last composed only by him, providing another possible explanation for his appearance in the notated record at this time. The notation of *Weather Bird Rag* and *Dipper Mouth Blues* by Lillian is telling, since she was not the co-composer of either one.

[23] Chevan 1999, 299, has parallel transcriptions of the manuscript and the recorded solo. See also Gushee 1998, 298, on the comparison between lead sheet and recorded performance. In the third and final statement of the chorus, Armstrong does deliberately vary each statement of the core melodic gesture, in traditional jazz variation style—or "ragging the tune," as they said in early New Orleans.

24 Arthur Lange (1926, 207–8) describes a popular-song form that resembles Armstrong's: "The average popular song consists of two strains, viz. 'verse' and 'chorus.' Sometimes a third strain is added, commonly known as 'patter,' which if musically interesting, may be incorporated in a dance arrangement. Verses vary in length, and are from sixteen to thirty-two measures long, whereas, the average chorus is thirty-two measures long." Lange also explains (p. 209) that "the patter may take the place of the third chorus"—the third statement of the chorus in a repetition scheme—and (p. 211) that "the third chorus may be properly termed 'arranger's chorus,' because, in this chorus, the arranger may take any liberty, and let his imagination take vent." There are many references to patter in black newspapers, most of them associated with comedy, dance, and song without being too specific. Exceptions include this from the *Afro-American*, Nov. 19, 1927, p. 8: "Mike Bow and Willie Toosweet handle the blackface comedy in good style, using an unusually clean brand of patter, nothing unusual however for a Whitman show"; and this from the *Pittsburgh Courier*, Oct. 12, 1929, p. B3: "With the advent of the 'talkies' a new vocabulary has come into the picture studios and new terms are coined daily . . . some of the more picturesque terms follow: Patter Blender—one who writes the ad-lib talk or patter which gets the actor into his song."

25 I have benefited from the inquiries of John Howland and Jeffrey Magee into this issue. My aim is to go beyond Howland's conclusion (2009, 51) that "in this era, *jazz* was a catchall term that simultaneously referenced the syncopated music of Tin Pan Alley, Broadway, 'sweet' dance bands, symphonic jazz orchestras, and 'hot' jazz (black or white). This inclusive definition of jazz was part of a variety entertainment culture that regularly encouraged stylistic confluences." Certainly it is difficult to tease out the precise cultural-racial logic that shapes various usages, which are more or less vague, more or less general, more or less informed, and more or less articulate. But I am convinced that the deep assumptions of the period included such logic, even when masked by more "inclusive" usages (which are often invoked, especially in nonmusicological literature).

26 The close dates also indicate availability of a stock arrangement, an important topic for future research, as demonstrated by Magee (1995). Here are some recordings by white bands and singers that are close in time to those by Henderson: Jones and Whiteman: *Tell Me Dreamy Eyes*; Benson: *My Rose Marie*; Benson Orchestra, Bernie Cummins: *Words*; Benson, Charlie Fry and His Million-Dollar Pier Orchestra, International Dance Orchestra, Al Turk's Princess Orchestra, Kitty Irvin, Russo and Fiorito's Oriole Orchestra, Varsity Eight, California Ramblers, Five Birmingham Babies, Arkansas Travelers: *Copenhagen*; Jones: *One of These Days*; Lopez: *The Meanest Kind of Blues*; Wolverines, Tennessee Tooters, Ralph Williams and His Rainbow Orchestra, Frank Quartell and His Little Club Orchestra, Lampe's Orchestra from the Trianon Ballroom, Dave Harmon and His Orchestra: *Prince of Wails*; Ray Miller Orchestra, Whiteman, Bailey's Lucky Seven, Arkansas Travellers, Marion Harris, California Ramblers, Lewis James, Sam Lanin: *I'll See You in My Dreams*; Frank Crumit, George Olsen and His Music, Sam Lanin: *Why Couldn't It Be Poor Little Me*; Red McKenzie and His Mound City Blues Blowers: *Play Me Slow*; Whiteman, Ben Selvin, Bailey's Lucky Seven, Lucille Hegamin and Her Dixie Daisies: *Alabamy Bound*; California Ramblers, Ben Selvin, Isham Jones, Harry Reeser: *Swanee But-*

*terfly*; Bernie Cummins: *Poplar Street Blues*; Anthony Parenti's Famous Melody Boys: *Twelfth Street Blues*; Lopez, Lee Morse: *Me Neenyah*; Jimmy Joy's Baker Hotel Orchestra: *Memphis Bound*; Jack Stillman's Oriole Orchestra: *When You Do What You Do*; Irving Post, Goofus Five, Ray Miller: *I'll Take Her Back If She Wants to Come Back*; Ted Lewis, Carlyle Stevenson's Bon Ton Orchestra, California Ramblers, Eddie Peabody, Whiteman, Reeser: *I Miss My Swiss*; Coon Sanders Nighthorse Orchestra, California Ramblers: *Alone at Last*. Information gathered from Lord 1992, Magee 1995, Pro-Quest database searches, and www .redhotjazz.com.

27 The information that Beiderbecke made the head arrangements comes from Mezz Mezzrow (1946, 79, 81), who was on the scene. Beiderbecke's participation as arranger and soloist in *Copenhagen* adds another layer of irony to the story, with Armstrong essentially receiving on the Henderson bandstand a creative accomplishment from the cornetist who would become his most successful white follower.

28 *Variety* noted the sudden "vogue in dance numbers for the hot order" in a November column (Magee 1995, 55). How much Henderson was following the lead of his white competitors is indicated in a *Variety* review (Oct. 8, 1924, p. 38) of the reopening of the Roseland, featuring Sam Lanin: "Sam Lanin, the Roseland ballroom veteran, has assembled a new dance orchestra that is a revelation to his contemporaries. For dance rhythm it need doff the mythical chapeau to nobody. Lanin for many seasons has enjoyed an enviable reputation as an orchestra leader with a band capable of producing ultra dance music. This year he has outdone himself. Having gone far and wide for his material, the western additions particularly bring to New York that rhythmic tempo so favored around Chicago and so little known around these parts." Henderson's "western additions"—Armstrong and Bailey—were clearly designed to outdo Lanin.

29 Based on my listening, Armstrong paraphrases the melody of each piece from his year with Henderson, except *Don't Forget You'll Regret Day by Day*, *My Dream Man*, and *Araby*. In *Why Couldn't It Be Poor Little Me*, however, his references to the tune are very slight. Paraphrase was not a new procedure for him; there are even a few recorded examples from his time with Oliver. See, for example, the transcription and analysis of solos by Armstrong and Oliver for *Froggie Moore* in Harker 2003, 148.

30 My guess is that this "little book" was a collection of *his* tunes, not tunes by Oliver; as I have argued in Chapter 3, Armstrong was probably the composer of *Dipper Mouth Blues*, to which Oliver added his famous solo, thereby making it possible for him to claim joint ownership of the evolving "piece." It seems less likely that Armstrong would have kept a collection of pieces by anyone else, and that he would have offered tunes by others to Redman.

31 It was standard practice for the hot soloist to play not first chair but second or third chair; the logic was to divide up the taxing demands of the respective jobs. In several comments (for example, 1966, 33), Armstrong hinted at his dissatisfaction about not being able to play first chair, that is, carry the lead. Drew 1950, 46; Armstrong 1971, 216; Henderson 1950; Hadlock 1965, 17; Gushee 1998, 300.

32 Henderson 1950a. An early interview made by Bill Russell with Armstrong (Armstrong WRC 1939) that touches on this topic is worth reporting: "Louis

said he started singing with the Henderson band. Used to scat around. I gathered that Henderson didn't give him much of a chance to sing in public. Louis thought some more and then said it was the Vendome theatre where he really began to sing. Used to sing a lot there. Sort of featured his singing. I said 'Louis when did you change from your cornet to trumpet?' He said, that was at the Vendome. The other fellows had those long trumpets and I had that short cornet and it didn't look right. He laughed at remembering that." And this from Armstrong LAHM 1970: "As Fletcher were concerned, singing was out the whole time I was in his band. He wouldn't listen to me sing nothing. All the singing that I did before I joined Fletcher Henderson's band went down the drain the whole time that I was with him."

33 Albertson 2003, 82. It would be wise to avoid making too much out of Smith's preference for Joe Smith over Armstrong, and instead approach it in the light of Doc Cheatham's comment (Cheatham IJS 1976): "We didn't appreciate so much playing with blues singers. . . . Not until Joe Smith, when he came throughout the circuit with Ethel Waters or Bessie Smith, one of those—I have to go back to that, then that's when he played with a plunger you know. He did all of his work with a plunger behind this blues singer. Then the musicians started waking up to see how—how it was a pleasure to play with the blues singers. This was done by Joe Smith. He made it interesting to the musicians to play with them."

34 Lyttelton 1978, 75, including a good analysis of the performance. *St. Louis Blues* is an example of Armstrong's collaborative ability at its finest—in addition to the many examples of collective improvisation, where the collaboration is imbedded in the texture. In most of his blues accompaniments from 1924–25, there was simply not enough preparation to reach this level.

35 *Defender*, Nov. 21, 1925, p. 8. Chicago bandleader Sig Meyer said (CJA n.d., box 86) that Peyton was "officious, talked down to people. 'I'll put my staff on it right away,' he would say, but he was the total 'staff.'" "He was high class and he was high brow," said Milt Hinton (COHP 1971), "he was bourgeois, a black bourgeois musician." Hinton also said that Peyton's musical penmanship was unbelievably neat and looked like printed music (Barker IJS). Further on Peyton, see Kenney 1993, 53–57; Hennessey 1994.

36 The *Broad Ax*, a conservative African-American weekly from Chicago, had an interesting spin on the term "chop suey" in its Sept. 18, 1926, issue (p. 7): "Jazz is a razz of aborted syncopation and instrumentation. . . . Its origins cannot be definitely described. It has no limitations. It is the 'chop suey' of the musical world . . . it is a blessing that Schumann, Mozart and Mendelssohn are not present to hear it, for they would think, indeed, that they had lived in vain." The use of "chop suey" here, as a put-down and as mongrel food that is superficially satisfying but ultimately malnourishing, certainly reflects an awareness of Armstrong's successful piece.

37 Darnell Howard (CJA n.d.), who worked at the Vendome with Armstrong, said that the typical schedule was 7:00 p.m. overture, hot number, and movie, then 10:15 overture, hot number, and movie, then on to the cabaret; see also Samuels COHP 1971. Armstrong wrote (1936, 84) that, after he moved from the Dreamland to the Sunset, he had this work schedule: "I surely began to work hard then, starting in at 7 every night at the Vendome, then going to the Sunset and

working through to 3 or 4 in the morning, rehearsing, planning new arrangements and all of that." Movies probably began at the Vendome at 2:00, with the orchestra starting work at 7:00. Leon Washington (COHP 1971) explained that "there were a lot of pit bands [in theaters]. I mean not all of them were large, but some of them had six pieces, seven like that. And some of the theatres had a piano player that would play in the afternoon until the band got there, and they had very good pianists during this particular period."

38 As Dave Peyton wrote (*Defender*, July 31, 1926, p. 7): "When the orchestra is through with their specialties the house empties considerably. The picture used to be the big card. Now it is the orchestra when it delivers." See also Altman 2004; Anderson 1988; Koszarski 1990.

39 "Our leaders must stop and think what they are doing when they use the phrase 'symphony orchestra.' It is wrong to apply it to dance combinations and small theater orchestras." Dave Peyton, *Defender*, Nov. 21, 1925, p. 6.

40 Armstrong 1966, 33. "Cornet" and "trumpet" continue to be used with almost equal frequency to describe Armstrong's playing throughout the period covered in this book. Armstrong's memorization of a solo from *Cavalleria rusticana* has been associated with New Orleans (Berrett 1992), but I find it highly unlikely that he heard the piece before playing at the Vendome. Certainly, none of the bands he played with up until this point performed it. The idea that New Orleans had a cosmopolitan, southern European musical atmosphere in which opera floated through the air like the scent of magnolia blossoms is highly remote from everything we know about Armstrong's experiences growing up there.

41 Randolph FDC 1973. As Eubie Blake observed (Feather 1976, 73), "In those days Negro musicians weren't even supposed to read music. We had to pretend we couldn't read: then they'd marvel at the way we could play shows, thinking we'd learned the parts by ear." On Armstrong reading music fluently, see also Nicholas HJA 1972; Havens 1992; Wilson 2001, 13; Jackson 2005, 117.

42 Tate hired New Orleanian cornetist Fred Keppard in 1923. But it is not clear that Keppard improvised jazz solos—at least, that kind of solo is not represented in the few recordings Tate made in that year. Ralph Brown (COHP 1971) said that in the beginning Tate did not have get-off (or "break-off") men. Buster Bailey (Russell 1994, 169) noted that Keppard loved to play *I pagliacci*.

43 My references to the magazine *Heebie Jeebies* include a continuous sequence of publications with three different names: *Heebie Jeebies: A Sign of Intelligence*, the *Light and Heebie Jeebies*, and the *Light: America's News Magazine*. I have identified some of the scrapbook clippings as *Heebie Jeebies* based on comparison of fonts and mention of the magazine in the articles. In December 1926, the magazine merged with the *Light* (*Courier*, Nov. 27, 1926, p. 11); by April 1928 the name had changed to the *Light: America's News Magazine*. The Chicago History Museum holds 18 issues of the three titles; one issue is at Yale's Beinecke Library; one issue is at the Missouri Historical Society; and a number of issues are held at the Schomburg Center for Research in Black Culture, New York Public Library. My suggestion that the scrapbooks held at the Louis Armstrong House Museum were compiled by Lillian is based on comparison of handwriting in the margins with lead sheets notated by her in the 1920s. The scrapbooks are extremely fragile. *Heebie Jeebies* circulated outside

of Chicago: references to the magazine pop up in the Norfolk *New Journal and Guide*, the *Baltimore Afro-American*, the *New York Amsterdam News*, and the *Pittsburgh Courier*, so more copies may still turn up. My thanks to Deborah Gillaspie, archivist at the University of Chicago Jazz Collection, for her help with this search. In July 1926 the magazine was sued by bandleader Sammy Stewart, who claimed that a fictional story entitled "Sammy and His Nude Cult" was a thinly veiled reference to him. Stewart lost the suit, which was covered in major African-American newspapers. In the late 1930s Armstrong wrote for another weekly called the *Harlem Tattler*; a few copies are now held at the Institute for Jazz Studies, Newark, N.J.

⁴⁴ Armstrong 1971, 212; Brown COHP 1971. The Vendome may well have included some kind of reduced staged version of the opera, for these were very common at the time (Altman 2004, 380); or there may have been a silent-film version. Armstrong said (Millstein HJA) that he knew the story and "just put it in spade life—colored life—where this guy in the story he fooled around with this man's wife and this cat finally picked up on it and stuck him in the back with a knife or somethin' like that. I could see if it was two colored cats diggin', he mightn't stick him in the back with a knife—he'd scratch him across the behind with a razor."

⁴⁵ My views on Armstrong and opera differ substantially from those advanced by Joshua Berrett (1992), who makes some valuable contributions but errs, in my opinion, in his use of evidence and in his primary conclusions. I would observe the following: (1) Too much is made out of Armstrong's only documented connection to opera in New Orleans—his ownership of a few phonograph discs. I find it unlikely that these purchases reflect a "taste that was formed in part by the environment in which he grew up" (Berrett 1992, 219). Instead, note how few African-American recordings were available for purchase in 1917, and, conversely, how prevalent recordings of arias were. (2) Though it is a marginal point for Berrett's article, it should be noted that the problematic document "Louis Armstrong and the Jewish Family" (published in Armstrong 1999), written near the end of his life after a life-threatening illness, is confused in both chronology and content; this document should always be used cautiously. For example, Armstrong writes there that he received his first cornet from this family in 1907, but there is so much earlier evidence in contradiction to this, from Armstrong and from others, that the statement has no value; certainly he did not play the cornet until he entered the Waif's Home. (3) It is troubling to read (in Berrett 1992) an account of Armstrong's early singing—and, indeed, an account of musical models that he "deeply internalized and fluently expressed in his brilliant improvisations"—and see no mention whatsoever to blues singing or church singing, the primary musical experiences that shaped him. (4) As I argue here, the pieces Berrett cites all fit perfectly at the Vendome Theater; to claim that his interest in this music is "fully consistent with what is known about Armstrong's *earliest preferences in music*" (emphasis added) is to willfully ignore what was an extensive and thorough immersion in the early preferences of a rich and strong array of African-American vernacular traditions (as argued in Brothers 2006). It is unlikely that he even heard these pieces before the Vendome, as he indicated (Armstrong 1966, 33): "Never [before the Vendome] played any classical music—*Cavalleria Rusticana*, reading music, turning sheets and

all that." (5) Vocal and instrumental styles associated with African-American church singing and blues are a far more likely source for many of the rubato and filigree techniques Armstrong favors than opera is.

46 There is also a report of Armstrong playing this tune at the Sunset Café, where he started working in spring 1926, having been lured from the Dreamland. Johnny St. Cyr explained (St. Cyr HJA 1958) that bands at different venues on the South Side often played the same repertory at the same time, since they wanted to keep up with current arrangements, as they were published. This made it easy for musicians to move in and out of bands, St. Cyr observed.

47 There are many reasons to draw out these issues, and two stand out. First, many writers who accept the African origins of jazz do so with little or no reference to specific musical features that are central to that connection. Second, it is still possible for a major scholarly press to publish a book in which the African origins of jazz are casually (and somewhat covertly) dismissed: see Sudhalter 1999, p. 749, n. 8.

48 A word about racially defined audiences. As already discussed, the Dreamland Café was characterized by the *Defender* as a "place of our own"; Milt Hinton (IJS 1976) said that the Vendome Theater was "all black"; and race records certainly targeted black markets. Yet many actors and musicians visited the Dreamland, and we know that Jack Teagarden was one white who purchased Armstrong's recordings. It is important not to be misled about the predominant ethnic makeup of a venue based on an exception, and this is especially true of white exceptions, for two reasons: first, whites, unlike blacks, could go anywhere they wanted to go and thereby instantly turn an all-black venue into a mixed one; second, whites, and especially white musicians, are exceptionally well represented in oral histories, giving a distorted picture.

49 Armstrong's two most compelling solos through May 1927, *Big Butter and Egg Man from the West* and *Potato Head Blues*, each clock around 192 beats per minute; compare that with the frantic performances with Erskine Tate of *Static Strut* and *Stomp Off Let's Go* from May 1926, both around 240. *Oriental Strut* moves at 188 and *Muskrat Ramble* at 182.

50 The information that Armstrong composed the lyrics for *Heebie Jeebies* comes from St. Cyr (Anderson 2007, 240). He did not get co-composer credit on the Hot Five discs, but that kind of omission was not uncommon. The same thing happened with *Don't Forget to Mess Around*, which is credited on the discs to Barbarin; co-composer credit to Armstrong is given on the copyright deposit now held at the Library of Congress (Chevan 1997, 474). In any event, typical contractual arrangements for race recordings generally did not grant royalties directly; rather, the composer sold rights to the company. Thus, Armstrong's quip about Atkins making a lot of dough did not hold for the sale of 40,000 copies of the Hot Five recording; the yield came with sheet music and recordings by others.

51 According to listings for these recordings at www.redhotjazz.com, the record labels note the "vocal chorus by Louis Armstrong" in all six performances from June in which he sings.

52 My dating of Venable's revue *Jazzmania* to July 1926 is based on the following conflation of datable appearances in Chicago of performers who were featured in it. The list of performers in *Jazzmania* is documented in two undated clippings

(transcribed below from Scrapbook 83, LAHM) from *Heebie Jeebies*; the datable appearances (noted in brackets) were drawn from newspapers and other scrapbook clippings. Clipping 1: "Sunset. Percy Vanable's [*sic*] latest production, 'Jazzmania,' which opened Thursday night at the Sunset Café, has been declared the fastest and most colorful show ever staged at this popular night club. The show is one riot of singing and dancing from the beautiful and impressive opening to the finale, in which Luis [sic; this is one of the earliest references to the nickname "Louie," which would stay with him for the rest of his life] Armstrong and Kid Lips, supported by the entire cast, features the "Heebie Jeebies" song. The show is built around a cast of stars including Brown and McGraw [July 10, July 26], Mae Alix [July 3, Aug. 7], Margaret Simms, Slick White [July 24], Kid Lips, Ralph Delaney, Ted McDonald [Aug. 7] and Chick Johnson [Aug. 14]." Clipping 2: "Sunset 'Jazzmania.' Percy Vanable's production now being featured at the Sunset, drew the largest crowd of the season last Saturday night. The proverbial sign 'Standing Room Only' might well have adorned the walls of the lobby as Mae Alix and Margaret Simms put over their song and dance numbers, Brown and McGraw executed their difficult steps and Luis [*sic*] Armstrong and Carol [*sic*] Dickerson's orchestra featured the 'Heebie Jeebies.'"

53 As Junius B. Wood (Wood 1916, 25) wrote in 1916, "Among the white patrons [of the Panama Café, at 35th and State] most conspicuous are the 'slummers,' largely of the class who kiss on the corner while waiting for street cars and whose terms of endearment would be considered cause for justifiable murder in the far west. Equally numerous but less noisy are the white men who strike up acquaintance with colored girls living in neighboring 'buffet' flats. There are also white women who associate with colored men. The waiters do a profitable brokerage business in arranging meetings."

54 The following quotations give a good sense why the depth of the primitivist view should not be underestimated. The first is from Dr. Frank Damrosch, director of the Institute of Musical Art in New York City (now the Juilliard School of Music), as published in *Etude* magazine in August 1924 (reprinted in Walser 1999, 44): "If jazz originated in the dance rhythms of the negro, it was at least interesting as the self-expression of a primitive race. When jazz was adopted by the 'highly civilized' white race, it tended to degenerate it towards primitivity. When a savage distorts his features and paints his face so as to produce startling effects, we smile at his childishness; but when a civilized man imitates him, not as a joke but in all seriousness, we turn away in disgust." The second quote is from composer Arthur Foote in the same issue (reprinted in Walser 1999, 45): "[It is odd that] after centuries of musical development we should be returning to the primitive."

55 Anderson (2007, 83–85) provides good coverage of the recordings and copyright. My hunch is that the lead sheet (facsimile in Anderson, p. 227) was notated by Barbarin (it is not in Armstrong's hand), which suggests that Barbarin composed the music, Armstrong the words. Barbarin's piece was recorded as an instrumental number in February 1926 by Austin and His Musical Ambassadors, and then as a vocal by the Hot Five in June, with Armstrong's lyrics; the lead sheet was received in Washington, D.C., on March 10. Valaida Snow introduced the dance—and perhaps the song—to the Sunset; she began a run there in May (*Defender*, Aug. 28, 1926, p. 7; *Courier*, May 22, 1926, p. 10). Alberta

Hunter recorded the song in September 1926. Cross-references to other dances were not unusual: see Banes and Szwed 2002, where the lyrics of Perry Bradford's *The Original Black Bottom Dance* (1919) are transcribed on p. 178, with Bradford referencing the Mess Around, the Black Bottom, and the Charleston.

[56] *Defender*, Aug. 28, 1926, p. 7. Valaida Snow's appearance at the Sunset in May 1926 and her connections to the Mess Around may have been the start of an interesting relationship with Armstrong. She was one of the more versatile women performers on the cabaret circuit. Hines said (Dance 1977, 63) that she "could sing, dance and produce a show. She could play trumpet, violin and piano. . . . Louis Armstrong had a fit when he saw her. 'Boy I never saw anything that great,' he told me." Armstrong welcomed her into the Sunset Orchestra to sit next to him and play second trumpet (Miller 2007, 42). Eventually she became an Armstrong imitator, calling herself "Little Louis" in England in 1934. Cross-gendered imitations like this were not unusual; for example, one Mae Fanning "stopped the show" at the Sunset in January 1927 with an act imitating Johnny Hudgins (*Light*, Jan. 8, 1927, p. 18).

[57] In August, Charles Cooke and Johnny St. Cyr composed their own song (Cooke writing the music and St. Cyr the words) to go with the dance; they called it *Messin' Around*. The *Defender* reported (Aug. 28, 1926, p. 7) that this tune was "written to the slow, draggy 'Messin' Around' rhythm" and that recordings were being planned by both Cooke and King Oliver. The song by Cooke and St. Cyr was also featured at the Vendome in August (Scrapbook 83, LAHM). It is interesting that Armstrong and St. Cyr wrote lyrics for these songs, which both reference New Orleans as the source of the dance.

[58] Quotation from Taylor 1987, 74. Alberta Hunter claimed to be the originator of the Black Bottom, and, according to *Heebie Jeebies* (Sept. 4, 1926, p. 16), she tried to copyright the dance in order to "protect 'her interests' through the law to restrain the promiscuous use of her dance invention. Miss Hunter is said to have had the step, hop, shake, or whatever it is, copyrighted." *Heebie* also reported that the *Chicago Daily News* planned on publishing lessons for the Black Bottom, and that the Daily News Service would be showing the dance at movie theaters. On crouching: Brothers 2006, 143–44; Thompson 1983, 125.

[59] Quantitative results from database searching of major newspapers (*Atlanta Constitution, Los Angeles Times, Chicago Daily Tribune, New York Times*) can be revealing. For the period 1920 through 1925 the words "black bottom" turn up in 16 different advertisements or articles; the number for 1926 through 1927 leaps to 605.

[60] *Courier*, March 12, 1927, p. 2; *Afro-American*, March 19, 1927, p. 9. The Sunset recovered, but early 1927 brought strife for two people close to Armstrong. In March, Hines sued his wife, Laura Hines, for divorce, claiming desertion. According to the *Courier*, they had married in Pittsburgh in April 1924. The article suggests that Hines's suit was prompted by alimony claims made by Laura. Joe Glaser, who had assumed ownership of the Sunset from his mother and would later become Armstrong's manager and close friend for many years, also experienced legal difficulties. In February he was arrested (*Chicago Daily Tribune*, Feb. 26, 1927, p. 3) for "attacking" a fourteen-year-old girl.

[61] Harker 2008, 93. Tap dancer Honi Coles (quoted in Dixon 2000, 104) said that black dancers "used to try and load their steps up to the point that they couldn't

be stolen." In other words, density of activity was part of the period's emphasis on short bursts of exciting entertainment, but it also became a defensive move, designed to prevent theft.

[62] Cheatham IJS 1976; Dance 1977, 48. The format became part of Armstrong's expanding array of entertainment niches. On Halloween night 1926 he and Brown and McGraw were scheduled to perform *Heebie Jeebies* in exactly the same way—they must have done so already at the Sunset—but the swarming crowd filled up the dance platform, leaving no room for the dancing duo (Scrapbook 83, LAHM). Rex Stewart remembered him later accompanying the dance team Dave and Tressie, and there is mention of the chorines doing taps to his solo breaks in a finale for a 1927 revue that Venable named *Jackass Blues* (CJA Steiner Collection, box 83, folder "Darnell Howard"; Dance 1977, 48; Harker 2007, n. 141).

[63] In a high-handed stroke of decontextualizing new criticism, the vocal duet was expunged from *Big Butter* in the *Smithsonian Collection of Classic Jazz*, leaving a truncated and purely (with emphasis on *pure*) instrumental piece; the instrumental solo was the "classic" part of the performance, in other words. I can remember how shocked I was when I eventually heard the complete recording, an experience that must have been shared by many for whom this otherwise wonderful collection provided an initial introduction to jazz history.

[64] The practice was surely standard. Charles McConnell (CJA): "As soon as [saxophonist Frankie] Trumbauer had 'set' an improvisation (often during rehearsal) he continued to use the same solo, note for note." For further discussion of jazz solos in the 1920s as composed rather than improvised, see Tucker 1991, 246 and 253; Magee 1992, 326–31; Harker 1999, 51. Not surprisingly, the same technique worked in other areas of entertainment. As actor Jimmy Cagney explained (Snyder 1989, 108), "Vaudevillians by persistent trial and error and unremitting hard work found out how to please . . . they spent years perfecting those acts so that they knew their jobs and they did their jobs without slighting either their talent or their audience." Mary Cass Canfield discussed (Snyder 1989, 104), in an article from 1922, "the comedian's carefully crafted image of spontaneity." In this regard, the Sunset Café and the Vendome Theater did not share much with the paid jam sessions of the 1940s, where expectations were quite different. Douglas (1995, 429) discusses the views of Gilbert Seldes, who may have been the white writer of the period most sympathetic to African-American jazz: "Black musicians might be 'geniuses' but they were 'wayward, instinctive and primitive' ones; nothing they did could count for much as long as they lacked, as he thought they did, 'mind,' the 'fundamental brainwork' needed 'to write out precisely what . . . [they] want us to hear.'"

[65] The two phrases are of different lengths and they work differently in the overall form of each solo. The phrase from *Chimes Blues* is the first four measures of a 12-bar blues chorus, while that from *Big Butter and Egg Man* is the first eight-bar phrase of a 32-bar chorus. That accounts for a fundamental difference in phrase construction: the phrase from *Chimes Blues* ends with a transitional gesture that leads into the next four-bar blues phrase, while the phrase from *Big Butter and Egg Man* brings closure. Holding a riff like this over chord changes was standard practice in the blues; for example, consider the famous *Royal Garden Blues*, or countless riff-based choruses from the swing era. The first phrase

of Armstrong's solo for *Muskrat Ramble*, recorded in February 1926, shows a similar conception (transcription in Anderson 2007, 76).

66 See Brothers 1994 for further discussion. As Lawrence Gushee points out (1998, 315): "Almost from the beginning, Armstrong had used such pitches [sixth, major seventh, and ninth] in a manner that seemed entirely natural, in distinction to such 'advanced' trumpeters as Beiderbecke and Nichols."

67 The report from the *Light*, Feb. 26, 1927, is a boxed feature on p. 22 entitled "Rating King Oliver." It runs: "While listening in over Station WEDC we heard Joe Oliver's Dixie Syncopators broadcasting between 11 p.m. and 2 a.m., from the Plantation Café. We are rating 'em as we heard 'em." The list then begins:

Jos. Oliver, cornetist . . . 25
Thomas Gray, cornetist . . . 29
Ed. Ory, trombone . . . 30
Junie Cobb, banjo . . . 30
Luis Russell, piano . . . 68
Darnell Howard, saxophone . . . 85
Rudy Jackson, saxophone . . . 86
Bonnie [*sic*] Bigard, saxophone . . . 89
Bert Cobb, bass . . . 92
Paul Barbarin, drummer . . . 98
Walter Burton, announcer . . . 100

If this seems like an indirect put-down of Oliver today, it probably was not so subtle at the time. Preston Jackson (2005, 85–86) discusses Oliver's decline around this time: "Things had begun to break bad for Joe Oliver. The Plantation closed and he was booked on the road and we heard he was coming to the Wisconsin Roof (early April 1927). . . . I liked Joe Oliver and began to feel sorry for him that his band was just not together and his teeth were beginning to bother him too but we felt our jobs were at stake and so we continued to pour it on. . . . It was sad to see how much he was struggling."

68 Scrapbook 83, LAHM. Another clipping from Scrapbook 83 reports that Armstrong was the "owner" of the "aggregation," Hines the conductor, with Mrs. Armstrong "officiating at piano." Armstrong may have turned away from conducting after a scathing review from Dave Peyton (*Defender*, March 19, 1927, p. 6). Hines once came off the stage at another venue and found that his smiling muscles had frozen into place; "I had gone too far," he explained (Dance 1977, 86–88).

69 *Alligator Crawl*, on the other hand, is much less polished and crafted, suggesting that it was created on the day of the recording. In many of these solos from May 1927, even those that are less polished, we can hear Armstrong working on gestures, figures, phrase patterns, and designs that surface in his more famous solos. It is hardly surprising that his stylistic language is consistent. The difference in quality has to do with design and confidence, both factors indicating sustained familiarity rather than the limitations of hasty improvisation.

70 *Amsterdam News*, July 7, 1926. Trumpeter Punch Miller (Miller IJS 1960) from New Orleans was asked about the history of stop time and explained that musicians took the practice from their accompaniments for tap dancers. "Every tap dancer that came up wanted *Sweet Sue* in stop time," Miller remembered. He also spoke about a musician named Georgie Boyd who wrote a piece that included

a stop-time chorus for clarinet solo. On the connection of stop-time dance to stop-time jazz solos, see also Harker 1999, 48–49. Harker (Harker 2008) also relates *Potato Head Blues* to stop-time dancing; my discussion is indebted to his work, though his approach to the analogy is more literal and more focused on the dancers Brown and McGraw. Harker quotes (2008, 111, n. 150) dance historian Heather Rees: "The spaces in the music [during stop time] are ideal opportunities for 'busy' tap sequences, rather like a musician's solo in jazz improvisation sessions"; and also Anita Feldman: "throughout the history of tap, dancers have competed for the 'fastest feet.' The audience waits for the moment when Stop-time comes in the music, and the tap dancer dazzles us with remarkable speed."

71 "Telling a story" is a common metaphor in jazz (Harker 1999), probably because of its flexibility. Not only instruments, but feet, too, could talk. John Bubbles tried to track the melody of *Ol' Man River* in his dance steps: "That smile would come from the people hearing what I'm doing," he remembered (Bubbles IJS). Bojangles Robinson liked to prepare the audience for what he was about to do: "Now I'm going to tell it" (Blesh 1946, 189). The talking drums of West Africa and the freak music of New Orleans are close at hand here. Armstrong spoke about continuity: "That clarinet is trying to tell a story—you can *follow* him" (Armstrong 1999, 165). Yet it would be a mistake to put too much weight on narrative structure in jazz storytelling. The metaphor ceases to be useful when taken to the point where melodic construction is parsed in terms like antithesis, development, climax, resolution, and denouement. Mutt Carey said that Armstrong "tried to make a picture out of every number he was playing" (Shapiro and Hentoff 1955, 46), which implies a more static conception less oriented toward linear structure and more involved with emotional ambience. Armstrong spoke about "seeing through" music to visual scenes in New Orleans that he remembered; for example, the 1927 *Potato Head Blues* reminded him of the Pelican Dance Hall in 1918 (Brothers 2006, 277). For Cootie Williams, telling a story clearly had more to do with emotional presence of the player than narrative structure: "It's not just to play the notes. Just like if you're reading a book and you're telling a story to kids or something. And when you're playing an instrument, which I try to tell a story when I'm blowing, in the same way" (Williams IJS n.d.). Basic to this are details of phrasing, shadings of loud and soft, distorted timbre, and attack, the markers that are fundamental to blues and jazz. Telling a story could mean nothing more than strong, individualized phrasing. Armstrong praised trumpeter Natty Dominique: "You've got that drive. You carries them with you—they've got to come with you" (Russell 1994, 150).

72 Dance 1969, 69. Consider these remarks from Armstrong (2005, 145): "Q: The highlife music of Ghana, did it stem from the jazz of America? A: No, we copied it from them. The beat. Tom-toms and drumbeats. I realized when I went down there that it was copied from them. When the slaves came, they brought the music with them and they've still got it. It brought me back to generations, my ancestors in Africa, in New Orleans. . . . I could see so many things that was brought from Africa. It brought back memories."

73 I am very grateful to Lesley Zlabinger, archivist at the Louis Armstrong House Museum, for her detective work on May Ann's death. Lesley calculated the date of July 6, 1927, based on indirect information from scrapbooks in the archive

and online death certificates housed by the Illinois Department of Public Health. See also Anderson 2007, 136, for an obituary from the *Defender*. There are some inconsistencies in accounts of the purchase of the house, but it seems likely that the couple bought it in late 1925, just before Armstrong returned to Chicago. "He walked in and said, 'You mean this is our house?'" Lillian remembered. "I said, 'Yes, it will be someday.' He said, 'You are a magician.'" Lillian remained in the house until her death in 1971. In the summer of 1927, Oliver was living five blocks away, at 209 East 46th Street, between South Michigan Avenue and South Prairie Avenue. Lillian and Louis also purchased lakefront property at Idlewild, an African-American summer gathering spot in Michigan. Riverside LP interview, 1936, 83; Scrapbook 83, LAHM; King 1967, 66; Armstrong 1966, 31; Armstrong 1999, 90, 65.

[74] Eddie Condon (1947, 85) described Beiderbecke: "The sounds came out like a girl saying yes." And Humphrey Lyttelton (1978, 137) compared Beiderbecke's solo for *Singin' the Blues* to the "perfect woman" in William Wordsworth's poem of that name. More recently, Richard Sudhalter (1999, 243) laid out a very different basis for the comparison, one dangerously close to centuries of racist ideology, with Beiderbecke contributing an intellectual dimension while Armstrong specialized in emotions: "[Beiderbecke's] phrasing—linear, compositional, less emotionally charged than Armstrong's but more layered, more complex—challenged the intellect as readily as the heart."

[75] *Put 'Em Down Blues* and *I'm Not Rough* were composed by Armstrong, *Ory's Creole Trombone* and *Savoy Blues* by Ory, *Struttin' with Some Barbecue*, *Got No Blues*, and *Hotter Than That* by Hardin (though Armstrong claimed authorship of both *Hotter Than That* and *Struttin' with Some Barbecue*—and I see no reason to doubt him; see Armstrong 1999, 25, for evidence of his lasting bitterness about the latter). *The Last Time* is credited to Ewing and Martin, who, as Anderson (2007, 149–52) explains, are Billy H. Ewing (a comedian who sometimes performed with Martin; *Defender*, March 6, 1926) and Sara Martin, a famous blues singer. Anderson reports that Lillian Hardin filed copyright for the same title in October 1927, and that Martin's recorded version differs from that of the Hot Five. In any event, Martin recorded frequently for OKeh, which probably accounts for the inclusion of this song in the Hot Five repertory, if, in fact, it was not composed by Hardin. *Once in a While* was composed by one William H. Butler; Anderson (2007, 165–68) suggests identification with the saxophonist by this name who played with Doc Cooke's band in Chicago, a band Johnny St. Cyr also played in.

[76] Armstrong said (1999, 135) that *Got No Blues* was "one of those quickies that was made up right there at the studio." It is also closely modeled on *Struttin' with Some Barbecue*, which encourages speculation that the latter was a well-established hit at the Sunset, the former an imitation designed to capitalize on its success.

[77] Bud Freeman (1970, 16): "You must remember that a few years before there wasn't any jazz; there was a thing we called ragtime. . . . Players who didn't have a feeling for jazz would take a series of 8th notes and play them dotted, like da-ta, da-ta, da-ta, ta. . . . Whereas Louie, out of his New Orleans background, or the riverboats, or sheer instinct, would take the same group of notes and give them a beautiful, graceful, powerful line of playing. . . . For instance if I may use an example, *Struttin' with Some Barbecue*, which he made up and first began to

play around 1927 . . . ladedadada da-do-deet-deet-doo. . . . There was always a drive to the playing, never the corny type of phrasing others were using; I am sure you will appreciate the difference." Freeman also told a funny story about this solo (1974, 16): "In the days in Chicago, before Louis Armstrong became world famous, he spent a great deal of time walking the streets of his neighborhood on the South Side. Louis was very friendly, and kind to everyone, especially pan handlers. One afternoon, as he strolled along 35th Street, he noticed a small crowd gathered around two street musicians. He stopped and listened and much to his delight, the trumpet player was playing Louis's improvised chorus of *Struttin With Some Barbecue.* At the finish of the number, Louis walked over to the street musicians and said: 'Man . . . you're playing that *too slow!*' 'How would you know?' they challenged. 'I'm Louis Armstrong . . . that's my chorus you're playing!' The next day the street musicians had a sign next to their tin cup. The sign read 'Pupils of Louis Armstrong.'"

[78] An ad for the Nov. 12, 1927, issue (p. 24) read: "Wanted/100 Charming Misses/They must dance well and possess individuality—charm—appearance/ the Opportunity to Earn from $30.00 to $75.00 Per Week Awaits You Apply Daily—10 A.M. to 3 P.M./Savoy America's Smartest Ballroom 47th and South Parkway Chicago."

[79] A clipping from Scrapbook 83, LAHM, lays out details of the "Louis Armstrong dance tour": Monday, Jan. 2, Harrisburg, Pa.; Tuesday, Jan. 3, Martinsburg, W.V.; Wednesday, Jan. 4, Richmond, Va.; Thursday, Jan. 5, Norfolk, Va.; Friday, Jan. 6, Newport News, Va.; Saturday, Jan. 7, Wilmington, Del.

[80] *Defender,* April 7, 1928, p. 6. Contributing to the decline of music at the Vendome was the death (the previous November) of Oliver C. Hammond, the owner who was credited with supporting Erskine Tate and his orchestra; *Light and Heebie Jeebies,* Nov. 12, 1927, p. 28. Hinton (1988, 27) has a good description of the "shopping center" that opened in 1927 and early 1928 at 47th Street and South Parkway, including a department store, a five-and-dime, a drugstore, a Chinese restaurant named the Chu Chin Chow, and the Savoy Ballroom.

[81] It is possible that the *Going Home* Armstrong played (*Defender,* April 21, 1928) was the spiritual *I'm Going Home* that is included in the famous publication *Slave Songs of the United States,* though that seems much less likely than Dvořák's tune, which was published as a song with words by William Arms Fisher in 1922. This would have been a natural choice for funeral ceremonies in churches like the Liberty Congregational. For description of a New Orleans funeral with music, see Brothers 2006, 85. A touching tribute to Powers was published in the *Light and Heebie Jeebies,* April 21, 1928, p. 2.

[82] Testimony: Shapiro and Hentoff 1955, 118; Jackson 2005, 87. Of the nine tunes recorded in late June and early July 1928, *Don't Jive Me, Two Deuces,* and *Knee Drops* were composed by Hardin; *West End Blues* by Oliver; *A Monday Date* by Hines; *Fireworks* and *Skip the Gutter* by Spencer Williams. All of those follow the pattern of local connections who signed away copyright to OKeh, thus explaining the presence of their pieces on the series (on the likelihood of an OKeh connection for Spencer Williams, see Chap. 5). That leaves *Squeeze Me* by Fats Waller and Clarence Williams (who had strong OKeh connections) and *Sugar Foot Strut* by Billy Pierce, Henry Meyers, and Charles Schwab.

[83] Armstrong, Lillian WRC 1938. The notes from the interview, taken by Bill

Russell, read: "Joe Oliver never played the West End cadenza. That came from some of the classical stuff that she taught Louis. . . . She spoke about the West End cadenzas and other things he got from the classical things." Compare with this from Earl Hines, speaking about Dizzy Gillespie and Charlie Parker in the 1940s (Hines 2005, 151): "Dizzy used to go to Charlie's dressing room and play out of his exercise book. Charlie would do the same. Play a lot of passages. They had photographic minds and they used to insert some of these passages in the things we were playing. But they were doing it in such an advanced way, especially the original tunes, that the average musician didn't know what it was all about." Jeffrey Taylor (1993, 95) compares figuration played by Hines on *Skip the Gutter* (June 27, 1928) with that of Chopin's Etude, Op. 10, No 4. Since *Skip the Gutter* was recorded the day before *West End Blues*, it is easy to imagine them exploring together the possibility of bringing into their music passages from classical technique. See also Schuller 1989, 272; Harker 2011, 156–58.

[84] People notate it today for study purposes, of course, and also because of the strange notion that seems to be part of jazz pedagogy that it is good training to notate the complicated jazz solos of the past. This teaching technique would have perplexed musicians of Armstrong's generation (and several generations following him, I'm sure), who learned all the famous solos by *ear* and would have shaken their heads at the idea of learning them through notation.

[85] The main exception here is the quiet call and response between Lonnie Johnson and Armstrong singing scat two-thirds of the way through *Hotter Than That*, which, as we have seen, was almost certainly created for the recording studio.

[86] *Sugar Foot Strut* seems to be another good candidate for having come directly from the bandstand of the Savoy Ballroom: (1) it is a fine demonstration of the new vocal style; (2) it is a strong performance, well rehearsed and organized; (3) it was a popular hit of the time, composed by Billy Pierce, Henry Meyers, and Charles Schwab, and thus seems to be an exception to OKeh's repertory policy.

[87] Perhaps the oddest of all of Armstrong's recordings from the 1920s is his performance (recorded June 26, 1928) with Lillie Delk Christianson of *Too Busy*, with Armstrong singing vocal obbligato behind Christianson's lead. (Christianson has sometimes been incorrectly identified as white in discussions of this recording.) Christianson tiptoes into her second chorus only to run up against an explosion of scat fill-in from Armstrong. Armstrong continues scatting as full-blown obbligato to produce a bizarre 20 seconds or so of music. This performance, like *A Monday Date*, was almost certainly inspired by *From Monday On*, recorded in January 1928 by Paul Whiteman and His Rhythm Boys and heard live by Armstrong in Chicago.

[88] Austin: McCracken 2000, 72; see also pp. 79–111 for musical examples. For other usages: Nellie Henry, niece of the recently deceased Florence Mills, shared (*Courier*, Nov. 26, 1927, p. 13) some of her aunt's private aspirations: "She yearned to be able to express that mother love in which she could croon over her own baby in its cradle, singing the soothing lullabies, the sobbing themes of her own African ancestry." For additional references, see "plantation songs" like G. H. Clutsam's *Croon, Croon, Underneat' de Moon* (1902). Also Frederick Donaghey, reviewer for the *Chicago Daily Tribune* (Nov. 11, 1928, p. H1): "Miss Marion Harris, liked here last season for her soft crooning of

blues. . . ." Also *Courier*, April 21, 1928, p. A8: "For days he moped about the roundhouse. Finally he commenced to croon to himself. With the innate musical instinct of his race he was trying to put the ache in his heart into song." Also *Afro-American*, April 23, 1927, p. 8: "Edna Thomas, 'the lady from Louisiana,' back from a two years' foreign tour, will make her first appearance since her return, April 24, at the Lyric, New York, at 8:45 p.m. in a recital of Negro spirituals and plantation croons." Also *Afro-American*, March 10, 1928, p. 9: "Abbie Mitchell . . . is successfully essaying a 'Mammy' role in the Broadway success, 'The Coquette.' . . . Abbie gets a chance to show the quality of that remarkable voice of hers, when as she starts to ascend the staircase she croons a spiritual." See also McCracken 1999, 368.

89 Teddy Wilson (2001, 104) on Earl Hines: "the technique he used gave great force to the solo piano in the big band before the days of electrical amplification. His octave technique was original, brilliant and clear, even above full ensemble backgrounds. When I first started playing, the microphone was beginning to be used on the piano, and all one had to do was turn up the volume control to be heard. Using the octave, instead of the individual fingers, involves utilizing hand touch and gives you much more power, so you can be heard in a hall where there is no amplification. By hand touch I mean the power of the whole hand behind the touch instead of just the individual finger. Hines pioneered and developed this technique and introduced it with tremendous dexterity so he could produce improvised piano solos which would cut through to perhaps 2,000 dancing people, just like a trumpet or a saxophone could." And further (p. 108): "The reason I do not use the extremely high volume of Hines and Waller is that I seem to be able to express myself well within a much narrower dynamic range."

90 The phrase "total unified conception" comes from Gunther Schuller (1968, 103), as a way to assess *Big Butter and Egg Man*. In the sweep of this 32-bar solo—I count 154 different notes in the transcription—Schuller identified a brief rhythmic figure of two notes repeated in five places. I hear the figure as a small sprinkling of musical patterning, one of the many small "conversations of notes" that come and go. For Schuller they are an example of Armstrong's keen regard for "musical logic and continuity" and the source of his greatness. My view is that Armstrong's primary focus is the fixed and variable model, which may be understood as a dimension of musical form. On the one hand, the fixed level of accompaniment, with its regular flow of harmonies, is coherent to the point of banality. Armstrong's solos dance on top of this plodding march, the perfect base for his quicksilver patterning. As long as the solo is connected to the fixed ground, it partakes of the musical logic of the chords. As suggested in Chapter 4, this is a common option for specialists in the African-American vernacular: to intensify or complement a given form with the right gesture at the right moment. The performer does not have to create a new form, but she or he can take advantage of the potentials of a given form. Local levels of musical patterning come and go, beautifully so, but the question is how systematic they are and ultimately how important any single one of them is. Filmmaker and historian Robert Altman (2004, 36, 51) has written about an "aesthetic of discontinuity" that conditioned popular theater, vaudeville, and films in the decades around 1900: "Today's assumptions about the importance of clearly integrating

all elements of a performance were not operative at this time," writes Altman, and the 154 driving notes of the *Big Butter and Egg Man* solo prove that claim. Read most sympathetically, efforts like Schuller's aim to counter the primitivist view that cultural production in jazz lacks form and order and is given over to the expression of primitive emotions. Assumptions like this sneak into analytical discourse to the present day. Consider this from author and musician Richard Sudhalter (1999, 745): "Tommy Ladnier, sitting alongside Joe Smith in Fletcher Henderson's mid-1920s orchestra, is deeply rooted in the special emotional urgency of the blues, whereas his section mate seems drawn to *song*, with its consciousness of form, tonal purity, precision of execution." The implication is that blues abandons precision and form in favor of emotional urgency. Against this, one can only state the obvious facts: first, blues was a protean musical idiom that manifested itself in many different ways; second, blues was very much a form; third, "purity" in music is a relative concept; fourth, blue notes are played and sung by great professionals with just as much precision as any other great professional brings to any other style. The topic indicates how integrally bound up micro-level musical analysis is with macro-level issues of culture and society, with race never far from the discussion. Additional critiques of this topic have been published by Gushee, Harker, and Howland.

[91] Garvin Bushell (IJS 1977) commented on the power of radio. He turned down a job at the Cotton Club in Harlem, even though it paid $1,100 per week for the band. "We had no idea the potential of radio, we didn't know about radio. . . . And had we known what radio could do we would have given them $1,100 a week instead of them giving us $1,100."

[92] Kenney 1993, 114. Charlie Carpenter (Dance 1977, 150) told a similar story about Hines: "I used to go places with Wallace Bishop, the drummer, where it was a borderline thing in a white restaurant. Sometimes, when we had sat down, we'd see Earl Hines looking through the window. . . . He explained how he felt about that kind of situation to me one time, and I give him credit: 'You went to Hyde Park High School, son. You went with all those white kids. . . . You were the star of the football team, and for two or three years there wasn't another Negro on it. You just got used to white people, 'cause you were always around 'em."

[93] Brothers 2006, 211. Earl Hines had a similar attitude. He was asked (COHP 1971) how he felt about white musicians "taking so much of your stuff, picking up a lot of your musical techniques, your ideas." His answer: "Oh we didn't pay any attention to that. No no, the idea is this, that you just keep on creating ideas of your own to play and actually I didn't know anybody was playing what I was playing until years later they began to tell me that. I never paid any attention to it because all I was doing was playing the way I felt, and on my recordings the same way, and I still do the same doggone thing. . . . I constantly play from the heart. I don't try to imitate anybody."

[94] It is easy to overstate this kind of thing. Jeffrey Taylor (1993, 141) has observed how, in Armstrong's two recorded performances of *Weary Blues*, one with Hines as pianist and the other with Lillian, Armstrong plays better on the one with Hardin, thus bringing into question the idea that "Hines's presence on a date invariably caused Louis to 'catch fire.'" This resonates with arguments made in the present study, that the quality of Armstrong's playing was dependent on a number of factors, such as his familiarity with the tune and tempo. Neverthe-

less, as Taylor and many others have pointed out, the creative dialogue that is evident on performances like the celebrated *Weatherbird* is certainly a reflection of the synergy between two great musicians.

[95] Facsimile in Chevan 1997, 486, and Gushee 1998. A new lead sheet was copied by Armstrong himself (facsimile in Chevan 1997, 487, and Taylor 1998, 23) and sent to Washington, D.C., in January 1929 as a follow-up to the December recording; the beginning of what Armstrong labels "4th Part" displays the same kinds of problems that he had in the rhythmic notation of *Cornet Chop Suey* five years earlier, as he took what may have been an improvised trombone break on the 1923 Oliver recording (Taylor 1998, n. 69) and incorporated it, with flawed rhythmic notation, into his lead sheet. A splendid transcription of the entire 1928 performance is given in Taylor 1993, 251. Taylor 1998 includes excellent analytical discussion of the performance; see the comments on pp. 30–32 for signs of lack of rehearsal.

[96] Armstrong, Lillian HJA 1959. Two of the titles given to these tunes were nicknames for Armstrong, *Papa Dip* and *Gate Mouth*; see also the excellent article by Bruce Boyd Raeburn, Jr. (2004). "That's not me, but I won't do it again," Armstrong quipped when confronted with the evidence of the recording (quoted in Raeburn 2004). Further on these sessions, see also Anderson 2007, 14. On a train much later, he hit Alpha and his fist "kept travelling through the double plate glass window. We knocked over the poker table and the chips went all over the floor. . . . It was a miracle. If God was ever with a person! I could have cut me right here [illustrating tendons]. There were other times when I'd have thrown her out of the hotel window if nobody had been around" (Armstrong WRC 1953).

[97] Here is Armstrong's commentary (Armstrong 1950, 24) on trombonist Charlie Green: "Long Green was all right but there was something in his playing—other than hitting those bell tones and he was strong and everything like that—but I always felt he didn't think about the music; his mind didn't function. All he was thinking about was: when is intermission so he can call home and see if his wife is still there." Consider also this from Armstrong (1970): "Joe Garland . . . he disliked bad notes the same as me. Like I mean you can't help it. I mean I ain't perfect either. That's why I hate 'em because I don't hear myself with 'em. That's why I try to make all my records with good notes at least and that's the way they all came out. I wouldn't let it pass. 'Oh that's all right let it go.' Bullshit! It had to be ok by me as long as the notes were right, whatever I attempted to do, high or low. Not thinking years and years from now when people simmer down with them ears to really listen and you can see, like a whole lot of musicians, the big names that recorded twenty years ago—goddamn!! . . . of course at that time they were putting their heart in it, and that's the way they feel . . . but you hear that shit twenty years later and my God, how did it pass the bar?"

[98] Don Redman in Williams 1962, 99; Singleton IJS 1975. The Savoy disappears from the *Light* around May 1928; they obviously cut back on advertising, which meant that the weekly column dedicated to the hall was also eliminated. The reason for the cutback may have been the swarming crowds that Armstrong brought in, which would be ironic since his success apparently cut off a good source for us about what he was doing. By July 7 he was leading his own band at the Savoy, playing in alternation with a band led by Dickerson (*Defender*, July 7,

1928, p. 6). But by September he appears to have folded back into Dickerson's band (*Defender*, Sept. 22, 1928, p. 6).

99 On the copyright and the published arrangement, see Chevan 1997, 206, 233, 420, and 497. The situation implies that Armstrong was again leading one of the bands at the Savoy, and that he asked Redman to visit and make the arrangements for his band. This suggests that all of the arrangements recorded on Dec. 5 and 12 were made by Redman and destined for the Savoy; they were probably still very new to the musicians. I have not been able to see a copy of the published arrangement, but from their recording made in February 1929, it sounds like Earl Hines and His Orchestra are playing a literal statement of Armstrong's solo, while Armstrong's December version is somewhat embellished. Armstrong's solo is transcribed by Schuller (1968, 128). *Beau Koo Jack* did not get recorded often, but apparently it did circulate; see Bernhardt 1986, 66.

100 Jeff Taylor (1993, 133) observes the similarities of Armstrong's tune to *The One I Love Belongs to Somebody Else*, by Isham Jones and Gus Kahn (1923).

101 Feather 1970, 35; Armstrong 1950a, 26. Armstrong also said (Herndon 1964, 72) that the Dickerson band, at the Savoy Ballroom in Chicago, imitated Lombardo's phrasing. But he immediately qualified that by adding that the Dickerson band "meantime . . . played THE HOTTEST MUSIC THIS SIDE OF HELL" (emphasis in original).

102 Armstrong's appearance at the Regal is dated in the *Chicago Tribune* April 29, 1929, p. 28; April 30, 1929, p. 36; and May 2, 1929, p. 34; there is also an undated clipping in Scrapbook 83, LAHM. Another undated clipping from Scrapbook 83 mentions that he was there for a week, that he was featured on stage with Peyton's Regal Symphonists, that Bob "Uke" Williams was the emcee (Williams began in early February), that the "king of jazz started to sing his favorite, *I Can't Give You Anything but Love*, in his own characteristic style, and the last chorus he burnt 'hot' with his penetrating cornet tones," that "after five healthy encores, [he] left the stage wringing wet and triumphantly retaining his crown as the king of jazz," and that he was going to Cincinnati for a one-night engagement on Tuesday, followed by a trip to New York to record. A notice in the *Defender* on May 25, 1929, places him in Cincinnati on May 7. Yet the reference to a trip to New York to record could be to the March 5 sessions, which would place this Regal appearance in late February. Information about the showdown with Reeves comes from Barker (1986, 129), citing an unnamed "witness," and is not dated, though the years 1928 and 1930 are both mentioned near this discussion; hence, it is my suggestion that the showdown with Reeves happened at this time. One contradiction between the two accounts is that Barker has Armstrong winning the contest not with *I Can't Give You Anything but Love*, but with *Chinatown*. On the Reeves-Armstrong rivalry, see also Harker 2011, chap. 6.

103 Schuller (1989, 161) transcribes without comment the solo from an alternate take that was not released until much later. The version released as OKeh 8669 and 41204 is the one that came out immediately, and my assumption is that it includes the trumpet solo that Armstrong played in Chicago. Schuller notes that "there are better solos" than the second take that he transcribes, and the primary take proves his point; the primary solo is transcribed in Ecklund 1995, 40. Charlie Holmes (Holmes IJS) remembered that it took an entire day to record

*I Can't Give You Anything but Love*, which was unusual. "Everything had to be perfect for him, according to the technicians," remembered Holmes, another indication of how OKeh was raising the stakes with Armstrong.

104 An intriguing remark from bandleader Sig Meyer suggests that an African-American tenor named Leon Diggs may have provided one precedent for Armstrong. Meyer said (Meyer CJA 1971) that Diggs "was the first to mix jazz singing with ballade singing."

105 The phrase "legitimate musician" remains part of jazz vocabulary today. Early uses may be seen in Peyton's columns for the *Defender*, for example, Aug. 10, 1929, p. 7. On *Great Day*, see also Magee 2005, 121.

106 As Gene Matthews, writer for the *Interstate Tattler*, put it in one column (April 5, 1929, p. 11), "I finally got into Connie's." A publication called *Nightlife* from 1931 (Shaw 1931, 75) explained that the clientele at Connie's was "wholly white." Other clubs seem to have aimed for at least some integration, perhaps with an eye toward the frisson of interracial intimacy, as documented again in an *Interstate Tattler* (May 10, 1929, p. 11) column: "Club Harlem, as usual, was pretty well packed, and quite a few ofays in the crowd. Danced with an ofay girl once. Nice little dancer, only she seemed to be trying to dance like colored people and kept hopping around." On segregation at Connie's, see Magee 2005, 236; Scott IJS 1979; Erenberg 1981, 257. Blake (in Huggins 1995, 339) implies that Connie's was integrated. Hughes (1986, 224) implies shifting policies, which may account for discrepancies.

107 Mezzrow 1946, 236. Garvin Bushell (1988, 55) said that "there was always a jungle number in the Negro shows . . . they'd always give the same reason to have some jungle music: tom-toms and hoochie-coochie."

108 Woll 1989, 72. According to the *Amsterdam News* (June 26, 1929, p. 13): "The dramatic department of the *Amsterdam News* has been searching zealously for the usual two tickets usually sent by producers or press agents of these shows, but so far he has been unable to locate the magnetic little pasteboards that admit we of sundown hue along with the white boys from downtown." William Hall in the *Interstate Tattler* (May 24, 1929, p. 9) discusses the reluctance of some established Broadway theaters to book colored acts because they tend to draw too many colored patrons, with some advice for the community to stay home: "we are doing the Colored performer an injustice when we crowd to a white theatre whenever a Colored performer appears. . . . Certainly, we want to do nothing to hinder their progress. . . . If our crowding white theatres hinders his progress, 'Give him a break.'"

109 Armstrong made two recordings on July 22, 1929, that provide a direct sonic connection to the dancing in *Hot Chocolates*. *Sweet Savannah Sue* was a number that featured the Bon Bon Buddies in a soft shoe (Morgenstern 1978). In fact, the tempo here is identical to that of the Ellington band's *Black Beauty*, as they accompany the celebrated "one man dance" in Dudley Murphy's 1929 film *Black and Tan*; the film is one of the great treasures of 1920s jazz. The up-tempo *That Rhythm Man* that Armstrong also recorded on July 22 was conceived for the first-act dance finale, "the best thriller I have found on Broadway . . . you are screaming, rocking and applauding like a savage," as the *Interstate Tattler* (June 28, p. 9) put it. *That Rhythm Man* was one of the first chances Zutty Singleton had to show what he could do on a recording, there having been only a few brief

moments to shine in the Chicago recordings where, even in electrical productions, he was often put on woodblocks (*Heah Me Talkin' to Ya?*, for example) or otherwise reduced for reasons of balance. In *That Rhythm Man* Singleton drives the band, vigorously and creatively, with off-beat accents similar to those that still define New Orleans street drumming. *That Rhythm Man* is a reminder of how incompletely most recordings reflect what actually happened in live performance.

110 *New York Times* (June 21, 1929, p. 17): "One song, a synthetic but entirely pleasant jazz ballad called *Ain't Misbehavin'*, stands out, and its rendition between the acts by an unnamed member of the orchestra was a high light of the premier." *Afro-American* (June 29, 1929, p. 9): "Louis Armstrong does a specialty just before the opening of the second half."

111 I imagine that the white Hudson Theater audience reacted similarly to Leon René's Creole (I assume) mother when she first heard Armstrong sing scat. René told the story (Louisiana State Mint, vertical file Louis Armstrong) of Armstrong coming over to their house in Pasadena, in 1931, for dinner. Through the radio came a Guy Lombardo record. "Somewhere in the middle of the record Louie let out a burst of gravel tones 'Bop-o-dap-Du—Boo-La-Ba-do-da' that shook the room and stopped everything. My mother was so flabbergasted she just stood there with Louie's second plate of gumbo in her hand. She had never heard a musical break like that before. . . . After dinner we all went into the parlor to smoke and relax on the old antique chairs and sofa my parents brought from New Orleans."

112 Hints at the terms of this negotiation can be picked up here and there. The *New York Times* (June 21, 1929, p. 17): "it should be recorded that the newcomer [*Hot Chocolates*] has its moments of ingenuousness. But such moments are in the Broadway tradition rather than that of Harlem, and on the whole the diversion is an expert amalgam of naïve freedom and superficial skill." According to Frank Taylor (1987, 51–52), Alberta Hunter "called Sissle a dicty because he had an air of superiority coupled with a 'color complex.' He considered her too dark to be in his show [*Shuffle Along*], she said." Ethel Waters was likewise turned down for *Shuffle Along* because the casting director considered her "just a cheap honky tonk singer" (Taylor 1987, 52). See also Woll 1989, 109–13; Stearns and Stearns 1994, 146–48; Dixon 2003, 138.

113 Zora Neale Hurston (2006, 184): "I found the Negro, and always the blackest Negro, being made the butt of all jokes, particularly black women. They brought bad luck for a week if they came to your house of a Monday morning. They were evil. They slept with their fists balled up ready to fight and squabble even while they were asleep. They even had evil dreams. White, yellow and brown girls dreamed about roses and perfume and kisses. Black gals dreamed about guns, razors, ice-picks, hatchets and hot lye. I heard men swear they had seen women dreaming and knew these things to be true." See also the obvious humor in the performance by Blanche Calloway—with fine trumpet playing of Reuben "River" Reeves—in the Vocalion recording by Reeves and His River Boys of *(What Did I Do to Be So) Black and Blue* (advertised in the *Defender*, Oct. 26, 1929); also Hughes 1986, 234.

114 Singer 1992, 12. Razaf begins the verse with a minstrel reference to "old Ned": "Cold empty bed / Springs hard as lead / Pains in my head / Feel like old

Ned." Stephen Foster's 1848 song *Uncle Ned* was about a pathetic old man who became a stock figure in minstrel shows.

115  In 1928, the only other African-American musician OKeh experimented with similarly, as far as I can see, was Ellington. Four sides recorded by his orchestra were released on the popular series (*Black and Tan Fantasy*, *What Can a Poor Fellow Do*, *Jubilee Stomp*, and *Take It Easy*), while nine others were released on the race series. See *Catalogue for OKeh Electrical Records 1929* (held by the New York Public Library, Performing Arts Division); Laird and Rust 2004. My estimations of release times for Armstrong are based on where the catalogue numbers fall in relation to established artists whose recordings were probably released quickly. For example, I infer that *West End Blues* was released in the popular series soon after it was recorded, while *Skip the Gutter*, recorded a day earlier, was assigned catalogue numbers that imply a release three months later; this is based on the proximity of their catalogue numbers to recordings by Bix Beiderbecke made on July 7 and Sept. 21, 1928.

116  Various writers have speculated about the causes that lay behind changes in the repertory Armstrong recorded. They have, for example, looked at the racial identity of the composers of the tunes and wondered if Armstrong perhaps (1) bought into a vision of black autonomy during the early and mid-1920s by recording, in the overwhelming majority of cases, tunes and songs written by black composers; and (2) whether he then sold out when he shifted, in the early 1930s, to songs composed by whites. The numerical weight of the transition is impressive, though it is likely that the choices had nothing to do with racial identity and everything to do with the economics of the recording industry. All recordings during this period, regardless of who was doing them or when they were done, demanded that the choice of tune be guided by two primary concerns: How much does it cost? and What advantages will it bring? All other concerns were secondary. In the end, race didn't matter, and musical quality didn't matter very much, either. OKeh wanted the tunes copyrighted "in house," with no obligation to pay royalties to an outsider. If Armstrong didn't compose the piece himself, there were plenty of friends around town who were asking to have their pieces recorded. Studio musicians like Richard M. Jones, who had an ongoing gig with OKeh, worked this angle heavily. It was easy for a Crescent City buddy like Paul Barbarin to convince Louis to record *Come Back Sweet Papa*, and it is certainly no coincidence that he recorded Fats Waller's *Alligator Crawl* during Waller's brief tenure at the Vendome Theater. These kinds of close connections account for most of the Hot Five and Hot Seven numbers. In all cases, we can assume, the deal was sealed with very good terms for the recording company on the matter of copyright. Race never entered anyone's mind. The black orientation of composers in this series is thus an epiphenomenon; the connections were personal and pragmatic. When Armstrong arrived in New York City in the spring of 1929, things took a different turn, but not because there was a change in the twofold logic guiding choice of repertory. Immediately he stepped into African-American Broadway, its history, its marketing logic, and its composers.

117  A more direct antecedent for Carmichael was a story, one version of which was printed (originally in the *New Orleans Times-Democrat*) in the *Washington Post*, Feb. 19, 1893 (p. 12), as "When Aunt Harriet Died: A Silhouette of

Slavery Drawn Thirty Years After." Harriet, the article reveals, "had known slavery and freedom, and through all changes she had stood by 'Mistiss' [i.e., her mistress] and the old plantation." In the story, the mistress arrives while Aunt Harriet is on her deathbed and sympathetically attempts to administer medicine to her devoted slave. This reference should be added to the discussion of *Rockin' Chair* and Carmichael's songs by Roger Hewitt (1985). See also Moton 1929, 190. Hewitt's excellent article is the important rejoinder to the untenable claim by Richard Sudhalter (2002, 155) that "race, in this context, is less a political statement than a simple identification, not meant to carry social baggage."

[118] Here is a partial itinerary for early 1930, derived from newspaper notices and the scrapbooks at LAHM: Philadelphia, Jan. 2–4, Louis Armstrong and His Columbia Recording Orchestra, Shadowland, 20th Street and Montgomery Avenue; Washington, D.C., and Baltimore, Jan. 11–17, including the Standard, and Louis Armstrong and His Hot Chocolates Band, Howard Theater; New Albert Auditorium, Jan. 12; New York, Jan. 25–31, Loew's State Theater, Broadway at 45th; Chicago, Feb. 8–17, Regal Theater, Savoy Ballroom (this visit also included, on Feb. 9, a banquet held in honor of "three of the most distinguished colored artists in the world," Armstrong, George Dewey Washington, and Johnny Hudgins, with Armstrong playing a duet with Louis Panico); St. Louis, Feb. 22–23; New York, Feb. 26–March 26 (Feb. 26, Loew's State Theater; Feb. 26–March 14, Cocoanut Grove, 225 West 125th Street; March 23, Savoy Ballroom; March 26, Rose Danceland, 125th Street and Seventh Avenue); Detroit, April 7–13, Graystone Ballroom and Michigan Theater; Philadelphia, April 24, Pearl Theater and Strand Ballroom; Baltimore, April 28, New Albert Auditorium; Chicago, May 9–26, Tivoli, Cottage Grove at 63rd Street, Savoy Ballroom, Paradise Theater, the Extra Uptown.

[119] It is worth pointing out that Armstrong was not universally admired, even in 1930, in the African-American community. Frank Byrd in his column "Harlem Nite Life," (*Interstate Tattler*, Sept. 5, 1930, p. 10): "Some may like them, but this dept. finds no enthusiasm to spare for Louis Armstrong's new OKeh records. . . . 'Exactly Like You' and 'Indian Cradle Song' . . . not so hot."

[120] Armstrong had the good fortune to grow up in the heyday of vernacular-based dance music in New Orleans, and the coincidence of his musical maturity with the height of the race record phenomenon—and at one of the locations where the industry was well organized—was just as lucky. The flow of his life thus benefited, in a maximal way, from the cultural-social-economic dynamics of the Great Migration. In New Orleans, he was immersed in a sophisticated urban scene that nevertheless was also preindustrial; in his community, at least, the communal practices of the plantations, with emphasis on direct social interaction, still held strong. He then stepped into more competitive and commercially organized entertainment circles of the North, to which he responded with greater and greater control as a soloist; the industrial social organization of the North was ready to reward this achievement, and so was the commercial organization of the recording industry. It was not simply a matter of historical poetry that New Orleans jazz did not get recorded until it moved North, that it only gained documentation through commercial recordings at the very moment that it left the city and experienced a new set of pressures, causing it to change at the

very moment of its documentation. Less adaptable musicians like Fred Keppard initially refused to record. Armstrong, the most adaptable of them all, embraced the new environment.

121 Band leadership changed during Armstrong's stay there, with Vernon Elkins named as leader in newspaper reports from July, August, and October. Royal Marshal (1996, 37, and Bryant 1998, 40) said that Leon Herriford was leader "at the time he [Armstrong] was busted for having one measly marijuana cigarette" and that Herriford was replaced by Les Hite. Buck Clayton (IJS and Clayton 1987, 46) said that Armstrong's first recordings in Los Angeles were made under Herriford, who "was in the Cotton Club before Hite." The *Los Angeles Times* of Nov. 19, 1930 (p. A12) lists Armstrong as playing in Les Heydt's Orchestra [*sic*]. A report in the *Eagle*, Oct. 10 (p. 10; reference courtesy Steven Lasker), mentions Vernon Elkins's band closing at the Cotton Club. Thus, Elkins was leader until Oct. 10, Hite by Nov. 19, and Herriford sometime in between. See also Hampton 1993, 34; Zwicky 1970.

122 There are many references to Armstrong having originated scat in reviews from England, summer 1932 (Scrapbook 6, LAHM). For example: "Louis told me he was the originator of the 'scat' or 'Yo-do-deo-do' style of singing."

123 Zilner Randolph (IJS 1977) reported this story and said that Armstrong regretted holding Hampton back. Randolph also described a recording session when the sound engineer was motioning to him to play louder while Armstrong, simultaneously and in deliberate contradiction, motioned him to play softer, to stay in the background.

124 *Honey*, Rudy Vallée's big hit of 1929, clocking in at 120 beats per minute, may reflect the slow fox trot tempo (*Atlanta Constitution*, Oct. 6, 1929, p. J3; see also *Washington Post*, March 29, 1930, p. 3, and April 4, 1930, p. 3). Armstrong recorded seven numbers close to this tempo in 1929, two in 1930, and eight in 1931; these counts expand with five more numbers if we include a tempo around 138. On the slow fox trot, see McCracken 2000, 202; also *Chicago Daily Tribune*, Aug. 21, 1932, p. 4, and Aug. 14, 1934, p. 15. Most of the up-tempo numbers recorded by the Sebastian New Cotton Club Orchestra (*I'm in the Market for You, You're Lucky to Me, You're Driving Me Crazy!*) clock in around 180 beats per minute. (The exceptions are the multitempo *Just a Gigolo* and *Shine*, which would have been designed for the revue rather than for social dancing.)

125 There exist four documents, all dating from near the end of his life, that automatically give a strong and candid sense of Armstrong's personality, instantly cutting through the showman's persona that tends to dominate his public statements. Two were published immediately—Richard Meryman's 1966 interview for *Life* (Armstrong 1966; though this comes with a caveat, since Meryman removed his own side of the conversations, making the text read misleadingly like a monologue) and Larry L. King's 1967 profile for *Harper's*. "Louis Armstrong and the Jewish Family in New Orleans, La., the Year of 1907," which Armstrong began writing in March 1969 and thought of as a book, was published in 1999 (Armstrong 1999). The fourth document is a tape he made in the privacy of his living room (Armstrong 2008). He speaks for an hour, directly into the microphone, for his "posterity," as he liked to say, and he goes on at length and in great detail about the glories and comforts of marijuana. The beginnings

of the autobiographical sequel have been published as "The Satchmo Story," in *Louis Armstrong in His Own Words*.

[126] Armstrong 1999, 207. Also on file in the Library of Congress is a letter Armstrong wrote from Europe to Mezz Mezzrow, dated Sept. 18, 1932. Though marijuana is not explicitly mentioned, it is clear from statements like the following that this is what Armstrong is requesting Mezzrow to send: "see to your Boy being well fixed, because I wouldn't want to Run Short, because it might Bring me Down. No might in it, it would. Ha Ha." Stuff Crouch was also a steady supplier in a later period (Bigard IJS 1976), delivering bricks from Mexico.

[127] In a column entitled "Paris and People," ca. 1954, Art Buchwald wrote (Louis Armstrong HJA vertical file) of meeting Armstrong: "'Let's go up stairs, man, I'm beat,' he said. "But I'll get two or three Benzedrine pills under my belt and I'll feel all right."

[128] Gushee 1988, 292. This is reflected in historical study of Armstrong, for with 1929 and the move to New York City, close study of his music drops off dramatically. For the Chicago period, almost every trumpet solo and a number of vocal solos have been transcribed, which encourages analytical reflection and comparison; for the period beginning in 1929 there is far less work like this. Of course, as Gushee and others have observed, the falling off in analytical work also reflects bias against the supposed "commercial" orientation of this later period, with the "chamber jazz" of the Hot Five period valued over the big bands.

[129] Sometime during the summer of 1930, composer Eubie Blake sent Armstrong a copy of *Memories of You*, his new tune for Lew Leslie's *Blackbirds of 1930*. Back in December 1929, we noticed Armstrong doing a favor for his friend Hoagy Carmichael and recording *Rockin' Chair*. Examples like this appear not to have been very common in Armstrong's recorded oeuvre after he left Chicago, but here is another one, recorded by the Sebastian band in October.

[130] Wilbur 1948, p. 27: "As a listener Sidney [Bechet] has the intuitive ability to sense the value of any music he hears. I've never heard him say 'That's an awful tune.' He loves all music because he sees the way to play it." Albert Nicholas (Nicholas HJA 1972) remembered touring during the 1930s with a book of 40 arrangements. "In the band people wouldn't like one tune or the other but Louis Armstrong said all the tunes were good."

[131] Toni Morrison (quoted in Gilory 1993, 78) has said that "the major things black art has to have are these: it must have the ability to use found objects, the appearance of using found things, and it must look effortless." Armstrong certainly embraced the first two, though not the third, at least not completely.

[132] There are various signs of Armstrong's increasing reach. A search of six leading newspapers reveals no mention of his name at all until 1929, when an isolated OKeh ad for *St. James Infirmary* appeared in a March issue of the *Atlanta Constitution*; this was followed by three ads in April issues of the *Chicago Tribune* for appearances at the Regal Theater. As Bud Freeman (1974, 16) put it, "he had not become famous yet [in 1929], but of course every musician in the world had heard his recordings." The six major newspapers, searchable through ProQuest, are the *Atlanta Constitution*, *New York Times*, *Washington Post*, *Chicago Tribune*, *Los Angeles Times*, and *Wall Street Journal*. In 1930 the total number of mentions rises very slightly to six; that is where it stays in 1931 before

dropping to three in 1932 and one in 1933. These statistics are dwarfed by the attention he was getting in the African-American press during the same period: there are 29 mentions in 1929, 99 in 1930, 164 in 1931, 203 in 1932, and 155 in 1933. The searchable African-American newspapers are the *Chicago Defender, Philadelphia Tribune, Pittsburgh Courier, Baltimore Afro-American, New York Amsterdam News,* and Norfolk *New Journal and Guide.* White audiences were beginning to know who Armstrong was, but among black audiences he had become famous.

[133] Gunther Schuller, whose commentaries on jazz history have justifiably loomed very large, sums up the tragic view near the beginning of his chapter on Armstrong in *The Swing Era.* Schuller writes (p. 160) that "in early 1929 Armstrong began performing and recording exclusively with big-band backing—a state of affairs that, much to the dismay of his small-group fans, lasted unbroken until 1940." For the period covered in the present book, this collection of disappointed small-group fans is a complete fiction. As I have explained, Armstrong started playing arrangements in "big bands" in 1924 and never stopped; the Hot Five and Hot Seven recording series was an artificial enterprise designed on the cheap solely for the race record market. Likewise, there is no basis for thinking of Schuller's "second problem" (p. 161)—the change in repertory from ad hoc compositions created by him and members of his circle for the recording studio to mainstream popular hits—as a problem in any artistic sense. See also Gushee 1988, 303.

[134] The *Atlanta World* (Jan. 8, 1931) identifies John Collins as former general manager of the Keith Vaudeville Circuit.

[135] *Chicago Tribune,* Nov. 2, 1931, p. 25. It seems clear from dates and recollections that there was movement back and forth between these cities, so the sequence presented here is probably not complete. On Armstrong's performance at the Palace Theater in Chicago, see also *Defender,* Nov. 14, 1931, p. 5.

[136] Scrapbook 5, LAHM. More extensive description of his visual style comes from England, in reviews of his first tour there in summer 1932. For example (all from Scrapbook 6, LAHM): "Armstrong . . . is said to talk to the microphone when he broadcasts as if it were a human being. He grunts and spits at it. He wheedles, bullies, humours it until you positively expect it to 'up and biff him back'" (clipping identified as *Sunday Dispatch,* July 24). "Yet while he makes animal noises into the microphone which sends the sound to a loud speaker at the side, he makes love to the instrument as though it were a dusky belle! . . . Now and then he charges his all black orchestra like a drunken bull. Yet he caresses his trumpet like a lover—and then making it do things I never heard a trumpet do before, emits from it a rapid succession of notes which have nothing to do with the melody" (clipping identified as *Daily Herald,* July 25, 1932). "He perspires and his neck swells until you imagine that human endurance can go no further." "His energy is amazing. When not jazzing in front of Billy Mason's 'hot rhythm' recording band he is entertaining the audience with weird facial contortions." "At the outset he charges head down in the middle of the stage and addressing himself to a microphone, invites the audience to 'get a load of this song.' Then trumpet in hand, turning to his band, he gets right down to his job, rushing from one side of the stage to the other to call in trombone or saxophone player, dashing to the microphone to vociferate snatches of song,

into which he puts expression that ranges from pleas to threats, then breaking away to whoop what sounds like a war cry as he draws his attention of his audience to his trumpet playing." "Personally, I prefer to hear him on a gramophone recording, for on the stage he mixes 'showmanship' with his playing. A more restrained show would appeal better to his audiences who are apt to judge his playing by his fantastic gestures and vocal effects." "When introducing a new number, or expressing his thanks for the reception of one that he has just given, he grins, gesticulates wildly, and barks. The barking at times resolves itself into the phrase 'yes sir!' When starting a new number, Mr. Armstrong shouts into the microphone: 'I'll be glad when you're dead,' retires to a corner of the stage, gets 'set,' then with trumpet upraised hurls himself on the trombonist."

[137] Moton 1929, 187; *Defender*, Jan. 7, 1933, p. 22, and Jan. 21, 1933, p. 14. Musicologist Joshua Berrett (2004, 189) insists that "darky" was "perfectly acceptable during the 1920s and early 1930s." But the question, of course, is—acceptable to whom? Moton addressed the matter directly in *What the Negro Thinks* (187): "Only slightly less offensive [than 'nigger'] are the terms 'darky,' 'coon,' and 'shine,' all of them expressions of contempt for the personality of those to whom they are applied. . . . The Jews, the Irish, and other races have successfully banned such allusions to their own race from the press and from the stage. Negroes have the same feelings about the matter, though as yet they are powerless to do more in this direction than to appeal to the best instincts and the more delicate sensibilities of such of their white friends as indulge in the practice. . . . In all such practices Negroes discern a continuous propaganda for maintaining the superiority complex of the white man which in some quarters is deemed so essential for the maintenance of American civilization, and the inferiority complex in the Negro, without which he is regarded as a menace to the ascendency of the white man and the permanence of his institutions." See also *Defender*, Jan. 7, 1933, p. 22, which responds to Grafton S. Wilcox, managing editor of the *New York Herald Tribune*, who "didn't know that the word 'darky' was objectionable to members of the Race."

[138] African-American attitudes during this period toward racist lyrics occasionally poke through in letters to newspapers. In December 1931 (published Dec. 19, p. 15), one Velma Tacnean wrote to the *Defender* from 3746 Indiana Avenue in Chicago to protest a radio broadcast of the song *I Can't Get Mississippi off My Mind.* She had tuned to her favorite Sunday show, sponsored by a black-owned syndicate of funeral parlors, "expecting to hear something from our people to make me feel proud" and got this instead. Mississippi offers nothing to be proud of, she insisted. Several follow-up letters were published: "when you hear the strains of that song again, shed a tear, murmur a prayer, and don't forget us when you vote up there," wrote Nona Storye from Goodman, Mississippi (Jan. 2, 1932, p. 15). Another writer (Jan. 23, 1932, p. 15) complained that progress had been made and people should not be ashamed of their states of origin. Another (March 6, 1932, p. 14) suggested Tacnean should shift her energy to banning whites from singing *Mighty Lak' a Rose* and *When It's Sleepy Time Down South.*

[139] Film scholar Donald Bogle (1994, 167) makes this general observation about Armstrong's movie performances: "Part of his effect, perhaps part of his charm, is the way in which he seems to operate in a sphere of his own. Like so many

other black performers of the period, he has a persona strong enough to suggest for us another life apart from the seemingly benign yet racist world of the film. . . . There remains an irreducible part of Armstrong the actor, as there is of Hattie McDaniel and Eddie Anderson, that cannot be touched: there is a part of himself that he keeps unto himself." In that light, consider these words from Armstrong himself (quoted in Gitler 1985, 33): "When I go on the bandstand I don't know nobody's out there. I don't even know you're playing with me. Play good and it will help me. I don't know you're there. I'm just playing."

[140] A nice touch here is the presentation of the famous obbligato line, originally a piccolo part, now rendered by saxophones, which are in the sonic foreground. That is appropriate given the importance of this line in jazz history, though it runs counter to the priority of the main melody, which can barely be heard in the trumpet. As conductor, Armstrong turns around and seems to indicate the prominence of the saxes when they begin the obbligato.

[141] Rogers 1968, 218. Garvin Bushell (1988, 55) reports that "there was always a jungle number in the Negro shows [during the 1920s]."

# SOURCE NOTES

## Introduction

1 "He was just an ordinary-extraordinary man": Cheatham IJS 1976.

2 "Chicago was considered": Barker 1986, 71.

8 "Modernism will always rule": *Defender*, Nov. 14, 1925, p. 7.

## Chapter 1: "Welcome to Chicago"

13 August 8, 1922: On the date, see Wright 1987, 14; Harker (1997, 65) argues that the date of arrival was actually July 8.

13 basket of chicken: Armstrong 1954, 227–30; Armstrong 1966, 28.

13 "Hey hey boll weevil": Ma Rainey, *Bo-Weevil Blues*, recorded December 1923.

15 "the tremendous shore": Johnson quoted in Grossman 1989, 16.

15 porters, janitors, and domestics: Peretti 1992, 45.

15 some 50,000 African Americans: Drake and Cayton 1970, 58; Wang 1988, 102.

15 never heard his mentor called "King": Foster 2005, 40.

16 never seen a city like this: Armstrong 1954, 235; Armstrong 1966, 36.

17 when they start the cycle again: Spivey 1984, 40; Kenney 1993, 15.

17 The drive takes Louis past the red-light district: Ramsey 1939, 95; Miller 1946; Chilton 1987, 31; Miller 1946, 9.

17 the Creole Band from New Orleans: Gushee 2005, 118 and 119.

17 "They were the first to record": Armstrong 1966, 24.

18 Maybe he isn't good enough: Armstrong 1946, 40.

18 a painted canvas sign: Armstrong 1954, 232; Jackson 2005, 70; Shapiro and Hentoff 1955, 99; Armstrong 1999, 49.

18 shy ladies who lack escorts: Travis 1981, 66; Dodds 1992, 35; *Defender*, Sept. 1, 1923, p. 6, local edition; Freeman 1970, 15; Condon 1947, 111; Barbarin HJA 1957.

18 in traditional New Orleans format: Dodds 1992, 37; Armstrong 1999, 52. For Bill Johnson's biography, see Gushee 2005, 53–59 and 319, n. 67.

20 small group of women pianists: Armstrong's recollections of his entry into the Oliver band sometimes include reference to Lillian Hardin, but it seems clear that she did not join the band until months later. See Armstrong, Lillian 1963;

Armstrong, Lillian HJA 1959; Anderson 1994, 296; Armstrong, Louis 1936, 71; Jones and Chilton, 66.

20 keep track of the Chicago White Sox: Dodds HJA 1958; Armstrong 1999, 51; Dodds Jr. CJA 1969; Anderson 1990.

20 "He had a way of standing": Shapiro and Hentoff 1955, 99.

21 he scoots behind the bandstand: Armstrong 1999, 26, 51; Jackson 2005, 46; Jones 1989, 130–31; Armstrong, Lillian 1963.

21 until Dodds got the message: Dodds 1992, 15 and 33.

21 in the summer of 1918: Anderson 1994, 288, reviews some of the conflicting evidence for the date of Oliver's departure from New Orleans for Chicago. Armstrong—who took Oliver's place in Ory's band—was consistent in dating this to 1918; see Armstrong 1954, 136; Armstrong IJS 1954, 60; Armstrong 1999, 33; Jackson WRC n.d. To those reports I can add the earliest and strongest evidence, which comes from Jimmy Noone (WRC 1938), who accompanied Oliver on the trip. Shapiro and Hentoff 1955, 94.

22 rarely plays with an open horn: Dodds 1992, 38.

22 "With an ordinary mute": Shapiro and Hentoff 1955, 96; Barbarin WRC n.d.

22 "I never saw anyone": Bigard 1986, 29.

22 men in the hall threw their hats: Barbarin HJA 1957; Barbarin WRC n.d.; Wright 1987, 15; Garland HJA 1957. Paul Barbarin and Barney Bigard both believed that Paddy Harmon, who patented the Harmon mute, got the idea from watching Oliver, and that some of Harmon's millions should have gone to the creator himself. Bigard 1986, 29; Punch Miller HJA 1960a.

22 In Los Angeles they worked: Garland, IJS; Anderson 1994.

22 "Those are niggers!": Dodds 1992, 34.

23 easy to confuse the public: As late as 1927 a band from Chicago was named the Royal Creolians. "I always thought that name was funny," said Milt Hinton, "because as far as I know no one in the band was from New Orleans." Hinton 1988, 31; Ramsey 1939, 96.

24 clinging to their ethnically defining ways: Brothers 2006, 164–96.

24 Oliver's Creole Jazz Band was back in Chicago: Wright 1987, 12.

24 "You can stick your stinkin' feet": Hodes 1988, 30.

24 "If he ever gets here": Ramsey 1939, 94.

24 "It's my band": Dodds 1992, 35.

25 "Have a seat, son": Armstrong 1954, 232.

25 combs his hair in bangs: Travis 1981, 65; Collier 1983, 94.

25 canvas sign at the front entrance: Wright 1987, 28.

26 A reviewer from 1912: Gushee 1985, 402.

26 At the center of the Creole Band's act: This summary of the band's routine is drawn from different parts of Gushee 2005.

27 "It is an act that shows very clearly": Gushee 2005, 216.

28 "Louis is the plantation character": Down Beat, July 1, 1949, p. 13.

28 King Jones, master of ceremonies: On Jones, see Dodds 1992, 42; Armstrong 1999, 49; Kenney 1993, 20; Cheatham IJS 1976; Wright 1987, 28; Barker IJS; Dorsey, Thomas CJA n.d.

29 so has Ethel Waters: Shapiro and Hentoff 1955, 98; Wright 1987, 23.

29 "That fellow is just as big": Dodds 1992, 33 and 48.

29 "was in my estimation the whole worth": Armstrong 1999, 52.

29 a piece known as *Eccentric*: This was most likely a version of *That Eccentric Rag* by J. Russell Robinson (pub. 1912); see also Shapiro and Hentoff 1955, 42; Armstrong 1999, 52; Jackson 1994, 72.

30 "You would swear he was a white boy": Armstrong 1999, 52.

31 "The people came to dance": Dodds 1992, 35.

31 "a picture of rhythm": Freeman 1970, 15.

31 Oliver directs the music: Shapiro and Hentoff 1955, 115; Armstrong 1966, 28; Shapiro and Hentoff 1955, 95; Russell 1994, 72; Jackson, Quentin IJS 1976.

31 blues played at an extremely slow tempo: Dodds WRC n.d.; Bechet WRC ca. 1938; Russell 1994, 72 and 209; Sayles HJA 1959.

31 "The fastest numbers played by old New Orleans bands:" Kenney 1993, 45.

31 "play hot and at the same time": Chamberlain 2000, 10.

32 "We are making ourselves lithe and slim and healthy": Leonard 1987, 166.

32 "rear end like an alligator crawling up a bank": Stearns 1994, 24.

32 "correct dancing is insisted upon": Wright 1987, 28.

32 white reform organizations like the Juvenile Protective Association: Kenney 1993, 19, 71, and 79; CJA John Steiner Collection, box 84, copy of *Toddle New*, June 15, 1923.

32 "Get off that dime, man": Shapiro and Hentoff 1955, 99; Travis 1981, 66; Kenney 1993, 70.

33 "One more chorus, King!": Condon 1947, 111. Freeman (1970, 15) says that Oliver's band at Lincoln Gardens would play a single number for up to 20 minutes; see also Freeman 1994, 119–20. Souchon 1964, 28, describes how, in his experience, *High Society* entered the dance-band repertory in New Orleans. Moore HJA 1959.

33 "Hotter than a 45": Shapiro and Hentoff 1955, 99; Meyer, Sig CJA n.d.

33 the area forms a sort of barrier: Miller 1946, 27.

33 By the time of Armstrong's arrival ... stops by now and then: Armstrong 1999, 63, 50, and 33. Preston Jackson (2005, 56; see also Shapiro and Hentoff 1955, 97) said that Oliver was giving lessons to Panico around this time. Muggsy Spanier was still using a mute that Oliver gave to him during these years as late as 1961; Spanier HJA 1961; Peretti 1992, 92; Hodes 1977, 179. Armstrong WRC 1953. Dodds 1992, 37; Armstrong, Lillian 1963; Mares WRC ca. 1938.

34 "Well it looks like the little white boys is here to get their music lessons": Freeman 1970, 15; Freeman 1994, 119.

34 "A nod or a wave": Condon 1947, 111.

34 in front of Baby Dodds: Shapiro and Hentoff 1955, 117.

34 Spanier and a few others: Shapiro and Hentoff 1955, 116; Hodes 1977, 178; Miller 1946, 27; Armstrong, Lillian 1963; Banks 1980, 222.

34 "because New Orleans was so disgustingly segregated": Armstrong 1999, 33.

34 Lincoln Gardens is thriving: On the clientele at Lincoln Gardens, see Garland HJA 1957.

35 "They were always happy": Kenney 1993, 104 and 108.

35 "I never saw any white people": Wright 1987, 41, 45; Russell 1999, 312; Barbarin WRC; Kenney 1993, 20; Collier 1983, 94; Freeman CJA 1980.

35 Everyone knows ... they call them "alligators": Carmichael 1999a, 123. Paul Mares in Shapiro and Hentoff 1955, 123: "We [the New Orleans Rhythm Kings]

did our best to copy the colored music we'd heard at home. We did the best we could, but naturally we couldn't play real colored style." Dodds 1992, 61 and 25.

35 "They were guys": Shapiro and Hentoff 1955, 96.

35 stories about ringside musicians: Jackson 1994, 73; Dodds 1992, 37.

35 "The white man can write down": Travis 1981, 71.

36 "It got so I knew every phrase": Shapiro and Hentoff 1955, 116–17; Wright 1987, 262.

36 "We gave those fellows": Dodds 1992, 63.

36 "Should have been Freddie's": Armstrong LAHM Tape 495.

36 "We never went back": Bud Freeman IJS; Kenney 1993, 89–116.

36 up pops African-American jazz: Peretti 1992, chap. 5; Leonard 1962.

37 "The statistics of illegitimacy in this country": Leonard 1962, 34–36; Erenberg 1981, esp. chap. 3.

37 "Jazz brought about the downfall": Leonard 1962, 13.

37 "falling prey to the collective soul of the Negro": Leonard 1962, 12, 13, and 38.

37 a pattern that would become a twentieth-century archetype: Leonard 1962, 56.

38 feisty rejection of parental control: Peretti 1992, 98.

38 "this freedom of spirit that we whites didn't have": Freeman IJS; Kenney 1993, 107.

38 "I was not only hearing": Freeman 1974, 8.

## Chapter 2: Oliver's Band and the "Blues Age"

40 "had come up to Chicago": Russell 1999, 312, and Paul Barbarin WRC MSS 519 n.d.; Dress and pricing at Lincoln Gardens from Dorsey, Thomas CJA n.d.

40 "In Chicago an opportunity": Hansen 1960, 495.

40 Hinton eventually established a career: Hinton was interviewed many times: Hinton IJS 1974; Hinton IJS 1976; Hinton 1988; Hinton IJS n.d.

42 Booker T. Washington wrote: Washington 1907, 113.

42 "In 1910 a black man": Hinton IJS 1974. This kind of harassment does not seem to have existed in New Orleans, where, according to Preston Jackson (2005, 20), "on Rampart Street there were people there recruiting to come up to Chicago and work in the stockyards and the steel mills and they really were loading them in the box cars just like you would with horses or cows and they were leaving every day."

42 they shared with novelist Richard Wright: Wright 1998, 261.

43 Men worked in meat-packing and steel industries: Grossman 1989, 183–88; Hinton IJS 1974; Drake and Cayton 1970, 80 and 303.

43 Life on the South Side . . . capitalization of the word "Negro": Grossman 1989, 179; Lord 1976, 9; Drake and Cayton 1970, 65–73.

43 On the South Side it was possible: Drake and Cayton 1970, 80; Grossman 1989, 263; Kenney 1993, 5.

43 "Anybody I saw was black": Hinton IJS 1976. Hinton's first violin teacher was a white man who owned a store, and Hinton had a very positive relationship with him.

43 "sounded a little soft and pleasing": Hinton IJS 1976; Grossman 1989, 75; Hughes 1986, 103.

44 The *Defender*'s claim: Grossman 1989, 19.

45 "to better my position": Grossman 1989, 35; Hinton IJS 1976.

45 "A thousand percent better than we had in Mississippi": Hinton IJS 1976.

45 "lay down his burden of being a colored person": Jackson 1967, 46.

45 The word "freedom" . . . everywhere you turned: Grossman 1989, 259; Morton LC ca. 1938.

45 "They were a happy family": Armstrong 1954, 233.

45 "Is this my home boy?": Armstrong 1954, 233; Armstrong 1936, 70.

45 A guy from New Orleans . . . in town around this time: Armstrong IJS 1954, 120; Armstrong 1999, 48; Armstrong IJS 1954, 120; Russell 1999, 382; Elgar WRC 1970; Jackson 2005, 76; Jackson, Preston WRC n.d. Gushee (2005, 256) estimates that there were "perhaps 20 to 30 [New Orleans] players in various combinations rotating between the handful of cabarets that welcomed their music . . . in the first few years during and just after the war." Preston Jackson (2005, 27) said that the local union complained about the use of so many musicians from New Orleans, and that Oliver was brought up to face charges, which were eventually dropped for lack of evidence. See also Steiner 1959; Wang 1988; Kenney 1993, 12; Shapiro and Hentoff 1955, 79.

46 caste distinction between downtown Creoles of color and uptown Negroes: Integration between downtown and uptown musicians had already begun in New Orleans. See Brothers 2006, 9–30, and chap. 8; Armstrong 1999, 42.

46 a gesture of exclusion: Chilton 1987, 30.

46 a cliquish society that excluded musicians from other places: Bushell 1988, 35; Hinton IJS 1976; Wang 1988, 101; Shapiro and Hentoff 1955, 138; Chilton 1987, 28 and 32; Russell 1999, 383.

46 "The only time a New Orleans leader": Jackson 2005, 59.

46 The neighborhood was full . . . without leaving the building": Armstrong 1999, 53; Travis 1981, 55; Hinton 1988, 20; Armstrong IJS 1954, 120; Jackson 2005, 222–23; Jackson WRC n.d.

47 "You got to do a lot of blowing": Armstrong 1999, 49.

47 "let the youngster blow": Armstrong 1999, 53.

47 "nothing more clearly affirms one's 'class'": Bourdieu 1984, 18.

48 "Blues come out of the fields": Barlow 1989, 18.

48 "They were singing the blues in Mississippi and Louisiana": Barlow 1989, 27.

49 "Louis swings more telling a joke": Morgenstern 2004, 73.

50 Because of its associations . . . not shared by everyone: Smith 1964, 101; Grossman 1989, 150; Grossman 1989, 154. James Baldwin wrote about avoiding Bessie Smith's recordings "in the same way that, for years, I would not touch watermelon"; Baldwin 1961, 5; Harris 1992, 123.

50 W. C. Handy: This discussion of early sheet-music publications of blues relies heavily on the excellent study by Abbott and Seroff 1996.

50 publication of *St. Louis Blues*: Giddins 1998, 29.

50 Handy's success depended on his ability to highlight a few salient gestures from the vernacular: Several observers have insisted that Handy stole the entire composition of *St. Louis Blues*; see, for example, Foster 2005, 105; Abbott and Seroff 1996, 412. The same accusation has been made regarding a number of other songs by Handy; Morton 1994, 101; Russell 1999, 228. A good study of Handy is needed, for he is an important figure whose own remarks can be misleading.

When he says, for example, that blue notes were the product of "a deep-rooted racial groping for instinctive harmonies," he speaks as an outsider to the vernacular blues tradition, not as one of the "ordinary" people Sunnyland Slim knew in Louisiana and Mississippi who sang the blues. (Abbott and Seroff 1996, 404, have thus been misled and their conclusion that "improvising close harmonies was integral to the crystallization of the famous 'blue note'" reverses the historical dynamic; quotation from Handy taken from their discussion.) Handy's comment is similar to assertions by outsiders in New Orleans that blue notes in early jazz were the product of faulty instruments that could not be tuned. Both take African-American culture during this period as primitive, as a desperate imitation of European culture. The important point is that blues and blues melodic style evolved first as a *melodic* idiom; harmony was adapted to it. For more on Handy from this perspective, see Brothers 1997.

51 "organizer of the blues": *Courier*, Dec. 13, 1924, p. 9. In an analysis of Handy's borrowings, James Weldon Johnson wrote that "strictly speaking, it [*Memphis Blues*] is not a composition." Quoted in Abbott and Seroff 1996, 412.

51 blues songs as "colored folks' opera": Abbott and Seroff 1996, 419 and passim.

51 "Some time ago . . . lower classes of Race folks": *Defender*, June 26, 1926, p. 6.

51 Ma Rainey was one of the first: Information on Rainey from Bernhardt 1986, 24–26; see also Lieb 1981.

51 "She possessed her listeners": Dorsey quoted in Harris 1992, 89.

52 TOBA theaters eliminated the humiliation: Bushell 1988, 36.

52 three theaters catering to blacks: Travis 1981, 30.

52 "She, in a sense": Albertson 2003, 131.

52 tingling the spine of the enraptured patron: Travis 1981, 385.

52 "It [blues] gets down": Harris 1992, 96.

52 "digging, picking, pricking": Harris 1992, 98.

53 the aura of a life lived under special conditions: Peretti 1992, 123; Bernhardt 1986, 97.

53 In 1920, OKeh Records . . . marketed explicitly to African Americans: Bradford 1965, 114–29; Smith 1964, 103–5; Foreman 1968, 158; Albertson 2003, 24. The source for 18,000 is Perry Bradford (1965, 28), who should be regarded cautiously. My searches turn up no article in the *Norfolk Journal and Guide*, which Bradford claimed as his source. There is an advertisement in that newspaper on Jan. 22, 1921, referencing an article from the *Norfolk Ledger Dispatch*, but I have not been able to see the complete article.

53 "rough, coarse shouter": Foreman 1968, 61.

53 "she didn't get in between the notes": Bushell quoted in Williams 1962, 78.

53 Bessie Smith was initially rejected: Michael Harris citing Albertson 2003, 37–39 and 43.

53 Again, the white businessmen . . . build their careers: Albertson 2003, 46; Kenney 1999, 106, 119–20; Foreman 1968, 70; Kenney 1999, 129; Bushell 1988, 1.

56 Around age ten . . . from the plantations: Brothers 2006, 55–73; Lomax 1993, 77.

56 her husband listened to rail- and dockworkers: Oliver HJA 1959.

56 Armstrong said: Armstrong 1936, 26. Armstrong, Lillian WRC 1938; Jackson WRC 1938. There is room for suspicion about the consistent claims for an influence of Johnson on Armstrong in these 1938 interviews, which are summarized by Bill Russell on notes preserved at the Williams Research Center. It is likely

that Russell, who had already spoken with Johnson, was asking leading questions, as he often does on the taped interviews from the 1950s. On Armstrong's denial of influence from Johnson, see Armstrong 1999, 40–41 and 197–98. On the other hand, Ory also cited this kind of phrasing as Johnson's specialty; Russell 1994, 178.

56 "the strongest notes you can play": Foster 2005, 73.

56 Music can be heard . . . by ordinary people: Barbarin HJA 1957; Jackson 2005, 72–74.

57 Of these three terms . . . in 1955: Bechet 1960, 3; Brothers 2006, chap. 7; Armstrong 1955, 60.

58 Handy's band "was called": Foster 2005, 105.

58 "That was a rag": Zutty Singleton WRC ca. 1938.

58 "The word has been used for so many different things": Berrett 2004, 41.

58 "American dance music": Kenney 1993, 61–62.

58 "We hadn't heard groups in the East": Smith 1964, 123 and 129.

58 "There wasn't an eastern performer": Bushell 1988, 22; Williams 1962, 77; Morand HJA 1950.

58 With blues in their pockets . . . network of musicians: Jackson HJA 1958; Goodard 1979, 292. Hunter IJS 1976; Mitchell HJA 1959; Shapiro and Hentoff 1955, 77–79; McBride HJA 1959. Bushell 1988, 25. Ellington 1973, 47; Brown, Ralph COHP 1971. Kenney 1993, 102–16. Bushell 1988, 22. Hinton IJS n.d. Wettling 1945, 5; Compton HJA 1959; Freeman CJA 1980. Hinton IJS 1976; Washington COHP 1971; Smith HJA 1961.

59 "strictly" from New Orleans: Brown, Ralph COHP 1971; Russell 1999, 467.

60 Alberta Hunter suggested to Columbia Records: Taylor 1987, 56.

60 "When Joe Oliver went up": Foster 2005, 95.

60 In the spring of 1923 . . . "so we move on": Armstrong 1936, 79; Wright 1987, 16. Kennedy 1994, 36. Punch Miller HJA 1959. Bernhardt 1986, 54.

60 sign up bands on the spot: On these first sessions and the Gennett business, see Kennedy 1994, 28–30 and 114; Dodds 1992, 69; Russell 1999, 357; Davison IJS 1980; Dodds WRC n.d.; Moore HJA 1959. Wright (1987, 16) says that it is not clear whether the band made the recordings while on this tour or on a separate trip from Chicago, but Armstrong (1936, 16) plainly says that the recordings took place while on the tour. Kennedy (1994, 59) says without documentation that the band took a train from Chicago just to make the trip. Dodds (1992, 69) discusses making trips directly from Chicago, taking the train because there was no place for them to stay in Richmond.

62 Armstrong was overpowering Oliver's lead: Lillian Hardin Armstrong in Jones and Chilton 1971, 71; Dodds 1992, 69; Armstrong 1966, 37. George Brunis (HJA 1958) described something similar in a recording session with Gennett: his cornet was too loud, so the engineer had him "turn around and play to the wall."

62 Recordings were limited . . . with a bottle: Dance 1977, 26. Dodds 1992, 69.

62 In these brief, tinny recordings: Recordings of Oliver's band during 1923 have been reissued many times, most recently—and with excellent results—as *King Oliver Off the Record: The Complete 1923 Jazz Band Recordings* (Thurmont, MD: Off the Record, 2006; distributed by Archeophone Records, Champaign, IL).

63 they turned to the Original Dixieland Jazz Band: Noone in Dodds, John WRC ca. 1938.

63 "I'd never heard any white band": Mezzrow 1946, 51.

63 "I ain't gonna give these white boys my best stuff": Fess Williams in Wright 1987, 335; see also Brown, Ralph COHP 1971; also Buster Bailey in Shapiro and Hentoff 1955, 96. *I'm Not Rough*, the piece that earned him the crown of King at Lincoln Gardens in 1919, was not recorded, either.

63 Alberta Hunter remembered . . . credit for *Chimes Blues* to Oliver: Balliet 1977, 110. Connections with *Holy City* noted by Lyttelton 1978, 149; see also Sager 2006, 16 and 17. Lillian Hardin Armstrong (CJA n.d.) said she "conceived the idea of playing piano chords in chimes style against any blues to give the piano a chorus to be heard. I didn't know the tune had been published by Melrose."

63 both brought up with church music: See Brothers 2005, chap. 2 and passim.

64 even Oliver's wife Stella admitted: Oliver HJA 1959.

64 probably resembles the slap-pizzicato: Brooks 2002, 9.

64 the solo that quickly became identified with him: Wright (1987, 269) suggests that it is the most copied jazz solo ever.

65 "Once you got a certain solo": Armstrong 1966, 43. For an extended analysis of this phenomenon, see Harker 1999.

65 freak wah-wah effects: On the likelihood of hand manipulation, see Lyttelton 1978, 42.

65 This is the kind of playing . . . as Armstrong put it: Bushell 1988, 26. Bernhardt 1986, 95. Armstrong LAHA 1951a; Brothers 2006, 290, and endnote p. 364; Russell 1994, 138; Pleasants 1974, 101. Armstrong 1999, 38.

66 Oliver had put his name on it: Armstrong, Lillian CJA n.d.

66 had to advance from his corner position: Armstrong 1966, 37.

66 "As a kid it just came natural": Armstrong 1971, 214; Armstrong 1945, 13. Clarinetist Benny Waters (Waters 1985, 12 and 14) remembered his own sensitivity to chords developing as a child in precisely the same repertory of vocal quartets. Harker (2003, 143) analyzes Armstrong's arpeggiations in *Chimes Blues* and elsewhere as indicating influence from clarinet playing, but I see it as more strictly an indicator of precise interest in chords.

67 with some of the musicians playing a major chord and others a minor chord: The issue was signaled by Gunther Schuller (1968, 83), but Schuller's account is slightly misleading. It is not uncommon in pastiche pieces like this, with parts created by different people, for there to be slight changes in the chords, and I believe that this is precisely what has happened here. The choruses before Armstrong's solo do not involve the diminished chord in m. 6, and m. 2 is different as well; it is sometimes hard to get a clear impression of what is being played, but that much is clear. So Schuller's point that Armstrong is alone in getting the diminished chord correct is wrong—his is the only chorus that has a diminished chord prescribed for this measure. His point about conflict between F major and F minor in earlier choruses still stands, however.

67 When King Oliver . . . secondary concerns: Sudhalter 1999, 34. De Faut WRC 1970. Armstrong, Lillian WRC 1969.

## Chapter 3: Opposites Attract: Louis and Miss Lil

70 "But who was I to think": Armstrong 1999, 16.

70 "Louis, do you want to go over and meet Lil?": Armstrong 1936, 70.

70 They were not . . . she remembered: Dickerson 2002, 40. Hunter IJS 1976; Armstrong, Lillian 1963. Jones and Chilton 1971, 69.

70 "wasn't very much to look at": Armstrong IJS 1954, 36.

71 Once in New Orleans . . . in November 1922: Armstrong IJS 1954, 12. Armstrong, 1999, 87; Armstrong, Lillian CJA n.d. Armstrong 1936, 71.

71 Lillian's point of entry . . . relationship with Fisk: Jones Music Store: Armstrong, Lillian WRC 1938. Bergreen 1997, 181–82. Armstrong (1999, 203) believed that she had been valedictorian at Fisk University, and this claim has been repeated often. In an interview with John Steiner (CJA n.d.), Hardin said that she attended Fisk for two years.

72 In Memphis . . . she remembered: Armstrong, Lillian, 1963. Armstrong, Lillian WRC 1969; Armstrong, Lillian 2005, 140.

72 Through practicing . . . the improvising New Orleanians began: Armstrong, Lillian 1963. Armstrong, Lillian CJA 1960; Ed Garland WRC 1958.

72 She had memorized . . . extended considerably: Armstrong, Lillian WRC 1969. Smith: Smith 1964, 126.

73 Hardin managed to hide the situation: Armstrong, Lillian CJA 1960.

73 When Oliver took over . . . sheet music: Lil's enthusiasm for California may have had something to do with a bad marriage to singer Jimmy Johnson; see Hunter IJS 1976. Armstrong, Lillian 1963; Anderson 1994, 293–95. Bertha: aka Bertha Gonzales. Wright 1987, 14. Jones and Chilton 1971, 66. Preston Jackson (2005, 27) said that after Gonsoulin left Oliver's band, he replaced her first with Lottie Taylor, then with someone named Frances, and finally with Lil Hardin.

73 "From a musical standpoint": Armstrong, Lillian 1963.

74 Lil began to notice the pudgy second cornetist: Armstrong, Lillian 1963; Jones and Chilton 1971, 70; Armstrong 1936, 79.

74 "that ended the smelling session": Armstrong 1999, 54.

74 nighttime wanderings on the "stroll": For descriptions of night life in South Side Chicago around this time, see Smith 1964, 127; Samuels COHP 1970; Kenney 1993, esp. chap. 1; Sengstock 2000.

74 "You could stand on 35th and State": Howard CJA n.d.

75 "I made it my business": Kenney 1993, 13.

75 concentration of black-owned businesses: Travis 1981, 37; Smith 1964, 123. Drake and Cayton 1970, 82. Spivey 1984, 38–39; Samuels COHP 1971.

75 The stroll was "Wall Street and Broadway": Travis 1981 37; Kenney 1993, 15; Grossman 1989, 117.

75 Black musicians never . . . "knew Chicago like a book": Earl Hines: Hines COHP 1971. Smith 1964, 127. Knew Chicago: Armstrong 1946, 40.

75 At first, Armstrong . . . better tone: Keppard: Armstrong 1999, 66. Cheatham: Cheatham IJS 1976; Armstrong, Lillian 1963; Armstrong 1999, 25.

76 Keppard liked to create an air of intrigue: Cheatham IJS 1976, 114.

76 Louis and Lil . . . "singing like a choir": White musicians: Armstrong 1999, 66; Armstrong 1946, 42. Smith 1964, 126.

76 A little further down . . . "liquor music": Defender: Anderson 1994, 292. "much to the amazement": Waller 1965, 74; Hodes 1977, 177; Hunter IJS 1976; Oliver HJA 1959. "At one o'clock": Vincent 1995, 73.

76 One day in late 1922: Armstrong 1999, 183, 27.

77 The musical couple's favorite place: Armstrong 1999, 87. Anderson (1994, 292–93) reports that Bottoms was also part owner of the Chicago Whip, which explains the lavish coverage of the Dreamland there. On the Dreamland, see also Kenney 1993, 18; Hunter IJS 1976; Vincent 1995, 77; Garland HJA 1957.

78 Each solo entertainer ... lack of sophistication: "up": Shapiro and Hentoff 1955, 88. Aletha Hill: Garland WRC 1969. Hunter IJS 1976. "rocking the whole house": Armstrong 1946, 40. Also on Powers, Armstrong 1999, 54–55; Smith 1964, 129; Jackson 2005, 25.

78 "We did not really get together": This account of Armstrong's mother's visit is derived from Armstrong 1999, 87 and 57. On p. 57 Armstrong writes that May Ann's visit took place three months after his arrival in Chicago. But the chronology of his relationship with Lillian argues for a date in summer or early fall 1923.

79 "Now was my turn": Armstrong 1999, 59.

79 "that's what Louis wanted to be": Dodds, Warren WRC n.d.; Russell 1994, 20.

80 "It was real kicks": Armstrong 1999, 66.

80 "stay under" the lead: Armstrong 1966, 29: "I never blew my horn over Joe Oliver at no time unless he said, 'Take it!'"

81 "I felt that any glory": Armstrong 1999, 50.

81 "When a person's in the spotlight": Dance 1977, 54.

81 "I was so wrapped up in him": Armstrong 1999, 50.

82 "Only that ending was called 'jazz'": Jones WRC ca. 1938. On breaks in New Orleans, see Brothers 2006, 105, 148, 209, and 230.

82 "Without breaks": Morton 2005, disc 2, track 13.

82 "Joe broke them that night": Russell 1994, 37; Wright 1987, 335; see also Mitchell HJA 1959.

82 "The crowd would go mad over it!": Sager 2006, 14; Armstrong 1999, 50; Shapiro and Hentoff 1955, 102–03; Gleason 1974; Armstrong 1946, 40.

83 Barney Bigard said: Bigard IJS 1976.

83 It may not be mere coincidence: It is difficult to pin down release times of phonograph records, but the Blue Five recording of *Wildcat Blues* was advertised in the national edition of the *Chicago Defender* on Jan. 26, 1924, p. 6. For comparison of *Tears* with *Wildcat Blues*, see Brooks 2002, 60, citing Lyttelton.

84 felt well qualified to fill the rupture of the break: Armstrong 1966, 28.

84 His will to adorn: Hurston 1995, 224–27.

84 comes through again in his prose writings: Edwards 2002; Brothers 1999.

84 musical texture of early jazz: Brothers 2006, chap. 2.

84 The distinctive texture ... no drop in intensity: "every tub": Armstrong IJS 1965. Less often New Orleans musicians refer to "tailgate" style (Armstrong WRC 1954), a nod to the position of the trombone at the back of an advertising wagon. The connection: Armstrong 1999, 170.

85 Collective improvisation ... textural effect: "At all times": Dodds WRC n.d. Russell 1994, 72; Brothers 2006, 45; Brothers 2008. 1950s: See, for example, the performance of *Maple Leaf Rag* on *The Music of New Orleans,* vol. 4: *The Birth of Jazz* (Washington, DC: Smithsonian Institution, 2007).

86 Out of standard practices ... than Oliver did: Ramsey 1946, 28. Dodds 1992, 34. Gleason 1974. Barnes WRC 1968.

86 "Joe was always making suggestions": Dodds 1992, 38; Armstrong, Lillian HJA 1959; Wright 1987, 261; Russell 1994, 39.

87 "wanted everyone to blend together": Dodds 1992, 38–41; Nicholas HJA 1972; Dodds 1992, 36.

87 The rhythm section ... was valued: "She would": Armstrong 1999, 65. Armstrong 1994, 72; Garland IJS n.d.

88 When Armstrong wrote . . . two-beat feeling: Armstrong 1999, 65. Garland WRC 1958; Garland HJA 1958; St. Cyr HJA 1958.

88 A drummer could . . . keep things interesting: Williams 1979, 84. Shapiro and Hentoff 1955, 98. Wright 1987, 15.

89 do not give sufficient prominence to the cornets: Morgenstern 2006, 4. The problem is standard throughout the 1923 recordings, but for a particularly glaring example, listen to *High Society*. See Brothers 2006, 45, for further discussion of the central role of stating the lead melody prominently.

89 "few notes and with good rhythm": Spanier HJA 1961.

89 Lead melodies . . . noted Armstrong: Palmer HJA 1955. Armstrong 1971, 220.

89 Trombone, clarinet, and cornet . . . "in the windows": Condon in Peretti 1992, 113. Roy Palmer discusses options for the trombone in Russell 1994, 188. Mezzrow 1946, 114.

89 Armstrong claimed to admire: Armstrong 1999, 51.

90 even more exposed in the second strain: The Eurocentric musical tradition of band and dance music that the New Orleanians were familiar with has its own concept of an obbligato line, which is certainly where the term comes from. The practice comes out of traditional counterpoint. In counterpoint, too, there is delight in the coordination of independent melodies, which are held together not by the model of fixed and variable but by rules of simultaneously sounding consonances and dissonances.

90 Oliver provided one back in the early 1910s: Brothers 2009.

91 "I can't be a boss on that": Phillips WRC n.d.

91 A few comments here and there: Miles Davis's style of communicating with his band many years later was once described by a musician: "There were grunts, glances, smiles and no smiles. Miles communicated but not on a logical or analytical level." Lyons 1983, 261.

91 standard practice in New Orleans: Baby Dodds (1992, 36): "Somebody would suggest a number and we would play it and experiment with different keys to see which would sound the best."

92 "The only good thing about it": Armstrong 1999, 54.

92 "Once you got a certain solo": Armstrong 1966, 43. For an extended analysis of this phenomenon, see Harker 1999.

93 easy for the ear to pick out the layers: Brothers 1994.

93 Music of the African diaspora: Brothers 2006, 145–48; Wilson 1978.

94 "rhythm section provides transportation": Peretti 1992, 113.

95 "Notes I had never heard were peeling off the edges": Kenney 1993, 105.

95 Uptown African Americans . . . took it from there: *New York Clipper*, "Reviews of Disc Records," Abel, Sept. 14, 1923, p. 31; Wright 1987, 28. Kubik 1999, 43.

95 "One couldn't help but dance to that band": Dodds 1992, 36.

97 louder than his mentor's lead: Transcribed and analyzed in Schuller 1968, 80–84.

97 Condon succinctly described . . . African diaspora: Condon: Kenney 1993, 105. Chernoff 1979, 154.

97 Garvin Bushell remembered: Bushell 1988, 25.

98 The summer of 1923 . . . said Smith: Shapiro and Hentoff 1955, 98. Smith 1964, 123–25.

98 Lil bought a used car . . . left the scene: Armstrong, Lillian 1963. Armstrong 1999, 57.

98 The couple attended . . . left New Orleans: *Defender*, July 15 and 29, Oct. 21, 1922. Armstrong 1999, 55–56. Armstrong 1999, 87; Hunter IJS 1976.

99 In early June . . . seen the writing on the wall: Meyer, Sig CJA 1975. *Talking Machine World*: Wright 1987, 337.

99 "she was really *up* on things": Armstrong 1999, 61.

99 bafflement and even hostility: Armstrong 1999, 87ff and 64. The main competition may have been from Oliver. Oliver took romantic interest in Bertha Gonsoulin during their trip to California, according to Baby Dodds (WRC n.d.), and there appears to have been a New Orleans tradition of bandleaders regarding female pianists in this way. Pops Foster told a story about Oliver in the mid-1910s: Oliver set up Foster with a girl for pimping, but then became so jealous that he threatened to fire Foster; see Brothers 2005, 257.

99 On the June sessions . . . night after night: Wright 1987, 23. Facsimile of the lead sheet for *When You Leave Me Alone to Pine* in Chevan 1999, 488. *Defender*: Wright 1987, 27 and 28.

100 she would be looking out for him: Armstrong, Lillian 1963.

100 When he showed up . . . more than clothing: Budd Red: Armstrong, Lillian 1963. "He liked the way": Armstrong, Lillian 1963. First solo break comes in *Tears*: Brooks 2002, 61.

101 Lil said that the two of them . . . a name for himself?: Armstrong, Lillian WRC 1938; Armstrong, Lillian 1950. Oliver, Stella HJA 1959. Hodes 1977, 80.

101 "nice looking, stout, brown skin man": Armstrong 1999, 75.

102 he mailed a manuscript copy of *Cornet Chop Suey*: Carmichael 1999, 53. This book was apparently written by Carmichael in the early 1930s; the story is told slightly differently in the later autobiography cowritten by Carmichael and Longstreet (1999, 101). On the dates and authority of the two autobiographies, see Hasse 1999.

102 *Cornet Chop Suey* begins: The recording (Aug. 29, 1922) of *Bugle Call Rag* by the New Orleans Rhythm Kings begins with a solo bugle call. The recording (1921) of *Bugle Blues* by Johnny Dunn's Jazz Hounds is slower and does not begin with a solo, but the later (March 26, 1928) *Original Bugle Blues* by Johnny Dunn and His Band has the solo introduction. Williams never recorded *Bugle Blues*.

102 Armstrong did him one better: Brothers 2006, 265; Shapiro and Hentoff 1955, 23; Jackson 2005, 42.

102 To call a piece *Clarinet Marmalade* . . . widely shared pleasure: *Defender*, Jan. 6, 1923, p. 4; Taylor 1987, 47. Chinese food every night: Hinton IJS 1976.

103 "Improving my position" . . . the German guy as student": Garland WRC 1958; Russell 1994, 95 and 111. Noone WRC 1938; Dance 1977, 194; Shapiro and Hentoff 1955, 78. Peyton: *Defender*, Jan. 29, 1927, p. 6. Reeves FDC 1956. Ory: Russell 1994, 181; Ory HJA 1957.

104 This kind of training . . . classically trained girlfriend: Marable: Brothers 2006, 252; Russell 1994, 30.

104 Kimball Hall was . . . in 1925 and 1926: Warehouse: My thanks to Deborah Gillaspie for her help with this. Kimball Hall is #6 on this drawing: http://uic.edu /depts/ahaa/imagebase/intranet/chiviews/page173.html. Coverage: *Defender,* March 26, 1921; *Light and Heebie Jeebies*, Sept. 24, 1927, p. 18. Mrs. Gray: *Defender,* Oct. 31, 1925, p. 5, and April 1, 1922, p. 5. Hersal and George Thomas:

*Defender*, March 26, 1921, p. 9; see also March 26, 1921, p. 4; April 23, 1921, p. 5 (with a German teacher named Adolph Weidig); June 10, 1922, p. 5; July 17, 1926, p. 6. For more on Hersal Thomas, see Taylor 1993, 75–76. It is possible that Armstrong's lessons at Kimball Hall happened later, when he joined Erskine Tate.

104 Jones did say that Oliver studied harmony: Jones WRC ca. 1938. On Armstrong's command of solfège, see Randolph FDC 1973; Nicholas HJA 1972.

104 Armstrong said that he learned . . . eye of his fiancée: "wood shed": Armstrong 1936, 71; Ramsey 1939, 125. Anxious: Armstrong, Lillian WRC 1938. Confidence: Armstrong, Lillian 1950.

105 There are stories . . . picnics at St. Thomas Episcopal: "Cute guys": Brothers 2009, 26. Davis 1990, 60.

105 *Cornet Chop Suey* is a showpiece . . . the New Orleans–Chicago train line: "We were all very fast": Armstrong 1999, 133. "He's showing off": Barker 1986, 59. Brian Harker (2011, chap. 1) has explored a number of issues raised by this statement, and works with them in ways different than I do here. I find his insights into clarinet style as an alternative idiom for Armstrong useful (and I would extend those with consideration of Armstrong's history playing "second," which naturally involved more figuration; see Brothers 2009). But I think he exaggerates the importance of the clarinet as an obvious aural reference in Armstrong's construction of the piece, which ultimately leads him to see *Cornet Chop Suey* as a demonstration of novelty.

106 Lil and Louis had each . . . musically and romantically: *Sweet Lovin' Man*: Chevan 1999, 249–51, traces the history of this piece, with its various titles, copyright deposits, coauthors, and recordings. *I Wish I Could Shimmy*: Brothers 2006, 228.

106 Musicians in their circle . . . no reason to doubt Noone: "Have you got any": Oliver WRC 1930. Noone in Dodds WRC ca. 1938.

107 Armstrong once mused . . . paraphrases popular tunes: "there will be other tunes": Morgenstern 1965, 18. "no one created": Armstrong 1999, 38, 65. What did he mean by this: The question is raised by Gushee 1998, 292, which is one basis for the present discussion.

107 My guess is . . . this kind of appropriation, too: Wright 1987, 250–58, provides a list and discussion of Oliver's compositions. Morton and Oliver: Foster 2005, 96; Wright 1987, 340.

107 Recordings for Gennett and OKeh did not generate much cash: Kenney 1999, 118.

108 This was the chain . . . Lil's and Louis's compositions: He remembered: Armstrong 1999, 132. "We were": Dodds 1992, 36.

109 Lillian said that . . . he bragged: "all the fancy runs": Armstrong, Lillian WRC 1938; Armstrong, Louis WRC 1939; Miller HJA 1959; Jones WRC ca. 1938. "They came up whistling": Dodds 1992, 62. Bunk Johnson: Gleason 1961, 83, 86. Ory-Oliver band: Oliver HJA 1959. De Pass: De Pass HJA 1960. Jackson: Jackson 2005, 20 and 31; Jackson HJA 1958; Jackson WRC 1938.

110 "The thing that makes jazz so interesting": Leonard 1987, 102.

110 how much that played out in *Cornet Chop Suey*: Regarding the precision of chronology here, Lil told the story of Armstrong whistling different ways at different times. In the earliest version, as told to Bill Russell in 1938, she links the whistling to his frustration in playing Oliver's solo for *Dipper Mouth Blues*.

110 "She didn't want me to copy Joe": Jones and Chilton 1971, 76.

111 Each section is different in this way: The opening two bars of Armstrong's patter section were anticipated in his contribution, as second cornetist, to the end of *Buddy's Habit*, recorded in October.

112 He throws in harmonic variety: The diminished chord G-sharp, B, D occurs in m. 49 of Chevan's transcription (1997, 300).

112 "Where's that lead?": Armstrong quoting Oliver in Morgenstern 1965, 17.

113 Armstrong married . . . at 38th and Indiana: Parisian gown: *Defender*, Feb. 16, 1924, p. 9. Jackson: Jackson 2005, 59. Rice: Armstrong 1999, 65. Rented apartment: Conway 1971, 7.

114 If Oliver and the other musicians . . . hold at bay: Hunger: Hunter IJS 1976. "Gave me hell": Conway 1971, 7. Devout Christian: Armstrong 1999, 65.

114 Perhaps Louis's burgeoning . . . mostly about him: "He was just as sweet": Hunter IJS 1976. "If she hadn't run": Armstrong 1999, 50.

115 "I remember someone told me": Armstrong, Lillian CJA n.d.

115 "at the bottom of the ladder, holding it": Armstrong, Lillian 1950.

## Chapter 4: The Call from Broadway

116 to swing through the midwestern states: Armstrong 1999, 92.

116 The breakup . . . a few recording sessions: Armstrong 1999, 62–64. Dodds, John WRC ca. 1938.

116 When the checks came in: Dodds 1992, 48. Pops Foster (Foster 2005, 96) told a story about Oliver ordering uniforms for the band in New Orleans, at $12 apiece. He then wrote a letter to the band, masking it so that it appeared to be from the Western Uniform Company, with someone mailing it from Chicago, saying that the company had burned down and "we couldn't get our uniforms or our money back." "Joe never did pay me and died owing me money," insisted Foster. "That's why I'd never make records with him."

116 "King Oliver's men were always talking": Armstrong in Jones and Chilton 1971, 11; Armstrong, Lillian WRC 1938. Armstrong, Lillian 1963.

117 Zue Robertson eventually joined: Wright 1987, 39.

117 Armstrong believed . . . couldn't pull it off: Armstrong 1999, 62 and 63. *Chicago Defender*, June 21, 1924, p. 6, and June 28, 1924, p. 8, local editions.

117 Oliver started to loosen . . . middle of a performance: "he decided": Armstrong 1999, 64. Jones and Chilton 1971, 77; Armstrong 1999, 61. Brothers 2006, 231. "Help the ol' man": Armstrong 1999, 92 and 64. Chilton 1947, 6.

118 Rudy Jackson remembered . . . popular once again: Jones and Chilton 1971, 77. Chilton 1947, 5. Armstrong 1946, 42; Armstrong 1999, 72. Wright 1987, 39–41.

118 "ego and wounded vanity may hurt you": Reich HJA 2001.

118 "I told him I didn't want to be married": Armstrong, Lillian CJA n.d.

118 "Sitting by [Oliver] every night": Armstrong 1966, 29.

119 "Joe, this is the first time": Collins 1974, 36; Collins HJA 1958.

119 Lillian didn't want . . . unfortunate choice: Armstrong, Lillian 1963. Armstrong, Lillian WRC 1938.

119 In the summer of 1924 . . . one of them admitted: Jones WRC ca. 1938; Hennessey 1974, 24–26, 37; Kenney 1993, 113. Robinson CJA 1961. "A group of": *Defender*, March 3, 1923, p. 5; Shapiro and Hentoff 1955, 84; Jackson 2005, 57; Brown 1971. "Thought they were": Travis 1981, 65.

119 Armstrong gathered . . . about Stewart, bitterly: Armstrong, Lillian 1963; Jones and Chilton 1971, 78. Dance 1977, 68. Milt Hinton (Hinton IJS 1976) also talked about "blue veined" musicians with light skin who "hung together and got the better jobs" in Chicago; also Bernhardt 1986, 77, 138, 145, and 179. "I wasn't": Armstrong 1971, 211.

120 Lil suggested Ollie Powers . . . chance to shine: Taylor 1987, 36; Compton HJA 1959. "That's when": Armstrong, Lillian 1963.

120 Henderson first heard him: Allen 1973, 29; Henderson 1950a, 15; Armstrong 1936, 80; Singleton 1950.

120 Interestingly, Lillian stayed . . . he chortled: Armstrong 1936, 80; Armstrong, Lillian 2005, 143. "They were": Armstrong LAHM 1970.

121 His first rehearsal with Henderson: This account of the first rehearsal based on Henderson 1950 and Armstrong 1946, 42. "I had just": Henderson 1950a, 15.

122 After arriving in New York . . . appealing number for Henderson: "Your part's": Marshall 1943, 83. Osgood 1926, 110. On "high class" preferences of Black Swan Records, see Magee 2005, 22. As Garvin Bushell (1988, 25) put it in 1925, "Paul Whiteman had the premier orchestra in the States. No question about it. It's like when Muhammad Ali was champion: it was undisputed."

122 "When you was playing shows": Henderson 1950a, 15. Jones 1989, 133.

122 For the most part . . . his clunky shoes: Marshall 1943 in Hodes 1977, 83. Henderson 1950. Williams 1979, 96; Scott IJS 1979. Armstrong 1966, 31; Armstrong 1999, 205; Stewart 1991, 92–96. Armstrong 1936, 80.

122 Things would improve . . . he wrote bluntly: Armstrong 1970 and letter published by Jones and Chilton (1971, 211).

123 In the end . . . personification of that: Hinton IJS 1976. "a *machine* town": Russell 1999, 97–100.

123 more extensive introduction to the Harlem elite: I have drawn this description of the NAACP dance from a series of articles in the *Interstate Tattler, Pittsburgh Courier, Baltimore Afro-American*, and *Chicago Defender*; also Lewis 1993 and 1997. "Pinnacle of posh": Vincent 1995, 167. Hughes 1986, 94.

125 Du Bois's position was ascendant: Lewis 1993, 261.

125 "Keep in mind that when I was born": Travis 1981, 436.

125 Henderson (b. 1897) grew up in Cuthbert, Georgia: Early Henderson biography based on Magee 2005, chap. 1.

125 He was the deacon and superintendent: Harris 1992, 207.

126 his father continued to prohibit: Allen 1973, 3.

126 "classed with Rachmaninoff": Magee 2005, 19.

126 regarded by Du Bois as the perfect talented-tenth model: Lewis 2000, 9.

126 one of only around 2,000 African Americans: Lewis 1993, 644, n. 51.

126 Harry Pace: Allen 1973, 7; Magee 2005, 17. A recent overview of this part of Pace's career is given in Hurwitt 2000, esp. 214ff. See also Kenney 1999, 124.

128 Henderson became "musical director": Allen 1973, 10; Vincent 1995, 92 and 99.

128 "Was there ever a nation": Du Bois 1903, 45.

128 But for Du Bois . . . Hughes wrote: Vincent 1995, 145–46. Hughes 1986, 266.

128 "I had seen many of the important men and women": Barker 1986, 140.

129 Pace quickly realized . . . Waters remembered: Waters 1951, 141 and 147.

129 In summer 1922: Shih 1959; Hennessey 1973.

129 At a white Manhattan dance hall . . . in white Manhattan: Allen 1973, 41 and 86.

"made a nice": Williams 1979, 95. *Chicago Daily Tribune*, Jan. 18, 1924, p. 12; *New York Times*, Jan. 18, 1924, p. 7; Albertson 2003, 25. Magee 2005, 33–35 and 8.

130 In July 1924 Henderson . . . Henderson's strength: Magee 2005, 36. Armstrong 1936, 80. Charters 1962, 153. Allen 1973, 126. "Each section:" *Defender*, Feb. 27, 1926, p. 6.

131 In spite of the fact . . . "or anywhere else": Stewart 1972, 14. *Courier*, Nov. 1, 1924, p. 15. According to Bushell (IJS 1977), "there was no black band on radio then, outside of Fletcher Henderson, that was a big name jazz band." Allen 1973, 129. *New York Age*, April 4, 1925, p. 7. Allen 1973, 137; *Amsterdam News*, Sept. 9, 1925, p. 5; *Wall Street Journal*, Nov. 25, 1924, p. 3.

132 Jazz fans today may be surprised: For an earlier discussion along these lines, see Lyttelton 1978, 106.

132 "We have an opening": Allen 1973, 113.

133 five different usages of "jazz": Kenney 1993, 61–62.

133 "New Orleans hokum": *Defender*, Oct. 10, 1925, p. 6.

134 "to the vile instincts in human beings": Savran 2009, 194.

134 Irving Berlin's *Everybody Step*: Magee 2006.

135 A writer in *Etude*: Magee 2006, 698–700. Magee's identification of the bass pattern with blues can be strengthened by the view that the flat 4/4 accompaniment style was used for blues and church music in New Orleans and found its way into dance music there; see Brothers 2006, 43, 227, and 285.

135 "using the word 'jazz' and the word 'Berlin' as interchangeable terms": Magee 2006, 697.

135 "The simple fact is": Savran 2009, 70.

135 *Jazz was* . . . "We just called it great music": Osgood 1926, 27. Kenney 1993, 81 and 78. Deffaa 1990, 40.

135 Osgood nods briefly: Osgood 1926, 89.

136 the African-American antecedents had no importance at all: Sudhalter 1999 is a recent study that comes close to this position, even though it is not clearly articulated and only hinted at indirectly.

136 the most sublime blues chord ever heard: *Billboard*, May 31, 1924, p. 60.

136 "vulgarities and crudities": Rogers 1968, 221.

136 disdain for Henderson's early work: The paradox (but not this solution to it) is articulated by Magee 2005, 33. Magee is certainly right (p. 27) to critique the binary oppositions of writers like Panassié and Schuller and their reliance on formulas like "true and false jazz." The current discussion turns the analysis toward competing definitions of jazz.

136 Some insisted that symphonic jazz . . . like Henderson: A March 28, 1925, article in the *New York Age* is the earliest application of "symphonic jazz" to Henderson's band that I have seen. Howland 2009, 2.

138 Henderson, on the other hand . . . the Roseland Ballroom: "jazzy fox trots": *Defender*, March 29, 1924, p. 3. "nightly": *Afro-American*, May 30, 1924, p. 2.

138 Ever since the dance craze . . . in August 1925: Stearns and Stearns 1994, 95; Erenberg 1981, 153; Sanjek 1983. Osgood 1926, 42. Allen 1973,136.

139 the only black band to record these tunes: Two black bands with similar aspirations were those run by Sam Wooding, who recorded *Shanghai Shuffle* and *Alabamy Bound*, and Sammy Stewart, who recorded *Manda* and *Copenhagen*.

139 Like many bandleaders . . . cluttered and overblown: "The new": Berrett 2004, 49. "stodgy": Meyer CJA, box 83.

139 "He'd give me 16 bars, the most, to get off with": Armstrong LAHM 1970.

139 Henderson got what he wanted . . . the entire black community: Bushell 1988, 87. *Defender*, Feb. 27, 1926, p. 6; Aug. 27, 1927, p. 6.

141 Baby Dodds claimed . . . Armstrong remembered: Dodds 1992, 82. Scott IJS 1979; Allen 1973, 126. "Then I had": Henderson 1950a, 15.

141 The difference emerged . . . "that New Orleans stuff here": Reports on this performance from Allen 1973, 126; Henderson 1950a, p. 15; Armstrong 1946, 42. Scott IJS 1979; Scott's comment is not explicitly directed toward the performance of *Tiger Rag*.

142 "brassy, broad and aggressively dramatic": Baraka [Jones] 1963, 154.

143 In paraphrase solos: Transcription of the solo from *Go Long Mule* in Magee 2005, 77.

143 musicologist Jeffrey Magee has shown: The present analysis is an attempt to build on and extend the excellent work in Magee 1995.

144 "This arrangement is RED HOT as written": Magee 1995, 52.

144 He only needed to tweak the notated lines slightly: Oliver 1970, 64.

145 "an artistic reformulation of black folkways": Quoted and discussed, from a different point of view, in Magee 2005, 5.

145 With his strong, confident playing . . . he explained: "*so* good": Shapiro and Hentoff 1955, 206. Bernhardt 1968, 46; Bernhardt FDC 1974.

146 Smith's solo on *Alone at Last*: The recording was made by the Henderson band with white singer Billy Jones, under the name the Southern Serenaders, on Aug. 7 and released on the Harmony label. Presumably, the pseudonym was necessary to hide the racial integration of the session.

146 with Armstrong taking the riskier path: In her study of the 1920s, Ann Douglas (1995, 428) is trapped by much later images of Armstrong when she writes: "whatever the effort, even pain of performance, his aim was always to free the listener from worry and trouble, from any sense of the 'serious'; grinning, cajoling, grimacing, and alive, he wanted his considerable labor to appear the easiest, the most effortless in the world." Related to this is her incorrect suggestion (p. 427) that James Brown's self-promotion as "the hardest-working man in show business" reflects a sensibility that had no place in the 1920s and 1930s.

147 thinking in terms of a break: Armstrong had done the same thing earlier, with Oliver, in *Froggie Moore*. See the transcription of his solo in Harker 2003, 148.

147 In *Words*, a break effectively launches his solo: Transcription in Magee 1992, 135.

148 Moving in and out of phase: Brothers 1994.

148 superior sense of melodic coherence: Schuller 1968; Harker 1999; Gushee 1998, 294.

149 a hit at the Roseland: Drummer Kaiser Marshall claimed that when Armstrong left, the owner of the ballroom loaned him some money for a down payment on a house in Chicago; if that seems hard to believe, it probably indicates, at least, a level of success and appreciation. Marshall 1943, 85.

149 One milestone for the band . . . "made Fletcher Henderson nationally known": Condon 1947, 111. Allen 1973, 134.

150 the clearest harbinger of the Henderson band's future: Magee 2005, 90–96.

150 His year with Henderson . . . in New Orleans: Jones and Chilton 1971, 99. *Courier*, Aug. 29, 1925, p. 10.

151 There were also . . . heard Armstrong sing: Information in this paragraph from Marshall 1943, 83.

151 Henderson claimed . . . he concluded: Armstrong 1999, 64; Armstrong 1970; Reich HJA 2001; Armstrong IJS 1965. King 1967, 68; Armstrong IJS 1965. The biggest offender may have been Hawkins; see Scott IJS 1979. "big prima donna": Armstrong 1971, 211; Williams 1979, 97. "too much": Armstrong LAHM 1970; Armstrong 1971, 211. Armstrong, Lillian WRC 1938. "I personally": Armstrong LAHM 1970.

152 His year with Henderson . . . the fall of 1925: Magee 2005, 72–96, gives a good critique of the issue of Armstrong's impact. But see also the important counterview advanced in Spring 1993, 126–41, with special attention to micro-levels of rhythmic nuance, as coordinated with repertory. *New York Age*, March 28 and April 18, 1925. "considerable": Magee 2005, 84.

152 Armstrong was another . . . "Your boy, Rex": Stewart 1991, 89. Freeman CJA 1980.

152 Henderson worked hard . . . 2:00 or 3:00 in the morning: Scott IJS 1979. Bushell 1988, 36. Chilton 1987, 64; Waters 1985, 103. Scott IJS 1979; Marshall 1943, 85.

153 A favorite hangout spot . . . leave the building: Smith 1964, 159. Marshall 1943, 85; Barker IJS. Armstrong 1946, 42.

153 a source that is early: Goffin 1977, 204–5.

153 When Armstrong said . . . dissatisfaction with Henderson: Armstrong 1936, 80. "I knew": Armstrong LAHM 1970.

153 Just a week . . . three bluesiest players: "playing": Villetard 1984, n.p. Williams WRC 1970; Russell 1999, 356.

154 If Mamie Smith's singing . . . "play popular music": Bushell 1988, 23; Albertson 2003, 89. Scott IJS 1979.

154 "Your best bet is to keep your fill-ins rather simple": Sudhalter 1999, 503.

155 George M. Cohan wickedly nicknamed the building: On the Gaiety building, see Hinton IJS 1976; Hurwitt 2000, 196; Bradford 1965, 130.

155 Williams is credited as the composer: Co-composer credit is given to one Fae Barnes, and one can only guess if this is the Faye Barnes who sang more commonly as Maggie Jones.

155 Trumpeter Mutt Carey . . . took it all in: Brothers 2006, 269–71.

156 there was tension between them: Armstrong had several falling-outs like this in his later career, with, for example, Earl Hines, Zutty Singleton, Coleman Hawkins, and Benny Goodman.

156 The two solos that distinguish *Texas Moaner Blues*: Armstrong's solo is transcribed in Schuller 1968, 96. The "ubiquitous one" appears in mm. 2, 6, 10–12.

157 "were two of a kind": Foster 2005, 195.

157 Armstrong's solos with the Henderson band: Magee 1992, 326; Allen 1973, 128.

158 Clarinetist Paul Barnes: Barnes HJA 1959.

158 One of his personal favorites . . . "emancipated the jazz musician": Armstrong 1950, 24. "Emancipated": Jones and Chilton 1971, 99.

159 "Louie, I'll give you change for a thousand dollars": Albertson 2003, 90; Armstrong 1971, 211.

160 His solo on *Cold in Hand Blues*: Jones and Chilton 1971, 99. Teagarden had already heard Armstrong before he left New Orleans, playing *In the Land of Beginning Again* (Grant Clarke and George W. Meyer, 1918) with Fate Marable's band on the SS *Sidney*; Armstrong IJS 1965.

163 "I had never heard such a thing": Randolph IJS 1977.
163 varies phrase lengths: The solo is transcribed and discussed in Schuller 1968, 96.
163 he remembered the party: Armstrong 1999, 92; Armstrong WRC 1954.
164 Sidney Bechet bristled: Lewis 1979, 172.

## Chapter 5: "This Is What Really Relates to Us": The Dreamland Café, the Vendome Theater, and the First Hot Five Records

165 "His method of playing jazz": Scrapbook 6, LAHM.
165 Chicago was waiting for him: Anderson 2007, 16; Ory 1950a, 17; Ory CJA n.d.
165 His wife had been . . . about upstaging Oliver: Armstrong 1999, 94; Wilson 1968; *Defender*, Nov. 7, 1925, p. 8. Deffaa 1990, 18. Wilson 1968; Armstrong, Lillian 1963.
166 an article in the *Defender* announcing his return: Scrapbook 83, LAHM.
166 told a newspaper in Manchester, England: Scrapbook 6, LAHM.
167 "Our Own Place of Amusement": Scrapbook 83, LAHM.
167 Among South Side cabarets . . . "to cause complaint": *Defender*, March 15, 1924; Taylor 1987, 38; Kenney 1993, 17–19. The Dreamland Café should not be confused with the Dreamland Ballroom, a white ballroom where African-American orchestras sometimes played in the 1920s. "Residents": *Defender*, Oct. 18, 1924, p. 7, local edition, quoted and discussed in Kenney 1993, 19; Anderson 2007 11.
167 The word "class" . . . memory for decades: "to the queen's": *Defender*, June 28, 1924, p. 7. Dixon 2000, 46 and n. 12. "vulgar": *Defender*, Oct. 31, 1925, p. 6, local edition. *Defender*, Feb. 3, 1923, p. 4; *Chicago Whip*, Nov. 25, 1922, p. 5; Travis 1981, 66; Armstrong, Lillian WRC 1938. Taylor 1987, 39.
167 The enterprising hero . . . and Bill Bottoms: "our own": Vincent 1995, 72. Williams WRC 1970.
168 "Every now and then she'd make her breasts jump": Taylor 1987, 40.
168 The main presentation . . . in large spaces: Barker IJS n.d. Armstrong (1971, 91) mentions using a megaphone at the Vendome to sing *Heebie Jeebies*. Hunter IJS 1976.
168 the singers circulated between tables: Hunter IJS 1976; Jabbo Smith IJS 1979; Taylor 1987, 41; Bushell in Hentoff 1962, 74.
169 In both the main presentation . . . night after night: "You've got": Erenberg 1981, 183. Erenberg 1981, 113. Armstrong 1999, 125.
169 Singing and dancing . . . portion of the evening: "The entire": Scrapbook 83, LAHM. "Restaurant": Erenberg 1981, 215, 216–17.
170 "Now ladies and gentlemen" . . . trotting out a four-foot coach trumpet: "Now ladies": *Chinatown, My Chinatown*. "In those": Mezzrow 1946, 150. Kenney 1993, 50.
170 The words "eccentric" . . . "trick manipulations": For interchangeable usage of "novelty" and "eccentric," see Peyton, *Defender*, Feb. 27, 1926, p. 6; discussion of Armstrong's playing as eccentric in Harker 2008; Stearns and Stearns 1994, 231–32. "Louis has promised": *Defender*, Aug. 28, 1926, p. 6. "Louis has penned": *Defender*, April 16, 1927, p. 6. This is the earliest known placement of Hines at the Vendome; he probably followed Teddy Weatherford's departure.
171 "He was one of them fellas": Compton 1956.
171 In their pathbreaking account . . . describe jazz musicians: Stearns and Stearns 1994, 232 and 231.

171 "has a beautifully powerful rhythmic approach": Wilson 2001, 102–4.

172 "Behold now the days of super-speed": "Behold now": Drake and Cayton 1970, 78. "the new show": Kimball and Bolcom 1973, 173. "'Speed'": Salem Tutt Whitney, *Defender*, Dec. 4, 1926, p. 7. Erenberg 1981, 211.

173 "turned out to be a very popular tune": Armstrong 1999, 132–33.

173 Entertainers often integrated . . . cabaret-style comedy: McBride HJA 1959. "A show": Cheatham 1976, 160. "the Negro comedians": Dance 1977, 25. "The Boy": Louis Armstrong House Museum.

174 Musicians were rarely . . . "a class by himself": Hodes 1977, 10. Anderson 2007, 11. "ten deep": Armstrong 1999, 94; Ory 1950a, 17. Clipping: Scrapbook 83, LAHM.

174 Sociologists St. Clair Drake . . . community was all about: Drake and Cayton 1970, 78. "Things were": Armstrong 1946, 42.

175 Armstrong worked there: The end date is reported in the *Defender*, April 9, 1927, p. 6.

175 If Armstrong was embarrassed . . . "for that experience": "I like": Armstrong 1999, 95. *Defender*, Dec. 12, 1925, p. 7. "was my greatest": Armstrong 1999, 29. "I wouldn't": Armstrong 1946, 42.

176 The timing was perfect: Mitchell CJA 1969.

176 Of all the venues . . . a major draw: On movie theaters, see Carbine 1996; Hennessey 1974; Kenney 1993. "We sell": Koszarski 1990, 9.

177 African-American musicians . . . topped the list with fifteen: Kenney 1993, 56. *Pittsburgh Courier*, May 22, 1926, p. 10. Franz Jackson in Dance 1977, 248. *Defender*, Aug. 7, 1926, p. 7; the article is reproduced in Anderson 2007, 113; see also Carbine 1996, 41.

177 "the sensation of the time": *Defender*, June 28, 1924, p. 8.

177 There were plenty . . . the best musicians: Altman 2004, 291, 308, and 302. Anderson 1988, xviii.

178 Riesenfeld popularized . . . cultural packages: A list of overtures played by Riesenfeld is given by Anderson 1988, xxiv–xxvi. "No concert": Altman 2004, 316; see also Anderson 1988, xviii–xix.

178 What Riesenfeld did with 45 musicians: Armstrong 1999, 95; *Defender*, March 29, 1925, p. 7.

178 Bill Potter, writing in the *Defender*: *Defender*, Sept. 19, 1925, p. 6.

178 Tate was well suited . . . "band, you know": Jackson 2005, 218; Jackson, Preston WRC n.d.; on Tate's background, Hennessey 1974, 16. Saunders COHP 1971.

179 Musicians from New Orleans . . . "everything he does": St. Cyr HJA 1958. Howland 2009, 30. Altman 2004, 303. *Defender*, March 6, 1926, p. 6, and April 10, 1926, p. 6. Smith 1942, 46. Armstrong 1999, 29. Shapiro and Hentoff 1955, 107. *Defender*, June 19, 1926, p. 6.

180 Erskine's brother . . . a symphony orchestra: Scrapbook 83, LAHM; the font suggests that this clipping is from *Heebie Jeebies*. Armstrong 1971, 211. Armstrong 1966, 33; Hodes 1977, 80; Armstrong WRC 1939.

180 "Never [before] played" . . . "have any job": Jackson 2005, 93. Altman 2004, 309. Foster 2005, 118; Brothers 2006, chap. 11. "I really": Armstrong LAHA 1970. "I couldn't": Armstrong 1966, 33. Simeon HJA 1955.

181 Theaters that tried . . . conservatory-trained musicians: Altman 2004, 313 and 34. Anderson 1988, xxvi.

181 By the end of 1925 . . . the right ambition: *Defender*, July 3, 1926, p. 6. Armstrong 1971, 91. Brown COHP 1971.

182 A typical program of live entertainment: Regular advertisements in *Heebie Jeebies*.

182 "up-to-date manner": Scrapbook 83, LAHM; on Richardson, see also Cheatham IJS 1976.

182 hardly made with African Americans in mind: The point is made—though with a poor sense of context and with too much emphasis—in Carbine 1996, 21–26.

183 Tate's orchestra became . . . and newsreel to boot: *Defender*, July 3, 1926, p. 6. Anderson 1988, xviii.

183 Milt Hinton . . . as Hinton put it: Hinton IJS 1976; Kenney 1993, 126. Drake and Cayton 1970, 523. Apparently, music lessons were within easy reach of most people on the South Side. Hinton (IJS 1976) said that everyone in his community found lessons for their children, the girls on piano and the boys on violin.

183 There was apparently . . . in South Side Chicago: Samuels COHP 1971. This idea of "two sets of society" could be related to the division discussed by Drake and Cayton (1970, 524–25) between "respectables" and "shadies." Seating at the Vendome, *Defender,* Jan. 5, 1924, p. 7.

184 Orchestras were obliged . . . one of them remembered: *Defender*, June 5 1926, p. 6. "It became": Peretti 1992, 162–63.

184 It was a lot easier . . . wrote Peyton on May 14: "shouts vengeance": Anderson 1988, xix. "eccentric stop coupling": Dave Peyton, *Defender*, April 2, 1927, p. 8, and Aug. 13, 1927, p. 6. Victor Records issued two performances by Waller on organ and advertised them in the *Defender* (April 16, 1927, p. 3) with the comment, "Thomas Waller, popular organist, is now playing at the Vendome Theater in Chicago." Tenure was cut short: *Defender*, April 30, 1927, p. 6, and May 7, p. 6. "The old organ": *Defender*, May 14, 1927, p. 6.

184 Tate's orchestra was praised . . . "beautiful to watch him": Peyton: *Defender* April 24, 1926, p. 6. Brown COHP 1971; Randolf IJS 1977; Altman 2004, 347; Anderson 1988, xxx. *Defender* August 13, 1927, p. 6; Cheatham IJS 1976. Hines: Dance 1977, 35.

185 Music matched to the changing: Altman 2004, 380. Armstrong 1971, 91. Dance 1977, 35. Armstrong LAHM Tapes 295 and 96. *Heebie Jeebies*, May 8, 1926, p. 14.

185 "The audience were *still* applauding": Armstrong 1999, 29.

186 Armstrong played it so many times: Armstrong located the theme at the Vendome in an interview from 1953 (Armstrong WRC 1953). The piece has recently been identified by Vince Giordano, as reported in Sager 2009, 149–51. Regarding the likelihood that Armstrong played the tune from memory in 1933, consider these remarks from Barney Bigard (IJS 1976): "And you're talking about a man that can remember tunes of the past years and people of the past years. He had that memory. He was phenomenal. I've never seen anybody like that."

186 the Vendome played it after the movie: Armstrong 1999, 95; see also Altman 2004, 380; Anderson 1988, xvi.

186 The repertory had nothing . . . remembered Hinton: Hinton IJS 1976; Simeon HJA 1955; Brown COHP 1971. Scrapbook 83, LAHM. Altman 2004, 32. Hinton IJS 1976.

186 Tate's interpretive abilities . . . remembered Armstrong: Shapiro and Hentoff 1955, 107. Peyton: *Defender*, April 10, 1926, p. 6. Armstrong LAHM Tape 96.

186 *Cavalleria rusticana* . . . his expanding reputation: *Defender*, Nov. 7, 1925, p. 6. Armstrong 1966, 33.

187 Melodies from the light classics . . . at the Vendome: Altman 2004, 310. Armstrong 1999, 206; Hodes 1977, 81. Berrett (1992); on some of the pieces Berrett mentions, see Altman 2004, 32 and 310; Miller 2007, 19; Smith 1964, 68; Dominique HJA 1958.

188 It is possible that he was continuing lessons at Kimball Hall: The case that he took his lessons at Kimball Hall after he started work at the Vendome (rather than before he left for New York) could be built on three observations: first, Richard Jones, the source of the information, definitely knew him at this time; second, Tate had Reuben Reeves take lessons with a German music teacher when he joined the orchestra as a get-off man, and he could have made the same suggestion to Armstrong; third, Armstrong (WRC 1953) said that his experience with Tate was "better than paying money for music lessons," suggesting a link.

188 "no more boisterous, barrel house stuff": Armstrong 1999, 91.

189 Another special part . . . both always present: Armstrong 1999, 64. Armstrong 1971 91.

190 We know that . . . saxophonist Stump Evans: Dance 1977, 143. Cross dressing: *Light and Heebie Jeebies*, Jan. 8, 1927, p. 16; Tate CJA n.d. "The fans": Scrapbook 83, LAHM.

190 But his splashiest . . . "hundred or more patrons": An article in the *Light and Heebie Jeebies* from Jan. 8, 1927, says that Armstrong "'preached the Gospel' some weeks ago." A date of September 1926 is implied by the account in the *Defender*, Sept. 25, 1926, p. 6. Additional details from Dickerson, Killis CJA 1967. Eddie Condon (1947, 131) remembered seeing Armstrong at the Vendome "singing and 'preaching' as the Reverend Satchelmouth." The feature began as an instrumental number, according to a number of sources, but it may have become a vocal one. *Heebie*: Scrapbook 83, LAHM; see also Ramsey and Smith 1939, 129. *Defender*, Sept. 25, 1926, p. 6; Scrapbook 83, LAHM; Dickerson CJA 1967.

190 Another observer explained: Dickerson CJA 1967.

191 He also discovered . . . knew he would: Gabbard 2008, 148. In Chicago: Elgard CJA n.d.; Armstrong LAHM 1970; Armstrong 1971, 91; Armstrong, Lillian CJA n.d.

191 He started with high F . . . into the high range: Armstrong LAHM 1970. Carbine 1996, 29. Armstrong 1966, 39. Dance 1977, 92.

192 To see this . . . this extended control: Gabbard 2008. Drew 1950, 31.

192 Armstrong was funny . . . of his popularity: Earl Hines worked at the Vendome after Weatherford's departure, which happened sometime before Sept. 4, 1926 (*Defender*, p. 6); on Bertrand: Hinton 1988, 17. Randall COHP 1971; Tate CJA n.d. Cheatham: Deffaa 1990, 18. Armstrong 1999, 29 and 95; Hinton 1988, 17.

193 "swing tune": Armstrong 1999, 95.

193 "followed with another surprise" *Defender*, Feb. 20, 1926, p. 6.

193 "could be played as a trumpet solo": Armstrong 1999, 133.

193 The primary hot number . . . increasingly complex melodies: Cheatham IJS 1976. *Defender*, March 20, 1926, p. 6.

194 "I wanted to be able to play like Louis Armstrong": Cheatham IJS 1976.

195 "We were in the front row": Hampton 1993, 26.

195 Milt Hinton saw the Vendome . . . "making a success of it": Hinton IJS 1976 and 1974.
196 "The Philadelphia clubwoman is ashamed": Langston Hughes, *Nation*, June 23, 1926; published on the same day in the *New York Amsterdam News* (p. 16), the source of these quotations.
197 "white people danced": Dixon 2000, 214.
197 Musical details were bound up . . . place of power: Jackson: Jones 1988, 138–39. Brothers 2006, esp. chap. 9.
199 "You'll never be able to swing": Armstrong 1936, 48 and 68.
199 "The common people will give": *New York Amsterdam News*, June 23, 1926, p. 16.
200 "corrects the fiction that America is racist": Von Eschen 2004, 17.
200 full of stimulating cross-currents: Savran 2009, 90, 94; see also Howland 2009.
201 Armstrong even impressed . . . the qualifier "modern": Hinton IJS n.d.; Spivey 1984, 38. Peyton: Carbine 1996, 31; see also *Defender*, May 8, 1926, p. 6; June 5, 1926, p. 6; Aug. 7, 1926, p. 6; Sept. 23, 1927, p. 6. *Defender*, April 24, 1926, p. 6.
201 Novelist Richard Wright wrote: Berlin 2010, 29.
202 Eric Hobsbawm: Williamson 1960, 11.
202 Listening to jazz . . . explained the *New York Clipper*: DeVeaux 1989 is a good introduction to the early history of the jazz concert. "Those who": Kenney 1993, 78–79. But as Edmund Wilson (Wilson 1958, 114) quipped in January 1926: "In sitting through a whole evening of Whiteman, we cannot always rid ourselves of the feeling—which obtrudes itself also, and to a greater degree, in the case of Vincent Lopez—that we might enjoy the music more if we were eating and talking while we listened to it."
203 Armstrong was regarded . . . the jazz concert king: Peyton: *Defender*, Dec. 3, 1927, p. 8. Scrapbook 83, LAHM.
204 "The musicians didn't know": Armstrong, Lillian 1963.
204 "Pops, I don't need no rehearsal" . . . early and mid-1920s: "Pops": Hillman 1997, 10. To be precise, the comment as reported was addressed to Richard Jones regarding the sessions on Nov. 9, with Bertha "Chippie" Hill, not the sessions on Nov. 11. St. Cyr WRC 1969; St. Cyr HJA 1958; see also Anderson 2007, 240, and Smith 1964, 11.
205 "'What are you doing, writing a letter home?": St. Cyr HJA 1958.
206 What mattered, mainly: Kid Ory (Shapiro and Hentoff 1955, 109) said that the OKeh people "never told [Louis] what numbers they wanted or how they wanted them." On the other hand, it was made clear that the repertory had to fit race record marketing strategies. Lillian said (CJA n.d., box 78) that she wrote *My Heart* as a waltz, in 3/4 meter, but that the band recorded it in 4/4 because "Rockwell wouldn't have stood for us to spoil our reputation by playing a waltz." Armstrong said (Armstrong 1966, 37) this about the Hot Five sessions: "it was just pick up those cats and do it. And we didn't want no royalties, just pay me, man, give me that loot. Got $50 each for each session."
206 "it was all mixed together": Kenney 1993, 105.
207 "The records I made" . . . revisiting that atmosphere: Ory: Shapiro and Hentoff 1955, 109. Dodds 1992, 40. Armstrong IJS 1954, 61.
207 the differing business plans: On the interest in race record labels in having original material, see Kenney 1999, 133; Hennessey 1973, 60.

208 familiarity with the tunes from the Dreamland: It is impossible to pin down the dates precisely, but all five did work there at some point in the winter of 1925–26; see Ory 1950a, 17.

208 Armstrong uses the main pitches: A good analysis of the solo, with emphasis on Armstrong's use of St. Cyr's tune, is in Anderson 2007, 67–69.

209 This is eccentric . . . like petrified wood: Calloway 1976, 58. Manone 1948, 68.

209 From the first . . . vocal on *Heebie Jeebies*: Jasen and Jones 1998, 295. Johnny Dodds (WRC n.d.) said that "OKeh asked Louis to sing and that's why he did," which suggests that his singing had already been well received in public performance in Chicago. See Tucker 1991, 155, for discussion of *Georgia Grind*, compared with performances by Ellington, Perry Bradford, and Thomas Morris and His Seven Hot Babies. For a good summary of African-American speechlike singing, see Givans 2004, esp. 190–91.

209 *Cornet Chop Suey* . . . the home boy they once knew: Bigard IJS 1976; Frazier HJA 1972. Laplace 1988, 13; Davison CJA 1981.

210 Kid Ory is listed . . . played somewhere: Armstrong WRC 1954; Armstrong IJS 1965. Bigard (1986, 11 and 38) claimed that Ory could not read at all, which would place him in the vast majority of uptown African-American musicians from New Orleans. Preston Jackson (2005, 97) said that Ory was Armstrong's "idol on the trombone," and that when Jackson played with Armstrong in 1931, Armstrong tried to get him to imitate Ory. Trummy Young, who played with Armstrong in the 1950s, also closely attended to Ory's style, and with great admiration; see Dance 1977, 225. "Dixieland style is punch," said Young. "It's got to come on out. It's got to build. . . . I don't think anyone really knows it outside of Ory."

211 *Muskrat Ramble* was paired . . . "(meaning) 'money'": Armstrong WRC 1939. Armstrong 1936, 84. *Defender*, June 12, 1926, p. A6. Armstrong 1999, 132.

212 In one of several . . . one observer: Origins of scat: Brothers 2006, 94–95 and 331. Miller HJA 1959. Armstrong 1945, 11. Anderson 2007, 52. Red Happy Bolton: Russell 1994, 58 and 163–64. Manuel Manetta said that Bolton was a few years older than Armstrong; Manetta WRC 1968. On Bolton as dancer: St. Cyr HJA 1958.

212 Many signs . . . to indicate it: Armstrong, Lillian 1963. Ory CJA n.d. Bocage HJA 1960. For suggestions that scat had a more serious purpose, see Gabbard 2008, 105; Edwards 2002.

213 Humor aside . . . "into my voice": Talking blues: Williams, Mayo WRC 1970. Johnson: Dorsey, Thomas CJA n.d. Armstrong: Scrapbook 6, LAHM.

214 What distinguishes Armstrong's . . . a supposed mistake: Atkins borrowed heavily from *Heliotrope Bouquet* by Scott Joplin and Louis Chauvin (1907); Anderson 2007, 55; Collier 1983, 172. "The Heebie Jeebies": quotation from OED Online, "Heebie Jeebies," citing *Weekly Dispatch,* May 8, 1927.

214 The phrase "heebie jeebies" . . . a couple of happy minutes: Atlantic City: Smith 1964, 40. Appel 2002, 40; *Defender*, June 27, 1925, p. 16; *Washington Post*, Feb. 27, 1925, p. 10; *Afro-American*, Nov. 14, 1925, p. 16. The meaning of "heebie jeebies" was close to this definition of jazz from F. Scott Fitzgerald (1993, 42): "The word jazz in its progress toward respectability has meant first sex, then dancing, then music. It is associated with a state of nervous stimulation, not unlike that of big cities behind the lines of a war."

214 Atkins and Barbarin . . . brought them to the studio: Atkins knew Armstrong: Mason HJA 1960; Armstrong 1954, 186. Material from John Steiner's interview with Boyd Atkins, including a questionnaire filled out by Atkins, is in CJA, John Steiner Collection, box 78, folder "Boyd Atkins." Armstrong supplied: St. Cyr HJA 1958; St. Cyr WRC 1969.

215 There seems to be no doubt: Armstrong 1999, 131–32.

215 "There's fourteen million Negroes": Bradford 1965, 114–29.

215 If the scatted . . . heard on radio: Kenney 1999, 121; Banks 1980, 227. Scrapbook 83, LAHM. Kenney 1993, 124.

216 he was singing *Heebie Jeebies*: Megaphone: Scrapbook 83, LAHM; Armstrong 1971, 91. *Defender*, April 17, 1926, p. 6; Ory and Manetta HJA 1958; Russell 1994, 181.

216 On May 1 . . . crowed an OKeh ad: "big feature": *Defender*, June 12, 1926, p. A6; Miller 1946, 32; Kenney 1999, 121; Kenney 1993, 124. Contract: a newspaper clipping in Scrapbook 83 (LAHM) provides the following information: (1) that Armstrong had just completed a five-year contract with OKeh; (2) that OKeh (now absorbed into Columbia Phonograph Co.) was suing to stop him from jumping over to Victor, claiming rights to the option of an additional year; (3) that this was taking place while Armstrong was performing at Sebastian's Cotton Club in California. The clipping probably dates from the spring of 1932, when Armstrong returned to the Cotton Club; the *Amsterdam News* (April 13, 1932, p. 7) reported that he had just finished a five-year contract with OKeh. Armstrong made his final recording for OKeh on March 11, 1932. His next recording after that was for Victor, Dec. 8, 1932. Peyton: *Defender*, June 12, 1926, p. A5. *Defender*, June 12, 1926, p. A6. Kenney 1993, 124; *Defender* June 19, 1926, p. 6; Scrapbook 83, LAHM.

217 "We didn't rehearse much": Russell 1994, 181.

217 The Zulu theme was perfect: *Defender*, Oct. 30, 1926, p. 6. Lillian Hardin is credited as composer of *King of the Zulus*, and she notated the lead sheet in her tidy script. Interestingly, the title "Chief Bonco Boo" is crossed out on the lead sheet and "The King of the Zulus" entered below it, suggesting that the Zulu title was an afterthought. See also Anderson 2007, 100 and 231. LAHM owns a lyric sheet for "'King of the Zulus'—Blues," with verse, interlude, and chorus.

217 In July, Percy Venable . . . Armstrong's scatted dance: "The backward": *Afro-American*, Dec. 26, 1925, p. 5. Calloway's account of his first exposure to Armstrong (Calloway 1976, 58) places the event in summer 1927, and he is indeed documented in Chicago then (*Light*, June 4, 1927, p. 21). But the pieces he names fit summer 1926 better, suggesting that there may have been a trip to Chicago before he toured with the review *Plantation Days*. Earl Hines's discussion (Dance 1977, 49) of Calloway's first visit to the Sunset implies that he was not yet a professional singer. "All of": Calloway 1976, 58–59. "All the way": Leonard 1987, 94.

218 Summer contracts were . . . did it in scat: On the sheet music, see Anderson 2007, 52–54. Contractual information on the "orchestral roll" and piano rolls on file at LAHM. Sheet music for *Heebie Jeebies* at WRC; *Washington Post*, Feb. 26, 1928, p. F6. Ethel Waters advertised in *Afro-American*, Sept. 18, 1926, p. A6; Alberta Hunter advertised in *Amsterdam News*, Oct. 27, 1926, p. 13.

218 OKeh's coordinated strategies . . . "stop in Africa": Miss Tweedie: Sheet music,

WRC. "spent a lifetime": *Pittsburgh Courier*, Feb. 25, 1928, p. A6; see also *Washington Post*, Feb. 26, 1928, p. F6.

220 But the tune continued . . . "*Heebee Jeebees* [*sic*]": Bojangles: My placement of this event in January 1927 is based on Robinson's presence at the Palace at that time; *Defender*, Jan. 1, 1927, p. 7. Quotation: Scrapbook 83, LAHM. October: *Pittsburgh Courier*, Oct. 29, 1927, p. 10. Peyton: *Defender*, Dec. 31, 1927, p. 6. Alhambra: *Amsterdam News*, Aug. 14, 1929, p. 8.

220 "Aw, I am paid to *entertain* the people": King 1967, 68.

## Chapter 6: Melody Man at the Sunset Café

222 Armstrong's wife had . . . "fire me": "Look out": Armstrong, Lillian CJA 1960. "I would": Jones and Chilton 1971, 92.

222 In early April . . . "us young fellows?": Offer: *Defender*, April 10, 1926, p. 6. Hines remembered: Dance 1977, 45; Hines, Foster, and Deppe CJA 1961.

222 Here is another . . . bad behavior eventually: "I loved": Armstrong 1966, 35. Singleton IJS n.d.; Armstrong 1966, 35.

223 Armstrong started . . . every week, as usual: Wright 1987, 51, has Ory joining Oliver's Plantation band in late 1925, but by Ory's account (Russell 1994, 181; Ory and Manetta HJA 1958; Ory 1950a, 17), he worked at the Dreamland and then left when Louis did. On Ory at the Dreamland, see also Mitchell HJA 1959. "new departure": *Defender*, July 30, 1921, p. 7. Noone WRC 1938; Cheatham IJS 1976; Dance 1977, 48.

223 His friends Buster Bailey, Rudy Jackson, Honoré Dutrey, and Andre Hillare: Armstrong 1999, 72 and 75; Jackson HJA 1958; Russell 1994, 112.

223 Armstrong's arrival . . . Duhé's band in 1919: *Defender*, Sept. 12, 1925, p. 6; Jan. 30, 1926, p. 6; Jackson 2005, 57; Shapiro and Hentoff 1955, 84. Wright 1987, 48; Shoffner CJA 1958; Jackson 2005, 70; Shoffner HJA 1959.

224 "The mammoth King Oliver": Wright 1987, 60.

224 the 30-minute radio broadcasts: Howard CJA n.d.

225 Management at the Plantation . . . tapping a cymbal: The Plantation probably took its name and inspiration from the eponymous club in New York City, for which we have more information about the imaginative attempt to create an atmosphere of slavery. Wright 1987, 59; Russell 1999, 92: Frances Oliver WRC n.d.; Erenberg 1981, 254. Nicholas WRC 1970; Russell 1999, 321.

225 Jazz around 35th and Calumet . . . Peyton in the *Defender*: Jackson 2005, 70. "Close your": Condon 1947, 131; Ramsey 1939, 135. *Defender*, April 17, 1926, p. 6.

225 "All the white people, all the night lifers": Armstrong 1966, 35.

225 The white draw . . . on their days off: Wright 1987, 51–54 and 60.

226 African-American men acted as guides: Kenney 1993, 19.

226 "Outside the cabaret Negroes loiter in doorways": *Variety*, April 21, 1926, p. 45. Raid: *Pittsburgh Courier*, Jan. 1, 1927, p. A5.

226 "He had all the black guys": Hinton COHP 1971.

226 Rivalries for turf control: "Buddy": Freeman 1974, 5. Ory HJA 1957; Dance 1977, 33 and 47.

227 But it was also . . . the music business: Dance 1977, 172; Hinton IJS 1976; Washington COHP 1971; for an opposing view, see Kellery 1989, 91; Vincent 1995, 69. Armstrong 1966, 35. "this is": Dance 1977, 61. Greer: Sylvester 1956, 45.

227 Armstrong developed . . . secure their property: Cheatham: Deffaa 1990, 18. Dodds, John Jr. CJA 1969. Most of: Ory HJA 1957; Cheatham IJS 1976. Hines: Dance 1977, 61; Hines COHP 1971.

228 integration was one of the things that made Chicago's South Side cabarets different: Pianist Willie "The Lion" Smith (1964, 127): "there was a lot more mixing of the races in Chicago at that time than there was in New York." See also Kenney 1993, esp. chap. 1.

228 Evidence of black patronage . . . "the dancers frolic": Reeves 1961; Cheatham IJS 1976; Dance 1977, 52; Davison IJS 1980; Oliver WRC; Hinton IJS n.d.; Hinton IJS 1976. Cotton Club: *Amsterdam News*, July 6, 1927, p. 2; see also *Light and Heebie Jeebies*, Jan. 15, 1927, p. 25, for an article on the Jazzland Cabaret in Los Angeles, which had just converted from integrated to segregated patronage. *Defender*, July 10, 1926, p. 6.

228 Buster Bailey explained . . . "*Old Colored Joe* up there?": Shapiro and Hentoff 1955, 115. *Courier*, Feb. 5, 1927, p. A2. Armstrong, LAHM Tape 96.

229 places of white privilege: Wright 1987, 54 and 59–60; Hines COHP 1971; Dance 1977, 45; Armstrong 1966, 35.

229 a system of thought known as "primitivism": I have been influenced in this section by Togorvnick 1990; Clifford 1988; Leonard 1962; Levine 1988.

229 Even the most informed and sympathetic observers: Togorvnick 1990, 85–104.

230 novelist Mary Austin explained: Austin 1926, 476.

230 "a new genre, characterized by an improvement in technique": Sudhalter 1999, 34.

231 "a sort of primitive abandon": Tichenor 1930, 485.

231 The dominating side . . . social dynamics of the Sunset: Shapiro and Hentoff 1955, 116–17; Davison IJS. Dominique: Russell 1994, 150; Steiner, box 82; Dominique WRC 1952; Dominique CJA 1952.

232 "vicarious bohemianism": Erenberg 1981, 177, 127, and 139.

232 "Black men with white girls": Vincent 1995, 73.

232 The coveted tables were right next to the stage: Erenberg 1981, 125.

233 "A whole race" . . . sexual liberation was all about: Fitzgerald 1993, 42. Carmichael 1999a, 75. Allen 1931, 88–122; Taylor 1993, 51–52; Albertson 2003, 47; Jablonski 1961, 55; Erenberg 1981, 196.

233 Light-skinned female singers . . . "who is the wriggliest": Jackson 2005, 72; Calloway 1976, 59. Scrapbook 83, LAHM.

233 Mae Alix: Dance 1977, 49 and 143; Barker IJS, 5–19.

233 Twenty-four chorus girls . . . a lot of skin: Wright 1987, 59; Dance 1977, 45 and 48; Shapiro and Hentoff 1955, 108. Preston Jackson (2005, 70) gave this description of the Plantation: "The show would last an hour and a half or maybe two hours . . . the show girls would come out and dance ten or twelve choruses, then take an encore and come back and do about seven or eight more. . . . Jobs like the Plantation and the Sunset wore a trumpet player out. There was no 45 and 15 like now, but just one intermission a night." Hines: Dance 1977, 48; Shapiro and Hentoff 1955, 108.

234 The first option . . . "extreme 'Jazz Dances'": Anderson 2007, 53. "Hip dancing": Wright 1987, 59. "Supremacy": Levin 1985, 201.

235 The Mess Around . . . dance of the day?: *Defender*, Aug. 28, 1926, p. 8; Anderson 2007, 83–85, with lyrics from the song by Barbarin and Armstrong; Stearns and Stearns 1994, 107.

235 *Heebie Jeebies* scored an interview: Scrapbook 83, LAHM.
235 "Black Bottom" was slang: Moton 1929, 118.
235 the Black Bottom drew white attention: Stearns and Stearns 1994, 106; *Atlanta Constitution*, July 11, 1926, p. 4.
236 One can only . . . session on November 27: *Afro-American*, Sept. 11, 1926, p. 4. *Los Angeles Times*, Sept. 29, 1926, p. 8. Romania: *Chicago Daily Tribune*, Oct. 7, 1926, p. 7.
236 Several videos show . . . police reports, anyway: Kenney 1993, 70. Erenberg 1981, 250; Dixon 2000, 104.
236 In December 1926 . . . a public nuisance: *Courier*, Jan. 1 1927, p. 5. Glaser: *Chicago Tribune*, Dec. 26, 1926, p. 1; *Courier*, Jan. 1, 1927, p. 1. *Chicago Tribune*, Jan. 12, 1927, p. 14.
237 Venable designed a new show: *Courier*, Feb. 12, 1927, p. 3.
237 Armstrong himself was one . . . trumpeter Bobby Williams (thin): Armstrong 1966, 35. The date February 1927 is based on a story from the *Light*, Feb. 19, 1927, discussed below; characterizations from CJA Steiner, box 78, folder "Louis Armstrong"; Armstrong gives a similar account in Shapiro and Hentoff 1955, 111. Johnson: Williams 1979, 56.
237 I know of no video . . . "good instrumentalist": Brothers 2006, 141 and 231; St. Cyr HJA 1958. Smith 1964, 160.
238 "If you've been" . . . decades of his career: Glason: Snyder 1989, 109; also Smith 1964, 117–18. Abbott 2005.
238 The thrill for slumming whites . . . wrote *Variety*: "Slumming": Levin 1985, xiv, 170, 199; Woll 1989, 116. "white reform": Wright 1987, 72; also Vincent 1995, 75. Reeves 1961, 8. Hines: Dance 1977, 45. "grenades": Smith and Haskins 1983, 59; Preston Jackson in Jones 1988, 134; *Heebie Jeebies*, Nov. 7, 1925, p. 26. Prostitutes: Kenney 1993, 23. Wright 1987, 59, quoting *Variety*, April 21, 1926.
238 The list of white . . . "all over my face": List drawn from Howard HJA 1957; Armstrong LAHM 1967; Armstrong 1946; Russell 1994; Shapiro and Hentoff 1955; Condon 1947; Davison IJS 1980; Jackson HJA 1958; Jones 1988; Hines COHP 1971. Freddy Goodman: Dance 1977, 194–95. Sylvester 1956, 51. Hines: Dance 1977, 48. Freeman 1970, 17. Armstrong 1999, 112.
239 "It has been the custom": *Defender*, Oct. 23, 1926, p. 6.
239 But his words . . . "Makes me feel good": Spanier: Hubner 1944, 7. Davison IJS 1980. Armstrong 1966, 57.
240 "To me there's more natural suggestion": Mezzrow 1946, 27, 111, and 210.
240 Mezzrow's extreme position . . . Tichenor put it in 1930: "negroization": Douglas 1995. "stir the savage": Clark 2001, 34. Erenberg 1981, 140. Tichenor 1930, 485.
241 "I say the Negro is not our salvation": Seldes 1957, 98.
242 Percy Venable wrote a comic tune: Armstrong and Mae Alix also performed the song at the Vendome (Dance 1977, 143). In September 1926, the Sunset revue was called *Joymakers* (*Heebie Jeebies*, Sept. 4, 1926, p. 15). *Big Butter* was part of a cluster of pieces composed by Venable (most likely for the Sunset) and recorded by Armstrong in November 1926: *Sunset Café Stomp*, *You Made Me Love You* (not to be confused with the song of the same title by Monaco and McCarthy), and *Irish Black Bottom*.
243 Revues helped cabarets . . . social dance segment: Dominique: Russell 1994,

150. Armstrong (IJS 1965) said that the Sunset had two shows per night. Jackson 2005, 70.

243 Light classics . . . "Get rid of it!": Four weeks: Ory HJA 1957. Peyton: Ory HJA 1957; Russell 1994, 150. Barbarin: Shoffner CJA 1958 and Shoffner HJA 1959; see also Burton HJA 1959; Bigard 1986, 27. Hines's weak reading skills—if he was, indeed a weak reader; reports are contradictory—may have placed him in the same position at the Sunset, for there were apparently two pianists there when Armstrong joined. On Hines as a shaky reader, see Russell 1994, 148; for the contrary view, Dance 1977, 134 and 149. Penalties: Singleton CJA n.d.; Natty Dominique in Russell 1994, 150; see also Hines, Foster, and Deppe CJA 1961.

243 The Sunset hired Venable . . . "put on something, you know": Venable: *Defender*, Feb. 14, 1925; Dance 1977, 45–57; CJA box 87, folder V; *Light*, March 12, 1927, p. 21. Hines: Dance 1977, 45–46 and 57. Budd Johnson IJS. Sadly, Venable died early, his death perhaps brought on by drug addiction. Drug addiction: Budd Johnson IJS; early death: Freeman 1974, 15.

244 In spite of this lack . . . begun the previous April: Peyton: *Defender*, July 3, 1926. "With all": unidentified clipping, Scrapbook 83, LAHM.

245 *Big Butter* . . . first eight-bar phrase: Budd Johnson (IJS) reported that Armstrong was still playing *Big Butter and Egg Man* in his 1933 band. Since the philosophy of the New Orleanians was to stick with successful solos, it is likely that he was playing the same solo then that he played in 1926. Schuller 1968, 103–4; see also Hodeir 1956, 57.

245 banter back and forth: Dance 1977, 48; Armstrong 1966, 35.

245 The phrase "big butter and egg man" . . . $1,000 in a single night: Harker 2008; Berliner 1993, 101; Erenberg 1981, 200. Berliner 1993, 101; George S. Kaufman wrote a play titled *Big Butter and Egg Man*, which opened on Broadway in September 1925.

246 Danny Barker said . . . "'Hold it!'": Jackson 2005, 72. Hines: Dance 1977, 49.

247 "she was very cute": Dance 1977 48; Harker 2008, 83.

247 pushing the limits of speed: Cheatham IJS 1976; Harker 2008.

247 The background for kinetic-sonic synergy . . . movement of the body: Wilson 1978. Brothers 2006, chap. 2.

248 It's not surprising . . . could be heard: Accessories: Sengstock 2000 39; Russell 1994, 36; Singleton IJS 1975; Altman 2004, 41, 104. Foster 2005, 176. Bojangles Robinson once stopped in the middle of his routine to scold a drummer who was playing too loudly. Dance 1977, 54 and 86.

248 Earl Hines said . . . into every performance: Hines: Dance 1977, 48. Armstrong 1946, 42.

250 the miracle of Armstrong improvising melodic gems: Hodeir 1956, 58: "It is not unreasonable to believe that this improvisation of a genius opened a new chapter in the evolution of jazz."

250 "Even back in the old days": Armstrong 1966, 42.

250 the mistakes in rhythmic notation: On the challenges of rhythmic notation for the New Orleanians, see Brothers 2006, 127 and 237; also Brothers 2009.

251 a gang of hogs crying for corn: Dominique WRC 1952.

251 "their act was nothing without a trumpet": Dance 1977, 48; Cheatham IJS. The performance of *Big Butter and Egg Man* for the Sunset revue probably bore little

relationship to the Hot Five recording, aside from the vocal and trumpet solos; it is likely that the arrangements were completely different. Cheatham suggests that Brown and McGraw's act went on for quite a long time, wearing out the trumpet player. Traditionally, their routine would have been accompanied by stop time. Perhaps the most significant difference between my interpretation of Armstrong's development and Professor Harker's is that I attribute the special qualities of *Big Butter* to the fact that it was a special chorus that he worked out over many weeks, if not months, while his emphasis is on the impact of the dancers. It seems likely to me that few other special choruses were recorded in 1926; thus, the uniform appearance of commercial recordings is very misleading. The facts of the recording business make it difficult for us to track his development—and here I would point out, once more, the likelihood that *Big Butter and Egg Man* would not have been recorded at all unless Venable, the local and unknown composer, made a deal that was favorable to OKeh. Since most repertory pieces performed at the Sunset would have forced OKeh into less favorable royalty arrangements, we simply do not have recordings of what Armstrong regularly played. There is also the matter of tempo, with *Big Butter* clocking around a comfortable 192; compare that with the frantic *Static Strut* and *Stomp Off* from May, both around 240. The relatively relaxed tempo for *Big Butter* (like those for *Oriental Strut* at 188 and *Muskrat Ramble* at 182) favors his dense and varied conception.

252 André Hodeir: Hodeir 1956, 57.

253 The principle conditions the entire chorus: See Anderson 2007, 128, for additional examples.

256 Oliver apparently did the same thing: For an exception, see Salem Tutt Whitney in the *Defender*, July 10, 1926, p. 6; Shoffner HJA 1959.

256 The Plantation's emphasis . . . wrote Peyton in October 1926: Shoffner CJA 1973; Shoffner CJA 1958; Howard HJA 1957; Dixon CJA 1990. *Variety*: Wright 1987, 60; *Defender*, Oct. 9, 1926, p. 6.

256 Shoffner said: Shoffner HJA 1959.

256 The two cabarets . . . solo was finished: "I can play": Russell 1994, 152. The *Light and Heebie Jeebies* reported Oliver playing *Snag It* at the Plantation in the Jan. 8, 1927, issue (p. 17). Shoffner, Bob CJA 1973. Armstrong WRC 1954. Armstrong was given co-composer credit for *Wild Man Blues* in 1927, but he explicitly denied (Armstrong WRC 1970) having anything to do with the composition of the piece. A good explanation for the mistaken attribution is offered in Dapogny 1982, 231–32.

258 An even more magnificent outpouring: Howard CJA n.d.; *Down Beat*, March 15, 1941, p. 16; Freeman 1974, 15.

258 A hapless Johnny Dunn . . . slithered away in shame: Bradford 1965, 145; Williams 1979, 83; Drew 1950, 26; Bigard 1986, 30; *Defender*, Aug. 20, 1924; Stewart 1991, 47; Singleton, Zutty CJA n.d. The story of the contest with Dunn is sometimes placed at the Dreamland, which may have taken place in August 1924, when Dunn was in Chicago and Armstrong was working at that venue. But Hines and Singleton both were specific about it happening at the Sunset. Hines: Dance 1977, 50.

259 If Armstrong was . . . firm job offer: Armstrong: King 1967, 68; Armstrong 1966, 35.

259 His growing success . . . a year later: "Luis": *Light*, Jan. 8, 1927. The same issue (p. 16) has a story headlined "Luis Armstrong Scores Heavily with *My Baby Knows How* at the Vendome." *My Baby Knows How* was a popular hit composed by Benny Davis, Harry Akst, and Harry Richman, frequently recorded in 1926. In the Jan. 15, 1927, issue (p. 25), the *Light* references "Luis Armstrong's Sunset Recording Orchestra" at the Sunset. Dickerson: Dance 1977, 41–42 and 47; Dominique CJA 1981; Hines, Foster, and Deppe CJA 1961; Jackson 2005, 91. Warwick Hall: *Light,* Jan. 8, 1927, p. 23.

259 a promotion night: *Light*, Jan. 15, 1927, p. 25. On Feb. 12, the *Pittsburgh Courier* reported that Armstrong was still featuring *Big Butter and Egg Man*.

260 *Chicago Breakdown*: Taylor 1993, 142, transcribes parts of the ensemble.

261 *Alligator Crawl* . . . "Turn the Page!": Waller was documented at the Metropolitan Theater in the *Light*, March 12, 1927, p. 20, said to have arrived "last week"; he was placed at the Vendome "permanently" in the *Defender*, March 19, 1927, p. 6; at the Vendome in the *Light*, March 26, 1927, p. 20; "detained by the Chicago police" in the *Defender*, April 30, 1927, p. 6; and back in New York in the *Defender*, May 7, 1927, p. 7. Waller's legal difficulties, including the threat of imprisonment, were explained in the *New York Amsterdam News*, Dec. 7, 1927, p. 1, and in the *Defender*, Dec. 10, 1927, p. 6. "Man you can't": Dance 1977, 52.

262 "All we needed was a lead sheet": Ory quoted in Anderson 2007, 24.

262 But Armstrong's solos . . . of the swing era: See Garrett 2008, 83–120, for discussion of *Gully Low Blues* and *S.O.L. Blues*, with transcription of Armstrong's solo on p. 101. Eldridge: Shapiro and Hentoff 1979, 301.

263 Ralph Ellison considered: Ellison 1995, 329.

264 Those who knew this "strictly Negro" tradition: One indication that Armstrong understood the connection of stop time to dancing comes with his use of the term "patter" to describe the stop-time section of *Cornet Chop Suey*. There is need for more research on usages of "patter" in songs and tunes from this period. There was, of course, the "patter song," well known from Gilbert and Sullivan, from which a Broadway tradition developed. But Armstrong's usage here is probably independent of that, coming instead from dance-band arrangements with stop-time chorus called "patter." Harker 2011, 28; Anderson 2007, 62, n. 36; Howland 2009, 119.

264 The first few months . . . remembered Hines: *Defender*, May 7, 1927, p. 6; Harker 2008, 84. *Courier*, Jan. 28 and Feb. 12, 1927. Quotation and ad from the *Light*, Feb. 19, 1927, pp. 35 and 36. Buck and Bubbles are first placed at the Sunset in 1927 on Feb. 19 (*Light and Heebie Jeebies*) with references continuing on March 12 (*Courier*), March 19 (*Afro-American*), March 26 (*Courier*). Hines: Dance 1977, 48.

265 Armstrong shared . . . in New York City: Bubbles IJS. Mezzrow 1946, 237.

265 Bubbles was good . . . complexity, and originality: Stearns and Stearns, 1994, 214ff. Bubbles IJS.

266 Armstrong manipulates harmony: For more analytical detail, see Brothers 1994.

266 Breaks, snakes, and fill-ins . . . Eddie Rector, and John Bubbles: *Defender*, April 16, 1927, p. 8. *Defender*, April 16, 1927; Armstrong 1966, 38; Scrapbook 83, LAHM. As Salem Tutt put it in the *Defender* (Aug. 14, 1926, p. 6): "In show business, when a joedoke can buy a car, he has reached success." $600: Personal communication from Lawrence Gushee; the contract was dated Feb. 8, 1927.

267  Yet this stop-time solo . . . hearing the line unfold: Jimmy Maxwell IJS 1979. Correlated chorus: Sudhalter and Evans 1974, 100–101. Bud Freeman IJS n.d.

267  "stalks majestically across the beat": Lyttelton 1978, 120.

268  The high value . . . he ever took on: *Defender*, June 18, 1927, p. 6. "There never": Armstrong 1999, 52. Others agreed. Cornetist George Mitchell (Mitchell HJA 1959), who played at the Sunset and the Dreamland during these years, recognized that Armstrong could "handle the instrument better" than Oliver, "but the ideas . . . If Joe could have handled his instrument like Louis, well that guy . . . I liked Joe's ideas." Being original was part of the New Orleans ethos. Johnny St. Cyr (Russell 1994, 74): "The New Orleans style is based on originality." Abbey Foster (Russell 1994, 54): "Always make a style of your own." Jelly Roll Morton (LC ca. 1938) on Fred Keppard: "No end to his ideas, could play one chorus eight or ten different ways."

268  "I'm going out tonight": Carmichael 1999a, 227; Dance 1977, 49.

269  "I'm just an old" . . . "and my life": "I'm just": Photocopy of article in HJA, Armstrong vertical file, from *Daily Express*, May 4, 1956, n.p. 80 tunes: Chevan 1999, 208. "All them": quoted in Harker 1999.

270  "style of jazz the public has gone wild about": *Defender*, Feb. 27, 1926, p. 6.

271  "He plays on the beat": Williams 1979. "[Armstrong] works like a horse": Smith 1964, 123–26.

273  the tremendous explosion of twentieth-century creativity: Brothers 1997.

273  further innovations were possible: Brothers 1994.

274  Frank Teschemacher: Sudhalter 1999, 456.

275  "That's a broad question": Pond 2005, 27.

## Chapter 7: "Some Kind of a God"

276  "A musician in Chicago": Armstrong 1999, 74.

276  Armstrong and his orchestra appeared: *Defender*, June 4, 1927; Kenney 1993, 31. Calloway: *Courier*, June 11, 1927; *Afro-American*, June 11, 1927. Cab Calloway was criticized in the Oct. 22, 1927, issue of the *Light and Heebie Jeebies* (p. 28), while performing at the Plantation Café: "As master of ceremonies Calloway is a total failure—but this is covered up by a good review."

277  "Oh what a sweet and helpful girl May Ann was": King 1967, 66.

277  Armstrong insisted that all twelve members of his orchestra be hired: *Defender*, July 30, 1927, p. 8; Kenney 1993, 34.

278  "a scream": *Courier*, Oct. 29, 1927; *Afro-American*, March 26, 1927; Scrapbook 83, LAHM.

278  In late August . . *Chicago Breakdown*: *Defender*, July 23, Aug. 6, Aug. 20, Sept. 24, 1927; Scrapbook 83, LAHM; Miller 2007, 34; Armstrong 1999. "a good blues": Armstrong 1950, 24.

279  In September . . . musicians in the orchestra: *Defender*, Sept. 3, Sept. 12, Sept. 17, 1927; Scrapbook 83, LAHM; *Courier*, Oct. 29, 1927. *Defender*, April 7, 1928.

279  he still performed comedy: Armstrong 1946, 43.

280  "one of his freakish, high register breaks": *Defender*, Sept. 17, 1927, p. 6. "Nice, sweet arranging": Scrapbook 83, LAHM.

280  In early November . . . the Sunset Café: *Chicago Tribune*, Nov. 6, 1927. "You take": Shapiro and Hentoff 1955, 159.

280 Beiderbecke stopped by... "on the blues": Carmichael 1999a, 114; Hines COHP 1971; Dance 1977, 48; McHargue HJA; Carmichael 1999, 53. "We sat": Levinson 2005, 25. Wettling WRC ca. 1938; Shapiro and Hentoff 1955, 159. Manone 1948, 61.

281 "His intervals were so orderly": Deffaa 1990, 77. See the analysis of *Singin' the Blues* in Brooks 2000, chap. 5, including an interesting comparison with Armstrong.

281 Beiderbecke owed something... at age twenty-eight, in 1931: Dance 1977, 48. Mezzrow 1946, 157; Carmichael 1999a, 91; Dance 1977, 48. Gabbard 2008, 161.

282 slapped together at the last minute: Armstrong 1999, 133–34.

283 *Cornet Chop Suey*... who had moved north: Manone 1948, 61; Hodes CJA n.d.; Armstrong 1999, 131. Major 1994, 22; advertisement reproduced in Anderson 2007, 156. Cakewalk: Cheatham IJS 1976. "Struttin' time": Hunter IJS 1976–77.

284 "Lonnie was the only guy": Foster 2005, 106.

284 Armstrong said: Armstrong 1999, 136. Perhaps OKeh was encouraged to do this by the success of the Trumbauer, Beiderbecke, and Lang recording of *Wringin' and Twistin'*, from September 1927.

284 Armstrong immediately... widely known *Tiger Rag*: Ory 1950a, 17; Anderson 2007, 181–87. Armstrong 1999, 136. Anderson 2007, 175.

285 often talked about in the press: Scrapbook 83, LAHM.

285 many listeners have heard: James Lincoln Collier (1983, 187), for example, wrote that he was "as certain as one can be about these things that the growing mood of sadness [first heard in *Savoy Blues*], leading up to the classic 'West End Blues,' sprang from the death of his mother." See also Black, Charles L., Jr. 1979, 66–73.

286 Compton wrote a letter: *Defender*, Dec. 24, 1927, p. 6.

286 By December 3, 1927... sessions with OKeh: *Defender*, Dec. 3, 1927, p. 6. Armstrong 1946, 43. Dance 1977, 54.

286 Singleton was working: Singleton WRC ca. 1938. "Highbrow district": *Defender*, Dec. 10, 1927, p. 7.

286 "little corporation": Singleton WRC ca. 1938; *Defender*, Dec. 31, 1927, p. 6; Dance 1977, 55; Armstrong 1946, 43; Smith 1942, 46; Armstrong 1999, 99; *Courier*, Dec. 17, 1927, p. A4.

287 "Man we didn't"... Singleton admitted: Singleton WRC ca. 1938; Singleton IJS Reels 4, 5, and 6. *Defender,* Dec. 31, 1927, p. 6.

288 Armstrong reasoned... "all three of us": Dance 1977, 53. "Things gotten": Armstrong 1999, 99. Hines, Foster, and Deppe CJA 1961.

288 Finally, a decent offer... he grumbled: *Defender*, Feb. 18, 1928, p. 6. *Defender*, March 10, 17, and 24, 1928, p. 6. Kenney 1993, 162; *Light*, Jan. 14, 1928, p. 22.

289 Carroll Dickerson... "really took over": Singleton WRC ca. 1938; Hines, Foster, and Deppe CJA 1961. Dance 1977, 54 and 145. Saunders COHP 1971.

289 The heavily funded Savoy... with eccentric dancing: On the Savoy, see Kenney 1993, 162; Travis 1981, 79–94; *Light and Heebie Jeebies*, Nov. 19, 1927, p. 2, Nov. 26, 1927, p. 21, Dec. 3, 1927, p. 28. Ethel Waters: *Defender*, Dec. 3, 1927; *Light and Heebie Jeebies*, Nov. 26, 1927, p. 21; Dec. 3, 1927, p. 28.

290 Like many large... black: *Light and Heebie Jeebies*, April 7, 1928, pp. 4 and

14; April 14, 1928, p. 4. Scrapbook 83, LAHM. *Defender*, April 14, 1928, p. 7; April 28, 1928, p. 6; May 12, 1928, p. A2. Scrapbook 83, LAHM, clipping dated April 21, 1928; *Afro-American*, Dec. 1, 1928.

290 One promotional article . . . the crowd's shoulders: Promotional article: a clipping from the house publication *Savoyager*, Scrapbook 83, LAHM, with information that WMAQ picked up nightly broadcasts from 11:00 p.m. to 1:00 a.m.; see also Jackson 1994, 76: "All they had to do was play *Savoy Blues*, *Some of These Days*, and the *St. Louis Blues* and the fight was over." *Liebestraum*: Freeman 1970, 17. Paul Whiteman's Orchestra recorded their own version in December 1928. *Defender* May 5, 1928, p. 6. Hodes 1977, 74; Hodes CJA n.d.

290 sudden death of Ollie Powers: *Defender*, April 21, 1928, p. 3.

291 In early May . . . "a serious matter?": *Defender*, May 12, 1928, p. 6; Travis 1981, 240. *Defender*, June 23, 1928, p. 6; June 30, 1928, p. 6; quotation from July 14, 1928, p. 6; Aug. 4, 1928, p. 6. Mencken in *New York Tribune*, July 17, 1927; quoted in Howland 2009, 4. Lyricist Andy Razaf responded directly (*Amsterdam News*, Aug. 10, 1927, p. 11), holding up Will Marion Cook and especially James P. Johnson as strong African-American composers. See also *Heebie Jeebies*, July 23, 1927, p. 26; July 30, 1927, p. 21; Aug. 6, 1927, p. 6. See also Moore 1985, 94–98.

291 "slaughtered all of the ofay jazz demons": *Defender*, July 14, 1928, p. 6.

292 Armstrong's display of individual power: Gabbard 2008.

293 "brassy, broad and aggressively dramatic": Baraka [Jones] 1963, 154.

294 Oliver was in Chicago: Wright 1987, 264; Hodes, Art CJA n.d.

295 "When Louis started blowing": Wettling in Shapiro and Hentoff 1955, 118.

296 Armstrong "had to stand back" . . . until June 1928: "had to stand": Travis 1981, 385. "There was": Shapiro and Hentoff 1955, 245.

297 *A Monday Date*: Hines told a different story about the origins of the title; Dance 1977, 53.

297 In late December . . . during his youth: *Tattler*, Dec. 27, 1929, p. 16. *Afro-American*, June 13, 1925, p. 4.

298 "For a picture of some pretensions": *Los Angeles Times,* Feb. 19, 1928, p. C11.

298 *West End Blues* . . . Armstrong's performance: Holiday 2006, 9–10. Recording studio: Albertson 1982, 189.

299 After the vocal-clarinet . . . remembered Wilson: Scrapbook 83, LAHM. *Melody Maker*, November 1929. Wilson, Teddy 2001, 102; Dance 1977, 183.

300 "It was sort of a special deal": Singleton IJS 1975. With Dickerson, Armstrong, and Singleton involved, this could only have been while all three were working at the Savoy Ballroom.

301 "the meaning used to change": Holiday 2006, 10.

301 "*West End Blues* was his real beginning": Carmichael 1999a, 204.

301 Quite a few musicians . . . "as nothing had before": Jackson FDC 1973; Smith, Jabbo HJA 1961; Laplace 1988; Travis 1981, 240; Elgar CJA n.d. "he had": trumpeter Fred Gerard in Laplace 1988, 18. On other trumpeters copying Armstrong's *West End Blues*, see Quentin Jackson IJS 1976. Stuff Smith: Barnett 2002, 12 and 19. Feather: Kenney 1999, 20.

302 When he first arrived . . . treasures of jazz history: Dance 1977, 18–34; Gleason 1961, 107–10. Armstrong LAHM 1967.

302 Hines convinced Armstrong . . . notebound playing: The September date for

Hines at the Vendome is my inference, based on a clipping in Scrapbook 83, LAHM, which mentions Chick Johnson (who was in Chicago Aug. 14, 1926), St. Cyr and Cook's song *Messin' Around* (composed in 1926), Tate's vacation, and Hines's participation at the Vendome. See also Armstrong 1936, 84; Dance 1977, 140.

302 "He was always a trouper": Dance 1977, 49.

303 Hines sat down and started playing: Manone 1948, 63.

303 When Singleton arrived . . . "paid the bills": Gleason 1961, 108. Dance 1977, 54. Armstrong 1966, 35.

303 The three friends rented an apartment: Armstrong 1999, 100; Jackson 2005, 87; Hodes 1977, 13; Herndon 1964, 72.

303 Their social world . . . "or you weren't": Washington COHP 1971; Singleton HJA 1969; Dance 1977. Singleton HJA 1969. Scott IJS 1979; Washington COHP 1971.

304 "Every professional musician": Magee 2005, 161.

304 White musicians flocked: Davison CJA 1981. Hodes 1977, 13, 74; see also Hodes 1944, 7; Washington IJS; Davison CJA 1981.

304 Spanier, Stacy, Teschemacher . . . or with him: "Yeah": Hodes 1977, 174. Soper CJA 1983; Davison IJS.

304 For one thing . . . "pretty much": Browne COHP 1971. Kenney 1993, 33.

305 "it was just a bunch of people": Hodes 1977, 27. Armstrong, Lillian WRC 1938; Hodes 1977, 27. Wright, Richard 1998, 273.

305 Robert Moton . . . "stay there": Moton 1929, 227. Bushell 1988, 44.

306 Did he . . . readership was facing: Saunders COHP 1971. On whites stealing black music, see Hinton COHP 1971; Brown COHP 1971; Kenney 1993, 111; *Defender*, Oct. 9, 1926, p. 6, and Oct. 23, 1926, p. 6; Barker IJS; Hines COHP 1971; Dodds 1992, 63.

307 Armstrong's experience . . . "really tough skin": Barker and Hinton IJS.

307 both very fond of marijuana: Soper CJA 1983; Dance 1977, 146.

308 Marijuana usage . . . cost two dollars: Armstrong 1999, 112; Dance 1977, 146. Mezzrow 1947, 51, 71–74, and 92–94.

308 The recording . . . chuckle over the title: Old New Orleanian trick: Howard, Paul WRC 1969. House parties: Cheatham IJS 1976.

308 Armstrong spent . . . lay there, grinning: Scrapbook 83, LAHM. Jackson 2005, 87; Armstrong 1999, 100.

308 Basketball . . . home in bed: Armstrong 1999, 100. Armstrong LAHM Tape 202.

309 In September . . . $1 at the door: *Defender*, Sept. 15, 1928, p. 6; Ramsey 1939, 137; Singleton WRC ca. 1938; Dance 1977, 146; Singleton IJS 1975. Russell 1999, 486; Singleton HJA 1969; Armstrong, Lillian WRC 1969. Scrapbook 83, LAHM; *Afro-American*, Dec. 1, 1928.

309 Armstrong said . . . " 'Zuttyface' ": Armstrong 1999, 74; Hinton IJS 1976. Dance 1977, 80, 143. Browne COHP 1971; Hines COHP 1971. Cheatham IJS 1976.

310 not really trained in blues: Taylor 1993, 35.

311 "Earl is a very difficult person to play with": Dance 1977, 290; see also Wilson 2001, 102–4.

311 What is especially . . . another direction: "Poor old": Peretti 1992, 117. Foster 2005, 198.

311 But with Hines . . . in early jazz: Taylor 1993, 216. Jeffrey Taylor argues (per-

sonal communication) that the standard discographical entry for these solo sessions—Dec. 8—is almost certainly incorrect. More likely, the sessions took place earlier. Taylor (1993, chap. 6) gives a good discussion of these pieces, with excellent transcriptions; see also Taylor 1992, esp. p. 71, with transcription and discussion of *Savoyagers' Stomp*.

312 The two of them . . . "the closer you become": "We were": Dance 1977, 52; see also Dance 1977 183; Freeman 1994, 121; Hines 2005, 151. See Taylor 1992 for precise discussion of Armstrong's influence on Hines. Anita O'Day: Leonard 1989, 29.

313 There are many examples: See, for example, Taylor 1993, 152, for transcription and analysis of *Sweethearts on Parade* and pp. 153–58 for *Skip the Gutter*.

313 Hines made it clear: Taylor 1998, 22.

314 it would have surprised everyone involved: Taylor 1993, 160.

314 "Louis had some ideas": Taylor 1998, 22.

315 Armstrong carries the lead: Taylor (1993 and 1998) cites many instances of these kinds of fleeting connections. For a fine example, see p. 263 of Taylor 1993, mm. 2–4 of C3. Note that it is Hines who generates the effect, as he does throughout the piece, with Armstrong more or less stating his lead and Hines commenting and providing the conversational glue.

315 This is the kind of moment: This could have been a mistake, of course. The moment recalls one of the most famous misentries in jazz, Count Basie's entrance in a break designed for Lester Young in *Lester Leaps In*. See Schuller 1989, 249–50.

317 That musicians hold powers . . . *Tight Like This*: Smith 1964, 53. Billy Eckstine: Dance 1977, 241. For other discussions of Armstrong and sexuality, see Gabbard 2008 and 1995; Raeburn 2004. On the general topic of jazz and sexuality, see Tucker 2000; Smith 2008; DeVeaux 1997, 103; Wilmer 1977. Additional primary sources include Singleton IJS 1975; Deffaa 1990, 37; Bushell 1988, 46.

317 James Baldwin insisted . . . sex is irrelevant: Baldwin 1961, 188. Mailer 1970.

318 "Ever since I was a little boy": Armstrong 1999, 95; on the masculine world of Armstrong's teens, see Brothers 2006, chap. 9.

318 What got the ladies . . . "makes you produce jazz": Hines COHP 1971. Johnson: Davin 1995, 332; Williams 1962, 57–61. Smith 1964, 118. Cootie Williams: Wilmer 1977, 199.

318 Percussionist Art Lewis . . . in 1938: Lewis: Leonard 1987, 59. Armstrong 1999, 95, 99.

319 Apparently, things weren't . . . "that's my life": Armstrong 1999, 97. Millstein n.d.

319 His nephew Clarence: Armstrong 1946, 41; Armstrong 1999, 89.

319 It was a comic number: Armstrong 1999, 134. Spousal-abuse songs like this were not uncommon during this period. Percy Grainger made a specialty of them, with *You've Got to Beat Me to Keep Me*, *Tain't Nobody's Business If I Do*, and *Mistreatin' Daddy*.

320 As a child . . . according to Armstrong: "That taught": Armstrong 1999, 60 and 95. Raeburn 2004, 12.

321 "poor girl, not near as fortunate as Lil": Armstrong 1995, 95.

321 "I became" . . . *Tight Like This*: Armstrong 1995, 95. Dorsey CJA n.d.

322 "It is only within the last two or three years": Osgood 1926, 249.

323 "fucking rhythm": Gabbard 1996, 143, and 1995, 110.

323 "eccentric piano": *Defender*, Oct. 6, 1928, p. 6, giving Hill's address at 457 East 47th Street and reporting that he is playing in a band led by Jimmy Wade.

324 The *Light* announced the wedding: *Light*, June 23, 1928, front cover; see also *Defender*, May 26, 1928, p. 7, and June 23, 1928, p. 6. On Marshall "Garbage" Rodgers, see also Scrapbook 83, LAHM; *Courier*, July 28, 1928, p. A2; Aug. 18, 1928, p. A1; *Afro-American*, Sept. 15, 1928, p. 9; Jan. 31, 1929, p. 9. Other references to the phrase: *Defender*, Sept. 29, 1928, p. 7; Oct. 20, 1928, p. 7; Dec. 6, 1930, p. 15; *Afro-American*, Oct. 5, 1929, p. A14. The wedding event was apparently problematic; see *Light*, July 14, 1928, p. 2. A scrapbook reference (item 25) refers to Armstrong performing *Heah Me* over the radio, which probably places the performance at the Savoy. The recording was advertised quickly, in a January 1929 issue of the *Afro-American*.

## Chapter 8: The White Turn

326 "Honey, colored people": Bernhardt 1986, 165.

326 "You follow the people": Huggins 1995, 338.

326 "one of the swellest white night clubs": *Defender*, Oct. 13, 1928, p. 6; Herndon 1964, 72–73.

326 As impressive . . . their shared apartment: *Defender*, Oct. 23, 1926, p. 6. Feather 1970, 35; Jackson 2005 196; Armstrong 1950a, 26.

326 It was even possible . . . say to Hines: *Light and Heebie Jeebies*, April 28, 1928, p. 14. Union: Spivey 1984, 39; see also Banks 1980, 227–28. South: Hinton IJS 1976; Hinton IJS 1974. Hines COHP 1971.

327 he was not alone: Bud Freeman (IJS n.d.): "Now we in jazz do not use categories. We do not put people into categories. . . . We don't call a man a modern drummer or an avant garde drummer or a dixieland drummer. A man can either play or he cannot. This is what it's about and only musicians know this, not critics, I'm sorry to say."

327 The appreciation . . . in October 1928: Surfing: Washington CJA 1965. Lombardo: Dance 1977, 63.

328 When the Regal . . . Plantation and Sunset: *Light*, Feb. 11, 1928, p. 2; see also Feb. 25, 1928, p. 4. Hinton and Berger 1988, 27. *Defender*, April 7, 1928, p. 6. Peyton was hired to do the original contracting for the Regal; CJA Steiner Collection, box 87, article "The Fess Williams Story."

329 A review of his performance: Scrapbook 83, LAHM. The undated article references an upcoming visit to Cincinnati, which is probably the one that took place on May 17, thus providing a terminus ante quem for the article.

329 It is no surprise . . . until now: Peterson 1993, 37. Composer credit for *I Can't Give You Anything* went to Dorothy Fields and Jimmy McHugh, but it has been argued that Fats Waller was the actual composer; see Givan 2004, 213, n. 24; see also Winer 1997, 26–37. Advertisement in *Interstate Tattler*, Feb. 29, 1929, p. 10. Recordings include Red Nichols (May 1928), Martha Copeland (May 1928), Paul Whiteman (June 1928), Ben Selvin (June 1928), Annette Hanshaw (July 1928), Abe Lyman (November 1928).

329 The visit was organized: Armstrong (1999, 100) explained it this way: "So I was still signed up to the OKeh Record Co. But Mr. Fern turned my Contract over to Mr. Tommy Rockwell whom was stationed in New York. And at the same time Mr. Fagan was coming up short with our money, Mr. Rockwell

sent for me to come to New York immediately to make some records and also book me into a show called 'Great Day' produced by Vincent Youmans." It is possible that the Savoy Ballroom of Harlem sponsored the visit. Armstrong's performance there was announced in the *Interstate Tattler* as early as Feb. 22, 1929, p. 11.

331  Ethel Waters parodied him: Freeman 1970, 17; Carmichael 1999a, 202; Cheatham quoted in Goddard 1979, 292. See also Douglas 1995, 336.

332  Kaiser Marshall remembered: Marshall 1943, 85.

332  Rockwell used the Luis Russell Orchestra: Singleton IJS 1975.

332  The rhythm section . . . of those qualities: Foster: Russell 1994, 106. "Jazz is": Foster 2005, 90.

333  This brief visit . . . weeks in a row: *Defender*, March 16, 1929, p. 6, and March 23, 1929, p. 4; Holmes IJS n.d. Armstrong 1999, 100; Armstrong 1966, 38. *Chicago Tribune*, April 29, 1929, p. 28; April 30, 1929, p. 36; May 2, 1929, p. 34. Early May also included a brief trip to Cincinnati for a one-night stand on May 7 at the Paradise Ballroom. The hall was so jammed that there was no room to dance, "but the crowd was happy to listen to the wonderful music," reported the *Defender* (May 25, 1929, p. 6).

333  In fact . . . headed for New York City: On the Plantation, *Defender*, March 24, 1928, p. 6. What the *Light* repeatedly called the "Carroll years" was a reference to citywide crackdowns on cabarets and their relentless bootlegging. Hines: Dance 1977, 52; Levin 1985, 195. "Could I have": Davison CJA 1981. Hennessey 1974, 30; Hinton IJS n.d.; Anderson 1988, xliii. Headed for New York: Leonard 1962, 105; Mezzrow 1946, 164; Jones 1988, 134; Kenney 1993, chap. 6; Bud Freeman IJS n.d.

334  His next move: On the movie, *Defender*, April 13, 1929, p. 6.

334  They decided . . . she once admitted: Armstrong 1999, 100 and 105; Armstrong 1946, 43. Singleton WRC ca. 1938. Recital: Scrapbook 83, LAHM; *Defender*, May 25, 1929, p. 6; Barrett 2004, 73. According to the *Defender* of June 15, 1929 (p. 6), Lillian planned to pay "a short visit" on Louis in New York soon, and on June 8 the *Defender* reported that she had supervised "the costumes, the stage settings and the music" for a recital of the Mary Bruce Dancing school in Chicago. Armstrong, Lillian IJS n.d.

334  the musicians wound their way: Accounts of the trip: Singleton 1950; Jones and Chilton 1971, 103; Armstrong 1946, 43; Ramsey 1946, 33; Armstrong 1999, 105; Singleton WRC ca. 1938.

335  An irritated Rockwell . . . the fall of 1924: Armstrong 1946, 43. "the decision": Jones and Chilton 1971, 103. Magee 2005, 121.

335  stopped by the Rhythm Club: *Amsterdam News*, March 6, 1929, p. 7, for "negotiations" with Aaron Douglas to decorate; opening cited *Defender*, March 16, 1929, p. 6; April 27, 1929, p. 6; July 13, 1929, p. 6. Singleton WRC ca. 1938.

335  "caste system": Magee 2005, 30; Barker IJS, 3–22; Howland 2009, 21.

336  Several musicians left . . . bantering back and forth: Danny Barker in Williams 1962; Barker 1986, 113–19; Smith WRC 1970; Smith 1964, 159; Higgenbotham IJS; Singleton HJA 1969; Nicholas WRC 1970; Hinton IJS 1976.

336  The first job Armstrong and the Dickerson band landed: Singleton 1950; Singleton WRC ca. 1938; Singleton IJS 1975.

337  Next the band opened . . . white audiences for him: Singleton WRC ca. 1938.

The *Defender* (June 22, 1929, p. 6) reported that Armstrong and the Dickerson band were to begin work at Connie's on June 24.

337 Clyde Bernhardt: Bernhardt 1986, 64.

338 "heat wave": Hughes 1986, 226–27; Lewis 1979, 162–63; Huggins 1995, 339.

338 "spellbound": Howland 2009, 231.

338 The Cotton Club . . . "there's no mixing": Huggins 1995, 339; see also Waters 1951, 34. "Nobody wants": Lewis 1979, 209.

338 "crafty night people": Barker 1986, 134–38; Barker IJS.

338 The familiar primitivist package . . . dark and exotic: Johnson: Erenberg 1981, 233. Durante: Lewis 1979, 208.

339 It was the familiar mix . . . were asleep : "The whole": Saul 2003, 37; Calloway 1976, 121 and 178. Erenberg 1981, 255.

339 Connie's Inn . . . Lafayette Theater: Armstrong 1936, 89. Bernhardt 1986, 70.

339 Locals gathered in the alley: Mezzrow 1946, 208.

340 The assignment . . . "among Negro women": *Amsterdam News*, June 26, 1929, p. 13; Armstrong 1999, 105; Mezzrow 1946, 209. *Afro-American*, Sept. 28, 1929, p. A8.

340 Armstrong characterized as a slow fox trot: Armstrong 1999, 105.

341 The crowds . . . "Musicians of New York": Smith 1964, 170; Dixon 2000, 100. *Defender*, Aug. 10, 1929, p. 6; Armstrong 1999, 105.

341 Connie Immerman . . . made his mark: "a little fat guy": Quentin Jackson IJS 1976. Singer 1992, 2.

341 "All-colored" shows: Waters 1951, 217; Stearns 1994, 140–42; Woll 1989, 112 and 136.

341 When Rudolf Fisher . . . "some good comedy": Howland 2009, 23. Hughes 1986, 223. Stearns and Stearns 1994, 134; Goddard 1979, 290. "Just enough": Miller 2007, 37.

342 *Shuffle Along*'s combination . . . to be illiterate: Kimball and Bolcom 1973, 133 and 116; Savran 2009, 124. Blake: Savran 2009, 121.

342 *Shuffle Along* was packed . . . during the 1920s: *Interstate Tattler*, June 14, 1929, p. 16. Stearns and Stearns 1994, 133. Blake: Huggins 1995, 337.

343 Black patrons . . . exclusionary practices: *Interstate Tattler*, June 28, 1929, p. 9. Stearns and Stearns 1994, 141.

343 whites did not go to theaters: Though some came close; see Woll 1989, 109.

343 For while the music . . . "on a bet". "You see": Kimball and Bolcom 1973, 238. White critic: Kimball and Bolcom 1973, 180.

344 "Jimmy Johnson had the band lay out": Bradford 1965, 137; see also Gilbert Seldes quoted in Spring 1993, 210.

345 "The two greatest Negro songs": Woll 1989, 97 and 112; Peterson 1993, 272.

345 With *Blackbirds of 1928* . . . Immerman's *Hot Chocolates*: Woll 1989, 124; Stearns and Stearns 1994, 149–55 and 181. Mills: *Variety*, June 26, 1929, p. 55; Woll 1989, 131.

345 Immerman hired . . . a cast of 85: *Interstate Tattler*, Feb. 22, 1929, p. 11; *Variety*, June 26, 1929, p. 55; *Amsterdam News*, May 29, 1929, p. 12. The *Defender* (June 15, 1929, p. 6) reported that Ethel Waters was "engaged" to star in *Hot Chocolates*, but her appearance apparently did not come to pass. Stearns and Stearns 1994, 153; *Variety*, June 26, 1929, p. 55.

345 "It is distinctly" . . . graceful adagio routine: *Variety*, June 26, 1929, p. 55. For

other reviews emphasizing dancing, see *Amsterdam News*, June 26, 1929, p. 13; *Afro-American*, June 29, 1929, p. 9. "every muscle": *Afro-American*, June 29, 1929, p. 9. Cook: *Interstate Tattler*, June 28, 1929, p. 9; *Afro-American*, Sept. 28, 1929, p. A8; Scrapbook 83, LAHM (handwritten "New York Evening Graphic Oct. 31, 1929"). Calloway: *Courier*, Nov. 23, 1929, p. A3; Travis 1981, 224. "Not only": *Interstate Tattler*, June 28, 1929, p. 9, and June 14, 1929, p. 16; *Defender*, June 15, 1929, p. 6.

346 "The dancing" . . . the *Evening Graphic*: *Interstate Tattler*, June 28, 1929, p. 9; *Norfolk Journal and Guide*, July 13, 1929, p. 9; *Variety,* June 26, 1929, p. 55; July 31, 1929, p. 54. "Blacker than": *Variety*, July 31, 1929, p. 54. Scrapbook 83, LAHM (handwritten "New York Evening Graphic Oct. 31, 1929").

346 lewd double entendres: *Interstate Tattler*, June 28, 1929, p. 9; *Afro-American*, June 29, 1929, p. 13; *Interstate Tattler*, June 14, 1929, p. 16.

346 "The show in the Hudson" . . . *Blackbirds of 1928*: *Amsterdam News*, June 26, 1929, p. 13. Mezzrow: Shapiro and Hentoff 1955, 256. Armstrong 1936, 91. *Variety*, June 26, 1929, p. 55; Woll 1989, 132.

347 At the Hudson . . . sing between acts: People hung: Trail 1971, 3. Dunn: Williams 1979, 83 (Bushell) and 98 (Redman); see also *The Official Theatrical World of Colored Artists 1928* (WRC MSS 519, folder 81), which has a large display ad for Johnny Dunn, reading, in part, "Creator of the WahWah/Sensation for 'Blackbirds' European Tour." Smith also sang in *Pansy*, in May 1929, from the stage as herself; Peterson 1993, 180 and 267; Stearns and Stearns 1994, 153.

347 "decided sensation": *Interstate Tattler*, June 28, 1929, p. 9, and Sept. 6, 1929, p. 11; *Afro-American*, Sept. 28, 1929, p. A9.

348 Armstrong once described . . . Bessie Smith: "On the first": Collier 1983, 287. Gillespie 1979, 303.

350 In an insightful . . . "for the public": Giddins 2001, 9. Armstrong 1966, 41.

350 "Bo's face" . . . films and fortune: Stearns and Stearns 1994, 188 and 156.

350 "He always did things in eight bars": Al Minns quoted in Stearns and Stearns 1994, 187.

351 Armstrong complained: Jones and Chilton 1971, 86.

351 "The best scenes": Woll 1989, 119.

352 "When you get people relaxed": Gillespie quoted in Leonard 1986, 154. And consider Ralph Ellison, writing about the role of laughter as an immediate way to defuse tension: "If you can laugh at me, you don't have to kill me." O'Meally 2003, 124.

352 the first lines of the verse: Singer 1992, 217.

353 "Lokka here, my Man Tan's coming off!": King 1967, 65.

353 "Way I sing it now ": Armstrong 1966, 42.

354 Ellison framed it in *Invisible Man*: Ellison 1947, 6–10.

354 reception history of *Black and Blue*: Katz 2004, 14.

354 One critic found . . . "the things I was doing": *Variety*, June 26, 1929, p. 55; *Interstate Tattler*, Aug. 9, 1929, p. 11. Armstrong 1966, 40.

355 At Connie's . . . happened in print: *Defender*, Aug. 24, 1929, p. A3. *Amsterdam News*, June 26, 1929, p. 12.

355 He tripled up there: *Amsterdam News*, June 19, 1929, p. 13.

355 seminudity: Dixon 2000, 79.

355 John Bubbles . . . Willie "The Lion" Smith: Bubbles IJS n.d. "In Harlem": Dixon 2000, 79. Smith 1964, 196.

356 a performance on October 8: *Amsterdam News*, Oct. 2, 1929, p. 8, and Oct. 9, 1929, p. 9; *Defender*, Oct. 19, 1929, p. 6.

356 The Lafayette . . . he didn't: Dominique CJA 1952. Armstrong 1966, 40; marijuana: Mezzrow 1946, 236; Clayton IJS n.d. Holiday: Shapiro and Hentoff 1955, 198.

356 In September he performed: *Defender*, Sept. 7, 1929, p. A3.

356 "I believe" . . . 16 times previously: Armstrong 1936, 91. 22 times: Crawford and Magee 1992, 71–72.

357 he remembered: Harker 2011, 93.

361 At some point . . . Singleton remembered: The *Interstate Tattler* (Nov. 22, 1929, p. 11) has an ad for Louis Armstrong and His Connie's Inn Orchestra playing for a "breakfast dance" from 3:00 to 8:30 a.m. on Thanksgiving morning at Rockland Palace, 155th Street and Eighth Avenue. Armstrong 1999, 105. Singleton IJS 1975.

361 Rockwell started booking . . . New Year's Eve: Keepnews 1950, 25; Armstrong 1999, 105. 1928: Kenney 1999, 173. Ferrer: Armstrong LAHM Tape 17. *Philadelphia Tribune*, Dec. 26, 1929, p. 6.

361 The Russell band . . . he said: A good discussion of Allen's musical debt to Armstrong is in Lyttelton 1978, 193. Armstrong LAHM 1970.

363 "Poor Russell": Holmes IJS n.d.

364 "Compared with the Hot Five": Lyttelton 1978, 135.

365 there is no discernible change: See the good discussion of this performance in Eisenberg 1987, 156.

365 Breaking into . . . "rhythm of the jungle": Hines: Dance 1977, 62. *Defender*, Dec. 5, 1931, p. 5.

365 It was a get-ahead decade . . . the only African American: Foster 2005, 167. "December Records," *Time*, Dec. 15, 1930, p. 28. Scrapbook 83, LAHM.

366 a report from Baltimore: *Afro-American*, Jan. 18, 1930, p. A9.

367 gathered mixed reviews: Scrapbook 83, LAHM; see also *New York Morning Telegraph*, January 1928, p. 7, reference courtesy Steven Lasker and Ken Steiner.

367 On January 24 . . . "than the orchestra": Scrapbook 83, LAHM (identified as *Daily Mirror*, Monday, March 24, 1930). New stunt: Scrapbook 83, LAHM.

368 "I just try": Scrapbook 6, LAHM.

368 he offered $5,000 cash: Scrapbook 83, LAHM.

369 *Tiger Rag* was recorded: Crawford and Magee 1992 list 16 recordings of *Dinah* before Armstrong's, and 56 recordings of *Tiger Rag*.

369 Again musical quotations . . . recorded performances: *Tiger Rag*: St. Cyr HJA 1958; Morton 2005; Szwed 2005, 36–41. Quotes: Berrett 1992, 224.

370 recordings shaped jazz history: This section benefits from Katz 2004 and Eisenberg 1987.

372 as Clyde Bernhardt and Louis Metcalf tell us: Shapiro and Hentoff 1955, 206. Bernhardt 1968, 46; Bernhardt FDC 1074.

373 "It would have been impossible": Wright 1998, 250.

373 "the way he carried himself": Jones 1988, 138–39.

374 The recordings lost . . . "emancipated the jazz musician": Watts HJA 1963. Johnson IJS n.d. Cootie Williams IJS 1976. Price: Jones and Chilton 1971, 99.

375 Shoeshine boys on Royal Street: Barker 1986, 59; Manone 1948, 99.

376 A trip to Paris was announced: Scrapbook 83, LAHM.

376 the chance to make a movie: *California Eagle*, July 11, 1930, p. 8.

## Chapter 9: The Rosetta Stone

377 "[Armstrong] found the Rosetta stone": Quoted in Stanley Crouch, "The Colossus," *The New Yorker*, May 9, 2005, p. 64.

377 Armstrong left Chicago . . . he quipped: Information on the arrival from Dickerson 2002, 158; Armstrong 1999, 117; see also the regular columns for the *Defender* ("Coast Breezes") and *Afro-American* ("Movie Gossip"). Arrival dated Wednesday, July 9, in the *California Eagle* (July 11, 1930, p. 1); reference courtesy Steven Lasker. Hinton IJS 1976. "The Lord": Armstrong 1999, 107–8.

377 The Dunbar . . . starring Amos 'n' Andy: Du Bois: Bogle 2005, 77. Jones and Chilton 1971, 115.

378 What lured him . . . "his own song style": Scrapbook 83, LAHM. Also on Sebastian's, see Bryant 1988. Quote from Scrapbook 83, LAHM, clipping identified as *Los Angeles Evening Herald*, July 10, 1930.

378 Sebastian's Cotton Club . . . as you approached: There is much evidence about the segregated policy of the Cotton Club, including this from a clipping in Scrapbook 83, LAHM, dated Aug. 22, 1930: "Vernon Elkin and his orchestra with Louis Armstrong as the star trumpet are playing at Sebastian's Cotton Club, which caters exclusively to white trade." See also *California Eagle*, Aug. 15, 1930, p. 10, and Oct. 31, 1930, p. 1; also *Defender*, Oct. 28 (local edition, page unidentified; photocopy courtesy Steven Lasker). Armstrong, Lillian 1963. Royal 1996, 36.

379 Dickerson was supposed to yell out: Royal 1996, 44.

379 Forty entertainers . . . according to one clipping: *Defender*, Aug. 16, 1930, p. 5, and Jan. 10, 1931, p. 5. Scrapbook 5, LAHM, clipping identified as *Defender*, July 19.

379 He brought . . . Red Top taxis: "took over": Scrapbook 83, LAHM, clippings identified as *Los Angeles Evening Herald*, July 21, 1930, and July 18, 1930. Taxis: Scrapbook 83, LAHM, clipping identified as *Los Angeles Evening Herald*, July 26, 1930.

380 The Cotton Club . . . Lillian's clipped articles: "the newly found rich": Bryant 1998, 38. Armstrong LAHM Tape 202. Armstrong 1961, 82. "Patrons have": Scrapbook 83, LAHM.

380 "The few [white] parties I did go to": Armstrong 1961, 82.

380 The band included . . . "their instrument": "I discovered": Armstrong 1999, 106. Hampton 1993, 37. "When I sing": Dance 1974, 268. Cootie Williams IJS 1976. Armstrong 1999, 118.

381 You can almost hear him: The performance is partially transcribed in Armstrong 2003, 6–7. Rodgers continually inserts two-beat measures into the flow of otherwise regular blues phrases, and he does so differently in each chorus.

382 "He rarely has more than a rough idea": "Black Rascal," *Time*, June 13, 1932 (accessed online, n.p.).

382 This scat solo . . . in Culver City: Clayton IJS n.d. Armstrong 1999, 106; Dance 1974, 270.

382 The new show . . . higher still: Scrapbook 83, LAHM, clipping identified as *Los Angeles Evening Herald*, July 29, 1930. Armstrong, Lillian 1963.

383 In August . . . the youngster play out: Scrapbook 83, LAHM, clipping identified as *Los Angeles Evening Herald*, July 29, 1930. Overloading: Travis 1981, 506. James: Havens 1992, 8.

384 The crooners . . . did not exist: Gellhorn 1929, 311. In 1941 (Armstrong IJS 1941), Armstrong was asked to list some of his favorite recordings, and the two from this California period that he mentioned were *Confessin'* and *Memories of You*. For the possibility: good discussion of this phenomenon in Magee 2005, 138 and 183.

384 "I just stopped still": Clayton and Elliot 1987, 44.

384 African Americans got . . . "for blues in addition": "The finest": *California Eagle*, Aug. 29, 1930, p. 11, Scrapbook 83, LAHM. "He not only": Scrapbook 83, LAHM, clipping identified as *Los Angeles Evening Herald*, July 21, 1930; see also *Los Angeles Daily News*, July 26, 1930, p. 23; July 28, 1930, p. 6; Aug. 25, 1930, p. 21 (references courtesy Steven Lasker).

384 Life was good . . . as souvenirs: Mosby: *California Eagle*, Aug. 25, 1930, p. 6. Miniature golf: Scrapbook 83, LAHM. Handkerchiefs: Dance 1974, 270.

385 "paving the way for the Race": *Defender*, Jan. 10, 1931, p. 5.

385 Armstrong began . . . Ellington's reputation: *Afro-American*, Feb. 21, 1931, p. 8. Bogle 2005, 106.

385 Disappointingly . . . survive today: *Variety:* Bogle 2005, 106. *Los Angeles Times,* Dec. 19, 1930, p. A9. Steven Lasker has kindly provided me with an unidentified advertisement that reads: "A real American Jazz Band of lively colored folk appear as an attraction at an elaborate English house party in 'Ex-Flame,' the modernized version of 'East Lynne,' produced under the direction of Victor Halperin for Liberty Productions. Louis Armstrong and his band provide the uproarious music to which Neil Hamilton, Marian Nixon, Norman Kerry, Judith Barrie and others of an extremely well chosen cast make merry. Begins today at the Pastime Theatre." *Chicago Daily Tribune*, Jan. 23, 1931, p. 20. Reviews in *Daily Reporter*, Oct. 23, 1930, p. 4 (courtesy Steven Lasker); *Defender*, Dec. 27, 1930, p. 5.

386 he especially admired: Clayton and Elliot 1987, 44.

386 "They have a new": *Afro-American*, Feb. 22, 1930, p. 8, and Feb. 15, 1930, p. 8.

386 Trombones are built . . . drug addiction: Clayton and Elliot 1987, 45. On glissing in New Orleans, see also Chilton 1987, 49.

387 On the drive downtown . . . broadcast that night: Armstrong WRC 1953; Jones and Chilton 1971, 113. *Variety*, Nov. 19, p. 57, and Nov. 29, 1930, p. 5; photocopies of these and other documents related to the trial courtesy Steven Lasker. Red Mack: Clayton and Elliot 1987, 46.

387 As noted in Chapter 7 . . . "very much": Dance 1977, 146; Peretti 1992, 139. *Muggles,* recorded Dec. 7, 1928, is the enduring testament to this beginning. Foster 2005, 188. Armstrong 1999, 114. Armstrong WRC 1953.

389 When he joined . . . Armstrong toured: Often-repeated claims: for example, Martin Booth, *Cannabis: A History* (New York: Doubleday, 2003), 138. Dodds 1992, 43. The whites: Keller 1989, 86; Meyer CJA 1965, 1971, 1974; Jess Stacy in Feather 1976, 84; Carmichael 1999, 53, and 1999a, 89 and 101; Bud Jacobson in Banks 1980, 229; Shapiro and Hentoff 1955, 141; Hammond 1977, 106.

389 By the time . . . distributed by whites: Assassin: Reproduced in David Musto, ed., *Drugs in America: A Documentary History* (New York: New York University Press, 2002), 433. *Norfolk Journal and Guide*, Oct. 11, 1930, p. 9. *California Eagle*, Nov. 2, 1930.

389 Armstrong's trial . . . "drive away smiling": Information from *California Eagle,*

March 13, 1931, p. 1, and March 27, 1931, p. 1; *Defender*, March 21, 1931, p. 1. Jones and Chilton 1971, 115.

390 Transcripts . . . moved to Chicago: The transcripts were discovered by Steve Lasker and are discussed and quoted in Teachout 2009, 157–58 and 413–14. Jones and Chilton 1971, 114.

390 As the decades passed . . . Russell in 1953: Armstrong 1999, 114. Armstrong WRC 1953.

390 He thought of marijuana . . . he explained: Armstrong WRC 1953; Jones and Chilton 1971, 113; Armstrong 1999, 75. Hammond 106; Armstrong 1999, 112.

391 Marijuana was . . . preferences were clear: Armstrong 1999 112, 114, and 25; see also Armstrong WRC 1953. Quotations from Armstrong, except Carroll Dickerson, from Natty Dominique. Armstrong WRC 1953; Freeman IJS n.d.; Smith 1964, 259; Dominique CJA 1981. Mezzrow 1946, 94. Hinton IJS 1976; Armstrong WRC 1953; Armstrong 1999, 68.

391 The legal status . . . Gertrude Michael sang: Keller 1989, 86; Feather 1976, 84. Budd Johnson IJS n.d.; Dance 1977, 211–12.

391 Armstrong wasn't . . . King Louis: "Anybody from": Jones and Chilton 1971, 113. Hammond 1977, 106. Budd Johnson IJS n.d.; Dance 1977, 211–12. He and Billie: Clarke 1994, 203.

392 Budd Johnson had the idea: Randolph IJS 1977.

392 Cab Calloway's famous *Minnie the Moocher*: Hinton IJS 1976.

393 He was adamant . . . the association: Armstrong WRC 1953; Armstrong 1971, 218. Before and after: See also Budd Johnson IJS n.d.

393 Hammond detested: Hammond 1977, 106.

393 Hoagy Carmichael . . . "write those songs?": Carmichael 1999a, 175–76; see also Hinton IJS 1976; Barker 1986, 137. Mezzrow 1946, 74. Carpenter: Dance 1977, 146.

394 What can definitely . . . he grumbled: Bill Robinson: Fox 1960, 96. Professional: For testimony specific to 1931, see Havens 1992, 7. Baldwin 1961, 199. Gillespie: Dance 1977, 260. Armstrong 1999, 114.

395 An early description . . . in his community: Epstein *Sinful Tunes and Spirituals*, 302. Givan (2004, 188) also relates Armstrong's vocal performances from the early 1930s to the African-American vernacular tradition, with reference to Jeannette Robinson Murphy's discussion, in 1899, of "Negro melodies" in which "around every prominent note [the singer] must place a variety of small notes, called 'trimmings,'" and "must also intersperse his singing with peculiar humming sounds." Duhé: Brothers 2006, 156, 157, and chap. 7.

395 Ragging the tune: On the usage of "ragging the tune" and its relationship to ragtime, see Brothers 2006, chap. 7.

395 "in typical Negro fashion": Scrapbook 83, LAHM.

396 "Riffing": From a 1962 interview conducted by Pat O'Daniels for *Lyke* magazine (p. 54): Q: "Could you explain a little about what 'scat' is?" A: "Oh it's nothing. . . . They used to call it 'riffing,' you know, 'rif.' It's from the South, you know, there's no worry about style or sound or anything."

397 "blubbering, cannibalistic sounds": Carmichael 1999, 140; Leonard 1987, 95. Appel (2002, 154) points out that Armstrong's additions of address to "mama" in songs like *Exactly Like You*, *Star Dust*, and *Georgia on My Mind* identify a black female, rather than white.

397 Verbal and musical departures: It would be difficult to quantify, but there often seems to be a loose correlation between the degree of departure from the melody and degree of departure from the words. When the departures are relatively light (for example, *I Surrender Dear*), he blurs words, and when they are complete, he scats, though the correlation is certainly not consistent.

397 Scat combines with melodic invention: Givan 2004; Edwards 2002; Panassié in Berrett 1999, 70.

397 "Negroes, too, could live": Wright 1998, 271.

398 White crooners . . . "at his own pleasure": See McCracken 1999, 378, on the passive role playing of the crooners. "Tenderly": McCracken 1999, 377. Scrapbook 83, LAHM.

398 "Whatever the Negro does": Hurston 1995, 224–27. Vallée: Armstrong 1936, vii.

400 "white Americans seem to feel": Baldwin 1967, 56.

400 to create the illusion of direct access: Taylor 2002, 438, quoting Herman S. Hetinger from 1933: "The real success of crooning has been not in its musical aspects, but in the personal touch and atmosphere of romantic intimacy which the crooner has been able to build up through his distinctive delivery."

401 "divine details": John Updike, Introduction to Vladimir Nabokov, *Lectures on Literature* (New York, Harcourt, 1980), xxiii.

403 In this case . . . often been noted: Sudhalter 2002, 108–13. Carmichael 1999a 227; Dance 1977, 49.

404 The simple gestures: Schuller 1989, 173–76. My discussion is of the take Schuller identifies as "take 2" (OKeh W 405061-4).

407 "a beautiful romantic song": Armstrong 1936, viii.

407 This music is . . . the same way: Savran 2009, 149ff. Seldes: Douglas 1995, 38.

407 But ragging . . . its main thesis: "into spade's life": Millstein n.d. Appel 2002.

408 "ultra modern": An American precedent is R. D. Darrell, writing in *Phonograph Monthly Review*: "Strawinskites and Bartokians will find more than a trace of their cherished modern feeling right here [in *A Monday Date* by Armstrong and Hines]" (December 1930, quoted in Collier 1988, 37). References from Scrapbook 6, LAHM, some of which can be only partially identified: Dudley Leslie, *Evening News*, July 22, 1932; handwritten "Leeds Oct. 15"; *Daily Herald*, July 25, 1932; *Daily Express*, July 20, 1932.

409 His was advertised . . . in the business: *Defender*, Nov. 14, 1931, p. 5. *Time*, "Black Rascal," June 13, 1932 (accessed online, n.p.).

409 Records had become . . . modern scale: Crooners and radio: McCracken 1999 and 2000. "Are your": Quoted and discussed in Taylor 2002, 425.

410 When Armstrong arrived . . . stunning modernity: *California Eagle*, July 11, 1930, p. 8; *Defender*, July 19, 1930, p. 5. *California Eagle*, March 13, 1931, p. 1: "His bizarre method of playing the trumpet and his individualistic interpretation of popular songs have won him wide following among night club followers and radio fans, who listened in great numbers to his nightly broadcasts." Armstrong 1999, 107. Radio broadcasts were reported from midnight to 1:00 a.m.; "Louie Armstrong to 3:30. KMIC"; and "KMIC Sebastian's Orchestra to 2:30." Photocopies of newspaper clippings courtesy Steven Lasker. Leonard 1962, 94.

410 Did Armstrong have . . . he once quipped: Bud Freeman 1974, 16. On this topic, see also Gushee 1998. Berigan: Dupuis 1993, 22. Maxwell IJS 1979;

Dance 1974, 149. Gonella: Dixon 2000, 99. Pinkett: Barker 1986, 132. Armstrong WRC n.d.

411 With his voice . . . *Riffin' the Scotch*: Selby: Singleton IJS 1975. Boswell: Scrapbook 83, LAHM. Crosby: Armstrong 1936, ix.

411 "made his greatest recordings": Hammond 1977, 107.

412 "Louie Armstrong's boys": *Defender*, May 16, 1931, p. 5, and June 20, 1931, p. 5. *California Eagle*, March 27, 1931, p. 9.

412 On Sunday . . . stayed in California: "That moment": Jones and Chilton 1971, 116. *Louisiana Weekly*, March 28, 1931, p. 1.

412 The South Side . . . as his chef: Drake and Cayton 1970, 83. *California Eagle*, March 27, 1931, p. 10; Armstrong 1999, 107. Dance 1977, 146; Freeman CJA 1980.

413 Meanwhile . . . noted the *Defender*: Jackson 2005, 94; Havens 1992, 6. Jackson FDC 1973. Armstrong 1936, viii. *Defender*, Jan. 31, 1931, p. 5.

413 On April 8 . . . design of his solos: This paragraph is based mainly on a clipping from Scrapbook 83, LAHM, entitled "Bright Spots" by Charlie Dawn; also Freeman 1970, 17; *Defender*, April 11, 1931, p. 5; Jackson 2005, 97. On *Tiger Rag*, see also Dance 1977, 146; Havens 1992. Panico: Jackson 2005, 97.

414 "Come to think of it": Armstrong 1999, 108–9.

414 The Show Boat . . . years later: Havens 1992, 6; Travis 1981, 240. Hinton 1988, 49. Jackson 2005, 97. Quoted in Teachout 2009, 162, with a fuller version of the story.

415 Frankie Foster . . . in one newspaper: King 1967, 67; Armstrong 1999, 110; Jones 1988, 135; Scrapbooks 5 and 83, LAHM; *Chicago Tribune*, April 19, 1931, p. 3, and April 22, 1931, p. 3; *Defender*, April 25. "The more": Scrapbook 5, LAHM.

415 But the pressure . . . train for New Orleans: Shapiro and Hentoff 1955, 130; Jackson 2005, 97; *Defender*, May 16, 1931, p. 5; Jackson HJA 1958. Jackson 2005, 100.

415 Plans were to go . . . was not easy: Travis 1981, 240; Hinton IJS 1976. "You needed": King 1967, 67. "Always": Armstrong 1999, 160.

416 The irony was: Armstrong 1999, 33.

## Chapter 10: Sleepy Time Down South

417 "Music is such a tremendous proposition": Morton quoted in Lomax 1993, 237.

417 The cultural impact . . . "was over": Laird and Rust 2004, 74. Stearns and Stearns 1994, 158. Fitzgerald 1993, 46.

417 "King was no business man": Wright 1987, 161–78 and 336; Stella Oliver HJA 1959; Simeon HJA 1955; Moore HJA 1959; Bernhardt 1986, 96.

418 "I watched all that": Armstrong 1950b, 30.

418 He and his band arrived: Details of the New Orleans visit from the following sources: Armstrong 1936, 96; Scrapbooks 5 and 83, LAHM; *Louisiana Weekly*, June 13, 1931, p. 1; Armstrong 1961; Havens 1992, 8; Jackson 2005, 103; Jackson HJA 1958; Jackson 1994, 76; Jackson FDC 1973 and 1973a; Jones 1988, 135; Randolph IJS 1977; Jones and Chilton 1971, 122ff; Bob Watts HJA 1963.

418 Collins and Armstrong . . . Huey Long: Jackson 2005; photocopies of court depositions held by Louis Armstrong House Museum. Hogan Jazz Archive,

"Louis Armstrong" vertical file; Scrapbook 5, LAHM, clipping from *Morning Tribune*, June 9, 1931, "The Spotlight" by Mel Washburn.

420 On the first night: Jackson 2005, 104.

420 "Virtually all" . . . Armstrong confessed: Scrapbook 83, LAHM. Jones and Chilton 1971, 123.

421 In late June: *Defender*, July 4, 1931, p. 5; Hodes 1977, 81; Scrapbook 5, LAHM.

421 "Randy, pick out a set": Zilner IJS 1977.

422 One night at Suburban Gardens: Jackson FDC 1973a; Jackson 2005, 104.

422 Bud Freeman talked: Freeman IJS n.d.

423 "This is *my* band": Jackson 2005, 104; Jackson HJA 1958.

423 Loyal to his friend . . . an incalculable degree: Jackson 2005, 104. Jackson 1994, 76. Jackson HJA 1958.

424 "That happened the whole three months": Jones 1988, 138.

424 On August 23 . . . off the mound: Scrapbook 5, LAHM. *Louisiana Weekly*, Aug. 29, 1931, p. 9.

424 The summer of 1931 . . . young musicians: Four areas: Brothers 2006, 266–68, with further literature cited there. Jackson FDC 1973a; Jackson 2005, 104; Bethel 1977, 82.

424 Efforts were made . . . had intervened: *Louisiana Weekly*, June 13, 1931, p. 5; Scrapbook 5, LAHM. *Louisiana Weekly*, July 4, 1931, p. 7. Jones and Chilton 1971, 126; Jackson 2005, 107.

425 "I had never seen such a superb act": Jackson FDC 1973a; Zilner IJS 1977.

425 He had been entertaining: Scrapbook 5, LAHM, clipping identified as *Item-Tribune New Orleans*, June 14, 1931.

425 Collins's southern tour . . .teenage novices: Jackson FDC 1973; Havens 1992; Jones 1988, 138; Jackson 2005, 107; Scrapbook 5, LAHM; Randolph IJS 1977; Armstrong 1971, 213. Armstrong 1961, 81. Jackson CJA n.d.

426 First stop was . . . Houston, 3,000: Scrapbook 5, LAHM. Jones 1988, 138. *Afro-American*, Dec. 26, 1931, p. A9.

426 Ralph Ellison heard him play: Ellison 1995, 314. Ellison dated the appearance to 1929, but that seems unlikely. Stratemann (1996, 22) places the band in Tulsa Sept. 9–13, 1931.

426 They gave two . . . "can't read or write": Jackson FDC 1973. Smith 1964, 199.

427 "Steam whistle power": Black 1979, 67.

427 After Tyler . . . "they'd ever talked to": Johnson IJS n.d. Armstrong 1971, 218.

428 Oliver had been touring: Moore 1945, 10; advertisement for Sept. 19, 1931, in Scrapbook 5, LAHM.

428 The scene was tense . . . waiting for them: Havens 1992, 9; Jones and Chilton 1971, 213. Scrapbook 5, LAHM.

429 Back in Memphis . . . "Dig this Mezzeerola!": Jackson 2005, 107. Mezzrow 1946, 235; Jackson FDC 1973.

429 The *Defender* reported: *Defender*, Oct. 17, 1931, p. 5.

429 "There isn't the shadow": Scrapbook 5, LAHM.

430 Lee Collins saw them: Collins 1974, 71.

430 where she lived until the end: Armstrong WRC 1954.

432 "One feels that a Negro's expression": Tichenor 1930, 489.

433 "According to the crowd": Scrapbook 83, LAHM.

433 "Very good for a cabaret": Scrapbook 5, LAHM.

434 His ascent . . . "Yes sir": "not only": Scrapbook 83, LAHM, clipping dated Nov. 5, 1931. Sullivan: Scrapbook 5, LAHM, clipping identified as *New York Evening Graphic*, Oct. 9, 1931. Oberstein: Photocopy of legal transcripts at LAHM.

435 Then came . . . his big band: Eldridge: McCarthy 1978, 23. Wilson: Dance 1977, 183; Dixon CJA 1990.

435 Charlie Carpenter remembered: Dance 1977, 148.

436 Then the band settles . . . this performance: James: Havens 1992, 8; Jones 1988, 138. Barker 1986, 153.

436 Two Chicago sessions . . . during these years: *Courier*, April 9, 1932, p. 9. *All of Me* is partially transcribed and analyzed in Givan 2004.

436 "Louis stopped the show": Jackson 2005, 109.

437 "When he finished": Jackson HJA 1958; Jackson 1994, 76.

437 "The reason, I believe": Jones 1988, 138.

437 making two short films: Stratemann (1996, 23) estimates the movie-making dates to "either mid-to-late January or the second half of February, 1932."

439 Buck Clayton remembered: Jones and Chilton 1971, 132.

439 closely associated with *Shine*: Johnson IJS n.d.; Dance 1977, 211–12; Harker 2011, 107. John Hammond (*Melody Maker*, April 1932) describes musicians attending the Lafayette Theater and bringing lunch, dinner, and marijuana, staying for all four shows to watch Armstrong perform high-note stunts with *Shine.*

439 "what he can do": Appel 2002, 140–43; Scrapbook 5, LAHM.

440 "It is an act that shows": Gushee 2005, 216.

440 "When I was coming along": King 1967, 66.

440 In *Sleepy Time* . . . at Sebastian's: Lyrics of *Carolina Sunshine* in Cox 2011, 17–18. Pasadena: Louisiana State Mint, clipping dated May 7, 1979; also "A Story of 'When It's Sleepytime Down South' (In memory of the late LOUIS 'Satchmo' Armstrong)" by Leon René, both in vertical file "Louis Armstrong," HJA.

441 "Louis Armstrong Scores Again": Scrapbook 5, LAHM.

441 watermelon smile: Armstrong WRC 1953.

441 Thurgood Marshall: Armstrong WRC 1954; vertical file "Louis Armstrong," HJA, clipping from *Melody Maker* dated Oct. 12, 1957; Gillespie 1957, 55.

441 "With one or two" . . . occurred to him: Moton 1929, 204; see also Bushell 1988, 55, on plantation songs. Armstrong 1971, 218.

442 Reconciliation of North and South: For this general theme, see Cox 2011, 16, citing further sources.

442 The fun of . . . say anything more: "appeal": Cox 2011, 34. Ed Sullivan, *Washington Post*, Sept. 13, 1935, "Broadway: Talk of the Town" column, p. 13.

443 the first in the Paramount series: Stratemann 1996, 11.

444 Critics have seen: Murray 1976, 31; Gabbard 2008, 103.

445 When they filmed Cab Calloway: Erin McKinney, paper for liberal studies class, Duke University.

445 ultimate marker of African primitivism: Torgovnick 1990, 147.

446 "Sometimes it is all a huge joke": Moton 1929, 219.

447 "musical octoroon": Hurston 2006, 280.

447 "barbaric indigo dance tunes": *New York Clipper*, Sept. 14, 1923, p. 31; Wright 1987, 28.

448 "Music is such a tremendous proposition": Lomax 1993, 237.

449 "culture that both psychologically and physically": Early 1984, 94.
450 "hotbed of dark, uneducated": Edmond Souchon, typed and unpublished memoir (Louisiana State Museum, New Orleans, n.d.), p. 73.
451 "Musicians don't talk about music much": Higgenbotham IJS n.d.
451 Leonard Bernstein: *Satchmo the Great* (New York: Columbia Records, 2000), CD track 22.
451 You can see . . . melodic design: "He can: Green 1970, 4; McCarthy 1978, 22. Hines: Dance 1977, 23.
452 White musicians . . . culturally and socially: Mezzrow 1946, 151. Freeman: Banks 1980, 227.
454 "the average layman does not understand": Bernhardt 1986, 97. Eli Oberstein, executive at RCA Victor, deposition taken March 1, 1932; photocopy of legal transcripts at LAHM.
454 "an endless succession": Scrapbook 5, LAHM, clipping identified as *Ohio State Journal* (Columbus), Oct. 18, 1931.
458 "that's what they hired me for": Armstrong 1971, 91.
460 His modern versions . . . "and its effect": Sousa: Patrick Warfield, ed., *Six Marches* by John Philip Sousa, vol. 21, *Music of the United States* (Middleton, WI: A-R Editions, 2010), lii. Scrapbook 6, LAHM.

# INDEX

Page numbers in *italics* refer to illustrations.
Page numbers beginning with 489 refer to endnotes.

Adams, Stephen, 63
Adams, Wilhelmina, 125
Africa, 3, 6–7
    diaspora of, 38, 93, 97, 272, 449
    music of, 6, 92–95, 142, 196, 269–70
    sub-Saharan, 6, 95
*Africana*, 351
African-American music:
    church-based, 4, 5, 41–42, 48–49, 52,
        63–64, 67, 84–85, 133, 191, 248, 395
    communal participation in, 4, 97, 134,
        191, 450
    diminished chords in, 5, 66
    fixed and variable format in, 6–7, 9, 11,
        68, 92–97
    group identity strengthened by, 6, 128
    harmonies of, 5, 27
    heterophony in, 4–5, 6, 67, 84–85, 330,
        386
    history of, 141
    integration of movement with, 242, 252
    pitch bending in, 4, 6
    "release and return" of, 231
    rhythmic intensity of, 4
    vernacular principles of, 4, 7, 8, 9, 10, 11,
        48–49, 53, 67, 68, 69, 80, 92, 107, 128,
        131, 135, 162, 166, 189, 196, 199, 200,
        224, 247, 252, 255, 273, 371, 409, 454
    vocal traditions of, 4, 5, 27, 134
    *see also* bebop; blues; Dixieland; jazz;
        ragtime
African American press, ix, 27, 138, 343
    *see also specific publications*
African Americans:
    achievement and "self-improvement" of,
        10, 40, 43, 44–45, 103–5, 114, 453

"Aunt Jemima" image of, 442–43
    dark-skinned, 1, 3, 80, 115, 189
    economic exploitation of, 230
    Great Migration from South to North
        by, 3, 8, 13–15, 32, 39, 40–42, 44–45,
        48, 50, 51, 53, 60, 79–80, 109, 115,
        190, 325, 370, 374, 440, 452–53, 515
    higher education for, 125–27
    light-skinned, 20, 23, 29, 30, 71, 78, 120,
        145, 170, 233
    lynching of, 15, 42
    oral tradition of, 4, 107, 109, 162
    ornamentation and embellishment val-
        ued by, 84, 95, 398
    social discrimination among, 120, 121,
        170
    stereotypes of, 42, 229–33, 342, 416,
        441–43, 448
    "talented tenth" of, 123–31, 137, 139,
        141, 148, 150, 163, 166, 191, 335, 355
    terminology for, 43–44
    "Uncle Tom" image of, 42, 239, 342,
        441
    upwardly mobile working class of, 196
    white culture vs. culture of, 8, 9–10,
        305–7, 397–98
    *see also* racism; slavery
African Baptist Church, 395
African Methodist Episcopal (AME)
    Church, 125–26
*After You've Gone*, 357, 365–66, 447
*Ain't Misbehavin'*, 153, 211, 249, 359, 367,
    396
    LA's vocal on, 346–48, 351–54, 356–58,
        407, 513
Alabama, 42, 84

*Alabamy Bound*, 148–49
Albert, Don, 427
Albert, May Ann (mother), 4, 13, *16*, 48
  death of, 276–77, *277*, 504–5
  LA's relationship with, 71, 78–79, 99,
    114, 276–77, 319, 320, 390
  Lillian Armstrong and, 79, 99, 276
alcoholism, 282, 391
Alexander, Charlie, 413
Alhambra Girls, 220
Alix, Mae, 78, *233*, 237, 242, 244, 246, 252,
  260, 265, 276
*All Alone*, 193
Allen, Henry "Red," 210, 361–62, *362*, 374
*Alligator Crawl*, 261–62, 503, 514
*All of Me*, 436
*Alone at Last*, 146, 148
Al Turk's Princess Orchestra, 144
American Federation of Musicians, 419
*American Mercury*, 338
Amos 'n' Andy, 378, 385
*Amsterdam News*, 130, 346, 354–55, 493,
  503, 512
Anderson, Charles W., 124
Anderson, Connie and Eddie, 379
Anderson, Gene, 303, 334
Anslinger, Harry, 389
anti-Semitism, 448
*Anybody Here Want to Try My Cabbage*,
  158
Appel, Alfred, 408, 439
Arban cornet method, 104
Arkansas, 425, 428
Armstrong, Alpha Smith (third wife), 115,
  318–19, *320*, 321, 334, 377, 430, 510
Armstrong, Beatrice (sister), *16*, 390
Armstrong, Clarence (nephew), 319, 321
Armstrong, Daisy Parker (first wife), 71,
  99, 188, 320, 492
Armstrong, Lillian Hardin (second wife),
  *37*, 68, 69, *96*, 153, 164, 182, 276, *431*
  classical piano training of, 10, 66, 70, 72,
    115, 126, 179
  courtship of LA and, 74–80, 98–101,
    105, 109–10
  death of, 430
  divorce of LA and, 430
  engagement and marriage of LA and,
    83, 99, 113–16, *113*, 325
  fashionable clothes of, 70, 71, 113
  first marriage of, 70, 99
  in Hot Five and Hot Seven, 165, 204,
    206, 260
  LA guided and influenced by, 100–101,
    105, 110, 113–15, 118–21, 141, 165–

  66, 176, 191, 222–23, 291, 292, 312,
    314, 430
  LA's co-compositions with, 99–100, 106,
    110, 111, 319–20, 430, 457
  LA's first meeting with, 70, 71, 114, 321
  marital friction of LA and, 115, 120–21,
    222, 318–21, 377, 430
  physical appearance of, 70, 71
  piano playing of, 10, 66, 68, 70, 72–74,
    86–88, 95, 97, 101, 158, 165, 334, 381,
    395, 430
  refinement of, 114–15, 319
  singing of, 209, 319
Armstrong, Louis, *16*, *37*, 43, *55*, *96*, *147*,
  *320*, *336*, *362*, *399*, *461*
  acting talent of, 441
  adaptability of, 164, 274, 410–11, 418,
    516
  African cultural heritage of, 3, 6–7,
    92–94, 196, 269–70, 275
  ambition of, 182, 202
  arrests and jailing of, 387, 389–90, 412,
    428
  artistic discipline and work ethic of,
    10–11, 141, 312, 394
  birth of, 4, 43, 56
  black criticism of, 439–41
  career advancement of, 69, 98, 141, 430,
    441, 449, 452
  childhood and adolescence of, 4–6, 25,
    56, 63, 65, 66, 102, 103, 118, 126, 189,
    197–98, 200, 212, 222, 237, 276–77,
    301, 312, 317–18, 321, 327, 402, 449
  clothing styles of, 25, 100, 122, 438
  collage decorations of, 84, *85*
  comedy routines and humor of, 118,
    173–74, 190–91, 246, 279, 349, 352–
    53, 407, 435, 438–39
  competitive nature of, 8, 110, 159, 255,
    260, 291–92, 365
  compositional skills of, 9, 64, 69, 83,
    99–103, 106–12, 149, 155, 204, 217,
    251, 263–64, 272, 300–301, 313–14,
    316, 319–20, 457–58
  conducting by, 263, 520
  confident persona of, 2, 3, 149, 163, 197,
    373, 410–11
  copyrights of, 102, 108–9, 111–12, 250,
    269, 430, 457–59
  cornet virtuosity of, 1–2, 4–5, 13, 15, 20,
    45, 174, 175, 198, 207
  dancing of, 237, 318, 356
  dark skin of, 1, 3, 115, 189, 224, 239,
    246, 441
  death of, 3, 430

distinctive solo playing of, 90, 100–101, 110, 139, 142–51, 191–95, 198, 200–201, 206–7, 374–76

early church singing of, 4, 63, 84, 247–48, 276, 312

efforts to succeed in white market by, 9, 11, 141, 274, 327, 360, 363, 365–66, 408, 411, 441–43, 460

European trip of, 431–32

fifty-year career of, 2–3

fill-ins and obbligatos of, 90, 97, 147–49, 154, 158, 160, 162–63, 257, 266, 270, 274

first cornet of, 4, 5, 421

first interracial recording session of, 332

first musical job of, 56, 426

first recorded solo of, 456

fixed and variable format central to music of, 6–7, 9, 11, 148, 162, 163, 172, 197, 211, 250, 270–75, 394, 453

formal education of, 3

formidable musical intellect of, 10–11, 253–54, 301, 451, 461

full rounded tone of, 142, 269

hair style of, 25, 70

harmonic command of, 66–67, 198, 253–55, 269–73, 406

high-note playing of, 9, 191–92, 198, 211, 246, 253–54, 259, 267–68, 299, 337, 357, 369, 371, 382–83, 432, 435, 437

illnesses of, 309, 498

improvisation of, 197, 198, 238, 242, 250, 283–84, 350

income of, 1, 24, 165, 174, 183, 191, 223, 291, 309, 355, 379, 409, 429

innovation and talent of, 1, 5, 6–9, 11, 56, 74, 83–84, 106, 149, 171, 198–99, 203, 452

instructional books published by, 266–67

as "jazz concert king," 203–4, 248, 290

as largest selling artist on records, 434

late-life persona of, 189, 306

letter-writing of, 78–79, 106–7

loyalty and generosity of, 113, 120, 423–24

marijuana use of, 307–8, 377–78, 387–94, 428–29, 516

as master of modernism, 8–11, 106, 148, 164, 174, 196, 242, 268, 350, 354, 376, 394–96, 407–8, 453–55, 460

mature musical style of, 6–9, 40, 92, 94, 98, 112, 118–19, 164, 166, 189, 191, 198, 200, 324

melodic creativity of, 7, 9, 111–12, 148–49, 157, 196, 210–11, 242, 250, 257, 269–72, 275, 330, 372, 374–75, 401, 449, 455–56, 459–62

memoirs of, 321, 388, 517

multidimensional skills of, 150, 166–68, 170–72, 197–99, 237–38, 272, 275, 394, 459

musical dialogue of, 312–13, 400–401, 406, 448

musical quotations of, 349–50, 369, 432

musical training of, 4–10, 24, 45, 56, 65–67, 69, 80, 81, 83, 97–98, 103–5, 109, 110, 118–19, 141, 149, 188, 283, 292–93, 418

musicians influenced by, 152, 163, 194, 200, 231–32, 239–40, 251, 262, 271, 374, 380, 403–4, 410–11, 435

nicknames of, 24, 25, 490

performance video of, 431–32, 444

playful verbal "mugging" of, 151, 204–5, 238

popularity of, 174, 192, 194, 238, 244, 249, 419

prose writings of, 84, 170

quick fingers of, 9, 102, 103

radio broadcasts of, 1, 9, 150–51

ragging the tune by, 393, 395–96, 400–401, 403, 406–8, 412, 448, 454, 460, 493

reading of music by, 122, 180–81, 198, 291, 418

recordings of, 1, 7–9, 28, 50, 62, 81, 83, 84, 97, 194, 369–76, 375, 381–82, 409–10, 434–36

scat vocals of, 209, 211–18, 220, 242, 298, 349, 351–52, 367–68, 375, 382, 396–98, 439

sexual life of, 317–19, 430

smiling of, 239, 303, 439

social tensions of, 120, 121–23, 390

sports activity of, 308–9, 424

stature and physique of, 3, 25, 153, 237, 308–9

strong initial attacks of, 142, 197, 242

study of the "classics" by, 10, 141, 198

stylized facial expressions of, 169

success and fame of, 3, 114–15, 118, 122–23, 303–4, 309, 365–66

touring of, 1–2, 40, 84, 116–18, 288, 366, 415, 425–31, 433–37

trumpet virtuosity of, 2, 7, 9, 180–81, 190–92, 217, 221, 263, 323, 331, 340–41, 349, 352, 364–65, 384, 410, 434, 435–36

Armstrong, Louis (*continued*)
  unique singing style of, 2, 7, 8, 9, 118,
    151, 166, 169, 174, 182, 189–90, 197–
    98, 211–21, 236, 237, 263, 278–79,
    296–99, 326, 329–32, 346–48, 351–54,
    356–61, 365–68, 383–84, 396–403,
    434, 438–39
  use of mutes by, 101, 402
  vernacular values of, 3–4, 7–9, 10, 11,
    69, 141, 145, 166, 189, 196, 200, 224,
    354, 454–55
  whistling of, 109–10
  white admirers and friends of, 38, 174,
    304–7, 326–28, 365–66, 380, 451
  youthful shyness of, 71, 78, 119
Armstrong, Willie (father), *277*
Ash, Paul, 218, 286, 326–27
Association of Trade and Commerce, 124
Atkins, Boyd, 211, 213, 214, 218–19, 308
Atkins, Eddie, 180
Atlanta University, 125, 126–27, 129
Atlantic City, N.J., 53, 214
*Auld Lang Syne*, 421
*Aunt Harriet Becha Stowe*, 363
Austin, Gene, 298, 400
Austin, Mary, 230–31
Austin, Obie, 386
Austin, Tex., 426, 427

*Baby Face*, 182
Bach, Johann Sebastian, 135, 267, 366
*Backwater Blues*, 52
Bagnall, Robert W., 124–25
Bailey, Buster, 22, 35, 103, 117, *117*, 141–
    42, 145, 154, 163, 223, 228, 297
  growl clarinet technique of, 142
Bailey, Joe, *399*
Bailey, Mildred, 238
Baker, Houston, 145
Baker, Josephine, 342, 344
Baldwin, James, 317, 394, 398, 400
Baltimore, Md., 434
  Royal Theater in, 435
*Baltimore Afro-American*, 125, 138, 385,
    386, 426, 494, 498, 501, 508
bands, 5, 272
  contests between, 5, 8
  dance, 5, 26, 31–33, 58–60, 63, 88, 90,
    115, 130, 135, 138–39, 272
  marching, 4–5, 21, 32, 85, 248, 395, 438
  minstrel, 23
  pick-up, 153–54, 163
  swing, 165
  white, 10, 17, 23–24, 57, 58, 63, 76, 129–
    31, 138–41, 143–44, 151, 286, 494–95

banjos, 18, 61–62, 64, 88, 123
Baraka, Amiri, 48, 142, 293, 365
Barbarin, Paul, 35, 40, 207, 214, 217, 235,
    243, 256, 332, *362*, 500, 514
Barker, Danny, 2, 52, 123, 128, 246, 307,
    329, 336, 338, 436, 511
Barnes, Paul, 158
*Barney Google* comic strip, 214
Barrymore, John, 185
Basie, Count, 31, 317
*Basin Street Blues*, 325, 359
Beatles, 10, 11
*Beau Koo Jack*, 323–24, 364, 415, 511
bebop, 89, 97
  improvisation in, 251
Bechet, Sidney, 17, 57, 91, 153, 164, 196,
    344, 417–18, 517
  confidence and virtuosity of, 83, 159
  European move of, 157
  first successful recording of, 83
  influence of, 64
  jazz breaks and obbligato of, 83, 159
  LA and, 83, 155–59
  New Orleans sound of, 59
  rivalry of LA and, 83, 156
  on soprano sax, 98
Beethoven, Ludwig van, 10–11, 136, 178,
    366
Beiderbecke, Bix, 61, 143, 218, 238, 280–
    82, 313, 364, 391, 403, 495, 505
  LA's influence on, 267–68, 281
  premature death of, 282
Bell, Jimmy, 279–80
Belt, Madeline, 346
Benjamin, Walter, 354
Bennett, Eloise, 278
Ben Selvin's Famous Moulin Rouge
    Orchestra, 130
Benson Orchestra, 131, 138, 144
Berigan, Bunny, 154–55, 410
Berlin, Irving, 78, 134, 135, 193
Berlioz, Hector, 393
Bernhardt, Clyde, 60, 65, 146, 326, 372, 454
Bernstein, Leonard, 451
Berquist, Whitey, 239
Berton, Vic, 387
Bertrand, Jimmy, 180, 186, 192
*Bessie Couldn't Help It*, 361
Best, Edward, 124
Betty Boop cartoons, 437, 444–46, 447, 454
*Between the Devil and the Deep Blue Sea*,
    436
Bigard, Barney, 22, 83, 209
*Big Butter and Egg Man*, 174, 190, 221,
    237, 242–43, 244–45, 247–50, 259,

266, 278, 281, 286, 348, 352, 371, *375*, 438, 508–9
  LA's famous trumpet solo in, 243, 245, 249–55, *252*, 260, 263, 374, 459, 460
*Billboard*, 342
Bill Brownie's Boys, 386
Billups, Pope, 124
Binga, Jesse, 75
*Birth of a Nation* (film), 443
Bix Beiderbecke and His Rhythm Jugglers, 61
Black, Charles L., Jr., 427
Black, Clarence, 290, 309
*Black and Tan* (film), 378
*Black and Tan Fantasy*, 300, 489, 514
*Blackbirds of 1928*, 329, 345, 347, 350, 354
Black Bottom, 234–37, 241, 501
*Black Boy* (Wright), 305
*Blacker the Berry, The* (Thurman), 352
Black Swan Records, 53, 127–29
  Henderson as musical director at, 128
Blake, Eubie, 73, 155, 326, 338, 341–44, 347, 351, 398, 497, 517
Bleyer, Archie, 304
*Blue Again*, 413
Blue Five, 83
blue notes, b, 149, 154, 156, 197, 258, 281, 372, 448
blues, 15, 47–56, 76, 370
  AAB standard form of, 51, 58, 64, 90, 155
  adaptations of, 50–54
  additive rhythm in, 94, 134
  black opposition to, 50
  call and response in, 90
  as "colored folks' opera," 51–52
  commercial explosion of, 127
  "crooning," 298
  delta tradition in, 49
  diminished chords in, 66
  dragging behind the beat in, 65, 94
  flexible concepts of, 57–59
  gutbucket, 52, 57
  harmonies of, 5, 66–68, 134, 136, 156
  heightened emotion in, 48–49, 52–53
  heterophony in, 67
  "hot," 65
  improvisation in, 5, 11, 49, 59, 72, 83, 131
  intense vibratos in, 68
  irregularly placed accents in, 94
  LA's playing of, 4, 5, 11, 47, 50, 56, 62–67, 115, 282–83, 292–95, 393, 438, 455
    lowdown, dirty, 56
  New Orleans style, 47–48, 54–60, 65–69, 72, 133
  obbligato lines in, 5, 49, 90
  origins of, 48–50
  ornamentation in, 49, 52, 65, 84
  pastiche approach to, 64
  performer-centered, 51–54, 59–60, 69, 81–84, 91
  phrasing and fleeting rhythmic patterns of, 49, 56, 57, 118–19, 188–89
  pitch bending and "blue notes" of, 49, 50–52, 56, 57, 64, 65, 68, 112, 134–35, 149
  playing by ear in, 36, 49, 59, 68, 73, 86–87, 91, 92, 133
  popularity of, 51, 57
  publication of, 50–52, 59
  recordings of, 50, 53–54, 60–67, 129
  slow tempos of, 31, 51–52, 57, 58, 154, 156, 162, 163, 256, 295, 308, 455
  strong initial attacks in, 68, 118–19
  "talking," 213
  unequivocal black identity of, 49
  vocal style of, 5, 49, 51–52, 59–60, 65–66, 129
  on wind instruments, 54–56, 62–67, 156
"blues people," 48
blues singers, 52–54, 59–60, 129
  LA's playing for, 153–55, 158–63, 165
  *see also specific singers*
blue tritone dissonance, 144
*Blue Turning Grey Over*, 365, 367
*Blue Yodel Number 9 (Standin' on the Corner)*, 381
B-Minor Mass (Bach), 135
Bocage, Peter, 212
"Bodidly," 29
*Body and Soul*, 386, 398, 406–7
*Bogalousa Strut*, 283
Bolden, Charles "Buddy," 293
  blues playing of, 56, 69, 90–91, 110
  popularity and fame of, 56
Bolton, James "Red Happy," 212, 237, 491–92
Bordoni, Irene, 367
*Borneo*, 313
Boston, Mass., 489
  Metropolitan Theater (Wang Theater) in, 436–37
  Paul Revere Hall in, 437
Boswell Sisters, 220, 411
Bottoms, Bill, 77, 167–68
Bourdieu, Pierre, 47–48

Bradford, Perry, 53, 54, 155, 163, 165, 215, 258, 344, 501
Brahms, Johannes, 267
Branen, Jeff, 278
Braud, Wellman, 103
Briggs, Peter, 260, 308
Brooks, Harvey, *399*
Brooks, Shelton, 155
Broomfield, Leroy, 182, 379
Brown, Herbert, 247, 267
Brown, Lawrence, 380, 382
Brown, Ralph, 59, 185, 187
Brown, Scoville, 305, 309
Brown and McGraw, 203–4, 235, 246–47, 248–49, 251–52, 264, 276, 290, 502, 504
Brown Brothers, 235
*Brown v. Board of Education*, 427
Brymn, Tim, 344
Bryson, Prentice A., 276
Buck and Bubbles, 244, 247, 264–65, 312, 355
*Buffalo Express*, 410
*Bugle Blues*, 98, 101, 102
*Bugle Call Rag*, 101, 102, 105
bugle calls, 101–2
Bunny Hug, 18
Burke, Ceele, 384
burlesque, 167
Bushell, Garvin, 53, 58–59, 65, 88, 97, 152, 177, 509, 512, 520
    on Henderson, 139–41
Butterbeans and Susie, 238
*Butterfly Fantasy*, 279–80
*Bye and Bye*, 147
*By the Waters of Minnetonka* (Lieurance), 122

cabarets, 28, 53, 113, 130, 165–74, 182, 189, 203, 231
    "black and tan," 22–23, 34, 40, 228, *229*, 232–33, 238–44, 338–43, *340*, 489
    integration in, 226–29, 232–33, 238
    liberation and hedonism in, 232–38, 240–41
    white patrons of, 33–39, 63, 82, 143, 226, 238–39
cakewalk, 283
*Cake Walking Babies from Home*, 158–59
California, 21, 22–24, 30, 73, 86, 325, 360, 376–87, 410, 412, 437
*California Eagle*, 389, 410
California Ramblers, 138, 144
call and response, 90, 143–44
Calloway, Blanche, 165, 218, 278, 513

Calloway, Cab, 165, 276, 278, 308, 339, 346, 392, 403, 411, 422, 447
    dancing and scatting of, 445
    on LA, 218
Campbell, Dick, 379
Campbell, E. Simms, 391
Campbell, Floyd, 291
*Camp Meeting Blues*, 107
*Canal Street Blues*, 61, 63–64, 90
    LA and Oliver as co-composers of, 64, 106, 107, 457
*Can't Help Lovin' Dat Man*, 239–40
Capone, Al, 226, 415
    LA and, 227
Carey, Mutt, 155
Caribbean Sea, 28, 92
Carmichael, Dorothy, 268
Carmichael, Hoagy, 35, 233, 238, 393, 443
    compositions of, 268, 360, 362–63, 367, 396, 403–7, *405*, 515
    on LA, 102, 281, 301, 331–32, 397, 403–4
*Carolina Stomp*, 150
*Carolina Sunshine*, 440
Carpenter, Charlie, 393, 412, 435–36, 509
Carpenter, John Alden, 134
Carr, Mancy "Peek," 292
Carroll Dickerson's Orchestra, 101, 205, 216, 244, 255, 290, *294*, 308–9, 334–37, 340, 347, 491, 510–11
Carroll Dickerson's Syncopators, 259
Carter, Bennie, 333
Carter, William J., 124
Carter Temple CME Church, 276
Casa Loma Orchestra, 436–37
Castle, Irene and Vernon, 32, 235
Cato, Minta, 434
*Cavalleria Rustican* (Mascagni), 180, 186–87, 188, 438, 497, 498
Cayton, Horace, 174, 183
Celestin, Oscar "Papa," 91
Chambers, Elmer, *147*
*Changeable Daddy of Mine*, 158
Charleston (dance), 135, 163, 169, 182, 184, 218, 233–37, 240, 244, 258, 338, 343–44
*Charleston Rag*, 214
Charlie Davis and His Orchestra, 143
Charlie Elgar's Creole Band, 23
Charlie Johnson's Paradise Ten, 386
Chauvin, Louis, 219
Cheatham, Adolphus "Doc," 7, 75, 173, 192, 227, 331
    on LA, 248, 251, 309
*Check and Double Check* (film), 378, 385

Chicago, Ill., 2, 7–8, 13–39, 436
  African-American community of, 16–17,
    43, 46–48, 74–75, 174, 183
  after-hours clubs in, 176
  Apex Club in, *14*, 194, 225
  Arlington Restaurant in, 79
  Big Fat Mammy from Alabama in, 283
  Black Hawk Grill in, 277
  black-owned businesses in, 75, 77–78,
    165–71
  Café de Paris in, 276
  Chicago Theater in, 280
  City Hall in, 113
  classical music teachers in, 103–5
  Club Baghdad in, 286
  Coliseum in, 215–16, 278–79
  Columbia Hotel in, 75
  Congress Hotel in, 278
  crime and prostitution in, 226–27, 238
  Deluxe Café in, 194
  Drake Hotel in, 36, 99, *179*
  Dreamland Café in, *14*, 21, 70, *71*, 73,
    77–78, 102–3, 120, 165–71, 175–76,
    183, 189, 203–6, 208–9, 453, 459
  Edelweiss Gardens in, 75–76
  Edgewater Beach resorts in, 36
  Ed Victor's Barber Shop in, *14*, 46
  Eighth Regiment Armory in, *14*, 203–4,
    217
  Elite Café #1 in, *14*, 17
  Erlanger Theater in, 76–77
  Fiume Café in, *14*, 76
  garment industry in, 43
  "Gold Coast" of, 99
  Granada Inn in, 326–28
  Grand Theater in, *14*, 17, 52
  Hotel Sherman in, 327
  Ideal Tea Room in, 113
  Jackson's Music Shop in, 17
  job opportunities in, 15, 40, 43, 45
  Jones Music Store in, *14*, 72
  Kelley's Stables in, 194
  Kimball Hall in, 104, 105, 141, 188, 198,
    283, 292–93, 493
  LA's 1922 arrival in, 3, 7, 15–17, 39, 49
  LA's 1925 return to, 113, 163–65, 430,
    458
  Liberty Congregational Church in, 291
  Lincoln Cemetery in, 276
  Loop in, 104, 277, 280, 413
  meatpacking industry in, 15, 43
  Mecca Flats in, *14*, 46, *47*
  Metropolitan Theater in, *14*, 261, 279–
    80, 286, 288
  Monogram Theater in, *14*, 52, 177
  movie theaters in, 175–97, *175*, *195*
  Nest Club in, 225
  New Orleans musicians in, 15, 17–28,
    *19*, 43, 46, 54, 58–59, 62–63, 103, 123,
    194
  night life in, 16–17, 74–79
  1919 race riots in, 43
  1925 battle of the bands in, 8
  Palace Theater (Cadillac Palace) in,
    430–32
  Pekin Theater and Cabaret in, *14*, 17,
    76, 103
  Phoenix Theater in, 52
  Plantation Café in, *14*, 194, 222–28, 232,
    235–38, 241, 255–56, 259, 334
  police in, 236–37
  racial conditions in, 33–39, 42–45
  racial integration in, 33–39, 76, 226–29,
    232–33, 326–28, 404–6
  red-light district in, 17
  Regal Theater in, *14*, 328–29, 366, 412
  Roosevelt Theater in, 327
  St. Thomas Episcopal Church in, 98–99,
    105
  Savoy Ballroom in, 283, 285, 287–97,
    *289*, *294*, 303–4, 307–10, *310*, 324,
    327–30, 366, 387, 433, 438, 453
  Schiller's Café in, 17, 98
  Show Boat in, 413–15, 433
  South Side of, 11, *14*, 18, 38, 43–44, 59,
    68, 70, 77, 102–3, 130, 131, 141, 168,
    178, 190, 194, 224, 412
  South State Street in, 16–17, 21, 46, 52,
    72, 74, 76, 77
  steel industry in, 15, 43
  Sunset Café (Grand Terrace) in, *14*,
    34, 101–2, 209, 216–17, 220–34, *224*,
    236–44, *261*, 274–75, *286*, 317, *372*,
    434, 438, 453, 459
  Trianon Ballroom in, 202
  12th Street Railroad Station in, 15
  urban sophistication of, 8
  Vendome Theater in, 8, *14*, 17, 52,
    166, 175–97, *175*, 199–204, 206–7,
    242, 246, 261–63, 268, 273–75, 288,
    318–19, 370–71, 405–6, 434, 438, 453,
    458
  Vincennes Hotel in, 276, 288
  Warwick Hall in, *14*, 259, 286–87, *287*
  *see also* Lincoln Gardens
*Chicago Breakdown*, 260–62, 279, 312
Chicago College of Music, 334
*Chicago Daily News*, 172, 501
*Chicago Daily Tribune*, 430, 490, 501, 507,
  511, 518

*Chicago Defender*, 15, 37, 40, 42, 44, *44*,
    50, 54, 75, 76, 98, 102, 167, 173,
    235–36, 307, 439
    on LA, 100, 166, 326, 356, 387, 413, 429
    music reviews in, 17, 32, 51, 53, 100,
        104, 119, 130–31, 138, 141, 166, 178,
        344, 346
Chicago Symphony, 103
Chicago *Whip*, 50
Chicago White Sox, 20, 179
*Chimes Blues*, 7, 61, 63, 86, 90, 107, 148,
    272, 502
    LA's solo on, 64, 66, 69, 83, 112, 143,
        172, 194, 250, 253, *253*, 255, 456
*Chinatown, My Chinatown*, 435, 445–46,
    511
Cincinnati, Ohio, 430, 433
    Albee Theater in, 429–30
    Palace Theater in, 441, 444
Cincinnati *Enquirer*, 430
civil rights movement, 3, 28, 427
Civil War, U.S., 27, 450
Clarence Jones's Orchestra, 279–80,
    288–89
Clarence Williams's Blue Five, 83, 155–59,
    165
*Clarinet Marmalade*, 102, 105, 106, 184
Clayton, Buck, 382, 384, 386–87, 439, 516
Cleveland, Ohio, 433, 454
Cohan, George M., 155
*Cold in Hand Blues*, 160–61, 332
Cold War, 3
Cole and Man, 182
Coleman, Bill, 151
Coleridge, Samuel Taylor, 393
Coles, Charles "Honi," 171, 350, 501–2
Collins, Chief, 237
Collins, Johnny, 413–15, *414*, 418–19,
    422–23, 425–26, 428–29, 434, 446
Collins, Lee, 105, 119, 430
Collins, Mary, 428
Colored Waif's Home for Boys, 418, 421,
    *421*
    LA sent to, 102, 276–77, 498
Coltrane, John, 292
Columbia Records, 60, 130, 159, 319–20
Columbia University, 126, 427
Columbus, Ohio, 415, 433, 454
*Come Back Sweet Papa*, 207, 216
Compton, Glover, 59, 171, 286
Condon, Eddie, 33–34, 239, 332, 391, 505
    on King Oliver band, 34, 88, 89, 95, 97,
        149, 206
    on rhythm, 94

Conover, Willis, 200
contests, 5, 8, 98
    Charleston, 233, 237, 240
    cutting, 83, 102, 105, 110, 112, 159, 173,
        191, 203
    singing, 151
    talent, 118, 158
    whistling, 110
Cook, Albert, 103
Cook, Louise, 340, 345–46
Cook, Sherman, 424, 426
Cooke, Sam, 8
Cooper, Ralph, 264
Copenhagen, 44, 431–32
*Copenhagen*, 143–46, 297, 351, 454, 495
    LA's hot solos in, 144–46
*Copyin' Louis*, 365
Corea, Chick, 275
*Cornet Chop Suey*, 100–101, 102–4, 105–6,
    193, 203, 242, 264, 430, 458–59
    buglelike introduction of, 111, 112
    copyrighting of, 102, 108, 109, 111, 112,
        250, 269
    as a creative breakthrough, 109, 112
    LA's composing of, 108–12, 193, 263
    LA's solo in, 102, 112, 158, 266
    melodic variety in, 111–12
    musical form of, 110–11
    notated breaks in, 111, 250–51
    recording of, 108–9, 110–11, 202–10,
        372
Coward, Noel, 237, 258, 371
Cox, Baby, 346
Craven, Luther "Sonny," *399*
Crawford, Joan, 236, 298
Crawley, Wilton, 278
*Craze-O-Logy*, 239
*Crazy Blues*, 53, 154, 215
Creamer, Henry, 278
Creath, Charlie, 429
*Creation, The* (Haydn), 98
Creole Band, 23, 30, 56, 438, 440
    blackface minstrel shows of, 26–28, 38,
        39
Creoles, 22–24, 104, 197, 275, 379
    distinction between Negroes and,
        22–23, 46
    French patois of, 23, 24, 46
*Crisis*, 125, 128
"crooning," 297–98, 398, 403, 405, 453
Crosby, Bing, 151, 239, 400, 403, 404,
    411
    LA and, 363, 380
Cruze, James, 380

Cullen, Countee, 125
Curl, Langston, 321–22
Cuthbert, Ga., 125–26

Dabney, Ardelle Mitchell, 124
Dabney, Ford, 124
*Daily Herald* (London), 408–9
Dallas, Tex., 426–27
Damrosch, Frank, 500
dancing, 93, 151
  buck and wing, 264
  chorus line, 216, 233–34, 243, 337,
    339–40, 342–43, 345
  contortionist, 171, 342
  quick tempos for, 172–73
  shimmy, 76, 78
  tap, 247–48, 265, 346
  team, 170, 171, 182, 203–4, 234, 235,
    238, 246–47, 251–52, 264–65
  trumpet accompaniment to, 248–49,
    *249*, 251–52
  vernacular, 88, 203
  *see also specific dance styles*
Dancing Masters of America, 236
Davis, Charlie, 143–44, 342
Davis, Miles, 105, 365, 401
  on LA, 271
Davis, Peter, 5, 418
Davison, Wild Bill, 35, 210, 239, 304–5
De Droit, Johnny, 419
Deep South, 3, 8, 80, 103, 134, 204, 224,
    247, 263, 270, 429
  bollweevil epidemic in, 13–14
  cotton pickers in, *41*, 51
  floods in, 13
  lynchings in, 15
  slave plantations of, 4, 23, 26, 27–28, 30,
    48, 50, 53, 56, 57, 59, 66, 67, 95, 131,
    *272*, *283*, 440, 442, 450
DeFaut, Voltaire, 67–68
De Paris, Sidney, 386
De Pass, Lillian, 110
Depression, Great, 2, 3, 366, 383, 417–18,
    442
Desmond, Mrs. Binga, 124
Detroit, Mich., 419, 421–22
Dickerson, Carroll, 222–23, 243, 244, 255,
    259, 287, 289–90, 300, 333, 335, 348,
    355, 357, 391
Dickerson, Dudley, 379
Diggs, May "Miss Snakehips," 384
Dill, Augustus Granville, 125
*Dinah*, 368–69, 371, 411, 413, 431, 432
*Dinah* (Bechet and Brymn), 344

*Dipper Mouth Blues*, 58, 61, 101, 109, 143,
    301
  LA and Oliver as co-composers of, 69,
    106, 457, 490
  Oliver's solo on, 64–65, 66, 69, 252, 458,
    490, 495
  recordings of, 64–65, 90, 95, 149
d'Ippolito, Vic, 151
*Dixiana* (film), 385
Dixieland, 57, 256
Dixie Stompers, 193
Dixon, Mort, 280
*Doctor Jazz*, 256
Dodds, Johnny, 20, *37*, 59, 69, 92, 116–17,
    144, 227, 489
  breaks and obbligatos of, 90
  funky blues playing of, 20, 64
  in Hot Five and Hot Seven, 165, 206–7,
    260
  on Oliver, 86–87
  personality of, 20
Dodds, Warren "Baby," 20–23, 31,
    34–36, *37*, 59, 79, 95, 110, 116–17,
    141, 389
  on collective improvisation, 85
  drinking of, 21, 62
  in Hot Seven, 260
  on LA, 79, 108
  percussion instruments of, 62, 88–89
  "shimmy beat" and counterrhythms of,
    29, 64
  solo breaks of, 82
Dodge, Roger Pryor, *249*
Dominique, Natty, 232, 243, 256, 356, 430,
    504
*Don't Forget to Mess Around When You're
    Doing the Charleston*, 214, 235, 332,
    499
*Don't Jive Me*, 359
Dorsey, Jimmy, 239, 280
Dorsey, Thomas A., 51–53, 91, 321, 492
Dorsey, Tommy, 239, 280, 422
Douge, Robert F., 124
Douglas, Aaron, 335
*Down by the Levee*, 302
*Down Hearted Blues*, 54
*Down Home Blues*, 129
Drake, St. Clair, 174, 183
Dreamland Syncopators, 167
drum ensembles, 92–94
  in New Orleans, 93
  in West Africa, 93–94, 95
Du Bois, W. E. B., 125–28, 235–36, 377,
    450, 454

Duhé, Lawrence, 21–22, 223
  Lillian Armstrong and, 72–73, 395
Dunn, Johnny, 59, 258–59, 347
DuPont, Floyd, 218
Durante, Jimmy, 338–39
Dutrey, Honoré, 21, 23, 37, 89–90, 148,
  207, 223, 260
  band of, 116–17
Dvořák, Antonin, 291
dynamic markings, 122

Eagle Band, 20
Earl Hines and His Orchestra, 324, 511
Early, Gerald, 449
East St. Louis Toodle-Oo, 300
Eccentric, 29–30, 36, 63, 83, 171
eccentric acts, 170–72
Eckstine, Billy, 317
Edie, Irene, 278
1812 Overture (Tchaikovsky), 280
Eldridge, Roy, 262, 410, 435
Ellington, Duke, 31, 59, 137, 139, 145,
  275, 291, 292, 336–37, 354, 378, 385,
  422, 447, 489
  LA and, 384
  sophisticated style of, 200, 300
Ellington Band, 367, 376, 378, 409, 512
Ellington Orchestra, 346, 380, 385
Ellis, Seger, 358, 400
Ellison, Ralph, 263–64, 426, 462
Emerson Race Records, 138
England, 326
  LA's first trip to, 408–9, 415
Entertainer, The, 111, 266
Erenberg, Lewis, 232, 240–41
Esquire, 268
Etude, 135, 500
Europe, James Reese, 270, 335
Evans, Paul "Stump," 180, 192
Evening News (Manchester), 165, 166
Everybody Loves My Baby, 151, 157–58
Everybody Step, 134, 135
Every Day's a Holiday (film), 448
Exactly Like You, 365, 368, 379, 515
Excelsior Brass Band, 20, 21
Ex-Flame (film), 376, 443
Experiment in Modern Music, 202

Fanning, Mae, 237, 501
Feather, Leonard, 302
Federal Bureau of Narcotics, 389
Federal Council of Churches of Christ in
  America, 124
Ferguson, Jimmy, 278
Ferrer, José, 361

Fetchit, Stepin, 378, 385
Fields, Dorothy, 345, 368
Fifty Hot Choruses for Cornet (Armstrong),
  266–67
Filo, 45–46, 47
Fiorito, Ted, 146
Fire in the Flint, The (White), 125
Fireworks, 364
Fisher, Rudolf, 338, 341
Fisk University, 70, 71, 72, 80, 120
Fitzgerald, F. Scott, 48, 233, 417
flappers, 9
flatted thirds, 144
Fleischer brothers, 444–46
Fletcher Henderson and His Famous Club
  Alabam Orchestra, 130, 138
Fletcher Henderson Orchestra, 120–23,
  137, 205, 278–79, 335, 437, 489
  gradual turn to jazz in, 132, 141–51,
  224
  LA as third cornet in, 121, 124, 132,
  138–41, 496
  LA's solos in, 121, 139, 142–51, 157,
  170–71, 456
  musicians of, 141–42
  recordings of, 121, 138–39, 143–44,
  147–51, 193
  rehearsals of, 121–22, 142, 335
  sections and written arrangements of,
  121, 122, 131, 132, 383
  touring of, 141, 151
Floyd Campbell's Orchestra, 291
For No Reason at All in C, 364
Foster, Frankie, 415
Foster, Pops, 56, 58, 60, 157, 248, 284,
  311, 361–63, 362
  bass playing of, 56, 332, 362
  on LA, b, 388
Foster, Stephen, 26, 514
Four Covens, 385
Four or Five Times, 322
Four Sons (film), 298
Fox, Ed, 237
fox trot, 78, 122, 135, 138, 213, 283, 340,
  383, 401
Frankie Trumbauer and His Orchestra,
  281
Frazier, Josiah, 209–10
"freak music," 5–6, 21, 36, 69, 109, 156,
  278
  of King Oliver, 21, 22, 29–30, 58–59,
  64–65, 101, 171, 199, 213, 260, 458
  use of mutes in, 22, 29, 65, 171, 199
Freeman, Bud, 31, 33, 35, 36, 38, 152, 331,
  422, 452

on LA, 49, 239–40, 258, 267, 283, 410, 413, 505–6
Freud, Sigmund, 241, 393
Friars Society Orchestra, 230–31
*Froggie Moore*, 492, 495
*From Monday On*, 280, 297, 507
Frost, Arthur Burdette, 442

Gabbard, Krin, 192
Galveston, Tex., 426, 428
Garland, Ed "Montudie," 88, 103, 311, 489
Garvey, Marcus, 236
Gauguin, Paul, 233
Gellhorn, Martha, 384
Gennett Records, 36, 60–65, *61*, 68, 74, 81, 100, 101, 107, 116
Georgia, 40, 60
*Georgia Grind*, 208, 214
Germany, Nazi, 448
Gershwin, George, 9–10, 58, 119, 135, 291, 300, 336, 349–50, 457
Gershwin, Ira, 200
Giddins, Gary, 350
Gillespie, Dizzy, 28, 137, 348–49, 394, 441
Glaser, Joe, 286
    LA's finances managed by, 100, 237, 388, 501
Glason, Billy, 238
*Goddess of Rain*, 345–46
*Going Home*, 291
*Go Long Mule*, 143, 147, 148, 210
Gonella, Nat, 410
Gonsoulin, Bertha, 20, 73
Goodman, Benny, 33–34, 59, 103, 238, 239, 422
Goodman, Freddy, 239
*Good Time Flat Blues*, 158, 160
Goofus Five, 218
Graham, Billy, 52
Graham, George, 380
Grant, Ulysses S., 420–21
Gray, Jack, 104
Gray, Mrs. W. T., 104
*Great Day* (Youmans), 334–35
Greely, Aurora, 379
Green, Charlie, 142, 145, *147*, 154, 510
Green, Lil, 326
Greene, Gene, 212
Greer, Sonny, 227
Griffith, D. W., 443
Grofé, Ferde, 122
Guinan, Texas, 245–46
guitars, 49, 72, 88, 93, 284, 412
Gulf of Mexico, 449

*Gully Low Blues*, 262
*Gut Bucket Blues*, 40, 48, 161, 204, 218, 283, 314, 436
Guy Lombardo and His Royal Canadians, 326–28, 400

Haas, John F., 237
*Half-Century Magazine*, 75
Hall, Adelaide, 276, 342
Hall, Bert, 335
Hall, John, 385
Hall, Tubby, 59, 73, 237, 308, 413
*Hallelujah*, 278
*Hallelujah* (film), 378, 385
Hammond, John, 393
Hampton, Lionel, 194–95, 226, *399*
    LA and, 380, 382, 383, 402
Handy, W. C., 50–52, 54, 59–60, 64, 126–27, 154, 155
    band of, 58, 258
    published music of, 50–51, 59, 134, 161–63
Hardin, Dempsey, 71–72, 73, 114, 120, 319
Harker, Brian, 247
Harlem, 122, 126, 128, 141, 142, 146, 166, 171, 231, 337–41
    Alhambra in, 220
    Amsterdam Club in, 153
    Connie's Inn in, 337, 339–41, *340*, 343, 345, 354–55, 414, 419
    Cotton Club in, 228, *234*, 338, 339, 341, 345
    elite social occasions in, 123–25
    Lafayette Theater in, *140*, 152, 339, 355–57, 410, 435
    musical scene of, 126, 152–54
    New Manhattan Casino in, 123–24, *140*
    Rhythm Club in, *140*, 153
    Savoy Ballroom in, 333, *333*, 337
    Small's Paradise in, *149*, 163–64
    "Striver's Row" in, 131
    white tourism in, 338–41
Harlem Renaissance, 128, 145
Harlem Symphony Orchestra, 166
*Harlem Tattler*, 297
harmonicas, 93
harmoniums, 161–62
harmony, 149
    LA's command of, 66–67, 198, 253–55, 269–73, 406
    barbershop, 26–27, 395, 437
    blues and jazz, 5, 66–68, 134, 136, 156
    disregard of, 67–68, 73, 86, 95
    European, 93, 94
Harper, Leonard, 345

Harris, Charles, 190, 193
Harris, Jimmy, 279, 333
Harris, Joel Chandler, 442
Hart, William, 104
Hawkins, Coleman, 142, 154, 273, 406–7
Haydn, Joseph, 98
Haynes, Elizabeth, 124
Haynes, George F., 124
*Heah Me Talkin' to Ya?*, 324, 333, 367, 513
*Hearts in Dixie* (film), 385
*Heebie Jeebies*, 174, 190, 203–4, 208, 220–21, 245, 246, 249, 259, 278, 296, 297, 370, 459
   scat vocals on, 209, 211–18, 220, 242, 263
Heebie Jeebies (dance), 234
*Heebie Jeebies Dance*, 216, 218–19, *219*
*Heebie Jeebies* weekly, 170, 182, 186, 190, 204, 214, 217, 235, 244, 497–98
*Hello Dolly*, 220, 274
Hemingway, Ernest, 37–38
Henderson, Fletcher, Jr., 113, 120–27, *127*, 270, 274, 291
   blues accompanying of, 129
   childhood of, 125–26
   classical piano studies of, 126, 131, 179
   education of, 125, 126–27, 129, 130
   fame of, 126, 149
   jazz career of, 126, 129–32, 138, 141–51
   LA and, 120, 123, 131, 141, 163, 170–72, 176, 198, 207, 245, 278–79, 309, 351, 355, 430, 458
   white orchestras emulated by, 131–32, 139–41, 143, 152, 203
Henderson, Fletcher Hamilton, Sr., 125–26, *127*, 129
Henderson, Katherine, 295
Henderson, Mrs. Fletcher, 124
Henderson's Rainbow Orchestra, 124
Henry, Charles "Sunny," 97
Herbert, Victor, 344
heterophony, 4–5, 6, 67
   church, 84–87
   definition of, 4
*Hi De Ho*, 218
Higginbotham, J. C., 362, *362*, 451
*High Society*, 32–33, 102, 105, 106, 119, 402, 420, 435, 445
*High Society Blues* (film), 382
Hill, Alex, 324
Hill, Bertha, 165
Hill, Teddy, *362*
Hillare, Andre, 223
Hill, Letha, 78, 337

Hines, Earl, 62, 75, 120, 170, 173, 180, 192, 257, *261*, 365, 499
   on accompanying, 81
   on cabarets, 227, 233–34, 238, 239, 243, 247
   conducting of, 184–85, 244, 260, 394
   on LA, 234, 246, 249, 251, 259, 302–3
   LA and, 222–23, 260–61, 263, 281, 286, 288–89, 292, 302–18, 451–52
   piano style of, 171–72, 260–61, 295, 299, 302, 310–17, 325, 508
Hines, Laura, 501
Hinton, Hilda, 41, 43, 46, 183, 196
Hinton, Milton, 40–45, 59, 123, 186, 196, 226, 309, 377, 414, 448
   childhood of, 40–43, 183, 196
   on LA, 195, 199, 201, 293, 307
Hite, Les, 379, 385, *399*, 412, 516
*Hitting the High Spots with Louis Armstrong*, 382
Hoagy Carmichael and His Pals, 403
Hobson, Homer, *336*
Hodeir, André, 252
Hodes, Arthur, 239, 290, 296, 304–5
*Hold That Tiger*, 184
Holiday, Billie, 298–99, 301, 356, 368, 392, 399–400, 411, 413
Hollywood, Calif., 380, 385
   Cocoanut Grove in, 411
Holmes, Charlie, *362*, 363, 489, 511–12
*Holy City*, 63–64, 90, 489
Holy Roller churches, 236
*Home*, 436
homosexuality, 45
*Honeysuckle Rose*, 436
Hooper, Louis, 152
Hoover, Herbert, 389
Hopkins, Lightning, 48
Hoskins, Allen (Little Farina), 385
Hoskins, Mr., 49
*Hot Chocolates*, 341, 345–47, 352–55, *353*, 434, 512
*Hotter Than That*, 282, 284–85, 312, 315, 332, 352, 382, 507
House of Representatives, U.S., 43
Houston, Tex., 426
Howard, Darnell, 74, 496
Howard Normal School, 125–26
*How Come*, 347
Hudgins, Johnny, 248, 515
Hughes, Howard, 379, 382, 434
Hughes, Langston, 128, 196, 199–200, 297–98, 338, 341
   on LA, 203
*Hungarian Rhapsodies* (Liszt), 314

Hunter, Alberta, 53, 58, 60, 78, 102–3, 154, 158–59, 167, 218, 513
    on LA, 63, 70, 114
*Hunt in a Black Forest, A* (Voelker), 278
Hunton, Addie W., 124
Hurston, Zora Neale, 84, 398, 447, 513

*I Ain't Gonna Play No Second Fiddle*, 163, 279
*I Can't Believe That You're in Love with Me*, 367
*I Can't Give You Anything but Love*, 329–32, 345, 349, 356–57, 359, 368, 383, 386, 396–97, 460, 511
*I Covered the Waterfront*, 431
*I'd Love to Have Somebody to Love Me*, 244
*If I Could Be with You (One Hour Tonight)*, 384, 401–2, 413
*I Got Rhythm*, 436
Ike Dixon Amusement Company, 288
*I'll Be Glad When You're Dead You Rascal You*, 1–2, 413, 429, 434
*I'll Be Glad When You're Dead You Rascal You* (film), 437, 443, 444–47, 446
Illinois, 60
*I'll See You in My Dreams*, 148
*I'll Take My Stand: The South and the Agrarian Tradition*, 442
*I'm a Ding Dong Daddy (from Dumas)*, 382
*I'm Confessin' That I Love You*, 384, 397, 401, 413, 432
*I'm in the Market for You*, 382, 516
*I Miss My Swiss*, 150
*I'm Just Wild About Harry*, 342
Immerman, Connie, 340, 341, 345, 347, 354–55, 429
Immerman, George, 341
*I'm Not Rough*, 22, 284
*In a Mist*, 282
*In Bamville* (Sissle and Blake), 344, 347
Indiana, 60, 74
*Indian Cradle Song*, 340–41, 349, 368, 515
*I Need Lovin'*, 278
*In Shadowland*, 357
Interracial Commission on Race Relations, 43
*Interstate Tattler*, 124, 343, 346, 347, 512
*In the Evening by the Moonlight in Dear Old Tennessee*, 440
*Invisible Man* (Ellison), 354
*Irish Black Bottom*, 214, 236, 246, 438
*Irish Fantasy*, 290
Isham Jones and His Orchestra, 131, 138
*I Surrender Dear*, 413

*It's Getting Dark on Old Broadway*, 343
*It's Tight Like That*, 321–22
*I Wish I Could Shimmy Like My Sister Kate*, 106, 155

Jackson, Charlie, 117, *117*
Jackson, James, 103
Jackson, Jigsaw, 171
Jackson, Mahalia, 45, 48
Jackson, Oliver, 311
Jackson, Preston, 1–2, 46, 58, 91, 110, 122, 225, 243, 413–14, 426, 492, 503
    on LA, 197, 426, 429, 436–37
    in LA's band, 113, 422–23, 426–27
Jackson, Rudy, 117, *117*, 223
    on LA, 118
Jackson, Tony, 17, 45
Jacobson, Bud, 215, 389
James, George, 383, 414, 428–29, 436
jam sessions, 251, 281–82, 315, 328
jazz, 4
    African roots of, 6–7, 92–95, 134
    birth of, 109
    Chicago, 28–39, 97
    collective improvisation in, 5–6, 8, 59, 84–87, 90, 92–93, 95, 133–35, 143–44, 147–48, 206, 250, 284–85, 312, 331, 363–64, 370, 372
    competition in, 5, 8, 83, 97, 98
    composed, 135, 136
    "cool," 364
    criticism of, 37–38, 133, 134, 135, 136
    crossing racial lines in, 33–39, 134, 150, 198, 200
    dancing to, 171, 208, 214, 224, 234–37, 256
    definitions of, 132–38, 144, 447, 457
    dissonance in, 201, 255
    evolution of, 136–38
    fixed and variable model of, 6–7, 9, 11, 68, 92–97, 119, 148, 162, 448
    four-beat style of, 87–88
    free, 97
    harmonic dislocations in, 254
    historical concepts of, 7, 9–10, 200, 230
    "hot," 31, 33, 57, 65, 139, 141–51, 192–95, 364, 402, 456–57
    impact of LA on development of, 7, 11, 66, 94, 251, 264, 269–75
    LA as central figure in, 376
    listening to, 202–4, 208, 248, 433, 460
    memorization in, 36, 49, 91, 372, 410
    modal, 97
    modern, 201, 203
    moral concerns about, 37–38

jazz (*continued*)
  musical riffs and chord changes in, 35
  New Orleans style, 17, 31, 32, 35,
    54–60, 62, 67, 82–83, 87–95, 102, 105,
    109, 119, 201–2, 208, 395
  plurality of rhythms (polymeters) in, 6,
    73
  rhythmic hierarchy of, 6
  sexuality and, 38, 232–33, 238, 317–19,
    321–23, 330
  social pressures of, 68
  standard length of numbers in, 33
  styles encompassed in, 57, 132–38
  "sweet," 327–28, 364, 365
  symphonic, 136–38, 152, 201, 203
  syncopation in, 134
  tempos in, 31–32
  tension between accessibility and explo-
    ration in, 146
  as a term, 57, 58, 82, 132–38
  up-tempo, 57
  vaudeville and, 26–30, 117–18
  white, 7, 9–10, 23–24, 33–39, 57, 58, 63,
    76, 129–31, 134, 135, 137–41
  white "alligators" appropriation of,
    23–24, 35–39, 63, 143, 239–40, 242,
    306–7, 365, 372, 389
jazz age, 48, 233, 366
jazz breaks, 81–84, 90
  dance connection to, 82
  definition of, 81–82
  duet, 82–83, 117, 248
  of LA, 82–84, 100, 111, 117, 142, 146–
    47, 149, 172, 257, 266, 292
  notated, 111
  of Oliver, 82–83, 117
  solo, 29, 81–84
*Jazzmania*, 217–18, 245, 499–500
*Jazzmen* (Russell), 493
*Jazz Modernism: From Ellington and Arm-
  strong to Matisse and Joyce* (Appel),
  408
jazz orchestras, 132–38
Jersey City, N.J., 435
Jews, 409, 448
  as mediators between Africa and
    Europe, 135
  in popular music, 135, 291
Jim Crow legal system, 3, 27, 307
Joe Oliver's Dixieland Syncopators,
  255–56, 503
Johnny Dodd's Black Bottom Stompers,
  257, 263
Johnson, Bill, 17, 18–20, 29–30, 37, 76–77,
  150, 213, *362*, 490

  banjo playing of, 18, 61–62, 64, 491
  influential bass style of, 26, 59, 62, 64
Johnson, Budd, 243, 374, 391, 392, 427–28
Johnson, Bunk, 90, 106–7, 109
Johnson, Chick, 244
Johnson, Jack, 46
Johnson, James P., 129, 163, 214, 237, 318,
  341, 344, 401–2
Johnson, James Weldon, 15, 125, 128, 264,
  338–39
Johnson, Jimmy, 278
Johnson, Joe, 105
Johnson, Lonnie, 216, 282, 284–86, 312
Johnson, Margaret, 154, 158
Johnson, Marvin, *399*
Johnson, Otis, *362*
Johnson, Walter, 192, 308
*Joker, The*, 280
Jolson, Al, 167
Jones, Billy, 150
Jones, Calwell "King," 22, 28, 32, 37
Jones, Charlie, *399*
Jones, Clarence, 279–80, 288–89
Jones, Clifford "Snags," 117, *117*
Jones, Dave, 29, 418
Jones, Isham, 33, 58, 131, 133, 135, 222
Jones, Joseph, 418
Jones, Maggie, 154, 158, 160
Jones, Reverend, 42
Jones, Richard M., 81–82, 91, 104, 165,
  204, 216, 381, 392, 489, 514
Joplin, Scott, 11, 106, 109, 111, 219, 264,
  266, 274, 275, 371, 401, 457, 459
jukeboxes, 220, 410
*Just a Gigolo*, 439, 516
*Just Like a Butterfly That's Caught in the
  Rain*, 279–80
Juvenile Protection Association, 32, 235,
  236–38

Kahn, Gus, 222
Kaminsky, Max, 281
*Katie's Head*, 106
Keith Vaudeville Circuit, 429, 433
Kentucky, 59, 429
Kentucky Derby, 415
Keppard, Fred, 17, 36, 42, 46, 63, 91, 101,
  303, 371, 516
  cornet playing of, 67–68, 75–76, 194,
    308, 497
  LA and, 75–76
*King of the Bungaloos*, 212
*King of the Zulus*, 217
King Oliver and His Creole Jazz Band, *30*,
  149, 224–25, 428, 447

admiration of white musicians for,
    33–39, 57
blend of music and entertainment by,
    26–30
break up and rebuilding of, 116–19, *117*
competition in, 97
Eddie Condon on, 34, 88, 89, 95, 97,
    149, 206
fast tempos of, 31–32
harmonic precision lacking in, 67–68,
    73, 86, 95
LA as second cornet player in, 20, 24,
    47, 62, 69, 74, 80–81, 90, 97, 115,
    117–19, *117*, 121, 389
LA's solo debut with, 54, 56
Lil Armstrong's role in, *37*, 66, 68,
    73–74, 86–88, 90, 91, 95, 97, 115, 117,
    *117*, 119
main melody instruments of, 89–91,
    94–95, 117
musicians in, 18–21, 29–33, *37*, 103,
    117, *117*, 141
Oliver's leadership of, 86–91, 97
recordings of, 32–33, 58, 60–67, 68, 74,
    80–81, 86, 88–91, 94, 95, 97, 99–104,
    116, 155, 206
rehearsals of, 91–92, 117
rhythm section of, 87–89, 94
singers featured with, 28–29
success of, 86–87
touring of, 21, 22–23, 60–61, 73, 74,
    116–18
white criticism of, 67–68
*see also* Lincoln Gardens
King Oliver's Dixie Syncopators, 294–95
KMIC radio, 410
*Knee Drops*, 364
*Knockin' a Jug*, 332
KPVD radio, 410
Krupa, Gene, 59, 389
Kubik, Gerhard, 95
Ku Klux Klan, 2, 60, 231, 443

Ladnier, Tommy, 101, 279, 391, 509
*Lady Be Good*, 436
LaGuardia, Fiorello, 342
Lake Ponchartrain, 293, 424
Langston, Tony, 53
Lanin, Sam, 130, 131, 132, 138, 151, 495
Larenzo, 4, 56
*Last Time, The*, 282
Latin language, 125, 126, 127, 129
*Lazy River*, 396
Lennon, John, 393
Leslie, Lew, 329, 344–45, 347

Le Tang, Mrs., 124
Levette, Harry, 378, 385
Lewis, Art, 318
Lewis, Ted, 328
Library of Congress, 390
*Liebestraum* (Liszt), 290
Lieurance, Thurlow, 122
*Light*, 187, 328, 503
*Light and Heebie Jeebies*, 244, 259, 265,
    287, 308, 327, 497, 506
Lillian Hardin's Dreamland Orchestra, 205
Lincoln Gardens, 11, *14*, 15, 116–17, 121,
    381, 438
    black audiences at, 28, 40, 201–2
    crystal ball in, 18
    floor show and dancing at, 25–26,
        28–33, 34, 47, 172–73
    interior of, 18, *25*
    King Oliver and His Creole Jazz Band
        at, 18–40, 45, 47–48, 56, 60, 63, 67–69,
        73, 74, 76, 78, 88–92, 97, 100, 112,
        119, 143, 206, 248, 452
    white musicians ringside at, 33–39, 63,
        82, 143, 226, 242, 420
    whites only "midnight ramble" at, 35,
        225
Lindsey, Joe, 424, 426
Lindy Hop, 383, 491
Lips, Kid, 218, 245, 246, 247, 500
Liszt, Franz, 290, 314
*Little Ida*, 182
*Little Joe*, 438–39
Little Rock, Ark., 428
*Livery Stable Blues*, 136
*Liza*, 336, 344, 436
Locke, Alain, 125
Loew, Marcus, 176
Loew's Theaters, 334, 367, 380, 384
Lombardo, Carmen, 400
Lombardo, Guy, 326–28, 357, 366, 403,
    513
London, 408–9
    Palladium in, 409
*Lonesome Blues*, 295
*Lonesome Road, The*, 392
Long, Huey, 419
Longshaw, Fred, 159, 161–62
Lopez, Carmen, 244
Lopez, Vincent, 130, 131, 132, 138, 151,
    270, 274, 366
Los Angeles, Calif., 22, 373, 377–87, 410,
    430
    Apex in, 378
    Appomattox Country Club in, 384
    Dunbar Hotel in, 377–78, 384, 389

Los Angeles, Calif. (*continued*)
  Frank Sebastian's Cotton Club in,
    378–84, 386–87, *388*, 392, *399*, 402–3,
    408, 411, 412, 439, 440
  Loew's State Theater in, 384
Los Angeles *Evening Herald*, 378, 384
*Los Angeles Times*, 236, 385
Louis Armstrong and His Hot Five, 165,
    430, 438
  musicians in, 165, 204–7, *205*, 210, 242
  recordings of, 155, 160–61, 166–67,
    204–19, 236, 238, 239, 242, 262, 263,
    282–86, 288, 295–97, 303, 363–64,
    372–76, 411, 490
Louis Armstrong and His Hot Seven, 257,
    259, 260–63, 364, 411, 435
  musicians in, 260
Louis Armstrong and His Hot Six, 287–88
Louis Armstrong and His Orchestra, 1–2,
    323, 364
  musicians in, 113
  recordings of, 308, 337, 392
Louis Armstrong and His Savoy Ballroom
    Five, 317, 323, 324, 364
Louis Armstrong's Chocolate Drop
    Orchestra, 355
*Louis Armstrong's 50 Hot Choruses for
    Cornet*, 170
Louis Armstrong's Jazz Four, 165, 490
*Louis Armstrong's New Orleans* (Brothers),
    3, 57
*Louis Armstrong's 125 Jazz Breaks for Cor-
    net*, 170
Louis Armstrong's Sunset Stompers, 244,
    *257*, 259, 276–79
Louisiana, 46, 48, 67, 95, 235, 425, 428,
    440
*Louisiana*, 356–57
*Love Supreme, A*, 292
*Love Will Find a Way*, 72–73
Lovie Austin and Her Blues Serenaders,
    214
Luandrew, Albert (Sunnyland Slim), 48
Luis Russell Orchestra, 332–33, 361–63,
    *362*, 367
Lyles, Aubrey, 341–42
Lyttelton, Humphrey, 163, 267, 364, 489,
    496

*Mabel's Dream*, 97, 159
Mack, Baby, 379, 385
Mack, Cecil, 344
Mack, Red, 387
*Madama Butterfly* (Puccini), 280
Magee, Jeffrey, 143

Mahler, Gustav, 177
*Mahogany Hall Stomp*, 150, 332–33
Mailer, Norman, 317, 322
Majors, Florence, 18, 91
Malcolm X, 197
*Mammy's Little Coal Black Rose*, 167
*Manda*, 142
*Mandy*, 254, 266
*Mandy Lee Blues*, 61
*Mandy Make Up Your Mind*, 148
Manone, Wingy, 33, 239, 281, 304
*Maple Leaf Rag*, 82, 111
Marable, Fate, 104, 180, 189
Mares, Paul, 24, 33, 36
"Marijuana: Assassin of Youth"
    (Anslinger), 389
Marshall, Kaiser, 122, 332
Marshall, Thurgood, 441
Martin, David, 124
Martin-Smith Music School, 124
Mascagni, Pietro, 186–87
Matisse, Henri, 408, 409
Maxwell, Jimmy, 267, 410
MCA Agency, 117
McCartney, Paul, 393
McClendon, Dotty, 244
McCutcheon, Joe, 179
McGraw, Naomi, 247
McHargue, James "Rosy," 67–68, 239
McHugh, Jimmy, 341, 345, 367, 368
McKendrick, Mike, 413, 422–23
McKinney, Nina Mae, 378, 385, 389
McKinney's Cotton Pickers, 290, 321–22,
    412, 415
McPartland, Jimmy, 33
Meers, Paul, 346, 355
Meers, Thelma, 346, 355
*Melancholy Blues*, 263
*Melody Maker*, 299
Melrose Music Company, 266–67
*Memories of You*, 366, 383, 384, 386, 398,
    517
"Memphis," 57
Memphis, Tenn., 42, 51, 58, 59, 72, 103,
    258, 381, 428–29
  Peabody Hotel in, 1–2, 429
*Memphis Blues* (Handy), 50
Memphis *Commercial Appeal*, 428
Memphis Police Department, 1–2, 428, 444
Mencken, H. L., 291
Menelik II, Emperor of Ethiopia, 291, 405,
    438, 446, 448
Mess Around, 234–35
Metcalf, Louis, 146, 149, 372
Metropolitan Opera House, 131

Meyer, Sig, 99, 139, 389, 496
Mezzrow, Mez, 63, 89, 170, 238–41, 282,
    340, 346, 391, 393, 452, 495
    autobiography of, 240, 388
    LA and, 38, 218, 307, 389, 429
MGM Studios, 380
Michael, Gertrude, 391
microphones, 65, 284, 370
    LA's use of, 9, 296–98, 296, 330, 347,
    358, 393, 400, 516, 519
Mid-Summer Follies, 182
Mike, Gladys, 324
Miley, Bubber, 58–59, 249, 300, 489
Miller, Flournoy, 341–42
Miller, Punch, 60, 212, 261, 302, 503–4
Miller, Ray, 193
Miller and Lyles, 215, 341–42, 385
Mills, Florence, 342, 345
Minnie the Moocher, 392
minstrel shows, 23, 26–28, 38, 39, 51, 169,
    220, 241, 381, 438, 453
Miss Cleo Mitchell and Her Fast Steppers,
    29
Mississippi, 40–41, 45, 60, 67, 95, 183,
    425, 428
    "delta" region of, 48
Mississippi Mud, 288
Mississippi River, 420, 449
    LA's playing on riverboats in, 11, 15–16,
    29, 34, 71, 104, 106, 121, 180, 189,
    198, 199, 214, 313, 418
Mitchell, George, 69, 319
Mole, Miff, 239
Monday Date, A, 297, 303, 311, 364, 507
Monk, Thelonius, 401
Montgomery, Little Brother, 428
Mood Indigo, 292
Morton, Jelly Roll, 17, 26, 45, 46, 56, 103,
    168, 303, 309, 438
    compositions of, 86, 107, 257, 260
    on LA, 212
    on music, 82, 336, 417–18, 448–49
    piano playing style of, 72
Mosby, Curtis, 378, 384
Moton, Robert, 305–6, 439, 441, 446, 519
movies, 412, 417
    LA in, 28, 376, 385, 415, 437, 443–45,
    448, 454, 519–20
    orchestral accompaniment to, 176–78,
    184–89
    racist, 28, 182–83, 437, 443–45, 448, 454
    silent, 176–78, 184–89
    talking, 9, 334, 376
Mozart, Wolfgang Amadeus, 245, 250,
    252–53, 255, 334, 455, 496

Muggles, 308, 392
Muse, Clarence, 385, 440
musical arrangements, 92, 119, 121, 122,
    137, 150, 151, 164, 206, 383
    commercial "stock," 91, 139, 193, 243
    published, 143–44
musical notation, 5–6, 10, 20, 35, 49, 50,
    52, 92, 106–11, 121, 381, 430, 457–58
    of breaks, 111
    lead sheets in, 108, 111–12, 250, 371,
    459
    reading of, 122, 180–81, 198, 243, 261,
    291
Music Trades Convention, 99
Muskrat Ramble, 208, 210–11, 216, 218,
    251, 254, 266, 459, 503
My Baby Knows How, 190
My Blue Heaven, 298
My Daddy Rocks Me, 192
Myers, Alonzo, 124
My Heart, 204, 206
"My Old Kentucky Home," 26
My Rose Marie, 142, 143
My Sweet, 367–68

Nabokov, Vladimir, 401
Nail, John, 124, 128
Naitland, Johnny, 413
Nation, 230
National Association for the Advancement
    of Colored People (NAACP), 191,
    236, 439, 441
    annual ball of, 123–25
    Women's Auxiliary of New York branch
    of, 123
National Association of Colored Women,
    124
National Association of Negro Musicians,
    124
Native Americans, 38
Navy, U.S., 21
Nearon, Leo Fitz, 124
Negro Baseball League, 303
Nelson, Willie, 393
New Haven, Conn., 436
New Negro, The (Rogers), 447
New Orleans, La., 2, 3, 23, 29, 40, 41,
    45–46, 325, 373–74, 437–38
    African-American dance halls in, 31, 32
    antebellum, 27
    Astoria Gardens in, 418, 424–25
    as Big Easy, 449
    Bourbon Street in, 225
    Bywater neighborhood of, 425
    Canal Street in, 104

New Orleans, La. (*continued*)
  Congo Square in, 93, 450
  Country Club in, 198
  early jazz in, 17, 31, 32, 35, 54
  funeral processions and parade bands
    in, 4–5, 15, 26, 32, 85, 198, 213, 291
  Funky Butt Hall in, 32, 438
  Heinemann Park in, 424
  honky tonks of, 4, 56, 437
  Industrial Canal in, 425
  Jefferson Parish, 418
  LA's early years in, 4–6, 11, 97, 115, 129,
    197–98, 438
  Mardi Gras Rex parade in, 217
  Orpheum Theater in, 169
  Patterson Hotel in, 418, 423–24
  post-Reconstruction in, 437
  Pythian Temple Roof garden in, 425
  racial and national mixing in, 449
  railroad stations in, 13, 418
  Rampart Street in, 418, *419*
  Robert Charles riots of 1900 in, 43
  St. Raymond Park in, 424
  segregation and prejudice in, 34, 43,
    415–16
  Seventh Ward of, 104
  Storeyville prostitution district of, 11,
    20, 46
  Suburban Gardens outside of, 418–25,
    *423*, 429, 433, 437, 453
  trolley line in, 293
  U.S. Army Supply Base in, 425
  whistling in, 110
New Orleans Black Pelicans, 424
New Orleans Creole Band, 17, 23
New Orleans Rhythm Kings, 33, 36, 63, 106
*New Tiger Rag*, 430–31
*New World Symphony* (Dvořák), 291
New York, N.Y., 43, 113, 115, 120, 317, 325
  Aeolian Hall in, 202, 349
  Audubon Theater in, 336–37
  black Broadway shows in, 72–73, 241,
    329, 341, 345–47, 352–55, *353*, 417,
    434, 512, 513
  Broadway in, 120, 138, 150, 155, 241,
    248
  Carnegie Hall in, 178, 317
  caste system of black musicians in, 335
  Chrysler Building in, 9
  Clef Club in, 335–36
  Club Alabam in, 130, *140*
  Columbus Circle in, 159
  El Fay Club in, 245
  Fifth Avenue in, 152
  Gaiety Theater Building in, *140*, 155

  Hudson Theater in, 141, 345–53, 360
  as jazz center, 142, 159
  LA in, 120–23, 333–60, 430
  Liberty Theater in, 329, 345
  Lincoln Center in, 159
  Loew's State Theater in, 367, 380
  Rhythm Club in, 335–36
  Rialto Theater in, 177–78
  Rivoli Theater in, 177–78
  Roseland Ballroom in, 120, 130–32, *133*,
    138–39, *140*, 141–42, 145, 149–52,
    155, 206, 245, 438, 453, 495
  63rd Street Music Hall in, 341–44
  Terrace Gardens in, 129–30
  Times Square in, 130
  Windsor Theater in, 345
  Ziegfeld Theater in, 355–56
  *see also* Harlem
*New York Age*, 131, 152, 335
*New York Clipper*, 95, 132, 203, 447
*New York Daily Mirror*, 131, 367
*New Yorker, The*, 350, 447
*New York Evening Graphic*, 346, 434
New York Philharmonic, 451
*New York Times*, 130, 138, 513
Niagara Falls, 335, *336*
Nicholas, 45–46
Nicholas, Albert, 87, 332, *362*, 489, 517
Nichols, Red, 239
Nicodeemus, 237
*Night-Club Map of Harlem*, 391
*No*, 325, 359
Noone, Jimmy, 21, 59, 103, 106–7, 194
*No One Else but You*, 325, 359
Nootsy, 70–71, 79, 320
Norfolk, Va., 53

obbligato, 5, 49, 90, 94, 97, 145, 159
Oberstein, Eli, 434, 454
O'Brien, Floyd, 215, 304
O'Day, Anita, 312
*Of All the Wrongs You Done to Me*, 157
Ohio, 60, 119, 223
Ohio State University, 415
OKeh Cabaret and Style Show, 216
OKeh Records, 53, 64–65, 100, 107, 127,
  159, 165, 204–16, 218–19, 239, 260,
  262–63, 282–86, 357–60, 368–71,
  381–82, 431, 434
Oklahoma, 425–26
Oklahoma City, Okla., 426
*Old Black Joe*, 26–27, 30, 38, 39, 228
*Old Man Blues*, 385
Oliver, Joe "King," 11, *37*, 48, *55*, *87*, 133,
  192, 194, 371

adolescence of, 56
band leadership of, 86–91, 97
character and personality of, 20–24, 80, 86–88, 116–18
composing of, 64, 69, 106, 107, 294–95
cornet playing, 29, 33, 56, 63–65, 69, 80–83, 100, 150, 187, 190, 252, 255–57, 268
death of, 418
freak music style of, 21, 22, 29–30, 58–59, 64–65, 101, 171, 199, 213, 260, 458
gum disease and deteriorating playing of, 89, 243, 255, 259
jazz breaks of, 82–83, 117
LA's break with, 112–13, 114, 118–19, 120
LA's co-compositions with, 64, 69, 106, 107, 149, 265, 457–58
LA's cornet duets with, 63–64, 82–83, 91, 98, 117
LA's musical training with, 5, 7–8, 24, 45, 65, 69, 80, 81, 83, 97–98, 107, 109, 110, 118–19, 143, 268, 325, 455–56
LA's relationship with, 70, 78–83, 98, 100, 107, 112–13, 117–19, 222–23, 225, 255–56, 417–18
popularity and fame of, 24, 40, 60, 68, 101, 109, 131, 149
sacred and secular music mixed by, 63–64
skill and creativity of, 29–31, 33, 59, 63–65, 255–57
use of the term "Creole" by, 22–24
see also King Oliver and His Creole Jazz Band
Oliver, Stella, 17, 45, 119
on King Oliver, 56, 64
Oliver-Ory Band, 18, 22
Ollie Power's Harmony Syncopators, 101
Ol' Man River, 265, 345
125 Jazz Breaks for Trumpet (Armstrong), 266–67
One I Love (Belongs to Somebody Else), The, 222
Onward Brass Band, 90
Orendorff, George, 386, 399
organized crime, 226–27, 414–15, 418, 433
Oriental Strut, 208–10, 216, 218, 251, 264, 459
Original Creole Band, 23
Original Dixieland Jazz Band (ODJB), 136
black music adopted by, 24, 134
popularity and success of, 17, 23–24, 63
recordings of, 17, 36, 57, 63, 102, 134
Original Indiana Five, 218

Ormandy, Eugene, 187
Orpheum circuit, 117
Ory, Kid, 22, 56, 103–4, 165, 174, 217, 223, 227, 260, 417–18
compositions of, 282–85
in Hot Five, 206–7, 210, 212, 215, 262, 282–85
on LA, 212
Ory Band, 20, 21, 189, 207, 223
Ory's Creole Trombone, 282
Osgood, Henry, 122, 135–36, 138
Our Gang films, 385
Overton, Anthony, 75

Pace, Harry, 53, 126–29, 154
Pace and Handy Music Company, 126–27, 154
Page, Oran "Hot Lips," 374
Palmer, Roy, 89
Panico, Louis, 33, 413–14, 515
Paramount Pictures, 437, 443–44, 446–47
Paris, 286, 376
Pasadena, Calif., 440–41, 513
Paul and His Pals, 426–27
Paul Whiteman and His Orchestra, 138, 280, 327
Paul Whiteman and the Rhythm Boys, 280, 507
Peanut Vendor, 413, 425
Pennies from Heaven (film), 448
Pennington, Ann, 235
Peoria, Ill., 27
Perez, Manuel, 90
Perkins, Bill, 399
Perry, Katherine, 278
Petit, Buddy, 5, 66, 90, 105, 424, 490
Petrouchka (Stravinsky), 135
Peyton, Dave, 8, 40, 51, 68, 103, 130–31, 133, 141, 180, 183–84, 186, 220, 239, 256, 270, 286, 497
arrangements of, 243
conducting of, 187, 223, 328–29
on LA, 166, 170, 191–93, 201, 203, 216, 266, 268, 273, 280, 290–91
Philadelphia, Pa., 366, 429
Pearl Theater in, 434
Philadelphia Orchestra, 187
Phil Romano and His Rainbow Orchestra, 130
Picasso, Pablo, 408
Picou, Alphonse, 102
Pinkett, Ward, 410, 453
Piron, Armand, 106, 155
Pittsburgh, Pa., 75
Duquesne Garden in, 151

*Pittsburgh Courier*, 51, 131, 151, 436, 494, 518
player pianos, 176
  piano rolls for, 72, 129, 218
playing by ear, 36, 49, 59, 68, 73, 86–87, 91, 92, 133, 255, 381
*Play That Thing*, 101
Plunkett, Vincent, 278
polka, 150
Pollack, Ben, 280
*Pool Room Papa*, 346, 352
*Poor Little Rich Girl*, 194, 237, 371
  LA's solo on, 258, 259
popular music, 43, 146, 154, 267, 270, 271–72, 297
  Broadway show tunes as, 72–73, 134
  dancing to, 138
  domination of 4/4 time in, 88
  jazz versions of, 9, 11, 107, 134
  Jewish talents in, 135
  LA's transformation of, 9, 11, 354, 365, 368, 383, 394, 396, 408, 411–12, 459–60
  publication of, 138
  recordings of, 72
post-Reconstruction, 437, 449, 450
*Potato Head Blues*, 265–68, 281, 352, 404, 504
  LA's solo in, 83, 261, 263–64, 266–68, 272, 460
Potter, Bill, 178
Powers, Ollie, 78, 101, 120, 168, 290–91
Preer, Evelyn, 379
*Pretty Baby*, 17
Price, George, 367
Price, Sammy, 158, 374
primitivism, 229–33, 239, 240, 241, 242, 268, 272, 337–38, 343, 374, 448, 451
Prince, Henry, *399*
Prince, Morgan, 26
Prohibition era, 226
  bootleg whiskey in, 229, 390
Puccini, Giacomo, 280
Pullman porters, b, 42, 75
Purdue University, 27
Purvis, Jack, 365
*Put 'Em Down Blues*, 282

QRS Records, 311–12, 315

race records, 53, 130, 133, 138, 153, 155, 157, 204–11, 263, 355, 360, 376, 383, 438, 453
  blues as staple of, 204–5, 372
Rachmaninoff, Sergei, 126

racism, 137, 200
  blackface minstrel shows and, 26–30, 453
  condescension and prejudice inherent in, 38, 229–33, 239, 240, 354
  cultural, 437–39
  in films, 28, 182–83, 437, 443–45, 454
  LA's encounters with, 1–3, 28, 328, 416, 419–20, 425–28, 437
  stereotypes of, 229–33, 416, 441–43, 448
  vigilante terrorism of, 15
  violence and rioting of, 43, 390
  *see also* Jim Crow legal system; segregation; slavery
radio broadcasts, 1, 9, 131, *179*, 220, 290, 291, 300, 309, 334, 378, 387, 409–10, 419–20
Raeburn, Bruce Boyd, 321
rags-bottles-and-bones men, 56, 57, 197–98, 201, 437–38
ragtime, 4, 26, 57, 58, 65, 72, 95, 106, 109, 275, 401
  dances in, 32, 230
  syncopation and additive rhythm in, 94
*Ragtime Dance*, 264
Rainey, Ma, 29, 51–52, 54, 154, 155, 258
Randolph, Manda, 220
Randolph, Zilner, 163, 421–22, 425, 435, 516
Ray Miller and His Orchestra, 131
Razaf, Andy, 345, 352, 434, 513–14
RCA Victor, 434
*Reckless Blues*, 162
Rector, Eddie, 237, 264, 267
Redd, Bud, 18, 74, 100
Red Heads, 218
Redman, Don, 130, 143, 145, 149–51, 212, 314, 321, 323–25, 352, 392, 415, 490, 510–11
Reeves, Reuben, 103, 238, 328–29, 513
Rena, Kid, 105–6, 151, 210, 418
René, Leon and Otis, 440–41, 513
*Reveille*, 101, 102
*Rhapsody in Black and Blue* (film), 437, 443, 444
*Rhapsody in Blue* (Gershwin), 119, 234, 291, 300, 349–50
Richardson, Jazz Lips, 276, 346, 378
Richardson, Walter, 182, 378, 385
Richie, Martha, 379
Richmond, Va., 60, 63, 421
Riesenfeld, Hugo, 177–78
*Riffin' the Scotch*, 411
*Riverside Blues*, 91
RKO Pictures, 378, 385

RKO vaudeville-movie circuit, 429, 433–34, 437, 455
Roach, W. H., 124
roaring twenties, 245–46
Robertson, Zue, 117, *117*
Robeson, Paul, 340
Robichaux, John, 21
Robin, Leo, 278
Robinson, Bill "Bojangles," 11, 76–77, *77*, 155, 220, 230, 247, 259, 336, 338, 345, 353
 films of, 385
 LA and, 394
 stage presence and professionalism of, 350–51, 394, 438
Robinson, Fred, 292, 334
Robinson, J. Russell, 345, 392
rock and roll, 242
*Rockin' Chair*, 359–60, 362–63, 413, 515
Rockwell, Tommy, 319, 419, 429, 434
 LA managed by, 329–31, 333–37, 358–59, 366, 376, 378, 414
Rodgers, Jimmie, 381
Rogers, A. J., 447
Rogers, Marshall "Garbage," 324, 333, 367
Roland, Ruth, 436
Rolfe, B. A., 151, 191, 357, 366
Rollins, Sonny, 377, 399
Roppolo, Leon, 307–8, 389, 392
Roseland Orchestra, 124
Ross, Allie, 130
Rosseau, Myrner, 384
Royal, Marshall, 380
*Royal Garden Blues*, 106–7, 193, 502
Royal Gardens, *see* Lincoln Gardens
*Runnin' Wild* (Johnson and Mack), 344
Russell, Luis, 103, 207, 332, *362*
Russell, William, 390, 493, 495–96, 506–7
Russia, 448
Rutledge and Taylor, 379

Saar, Louis Victor, 334
St. Cyr, Johnny, 31, 179, 489, 499, 501
 in Hot Five and Hot Seven, 165, 204–5, 208, 215, 260
St. Louis, Mo., 51, 291, 309, 391–92, 433
 Chauffeur's Club in, 429
 St. Louis Theater (Powell Hall) in, 429
*St. Louis Blues*, 50–52, 161–63, 252, 295, 309, 337, 349, 360, 362, 367, 369, 371, 415, 447
*St. Louis Tickle*, 72
*St. Martin's*, 395
Salemme, Antonio, 340
Sam Lanin Orchestra, 130, 151

Sam Morgan's Jazz Band, 283
Samuels, William, 183
San Antonio, Tex., 426, 427–28
Sanctified Churches, 84–86, 114, 191, 437
San Francisco, Calif., 21–23, *30*, 438
 California Theater in, 22
Saunders, Red, 179
*Save It Pretty Mamma*, 325
*Savoy Blues*, 282–86, 290, 293, 315, 324, 352, 405
Sayles, Emmanuel, 31
*Scandals*, 235
Schoepp, Franz, 103
Schubert, Franz, 245, 250, 252–53, 255
Schuller, Gunther, 245, 252, 411, 508–9, 511, 518
Schuyler, George, 123
Scott, Harold, *399*
Scott, Howard, 142, 154, 156, 303
*Screamin' the Blues*, 158
*Sea Beast, The* (film), 185
Sebastian, Frank, 378–79, 383, 389–90, 412
Sebastian New Cotton Club Orchestra, 382, 386
Secret Nine baseball team, 424
See, Hilda, 431–32
segregation, 189, 240
 elimination of, 43
 in New Orleans, 34, 416
 performing and touring under conditions of, 1–2, 3, 36, 52, 60, 131, 145, 228, 327, 378–79, 416, 426–27
 "separate but equal" concept and, 231
 "White" and "Colored" signs in, 42
Selby, Norman, 411
Seldes, Gilbert, 241, 407, 502
*Seven Lively Arts, The* (Seldes), 241
*Shanghai Shuffle*, 143
sharecroppers, 42, 54
sheet music, 5, 20, 50, 54, 72, 73, 107–8, 366, 371
 memorizing of, 91
 sightreading from, 72
*Sheik of Araby, The*, 98
*Shine*, 432, 439
Shoffner, Bob, 103, 243, 256
Shostakovich, Dmitri, 448
*Show Girl*, 337
*Shuffle Along* (Sissle and Blake), 72–73, 341–45, 351, 513
Simms, Margaret, 233
Simons, John Henry, 98
Sims, Joe, 212
Sinatra, Frank, 398–99
 LA and, 363

*Singin' the Blues*, 281, 505
Singleton, Zutty, 58, 59, 300, 334, 337, 340, 361, 512–13
    LA and, 286–89, 303, 305, 308, 318, 326, 333
Sioux City, Iowa, 27
Sissle, Noble, 73, 341, 343–44, 347, 513
*Skip the Gutter*, 313, 315–16, 364, 507, 514
slavery, 38, 41, 105, 437, 452
    drumming suppressed in, 93
    ecstatic worship associated with, 125–26
    Middle Passage and, 449
    musical and social legacies of, 3–6, 26–28, 59, 67, 92–94, 305, 339, 354
slide whistle, 99
slow drags, 31, 256
Smart, Byron, 403
Smith, Bessie, 52–54, 59–60, 65, 154, *161*, 252, 258, 295, 298–99, 301, 347, 373, 399
    LA and, 50, 153, 159–63
Smith, Clara, 154
Smith, Florence, 321
Smith, George, 243
Smith, Hazel, 295
Smith, Jabbo, 301–2, 415
Smith, Joe, 146, 148, 151–52, 154, 160, 248, 274, 347, 496, 509
Smith, Leroy, 270, 339
Smith, Mamie, 53, 154, 182, 215, 258
Smith, Stuff, 302, 392
Smith, Thomas "Sugar Johnny," 21
Smith, Trixie, 154
Smith, Willie "The Lion," 50, 58, 72, 75, 76, 194, 237, 271, 317–18, 336, 427
    on LA, 98
*Smithsonian Collection of Classic Jazz* (Williams, ed.), 245
*Snag It*, 256
*Snake Rag*, 81, 107
Snow, Valaida, 235, 500–501
*Sobbin' Blues*, 99–100
*S.O.L. Blues*, 262
*Some of These Days*, 290, 357–58, 367
*Song of the Islands*, 367, 379, 380
Soper, Tut, 239
*Sophisticated Lady*, 317
*So This Is Jazz* (Osgood), 122, 135–36
Sousa, John Philip, 460
South, Eddie, 327
Southern Serenaders, 150
Soviet Union, 448

Spanier, Muggsy, 33–34, 89, 231–32, 239, 304–5
*Spanish Shawl*, 193
spirituals, 4, 230, 236
Spurrier, Esten, 267
*Squeeze Me*, 297, 506
Stacey, Jess, 239, 304, 389, 391
*Star Dust*, 323, 403–7, *405*
    AL's performance of, 404–7
Staten, Georgie, 244
*Static Strut*, 193, 210, 459
Stearns, Jean, 171
Stearns, Marshall, 171, 230–31
Stewart, Rex, 131, 152–53, 335, 502
Stewart, Sammy, 119–20, 145, 191, 223–24, 291, 498
*Stomp Off, Let's Go*, 193, 210, 459
stop time, 111, 208, 264, 265–67, 272, 504
*Stoptime Rag*, 264
Stowe, Harriet Beecher, 363
Strauss, Richard, 448
Stravinsky, Igor, 10, 11, 135, 393
Stringbeans and Sweetie May, 213
Strong, Jimmy, 292
*Struttin' with Some Barbecue*, 282–83, 286, 315, 352, 364, 505–6
Sublett, John William "Bubbles," 264, 267, 268, 355–56, 504
*Sugar Foot Stomp*, 149–50, 193, 205, 297, 301, 507
Sullivan, Ed, 434, 443
Sullivan, Joe, 239, 280
*Sunset Affairs*, 278
*Sunset Cafe Stomp*, 214
*Sunset Gaieties*, 244, 264–65
Supreme Court, U.S., 231, 427
Swaffer, Hannen, 408–9
*Sweet Baby Doll*, 104
*Sweethearts on Parade*, 327, 384, 400, 402, 404, 406–8
*Sweet Lovin' Man*, 100, 106
*Sweet Sue—Just You*, 392
swing, 57, 193, 210
    four-beat style of, 88
swing era, 31, 39, 88, 262, 411
syncopation, 94, 134–36, 147, 201, 457

*Take Me to the River*, 301
*Talking Machine World*, 54, 99, 100
tango, 51, 135
Tansur, William, 395
*Tan Town Topics*, 341, 345
*Taps*, 102

Tate, Erskine, 175–76, 178, *179*, 180, 183–86, 188, 190–94, 203–4, 205, 290, 499, 506
Tate, James, 180, 182
Tatum, Art, 171, 273
Taylor, Cecil, 110
Taylor, Eva, 154
Tchaikovsky, Peter Ilyich, 280
Teagarden, Jack, 160, 332, 391, 422, 499
*Tears*, 83–84, 105, 146, 172
   LA and Lillian Armstrong as co-composers of, 83, 100, 110, 111, 430, 457
   recording of, 110, 490–91
*Tell Me Dreamy Eyes*, 142, 147
Terrell, Pha, 392
Teschemacher, Frank, 59, 218, 238, 274, 304
Texas, 158, 160, 425–28, 433
*Texas Moaner Blues*, 155–57
Texas Rangers, 427
*That Eccentric Rag*, 29
*That Rhythm Man*, 512–13
*That's When I'll Come Back to You*, 319
*That's Why Darkies Were Born*, 345
Theater Owners Booking Association (TOBA) circuit, 17, 52, 434, 489
*Them There Eyes*, 413
Thibeau, Tom, 35
Thomas, George, 104
Thomas, Hersal, 104
Thomas, Hociel, 165, 489–90
Thompson, "Big Bill," 276
Three Classy Misses, 278
Thurman, Wallace, 352
Tichenor, George, 231, 241, 432
*Tiger Rag*, 141–42, 284, 368–69, 371, 383, 413, 420, 430, 432, 437
*Tight Like This*, 317, 321–24, 330, 356
*Time*, 366, 382
Tin Pan Alley, 149, 495
*Tin Roof*, 389
*TNT*, 150
Todd, Clarence, 158–59
Toomer, Jean, 125
Tough, Dave, 33, 38, 59, 391
*Traffic in Harlem*, 346, 352
Treaty of Versailles, 84
*Trip Through Southland, A*, 288
*Tristan und Isolde* (Wagner), 136
Trumbauer, Frank, 281, 313, 364, 502
Tucker, Earl "Snakehips," 345, 385
Tucker, Sophie, 169, 357
*Turkey in the Straw*, 395
Tuskegee Institute, 305

Tuxedo Brass Band, 91
Tweedie, Tinah, 218
Tyler, Tex., 427

Ukelele Ike, 212
Uncle Remus Tales, 442
*Uncle Tom's Cabin* (Stowe), 363
*Underneath the Moon*, 278
United States:
   biracialism in, 23
   European immigration in, 13, 36–37
   illegitimacy statistics in, 37

Vallée, Rudy, 366, 367, 398, 400, 401, 407, 413, 434, 516
Vanderhurst, Sammy, 244
*Variety*, 130, 152, 169, 172, 224, 226, 235, 238, 247, 256, 345, 347, 385
vaudeville, 26–30, 38, 51–52, 54, 117–18, 151–52, 158, 167, 187, 238, 241, 243, 367, 407, 417
Venable, Percy, 236, 242, 252, 254–55, 329, 371
   revues produced by, 17, 243–46, 250, 258, 277–78, 290, 499–500, 502
Vendome Theater Symphony Orchestra, 175–87, *179*, 205
Venuti, Joe, 327
vibrato, 119, 157, 231
Vicksburg, Miss., 40–43, 46
Victorian values, 240, 407
Victor Records, 63, 381, 434
Victory Life Insurance Company, 75
Victor Young Orchestra, 404
Vidor, King, 378
Vincent, U. Conrad, 124
Vincent Lopez's Orchestra, 130, 151
violins, 20, 136, 179, 183, 196
*Virtuoso, The*, 314
Vitaphone system, 220, 334
Vocalion, 130, 138, 320
Voelker, George, Jr., 278
Voice of America, 200
voting rights, 45, 230

Waco, Tex., 427
Wade, Jimmy, 323
Wagner, Richard, 136, 178, 298, 409
Walker, A'Lelia, 125
Walker, Ruby, 160
Wallace, Sippie, 154, 158
Waller, Fats, 158, 171, 184, 341, 344, 345, 346, 348–49, *348*, 408, 434
*Wall Street Journal*, 131

waltzes, 122, 135, 182, 344, 422
Ware, Edmund A., 125
Washington, Albert, 308
Washington, Booker T., 42, 54, 125
Washington, D.C., 106, 108, 112, 124, 250,
  269, 366, 371–72, 429, 434, 459
  Howard Theater in, 435
Washington, Ford L. "Buck," 264, 265,
  367–68
Washington, Leon, 59, 497
*Washington Post*, 218, 443, 514, 516
Waters, Benny, 135, 152
Waters, Ethel, 29, 81, 129, 139, 218, 290,
  295, 299, 331, 338, 340, 345
Watts, Bob, 374
*Way Out West* (film), 384
WCFL radio, 290, 309
*Weary Blues*, 262–63, 509
*Weary Blues, The* (Hughes), 297–98
*Weather Bird Rag*, 106, 108, 111–12, 272,
  313–17, 457, 490, 510
Weatherford, Teddy, 180, 192
Weatherly, Frederick, 63
Webb, Chick, 333
*West End Blues*, 107, 157, 158, 217, 262,
  292–95, 298–302, 308, 312, 324–25,
  358, 371, 400, 413, 415, 438, 507, 514
Westmoreland, Lillian, 237
Wettling, George, 33–34, 59, 239, 281,
  295, 304, 391
*What a Friend We Have in Jesus*, 82
*What Did I Do to Be So Black and Blue*,
  346, 352–54, 438, 513
*What'll I Do*, 78
*What the Negro Thinks* (Moton), 305–6
*When It's Sleepy Time Down South*, 28,
  413, 432, 440–44, 447–48, 519
*When It's Sleepy Time Down South* (film),
  28, 448
*When You Leave Me Alone to Pine*,
  99–100, 457
*When You're Smiling*, 327, 357–58, 367,
  379, 410, 421
*Where Did You Get Those Eyes*, 182
*Where Did You Stay Last Night?*, 99, 100,
  457
White, Lulu, 20
White, Slick, 244, 278
White, Walter, 125, 126
Whiteman, Paul, 9–10, 34, 119, 122, 132,
  135, 138–39, 152, 202–3, 238, 270,
  274, 280, 291, 297
  fame of, 326–27
  on LA, 434

white reform organizations, 32, 238
white supremacy, 231, 240, 416, 442
Whitlock, Frankye Marilyn, 378
Whitney, Salem Tutt, 228, 440
Whyte, Zack, 429–30
WIBO radio, 413
Wichita Falls, Tex., 426
*Wildcat Blues*, 83
*Wild Man Blues*, 257–58, 262, 266, 267,
  295
Willems, Jos, 441
Williams, "Black Benny," 415–16, 492
Williams, Bobby, 98, 101–2, 223, 237, 492
Williams, Clarence, 43, 83, 106–7, 193,
  294, 355, 506
  LA and, 153, 155–59
Williams, Cootie, 318, 374, 378, 380, 504
Williams, Fess, 82, 328
Williams, Martin, 245
Williams, Spencer, 332
*Willie the Weeper*, 262
Wilson, Edith, 346, 352–55
Wilson, Teddy, 171–72, 209, 299, 435, 508
Winchell, Walter, 367
Wolverine Orchestra, 143–44
Woodbridge, Hudson, 321
Wooding, Sam, 154
Woods, Harry McGregor, 279–80
Woods, Tommy, 342
*Words*, 142, 147
World War I, 50, 101
World War II, 3, 50
Wright, Minnie T., 186
Wright, Richard, 42, 201, 305, 372–73,
  397–98
WSNB radio, 419–20
W. W. Kimball Company, 104
Wynn's Creole Jazz Band, 302

Yale University, 427
*Yes! I'm in the Barrel*, 204, 206
Youmans, Vincent, 278, 334
Young, Lester, 267, 364
Young, Oscar, 113
Young Women's Christian Association
  (YWCA), 124
*You're Driving Me Crazy*, 398, 516
*You're Lucky to Me*, 386, 516
*You're Next*, 208, 218

Ziegfeld, Florenz, 169–70, 243, 337
*Zippity Do Dah*, 4
Zulu Social Aid and Pleasure Club, 418,
  424